SDL '99
THE NEXT MILLENNIUM

SDL '99
THE NEXT MILLENNIUM

Proceedings of the Ninth SDL Forum
Montréal, Québec, Canada, 21-25 June, 1999

edited by

Rachida DSSOULI
UNIVERSTITY OF MONTRÉAL

Gregor v. BOCHMANN
UNIVERSITY OF OTTAWA

Yair LAHAV
SDL FORUM SOCIETY,
ECI TELECOM LTD

1999

ELSEVIER
Amsterdam • Lausanne • New York • Oxford • Shannon • Singapore • Tokyo

ELSEVIER SCIENCE B.V.
Sara Burgerhartstraat 25
P.O. Box 211, 1000 AE Amsterdam, The Netherlands

First edition 1999

Library of Congress Cataloging in Publication Data
A catalog record from the Library of Congress has been applied for.

ISBN: 0-444-50228-9

⊗ The paper used in this publication meets the requirements of ANSI/NISO Z39.48-1992 (Permanence of Paper).
Transferred to digital print on demand, 2006
Printed and bound by CPI Antony Rowe, Eastbourne

Introduction

With the new millennium starting soon, it is time to consider what has been achieved in the past and to plan future developments for the time ahead. In the context of the SDL Forum, we are concerned with two languages, namely MSC (Message Sequence Charts) and SDL (Specification and Description Language), which appear to have a promising future.

The development of MCS, the younger language, goes back to a paper presented by Ekkart Rudolph and Jens Grabowski at the SDL Forum in 1989. It is now an ITU-T standard (Z.120) used in conjunction with SDL, but it is also well known in the context of object oriented analysis and design, were MSC or similar notations are used in several leading methodologies.

The SDL has evolved over the last 20 years through successive versions of the ITU-T standard Z.100. The first version came out in 1980 and included already the typical graphic notation for describing state transitions. The first SDL Forum was held in 1981 and the first tool support also appeared during the eighties. During that time, the language was essentially used as a description language, but over the years the language was extended to include data and object-oriented aspects which enable the construction of tools for simulation and code generation. In addition, present-day tools allow for systematic verification and tests, and allow to check the correctness of an SDL design in respect to requirements given in the form of MSC scenarios.

Since its early development, SDL has been used in the writing of standards by the ITU-T. In most cases, the SDL descriptions were annexes to the standards, the latter written in natural language, complemented with diagrams, tables and other formalisms. In recent years, there has been a change in attitude and the MSC/SDL models have sometimes been included in the normative part of the standard and given precedence the textual part in case of conflict between the text and the formal MSC/SDL model. This approach was first introduced by ETSI. It should also be noted that the ITU-T, conscious of improving the quality of their standards, consider the idea of adding MSC/SDL experts to the ITU-T staff in order to support the standards developers.

At the end of this year, new versions of the two languages (MSC-2000 and SDL-2000) will be approved by the ITU-T Study Group 10. These new versions can be considered as major releases. The new version of MSC will include data definitions, timing and other additional features. The new version of SDL will include new features for data algorithms and new object oriented schemes for data and dynamic gates. But it is also important to note that the languages are being harmonized with other up-to-date languages and notations, such as UML and State Charts.

Today, the SDL Forum Society (http://www.sdl-forum.org) is responsible for disseminating information on SDL and MSC and for promoting these languages. The society organizes the SDL Forum every two years. Last year, the society also introduced a new series of SDL/MCS workshops to be held in between the SDL Forum meetings. The first of these workshops was held last June in Berlin, Germany and attracted 120 participants. The next workshop is planned in the year 2000.

This book represents the proceedings of the 9th SDL Forum which will be held in Montreal, Quebec, Canada, during the week of June 21-25, 1999. This is the first SDL Forum held outside Europe. The choice of Montreal is not a big surprise. Montreal and the nearby Ottawa are internationally important centers for the telecommunications and multimedia industries. The Forum is organized by the University of Montreal, the SDL Forum Society and Nortel Networks. The University of Montreal is well known for its research in the area of formal description techniques, and specifically on methods for test development from SDL specifications. Nortel Networks is one of the world leaders in telecommunications and has been using SDL in various divisions. However, it is important to note that this geographical area includes several other universities and many industries which are very active in telecommunications, distributed applications and software engineering, and consider the use of SDL in their respective context.

The 9th SDL Forum presents papers on the past and future development of the MSC and SDL languages, on experience with the use of these languages in industrial development projects, on tools and techniques for using these languages in the software and hardware development process and other aspects of these languages. The Forum also includes two tracks of tutorials giving newcomers and specialists an opportunity to broaden their knowledge. Tool demonstrations allow the participants to familiarize themselves with the latest tool developments.

We would like to thank the authors for submitting their papers, and the members of the program committee and the other reviewers for the careful reading of the manuscripts and their help in selecting the conference program. The program of the conference is based on their work. We would also like to thank the local organizing committee Lucie Lévesque, A. En-Nouaary, N. Sabeur, N & M Elqortobi, A. Elqortobi and the Support Team of the Département d'informatique et de recherche opérationnelle at the University of Montreal who have been indispensable for putting this conference together. Finally, we mention the generous sponsorships from Nortel Networks, University of Montréal, CS Verilog, Telelogic, France Telecom, Motorola, Cinderella, CRM, CRT, CRIM, and the Université du Québec ETS and le Ministère de l'Éducation du gouvernement du Québec.

Rachida Dssouli, University of Montréal
Gregor v. Bochmann, University of Ottawa
Yair Lahav, SDL Forum Society, ECI Telecom Ltd

TABLE OF CONTENTS

Program Committee

Chair persons:

Rachida Dssouli (DIRO, Université de Montréal, Canada)
Gregor v. Bochmann (SITE, University of Ottawa, Canada)
Yair Lahav (SDL Forum Society Chairman, ECI Telecom Ltd, Israel)

Program Committee

El Mostapha Aboulhamid
Ai Bo
Gregor v. Bochmann
Rolv Braek
Ana Cavalli
Pierre Combes
Rachida Dssouli
Jan Ellsberger
Anders Ek
Hakan Erdogmus
Michael J. Ferguson
Joachim Fischer
Qiang Gao
Øystein Haugen
Dieter Hogrefe
Gerard J. Holzmann
Claude Jard
Ferhat Khendek
Yair Lahav
Philippe Leblanc
Nikolai Mansurov
Sjouke Mauw
Birger Moller-Pedersen
Ostap Monkewich
Andrij Neczwid
Anders Olsen
Robert L. Probert
Rick Reed
Nathalie Rico
Ekkart Rudolph
Amardeo Sarma
Hasan Ural
Louis Verhaard
Daniel Vincent
Yasushi Wakahara
Thomas Weigert

Local organizing committee

Lucie Lévesque (DIRO), Nasser Sabeur (DIRO),
Abdeslam En-Nouaary (DIRO), Daniel Ouimet (CRM),
Abdelkader Elqortobi (DIRO), and the Support Team of Département d'informatique
et de recherche opérationnelle of the University of Montreal

Additional Reviewers

D. Amyot
M. Barbeau
R. Castanet
R. Dijkerman
J. Drissi
F. Dubois
A. Ek
K. El-Fakih
A. En-Nouaary
A. Engels
L. Feijs
J. Grabowski
S. Heymer
M. Ionescu
Y. Iraqi
T. Jeron
G. Juanole
A. Kerbrat
I. Khriss
B. Koch
N. Landin
J.-L. Raffy
M. Reniers
C. Rinderknecht
J.L. Roux
A. Salah
M. Schmitt
M. Tabourier
C. Viho
F. Zaidi

Session I

Applications I

Session I

Applications I

SDL'99 : The Next Millennium
R. Dssouli, G.v. Bochmann and Y. Lahav, editors
©1999 Elsevier Science B.V. All rights reserved

3

IN Service Prototyping using SDL Models and Animation

Miguel Alabau, Pierre Combes, Béatrice Renard
France Telecom - BD Cnet DAC/PRI

38, rue du Général Leclerc, 92794 ISSY-LES-MOULINEAUX Cédex 9, FRANCE
E-mail:
pierre.combes@cnet.francetelecom.fr,
miguel.alabau@cnet.francetelecom.fr
beatrice.renard@cnet.francetelecom.fr,

ABSTRACT

This paper describes a environment for service prototyping based on the graphical animation of the service logic. It is based on SDL models of services and network. It aims at simulating and animating the service behaviour from different actors points of view, mainly from the user and subscriber points of view. Applied at different steps of service creation, from the elaboration of the first idea of a new service to the validation of the service logic design, taking into account architectural constraints, this simulation and animation environment helps to guarantee the validation of service requirements between service provider, service developer, subscriber and users. The environment presented here allows the validation of different service domains: call processing but also management scripts.

Keywords: Intelligent Network, Service Prototyping, Service Validation, Simulation, Animation, SDL, MSC

1 Service Validation and Service Animation

Service creation involves numerous actors (service and network provider, service developer, service subscriber, users) and follows a specific process divided into different activities (requirements gathering and analysis, specification and rapid prototyping, service design, coding and final testing).

The will for introducing quickly and customising new services necessitates to insist on careful service validation tasks to ensure that the service satisfies the needs of the different actors [3]. It should be performed at different steps during the creation of the service. In particular, user and subscriber needs have to be validated as soon as possible to fix very early service functionalities and some ergonomic aspects. The validation of the requirements has also to be performed during the design activity where the service logic is refined depending on architectural or platform constraints (including existing building blocks).

This paper presents how the integration of service simulation and animation in a Service Creation Environment will allow:

- to easily *play* with the service specification in order to elaborate and quickly modify the service requirements, specially the ergonomic aspects,
- to validate with service subscribers and users the service specification, using a comprehensive graphical view of the service behaviour,
- to validate that the service design is still conform to the subscriber and user requirements,
- to obtain a basis for the contracts between different actors (e.g., service developer and provider, service provider and subscriber) with animation scenarios and MSC [10] that are derived from the specification.

The proposed environment is based on formal SDL model, which ensures that the animation is obtained from a specification semantically clear. It also guarantees the consistency between the different refined models.

The methodology presented here focuses not only on real time aspects; it allows to validate in a same environment service data, real time service logic and management scripts.

The paper is structured as follows:

- Section 2 describes the animation tool, its main graphical features, its dependencies with an SDL model and how it communicates with the simulator,
- Section 3 presents how the environment helps to validate service management scripts based on SDL specifications; in particular, the modelling of a *French Videotex* service is presented,
- Section 4 describes the complexity of the Intelligent Network and how it should be modelled in order to analyse and validate the behaviour of a service logic distributed on the different network entities,
- Section 5 describes the benefits provided by the use of SDL96 for the construction of such a model,
- Section 6 is dedicated to the application of simulation and animation to the service interaction problem, focusing on the use of the methodology as a step towards the resolution.

2 An Animation Tool Based on SDL Models

The animation tool allows to dynamically present different elements of an SDL model (processes, procedures, channels, messages) as graphical objects such as icons, links, sounds, gauges (see figure 1). An animation can evolve step by step or continuously.

During the simulation of the underlying SDL model using the ObjectGeode simulator [1], the aspect of the graphical objects evolves according to the model execution. For example:

- a user terminal will be described by different icons depending on its type and its state: fixed, mobile, onhooked, ringing state, conversation, receipt of a message,
- graphical links representing interfaces between objects can be animated when a message occurs and become visible/invisible, blink or appear with a different colour,
- messages received by a terminal can be animated as graphical labels or sounds,
- labels can be displayed and present the value of variables of the model,
- icons representing service constituents can appear, disappear depending on their invocation during the service logic execution.

The animation tool interface allows a user to send requests to the simulator, clicking the icon representing for example a terminal and selecting one of the possible actions at this animation step: offhook, onhook, dialling a number, pushing a button, selecting a text, talking. On the same way, variables of the SDL model can be accessed during the animation and their values can be modified. It is also possible to specify to stop the animation when it reaches a specific state or when a specific message appears. Finally when observers are used during the simulation to verify some specific properties, it is possible to animate them e.g., as lights which become orange when they evolve and red when they reach a success or error state.

The associations between the SDL model elements and the graphical objects are done via configuration files. Different configurations can be created for the same SDL model which allow to animate different aspects of the service model by means of different windows (a userview with terminals, network and protocols aspects, a service logic view by constituent aggregation) without modifying the SDL model.
Scenarios obtained during the animation of the SDL model can be recorded and replayed on a version of the tool independent of the ObjectGeode environment. It is thus easy to show them on a personal computer.

The architecture presented below shows how the tools communicate. The animation tool sends requests to the simulator and receives answers via the tool software bus. The graphical aspect of the animation changes according to the answers and a variable of the SDL model is modified by a request.

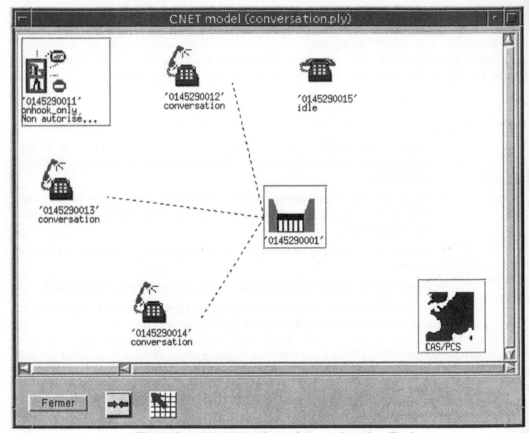

Fig 1. Graphical Interface of the Animation Tool.

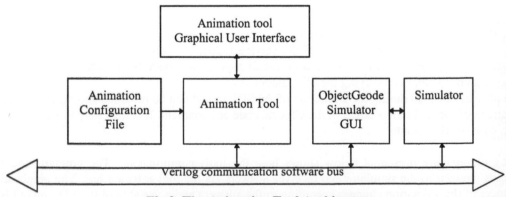

Fig 2. The Animation Tool Architecture.

3 Animation of Management Scripts

The animation tool was advantageously used to animate *vocal* and *French Videotex* management scripts.

The basic principle of such scripts, more precisely the logic of dialogue sequencing, is quite simple. A script is constituted by different phases, each of them being a sequence of different steps. A step consists in:

- for the *vocal* services, to play an *audio film* and the possibility for the user to dial some choice,
- for the *French Videotex* services, to display a page and the possible buttons provided to the user.

The result of an action performed by the user will trigger another step.

Scripts themselves are quite complex, due to the great number of possibilities offered to users (nominal and erroneous choices), to the complexity of feedbacks and controls, and to the intrinsic complexity of some service subscriber profiles.

The most common representation of these scripts is the textual form, and reading a complete dialogue often needs to switch from one page to another one, which makes them not so easy to understand.

The use of SDL to model such scripts is really efficient to ease their validation. In fact, only few functionnalities of the SDL language are needed: one step is modelled by one SDL procedure, and service logic is a succession of procedure calls and decisions performed when the procedure returns and corresponding to user choices (see figure 3). Moreover, reuse aspects were introduced, allowing to use some basic procedures for the modelling of other management scripts. The simplicity of the scripts allows a non specialist of SDL to easily and quickly specify and modify them.

The animation of such dialogues has allowed to play scripts entirely and to have a much better perception of the service than the textual form. Therefore we have obtained feedbacks from the users: is it the best sentence? The best word? Is this choice proposed in the good context (compared with the preceding pages)? It has allowed to discover some incompleteness of the script and some redundancies.

As an example, we have discovered an incompleteness in the handling of erroneous PIN number when specifying the call forwarding service. On one of the first page of the service it was asked the phone number you wanted to forward. On a page after, it was asked your PIN. If the phone number you had dialled were wrong (and thus, the PIN too), the message which appeared only said that the PIN was not correct without specifying the phone number you had dialled. This incompleteness can make you enter three times your PIN and prevent you from accessing your service until you ask to your provider to make it available again. If the phone number were specified in the message, of course you had found your mistake.

During the validation step, modifications were introduced very quickly and had spared several versions of textual specification.

8

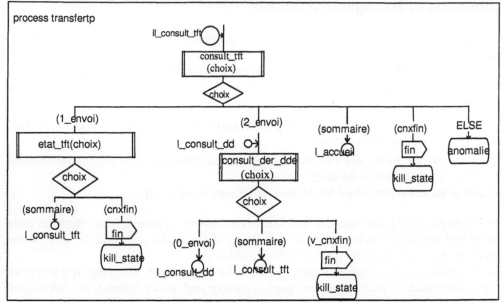

Fig 3. Scheme of Logic of a French Videotex Call Forwarding Service.

Animation was used to validate scripts and also to analyse the perception of final users very early in the development of the management service. Such analysis has allowed to modify the service logic (corrections and simplifications of dialogues) very early in the service development process.

4 Intelligent Network SDL Model

4.1 Intelligent Network Distributed Functional Plane Model

A major obstacle in real service development is to obtain a common agreement between service provider and service developer just before the real development phase. To reduce time in service life cycle, we need to produce a service specification which can be the basis of contracts between the service provider and the service developer. Such specification:

- should take into account the distribution of the service logic in the different entities of the network (and consequently in the different platforms),
- should allow the analysis of the feasibility of the service development,
- should be validated easily by the service provider, focusing on user and subscriber point of view,
- should also reduce the time in the final validation steps (unitary tests, integration steps), by test generation and analysis of the test coverage and traceability between test and specification.

In order to reach such objectives, we need to develop a model of the intelligent network architecture. The IN architecture aimed at easing the introduction of numerous new services in the network with short delays[12]. As examples of IN services, we can mention freephone, credit cards, voice mail, universal personal telecommunications, premium rate, conference call, virtual private network. The IN architecture is based on the separation between the service control and the call control.

- A specific node, the Service Control Function (SCF) contains and executes the service logic and communicates with the switching system to indicate it how to resume the basic call.

- The Call Control Function (CCF) provides the basic call processing and control (with a modelisation of originating and terminating basic call state machine), and the Service Switching Function (SSF), associated to the CCF, provides the capability for the CCF and the SCF to interact (notions of detection point and service triggering mechanisms).

- The communication between the entities SSF and SCF is performed through a standardised interface (INAP) as illustrated by the figure 4.

In theory, the service logic is mainly deployed on the SCF, however some service scripts may also be deployed in other network entities as Specialised Resource Function (SRF), such as intelligent peripherals (IP) for service features related to the user interface.

The construction of an SDL model including these different network entities allows to analyse in a consistent way the service execution from the different interfaces, and in consequence to obtain trace and test sequences with a clear relationship with the subscriber and user point of view.

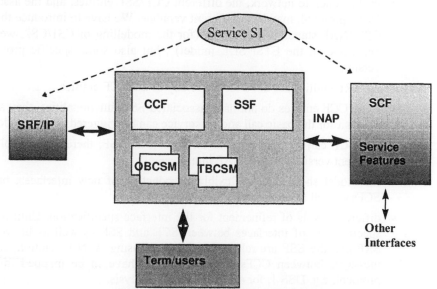

Fig 4: A Intelligent Network model

4.2   A Configurable Model

In the terminal view (SDL block) different kinds of terminals can be introduced (normal phone, mobile phone, audio conference bridge). These SDL block and terminal processes are easily configurable by a set of predefined data and variables, which can be modified from the simulator interface or also directly from the animator interface.

Therefore, a user of the animation tool can easily modify some characteristics of the terminal block (phone feature capabilities, line access, calling party category, number of terminals), with the possibility for the associated graphical icons to be modified. Such flexible possibilities of model configuration allow to play different simulation scenarios according to different terminal and line access capabilities, and to provide and record the associated animation and trace scenarios.

4.3 Towards a Complete IN Model

The model presented before corresponds roughly to the distributed functional plane of the Q12xx recommendation [12]. The wish to analyse service execution in a real and concrete way forces us to build a more complete model. Indeed, the Intelligent Network is more complex and closer to the figure 5. A basic call between two users go through a sequence of entities as Call Control Agent Function (CCAF) and different CCF, corresponding to the sequence of switching nodes. We have also to distinguish CCF as local exchanges and transit exchanges, and service triggering can be done in these different CCF nodes (we consider in this paper only the fixed telecommunication network).

The wish to build such an SDL model needs to take into account that:

- in the concrete network, the different CCF/SSF entities, and the associated INAP protocol, may have different versions. We have to introduce the CS1, CS2 INAP standardised version (for the modelling of CS1/CS2, we based our work on the ETSI SDL model) , but also some specific proprietary versions,

- the SRF entities are not attached to any of the CCF entities,

- some CCF entities do not have associated SSF functionalities, they are just a transit for the basic call and no service can be triggered in such nodes,

- one SCF can be connected to different CCF/SSF, therefore possibly with different versions of the INAP interfaces,

- the model should allow flexible introduction of new interfaces, between SCFs as well as between SCF and SRF,

- different levels of refinement for the interface specification. Until now the specification of interfaces between SCF and SSF as well as between the SRF and the SSF are relatively complete, using ASN.1 notation, whereas messages between CCFs are abstract and have to be mapped to a real protocol, e.g. DSS 1, for a more concrete analysis.

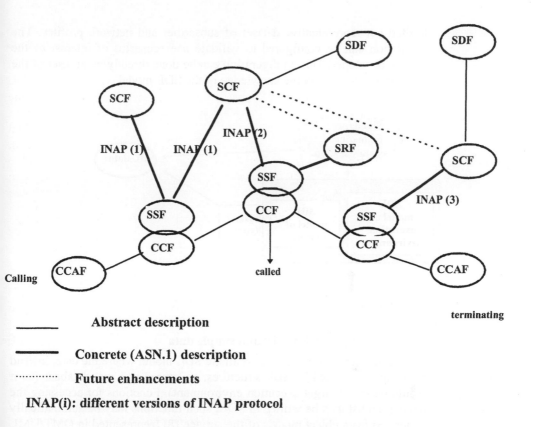

Abstract description

Concrete (ASN.1) description

.... Future enhancements

INAP(i): different versions of INAP protocol

Fig 5: A complete network model

4.4 Service and Subscriber Data

Telecommunication services may exhibit a large number of different service behaviours due to diverse combinations of service features with service data. For example, virtual private network services when associated with various service features will involve the validation of many different use scenarios depending on subscriber or network profiles. Validation may involve the identification of national or international private network locations, the use of mobile or fixed terminals, the identification of terminal characteristics, etc. Subscriber service profiles may also be very complex, allowing different filtering and forwarding features, related to terminal category, calling number, called number or call back features, all of these depending on date and hour.

All these service behaviours defined by so many different datasets cannot be exhaustively validated. The validation of such complex services should thus be done in two steps:

- the first step involves validating an «abstract» SDL model where the service and target execution environment are modelled entirely in SDL, including a limited but representative dataset of subscriber and network profiles. The simulation can be configured to validate use scenarios of interest to the service developer. This configuration can be done directly by an user of the animation tool without the knowledge of the SDL model.

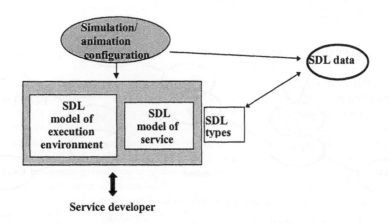

Fig 6: SDL model and simple data

- the second step involves a more realistic SDL model where the data, instead of being represented by SDL structures, are stored in a real database (as it would be in the target execution environment). Functions for accessing the database must then be written in SDL; such functions may be automatically generated from object models of the service [8] (represented in OMT/UML [11] or class-relation [13]) since many object modelling tools now provide such code generation features.

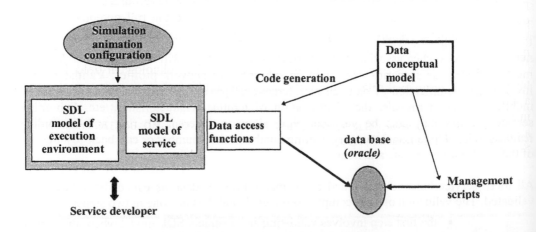

Fig 7: SDL model and concrete data base

This second step comes closer to validating a more realistic execution of the service, since simulation can then examine how the service reacts when real datasets are modified dynamically. Note that in both steps, the same SDL model of the service and the target execution environment, are used.

The model should be structured so that the service logic, the execution environment, and the data and its access functions are modelled reasonably independently (see section 5.2).

An interesting application of such an environment is to validate with the same tools the management scripts of a service, and the corresponding call processing behaviour.

5 Benefits that can be obtained from using SDL92/96

The Intelligent Network may be seen as a functional model that can be used to implement flexible and scaleable telecommunication systems. A simulation model of the IN is a kind of high-level implementation of the IN itself, hence it must be tailored in such a way that a change in the implementation is performed at a lower cost.

The SDL92/96 language [9] has powerful description features that can be used for IN formal descriptions. These features are concerned essentially with object orientation . In the following sections we describe how to build flexible and scaleable system behaviours (i.e. program control) and protocols (i.e. program data). We also show how to separate the problems which concern algorithms from those which concern data structures, in order to make an implementation more flexible.

5.1 System behaviour

Blocks vs. processes

The IN functional plane defines a set of concurrent functional entities that cooperate to provide services (see section 4.3). For the sake of clarity, each functional entity is decomposed itself into a set of parallel processes. It could be possible to use only one SDL block containing only processes, but the description would be rather hard to read and maintain.

By devoting one block to every functional entity, system structuring is better performed in terms of readability and maintenance. Every functional entity is mapped into a point which is a virtual machine dedicated to the functional entity. The SDL blocks of a decomposition are, in fact, these points . However, it is possible to group together several functional entities into a same block in order to simulate or emulate a mechanism in the network. For instance the SSF appears in the french IN in two places:

- inside the user switching equipment, grouped with the CCF,
- inside switching equipments devoted to transport and routing.

Types vs. instances

Of course, the use of blocks and processes rather than only processes for system description compels oneself in using types because instances of blocks do not exist. But the main reason, in fact, is that refinement of behaviours can be performed only on types, as it is described in the next section.

As a consequence, the manner to designate the receivers in communications is changed, since it is not possible from within a process type (or a process contained in a block type) to know all the processes that would communicate with this process.

Specialisation of behaviours

Hence a systematic description in terms of types (system, blocks, processes) may be used if some parts of the description are to be specialised in some future, and also for the sake of clarity (uniqueness of the programming model used for the description).

Specialisation in SDL can be performed by inheriting properties from types. The first way to do it is by adding properties to the inherited type. This is the case, for instance, if a process is added to an inherited block type. The second manner to perform specialisation is to modify a predefined abstract behaviour (which is declared in SDL as virtual).

For instance, when switching from CS1 to CS2, a specialisation of the first kind may consist in adding the handling of some signal in a given state of a process. At the same time, one given implementation may consider that, for a given signal, the processing of one signal might be more complete (or different) in CS2 than in CS1. Such a case requires the concerned transitions to be virtualised in order for them to be modified.

5.2 Signalling and external data structures

ASN.1 enhancements vs. SDL data

ASN.1 features of Z.105 provide additional flexibility to SDL descriptions. Of course, all the ASN.1 features accepted by SDL can be described in a pure Z.100 syntax, however they represent a convenient way of protocol signalling description since ASN.1 involves constructors like choice, default valued and optional fields in structures, and so on. As ASN.1 descriptions are commonly used for protocol specifications, such descriptions can be easily incorporated into SDL programs.

Composite vs. simple types

When passing parameters (in communications or procedure calls), it is a better choice to transmit a lesser number of complex parameters rather than a high number of simple parameters. A signal in the network is generally made up of lots of pieces of data. It is an evidence that providing a type for such a signal and a complete description of its contents increases readability. Flexibility of the program is also enhanced, since the interfaces are independent from any evolution of the signal structure.

If any parameter is modified or added to the signal description then the only changes that have to be done are in the implementation of the sender and receiver processes, but no link description is to be modified. When used in conjunction with virtuality, it means that only short pieces of code have to be added to an existing inherited description.

Procedural interfaces for accessing external data

As said previously in the paper (see section 4.4), services commonly use remnant data (user or service profiles, for instance) which are kept in databases. When using data modelling tools (e.g. Objecteering [13]) access functions to the data may be generated automatically by the tools. The signatures of these functions may depend on the tool itself, which in turn introduces this dependency inside the IN service itself. Such a drawback can be simply overcomed by developing a procedural interface for accessing external data. This interface can be isolated inside an SDL package; hence a change in the database itself has lesser impact on the service (only the procedure bodies contained in the package are to be changed, but the interfaces remain unchanged). By this way flexibility and maintainability are preserved.

Of course, the counterpart of such advantages is for the designer to have to define a general and complete set of procedures for accessing the external data.

6 Application to service interaction

A SDL and MSC environment for service interaction detection has been previously developed [2,4,7] and has allowed to detect a great number of interactions. It is based on the simulation and validation of each service introduced alone in the SDL environment, and on the detection of interactions by requirement violation when several services are introduced in the model. The different service requirements being expressed as properties on the model with help of observers [1,5].

Such previous work was done based on exhaustive simulation and satisfaction-on-a-model approach [4]. Even if it were applied to a realistic set of service feature [4] and allowed to detect many interactions, it is far away from the real and concrete world. In another way, with the models described in this paper, exhaustive simulation is no more possible, due to the size of the model (too many service data, more concrete protocol specification).

The objective here is to identify and analyse in a more complete and concrete way the behaviour of different services introduced in the network, in particular we can analyse service interaction due to architectural constraints. It could be done after a more abstract and formal detection method, allowing the identification of potential interaction problem due to specific service feature combination and service configuration and scenario.

However the notion of observers to specify service properties and the validation of the correctness of the properties during simulation is still used. Moreover the visual animation of the observers (as lights, for example) may help the identification of service interaction.

The results of simulation and animation with such methodology will be a clear and understandable description of the interaction problem: the service features involved, the cause of the interaction problem (logical or architectural), the actors involved, the scenarios corresponding to the desired service behaviour, and the scenario corresponding to the identified interaction. It will help to give criteria to initiate a resolution process.

Such a more complete model allows also to introduce in the protocol specification the signalling parameters introduced in the normalisation for service interaction handling. Such parameters which allow to exchange information from a network entity to another network entity, and thus from a service logic in one SCF to another service logic in another SCF, should allow the resolution of some interaction problems.

7 Conclusion

This paper presented a environment for service validation based on the construction of SDL network model and on the use of simulation and animation tools. The elaboration of the SDL models, and the use of SDL96 features, allow to adapt this environment to specific service domains: management script and rapid prototyping alone, call processing prototyping alone, or integrated view by management and call processing execution on the data model.

A great interest of such environment is also to enable reusability when prototyping different services, by reusing service feature (component) specification. It allows easy modification of an existing specification (modification of an existing feature or introduction of a new service feature), and the quick comparison between the initial service execution and the modified service execution. The use of the simulation and the animation tool provides a comprehensive view of the ergonomic aspects of the service behaviour and will ensure that the same service feature will have the same user behaviour, even if it used by different services (as authentication features).

Even if the environment presented here allows to cover different phases of the service life cycle, more work should be done on test generation. We do not argue for complete and automatic test generation but for more pragmatic techniques, focusing our interest on coverage analysis and traceability between test sequences and specification.

We plan to enhance our validation environment by introducing in the animation tool the possibility to animate scenario description (based on the MSC notation or a subset of the UML notation).

Bibliography

[1] B. Algayres, Y. Lejeune, F. Hugonnet, GOAL: Observing SDL behaviors with GEODE, in Proceedings of the 7th SDL forum, Oslo, September 1995.

[2] B. Renard, P. Combes F. Olsen, An SDL/MSC Environment For Service Interaction Analysis, in Proceedings ICIN96

[3] P. Combes, B. Renard, Service Validation, Tutorial of the SDL forum, 1997.

[4] P. Combes, S. Pickin, Formalisation of a user view of network and services for feature interaction detection, in Proceedings of Feature Interaction in Telecommunication Systems, IOS Press, 1994.

[5] I. Aggoun, P. Combes, Observers in the SCE and the SEE to detect and resolve service interactions, in Proceedings of Feature Interaction in Telecommunication Systems IV, IOS Press, 1997.

[6] C. Capelmann, P. Combes, J. Petterson, B. Renard and J.L. Ruiz, Consistent Interaction Detection - A Comprehensive Approach Integrated with Service

Creation, in Proceedings of Feature Interaction in Telecommunication Systems IV, IOS Press, 1997

[7] K. Kimbler, Addressing the Interaction Problem at the Enterprise Level, in Proceedings of Feature Interaction in Telecommunication Systems IV, IOS Press, 1997.

[8] Y. Chevalier, K. Milsted, N. Renaud, Service Data Component, in Proceedings of ICIN 1998.

[9] SDL 96, Z100 - Addendum, ITU, Geneva, Switzerland, 1996.

[10] MSC, 96, ITU Z120 Message Sequence Charts (MSC), ITU-T, Oct 1996.

[11] J. Rumbaugh and al., Object Oriented Modelling and Design, Prentice-Hall, 1991.

[12] UIT-T, New recommendations Q1200--Q series: Intelligent Network Recommendation, UIT.

[13] P. Desfrays, Object Engineering: the fourth dimension, Addison-Wesley, 1994.

SDL'99 : The Next Millennium
R. Dssouli, G.v. Bochmann and Y. Lahav, editors
©1999 Elsevier Science B.V. All rights reserved

SDL Framework for Prototyping and Validation of IN Services

Kristofer Kimbler[a], Carl-Henrik Hagenfeldt[a], Niklas Widell[a],
Jan Ellsberger[b] and Gustav Bergman[c]

[a]High Definition Systems AB,
IDEON Research Park, SE-223 70 Lund, Sweden

[b]L.M. Ericsson A/S,
Sluseholmen 8, DK-1790 Copenhagen V, Denmark

[c]Telelogic AB,
P.O. Box 4128, SE-203 12 Malmö, Sweden

Service Creation Environments (SCEs) for Intelligent Networks provide very limited support for service requirements analysis, specification and validation. This makes the service creation process long and costly. To shorten time-to-market for new services, High Definition Systems AB developed an environment, called INAP Wrapper, that supports IN service prototyping and validation at the early stages of service creation. The environment is based on Telelogic Tau and built around the standard SDL specification of the INAP CS1/2 protocol developed by ETSI [1]. This paper presents the SDL framework for service logic prototyping and the capabilities for service behaviour animation provided by INAP Wrapper.

1. INTRODUCTION

Growing competition on telecom markets increases the pressure on service providers to respond quickly to growing market demands. Unfortunately, after more than ten years of experiments with Intelligent Networks (IN) [2], the time-to-market for new services still exceeds the customers' expectations.

Thanks to the capabilities of commercially available Service Creation Environments (SCEs) the actual design of the IN service logic can be accomplished even within a few weeks, but the whole creation process starting from the market needs analysis and ending with a ready service product takes usually several months or even years.

This situation is mainly caused by the lack of tool support for service requirements analysis and poor validation and testing capabilities of the SCEs. This decreases the probability of eliminating service specification errors and undesired service interactions [3] at the early stages. Since, too many errors have to be corrected during the testing phase the whole service creation process becomes much longer than it could be. Moreover, the typical service testing process is manually-driven. This concerns the lack of automation both in the test-case generation and in the service testing as such.

In consequence, the existing SCEs support the service logic design that is only a minor part of the whole service creation process (10 to 20% of the service development cycle) as shown in the Figure 1 below.

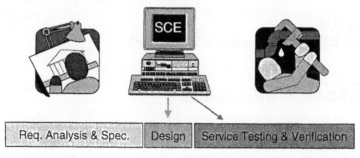

- Lack of tool support
- No early service validation
- Limited customer feedback

- Limited support in SCE
- Manual testing process
- Too many error corrections

Figure 1. IN service creation process

By validating service products early in the development process, service providers can quickly assess whether or not services being developed will demonstrate expected properties and will satisfy the users. Several techniques such as rapid prototyping, executable specification, animation, simulation, or model checking can be used for this purpose.

There is a need for tools, such as SCF3[1] environment from Bellcore [4], that complement the capabilities of the SCEs by supporting the specification and early validation of service requirements. Unfortunately, it is very hard to find more examples of commercially available tools of this kind.

2. INAP WRAPPER

To fill the gap left in the service creation process by the SCEs, High Definition Systems AB developed an environment called INAP Wrapper that provides capabilities for the prototyping, simulation and validation of IN-based services at the early stages of their development.

1.SCF3 is a trademark of Bellcore

INAP Wrapper is based on the Telelogic Tau tool suite [5] and the standard SDL model of the INAP CS1/2 protocol developed by ETSI [1]. The environment includes:

- SDL framework for IN service logic prototyping,
- executable SDL model of CS1/2 INAP and switched network,
- service, user profile, and network configuration management,
- service logic and IN-platform simulation (SCF, SSF, and CCF),
- service behaviour animation on the user and protocol levels.

The architecture of the INAP Wrapper environment is shown in Figure 2.

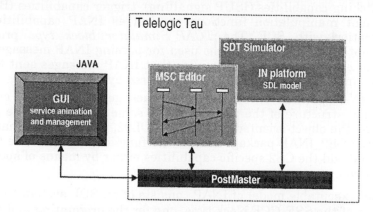

Figure 2. Architecture of INAP Wrapper

INAP Wrapper utilises the graphical editors, analysers and simulators of Telelogic Tau. These capabilities are used for adding new service prototypes to the SDL model as well as for simulating them. Both SDL and Telelogic Tau are widely used in the telecom industry, which should facilitate the incorporation of the INAP Wrapper into the service creation processes of service providers.

To facilitate service validation, the INAP Wrapper provides a GUI that animates the service and network behaviour at the user level. The GUI is used as an input device to the simulated IN system (e.g. dialling a number and other user actions). The GUI also includes functions for the management of prototyped services, user profiles, and a simulated network. The GUI is implemented in Java which makes it (fairly) platform independent.

3. SDL MODEL OF THE IN PLATFORM

The core of the INAP Wrapper is the executable INAP CS1/CS2 specification in SDL92 and ASN.1 developed by ETSI [1]. In order to implement a comprehensive *service prototyping framework*, the ETSI specification has been complemented by a number of SDL blocks simulating Switched Telephone Network, Service Management System and Service Control Function (SCF).

3.1. ETSI model of INAP CS1/2

The executable SDL specification of the INAP protocol created by ETSI covers parts of the IN standards [2] including Service Switching Function (SSF) and Call Control Function (CCF) as well as the subset of the TCAP protocol relevant to IN. The specification consists of three main parts.

1. *The ASN.1 definitions* contain the definitions of the arguments to the INAP operations as well as the various data types and constants used internally in the INAP specification. These definitions are used in the whole SDL system.

2. *The CS1_INAP package* provides the SDL specification of the CS1 INAP protocol. The package contains two block types, one implementing the SSF and CCF and the other implementing the TCAP. The *SSF_CCF block type* provides basic switching capabilities (ISUP signalling), trigger capabilities (BCSM) and call segment manipulation functions as well as INAP capabilities for the communication with SCF. The *TCAP_Simulator block type* provides the implementation of TCAP operations used for passing INAP messages between the SSF/CCF and the SCF. This implies that INAP messages sent to the SCF are packed into TCAP operations to be processed by the SCF.

3. *The CS2_INAP package* extends the CS1 package with the CS2 capabilities. The internal structure of the package is the same as for CS1. The package is made using the object-oriented features of SDL92, which means that the block types in the CS2_INAP package inherit the functionality from the CS1_INAP package and add the CS2 specific capabilities either by means of specialisation or redefinition.

The actual executable model of INAP consists of an SDL system that contains two instances of the SSF_CCF block type, one for the originating and one for the terminating side of the call, as well as an instance of the TCAP_Simulator block as shown in Figure 3. To be strict, there are two systems of this structure, one for CS1 and one for CS2.

Three internal channels interconnect the system blocks:

- *CS2_INAP_A / B* - INAP messages sent between SSFs and the TCAP Adapter,
- *IBI2* - ISUP operations sent between the originating and terminating CCFs.

Besides, the system has three *open interfaces* implemented as SDL channels connecting the blocks to the environment:

- *SCF* - the TCAP operations containing INAP messages sent to SCF,
- *SigCon_A / B* - the ISUP operations sent to and from the switched network,
- *MGT* - the TDP management operations sent from the management system.

The presence of open interfaces in the model implies that in order to simulate IN services in the ETSI model, the necessary signals have to be sent to the SDL system from the environment on all three interfaces. Considering the complexity of the TCAP, INAP and ISUP signalling, the simulation of call and service processing in the ETSI model is not a trivial task at all.

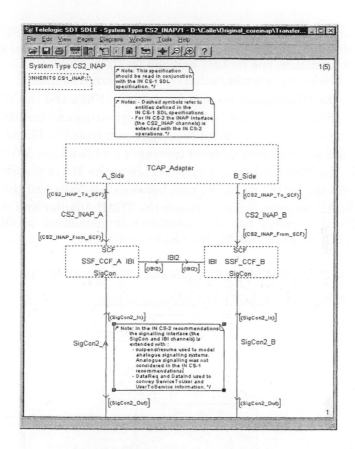

Figure 3. ETSI Model of INAP CS2

3.2. INAP Wrapper model of IN platform

In order to provide a service prototyping framework running on a simulated IN platform, the ETSI model of INAP has been extended by a number of SDL blocks simulating such functions as:

- *Service Control Function (SCF)* - service logic invocation and execution,
- *Telephone Switched Network (NET)* - terminal handling and call processing,
- *Management System (MS)* - service activation and network configuration.

These three additional SDL blocks together with the GUI blocks "wrap" the INAP model and make its simulation much simpler and user friendly.

The original ETSI model of INAP supports simulation of one originating call instance at a time. It does not provide for the individual arming of TDPs and activation of services per user (terminal). These constrains are not so important as long as the model serves for the protocol specification, which was its original application. However, they limit its applicability for service prototyping. Therefore, the call reference value handling and the TDP management had to be improved in the INAP Wrapper model.

24

The structure of the resulting model of IN platform is shown in Figure 4. As for the ETSI model, the INAP Wrapper system actually contains two systems with the same block structure, one for CS1 and one for CS2.

The system blocks are interconnected by nine internal channels:

- *INAP_A/B* - the INAP messages sent between the SSFs and the TCAP Adapter,
- *IBI* - the ISUP operations sent between the originating and terminating CCFs,
- *MS_SCF* - the service management messages sent from the MS to the SCF,
- *MS_NET* - the network management messages sent from the MS to the NET,
- *MGT_A/B* - the TDP arming messages sent from the MS to the SSFs,
- *SigCon_A/B* - the ISUP operations sent between the SSFs and the NET,
- *SCF* - the TCAP operations sent between the TCAP Adapter and the SCF.

Additionally, the system has two interfaces implemented as SDL channels (MS_GUI and SC_NET) connecting the blocks to the GUI

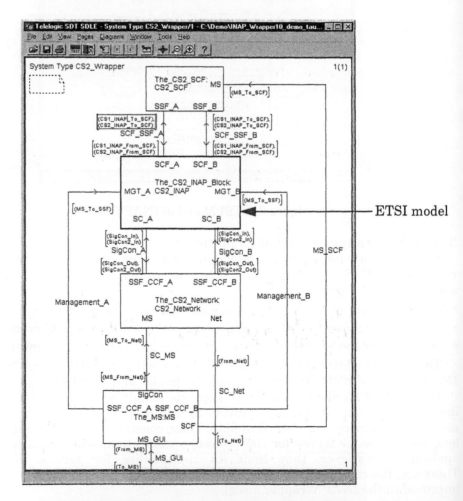

Figure 4. INAP Wrapper model of IN CS2 platform

4. SERVICE PROTOTYPING FRAMEWORK

INAP Wrapper is an open-ended environment. This means that the users can easily add new services and features (or rather their prototypes) into the SDL model and extend the capabilities of the model and the GUI. For instance, for a service that requires large volumes of data, an interface to an external database can be implemented in Java and SDL and added to the environment. To facilitate the process of adding new services into the model, INAP Wrapper provides a generic service prototyping framework.

The service prototyping framework is the crucial element of the INAP Wrapper environment. The logic of prototyped IN services can be specified in the SDL language and added to the simulated SCF, which corresponds to the service deployment in the real IN platform. Such newly deployed services also have to be defined in the INAP Wrapper management system and then activated and parameterised for particular users (see Section 5.2).

The framework consists of a number of SDL processes (or rather process types) located in the SCF_Simulator block type. The framework facilitates introduction of new services to the model by providing processes managing the service data and service logic interworking with the SSF, as well as a generic process type that can be specialised in order to implement the logic of particular services.

In the remaining subsections we will discuss the structure of the service prototyping framework and the procedure of introducing new services.

4.1. Prototyping framework architecture

The service prototyping framework is located in the SCF_Simulator block. shown in Figure 5, models the behaviour of the SCF and services. It consists of:

- service logic prototypes,
- generic signalling interface manager,
- database containing service parameters.

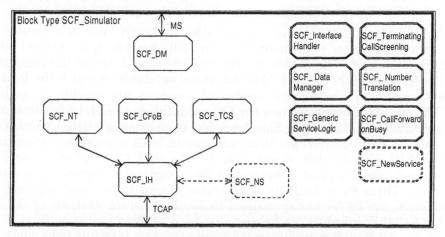

Figure 5. Structure of the service prototyping framework

The SCF_*SERVICENAME* (e.g. SCF_NumberTranslation, instantiated as SCF_NT) process types contain the SDL specifications of the service logic "deployed" in the system (we also call them *service prototypes*). Each IN service is represented by a separate SDL process type. Such a service logic process type is instantiated by the SCF_InterfaceHandler for every invocation of the service (i.e. after having received an InitialDP operation) and then fully controls the service processing. The service logic process instances communicate with the SSF through the SCF_InterfaceHandler.

The *SCF_InterfaceHandler* (instantiated as SCF_IH) process type has a number of functions. It acts as an interface to the SSF, and thus it is responsible for dispatching the INAP operations (or rather TCAP messages containing these operations) between the service logic processes and the SSF. It is also responsible for invoking the appropriate service logic when receiving an InitialDP operation from the SSF. The SCF_InterfaceHandler also provides the dialogue management as required by the TCAP Adapter. This involves adding new TCAP dialogues and mapping them to the corresponding service logic instances.

The *SCF_DataManager* (instantiated as SCF_DM) process type is a simple database storing service parameters dispatched to it by the MS. The database contains data, in a generic format, per service and user profile. The service parameters are sent to the SDL model when services are activated in the *Profile Windows* in the GUI (see Section 5.2). They are retrieved by the service logic instances through remote procedure calls (RPCs). This process also provides conversion procedures that translate generic service data into various formats.

4.2. Service prototyping process

Adding a new service into the INAP Wrapper model involves a number of steps:

1. creation of the service logic process,
2. deployment of the service logic in the SCF,
3. definition of the service in the management system,
4. activation and parameterisation of the service for particular users.

In the first step, the service logic specification (prototype) has to be *created*. The service specification is implemented as an SDL process type, located in the SCF_Simulator block (see Figure 5). The process should model the complete or partial behaviour of the service. More advanced solutions in which the logic of a complex service is modelled by a number of processes, are possible as well. The INAP Wrapper framework utilises the OO capabilities of SDL to facilitate rapid service prototyping. The SCF_Simulator block includes a virtual service type called *SCF_GenericServiceLogic* that implements basic capabilities necessary to create an SDL specification of service logic. The *SCF_GenericServiceLogic* type may be specialised (through inheritance) for a particular service, such as Call Forwarding, Three Party Call, etc. The service process types resulting from such specialisation can be further specialised to obtain different variants of the same service, e.g.Call Forwarding can be specialised to Call Forwarding on Busy.

In the second step, the newly created service process type has to be "deployed" in the simulated SCF. This means that the definition of the service process has to be added to the SCF_Simulator block and connected to the SCF_InterfaceHandler process by a signal route. Through the route the INAP operations are received from and sent to the simulated SSF. Since the TCAP protocol is applied for the communication between the SSF and the SCF, the service logic processes extract the INAP operations from the received TCAP messages and pack outgoing INAP operations into TCAP messages.

Moreover, the invocation (create statement) of the newly added service process has to be introduced into the SCF_InterfaceHandler process. This can be achieved either by the modification of the existing process graph or by the specialisation of the transition that follows the reception of the INAP operation (virtual input!). When steps one and two are completed, the SDL model has to be analysed again.

In the third step, a newly deployed service has to be *defined* in the service management function provided in the INAP Wrapper GUI (see Section 5.2). Except for giving the service its *name* and *acronym*, this activity comprises the selection of the *service key* that will represent the service in the INAP operations and the *TDP* in which the service will be triggered. Please note that this operation only defines the new service in the Management System (in the GUI) and does not update any data in the SDL model.

Finally, the new service has to be *activated and parameterised* for particular users (terminals). This is done in the user profile management function provided in the INAP Wrapper GUI (see Section 5.2). As mentioned earlier, INAP Wrapper allows for flexible activation and parameterisation of the services. This means that one service can be activated with different parameters for different users as well as that a number of different services can be activated for one user. The services can also be deactivated and their parameters can be modified as needed.

The activation of a service in the GUI results in sending the service parameters to the Management System (MS) block in the SDL model. The parameters are then dispatched to the SCF_Simulator and eventually stored in the SCF_DataManager process. Likewise, the service triggering information is sent to the MS block, dispatched to the originating or terminating SSF_CCF block, and stored there.

5. SERVICE SIMULATION AND ANIMATION

The INAP Wrapper SDL system as such is self-contained and could, in theory, be simulated strictly from the SDT Simulator UI. In practice this would not be very convenient and practical. First, it would require that the user manually sends the signals from the Simulator UI to the SDL system. This is a tedious and error-prone process that requires the user to have detailed knowledge of the signal interface between the SDL system and the environment.

Second, the only way of showing the dynamic behaviour of the simulation is to generate an MSC trace from the simulation. Considering the complexity of the system, these MSC traces might become huge and hard to understand.

5.1. Graphical user interface to SDL model

In order to enable effective and efficient validation of service prototypes INAP Wrapper provides a Graphical User Interface (GUI) for the simulated model of IN platform. The GUI includes the capabilities for network and service simulation and animation at the user level, which makes the usage of the INAP Wrapper much more easy and user friendly. The GUI also contains the functions for managing services and user profiles.

The INAP Wrapper GUI has been implemented in Java, which makes it platform independent. The Java application communicates with the SDT Simulator through the *PostMaster* (a module of Telelogic Tau that links different tools included in the environment) as shown in Figure 2.

5.2. User-level animation

The simulated network is represented in the GUI by two types of windows:
* *Network window* showing the overall network state,
* *Terminal window* showing the state of one terminal.

The network window symbolically presents the simulated network and the activated telephone terminals (see Figure 6 below). Since it reflects the state of the SDL system, it can be perceived as an animation of service and network behaviour on the user level. The number of the terminals can be selected during the system start-up.

By clicking on a selected terminal icon in the network window one can open a terminal window. Each terminal has its own window associated with its icon in the network window. The window represents the sate of a telephone terminal.

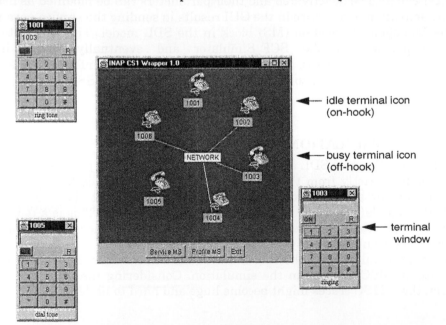

Figure 6. Graphical representation of telephone network and terminals

The service and network animation at the user level can be used for early service validation. Today, the customer can see for the first time how an IN service works after the service has been implemented. This usually takes several months after the preliminary service requirements have been specified. By animating the prototyped services the designers can assess much earlier if the service behaviour fulfils the requirements. The animated service prototypes can be also directly demonstrated to the customers and the end users. Such demonstrations can provide quick feedback and contribute to the improvement of the service requirements specification. In consequence, the quality of the service (as a measure of the user's satisfaction) will be also improved.

INAP Wrapper enables simultaneous simulation of different services in different configurations and with different parameters. This capability can be utilised for detecting undesired service interactions [3]. The service designers can simulate scenarios including different services or different instances of the same service in order to see if the required service properties are not violated.

5.3. System-level animation

The system-level details of the IN call processing and service execution can be observed in the MSC Editor (part of Telelogic Tau) as shown in Figure 7. The MSC Editor receives the INAP, TCAP and ISUP messages (with parameters) generated during simulation, and produces on-line a Message Sequence Chart (MSC).

This feature can be used for the validation of particular INAP designs (in SDL) and for training in the INAP protocol. The generated MSCs can also be used as test purposes for the AutoLink tool (part of Telelogic Tau). From the MSCs, the tool can automatically generate test cases in TTCN that can then be applied for the testing of the actual service product.

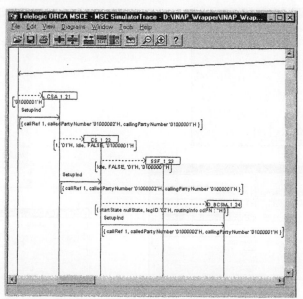

Figure 7. MSC generated from service simulation

5.4. Service management functions

The network window also contains a number of buttons for activating the management functions of the INAP Wrapper GUI. By pressing the *Profile MS* button in the network window, the *Profile Management* window can be opened, see Figure 8. This window lists all terminals in the simulated network together with their corresponding telephone numbers.

By clicking on the *Profile* button next to a telephone number the user *Profile* window will appear. The window displays all services available to the user. A service is activated or deactivated by clicking the toggle box left of the service name. Service data is entered in the text box to the right of the service name. When all required modifications of the service profile are done, they have to be confirmed by pressing the *Commit* button. This causes the services to be activated/deactivated in the SDL model (see Section 4.2).

By pressing the *Service MS* button in the network window, the *Service Management* window can be opened, see Figure 8 below. This window lists all services defined in the system. The actual service logic must have been added previously ("deployed") in the SDL system.

A new service can be defined by pressing the *Activate Service* button. The *Add Service* window enables the user to define a new service in the system by entering the service key, service name, service acronym and service TDP in the corresponding input fields. The TDP is chosen from a list of all available TDPs and specifies which TDP should be armed in order to invoke the service. When all parameters are entered, the new service is added by pressing the *Commit* button. The service will then appear in the list displayed in the *Service Management* window.

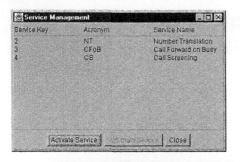
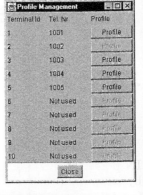
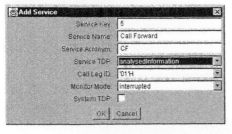

Figure 8. Service and user profile management functions

6. CONCLUSIONS

The existing SCEs offer limited support for the specification and validation of IN services. Since the early stages of the service creation process remain unsupported they are costly and time consuming. This is a concern to both telecom vendors and network operators that develop IN services.

The INAP Wrapper environment provides capabilities for IN service prototyping and validation. The environment is based on the standard SDL model of the INAP CS1/2 extended by the simulated switched network, service management, and service control function.

The service prototyping framework of INAP Wrapper makes the introduction of new services into the SDL model relatively easy. The user friendly GUI allows for animation of service behaviour at the user level and provides service and network management functions. The open-ended character of the environment allows the users to extend the capabilities of both the SDL model and the GUI.

Though INAP Wrapper was originally designed to facilitate IN service *prototyping and validation*, it may be used for various other purposes such as:

- *Service interaction detection.* Undesired service interaction can be detected by using the INAP Wrapper's capability of the parallel simulation of different services or different instances of the same service.

- *Service demonstrations for customers.* The animation capabilities in the GUI can be used as a means of demonstrating new services to prospective customers in a comprehensible way. This gives quick feedback to the service designers, which might be regarded as a part of early service validation.

- *Automated test-case generation.* With the help of the AutoLink tool, TTCN test cases can be automatically generated from the MSCs that have been produced during the service simulation. Such test cases can then be applied to test the actual IN services.

- *Validation of INAP CS1/2 design.* The INAP Wrapper modules surrounding the INAP model can be used to validate a real design of INAP CS2 in SDL. This also includes validation of the SDL specifications of the INAP protocol for particular IN platforms.

- *INAP CS2 training.* The INAP Wrapper system can be used as an educational tool for the INAP protocol and the whole IN concept. A good and quick way to learn the protocol is to simulate the SDL model of IN services and platform and analyse the MSC traces.

The further development of the INAP Wrapper will aim at covering the whole IN platform by adding an SDL model of the SRF (user interaction functions) and by extending the model of the SCF. Besides, it is planned to develop SDL models (prototypes) of typical IN services such as Freephone, Credit Cart Calling, or Virtual Private Network.

High Definition Systems also plans to start the development of similar environments for the IP telephony and other future service platforms.

REFERENCES

1. EN 301 140-1: *Intelligent Network (IN); Intelligent Network Application Protocol (INAP); Capability Set 2 (CS2); Part 1: Protocol specification*, ETSI, March 1998.

2. ITU-T Q.122x-series. *Recommendations for Intelligent Network, CS-2*, ITU-T, March 1993.

3. K. Kimbler and W. Bouma editors. *Feature Interaction in Telecommunications and Software Systems V*, IOS Press, 1998.

4. J. Cameron, K. Cheng, S. Gallagher, J. Lin, P. Russo, D. Sobirk. *Next Generation Service Creation: Process, Methodology and Tool Integration,* in Feature Interaction in Telecommunications and Software Systems V, IOS Press, 1998.

5. Telelogic Tau 3.4, Telelogic AB, 1998

GLOSSARY

ASN.1	Abstract Syntax Notation One
BCSM	Basic Call State Model
CCAF	Call Control Agent Function
CCF	Call Control Function
CS1	Capability Set 1
CS2	Capability Set 2
DP	Detection Point
ETSI	European Telecommunications Standards Institute
GUI	Graphical User Interface
IN	Intelligent Network
INAP	Intelligent Network Application Protocol
IP	Internet Protocol
ISUP	ISDN User Part
MSC	Message Sequence Chart
OO	Object-Oriented
RPC	Remote Procedure Call
SCE	Service Creation Environment
SCF	Service Control Function
SDL	Specification and Description Language
SRF	Special Resource Function
SSF	Service Switching Function
TCAP	Transaction Capabilities Application Part
TDP	Trigger Detection Point
TINA	Telecommunication Information Network Architecture
TTCN	Tree and Tabular Combined Notation

SDL'99 : The Next Millennium
R. Dssouli, G.v. Bochmann and Y. Lahav, editors
©1999 Elsevier Science B.V. All rights reserved

Evaluating an SDL Framework for AXE Development

Stein Erik Ellevseth, Birger Møller-Pedersen

stein.erik.ellevseth@ericsson.no, birger.moller-pedersen@ericsson.no

Applied Research Center, Ericsson AS, P.O.Box 34, N-1361 Billingstad, Norway

Abstract

The paper presents a framework approach to the specification of AXE applications in SDL. AXE is the widely used public switching system developed by Ericsson. The framework captures the application specific and target specific properties of AXE applications by packages of predefined SDL types. The AXE developer will, building on top of these types, work in an AXE framework and work in pure SDL extended with types. It is also indicated how certain kinds of design rules can be represented in the framework. The concept of framework is based upon previous experiences with SDL, where code generation to Plex from SDL is controlled by directives. The experiences achieved so far are limited but nevertheless encouraging in achieving efficient reuse of common functionality. The scope of the evaluation have been on making simulation models. Future work will be on code generation and targeting to alternative platforms. In a re-engineering context, the concept of an SDL frameworks forces the designer to think in terms of design instead of documenting the implementation by the use of SDL. The latter is the usual process when an application system is re-engineered from target code to an SDL description.

Keywords: SDL, framework, reuse, reverse engineering.

1 Introduction

Introducing SDL into organisations like the AXE development is a process of moving from an implementation oriented development to design orientation. The first natural step for an existing product and/or existing team is to document existing software using SDL by regenerating the system from design documentation and the Plex code. This is not always a straight forward process. Phrases like *It is easier to program PLEX in PLEX than in SDL* and *SDL is not a very efficient programming language* is a very common experience from first time SDL users. Products tend to establish their own concepts of implementation based on the concepts offered from the programming language in use. Although large parts of the Plex code can be regenerated, the use of directives may lead to unreadable SDL specifications, and secondly may lead designers to think in implementation in terms of Plex instead of SDL.

The identification, definition and packaging of AXE concepts in SDL seeks to avoid these problems. The SDL language have tried to capture the most common needs for designing reactive system and can also be seen upon as *best practice*. Learning to use these concepts is a cumbersome process which needs attention, training and support. However, by defining a framework of common functionality, several obstacles can be overcome.

The framework approach can be applied to any level of design. In [1] it is applied on system level. In this paper the approach is applied to parts of a system, the reason being that the approach is evaluated in a configuration where complete systems are not made, but rather parts of existing systems.

The evaluation project define a subset of AXE infrastructure and behaviour to be included in the first version of the AXE SDL Framework to be evaluated. It contains types of services, processes and blocks as building blocks to build AXE applications. Most of the behaviour is encapsulated in services in order to be able to easily configure.

2 What is a Framework?

The difference between a library and a framework is well-known: While a library is a collection of related classes, a framework embodies a generic design with some default functionality. Specific applications are obtained by specialising the framework. Frameworks has greater potential for large-scale re-use, but they are harder to make than libraries.

Libraries and frameworks are usually associated with programming languages. When specification or modelling (e.g. in UML) is applied prior to implementation, this does normally not include the design of the whole application. This is first done in the implementation language, with the implication that framework-thinking is only relevant then. This paper reports from an experiment on defining frameworks at the specification/modelling level.

An application will have mainly two aspects: application- and infrastructure (platform- implementation)- specific aspects. Frameworks can be made in order to capture either of these, or both, in such a way that any of these can be specialised. Specialising the application-specific aspects give a new application with the same infrastructure part.

Application specific and infrastructure specific parts of a system can be defined in a framework of types encapsulating structure and behaviour. It is not obvious for the first time because of the overhead of making the framework reusable. However, productivity should increase every time the framework is being reused. Verification can be simplified by doing it once for the framework and not in every delivered instance of systems.

SDL systems contains concepts of application specific and infrastructure specific character which can be defined in a framework. A framework for a whole family of applications with the same structure can be defined by a *system type* in SDL, and a specific application of the framework by a *subtype* of the system type. The framework will have *virtual types* for those components that should be adapted to specific applications of the system type. These virtual types will be *redefined* when the framework is used as a supertype when defining the system type for a given application.

The same techniques can, however, also be applied to parts of systems. In SDL this means to blocks. A block in SDL captures structure by means of interconnected sets of processes, and behavior by means of these processes. The types of these process types can be defined as virtual types, so that they can be redefined for special applications, maintaining the structure imposed by the block type.

The framework being investigated in the AXE Framework approach is a framework that shall make it possible to port SDL applications from one platform (e.g. for simulation) to another platform for code generation - without changing the SDL application specifications. This kind

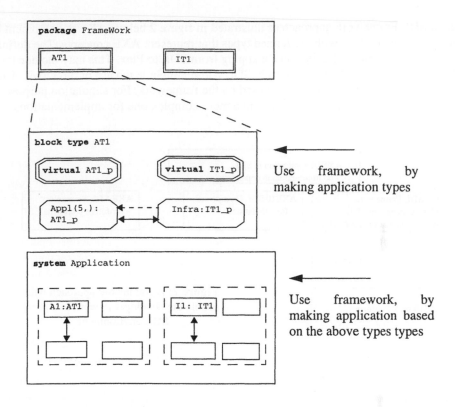

Figure 1: A framework as a package of block types with inherent structure

of framework is more or less a collection of types. The applications as such do not have a common, fixed architecture coming from the framework, but parts of the applications may have fixed architecture.

Even though the framework is just a collection of types, we still want special frameworks for the different situations. On the other hand, as seen from the applications, these special frameworks shall provide the same types, with the same names and interfaces, as the general framework.

3 The approach

The purpose of the AXE SDL Framework is to support and simplify design of AXE10 applications using SDL by providing support for necessary common AXE10 mechanisms and design rules. This is done in a way that simplifies the task of application designers, enabling applications to be fully designed, simulated and analysed using SDL. When the verification of the system is completed, the implementation is made that finally enables automatic generation of performant Plex code.

With an SDL Framework approach as illustrated in figure 2 below, AXE development is done in pure SDL "extended" with predefined types that represent AXE concepts. The definition of the AXE SDL Framework relies on a mapping from SDL to Plex. This may include the use of SDL directives, but AXE applications in SDL will *not* include the use of directives. The developer will define the AXE application based on the framework. For simulation purpose the developer will use a simplified variant and a more complex one for implementation.

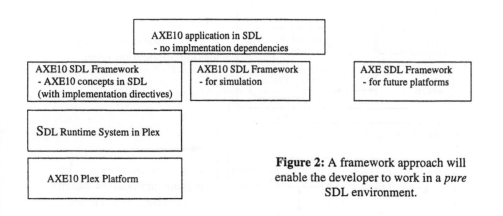

Figure 2: A framework approach will enable the developer to work in a *pure* SDL environment.

4 The principles

Application Modules, the AXE structuring concept, contains a structure of blocks in which behaviour in an AXE system is encapsulated. This is also the scope of the SDL Framework for AXE development. There are common functionality in these blocks which are described as Design Rules which each designer have to include during design and implementation. By capturing the commonalities in a framework the design, implementation and verification can be simplified significantly.

A typical application will have several concepts which formal languages normally do not have mechanisms for. Such functionality is related to common behaviour for several processes like creation and allocation of individuals, initialization at start-up, configuration of size of resources, addressing and selecting (addressing) individuals during processing. In traditional system development, specific guidelines will be developed to handle these. However, they very often will be implemented different between systems and also inside systems.

The traditional AXE implementation model for handling individuals are as collection of records in arrays, as illustrated in figure 3. This solution is very common, and simplify the selection of individuals by the use of traditional techniques like scanning, indexing and hashing. However, a large system based on this principle can be very complex and difficult to understand.

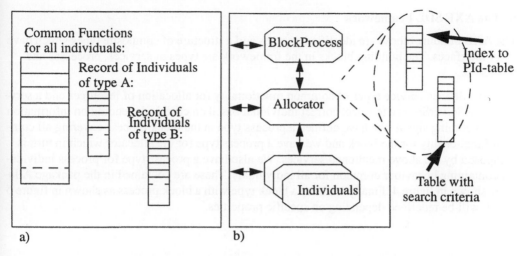

Figure 3: a) A part of a system of common functionality and records of individuals encapsulated in an AXE block. b)In SDL common functionality of the block is encapsulated in the block process and in the allocator for each individual process set.

An SDL system as illustrated in figure 3 encapsulates the individuals in a process set together with behaviour related to this individual.

In the AXE block the *Block process* encapsulates all common functionality in the block related to routing of incoming messages to the correct type of individual, Start/Restart functionality, System Configuration, etc. The *Allocator process* will contain common functions to create, allocate and identify individuals and manage individuals of the same kind. There will be information mapping indexes to PId´s and vice verse. In addition, information to select an individual based of application specific criteria will be stored in the Allocator. The *Individual processes* will contain the behaviour specific for the application.

38

5 The AXE SDL Framework

The AXE building blocks are identified as types and a structure of composite types which have strict interfaces. The building blocks in the framework are types of services, processes and blocks.

We have defined service types of common functionality for allocation of resources and a service NameServerService to select correct individual based on criteria depending on information in the incoming signal. We have defined a process type in the block process covering all common functionality for the block and we have a process type for the allocator which in turn is composed by the above mentioned services. We also have a process type for process individuals containing behaviour common for all individuals. These are contained in the package Allocator shown in figure 4. Finally we have a block type with a block process as shown in figure 5 which will be redefined depending on specific properties.

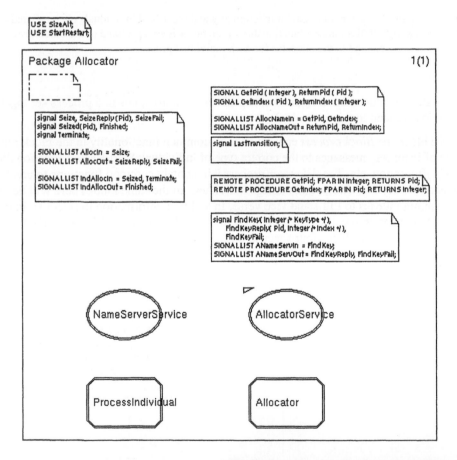

Figure 4: A framework will consist of types.
This is the contents of the Package Allocator

The AXE designer will be able to use these predefined types of blocks, processes and services. If these do not satisfy the requirements, new types can be defined by means of inheritance.

The fact that all AXE blocks have a special process is captured by the block type axe_block is illustrated in figure 5. As the definition of the block process depend on the actual block, it is defined as virtual, but minimal requirements on general signals coming to any AXE block are specified.

Further shown in figure 5 is gates that have been added. These have been designed for specific purposes. It is shown here that there are dedicated signal routes for specific properties like StartRestart (StaRe) and SizeAlteration (SAE). This principle is followed throughout the framework and the applications using the framework. However, in this application the block type is not used because not only the block type has to be redefined, but also additional functionality added. Therefore a complete new block process has to be defined, using the block type as a template in order to conform to the interface.

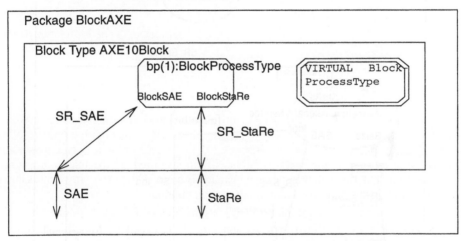

Figure 5: The general block type axe_block.

40

The figure 6 is illustrating how a process type Allocator can be a composition of the service types NameServerService and AllocationService. In this case the NameServerService is not connected to the environment, because it is not used in this application. If the signal routes were connected, the application had to connect the gates related to this service, which was not the case with this application.

The gates Seize, Ind, SAE and StaRe have been designed for specific purposes. Here the additional signal routes Seize and Ind are introduced, for seizure and allocation of individual processes which this allocator handles.

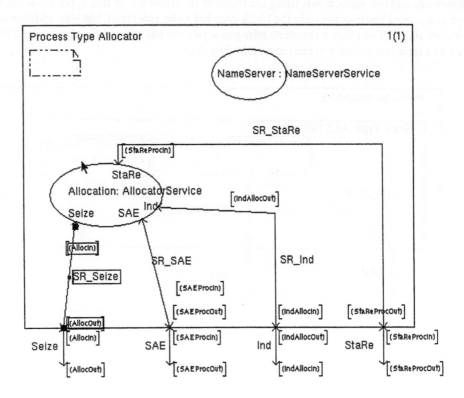

Figure 6: The process type Allocator with the service types with predefined allocation functionality. (Name server is not in use).

In figure 7 the contents of the service type AllocatorService is illustrated. This type is used by all allocator process types. The details of the content of the type is showing mandatory functionality wrt. initialization and seizure of individuals. The initialization can be redefined.

The gates Seize, Ind, StaRe, StaReInd, Name and SAE have been designed for specific purposes. The gate Seize is dedicated signals connected with seizure (allocation) of individuals while the Start-gate is dedicated start, restart and initialization of process sets and individual. It is useful to split into different gates because the connected channels and signal routes not always will be connected to a process type of the same kind.

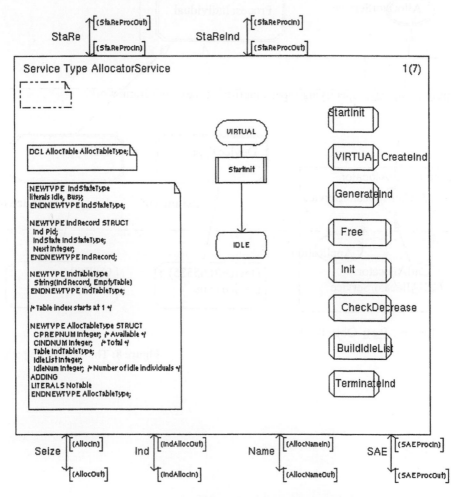

Figure 7: The service type AllocatorService with details

The figure 8 is describing describe the inheritance tree used in the use of this framework. Only parts of the framework is shown, and is illustrating how types in the framework are redefined and/or functionality is added, and finally making up the processes in the application. This way

42

of presenting inheritance will be needed in tools to support a framework approach in order for the user to have sufficient overview to understand the framework and the application.

Framework part: General types

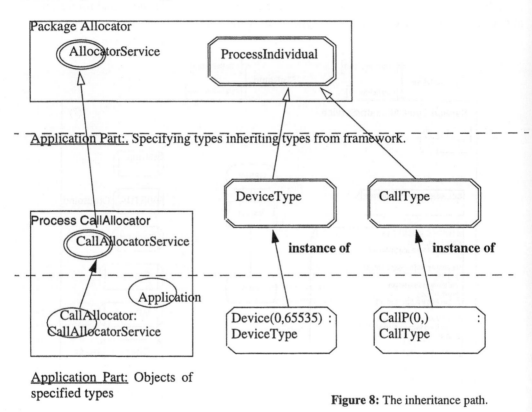

Application Part: Objects of specified types

Figure 8: The inheritance path.

6 The application

The application used utilized most of the framework utilities Block Process, Allocator, Process Individual as shown in figure 9 below.

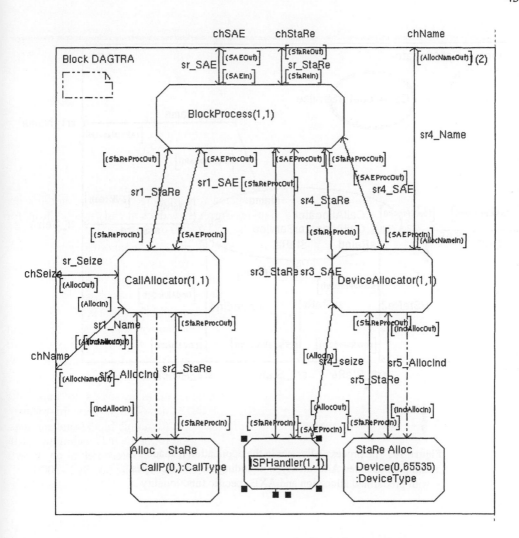

Figure 9: The structure of the application block DAGTRA.

The CallAllocator, DeviceAllocator is composed by redefining the procedure CreateInd in the service AllocatorService inherits from the framework (package Allocator). The process ISPHandler is a process which there is no types to reuse in this version of the framework.This process is containing the subscriber catalogue handling the identification, storing, changing and deleting subscribers connected to the system. If needed it may be available in future framework if and when general information can be encapsulated. CallType and DeviceType inherits the type ProcessIndividual not shown here from the framework (in the package Allocator) and are adding application relevant design.

44

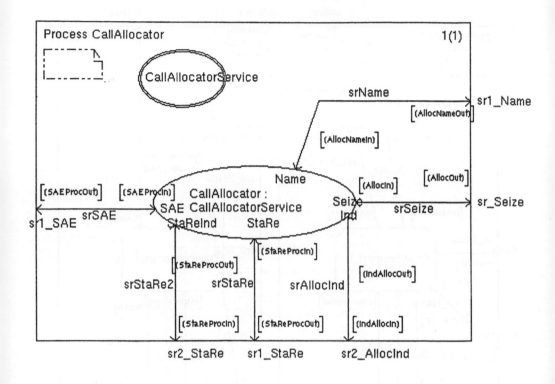

Figure 10: The process Allocator in the application is made by
making a dedicated Allocator type including the service types
with predefined allocation and AXE specific functionality

The figure 11 below shows how it is possible to redefine and add functionality to the service typ
AllocatorService. The service type which is being redefined is shown in figure 7. In fact it is red
fined and finalized which means it cannot be redefined after being finalized. The virtual procedure CreateInd is also finalized.

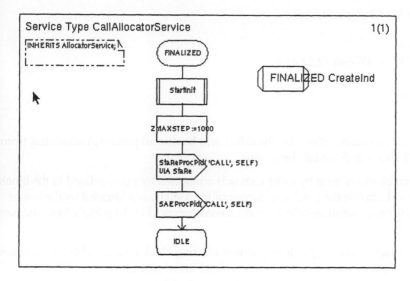

Figure 11: The service type CallAllocatorService

7 Design Rules

The introduction of types may also capture the design rules of the AXE software system. There are many obvious advantages implementing these in a framework. First, the designer do not need to take care of making sure that the design rules are followed. Second, the verification of whether the design rules have been followed is simplified through the verification of the framework. Third, this verification is done once for the system family instead for each instance deliverable. As an example consider the design rule for termination of forlopp adapted processes:

"If a block is forlopp adapted the individual processes should call the procedure FLLeave before terminating".

As a design rule, the developer has to remember to specify the following in all processes that are forlopp adapted:

> *process IP1;*
> ...
> *state WaitTerm*
> *input TERMINATE call FLLEAVE;*
> *endprocess*

The design rule may alternatively be represented by specifying the input transition as part of the FORLOPPadaptedProcess process type:

> *process type FORLOPPadaptedProcess;*
> ...

procedure FORLOPP_RESTART; ...

...

state WaitTerm
   input TERMINATE call FLLEAVE;
endstate;
endprocess type;

As SDL supports inheritance of behaviour, the effect will be that all processes inheriting from FORLOPPadaptedProcess will get this behaviour.

Addressing between blocks is done by using channels connected by gates defined in the block types in the framework. Inside the blocks, instances of individuals is addressed by the use of PIds. The allocator for each set of individuals have a nameserver to look up PId´s from indexes and vice verse.

The figure 9 shows that the block type already have a existing block reference because a block shall always have a block process. The allocators and the individuals, however, will vary, depending on the application.

8 Experiences, Benefits and Pitfalls

Designing applications based on SDL frameworks will ease design, reduce verification/validation/testing by simulation and code generation. Error rates will also be reduced through the use of predefined, verified functionality. Training can also be reduced because the need for detailed target information is not needed for all engineers. Only the knowledge of SDL and how to use frameworks will be needed.

In the framework, application specific and general functionality can be encapsulated in order to hide implementation details. This makes it possible for the designer to work in a pure SDL environment, learning details of the application by using the framework. It will be possible to do early verification and simulation of properties which are only available on the target platform.

However, due to the implementation orientation the maturity of reverse engineering to higher level of representation is usually done stepwise depending on knowledge. The following steps seems to be *natural* to follow:

1. Document legacy code based on implementation.

2. Make a formal design. Use the language as intended.

3. Use the formal design formally.

The first step is usually to use the SDL language as an implementation language. The use of frameworks forces the designer to think in terms of design and the effort in step 1 can be omitted or heavily reduced.

SDL frameworks do not give its benefits easily. Before it is possible to use it has to be created. This demand effort and qualified people both on the SDL language and on the AXE application technology it self. And it is not until the framework have been reused more than two or three times the effort to create it have been gained.

Incorporating AXE10 specific concepts in the framework and use these in the pure SDL application specification may imply carry over the AXE specifics to new platforms. This is possible if the AXE specific concepts are generalised. Notions like allocators and name servers are rather general, and are really not AXE specific. AXE specific concepts may not be valid on new platforms, or rather they would have another form or solution. However, the existing code generator will be modified to take care of this since Plex probably will not be supported on new platforms.

Instead of teaching people both AXE10, Plex and full SDL, they are taught SDL based upon the framework concept. The concepts in the framework will provide them with the concepts of AXE they need. They do not have to learn Plex, and the framework approach implies a certain way of using SDL, so people only have to learn that way.

The present version of the evaluated framework consists of the AXE specific functionality Start Restart and Size Alteration and the general functionality allocation and a nameserver. This is the basic functionality needed to start the system. A skeleton was made to be able run the start-up procedures and configure the size of the system by the AXE specific functionality SizeAlteration. This skeleton was used when the functionality from the application was added.

9 Further Work

The main goal of this project was to evaluate whether the concept of developing an SDL framework that encapsulates AXE specific properties is a feasible approach for design, simulation and analysis of AXE applications. The scope was therefore to make a prototype of limited AXE specific functionality use it on an existing AXE application described in SDL. The scope of this evaluation was therefore limited to simulation only.

Future work on this work will be on making a flexible code generator hiding directives in the framework and to add more AXE specific properties to investigate the usability, and finally to pilot in real environments.

It will be useful to develop packages for future platforms and target languages. When proved successful deployment through piloting in real projects will be done.

With Code generation to Plex and possibly to other embedded target platforms it is necessary to evaluate the efficiency of the re-engineered AXE specific properties and if the general mechanisms for identification and allocation of individuals is acceptable compared to the existing written in target language.

In order for this development approach to be flexible and efficient, improvements are needed both in the language, but most of all in the tools support.

10 Conclusion

SDL frameworks to capture AXE functionality can be very useful to capture common functionality and to verify its behaviour. The experiences so far are limited since this approach have not yet been used in a real project. However, real application modules have been used which already had been designed in SDL. Some of them was also executed (simulated in SDL). Observations from this stage in the evaluation show that the notion of a framework

48

forces the designer to regenerate the design architecture and lifting it up from a rather implementation and hardware-oriented description to make a design description which hides implementation details in the framework.

An SDL framework is a feasible approach and have the potential to be efficient for design and implementation. However, as always in the work of applying higher level of abstractions and the use of formal languages, there will be a trade-off between development efficiency and application efficiency.

References

1. Frameworks by means of virtual types- exemplified by SDL. Rolv Bræk, Birger Møller-Pedersen, FORTE/PSTV´98

Session II

Deriving SDL

)L'99 : The Next Millennium
Dssouli, G.v. Bochmann and Y. Lahav, editors
1999 Elsevier Science B.V. All rights reserved

'ew Results on Deriving SDL Specifications from MSCs[*]

. M. Abdalla[1], F. Khendek[1] and G. Butler[2]
)epartment of Electrical and Computer Engineering
)epartment of Computer Science
)ncordia University
·55, De Maisonneuve W., Montréal, Canada H3G 1M8
hendek/mm_abdal@ece.concordia.ca, gregb@cs.concordia.ca}

e have developed an approach for the derivation of SDL specifications from MSCs. The
chitecture of the target system is given with the MSCs as input to the derivation algorithm. In
is paper, we report on new results on this derivation and the *MSC2SDL* tool, which has been
erfaced with a commercial tool. We report on new issues related to multiple instances of a
ocess, multiple instances of a message from different processes, SDL process identifiers,
dressing schemes as well as the MSCs implementability issue and its implementation.

INTRODUCTION

e MSC (Message Sequence Charts) [1, 2] and SDL (Specification & Description Language)
languages are widely used within the telecommunications industry. MSC is used at the
quirement phase to capture the system requirements through message exchange scenarios
tween concurrent processes. SDL is used at the design phase to capture the (abstract or
tailed) system behavior and architecture. An important activity in the software engineering
ocess is the validation of each phase product against the previous phase product. In order to
oid or at least ease the validation process, we have introduced in [4] an algorithm for the
neration of SDL behavior specification from a bMSC. Contrarily to [10, 11], the derivation is
ven by the target architecture of the system. This architecture is given as input with the MSC.
e behaviors of the derived processes depend on the target architecture.

[5], we have reported about our initial results on the derivation of SDL specifications from
ASCs. We have presented few important issues, such as *compatibility* between the MSCs
mposing the HMSC as well as the *implementability* of the HMSC, that need to be considered.

is research was partly supported by the National Sciences and Engineering Research Council of Canada (NSERC) and
nds pour la Formation des Chercheurs et l'Aide à la Recherche du Québec (FCAR).

In this paper, we describe the *MSC2SDL* tool, which has been interfaced with ObjectGeode [*
We also report on the new theoretical development such as semantic differences between SI
and MSC, the implementability issue and its implementation. This paper is structured as follow
The next section describes the *MSC2SDL* tool. In the third section, we report about ne
important issues we had to deal with during the translation of bMSCs. Section 4 is devoted
HMSC, the implementability issue and its implementation within the tool. In Section 5, v
conclude.

2. MSC2SDL TOOL

The *MSC2SDL* tool (see Figure 1) works in a stand-alone workframe. We have interfaced the to
with ObjectGeode [9]. The *MSC2SDL* tool can be interfaced with any SDL/MSC tool, whi
follows the standard internal representation for graphical MSC/SDL specifications. *MSC2SI*
can be invoked from ObjectGeode project manager window. Our tool accepts ObjectGeo
internal representations for both MSCs and SDL architecture, and produces the correspondi
SDL behavior for the processes using the standard internal graphical representation.

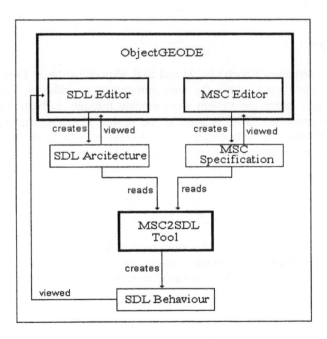

Figure 1. Interfacing *MSC2SDL* with ObjectGeode.

1e current implementation can handle any bMSC, which may contain *instances, exchange essages, conditions, timers, actions, coregions and instance creation*. The SDL architecture is ven as a normal SDL specification. However the behavior of the processes in this specification not defined. These behaviors are generated automatically. Through the following example, we 1ll describe the functionality of the *MSC2DL* tool. As input the tool takes an MSC specification shown in Figure 2 for instance and an SDL architecture as illustrated in Figure 3. These two ecifications are provided through the ObjectGeode MSC/SDL editors. The *MSC2SDL* tool rforms its functions on the files created by ObjectGeode for the internal representation of the SC and the SDL architecture. The *MSC2SDL* tool checks for consistency between the MSC ecification and the SDL architecture, i.e. for each MSC process there is a corresponding SDL ocess and there is a route to convey each MSC message between the corresponding processes. 1ce the consistency has been confirmed, the algorithm for the generation of SDL code from SC is performed [4]. It starts by creating the Event Order Table and the Occupancy Table [4].

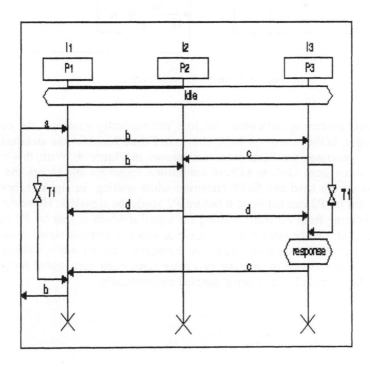

Figure 2. A bMSC example.

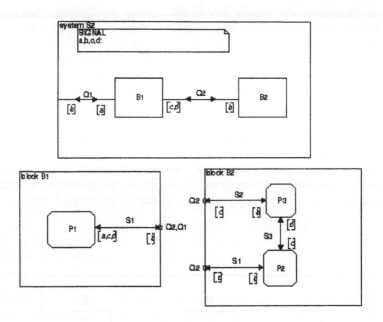

Figure 3. An SDL architecture.

Next, for each MSC process specification, the tool automatically generates the correspondir SDL process behavior. In the case of the MSC shown in Figure 2 and for the architecture given Figure 3, the tool generates the SDL processes shown in Figure 4. With this example, w illustrate the translation from MSC to SDL of conditions, messages and timers. As we can se for process *P1*, we do not need any *SAVE* construct while waiting for signal *a*, because both sent by *P2* and c sent by *P3* can not be sent before *P1* sends the signals *b*. However, we need save the signal *c* coming from *P3* while waiting for signal *d* which is sent by *P2* because thes signals are independent. On the other hand, we have to expect a timeout signal from *T1* at state *S1* and *S2*. For process *P2*, we have to save signal *b* coming from *P1* while waiting for signal sent by *P3*. In addition, we need to save the *PID* after consuming each signal for potential us Notice that the declarations in Figure 4 are generated automatically.

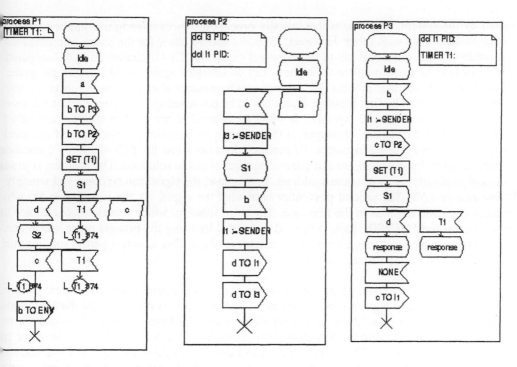

Figure 4. Derived SDL process behaviors.

MSC TO SDL TRANSLATION ISSUES

we have reported in [4], many of the MSC constructs are translated into SDL constructs in a straightforward manner. Among them, we list actions, conditions, instance creation and termination, message sending and receiving. However, few differences between these two languages, render the translation of certain concepts thornier than it may appear. In this section, we report on certain partly solved or unsolved problems.

Process instance identification and addressing

graphical MSC specification illustrates explicitly the message exchange between instances. The sender and receiver of any message are explicit in the MSCs without using any addressing or identification scheme. Unfortunately, it is not case for SDL. In the case where a signal can be sent to different instances, we have to specify explicitly the receiver. The SDL recommendation states that a process *Pi* instance identifier (*PID*) is known to another process *Pj* instance only after consuming a signal sent by that process *Pi* instance, through the predefined expression *sender*, except for the predefined identifiers such as *itself, offspring* and *parent* when *Pi* is not

created by the system. This means that initially process instances have to use implicit address
to communicate with each other. However, SDL-92 and 96 allow for the usage of process nar
as an address when the signal has to be addressed explicitly. This limitation in SDL compared
MSC may lead to an incomplete translation. Let us consider again the MSC example given
Figure 2, we can see that process *P1* instance sends message *b* to process *P3* instance and
process *P2* instance. The first message *b* sent has to be conveyed to *P3* instance while the seco
one has to be conveyed to *P2* instance. In order to assure that, we need to specify explicitly t
PIDs of *P2* and *P3* instances. However, at this point in its behavior *P1* instance did not recei
any message from *P3* or *P2* instances. *P1* instance does not know the *PID* of *P3* or *P2* instance
In order to solve this problem, we can enumerate three possible solutions. The first one is to se
the signal implicitly, i.e. without any address. In this case, the signal can be conveyed wrongly
P2 instance or *ENV*. The second possibility is to send the signal via the *signalroute S1*, whi
produces the same result as in the first case. The third solution, which represents our choice a
we use within the *MSC2SDL* tool, is to send the signal by using the process name which assu
that the signal is received only by one of the instances of *P3*. This is only a partial solution, sin
b can be received by any instance of process *P3*.

A similar situation may arise, when two instances of the same process or two different process
send the same signal to a given process instance. This situation is illustrated by the MSC shov
in Figure 5. In fact, while *P2* instance is waiting for signal *x* from process *P1* instance, it m
consume the signal *x* coming from process *P3* instance, which may be the first one to arrive ir
the input queue of process *P2* instance. *P2* cannot distinguish between the two *x* signals, sin
the *Sender PID* can be known only after consuming the signal (which can be the wrong signa
Although, this is a seldom scenario, a new construct in SDL which will allow for checking t
sender PID or another condition on signals in the input queue without consuming them, i
without side effect as in Promela [12], will be very useful for the modelling of distribut
systems.

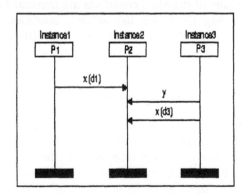

Figure 5. Indistinguishable signals.

2. Coregions

e have included MSC coregion with general order in our approach (it is not yet supported by bjectGeode MSC editor). Since coregions break the message sequence order, we had to extend r approach to handle coregions. We have introduced a new table (General Order Table or OT) to contain any order possible in the coregion. For illustration purpose, we have created a OT (see Table 1) for the coregion shown in the MSC in Figure 6.a. We build this table by eating a row for each event in the coregion. In each row, we add from the specification all vents that are preceded by the row event. If we consider for instance event e5 (X2) row, we can e that e5 precedes events e6, e7 which has been added to e5 row. In addition, since e6 is before n order) e8, we have added e8 to the e5 row.

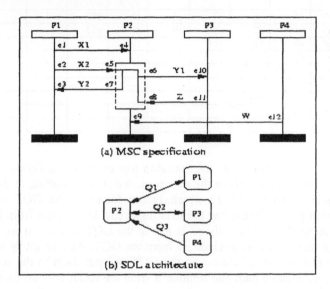

Figure 6. MSC specification with coregion and general order.

Table 1
General Order Table

Index	Entries		
e5(X2)	e6	e7	e8
e6(Y1)	e8		
e7(Y2)			
e8(Z)			

58

After the GOT, we create the Event Order Table (see Table 2) which remains the same as in [
except that we need to check the GOT for building event order row for each event in t
coregion. Let us consider event e6 (Y1) to illustrate our approach. From Figure 6.a, we can s
that *e6* precedes *e7*, but *e6* and *e7* are unordered with respect to each other (see Table
Therefore, we do not add *e7* or *e3* to *e6* row.

Table 2
Event Order Table

Index	Entries									
e1(X1)	e2	e3	e4	e5	e6	e7	e8	e9	e10	e11
e2(X2)	e3	e5	e6	e7	e8	e9	e10	e11		
e3(Y2)										
e4(X1)	e3	e5	e6	e7	e8	e9	e10	e11		
e5(X2)	e3	e6	e7	e8	e9	e10	e11			
e6(Y1)	e8	e9	e10	e11						
e7(Y2)	e3	e9								
e8(Z)	e9									
e9(W)										
e10(Y1)	e8	e9	e11							
e11(Z)	e8	e9								
e12(W)	e9									

From the GOT (see Table 1), we create the coregion tree as shown in Figure 7, which analys
the ordering sequence between events in the coregion. We start by putting at the top level of t
tree each index event (from the GOT) which is not found in the GOT entries. Then, v
recursively follow each path by excluding the existing events in this path from the GOT. For o
example, for instance we found that only *e5* is not in the GOT entries, so we put it in the fir
level of the coregion tree. Next, we exclude *e5* from the GOT. As a result of removing *e5* fro
the GOT, we found that *e6* and *e7* are not in the GOT, we put them in the second level of t
coregion tree. Then, we take *e6* path and remove it from the GOT, and we found that *e7* and
are not in the GOT. We put them in the third level of the coregion tree. Then, we take *e7* path an
remove it from the GOT. This will leave only *e8* in the GOT, which we put in the last level
coregion tree, and continue the process recursively.

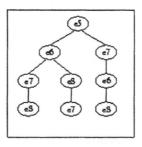

Figure 7. Coregion tree.

59

the next phase, we create the Occupancy Table (see Table 3) as in [4]. Finally, we translate the SC specification to its corresponding SDL behavior. The behavior of process P2 in our .ample is given in Figure 8.

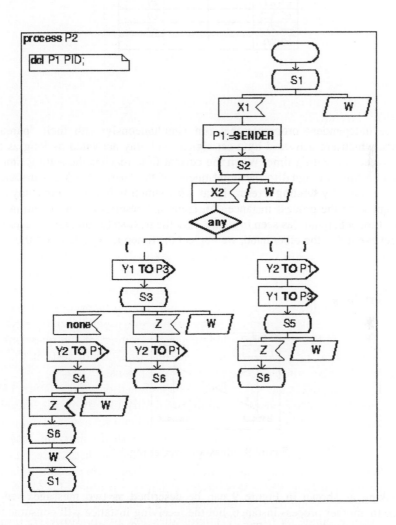

Figure 8. Process P2 for the example in Figure 6.

Table 3
Occupancy Table

	Q1	Q2	Q3
e4(X1)			e9
e5(X2)			e9
e8(Z)			e9
e9(W)			

3.3. Timers

SDL Timers are independent processes that run simultaneously with their "parent" proce
instance. Timers, which are activated by a set signal, will stay activated as long as the curre
time does not exceed the setting time. When the current time reaches the setting time, the tim
immediately send a timeout signal to the input queue of the "parent" process instance. We c
also deactivate the timer by sending a reset signal. This which will also remove any timer sigr
from the input queue of the process instance. So, from this description, after setting a timer, v
have to expect a timeout signal (as seen in figure 4) at the next states unless we reset the timer
receive a timeout event. On the other hand, we neglect the timeout expectation if the MSC did n
specify the event.

3.4. Message overtaking

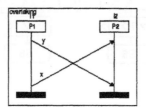

Figure 9. Message overtaking.

Message overtaking as shown in Figure 9 can be described as two messages sent from o
process instance to another process instance, but the receiving instance will consume them in t
opposite order of the sending order. This behavior breaks the general order rule. In order
handle it in our approach, we check for the existence of overtaking messages on each proce
specification, and made the appropriate save construct to save the earlier message for later use.

5. Deadlocks

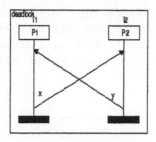

Figure 10. Deadlock.

ur translation algorithm works properly when the MSC specification and SDL architecture are
ee of syntax or semantic errors. However, like the tool presented in [7], we also detect
mantics errors such as deadlocks (see Figure 10). This detection is done during the creation of
e Event Order Table. When we encounter a semantic error such as a deadlock, the user is
ompted and the translation is cancelled.

6. Environment

our approach, we assume that the MSC Environment consists of several independent process
stances with their independent behavior. We can not assume or assure any order between the
essages sent by these instances in the environment. Therefore, we generate a *SAVE* construct
r every signal sent by the environment, for all the SDL states that precedes this environment
gnal.

7. Multiple instances of the same process

ur tool detects the presence of multi-instances of a process, and analyzes the differences among
eir behaviors. So far, we have found three different cases. The first case where all the instances
ve the same behavior, as in multi-clients-server architectures for instance. In this case, we
nerate only one process behavior. In the second case, the instances have completely different
SC behaviors, as for a sender-receiver scenario for a symmetric protocol. In this case, we
nerate alternative process behaviors that represent the different MSC behaviors for this process.
the last case, the instances have different behaviors in their specification. In this case, we have
merge the similarities of these specifications and keep as alternatives the other parts of their
haviors.

62

4. HMSC

We have extended our approach to handle High level MSCs (HMSCs). A HMSC provides graphical description for the (complete) system behavior. It integrates the bMSCs that descri partial behaviors of the system. Figure 11 shows an example of HMSC, in which the syste behavior consists of two alternative scenarios, *alt1* and *alt2* which are described with bMSCs *a* and *alt2* respectively.

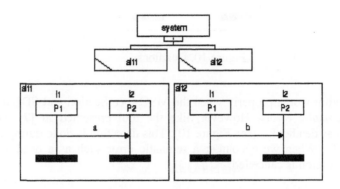

Figure 11. HMSC Example 1.

4.1. Distributed choice

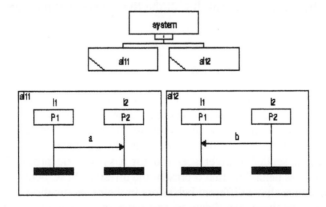

Figure 12. HMSC Example 2.

Figure 12 shows another example of alternative scenarios. We can distinguish three cases for t alternative scenarios. The first case is represented by process *P2* (in Figure 11) which selects o of the alternatives by receiving a distinguishing (sequence of) messages, in our example *a* or he second case is represented by process *P1* (in Figure 11) which triggers one of the alternative ths by sending a distinguishing (sequence of) messages, in our example message *a* or *b*. The ird case is represented by processes *P1* and *P2* (in Figure 12) where a process chooses an ternative by sending or receiving a message. This last case leads us to the well-known problem distributed choice [5, 7, and 8]. Our tool detects the distributed choice problem and prompts e user.

2. Implementability of MSCs

he implementability of bMSCs has been discussed in [6]. We have considered this issue for MSCs in [5]. We have shown that a given HMSC may not be implementable in certain SDL chitectures. In other words, we cannot find an SDL system, which has an equivalent behavior der these architectures. We have extended our tool with an implementability detection gorithm, which checks, during the translation, whether the given MSC is implementable in the ven architecture.

r illustration purpose, let us consider the HMSC given in Figure 13. In this example, the ternative scenarios are as follows: process *P1* instance sends the sequence *a.b* and receives *c*, or nds the sequence *b.a* and receives *d*. Process *P2* instance will select an alternative depending on e sequence of receptions. This scenario depends on the arrival order of the messages *a* and *b*, nich depends on the communication architecture of the system. If the messages are received in e sending order, then *P2* instance will follow the same alternative as *P1* instance. However, if e receiving order is different from the sending order (messages *a* and *b* taking different routes, r instance), then *P2* instance will select an alternative different from the one taken by *P1* stance. There is no way for *P2* instance to find out which alternative has been taken by *P1* stance. The resulting behavior of the whole system is not allowed by the HMSC. The HMSC in gure 13.a cannot be implemented in the architecture given in Figure 13.b.

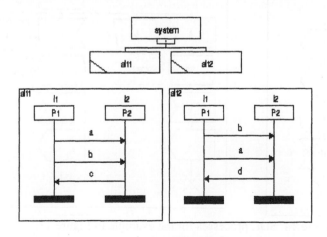

(a) *Alt* example.

64

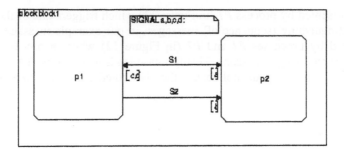

(b) SDL architecture.

Figure 13. Implementability of MSCs.

Such situations are detected during the translation, more precisely during the generation of SL processes. We consider each alternative as an independent MSC and say that the MSC is n implementable under the given SDL architecture, if at least one of the alternative branches has save a signal which is the distinguishing signal for another branch of the same alternativ Process *P2* given in Figure 14 is an example of such conflicts. During the translation, we need save the distinguishing signal of each branch. In this case, the translation is stopped and the us is prompted with the non-implementability error message.

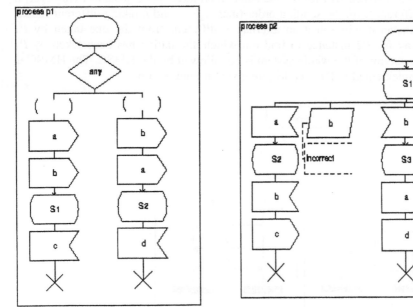

Figure 14. SDL processes for the example in Figure 13.

CONCLUSION

In this paper we have described our *MSC2SDL* tool. We use the standard internal representation for graphical MSC and SDL. Therefore, our tool can be interfaced with any MSC/SDL tool, which follows these standards.

We have discussed new issues we have met during the implementation of the tool. We are working toward the completion of our tool and transformation techniques. We will consider real case studies for the evaluation of our techniques and tool.

In the future, we will also investigate incremental construction techniques for SDL specifications. The current approach creates a new SDL specification from a given MSC and an SDL architecture. However, we can also assume that the SDL architecture is given with some initial behaviors for the processes, and the new MSC specification has to be added to these initial behaviors.

REFERENCES

ITU-T, "Recommendation Z.120 - Message Sequence Chart (MSC)", 1996.

E. Rudolf, J. Grabowski and P. Graubmann, "Tutorial on Message Sequence Charts (MSC'96)", Tutorial of the FORTE/PSTV'96 conference in Kaiserslautern, Germany, Oct. 1996.

ITU-T, "Recommendation Z.100-Specification and Description Language (SDL)", 1993.

G. Robert, F. Khendek and P. Grogono, "Deriving an SDL Specification with a Given Architecture from a Set of MSCs", in A. Cavalli and A. Sarma (eds.), SDL'97: Time for Testing - SDL, MSC and Trends, Proceedings of the eight SDL Forum, Evry, France, Sept. 22 - 26, 1997.

F. Khendek, R. Gabriel, G. Butler and P. Grogono, "Implementability of Message Sequence Charts", Proceeedings of the first SDL Forum Society Workshop on SDL and MSC, Berlin, Germany, June 29 - July 1, 1998.

A. Engels, S. Mauw and M. A. Reniers, "A Hierarchy of Communication Models for Message Sequence Charts", Proceedings of FORTE?PSTV'97, Osaka, Japan, Nov. 1997.

H. Ben-Abdallah and S. Leue, "Syntactic Analysis of Message Sequence Chart Specifications", Technical Report 96-12, University of Waterloo, Electrical and Computer Engineering, Nov. 1996.

8. F. Khendek, G. v. Bochmann and C. Kant, "New Results on deriving protocol specification from service specifications", in Communication Architectures and Protocols: AC SIGCOMM'89, pp. 136-145, Austin, Texas, Sept. 1989.

9. ObjectGeode, Verilog, Toulouse, France, 1996.

10. S.Somé and R. Dssouli, "An Enhancement of Timed Automata generation from Timed Scenarios using Grouped States", The Electronic Journal on Networks and Distributed Processing,1997, http://rerir.univ-pau.fr.

11. S. Somé, R. Dssouli and J. Vaucher, "Toward an Automation of Requirements Engineering using Scenarios". Journal of Computing and Information, Vol 2,1, 1996, pp.1110-1132.

12. G. Holzmann, "Design and Validation of Computer Protocols", Prentice-Hall, 1991.

SDL'99 : The Next Millennium
R. Dssouli, G.v. Bochmann and Y. Lahav, editors

From Timed Scenarios to SDL: Specification, Implemention and Testing of Real-Time Systems*

A. En-Nouaary[a], R. Dssouli[a] and F. Khendek[b]

[a]Département d'Informatique et de Recherche Opérationnelle, Université de Montréal, C.P. 6128, succursale Centre-ville, Montréal, Québec, P.Q. H3C 3J7, Canada
E-mail:{ennouaar,dssouli}@iro.umontreal.ca

[b]Department of Electrical and Computer Engineering, Concordia University, 1455 Maisonneuve Blvd. W., Montreal, Quebec H3G 1M8,
E-mail:khendek@ece.concordia.ca

Abstract

Nowadays, software systems are increasingly involved in safety-critical systems such as patient monitoring systems and air traffic control systems. Moreover, we witness the rapid development and deployment of new applications such as multimedia systems. The behavior of these systems are time-dependent. To be simulated, validated and implemented, real-time systems must be specified in a Formal Description Technique (FDT). In this paper, we propose a methodology to specify, implement, and test real-time systems. A system is first specified as a set of timed scenarios. These scenarios are integrated (via the tool REST [1]) to obtain a set of Timed Finite State Machine (TFSM), a variant of Timed Automata [2]. The resulting TFSMs are translated into SDL. After being validated, the SDL specification is used to generate automatically a partial implementation which is completed by the user. This implementation must be tested to assess its conformance to its specification. Timed test cases used to achieve this goal are generated from the TFSMs derived using REST.

Key-words : SDL, Timed Systems, Formal Description Techniques, Scenarios, Timed Automata, Testing.

1. Introduction

In the last three years, Formal Description Techniques (FDTs), namely Estelle [3], LOTOS [4] and SDL [5], have been developed for a standardized specification of communication protocols. The main goal of FDTs is to produce formal specifications that are unambiguous, clear, complete, and consistent. FDTs are also intended to help in analysis,

---

*This work was supported by NSERC Operating Grant (Dssouli) and IGLOO-NSERC Project.

simulation, validation, implementation and testing. SDL is the first standardized FDT and was developped for the following two main purposes:

- to describe the structure of a system to be constructed;

- to specify the required behavior of a system to be constructed.

SDL may be applied over a range of abstraction levels, starting from the very user-oriented, moving toward the very design dependent [6]. Moreover, SDL has two concrete syntax: a graphical syntax (SDL/GR) and a textual form (SDL/PR) which share the same abstract syntax. All these features make SDL very easy to learn and interpret and is so widely used in industries.

During the last two decades, SDL was widely used in specifying, simulating, validating and implementing communication protocols. The main behavior of these systems especially depends on the sequence of input/output events and data variables. However, nowadays, software systems are increasingly involved in safety-critical systems such as patient monitoring systems and air traffic control systems. Moreover, we witness the rapid development and deployment of new timed applications such as multimedia systems. SDL does not include sufficient real-time properties. So, it needs further extensions or a suitable manipulation to deal with timed systems.

In this paper, we present a methodology to specify, implement, and test real-time systems (see Figure 1). A real-time system is first described as a set of Timed Finite State Machine (TFSM). These TFSMs are incrementally derived from user's requirements given as scenarios. Then, the TFSMs are translated into SDL. Using commercial tools (e.g., SDT, ObjectGeode), the obtained specification is used to simulate, validate, and derive an implementation of the real-time system. This implementation may be incomplete; so it needs to be completed and refined by adding some behaviors. To assess its conformance to its specification, the implementation has to be tested. So, test cases are derived from the TFSMs. Once the test execution is done, a verdict is concluded and tells whether or not the implementation is conforme to its specification.

The remainder of this paper is organized as follows. Section 2 presents the requirements enginneering based on scenarios. Section 3 introduces the TFSM model and explains our approach to derive SDL specification from a set of TFSMs. Section 4 presents our method to generate timed test suite to test real-time systems. Section 5 is devoted to the test execution. Section 6 concludes the paper.

2. Scenario-Based Requirements Enginneering

Before describing how to translate an TFSM into SDL, we first start by explaining how to generate TFSM from a user requirements given in the form of timed traces.

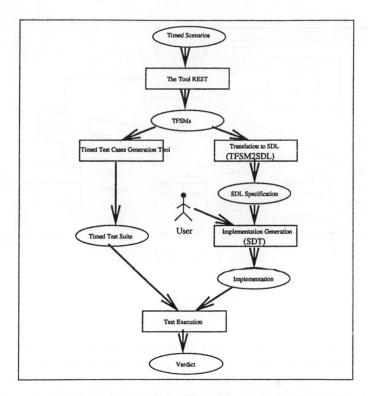

Figure 1: A Methodology to Specify, Implement, and Test Real-Time Systems

We have developped a tool (REST) that integrate scenarios [1]. Our methodology (Figure 2) consists of the following steps. The application domain definition concerns the enumeration and description of the system and environment features. It includes objects making the system and environment, and environmental factors relevant to the application (temperature, pressure, ...). A system component may be a physical unit (display, actuator, motor,...) or a piece of software doing specific functions, and may be composed of sub-components. A system component description includes its attributes and operations. At the beginning of a system requirement engineering process, an application domain definition is generally made by some elements known by users. This earlier definition is however generally incomplete and may be completed during scenarios acquisition.

Scenarios acquisition includes obtaining them from users and their syntactical analysis. They are described in a *semi-formal* language based on *structured english* or using a graphical representation. Our graphical langage is based on Message Sequence Charts. Our extention concerns addition of symbols for delays and conditions. We have constructed a graphical editor for scenarios description, and translation to textual representation. As

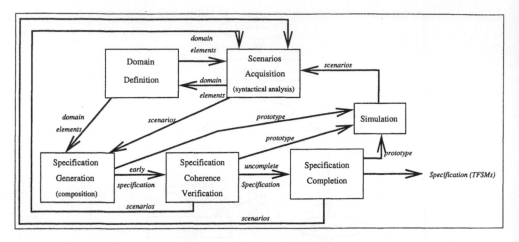

Figure 2: The Tool REST.

scenarios describe partial behaviors, and all of them may not be known at the beginning of the development process, scenarios are acquired one by one and the system whole behavior is constructed as one goes along. A scenario is expressed according to the constituents of the application domain. The syntactical analysis of scenarios uses elements of the application domain. Missing elements referred in scenarios, might however be added to the application domain description during scenarios analysis.

The specification generation activity analyses scenarios and merges their partial behavior with that obtained from scenarios previously acquired. This activity produces an early specification that includes all the scenarios.

In spite of an high abstraction degree and lack of details, an early specification can be used to show a system general behavior by prototype simulation. Prototyping is well used within a requirements engineering method based on scenarios, as it allows to reproduce all partial behaviors included in scenarios, and to uncover other behaviors following from them. Simulation may also induce users to modify their requirements, making changes in them to occur, and to be taken in account, earlier in the development process.

The specification generation do not make any assumption on the set of scenario used. Scenarios as partial descriptions, possibly gathered from different users, may include contradictions. The early specification obtained reflects the inconsistencies in the scenarios, and coherence verification aims at founding them. This activity may lead to a modification of some scenarios previously acquired.

The set of scenario provided may also not define completely the behavior of the system. A specification generated might lack important behaviors and the specification completion activity aims at adding these missing definitions. That may thus cause the acquisition of additional scenarios.

After obtaining an early specification or a complete specification, a corresponding SDL specification can be generated. Due to the lack expressiveness of time in SDL, a direct translation can not be achieved. For this reason, we have defined an operationnal semantic that is used to translate an TFSM into an SDL specification. This part will be presented in the next section.

3. From TFSM to SDL

Before describing our transformation from TFSM into SDL, we first define the TFSM model and mention all the known problems with specifying timed systems in SDL.

3.1. Timed Finite State Machine

A Timed Finite State Machine is a variant of Timed Automata [7,2,8] in which transitions are labelled with an input and output events. In other words, an TFSM is an extension of Finite State Machine (FSM) with clock variables and constraints over these variables to express the timing aspects of real-time systems.

Formally, an TFSM is a tuple $M = (I_M, O_M, L_M, l_M^0, C_M, T_M)$, where:

- I_M is a finite set of inputs,

- O_M is a finite set of outputs,

- L_M is a finite set of locations,

- l_M^0 is the initial location,

- C_M is a finite set of clocks,

- T_M is a finite set of transitions.

A transition of M consists of a tuple $(l, l', i/o, R, G)$, denoted in the rest of the paper with $l \xrightarrow{i/o,R,G}_M l'$, where l is the source location, l' is the target location, i is an input, o is an output, R is the subset of clocks to reset to zero within the transition, and G is a guard condition over clocks. The transition can be executed only if on input i, the values of clocks satify the guard G. In this case, the output o is produced, the clocks in R are reset to zero, and the machine changes its location to be l'. If the values of clocks do not satisfy the guard G, the input is ignored and the machine remains in its current location.

An example of TFSM is given in Figure 3. The machine has two locations named l_0 and l_1, one clock x, and two transitions. The transition from l_0 to l_1 is labelled with $In/Out1$,

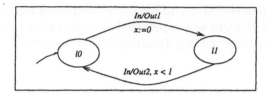

Figure 3: A Timed Finite State Machine.

has no guard condition, and reset to zero the clock x. However, the transition from l_1 to l_0 is labelled with $In/Out2$ and can be executed only if the value of clock x is less than 1.

Informally, the semantic of a TFSM M is as follows. Starting at the initial location, the values of clocks increase synchronously at the same speed and measure the amounts of time elapsed since they are last initialized. In a location, a transition can be taken if on an input, the values of clocks satisfy the guard of the transition. In this case, an output is produced, some clocks are reset to zero, and the machine possibly change its location. Otherwise, the input is ignored and the transition is not executed (the machine remains in its current location).

3.2. Real-time properties in SDL

SDL has a built-in real time mechanism, relying on an asynchronous timer mechanism [9]. However, its expressiveness is restricted with respect to the most important class of real-time requirements. In particular, we can not express directly in SDL any type of time constraints appearing in an TFSM using only timer mechanism. The SDL timer mechanism is asynchronous and is implemented using two constructs and two variables. An SDL specification can access the value of a global clock via a variable called **NOW** which always reflects the current time of the system. Another variable used in timer mechanism is the name of the timer itself (e.g. T_1) which is declared of type **timer**.

The construct **Set**($NOW + t$, T_1) sets the timer T_1 to a point of time which is t time units greater than the current moment of time. The set timer is managed by an *indepedent timer process*. This process continuously compares the value to which the timer is set with the current global time. When the value to which the timer is set is reached or exceeded, the timer process communicates the expiry by puting the signal T_1 in the input queue.

Once set, a timer can be *desactivated* by using the command **Reset**(T_1). As a consequence, either the timer process will be stopped if the value to which the timer is set is not yet reached, or the timer signal will be removed from the input queue if the timer expires before the **reset**.

Even if the timer mechanism is introduced to deal with timing aspects in SDL, its expressiveness remains restricted and has the following drawbacks [9]:

- The placement of the timer signal in the input queue takes some T_p time units,

- Since we can not make any estimation of the time it takes to consume all events in the input queue which have arrived earlier than the timer signal, the timer signal will be consumed some T_c time units after arriving at the input queue,

- The reaction to the timer signal will happen some T_r time units after its consumption.

Many researchers foccussed on how to remedy these drawbacks [9–11]. All the propositions are generally based on the extension of SDL language to cover timing aspects but they are not standardized.

However, in our methodology we do not extend SDL language but we give an operational semantic to timed system that helps enough to generate SDL specification from TFSM. This operational semantic facilitates timed system simulation, validation, implementation and testing.

3.3. Translation of TFSM into SDL

Being aware with the problems cited above and that concerns the timer mechanism, we give an operational semantic to timed systems described as a set of TFSMs. This operational semantic consists of the translation of each TFSM into an SDL block. So, a timed system will be described as a set of SDL blocks connected with each others by signal channels. The set of signals exchanged between two blocks B_i and B_j (respectively B_j and B_i) is computed as $I_{A(B_i)} \cap O_{A(B_j)}$ (respectively $I_{A(B_j)} \cap O_{A(B_i)}$), where $I_{A(B_i)}$ and $O_{A(B_i)}$ (respectively $I_{A(B_j)}$ and $O_{A(B_j)}$) are respectively the input and ouput actions of the TFSM corresponding to B_i (respectively B_j). Moreover, each SDL block is refined into two processes:

- A process *Control* that manipulates all the input and output actions exchanged with the environment.

- A process *Clock*, one per clock, that handles the clock variables.

Initially, the process *Control*, the only process active in the block, creates a *clock* process for each clock variable used in the TFSM. The communication between the *Clock* and the *Control* processes are realized via the exchange of the internal signals *Please-Value*, *GetValue* and *ResetClock*. When the control process receives an input from the environment, it tries to verify whether or not the input constraint is satisfied. So, it sends the *PleaseValue* signal to the involved clock processes asking for their clock values. By receiving this signal, each process computes the current value of its clock and gives it to the control process using the signal *GetValue*. To reset to zero a clock, the control process

74

sends the signal *ResetClock* to the corresponding clock process.

Notice that our model is well known in hardware and seems to be more suitable to implement time dependent systems. Indeed, the behavior of the system becomes more and more clear by expliciting the communication between the control and the clock parts. In addition, the clock part is very simple to implement and so allows us to avoid errors while implementing the system.

As an example, let us consider again the TFSM shown in Figure 3. This automata gives rise to the SDL block shown in Figure 4. The inputs and the outputs of the block are respectively the inputs and the outputs of the TFSM (i.e, the input is *In*, and the outputs are *Out1* and *Out2*). These events represent the interactions between the process *Control* and the environment. On the other hand, the communication between the process *Control* and the process *Clock* is realized via the internal signals {*PleaseValue, GetValue, ResetClock*}, as explained above.

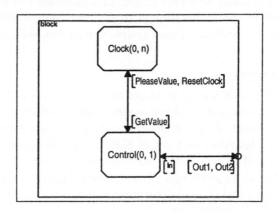

Figure 4: The SDL Block for the TFSM Shown in Figure 3.

Since our TFSM uses only one clock, there is only one clock process. Its behavior is shown in Figure 5. From state *Idle*, the process makes a spontaneous transition (i.e, the input *None*), registers the current time in the variable *Ti*, and goes to state *Wait*. In this state, the process can receive either the signal *PleaseValue* or the signal *ResetClock*. If it receives *ResetClock*, it must reset its clock to zero; so, it comes back to state *Idle* in order to update the variable *Ti*. If the process *Clock* receives *PleaseValue*, it calculates the current value of its clock (i.e, *V=Now-Ti*), sends it to the process *Control* via the signal *GetValue()*, and comes back to state *Wait*.

The *Control* process behavior is shown in Figure 6. From the initial state (i.e, state *Start*), the process creates the clock process for clock *x*, stores the clock process identifier

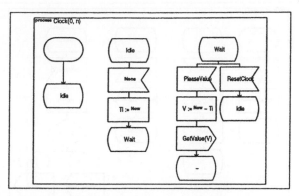

Figure 5: The Clock Behavior.

(i.e, *Offspring*) in the variable *Px*, and goes to state *l0*. In this state, when the process receives the signal *In*, it sends the internal signal *ResetClock* to the clock process *Px*, outputs the signal *Out1*, and goes to state *l1* . In *l1*, when the process receives the signal *In*, it tries to verify whether or not its guard condition is satified. So, it sends the internal signal *PleaseValue* to the clock process *Px* asking for the current value of clock *x*, and goes to state *Waitl1* to await the answer. In state *Waitl1*, when the process receives the current value of clock *x* (the internal signal *GetValue()*), it verifies the timing constraint of the transition. If it holds, it sends the output *Out2* and comes back to state *l0*; otherwise, it sends an error message (e.g, *"GuardViolated"*) and the process will be killed.

In addition to the above approach, there is another method to translate an TFSM into SDL. This solution is based only on timers. It consists of the transformation of the TFSM into another one by the introduction of timers. Constraints in TFSM are a conjunction of atomic formulas $(x\ op\ m)$, where x is a clock, $op \in \{<, =, >\}$, and m is an integer. Thus, each formulas $(x\ op\ m)$ gives rise to a timer. This timer is set to the constant m when the clock x is last initialized or reset to zero. To illustrate this approach, let us consider again the TFSM of Figure 3. Contrary to the operational semantic previously presented, we obtain one block which consists only of the process *Control*, as shown in Figure 7. Moreover, we use no extra internal signals for communication. The signals used in the specification are the input and output actions of the TFSM, and the timer's signals.

As for the operational semantic, the process *Control* always deals with the interactions between the system and its environment. Its behavior is shown in Figure 8. We use only one timer Tx since the constraint of the transition from the location l_1 to l_0 consists of one atomic formulas $x < 1$. The timer Tx is set to the value $Now + 1$ within the transition from l_0 to l_1 since this transition reset to zero the clock x. More specifically, the process *Control* bahaves as follows. From state *l0*, it receives the input *In*, sends the

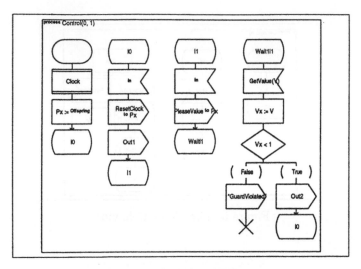

Figure 6: The Control Behavior.

output *Out1*, set the timer *Tx* to the value *Now+1*, and goes to state *l1*. In *l1*, the process receives either the input *In* or the expiry of timer (i.e, the signal *Tx*). If it receives *In*, it sends the output *Out2* and goes back to state *l0*; otherwise, it sends an error message (i.e, *"GuardViolated"*) and the process will be killed.

Even if the second solution is simple and uses only the real-time properties allowed by SDL, it requires many transformations and generates a large number of timers. Moreover, our methodology is intended to test real-time systems. Since the reset to zero of a clock is considered as an internal action, it is difficult to test a timed system without using a test architecture that explicits the reset to zero of a clock. We adopted the first translation of TFSM into SDL to generate timed test suite. So, the *observability* of the reset to zero of a clock is garanteed (the signal *ResetClock* at the interface of the process control).

4. Test Cases Generation for Real-Time Systems

Since we can not derive automatically a complete implementation for a real-time system from the SDL specification, the user has to complete the obtained implementation. So, he may introduce some errors when refining the implementation. Therefore, we need to test the implementation to assess its conformance to its specification. We have developed a tool [12] that generates timed test suite for real-time systems specified as an TFSM. Our approach (for a complete description, we refer the reader to [13]) consists of the following steps:

- The sampling of the semantic model (i.e, the region graph [2]) of the TFSM. This transformation aims to construct a subautomaton of the region graph, called Grid

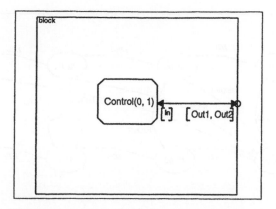

Figure 7: The SDL Block for the Solution Based on Timers.

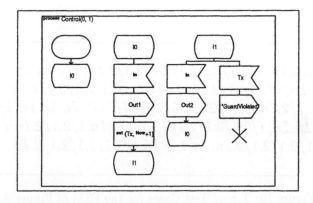

Figure 8: The Process Control for the Solution Based on Timers.

Automata [14,15], easily testable. Each state in the grid automata has an outgoing delay transition labelled with the same delay (the granularity of sampling). We use a granularity that depends only on the number of clocks in the TFSM [15]. If the TFSM uses n clocks with $n \geq 2$, the granularity is $1/(n + 2)$; otherwise, the granularity is $1/2$.

- The application of Timed Wp-Method [13] which is an adapted version of the Wp-Method [16,17]. The Timed Wp-Method is based on state characterization technique. Therefore, it allows to verify both the output and the target state of each transition.

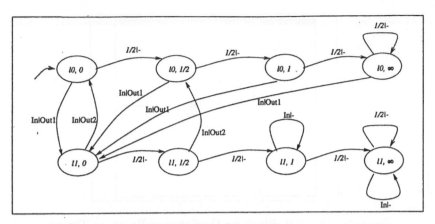

Figure 9: The Grid TFSM.

$In, 1/2.In, 1/2.1/2.In, 1/2.1/2.1/2.In, 1/2.In.In, 1/2.In$
$.1/2.In, 1/2.In.1/2.1/2.In, 1/2.In.1/2.1/2.1/2.In, In.In$
$, 1/2.1/2.In.In, 1/2.1/2.1/2.In.In, 1/2.In.In.In, 1/2.In.$
$1/2.In.In, 1/2.1/2.1/2.1/2.In, 1/2.In.1/2.1/2.In.In, 1/2$
$.In.1/2.1/2.1/2.In.In, 1/2.In.1/2.1/2.1/2.1/2.In$

Figure 10: Timed Test Cases for the FSM of Figure 9

To illustrate our approach, we consider again the TFSM given in Figure 3. We use a granularity of 1/2 to sample the region graph. The resulting automata is shown in Figure 9. For each state in this automata, we have an outgoing transition labelled with the delay 1/2 and a *null* output. The application of the Timed Wp-Method on the Grid TFSM of Figure 9 gives rise to the timed test cases shown in Figure 10. Here, we assume that the implementation has the same number of states as the specification. Notice that the delay 1/2 in test cases is interpreted as an input. It means that the tester must wait 1/2 units of time before applying the next input.

Compared to other methods [18,19,14,20], our approach is more practical and has a good fault coverage.

5. Test Execution

The test execution is the last phase in the test process and is done as follows. First, we have to choose a test architecture [21] to ensure the synchronisation between the Upper and Lower testers. Then, the timed test cases are submitted to the implementation. We conclude a verdict by observing the response of the implementation to each test case. If the output of the implementation corresponds to what is expected (i.e, the output derived from the specification), the implementation is said conforme to its specification; otherwise, it is said non conforme.

6. Conclusion

We presented a methodology to specify, implement and test real-time systems. First, a system is described as a set of scenarios. Each scenario represents the requirement of a user of the system. Then, these scenarios are integrated, via the tool REST, into a set of communicating TFSMs. These TFSMs are translated into SDL using a specific operational semantic. We mentioned that this operational semantic is not the only manner to obtain SDL specification from TFSMs. We presented another solution based on timers. The obtained SDL specification is used to simulate, validate and derive an implementation for the timed system. To test this implementation with respect to its specification (given as TFSMs), we showed how to generate timed test cases from the TFSMs.

As future work, we plan to study in detail the test execution inorder to complete our methodology.

REFERENCES

1. S. S. Some, R. Dssouli, and J. Vaucher, "From scenarios to timed automata: Building specifications from users requirements," in *Proceedings of the 2nd Asia Pacific Software Engineerin Conference (APSEC'95), IEEE, December,* 1995.
2. R. Alur and D. Dill, "A Theory of Timed Automata," *Theoretical Computer Science,* vol. 126, pp. 183–235, 1994.
3. ISO, "ESTELLE — A formal description technique based on extended state transition model," International Standard 9074, International Organization for Standardization — Information Processing Systems — Open Systems Interconnection, Genève, Sept. 1988.
4. ISO, "LOTOS: A formal description technique," tech. rep., International Organization for Standardization, 1987.
5. CCITT, "CCITT, Specification and Description Language (SDL), Recommendation Z.100," International Standard Z.100, CCITT, Genève, 1993.
6. F. Belina, "The CCITT-Specification and Description Language SDL," *Computer networks ans ISDN systems,* vol. 16, no. 4, pp. 331–341, 1989.
7. R. Alur and D. Dill, "Automata for modeling real-time systems," in *Proceedings 17th*

ICALP, Warwick (M. Paterson, ed.), vol. 443 of *Lecture Notes in Computer Science*, pp. 322–335, Springer-Verlag, July 1990.

8. X. Nicollin, J. Sifakis, and S. Yovine, "Compiling Real-Time Specifications into Extended Automata," *IEEE transactions on Software Engineering*, vol. 18(9), pp. 794–804, September 1992.

9. S. Leue, "Specifying real-time requirements for sdl specifications - a temporal logic-based approach," 1994.

10. C. Dou, "A timed-sdl for performance modeling of communication protocols," *IEEE*, pp. 1585–1589, 1995.

11. F. Bause and P. Buchholz, "Protocol analysis using a timed version of sdl," in *Proceedings of Formal Description Techniques, III* (J. Quemada, J. Manas, and E. Vazquez, eds.), North-Holland, 1991.

12. F. Belqasmi, *Génération de Tests pour les Systèmes Temps-Réel*. Rapport de Stage, ENSIAS, Université Mohammed V et DIRO, Université de Montréal, June 1998.

13. A. En-Nouaary, R. Dssouli, F. Khendek, and A. Elqortobi, "Timed Test Cases Generation Based on State Characterisation Technique," in *19th IEEE Real-Time Systems Symposium (RTSS'98), Madrid, Spain*, December, 2-4 1998.

14. J. Springintveld, F. Vaadranger, and P. Dargenio, "Testing Timed Automata," Technical Report CTIT97-17, University of Twente, Amesterdam, 1997.

15. K. Larsen and W. Yi, "Time abstracted bisimulation: Implicit specifications and decidability," in *Proceedings Mathematical Foundations of Programming Semantics (MFPS 9)*, vol. 802 of *Lecture Notes in Computer Science*, (New Orleans, USA), Springer-Verlag, Apr. 1993.

16. S. Fujiwara, G. Bochmann, F. Khendek, M. Amalou, and A. Ghedamsi, "Test Selection Based on Finite-State Models," *IEEE Transactions Software Engineering*, vol. SE-17, NO. 6, pp. 591–603, 1991.

17. G. Luo, G. V. Bochmann, and A. Petrenko, "Test Selection Based on Communicating Nondeterministic Finite-State Machines Using a Generalized Wp-Method," *IEEE Transactions Software Engineering*, vol. SE-20, NO. 2, pp. 149–162, 1994.

18. D. Mandrioli, S. Morasca, and A. Morzenti, "Generating Test Cases for Real-Time Systems from Logic Specifications," *ACM Trans. Computer Systems*, vol. 13, pp. 365–398, Nov. 1995.

19. D. Clarke and I. Lee, "Automatic Generation of Tests for Timing Constraints from Requirements," in *Proceedings of the Third International Workshop on Object-Oriented Real-Time Dependable Systems*, Newport Beach, California, Feb. 1997.

20. A. En-Nouaary, R. Dssouli, and A. Elqortobi, "Génération de Tests Temporisés," in *Proceedings of the 6th Colloque Francophone de l'ingénierie des Protocoles, HERMES, ISBN 2-86601-639-4*, 1997.

21. ISO, "Conformance Testing Methodology and Framework," International Standard IS-9646 9646, International Organization for Standardization — Information Technology — Open Systems Interconnection, Genève, 1991.

Session III

Language Extension

SDL'99 : The Next Millennium
R. Dssouli, G.v. Bochmann and Y. Lahav, editors
©1999 Elsevier Science B.V. All rights reserved

SDL Enhancements and Application for the Design of Distributed Services

Nils Fischbeck
Siemens AG, ICN WN AN AM46
Greifswald, Germany
nils.fischbeck@hgw.scn.de

Marc Born, Andreas Hoffmann, Mario Winkler
GMD FOKUS
Kaiserin-Augusta-Allee 31, D-10589 Berlin, Germany
{born I a.hoffmann I winkler@fokus.gmd.de}

Gregor Baudis, Harald Böhme, Joachim Fischer
Humboldt-Universität zu Berlin, Dept. of Computer Science,
Rudower Chaussee 5, D-12489 Berlin, Germany
{baudis I boehme I fischer}@informatik.hu-berlin.de

The complexity of telecommunication services has become increasingly high in recent years. Due to this complexity and the distributed nature of the services on one hand and the requirement to come up with a short time-to-market on the other hand, new methods, techniques and tools covering the whole service development phase are needed.
This paper is based on an integrated approach covering the fields of designing, validating and testing services and reusable service components. However, the focus here is mainly on the computational and engineering viewpoint. This paper uses ODL in connection with SDL to gain computational specifications which expose detailed behavior descriptions.
The paper introduces a new mapping from the ODP computational concepts to SDL which is based on SDL extensions currently in the standardization process. The new features are exception handling, remote procedure reject and associated timer. It is shown through a case study, how the readability and practicability of computational specifications improves through using this mapping. Furthermore, other nice-to-have extensions of SDL such as nested packages, interfaces and gate types and their benefits for modeling distributed systems are discussed.

1. MOTIVATION AND INTEGRATION

The Reference Model for Open Distributed Processing (RM-ODP) [8] describes an architecture for the design of distributed services where the basic idea is to split the design concerns into several viewpoints. This is in order to overcome the immense complexity of today's distributed systems by structuring the design process. Each of the ODP-viewpoints covers different aspects of the system which is to be designed. Though the RM-ODP itself does not define a concrete design methodology, there is a lot of ongoing work concerning this topic. One methodology which combines different description techniques to provide models for the viewpoints is described in [3]. A brief overview of this methodology is depicted in the following figure.

84

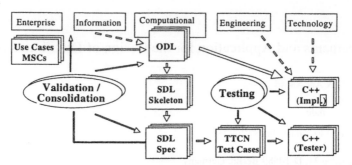

This methodology is mostly tool supported and has been applied to different projects dealing with the development of distributed telecommunication applications. In this methodology the following description techniques are integrated:

- Use Cases and Message Sequence Charts (MSC) for the enterprise viewpoint,
- Object Modeling Technique (OMT) for the information viewpoint,
- Object Definition Language (ODL) [7] and Specification and Description Language (SDL) [6] for the computational viewpoint,
- SDL for the engineering viewpoint,
- Tree and Tabular Combined Notation (TTCN) for test cases in order to check the service implementation.

The essential part of the methodology is the computational viewpoint which describes the structure as well as the functional behavior of the service to be designed. For that purpose a combination of ODL and SDL is used. ODL is a specification language based on CORBA-IDL designed for the development of computational viewpoint specifications of distributed services. The international standardization body ITU-T has established a new question (SG10/Q.2) to standardize this language. Aspects which can be expressed by using ODL include:

- The description of computational objects which support multiple interfaces. The different supported interfaces represent logically distinct functionality provided by the same object.
- The ability of objects to handle multiple instances of the same interface template. This allows the component to maintain client specific contexts.
- The ability to control the access and visibility of parts of the object's functionality.
- The possibility to describe the services/functionality an object needs from its environment. This feature allows to check the compatibility of interfaces on a static specification level.
- The ability to structure specifications using groups. Objects and groups which share a common property can be clustered in a group. Examples include implementation aspects as well as management issues.

Since ODL describes the structure of the service and the signatures only, additional information especially on the behavior and the connections between the component instances are needed. For this purpose the Specification and Description Language (SDL) has been chosen since SDL provides a formal and executable semantics. The state machine concept of SDL is very powerful to describe the externally visible behavior of the component's interfaces in terms of allowed sequences of operations. However, despite of the advantages of the application of SDL for the service design, practical experiences gained from several international projects have shown that SDL as it stands is not well-designed for the description of object-oriented systems. Since SDL has been developed for the specification of message-oriented telecommunication protocols, it suffers, for example, from the lack of an exception handling and from the absense of a native interface concept which are very essential for object-oriented systems.

To improve the modeling of ODP's computational concepts as well as the mapping of ODL to SDL new concepts for SDL are currently in the discussion. One of them is the exception handling concept which is quite stable and introduced here through a case study. Other new promising concepts are nested packages, gate types and interfaces where we introduce and discuss the basic ideas. Finally, the relation of the ODL/SDL based methodology for the development of distributed systems to current OMG standardization activities is discussed.

2. DEFINITION AND USAGE OF EXCEPTION CONCEPTS

The concrete syntax and semantics of exceptions for SDL is introduced in [9]. For better understanding the main ideas and syntactical constructs will be repeated here.

An exception can be defined wherever a signal can be declared in current SDL. This means that it can be defined at system level or even inside a block. The exception definition has only textual syntax, meaning that no graphical equivalent exists. The exception has a name and a list of parameters. In the following example an exception exc is defined which has one parameter of sort integer:

```
exception exc(integer);
```

An exception can be thrown with the raise-statement. This can be done not only inside a remote procedure call but even in a normal transition. The graphical syntax looks like in the following example:

```
exc(5)
```

To catch an exception one has to define exception-handlers. Exception-handlers have a name and must be attached to a process graph, a state, a stimulus (e.g. input), or an action (e.g. task). The association is done with a solid line with an arrow:

In this example a task is associated with an exception-handler with the name eh1. If an exception is raised the most specific exception-handler is selected first. If, for instance, an exception in a task is thrown, the exception-handler for the task is selected first, after that the exception-handler of the stimulus, the state and the whole process graph.

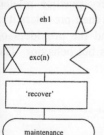

The exception-handler is searched for catch-statements for the raised exception. If such a statement is found, the transition following the catch is executed. Otherwise the next active exception-handler is searched. The next picture shows an exception-handler with a catch-statement for exception exc and a following transition with a task and a nextstate. The transition after the catch-statement is like any other transition in SDL. It is, however, not possible to continue after the place in the graph where the exception occurred with a resume.

With exceptions it is not only possible to allow a different user defined control flow. Some exceptions are predefined to allow the programmer to handle situations that lead in the current SDL to undefined behavior. The following exceptions are requested to be predefined: OutOfRange (a syntype range check fails), UndefinedValue (access to a variable with undefined value), and NoRevealer (viewed variable has no revealer).

A procedure definition must declare a list of all exceptions it can potentially raise. This simplifies the task of the programmer to know what exceptions can occur as result of a procedure call. If a procedure that is called remotely raises an exception, this exception is communicated back to the caller of the remote procedure. The exception is re-raised in the client process.

A new construct for remote procedure reject has been introduced. This allows the server specify that in certain states a remote procedure call will immediately raise an exception. The diagram beside shows an example in which the call of procedure op in the server will raise the exception exc. This exception will be raised on the client side.

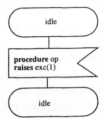

The proposal in [9] has also a solution to cancel remote procedure calls. It introduces associated timers for remote procedure calls. To a remote procedure call the programmer can associate a list of timers. On expiry of one of these timers an implicitly defined exception with the same name as the timer is raised. If a programmer wants to catch this exception he has to associate an exception-handler to the call, the stimulus, the current state or the whole process graph. The following diagram shows a remote procedure call with an associated timer t and an exception-handler that catches the implicit exception t.

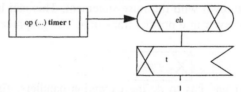

Although the proposed extensions to SDL are not yet confirmed with an ITU-T voting procedure it is very likely that they will be part of a new SDL language version. These extensions allow a mapping of ODL operations onto SDL remote procedures. An application of this new mapping is shown with a case study in the next section.

3. CASE STUDY USING EXCEPTION HANDLING

The starting point for the case study is taken from the retailer reference point specification [5] done by TINA-C. It describes a set of interfaces which contain interactions between a consumer and a retailer of a telecommunication service. This is a very practice related example. Due to the increasing amount of telecommunication services and their providers it is necessary to fix the interfaces between the consumers, the retailers and the providers of services. It is important, that this fixing does not only include signatures but behavior. The outcome should be an uniform access to the services of different retailers and providers.

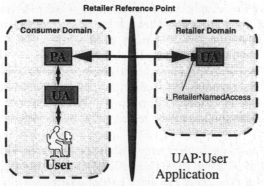

The figure shows the communication between the components defined by the TINA service architecture [4]. Within an access session which is the entrance to the TINA services the user communicates by the means of an appropriate user application via the provider agent with the user agent located in the retailer domain. The interface i_RetailerNamedAccess provided by the user agent has been chosen for the presented example and is shortened to four operations.

These operations are used to do initialization (setUserCtxt), to establish a TINA service (startService), to terminate a TINA service (endSession) and to close the connection to a service provider (endAccessSession). The detailed description of the operation's behavior is not of interest in the context of this paper and therefore it is not explained here. For reasons of simplicity the following specification example lacks the data type, exception and operation parameter definitions.

```
module Ret_RP {
    interface i_RetailerNamedAccess {
        void setUserCtxt (...) raises (e_AccessError, e_UserCtxtError);
        void endAccessSession (...) raises (e_AccessError, e_EndAccessSessionError);
        void startService (...) raises(e_AccessError,e_ServiceError,e_PropertyError);
        void endSession (...) raises (e_AccessError, e_SessionError);
    };
};
```

To describe the behavior of the interface the sequence of operation calls is needed together with the pre and post conditions determined by each operation. This order is summarized as follows: The initialization has to be done by using the setUserCtxt operation before calling any other operation. Following this, a service can be started with the startService operation and only when a service is established the endSession operation can be called. The operation endAccessSession is allowed in every case. If an operation is called with an invalid precondition, then an exception should be raised. This simple form of the overall behavior description of the interface should be specified without defining the concrete behavior of operations.

Considering the example of the case study, the new SDL features allow the following specification:

> **remote procedure** setUserCtxt;
> **fpar in** t_AccessSessionSecretId, **in** t_UserCtxt;

The operations are modelled as SDL remote procedures, which is the straightforward way.

The exceptions which can be raised are attached to the definition.

There is no need to define channels and signalroutes when the communication only takes place using remote procedures. However, channels may be considered as being useful, because with their help the configuration and relations of the entities can be shown graphically. Normally, this makes sense on the component level of a system.

On the client side, a time-out can be attached to remote procedure calls. This is essential for the description of distributed systems. The client has to be autonomous and must not block if the server does not answer an request. This property can be proven by validation of the specification. The implementation has to be tested to determine whether it fulfils the property or not.

Again, the definition of time-outs is very easy since they can be considered as being a special kind of exception. The difference to exceptions directly attached to the procedure is, that they are not raised by the server. The client can catch exceptions during it waits for the answer of a request. It is of special importance, that the client can perform different actions for each possible termination of the procedure. The normal SDL way to achieve this is by defining different transitions and nextstates for each of the terminations. As the following example shows, the exception states are exactly a straightforward model for the described purpose.

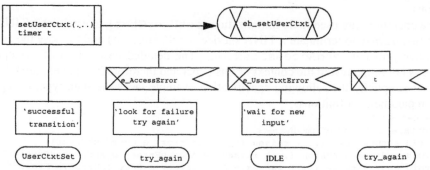

The most important new feature on the server side is, that the server can raise an exception and that exception is submitted to the client as a termination of the procedure. The exception must be contained in the raise specification of the procedure like any exception that the procedure can raise. Otherwise it would be possible that the client can not handle this exception because it is unknown.

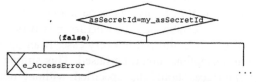

An important case of application for a formal specification of a server is to define the allowed sequences of operation calls. This can be done by applying the SDL state machine concept. The new SDL features allow to reject a call directly without executing the procedure. This increases the readability and avoids to have variables to store in which state the server is when it receives a call.

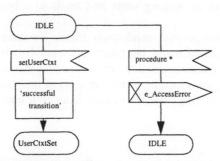

The graphically visible state machine is a great advantage of SDL compared with programming languages which mostly do not have such a concept.

If an exception is raised on the server side, the server should have a chance to change its state with respect to that exception. The possibility to do the state changes dependent on the procedure result is essential for the application of the state machine concept to the specification of the server. Looking on the example, if the operation setUserCtxt is performed successfully, the other operations are allowed (nextstate is UserCtxtSet), otherwise the state is the same as before (Idle).

However, since the exception is raised normally inside the remote procedure body and is transmitted to the client, there must be a semantics to allow the state change for the server process itself. This is achieved by attaching an exception-handler to the input part of the remote procedure call. In the case of an exception, the associated exception-handler is called and the actions specified there are performed. After that, the exception is re-raised and transmitted to the client. The following example shows the server side exception handling.

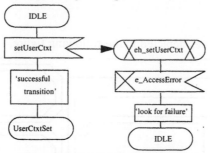

This section has shown, that the new exception features of SDL provide a suitable means for the behaviour description of the client and server sides of an object-oriented distributed system. The application of the state machine concept ensures a compact specification style, a good readability as well as the possibility to analyse and validate the specification. The new concepts prevent a procedural, less readable specification style which is similar to an implementation.

Although the new concepts discussed increase the expressive power of SDL in terms of enabling an adequate and compact modeling of ODP-like object-oriented distributed systems, there are some drawbacks still remaining. If SDL is used for the behavioral description of an ODP-like system specified by means of ODL, the names of signals, remote procedures etc. are often quite long since a global unique name has to be built from all enclosing scoping units of the ODL specification. The new SDL concept of nested packages introduced in the next

90

section avoids the flattening of scoping units and leads to a better readability of the SDL specification.

Furthermore, SDL does not provide an adequate means for describing multiple interfaces of an object. In the object-oriented world interfaces are used for structuring the operations an object provides to its environment as well as for controlling the visibility of and the access to the object's operations. The introduction of the concepts of interfaces and gate types into SDL enables the modeling of accessing objects via interfaces in a more adequate manner. This is discussed in Section 5.

4. NESTED PACKAGES

Nested packages provide a scoping concept similar to those of other specification languages and programming languages, particularly to that of ODL. They give the opportunity to logically structure a set of SDL definitions. Such a structuring is necessary due to the complexity of nowadays SDL specifications. The use of nested packages can lead to more readable and more comprehensible specifications.

Nested packages will become part of ITU's Z.100 standard and is introduced in [11]. They allow the definition of packages within other packages. Entities defined within those inner packages can be referenced from higher levels by qualification.

The scoping of ODL can be directly mapped onto SDL. This includes ODL's pure scoping construct module as well as the ODL scopes opened by group, object, and interfaces. Consider as an example the following ODL definition structure.

```
module mod{
   CO obj1{
        interface intf{...};
        ...
   };
   CO obj2{...};
};
```

This lead to an SDL structure as depicted in the following figure.

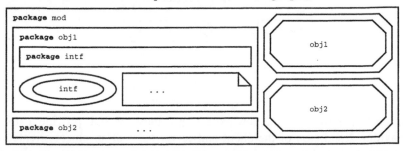

As for example the interface intf can be referred to from e.g. obj2 the former SDL package concept couldn't be used to reflect the scoping hierarchy. But now nested packages allow to see e.g. the service type intf from the top level. Note that a package is only used to reflect an ODL scope like e.g. obj1, so it serves as a container for the items defined within that scope, but not as a container for the entities that come along with the mapping of the same ODL construct, like the process type obj1, that will be defined on the same level as the package.

By the use of nested packages complicated naming rules with very long identifiers as well as a flat structure of the mapped specification can be avoided yielding a natural structuring of the SDL description.

5. INTERFACES AND GATE TYPES

In order to enable a better modeling of ODP's interface concept, the two SDL concepts SDL interfaces and SDL gate types [10] are presented here. In its closer sense SDL interfaces provide a generalization of SDL signal lists and signal sets. As a signal list groups a set of signals and identifies this group by a name, an SDL interface groups a set of signals, remote procedure names, and remote variables and again identifies this group by a name. In contrast to a signal list signals as well as remote procedures and remote variables can be defined within an interface. An interface is a scope unit and thus provides a name space for those definitions. Interfaces can be specialized and even multiple inheritance is possible. An interface name can be used where a signal list name can occur. Additionally, e.g. a process type can be declared to implement a specific interface. This implementation declaration resembles the concept of valid input signal set declaration, but here concerning interfaces. The main idea of the new interface concept is to describe the features that an entity like a process type or a service type shall implement and to provide a concept to enable typed communication.

SDL interfaces correspond to the ODP interface concept and cover some static aspects of typed communication. In conjunction with a broader concept for SDL gates including dynamic creation of blocks and services, which is also subject to the SDL standardization process and shall finally cover also some of the needed dynamic aspects, the interface concept yields a method to use SDL as description technique for RM-ODP's computational and engineering viewpoints. A concept for SDL gates is introduced in [10]. Here gate types play the role of interfaces. As within interfaces signals, remote procedures, and remote variables can be defined within a gate type. As with former SDL gates a direction is to be given to each of those definitions, so that a gate of the described gate type can have a signal flow in two directions--in contrast to the similar application with interfaces. Due to homogeneity with the SDL type concept, gate types doesn't support multiple inheritance, so here the interface concept goes further. The most important innovation coming with gate types is the renewal of the SDL addressing scheme. It is often required that clients have access to an specific interface instance, meaning here referring to a dedicated gate. To achieve this in an adequate manner each gate of a process has attached a set of a special kind of PId references. These gate references can be used for the communication.

Due to its broader approach we will refer to the gate type concept in the following paragraphs. So an ODL operation corresponds to an SDL remote procedure. With SDL gate types it is now possible to group the remote procedures that map ODL operations in a similar way as ODL does with its interfaces. Due to SDL gate types' lack of multiple inheritance the ODL inheritance of interfaces can't be adopted directly within SDL, here a similar multiple inheritance concept as SDL interfaces provide would yield a better mapping. The example interface i_RetailerNamedAccess now leads to an SDL gate type within the package

Ret_RP as follows:

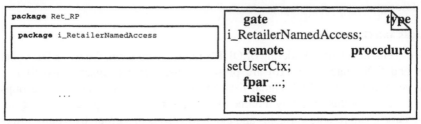

The package and the gate type are located on the same level. The package is used to map the scope of the ODL interface and the gate type is used to map the operations and attributes of an operational interface. The SDL gate type itself can now easily be used in a gate type expression for a gate of, for example, the process type that maps an ODL object template. Continuing with the example as part of the mapping there will also be a service type that would be used on the server side for a specification based on an ODL description. This service type now will be declared to implement the defined SDL interface.

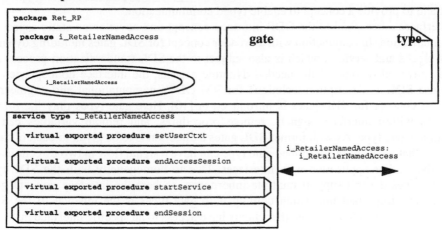

The service type can now be used to define the allowed sequences of operation calls. This can be done by applying the SDL state machine concept.

6. OUTLOOK: ODL-SDL INTEGRATION INTO THE OBJECT MANAGMENT GROUP (OMG) STANDARDIZATION PROCESS

In this section a brief overview on the possible usage and the requirements for a combined application of ODL and SDL for the description of distributed CORBA-based systems is given. A couple of requirements for description techniques for CORBA-based distributed systems standardized by OMG is briefly discussed. It is shown that there is a need for the new SDL concepts introduced in this paper if SDL in combination with ODL is to be used for the specification of distributed CORBA systems.

In the last three years the OMG had discussed many proposals to extend CORBA IDL by composition and multiple interface concepts, for which TINA-ODL gave the first ideas. Currently the OMG standardizes a new version of CORBA IDL which includes a component model. This model will support state required transactional integrity, security parameters, events, and implemented and required interfaces. A CORBA component will also support the concept of multiple interfaces, i.e. a single object will be able to control access to an object method based on the selection of an interface.

Under these circumstances the question for the relation between the two specification techniques (ODL, IDL in CORBA 3.0) by using a technique for describing behavior aspects (like SDL) will be an interesting one. A prognostic view is illustrated by the following diagram.

Using ODL a computational model of a distributed system can be specified, where objects,

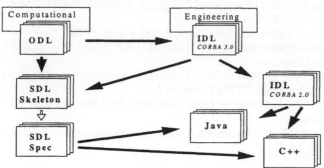

composed objects (groups) with (multiple) stream interfaces and (multiple) operational interfaces with their operations and exceptions are described. As a result of decomposition of these identified objects, we can get such objects with (multiple) interfaces which are the units of distribution in the real system. These units are identical with the components which should be described by the new version of CORBA IDL. One way to handle the mapping to all implementation languages supported by OMG is the definition of a complete language mapping to the existing IDL version.

The existing tool-supported mapping from ODL to SDL can now be extended to a component-based CORBA-IDL mapping. Then SDL can be used at different levels of object/component abstraction to describe behavioral aspects. For a simulation/interpretation of large distributed systems it will be very necessary to introduce in SDL interfaces of entities (system/block/process/service) which can be described by SDL or by real implemented CORBA components.

7. SUMMARY

The new introduced concepts of exception handling and nested packages in SDL which are already implemented by Humboldt University are essential to the mapping of the new languages ODL (ITU) and IDL (OMG, CORBA 3.0) to SDL, partially illustrated by a real case study. The expressive power of SDL for the description of object-oriented distributed systems has been enormously increased.

The need of a general interface concept in SDL in connection with a simplification/ unification of block/process/service is recognized in ITU not only under the pressure of new object-oriented technologies in the telecommunication area. The special request in alignment with OMG technologies concerns the support of multiple interfaces of one entity for communication. Furthermore the dynamic generation of interfaces is requested.

REFERENCES

[1]   OMG: *The Common Object Request Broker Architecture CORBA 2.2*, OMG, 1998.
[2]   Fischer J., Fischbeck N., Born M., Hoffmann A., Winkler M.: Towards a behavioral Description of ODL, TINA'97 conference.
[3]   Marc Born, Andreas Hoffmann, Mang Li, Ina Schieferdecker: Combining Design Methods for Service Development, accepted Paper for FMOODS'98, Florence, Italy.
[4]   TINA-C: Service Architecture 5.0, 1997.
[5]   TINA-C: Retailer reference Point 1.0, 1998.
[6]   ITU: SDL - Specification Description Language, International Standard Recommendation Z.100, Genf, 1996
[7]   ITU: ODL - Object Definition Language, Z.130, Genf, 1998
[8]   ITU-T Rec. X.901-X904 I ISO/IEC 10746-1-4: 1995, Open Distributed Processing - Reference Model Part 1-4
[9]   Humboldt-Universität zu Berlin: New Constructs for Exception Handling, SG10 meeting, Genf, März 1998, TD56 Revision 1
[10] E.Holz, J.Fischer: Introduction of Gate Tyes into SDL. Proc. of FBT'98 ,Cottbus,Germany
[11] Q.2/10 Rapporteur. Nested Packages. Temporary document TDI610, ITU Q.6/10 Internet Meeting, 1998

SDL'99 : The Next Millennium
R. Dssouli, G.v. Bochmann and Y. Lahav, editors
©1999 Elsevier Science B.V. All rights reserved   95

Modelling Interfaces in SDL with Gate Types

Eckhardt Holz

Humboldt-Universität zu Berlin, Dept. of Computer Science,
Rudower Chaussee 5, D-12489 Berlin, Germany

holz@informatik.hu-berlin.de

This paper proposes a type concept for gates. Its introduction is motivated by the concept of interfaces, which is extensively used for the specification and implementation of open and distributed systems. In the first place a pure syntactic extension for the current SDL gates is presented enabling the definition of gate types and type based gates. In a further step this is extended by new concepts for the communication between processes based on dynamic gate references. Gate references as an addressing scheme additional to PIds, can be created and deleted dynamically and serve as a model for the access to an interface. Finally a conclusion is given, summarizing also some further extensions.

1. Motivation

The decomposition of a system into objects which interact at their interfaces is a common baseline for all technologies for the design and implementation of open distributed systems. This holds as well for the abstract framework, the Reference Model of Open Distributed Systems (RM-ODP, [2]-[5]) as for more concrete architectures as CORBA [1], COM/DCOM or TINA [11].

Objects are dually characterized by their state and their behaviour. They are always encapsulated, that is, changes in an object's state can only occur as a result of an internal action or an interaction with its environment. Interfaces again are abstractions of the behaviour of an object consisting of a subset of the object's interactions and constraints on their occurrence. An object may support multiple occurrences of interfaces (of the same or of different types). In order for two objects to interact, they have first to obtain references to the respective interface instances, what is supported by the infrastructure.

These concepts are also reflected in the different languages for the computational specification of distributed systems, e.g. CORBA IDL or TINA ODL [12]. The computational languages provide means for the specification of interface types/templates (*interface* definition in ODL, IDL) and for object types/templates (*object* definition in ODL). On the other side, the concrete computational languages are missing features for the description of behaviour and the actual configuration of the system to be developed. To overcome this shortcoming different approaches to combine SDL and IDL or ODL have been made (cf. [5], [15] and other). These techniques start with a computational specification in IDL or ODL, map them to SDL-92 and add the behaviour specification at the SDL level. A major obstacle is however SDL's lack of concepts directly reflecting the concept of objects and interfaces. This implies that the ODP concepts themselves have to be modelled with SDL. Different combinations of blocks containing processes and being connected by channels are used instead of a single ODP construct, what implies additional specification overhead.

This paper revises the current concept of gates in SDL and extends it by a type concept similar to that for blocks and processes, and by a scheme to create and delete dynamically gate references. This gate type concept does directly reflect the interface concept of ODP and makes thus SDL more suitable for the specification of object-oriented open distributed systems. The dynamic creation and deletion of gate references correspond to interface references, whereas gates are ports or interaction points (i.e. locations where interfaces may occur).

2. Definition and Usage of Gate Types

Gate types are introduced by keeping the syntax and semantics for the existing gates. The current definition of gates in SDL has been extended to cover both, conventional and type based gates:

```
<gate definition> ::=
            <type based gate definition>
     |      <direct gate definition>
```

A <direct gate definition> follows the existing syntax for gates and is considered as a type based gate definition with an implicit gate type:

```
<direct gate definition> ::=
            gate <gate>
            [adding] <gate constraint> <end>
            [<gate constraint>]
```

The definition for typebased gates has a similar structure, however, the <gate constraints> are omitted, because they will be a part of the gate type definition.

```
<type based gate definition> ::=
            gate <type based gate heading> <end>

<type based gate heading> ::=
            <gate> :  [reverse] <gate type expression>

<gate> ::= [initial] <gate name> [<number of gate instances>]
```

The keyword **reverse** has been introduced to define a type based gate having an opposite information flow as defined in the gate type definition, i.e. the **in** and the **out** gate constraints are exchanged. **initial** and <number of instances> are explained in Section 3.

Type based as well as conventional gates can be defined in block, process or service types and represent connection points for channels and signal routes. Additionally to Z.100 they may also be defined for a system type. A typebased gate definition defines a gate according to the type denoted by <type expression>. The defined gate gets the properties of the type it is based on, its semantics follows the semantics of the conventional gates. Type based gates can be used as end points of channels or signalroutes and as a path element in the via clauses of output and remote procedure call statements.

Gate types themselves can be defined in a system, system type, block, block type, process, process type or in a package according to the required visibility level. A gate type definition may be virtual and may have formal context parameters (remote procedure, signal, remote variable, synonym or sort context parameter. As it is defined here, a gate type is only a syntactic construct. This implies that a static transformation can be used to map gate types and type based gate definitions on conventional gates. A gate type is defined according to the following textual syntax, a graphical syntax is not foreseen.

```
<gate type definition> ::=
              [<virtuality>]
              gate type {<gate type name> | <gate type identifier>}
              [<formal context parameters>]
              [<virtuality constraint>]
              [<specialization>] [<end>]
               <typebased gate constraint> <end>
              [<typebased gate constraint> <end>]
```

```
<typebased gate constraint> ::={<entity in gate type>}* <gate constraint>
```

If a gate type definition contains two `<typebased gate constraint>`s, they must have the opposite direction (**in** resp. **out**) and denote, whether an SDL unit with a gate of that type has a client role, a server role or both.

A gate type definition defines a scope unit, identifiers within a gate type definition are visible in the scope unit which contains that definition. This allows the inclusion of signal, signal list and remote variable/procedure definitions in a gate type:

```
<entity in gate type> ::=
                  <signal definition>
                 |<signal list definition>
                 |<remote variable definition>
                 |<remote procedure definition>
```

It is however required that an `<entity in gate type>` is used in at least one of the gate constraints of the gate type.

The excerpt of an SDL specification in Figure 1. demonstrates the definition of a gate type and its application. Block type `b1` as well as block type `b2`, both provide a gate based on the

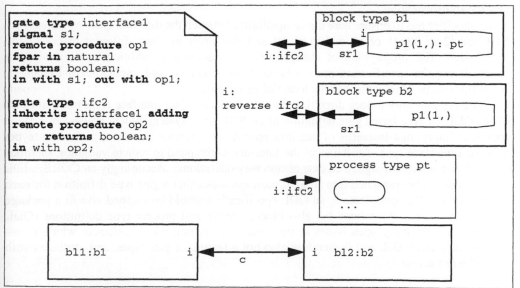

Figure 1.   Example based on gate types

gate type ifc2. However, b2's gate has been defined as a reverse gate. This ensures, that a channel connecting instances of both block types via their respective gates does fulfil the static requirements on the communication infrastructure. The same specification, but based on conventional gates only is given in Figure 2. This would also be the result of the application of

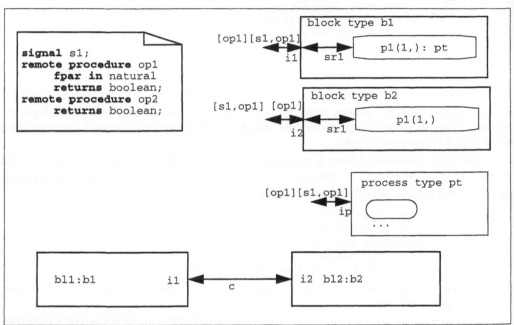

Figure 2.   Example based on conventional gates

the static transformation.

The specifier has to ensure here the compatibility between the different gates by himself (i1 of b1 and i2 of b2, i1 of b1 and ip of pt) and this often in many different places of the specification. The propagation of changes (e.g. introduction of additional communication means) during the specification process is therefore strenuous and implies textual changes, even if this can be limited through the usage of signal lists.

A gate type definition does directly reflect the concept of an interface (type) definition in IDL or ODL. A type based gate definition of an SDL unit (system, block, process or service type) does imply, that instances of that unit provide an interface (instance) according to the mentioned interface type. Attributes of the interface correspond to remote variables, methods to remote operations (or signals in case of one-way operations). Accordingly an CORBA-IDL specification can be translated into an SDL package containing a gate type definition for each interface in the IDL specification, an ODL specification would be mapped also in a package containing gate type definitions but also block, service and process type definitions (ODL objects). The remaining open issues in both cases are is multiple inheritance, which is not available in current SDL and is therefore also not a feature of gate types, and attributes with read and write access.

| **IDL** | ```
interface Broadcast
{
    void register(in Rcvr rcvr,in string id,in string nick);
    void registerWithCheck(in Rcvr rcvr,
        in string id, in string host, in string nick);
    void unregister(in Rcvr rcvr);
    StringSeq getRcvrNames();
    oneway say(in string text);
};

interface NickBroadcast : Broadcast
{
    readonly attribute long NoOfClients;
    void setNickName(in Receiver rcvr, in string nick);
    void getReceiverByNick(in string nick,out RcvrDesc desc);
}
``` |
| **SDL** | ```
gate type Broadcast;
    remote procedure register
        fpar in rcvr, charstring, charstring;
    remote procedure registerWithCheck
        fpar in rcvr, charstring, charstring, charstring;
    remote procedure unregister fpar rcvr;
    remote procedure getRcvrNames returns StringSeq;
    signal say (charstring) ;
in with
    register,registerWithCheck,unregister,getRcvrNames,say;

gate type NickBroadcast;
inherits Broadcast
adding
    remote NoOfClients integer;
    remote procedure setNickName fpar in rcvr, charstring;
    remote procedure getReceiverByNick
        fpar in nick charstring; in/out desc ReceiverDesc;
in with setNickName,getReceiverByNick,NoOfClients;
``` |

Table 1: IDL-SDL Translation based on gate types

3. Dynamic Gate References

3.1. General

The extended gate concept as described in the previous section is a pure syntactic construct. They are used to statically verify the signal lists attached to channels and signalroutes and the valid input signalset of processes. However, they don't play a role for the dynamic semantics. On the other hand it is often required to provide clients with a dedicated access to an interface (instance). To solve this problem each gate of a process has attached a set of references (values of type PId). These gate references may be used for the communication and can also be seen as additional PId's for the process owning that gate. The original PId value of a process can be conceived as a PId value related to an implicit gate having the complete input and output sets of the process as its gate constraints.

At most one dynamic gate reference can be created implicitly during the creation of a process instance, this is the gate marked with the keyword **initial**. After creating a process instance with an initial gate the creating process **offspring** and the created process **offspring** both have the same unique new PId value related to the initial gate, the created process **self** has the new unique PID value of the process instance itself.

It should be noted that although the set of references may be an empty set, the communication using just the gate itself is possible until its owning process ceases to exist. The reason to have this is compatibility with the current version of SDL. Gate references may be associated to type based gates as well as to non-type based gates. The maximum number of references associated with a gate may be limited by <number of gate instances>. If no limit is given the maximum number is unbounded.

3.2. Explicit Creation/Deletion of Gate References

Gate references are created by a <create request>. The definition has been changed as follows:

```
<create request> ::= create <create body>

<create body> ::=
   {<process identifier>|this}[<actual parameters>][from <PIdexpression>]
   |<gate identifier>
```

When the <create body> contains a <gate identifier> the create action causes the creation of a new PId value related to the gate denoted by <gate identifier>. The creating process **offspring** expression has this unique new PId (i.e. **offspring** is a reference to the new gate instance). If an attempt is made to create more gate References than specified by the maximum number of instances in the gate definition, then no new instance is created, the **offspring** expression of the creating process has the value Null and interpretation continues.

It should be noted that gate references may only be created for gates of a process. A <gate delete> makes a PId value related to a gate unavailable for further communication. After the deletion the gate reference has the value **null**.

```
<gate delete> ::= delete <PId expression>
```

<PId expression> must denote a PId value related to a gate of the process executing the gate delete, otherwise the gate delete does not change the PId value and the interpretation continues.

```
process type P;
gate initial g(2):ifc1;
        /* create one gate reference on process creation */
dcl mygate PId;
start;
   create g2;
        /* creation of a new gate reference */
   task mygate := offspring;
        /* mygate is the new reference to the gate */
   create g2;
        /* no new reference will be created because max number= 2 */
   create this;
        /* creates a new instance of the same process */
   task mygate := offspring;
        /* offspring is the initial reference of the created process */
...
```

Figure 3.   Dynamic creation of gate instances

The **from**-clause of a process creation has been introduced to provide the createe with a gate reference of the creator instead of the PId of the creator. This does change the semantics of **parent**: Its PId value is either the PId of the creating process or the gate reference submitted in the **from**-clause.

```
    process type p1 <process p atleast p2>;
       gate g (1) :gt;
       dcl mygate PId;
       start;
             create g;
             task mygate := offspring;
             create p from mygate;
             /* p's parent is the gate reference mygate */
             /* p does not know p1's PId (self) */
             ...
    endprocess type;

    process type p2;
       gate initial g;
       /* creators offspring is a reference to the initial gate of p2 */
       /* p2's offspring is also a reference to the initial gate of p2 */
       /* p2's self (PId of the process itself) is hidden to creator */

       ...
    endprocess type;

    process p (0 ,) : p2;
    process q (1,1) : p1;

    signalroute sr from p via g to q via g;
    ...
```

Figure 4.   Dynamic gates instances and process creation

3.3. Communication using Gate References

Being a PId value, gate references can be applied to denote a receiver of a signal or a remote procedure call in the same way as PId values of processes (i.e output <sig> to <gate reference>. However, compared to an output to a process-PId the following additional semantically restrictions do apply:

- a communication path from the sender to the receiver must exist (implicit or explicit),
- the communication path must end at the receiver side at the gate the gate reference belongs to, and
- the signal must be an element of the **in** gate constraint of that gate.

If these conditions and the conditions mentioned in Z.100 are fulfilled, the signal will be transmitted via the communication path to the process owning the gate reference. Otherwise the signal will be discarded. If a signal sent to a gate reference arrives at the receiving process, it will only be queued in the input port, when the gate reference is still valid (i.e. it has not been deleted). Signals to deleted gate references will be discarded by the receiving process.

Another solution instead of discarding the signal would be to throw an exception in these cases (e.g. unreachable gate or invalid gate reference). This would make the communication between processes using gate references more reliable.

Until now only the receiving process' gate reference is used for the communication. In many cases it however also desired to use a dedicated gate reference on the sender side (in a client role). To obtain this possibility, the syntax of the output statement has been extended by an additional clause:

```
<output> ::= output <output body>

<output body> ::=
            <signal identifier> [<actual parameters>]
            {, <signal identifier> [<actual parameters>]}*
            [from <PId expression>][ to <destination>]
            [via [all] <via path>]
```

The <PId expression> after **from** must denote a PId value related to a gate of the process performing the output. This PId becomes the **sender** within the receiving process. The gate belonging to the gate reference must be the starting point for the communication path from the sender to the receiver. A precondition for the sending of the signal is here the requirement that the signal must be in the **out** gate constraint of the gate. An example of the application of gate types is given in Section 4.

Currently no strong typing requirements are enforced for the communication using gate references, the only precondition is that the signal occurs in the in resp. out gate constraint of the referenced gates of the sender and receiver process. However, this could be strengthened to the demand that the types of the receiver gate and the sender gate are in a subtyping relation and the gates themselves defined in opposite directions to each other (using **reverse**).

The same extensions as have been made to the output have also been applied to remote procedure call and remote variables.

4. Application Case Study

The following example is a modification of the Daemongame specification given in Z.100. In contrast to the original specification only a single game process is used to handle all requests from the player (cf. overall structure in Figure 5.). Type based gates and gate references are used to ensure that only registered players may play and that replies are sent to the requesting process.

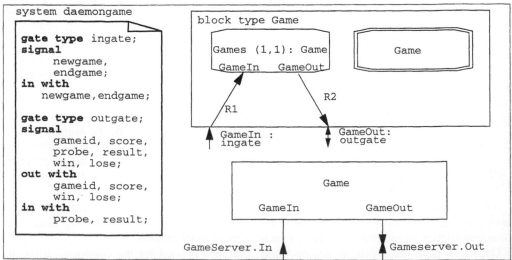

Figure 5.   Application example - overall structure

The behaviour specification of the process type game is given in the diagram in Figure 6. It has two tasks: the game itself and the registration/unregistration of players. For each player

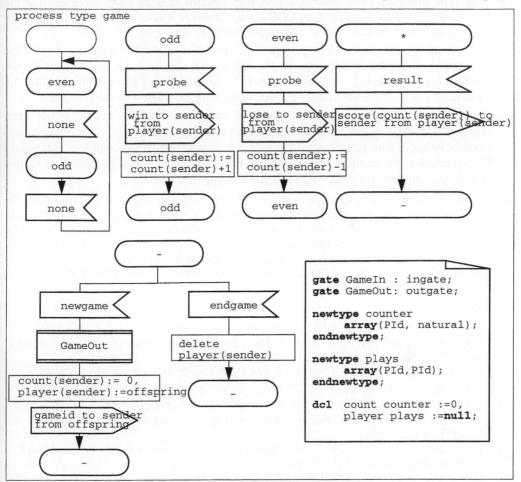

Figure 6.   Application example - behaviour specification

who registers with the signal newgame a new gate reference for the gate GameOut will be created. This gate reference will be used for the communication with that player and remains valid until the player sends an endgame signal. The game process answers all requests by players (probe, result) with the appropriate signals (win, lose, score). However, if a player is not registered, the signal will be discarded. This is due to the from clause in all output statements, which requires an existing and valid gate reference. It is neither possible for a player to play without registration nor to influence the game of another player.

If a player uses also gate references for the communication with the game, he may play multiple games at the same time. In this case the player registers with a gate reference instead of his PId.

5. Conclusion

The gate type proposal made here is a first step towards making SDL more apt for the description of distributed systems in an ODP-style. Currently it does already a good basis for the mapping of IDL to SDL. However, two major issues are still open:

- Multiple Inheritance: SDL does not support the concept of multiple inheritance, but for the description of interfaces this concept plays a crucial role (e.g. an interface being the combination of two other interfaces). It has to be investigated in more depth, whether the introduction of multiple inheritance for gate types only would be a possible solution.

- Due to compatibility reasons the concept of communication via gates has not been changed. This implies that a communication via that gate is always possible, independent whether or not a gate reference to that gate has been created. Although this is standard SDL semantics, for an more object/interface entered view it should be possible to allow communication only via gates with valid and existing gate references.

Despite these points, the gate type concept is applicable in many cases to make the specification more clear and does reflect concepts of ODP in a straight-forward manner. Proposals for the combination of gate types with other concepts (dynamic blocks and services, object-oriented data types) have been made in [18], the relation to the OOAD technique UML are explained in more detail in [17]. The gate type concept has been presented at an experts meeting of ITU-T Q.6/SG 10 and thus influenced also the interface concept of SDL-2000.

References

[1]   OMG: *The Common Object Request Broker Architecture CORBA 2.1*, OMG, 1997
[2]   ITU-T Rec. X.901 | ISO/IEC 10746-1: *Open Distributed Processing - Reference Model (RM-ODP) Part 1: Overview*, 1995
[3]   ITU-T Rec. X.902 | ISO/IEC 10746-2: *RM-ODP Part 2: Descriptive Model*, 1995
[4]   ITU-T Rec. X.903 | ISO/IEC 10746-3: *RM-ODP Part 3: Prescriptive Model*, 1995
[5]   ITU-T Rec. X.904 | ISO/IEC 10746-4: *RM-ODP Part 2: Architectural Semantics*, 1995
[6]   ISO/IEC CD 14750: *Open Distributed Processing - Interface Definition Language*, ISO/ITU-T DIS 1996
[7]   ITU-T Rec. X.950 | ISO/IEC 13235: *Open Distributed Processing - Reference Model ODP Trading Function*, ITU-T 1995
[8]   ITU-T Rec. Z.100: *SDL - ITU-T Specification and Description Language*, ITU-T, 1992
[9]   Rational: *UML Semantics V1.1*, 1997
[10]   Rational: *UML Notation Guide V1.1*, 1997
[11]   TINA-C: *Overall Concepts and Principles of TINA*, TINA-C 1994
[12]   TINA-C: *Object Definition Language - Manual Version 2.3*, TINA-C, 1996
[13]   TINA-C: *Computational Modeling Concepts*, TINA-C, 1996
[14]   A. Olsen: *Introduction of Gate Types in SDL*, ITU-T Temprary Document, Tele Danmark, 1997
[15]   E. Holz: *ODP Architectural Semantics in SDL*, ISO/JTC1/SC21 Input Doc., 1996
[16]   E. Holz: *Application of UML within the Scope of new Telecommunication Architectures*, GROOM Workshop on UML, Mannheim, Physica-Verlag, 1997
[17]   E. Holz: *Combined Application of UML and SDL*, GI Workshop UML, München, 1998
[18]   J. Fischer, E. Holz: *Introducion of Gate Types into SDL*, Proc. of FBT'98, Cottbus, 1998
[19]   E. Holz: *Application of UML in the SDL Design Process*, SAM-Workshop, Berlin, 1998

SDL'99: The Next Millennium
R. Dssouli ,G.v. Bochmann and Y. Lahav, editors

MSC and data: dynamic variables

A.G. Engels, L.M.G. Feijs, S. Mauw

Department of Mathematics and Computing Science,
Eindhoven University of Technology,
P.O. Box 513, NL–5600 MB Eindhoven, The Netherlands.
engels@win.tue.nl, feijs@win.tue.nl, sjouke@win.tue.nl

The extension of the MSC language with more advanced data concepts is one of the current topics of discussion in the MSC standardization community. A recent paper at the SAM98 workshop by two of the current authors [2] treated the extension of MSC with static variables. Feasibility of an approach to parameterize the MSC language with a data language was shown.

We have extended this research by studying the combination of MSC with a data language containing dynamic variables. Rather than giving a precise proposal of the way in which an actual data language must be added to the MSC language, we discuss options and problems. Choices have to be made, for example with respect to scope, use of variables, and the way of assigning variables. For some particular combination of the options mentioned above, we give a formal operational semantics of the combined MSC/Data language. It is argued that the interface between the data language definition and the MSC language definition should be explicit.

List of Keywords: Extension of existing language, Formal semantic models, MSC, Data, Variables.

1. INTRODUCTION

Quite high on the list of possible extensions for the language MSC [4] (Message Sequence Charts) is data. Currently, the language has hardly any data concept. At best, data can be expressed as a parameter of a message which is simply considered as a syntactical extension of the message name. Operations can be defined informally by means of actions. Again, this is considered as a purely syntactical concept.

There is clearly a need for a more extensive treatment of data. This is in line with the trend that MSC is becoming a language that is more and more useful for the complete description of system behaviour, rather than for displaying single traces. But also when using MSC for the visualization of traces, actual data values may be observed.

Since MSC is closely related to SDL [3], some things can be learned from the way in which SDL deals with data. The first formal data language integrated with SDL was based on algebraic specifications. These are known for having a very simple syntax and a clear semantical foundation. In practice, however, the functional style of an algebraic specification showed to be too difficult for people used to an imperative language. Therefore, an alternative data language, ASN.1 [5], was adopted. This enforced the development of a second recommendation, which exists next to the first one. Currently, the development of SDL2000 involves a redesign of the SDL data language.

This situation has several drawbacks. Both recommendations have a large overlap, and thus there is a maintenance problem. Furthermore it requires a new semantics definition. In which sense is the semantics dependent on the actual data language? And finally it is not clear what will happen if a new paradigm (such as Java) gets into the picture. Will a third recommendation be developed?

We clearly do not want these problems to occur when extending MSC with data. Therefore, we have initiated research on the extension of MSC with data. In a previous paper [2] we have discussed several issues related to the extension of MSC with a data language containing static variables. We have argued in favour of developing an explicit interface between the MSC behavioural part and the MSC data part. This would overcome some of the drawbacks mentioned above. Furthermore, we have designed such an interface, appropriate for two classes of languages, namely, algebraic specifications and constraint syntax languages such as ASN.1 [5]. In Section 2 we will summarize the results of this research.

In this paper, we study the extension of MSC with a language containing dynamic variables. These are variables whose value may change during "execution" of an MSC. This situation is clearly more complicated than the case of static variables. We mention some questions that arise: Which MSC constructs can be used for changing the value of a variable? What should be the scope of a variable? How often may a variable have a value be assigned to it? How to determine in which state an expression should be evaluated? How to handle references to undefined variables?

We will discuss all these questions, formulate possible answers and discuss their respective merits. As in [2] we aim at defining an interface between the MSC language and some data language with dynamic variables. However, we expect that a uniform interface cannot be defined. That is an interface which is suited regardless of the answers to the above mentioned questions. Nevertheless, we have studied such an interface for one particular combination of answers and we have roughly defined the operational semantics of this particular MSC/Data language.

This paper is structured as follows. In Section 2 we summarize the findings of [2]. Section 3 contains the description of a simple example showing the combination of Basic Message Sequence Charts with a basic data language. In Section 4 we discuss some questions concerning the extension of MSC with dynamic variables. The operational semantics of a combined MSC/Data language is sketched in Section 5. We will end with some concluding remarks.

Acknowledgments We thank Jan Friso Groote, Frans Meijs, Jaco van de Pol, Michel Reniers and all members of the MSC standardization group for their fruitful discussions on this topic.

2. STATIC DATA

In this section we summarize the findings of [2], which addresses the question how the MSC language could be extended with a data type formalism. It is argued that it may be better not to choose a particular data type formalism for standardization as a part of MSC, but instead set up the recommendation in such a way that the actual data language can be considered as a parameter. This leads to the research question of how to parameterize the MSC language with a data language. Starting from the idea that MSC is parameterized over some grammar with some semantical information, the latter research question is investigated in [2] by noting those properties of the data formalism that are required in order to formally define syntax, well-formedness and semantics of an MSC with data. As demonstrated in [2] it is indeed possible to define such an interface between MSC and data. As usual, the interface is a two-way contract; it describes both the required assumptions concerning MSC behaviour and the sets and functions to be provided by the data formalism.

In [2] it is found that this interface is sufficient for connecting quite distinct data formalisms to MSC. This is demonstrated by two case studies. The first case study is an algebraic data language. The second case study is a constraint syntax language which takes ASN.1 as a starting point and is based on the proposal from Baker and Jervis [1].

It is interesting to remark that [2] exploits a notion of variables too. In the setting of the present paper, they are a kind of static variables: the semantics is taken to consist of *all* possible behaviours of giving values to the variables.

3. EXAMPLE LANGUAGE

In this paper we will use a simplified data language to explain the various features of dynamic data in MSC. Our language will consist of:

- The data types of Naturals and booleans

- Variables x, y, z and $x_1, x_2, \ldots$ signifying naturals, and p, q, r and $p_1, p_2, \ldots$ signifying booleans

- The operators $+$, $\cdot$, $\wedge$, $\vee$, and $=$

It also contains variable declarations in the form *var x: Natural* or *var p: Boolean*, and assignments of the form $x := e$, with x a variable and e an expression. Variable declarations are placed in the MSC, near the MSC name. Assignments are made in local actions.

As said, we will use this example to show various proposals and choices. To get a first idea of how MSC with variables might look like, we show an example in Figure 1.

Intuitively what happens here is that x gets the value 1, $m(x)$, which thus should be $m(1)$ is sent and received, y gets the value 4, and $k(5)$ is sent and received.

For this simple example, clear and unambiguous semantics can be given. In more complex cases, with for example multiple assignments or restricted scopes, this may not be the case, and explicit choices have to be made. This is what will be discussed in the next section.

4. CHOICES

When designing a combined MSC/Data language, there are several choices with respect to the precise interaction of the two languages. We will first list the major issues and discuss possible answers in the next sections.

108

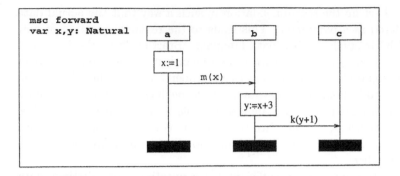

Figure 1. Example MSC with data

1. The extent to which the variables are behaving dynamically or statically.

2. The place where assignment of variables may take place.

3. The places where and the ways in which a variable is used.

4. The way undefined variables are handled.

5. What scope variables have, both regarding their extension over one, some or all instances and regarding their extension in time.

4.1. Static vs. dynamic nature of a variable

When talking about the dynamic nature of a variable, we are dealing with the liberty which we have in manipulating the data – the more dynamically variables are handled, the easier data can be manipulated. We distinguish four gradations here:

1. fully static variables

2. parameter variables

3. single time assignable variables

4. multiple times assignable variables

Fully static variables: In a fully static environment, the values of variables are either completely pre-determined, or not defined at all. In the latter case the semantics is taken to consist of *all* possible behaviours for *any* valuation of the various variables. This addition is the situation described in [2] and chapter 2 of the present paper.

Parameter variables: Parameter variables play a role within HMSC or MSC reference expressions, the idea being that one provides a value for one or more variables while calling the reference MSC. It can be used especially when the same behaviour needs to be described for different values for some of the actions, see for example Figure 2.

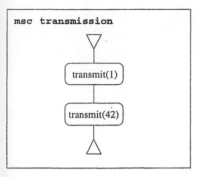 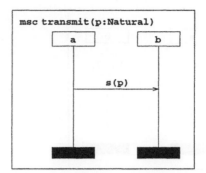

Figure 2. Example MSC with parameter variables

Intuitively, this means that the reference MSC *transmit* is called twice, but the first time with p equal to 1, and the second time with p equal to 42. Thus, first the message $s(1)$ is sent and received, then $s(42)$. Parametric data is semantically less complicated than the next two options of assignable variables. On the other hand, it is also less powerful. Of course, it would also be possible to include both options, resulting in an even greater power of expression.

Single time assignable variables: Here a variable can be assigned at any place in the MSC, but once it is assigned, it cannot get a new value, at least not within its current scope. So each time a variable is accessed, it will still have the same value. A problem here is what we should do with attempts to access a variable before it is given a value. We will go further into this question below. An example of an MSC with single time assigned variables can be found in Figure 1.

Multiple times assignable variables: This choice offers most expressiveness to the user. No restrictions apply; the variables can have their value changed at any time (provided they have been declared), and as often as is wanted. On the other hand, it is also the most complex one, thus possibly causing problems to those theorizing about the language and the tool makers. One problem is, that one sometimes would like to use an *old* value of a variable in the interpretation of an expression. See for example Figure 3 (assuming global variables). Intuitively it is clear that the sending of the message $m(x)$ uses the last assignment to x, and thus its current value. But what about its receipt? If that too would use the current value of x, we could have the trace $x := 1; s(m(1)); x := 2; r(m(2))$ (here s and r are used to denote the sending and reception of a message). But this would mean that the received message is unequal to the sent message. It would be more natural to let the final receipt be $m(1)$. This would imply that it refers to the value of x at some time in the past (namely, when the message was sent). Although it is not impossible to formulate a semantics that describes this, it is cumbersome, and the resulting semantics might become non-transparent.

Note that this same problem can also arise with single time assignable variables, if we allow access to the variable before it is used – what is important, is that there is an assignment between the two usages of the variable.

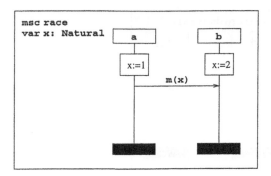

Figure 3. MSC with assignable variables and message

An even more complicated situation occurs when we consider multi-instance events. These are events that work on more than one instance but do not represent a point in time where all instances involved synchronize. One might think of conditions in this regard. There are proposals to use conditions as guards. This creates a problem when the truth value of a condition changes between the different times it is checked by the various instances. This problem will be described more extensively below, when we discuss the use of data in conditions.

4.2. Place of assignment

When having dynamic variables, one needs a construct to assign them a value. In the examples up to now, we have used local action for this purpose. Of course a new construct could be introduced to do so, but it seems both possible and preferable to use an existing construct for this, so that the language is not extended more than is necessary.

If we have static variables, no assignment takes place at all. Instead, all variables are quantified universally, that is, they can have *any* valid value, and a behaviour that corresponds to any value is a valid behaviour of the MSC. This is described in more detail in [2].

With parametric variables, we do have assignments, but they are necessarily part of the call itself, so again we have no options to choose from.

Thus, the only place where this question really comes up is with the (single or multiple times) assignable variables.

Apart from local actions, we could also use message inputs for assigning values to a variable. The idea is that a message which has received a value when sent, and has only a variable as its value when received, in that way sets the variable. This is shown in Figure 4. The variable x in the reference MSC is set by the fact that the actual value of the message $m(x)$ received from the environment is $m(3)$. One problem with this way of working could be that it may not be clear when a message receipt is a variable assignment and when it is not. For example, $m(3)$ could be unified with $m(x)$, but can $m(3 + y)$ be unified with $m(4)$, or even $m(x + 4)$?

Of course, some other MSC constructs could be used as an assignment, but we will not

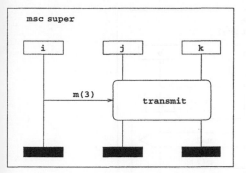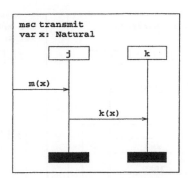

Figure 4. Message input as an assigning action

go into them here. Below when talking about data and conditions we will see one option in which conditions are used as assignments.

4.3. Place of referencing a variable

The next question we will discuss is the places and ways that a variable can be used. Basically, any place where now some string text appears in MSC which is not further specified, we could replace it with an expression in the data language. And such an expression could be, or could include, a variable.

This usage only requires evaluation of the expression. Such unspecified texts exist in local actions, messages, timers, and several other constructs, even instance names.

A more involved usage of expressions is in conditions. Currently, conditions do not have any dynamic meaning in the semantics of MSC. When data are added, they might be used as guarding conditions. To do so, one would put a boolean expression in the condition. The condition could then be passed only if the expression in it were true. For an example of this, see the left MSC in Figure 5. Instance a sends a message, containing the value of x, to instance b. If x equals zero, then the second alternative cannot be chosen, so it has to be the first, and instance b replies with message *zero*. If x does not equal zero, the first alternative cannot be chosen, and the second one will be, resulting in the message *nonzero*.

Unfortunately, we run into problems in cases like the one in the right MSC in Figure 5. Here, instance a gives x the value 0, then sends k, and arrives at the choice. It may now select the second alternative, change x to 1, and wait for $m(2)$ to arrive. However, it is possible that the right instance arrives at the choice of the alt-expression after x has been changed to 1, and then cannot pass the condition, at least not to the lower of the two choices where the left instance has gone. The question is: What should we do with such a case?

There are several options. We found at least the following, but this list is possibly not complete:

1. If we have only static and parametric data, or only single time assignable variables that cannot be used before their assignment, there is no problem.

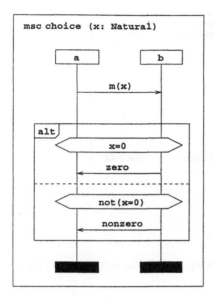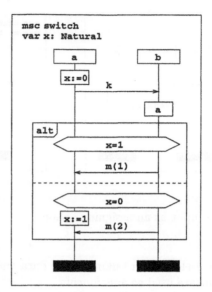

Figure 5. Using conditions as guards

2. Simply ignore this problem, and just go ahead with the semantics. This will cause the right MSC in Figure 5 to deadlock in the situation above, as the right instance will try to enter the second alternative, but cannot do so.

3. 'First one to pass the condition decides'. That is, the first instance going through the condition checks its truth value, and if it finds the condition to be true, then all instances can go through, no matter what the actual truth value at the time when they do so is.

4. Make a condition into a synchronization point. That is, all instances have to pass the condition at the same time. And thus, they have to evaluate the guarding expression at the same time, resulting in the same outcome.

5. Let each instance separately choose between the alternatives. In our example this would mean that whereas the left instance chose the lower alternative, the right one may still choose the upper one. We would like to advise against this alternative, though. It goes straight against the current MSC semantics, in which all instances do choose the same alternative. Another objection is that it solves the problem only when the condition guards a choice, not in other cases.

6. Make the assignments of variables in global conditions themselves, and let each instance remember its own copy of the variable, updating it when it goes through the condition. Although this does solve the problem, the working of variables may well differ much from people's intuitive ideas about them.

4.4. Handling of an undefined variable

In many cases it will be possible to refer to a variable while it does not have a value. It is not a priori clear how this should be managed. We will list several possible options:

1. Forbid this, and use static requirements to enforce this disallowance. This can be done if one uses a simple data language, and does not use complicated MSC structures (such as guarded loops), but if one uses a data language that is strong enough to function as a complete programming language, or if more complicated MSC functionalities are included, this may become difficult, or even impossible.

2. Detect the problem during dynamic evaluation. In this case we check runtime whether a variable is initialized. If not, we get a dynamic error (that is, semantically, a deadlock).

3. All undefined variables are regarded as universally quantified. That is, they can have any possible initial value. The semantics of the MSC is then the delayed choice of all possible behaviours for any initial value (or set of initial values). This is basically the same treatment as given to static variables in [2]. Thus, a dynamic variable is treated as a static one until its first assignment. A problem with this approach is that the number of alternatives could be infinite, and it is hard to give semantics for an infinite delayed choice, the resulting semantics without doubt being both ugly and hard to work with.

4. Each (type of) variable has a default value. Until its first assignment it has this default value. This way there are no undefined variables. We need to have a default value for each data domain, though.

The choice between these options will also be dependent on other choices. For example, the last two options, where the variable has some value before the first assignment, do not fit very well with the 'single assignment' dynamic variables. The reason that single assignment is simpler than multiple assignment, is that the variable will have the same value each time it is used. The last two solutions will remove this advantage, so we see no reason why, if they are used, one would prefer single assignments to multiple assignments.

4.5. Scope of a variable

A further point on which we can make different choices is in the definition of the scope of a variable. That is, once a variable has been declared, on which part of the MSC can it be used? This is the scope of that variable. Scopes might be nested, in which case the variables in the outer scope can also be used in the inner scope, unless a new declaration of the same variable has taken place. If a variable is used in two different scopes, then the two uses of the variable have nothing in common, and they should be regarded as two different variables that happen to share the same name.

We can distinguish two different dimensions to the scope: Block scope and architectural scope.

The block scope of a variable is a separated (framed) part of an MSC where the variable is defined. Such a separated part could be a complete MSC document, a single MSC, an MSC reference expression or an Inline expression. There might be more choices, but these seem to be the most logical ones.

114

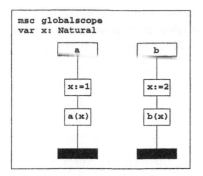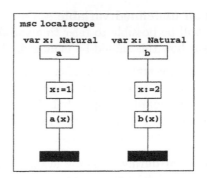

Figure 6. The difference between local and global architectural scope

Apart from this there is also the architectural scope. This gives the locality with respect to the instances in an MSC. We could define a variable to be defined on only one instance, or on all instances of the MSC. Possibilities in between, where a variable is defined on a number of instances (for example, the instances that reside on one processor), could also be considered, although it might be harder to find a syntax for that option.

The difference between (architecturally) local and global variables can be seen in Figure 6. On the left we see an MSC with a global variable x, on the right one with two local variables, both called x. The difference is that on the right, instance a will always do $a(1)$, as for this instance the value of x is 1, while the right instance will do $b(2)$, as for this instance the value of x is 2. On the left, where the variable x is global, it does not matter where the value of x has been changed, and thus both instances will use the last value of x, wherever it came from. Here $x := 1; x := 2; a(2); b(2)$ is a possible trace – at the time instance a executes $a(x)$ the value of x is 2, so that is the value that is used.

Of course one could decide to make all variables local, in that case the MSC on the left would act just like the one on the right, the creation of the variable x being shorthand for creating such a variable on all instances.

It might be argued that MSC is a language in which all communication is displayed explicitly, which implies that the introduction of a shared variable paradigm goes against the spirit of MSC. This would make the (architecturally) local character of variables the more logical choice. If one uses local variables, one does however also need a way to transport the value of a variable from one instance to another. A logical way to do so would be through messages - see however the problems that are mentioned about this in the 'place of assignment' subsection.

However, if this is chosen, one should also decide whether and how the value of a variable can be communicated from one instance to another.

5. SEMANTICS

As stated before, our aim is to parameterize the MSC language with a data language. To do so also requires to parameterize the MSC semantics. Included in such a parameterization needs to be an interface that specifies the information that is needed from the data language.

What exactly this interface looks like, depends on the choices made with respect to the issues raised above. For example, if one chooses to use default values to solve the problem of undefined variables, one needs these default values in the interface.

We will give example semantics for two choices, namely parametric variables with global architectural scope, and single-assignment dynamic variables with static check of undefined variables and global architectural scope. Several other choices will also be mentioned in short, giving an idea of how they can be elaborated as well as the problems this might cause.

5.1. General Interface

We first give a general idea about the interface that is needed, although some things will be added or removed depending on the exact choices that are made.

We would, in general, need 3 kinds of expressions:

- A set of declarations D, being the strings that represent variable declarations

- A set of assignments A, being the strings that represent (or can represent) assignments to variables

- A set of expressions E, being the strings that represent (or can represent) expressions

Apart from this we also need a set of possible variables Var, which in most cases will be a subset of E, and a semantic domain S, in which the expressions will be interpreted.

To define the semantics of the parameterized MSC language, we need the notion of a state. A state gives a snapshot of the values of all variables involved.

A state consists of:

- A set of defined variables $V \subseteq Var$

- A valuation function $\varphi : V \to S$, giving the values of the variables. The set of all valuation functions is called Φ.

Then, there need to be functions to interpret the various texts.

- For declarations: $d : D \to \mathcal{P}(\mathrm{Var})$ giving the variables that are declared by D

- For assignments: A set $A_V \subseteq A$ for each set of variables V, giving the set of assignments that may actually be used, given that only variables in V are defined, and a state transition function $\tau : \Phi \times A \to \Phi$. $\tau(\varphi, a)$ denotes the new state the MSC turns into when assignment a is executed in state (V, φ). Note that $\tau(\varphi, a)$ needs only be defined when $a \in A_V$, where V is the set of variables on which φ is defined.

- For expressions: A set $E_V \subseteq E$ for each set of variables V, giving the set of expressions that may actually be used, given that only variables in V are defined, and an interpretation function $I_\varphi : E_V \to S$, where V is the set of variables on which φ is defined. $I_\varphi(x)$ gives the value that x is interpreted to.

5.2. The Interface for our example

For our example language, the various elements of the Interface are described below.

- Var consists of all natural and boolean variables. Natural variables are x, y, z, $x_1, x_2, \ldots$; boolean variables are p, q, r, $p_1, p_2, \ldots$

- Natural expressions are formed from integers, integer variables, and the operators $+$ and $\cdot$, boolean expressions are formed from booleans, boolean variables, and the operators $\neg$, $\vee$, $\wedge$ and $=$ (the latter acting on natural expressions)

- D consists of all expressions of the form 'Var x: Nat', with x a natural variable or 'Var p: Bool', with p a boolean variable, and of lists of such expressions

- A consists of all expressions of the form $x := e$, with either x a boolean variable and e a boolean expression, or x a natural variable and e a natural expression

- E consists of all expressions of the form $a(x)$ with a a string of characters, and x a natural or boolean expression.

- S consists of the naturals, the booleans, as well as all expressions $a(x)$, with a some string and x a natural or boolean.

- $d(x)$ consists of all variables in x

- A_V and E_V consist of those expressions that contain only variables in V.

- The value of a natural or boolean expression e, given a valuation function φ is its numerical or truth value when each variable x in that expression is replaced by its value $\varphi(x)$. This value will be called $\varphi(e)$.

- $\tau(\varphi, x := e)$ is equal to φ with the value of x changed into $\varphi(e)$.

- $I_\varphi(a(x))$, with a some string and x some expression, equals $a(I_\varphi(x))$.

5.3. General Semantics

In a state (V, φ), all expressions must be in E_V and all assignments in A_V. Provided one uses variables with a well-defined scope, this should not be hard to check statically.

If the MSC is in a state (V, φ), all events such as $action(a, i)$ and $send(m, i, j)$, have as their "name" parts (i.e. a for an action and m for a message) an expression, which thus must be in E_V. The semantics for such an action are then equal to the semantics of $action(I_\varphi(a), i)$ and $send(I_\varphi(m), i, j)$, respectively in 'normal' MSC, apart from the two exception below:

- If we use assignable variables, using local actions as assignments, then a local action $action(a, i)$ may also have $a \in A_V$. In this case it causes a state change from (V, φ) to $(V, \tau(\varphi, a))$.

- If we use multiple times assignable variables, or single time assignable variables that can be used before their assignment, then to give the semantics of a message receipt, we need to use the state at the time the message was sent. We will discuss the problems this might result in, and how they might be solved, when discussing the extension of the semantics to other options.

Using the semantics of existing MSC, the semantics of MSC with data can now be described by (we will include the first but not the second exception):

$$\frac{x \xrightarrow{action(a,i)} x', a \in E}{(x, V, \varphi) \xrightarrow{action(I_\varphi(a),i)} (x', V, \varphi)}$$

$$\frac{x \xrightarrow{action(a,i)} x', a \in A}{(x, V, \varphi) \xrightarrow{action(a,i)} (x, V, \tau(\varphi, a))}$$

An operational rule like $x \xrightarrow{a} x'$ means that in an expression x one can do an action a, to end up in the expression x'. In the above rules, the interpretation of MSC with data (x, V, φ), is derived from that of MSC without data x – the step below the line can be taken if the step above the line can.

5.4. Parametric Variables

The interpretation to parametric variables as given below complies with the *call-by-value* principle used in many programming languages for instantiating the values of procedural parameters.

In parametric data, we do not have explicit assignments, so we can do away with A, and declarations will probably also not be necessary, as they are implicit as well. What remains are E, Var, E_V, and I_φ.

In parametric variables, we could have an MSC reference expression (most important example) refer to an MSC $msc\_name(e_1, e_2, \ldots e_n)$, with $e_1, \ldots, e_n \in E_V$, provided that MSC msc_name is defined as msc $msc\_name(x_1, \ldots, x_n)$, with $x_i \in Var$, $x_i \neq x_j$.

In this case the semantics of the MSC reference expression $msc\_name(e_1, \ldots, e_n)$ in a state (V, φ) can be found by pre-processing the MSC msc_name by changing expressions e into $I_{\varphi^*}(e)$, using the state $(V \cup \{x_1, \ldots, x_n\}, \varphi^*)$, where:

- $\varphi^*(x) = e_i$ if $x = x_i$

- $\varphi^*(x) = \varphi(x)$ if $x \notin \{x_1, \ldots, x_n\}$

Parametric variables are relatively simple, semantically speaking, which can be seen from the fact that pre-processing, as described above, is enough to describe the semantics. When we get to dynamical data, this will not be the case – we will have to use the state within the operational calculations

5.5. Single Time Assignable Variables

Our second example will use the following setting: single time assignable variables, static checks that unassigned variables are not used, architecturally global variables, and assignments in local actions.

Here it is important to use unique names for variables. To do this, each time we meet a declaration of an already used variable, we use a new name. Each action in the scope gets a list of which variable is actually used when some variable (like x) is meant.

That is, if we get a variable x in a scope, we define a fresh variable x_i, and everywhere within the scope, all actions get a pointer, saying that instead of the value of x, the value of x_i has to be checked. To be able to do so, the declaration of variables should be checked by the semantics at a time when it is clear what is and what is not the scope.

To do so, we need to 'rename' the variable within the scope, if it also has a meaning outside the scope. Thus, we will need to have renaming operators $\rho_{(x \mapsto y)} : E \mapsto E$ and $\rho_{x \mapsto y} : A \mapsto A$ for each pair of variables x and y, defining what is the result when x is replaced by y. Furthermore, to make everything work, Var should be (countably) infinite, and ρ should have certain nice properties, for example $I_{\varphi^*}(\rho_{x \mapsto y}(e)) = I_\varphi(e)$, when φ is not defined on y, and φ^* is given by adding $\varphi(y) = \varphi(x)$ to φ.

Suppose an MSC reference expression is called, which consists of a variable declaration D, and an MSC-part k. Then the semantics of MSC-reference expression (D, k) in a state (V, φ) is that of $\rho_{x_1 \mapsto y_1}(\rho_{x_2 \mapsto y_2}(\ldots(k)\ldots))$ in a state $(V \cup \{y_1, y_2, \ldots y_n\}, \varphi)$ (lifting ρ to MSC actions and expressions, then to a list of them, in the obvious way). Because the value of the new variables cannot be used until they have been assigned, how φ is extended to the new variables does not matter. $x_1, \ldots, x_n$ are the variables defined by D, that is, $v(D)$, and $y_1, \ldots, y_n$ are n unused variables.

Having done all this, we can then use the semantics as given in section 5.3.

5.6. Types

In the example language, there are variables in two types, natural and boolean. It is probably useful to add this concept to the MSC semantic interface, so we know that the expressions $x \wedge y$ is only legal if x and y are boolean expressions. Above we have used different sets of variables (p, q, r, $p_1, \ldots p_n$ for booleans and x, y, z, $x_1, \ldots x_n$ for naturals) to distinguish the two types, but in more realistic languages, one variable could be of more than one type, depending on the preceding declaration. Of course, which types exist, what their semantical interpretation is, and how the variables are given types, should be inherited from the data language. It has no actual relevance for the MSC language and its semantics. An exception could be the type of booleans, which would be the only allowable type if guarding expressions in expressions are added (see section 4.2); a similar treatment could also be given to naturals, which are used to give the number of times a loop must be passed, this could also be extended to include general expressions of the appropriate type.

Semantically, a semantic domain is asked for each possible type; their interaction is completely left to the data language. Using types would give a somewhat more complicated interface, which we will not give here.

5.7. Other choices

Above for two possible choices, the semantics have been discussed. We will now look at the other options, but in much less detail, giving only the main differences with our example settings in both the interface and the semantics.

Multiply assignable variables: Compared to singly assignable variables, the extra problem is in the situation that the value of a variable may change between the sending and the receipt of a message. Yet, the receipt should use the values as they were when the message was sent. To make this possible, one should add either to the process algebra expression or to the state, a list of messages that have been sent, and how they were interpreted. Then, when a message must be received, instead of looking up the current value, one should use the value given by this list. This method only works if one strictly keeps the uniqueness of message names. The semantics currently assume this uniqueness, but in the presence of loops, maintaining it is tricky.

Apart from this problem, multiply assignable variables can be given the same semantics that have been given to singly assignable variables.

Assignment in messages: One option here would be to make an incoming message expression correspond to an outgoing message expression, provided there is some assignment to variables that would allow it. The value of the variable after that would be any value for which the 'fit' would work. Still, there is the problem of when an incoming message is defining a value, and when it is merely using it. We do not see an immediately obvious answer to this question.

Guarding conditions: First, we need to define a set of Boolean expressions B, which have B_V and I_φ like normal expressions have E_V and I_φ, but necessarily have $\{\text{true}, \text{false}\}$ as their semantic domain. All conditions need to have a text which is a boolean expression in B_V. Where until now each condition could be gone through without changing anything, this now will only be true for conditions that evaluate to 'true'. If a condition evaluates to 'false', it acts as a deadlock.

The more detailed semantics for such a guarding condition, depends on what choice is made to deal with the 'changing value' problem, whether it be one of the five options we provide or yet another one.

Dynamical check of unused variables: The state now contains two sets of variables instead of one. One of these is the existing set V of defined variables, the other a set $V' \subseteq V$ of variables that actually have received a value. An action containing an expression may only be done when its expression is not just in E_V, but in $E_{V'}$. An action being disallowed is equivalent to making it a deadlock. For assignments, whether an assignment is allowed is dependent both on V and on V', resulting in $A_{V,V'}$ instead of A_V. If a variable gets assigned a value, it is added to V'.

Default values for unused variables: It is necessary to add the default variables for each variable (or, more likely, one default value for each variable type) to the interface. Apart from that, the problem of variable value changes, found in multiply assignable variables, also needs to be dealt with again; we propose the same solution.

Unused variables are universally quantified: We need the semantics to be the delayed choice of all possible 'default value' semantics. A problem here is that this may be a delayed choice of infinitely many options. Such an infinite operator makes things very complicated. Rules can probably be found for it, but most likely will be both ugly and unworkable.

Local variables: Instead of one set of variables V and one valuation function φ, we now have one set and one function for each instance in the MSC. The set and the function of the instance on which an action takes place are used to determine the semantics of that action. Of course message receipt is an exception, checking the instance from which the message was sent rather than the instance on which the action itself takes place.

When we have globally defined variables with local values, it seems logical to allow messages to make the value of a variable known to other instances. To allow this, we would need an extra interface function $c : E \to \text{Var}$, giving the variables whose values are sent when the expression is sent.

For each message, a 'snapshot' of the sender's state when the message was sent is remembered, and not only is this snapshot used to interpret the receipt of the message, but also for the variables in $c(e)$, the value on the receiving instance is set to the value they have in this snapshot.

6. CONCLUSIONS

In this paper we have argued that the extension of MSC with a data language shall be accomplished in such a way that the data language definition is a parameter of the MSC language definition. This will overcome maintenance problems of the recommendation and will make it possible to anticipate at the variety of data languages already used in conjunction with MSC.

In [2] we have shown feasibility of this approach for the case of a data language with static variables, using as our examples an algebraic specification language and a constraint syntax language. In the current paper we have extended this research to dynamic variables. Rather than giving a precise description of how to incorporate dynamic data variables in MSC, we have listed a range of questions and possible answers concerning the connection between MSC and a data language. Since most of the questions are orthogonal, in the sense that possible answers to one question do not restrict the answers to other questions, this gives raise to a large variety of options.

One such option is the following: variables can be assigned only once, static checks on the MSC guarantee that no references to uninitialized variables are made, variables are known to all instances, and only in local actions variables can be assigned a value.

For a number of such options we have experimented with defining the interface between the MSC language and the data language, and we have sketched a semantics of this combined language, based on such an interface. These experiments indicate that the parameterization approach is also feasible for dynamic variables. Of course, a more detailed treatment of the semantics of the combined MSC/Data language is dependent upon the design choices made by the MSC standardization group. However, the present paper gives an overview of both the possibilities and the problems from a semantic point of view.

REFERENCES

1. P. Baker and C. Jervis. Formal description of data. Experts meeting SG10, Lutterworth TDL16, ITU-TS, 1997.
2. L.M.G. Feijs and S. Mauw. MSC and data. In Yair Lahav, Adam Wolisz, Joachim Fischer, and Eckhardt Holz, editors, *SAM98 - 1st Workshop on SDL and MSC. Proceedings of the SDL Forum Society on SDL and MSC*, number 104 in Informatikberichte, pages 85–96. Humboldt-Universität Berlin, 1998.
3. ITU-TS. *ITU-TS Recommendation Z.100: Specification and Description Language (SDL)*. ITU-TS, Geneva, 1988.
4. ITU-TS. *ITU-TS Recommendation Z.120: Message Sequence Chart (MSC)*. ITU-TS, Geneva, 1997.
5. D. Steedman. *Abstract syntax notation one (ASN.1): the tutorial and reference*. Technology Appraisals Ltd., 1990.

Session IV

Testing I

)L'99 : The Next Millennium
Dssouli, G.v. Bochmann and Y. Lahav, editors
999 Elsevier Science B.V. All rights reserved

DL-based Specification and Testing Strategy for Communication Network Protocols

. Monkewich

ortel Networks, P.O. Box 3511 Station C, Ottawa ON K1Y 4H7 Canada

INTRODUCTION

a global, multi-vendor environment, product interoperability through nformance to international standards and specifications is of prime importance. It , therefore, essential to ensure that approved standards and agreed specifications 'e error-free and that product suppliers who implement the standards and ecifications carry out testing during the product development cycle to assess con-rmance. This would mean that in addition to implementing the standard or ecification, several thousand conformance test cases must be produced at fferent stages of development and executed against each implementa-tion. If this done by traditional means, it can add significantly to the product cost and crease the time to market.

urrent practice in protocol specification and testing is largely manual, based on atural language description and production of relatively few tests in relation to the umber of design requirements. The resulting specifications contain errors and nbiguities. The corresponding tests are not precisely traceable to the design ecifications.

more comprehensive, formalized process of specification, validation and testing is eded to reduce development cost, time to market and the incidence of field faults. his paper summarizes the main benefits offered by the formalized approach. The iantified results were obtained in two pilot projects using an SDL/TTCN-based ethodology in a product development setting. The formalized approach shows :omise of meeting the criteria of a design and development "best practice" process, ith a potential for improved market performance and profitability of product lines . the telecommunication industry.

1.1. Background

Currently, protocols are specified in natural language and contain errors a... ambiguities [1] which may not be detected until late in the design/produ... introduction cycle, making them costly to find and fix. Many development tasks a... done serially and can benefit from greater concurrency. Errors could be detect... early in the product development cycle beginning with the standard or t... specification itself. These benefits may be achieved through formalized techniqu... and the use of commercial tools.

Formal specification of protocols in machine-readable form is an essential first st... in making use of software tools. Once machine-readable specification is availabl... tools can be applied to generate the implementation code and valid conformance te... suites directly from the specification at lower cost and in shorter time. While sever... formal description techniques have been standard-ized, SDL [2] is preferred by t... industry, because it has good maintenance support and is widely supported l... software tool suppliers.

To demonstrate conformance to a standard or specification, it is required to execu... a set of test events in the form of protocol data unit exchanges between a tester ar... the implemen-tation under test. Sequences of test events are grouped into test cas... and sets of test cases into test suites. Each test case corresponds to a specific te... purpose reflecting a unique requirement in the specification. A test sui... corresponds to a set of requirements which fulfil the desired coverage of t... prescribed behaviour of the protocol. Such test suites are usually specified in t... standardized language, the Tree and Tabular Combined Notation (TTCN) [3] ar... may be converted into executable form by the use of a number of available TTC... compilers [4]. Test suites in TTCN can be generated from SDL protoc... specifications using commercial tools.

An Abstract Test Suite (ATS) expressed in TTCN, is a specification of a set of te... cases independent of any specific protocol imple-mentation or test platform. 1... minimize test suite errors, ATSs must be produced and validated from form... protocol specifications expressed in SDL. Complete ATSs with full coverage of t... specified conformance requi-rements, should consist of several thousand test cas... each, but are often reduced to about two hundred test cases to accommodate man... al test case production. When a large number of test cases are produced usin... manual techniques, the number of pervasive problems within the test suite... combination with protocol errors make the test suite unusable.

To test a medium-size protocol, a test suite that consists of several thousand te... cases may be required. This is well beyond the capability of manual test producti... methods. However, with software tools, it is possible to produce error-free te... suites from specifica-tions in SDL without limiting the number of test cases and te... coverage of the requirements.

tandardized ATSs are not available for most protocol standards. Up to now, due to ne cost of developing ATSs by manual methods, organizations seldom contributed rivately developed ATSs for standardization in ISO or ITU. Instead, ATSs were nade available under license in executable form. Executable test cases, however, annot be easily traced to determine consistency with the design speci-fication and ne small number of test cases did not provide the required coverage of the pecifications.

.2. Position

he longer an error remains undetected during the design/product introduction cycle, the more ostly and difficult it is to fix. Modern design methods reuse software, often of uncertain origin nd authors, and may import errors that cannot be easily discovered.

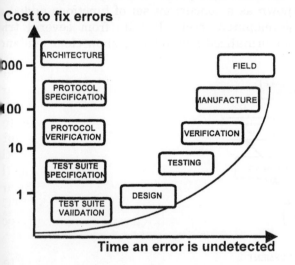

figure 1. Cost of undetected errors

igure 1 illustrates the increase in cost to fix an error if it is undetected through the arious stages of development, from protocol specifi-cation to the introduction of the roduct into the field.

his means that emphasis is required on "upfront" investment in specification, erifica-tion and testing. It is recommended that the product design community eview its development processes in the light of the available SDL/TTCN-based aethodology. The formalized process requires an early investment of resources to evelop error-free protocol standards and specifications which in executable SDL an be used to demonstrate the operation of the specification to the customer in rder to reach agreement on design. At the same time, the associated test suites in TCN should be produced.

126

Among the critical issues is the correctness of protocol and test specification, traceability of tests to the design specifications and the use of software tools [5].

It should also be understood that the process is based on a complex methodolog and requires skills to work with advanced commercial software tools. Design an development managers must have at their disposal well trained staff and mu make an investment in high-quality commercial tools.

2. THE FORMALIZED PROCESS

Figure 2 illustrates how the formalized process was integrated within th development environment. It is essential that each of these components considered in a combined context. The additional parts added by the process a shown as shaded blocks. They are shown as a concurrent set of functions added the serial process of the product development cycle. Results from several tri projects to quantify the benefits of the formalized methodology show clear eviden of the feasibility of this approach [6].

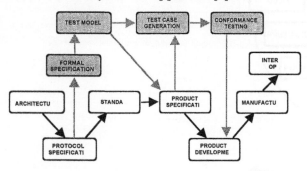

☐ SERIAL PROCESS OF THE CURRENT DEVELOPMENT
▨ PARALLEL FORMALIZED TESTING IS ADDED TO THE

Figure 2. Specification and testing integrat-ed with development

These components of the process and their interdependence are illustrated i Figure 3. This diagram closely resembles the recently adopted ITU-T process for th production of high-quality protocol standards.

In this process, a precise and unambiguous SDL specification is produced togethe with a suitable choice of related Message Sequence Charts (MSCs) [7]. This is dor with the aid of software tools and in conjunction with the natural languag specification. MSCs serve a useful role in specifying typical communicatic scenarios or specific requirements.

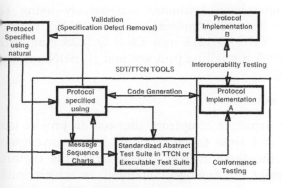

gure 3. The formalized process

he full process includes simulation and validation steps in which specification efects are detected and removed. Once the specification is verified, it can be used to :oduce two or more implementations to assess implementability and .teroperability of the specification and to produce and validate the conformance st suite.

onformance test suites are generated from the SDL specification [8] with the use ' commercial tools . As part of the process, the test suite generated is validated for rrectness and consistency with the specification, and can be standardized and ade available at the same time as the specification itself.

here are three main elements of the process which lead to specific benefits and lyback:

Machine-readable SDL form for standards and specifications.

Software tools for specification, mplemen-tation, verification and test generation.

Conformance testing integrated with the product development process.

)L is well suited for specification of communications protocols, reactive systems ich as switches and routers and distributed systems. It allows representation of 'stem behaviour to the desired level of detail while allowing the designer to make igineering decisions at the architectural level. MSCs provide a powerful means for rmally describing individual requirements that can be converted to SDL in order add proprietary features to the design specifications.

ie process applies to any system which requires specification and testing of the mplete protocol behaviour, verification of a single feature or simulation of the •eration of a complete systems.

128

Some examples of protocols that have been evaluated extensively using th
formalized process include Intelligent Network Application Part (INAP) protoc
Capability Set One Revised (CS-1R) ITU-T Q.1218 and CS-2 Q.1228 standard
Q.921 ISDN LAPD protocol, ATM Q.2931 Signalling protocol and B-ISDN point-t
multipoint capability ITU-T Q.2971 [9].

2.1. Best Practice and Time to Market

Best practice processes today use the principle of upfront increase in project tim
and people to reduce the total cost and time to market. An initial investmer
required to produce and validate specifications in SDL and generate the require
test suites aligns well with the concept of "front-end loading" in which initi
investment of 17% at the concept /design phase can result in a 30-50% savings a
the product development and deployment phases.

This is illustrated in Figure 4 which is based on a recent study done by th
University of West Virginia and the US Air Force.

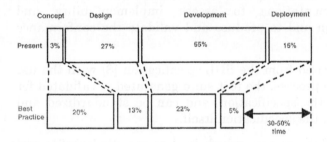

Figure 4. Impact on Time To Market

2.2. The New Process vs Current Practice

The cost of finding and fixing field errors is high. To find and fix one field fault
equivalent to $15,000 of engineering time; another $100,000 is required to retro1
the affected field units. For each field fault, about 1 month of development time
lost that could be used to develop new products [9].

Quantified data on the cost of production of formal specifications is varied an
strongly depends on the level of detail and the number of parameters included
the specification. As an example, it is estimated that a specification of the UNI 4
Signalling protocol (Q.2931) in SDL would take 1 person-year to develop.

Costs associated with test generation and the testing process are somewhat bett
quantified and may be summarized as in Figure 5. The figure represents a set
generic curves to illustrate the relative cost of manual and automated testing [9].

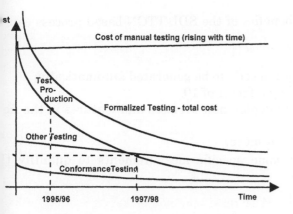

st

Cost of manual testing (rising with time)

Test
Pro-
duction

Formalized Testing - total cost

Other Testing

ConformanceTesting

1995/96   1997/98   Time

igure 5. Cost of testing with time

ne main cost component is the cost of computer assisted test case generation. This
·ocess, however, is becoming increasingly automated and new methods are being
·veloped.

uring the trial projects to quantify the benefits of the SDL/TTCN-based method-
ogy, some data from earlier projects that used manual methods was made
·ailable. This information, together with new data was used to shape the curves of
.gure 5.

me procedural information was also interesting. In testing, current practice relies
a testers that are not only difficult to use, but produce test data which requires
.man interpretation and analysis at the bit and byte level. Test logs required
·alysis to gain confidence that the test case verdicts were assigned correctly. When
st cases are in TTCN are derived form SDL, test case verdicts are assigned
rrectly and automatically requiring no further analysis by the human operator.

. some specific cases it was possible to make direct comparisons regarding testing
·ne. At the time of the pilot project, testers and test procedures used were capable
executing 10 test cases per day. This included analysis of test results to ensure
·aceability to specifications and verdict assignment. Under the pilot project, 200
TCN test cases derived from SDL were executed in less than 2 hours and required
· further analysis or verification of the verdicts. A further direct comparison was
·ade where 2 person months were required to execute 32 test cases using a modern
·ster. The equivalent 32 test cases, derived from SDL were added to a test suite of
·9 TTCN test cases and the entire test suite executed in about 2 hours.

me examples were found to compare the cost of producing the implementation
·de. In general, 100% of the implementation code can be generated automatically
·m SDL. If the resulting code is considered to be too large, subsequent manual
·justments may be required. This may reduce this number to about 60%.

The salient results quantifying the benefits of the SDL/TTCN-based process can b summarized as follows [6]:

- Reduce the cost of testing by 90%;
- Allow over 60% of the implementation code to be generated automatically;
- Reduce the cost of test generation by a factor of 10.
- Reduce time to market and time to deploy new services and features in the fie by 35-50%.
- Reduce product field faults by 80% or more.

Table 1 summarizes the results of some specific measurements to quantify th benefits of the formalized process [9].

Table 1. Benefits of the Formalized Process

Item	Current	Formal Process
Spec/Standard	268 errors (Q.2931)	Error-free
C code production	2 weeks	5 minutes
Test production	1 test case per day	12 test cases per day
Testing time	2 months	2 days
Test traceability to specifications	Poor	Exact
Coverage of Specifications	10%	100%
Future view	Worse with time	Continuously improving

2.3. Implementation of the New Process

It is recognized that the formal approaches are complex and require investment i time, resources and staff training. Expertise and capabilities in this area alread exist within different industry organizations. However, individual managers ofte must address their specific needs in isolation, unable to take advantage of disperse capabilities.

In general, the development groups do not describe their designs in SDL, althoug some have experimented with test case generation form available SDLs. In mo cases, the development groups purchase test cases from third party or generate te ises manually from natural language specifications. Under the current practice, ie development groups face the following problems:

standards which manufacturers implement contain errors and ambiguities;
there is a lack of specifications in SDL;
there is a lack of standardized TTCN test suites which are recognized in all markets;
test suites are limited in number and do not provide full coverage of specifications;
purchased executable test suites are not easily traceable to the specification;
the cost of purchased test suites is high
there is a lack of trained staff, capable of making use of the SDL/TTCN-based methodology.

ost leading telecommunications companies are aware of the problems surrounding ie current specification and testing practices.

the future, four main areas will need to be addressed. The quality of protocol andards will have to be improved. Training will need to be put in place to supply chnical staff trained in formal methods. Tool suppliers need to ensure that the ols are of industrial strength and quality. Communications sup-pliers must clude formalized techniques in among their best practice processes.

RELATED STANDARDS DEVELOPMENTS

September 1998, the ITU-T gave Recommendation status to a document entitled, *uidelines on the Quality Aspects of Protocol Related Recommendations*, which rongly supports the formalized process of Figure 3 as part of the development of U-T protocol Recommendations .

he *Guidelines*, which are now a supplement of Recommendation A.3, address the iteria of readability, completeness, correctness, consistency, unambiguity, iplementability and testability of standards [10]. It states that:

The quality of Recommendations is closely connected with the use of Formal Description Techniques (FDTs) and the use of computer-based tools. The main components of the quality process are formal specifications, validation of specifications and testing of prototype implementations.

his ITU-T commitment will make it possible to ensure that the new ITU-T protocol andards are error-free before the standards are approved.

arlier initiative within ISO/IEC JTC1 resulted in the development of ISO/IEC 646 conformance testing methodology and framework standard including the ecification of TTCN [11]. These principles are now being used within the ATM orum and elsewhere, and are an integral part of the formalized process.

ITU-T Study Group 7 (Data Networks and Open System Communications) ha approved the X.290 series of Recommendations on conformance testing methodolog and framework based on the ISO/IEC 9646 standard.

ITU-T Study Group 10 (Languages for Telecommunication Applications) is doir work in developing, maintaining and extending the SDL language and the metho ology for its use. The Study Group is also working on a testing methodology base on formal methods in conformance testing.

New work has been undertaken in SG 10 to produce a 3rd edition of the TTC standard for approval within ITU-T as Recommendation Z.140. This will include:

- resolution and implementation of the existing defect reports
- real-time testing
- performance testing
- simplification of TTCN

This work is expected to be completed by the end of 1999 with the help of inpu form the European Telecommunications Standards Institute (ETSI).

ITU-T SG11 (Switching and Signalling) uses formal SDL in accordance wi Recommen-dation Z.100 for the description of interface standards and continues move towards describing all interface standards in SDL. SG 11 has produce Q.1228 Recommendation which specifies INAP CS-1 and CS-2 models in executab SDL 92 form.

4. TRAINING

To provide research support and train workers, Nortel in partnership with Teleleg Inc., the University of Ottawa and Carleton University, has established two Nort *Advanced Communications Software Engineering Research and Trainir Laboratories*, one at each of the two universities in Ottawa.

The laboratories were established to address formal techniques for network protoc design and testing. The laboratories utilize tools from Telelogic and will devel new tools for the application of SDL and TTCN. The labora-tories provide graduat undergraduate and industry training supported by research and collaborati projects with other centers of excellence.

The laboratories will provide a source of potential hires trained in the use of tl SDL/TTCN methodology and tools and provide training for other Nortel staff.

5. FUTURE TRENDS

To remove the main roadblock standing in the way of wide acceptance of tl formalized process, it is necessary to make all protocol standards available :

xecutable SDL. This can be done during the standardization process where cost
iaring can reduce the up-front investment of producing the SDLs.

/ith the data network protocols gaining more attention in relation to the
raditional telecom-munications protocols, many of the relatively light-weight
iternet protocols may be expressed in SDL. This may be particularly appropriate
ith the newly formed liaison between ITU-T and the Internet Engineering Task
orce (IETF) and the potential for standardization of IETF Requests For Comment
RFCs) in ITU-T.

imilarly, opportunities exist to introduce the formalized methodology into the work
f the ATM Forum. The Forum is already a user of TTCN and the ISO/IEC 9646
esting method-ology and have recently expressed interest in SDL.

CONCLUSIONS

he benefits of implementing the new process based on formal techniques are clear.
owever, to implement the process, requires upfront investment of resources, staff
aining and industrial-strength tools.

commitment is required to produce SDL specifications and TTCN conformance
est suites. For this purpose, it is essential to utilize the standards community to
ie fullest extent. In a multi-vendor, global environment it is advantageous to have
ie recognized set of specifications and one set of tests worldwide. At the same
me, the cost may be shared by other interested organizations through their
ntributions to standards.

he expertise to develop specifications in SDL and test suites in TTCN currently
xists, but not in numbers sufficient to populate all development groups in the
idustry. Such expertise would have to be provided by the universities and phased
t over a period of time.

urrent and new tool producers need to be encouraged to continue with the
rolution of high-quality commercial tools and provide industry with maintenance
id training support.

EFERENCES

] Kim, M., *Implementation of B-ISDN Signalling Protocols using SDL,* 3rd
Annual Telelogic User Conference, San Francisco, November, 1997.

] ITU Telecommunication Standardization Sector (ITU-T), Recommendation
Z.100, *CCITT Specification and Description Language (SDL),* Geneva 1994.

] ISO/IEC 9646-3:1998, *Information Technology – Open Systems Interconnection –
Conformance testing method-ology and framework – Part 3: The Tree and
Tabular Combined Notation (TTCN),* Geneva 1998.

134

[4] Telelogic, *Telelogic Tau – Technical Presentation*, Telelogic Inc., Malm
Sweden, June 1998.

[5] ETSI, Making Better Standards - Practical Ways to Greater Efficiency ar
Success, Sophia Antipolis, France, May 1996.

[6] Monkewich, O. et al. *INAP CS-1R Test Suite from SDL*, internal report, Nort
Networks, Ottawa, September, 1998.

[7] Ellsberger, J. et al. *SDL, Formal Object-oriented Language for Communicatir*
Systems, Prentice Hall Europe, Hertford-shire, U.K, 1997.

[8] Prescott, P. et al., *Automated Test Case Generation Practitioner's Guide*, Be
Northern Research, BNR Project Report, Ottawa, 1996.

[9] Monkewich, O. et al., *Formalized SDL-based Specification and Testing*, 3
Annual Telelogic User Conference, San Francisco, November, 1997.

[10] ITU Telecommunication Standardization Sector (ITU-T), Supplement
Recom-mendation A.3, *Guidelines on the Quality Aspects of Protocol Recon*
mendations, Geneva 1998.

[11] ISO/IEC 9646-3:1994, *Information Technology – Open Systems Interconnectio*
– Conformance testing methodology and framework – Part 1 to Part 7, Genev
Switzerland, 1994.

[12] ETSI, *Use of SDL in European Telecommunications Standards - rules fe*
testability and facilitating validation, ETS 300 414, 1995.

SDL'99 : The Next Millennium
R: Dssouli, G.v. Bochmann and Y. Lahav, editors
©1999 Elsevier Science B.V. All rights reserved

Automated test generation from SDL specifications

Alain Kerbrat[a] , Thierry Jéron[b] and Roland Groz[c]

[a]Verilog, 150 rue Nicolas Vauquelin, BP1310, 31106 Toulouse cedex, France
e-mail: Alain.Kerbrat@verilog.fr   www: http://www.verilog.fr

[b]Irisa, Campus de Beaulieu, 35042 Rennes Cedex, France
e-mail: Thierry.Jeron@irisa.fr   www: http://www.irisa.fr/pampa

[c]France-Telecom-CNET, technopole Anticipa, 2 avenue Pierre Marzin, 22307 Lannion
Cedex France
e-mail: Roland.Groz@cnet.francetelecom.fr   www: http://www.cnet.fr

Automated test generation from formal specifications presents a lot of promises, either in cost control or test suite correctness. Some interesting tools begin to emerge, either prototypes or industrial strength tools. We present the result of the integration in *Object*GEODE of an industrial test generation tool [1]. This tool is based on two complementary test generation prototypes, TVEDA and TGV. TVEDA comes from the research laboratory France-Telecom-CNET, it provides for test purposes and test case generation, based on state space exploration combined with heuristics. TGV has been designed in the research laboratories Irisa and Verimag, it provides test case generation based on efficient, on-the-fly state space exploration techniques.

Keywords: test generation, conformance testing, SDL, TTCN, verification, static analysis

1. Introduction

Test generation is an area on which many companies are focusing in search of productivity and quality gains. Current industrial practices include at best semi automated test generation techniques, with all the cost and maintenance problems of an error prone process. This process should be fully automatically re-executable, with a complete understanding of the relationships between specification and tests, their meaning and their execution results.

Automating the test generation requires a precise and tractable description of the system to test. This is where using Formal Description Techniques such as SDL brings most of their benefits. In the telecommunications area, this approach has been developed first by giving a concrete framework to conformance testing [1], which is a necessary step to ensure the compliance of various implementations of a given protocol to its standards. Then this approach has been formalized further in order to facilitate the emergence of

---

[1]This work has been initiated and funded by France-Telecom

tools [18]. However, the interest into FDT based test generation tools has been mostly academic up to the middle of the 90s.

From two research tools to *TestComposer*

In this paper we present the result of the industrial transfer of two prototype tools. The resulting tool, *TestComposer*, is integrated into the *Object*GEODE toolbox from VERILOG.

The two prototype tools TVEDA and TGV offer complementary aspects of the test generation process. TVEDA's strengths are the analysis techniques of the FDT specification. These techniques allow to derive from the specification meaningful behaviors for the test, which are referred below as test purposes. On the other side, TGV applies powerful verification techniques to generate from these test purposes and the specification, the test cases which will constitute the final test suite. The combination of these two tools, integrated on top of the efficient *Object*GEODE's simulator, forms the new *Object*GEODE *TestComposer* tool. It comes as a replacement to the current *Object*GEODE's test generator TTCGEN.

In section 2, we present the principles and main features of each entry tool.

Section 3 is devoted to the architecture and working principles of the tool *TestComposer*. In this section, *TestComposer* functions will be demonstrated on the SSCOP protocol, this example being often used as support example for test generation tools.

2. Entry tools presentation

2.1. Tveda

TVEDA is a tool that was developed in France-Telecom-CNET (the R&D centre for France Telecom) over the years 1989-1995 (with a few minor improvements afterward). Its major aim was to provide people in charge of conformance testing in CNET (and related activities such as acceptance testing for protocols and services) with a tool to derive test suites suitable for the activity of test centres. The main features of TVEDA are the automatic generation of test purposes, its heuristic approach to the use of reachability analysis, and the wealth of pragmatic customizations that have been included to cater for the needs of many different applications within CNET.

TVEDA was delivered in several versions (from the very first prototype V0 in late 1989 to the last one V3 released in 1995) with strong differences in capabilities and underlying technology. In particular, SDL was introduced as an alternative input language in V2 (until then Estelle was the only input language). And only V3 implemented a semantic approach based on reachability analysis : all previous versions based test generation solely on syntactic transformations of the specification. However, in this paper, we refer only to the features of TVEDA V3, as this is the basis of what is integrated along with TGV into *Object*GEODE.

In the following subsections we provide a brief overview of the core ideas that are specific to TVEDA. More details will be found in previous papers on TVEDA, especially [16,5].

2.1.1. Empirical approach for test structure & TP generation

TVEDA was deliberately designed in opposition with traditional FSM-based techniques for test generation. Instead of concentrating on sound generation methods that can guarantee full fault coverage (under what test experts considered to be unreasonable assumptions on specifications and implementations), TVEDA was built on an empirical observation of the design methodology used by test experts for creating protocol test suites [16].

In particular, in TVEDA special attention has been paid to the TTCN output appearance emphasizing such aspects as test suite structure (e.g. grouping based on protocol functions, or control states etc), naming conventions for easier test identification, consistent use of test steps, comments (esp. associated to verdicts), automatic generation of the wording of test purposes in a meaningful natural language rendition, etc.

However, the most distinctive feature of TVEDA is the fact that it does not need test purposes as an input; instead, TVEDA can generate test purposes following the most common strategies used by test experts for protocols. Testing is usually based on the control structure of the EFSM representing a protocol specification. Typically, a test expert would design tests to cover each transition of this control structure. In terms of an SDL specification, a transition corresponds to a path from one state to the following nextstate. The usual approach followed is tantamount to branch coverage (covering every edge of a control flow graph) of the SDL graph.

TVEDA offers basically two strategies (each one has in fact variants) :

1. produce one test purpose and one test case for each transition

2. compute transition tours with a greedy algorithmic approach

In strategy 1, a typical TP would read : "Test that IUT responds B when it receives A in state S1. The IUT is expected to enter state S2"; and the corresponding test case is made of a first test step which refers to a preamble to reach state S1, followed by an output of A to the IUT, followed by an analysis of the possible responses (including B) and associated verdicts. In TVEDA V3, a postamble from state S2 is computed to reach the desired initial state.

2.1.2. Static analysis and use of reachability analysis

TVEDA V3 relies on bounded reachability analysis to compute preambles, postambles and test case kernels. In fact, we implemented two approaches [5], one based on symbolic execution and the other one on reachability analysis, but only the latter approach has been used in practical applications and will be integrated into *Object*GEODE. In TVEDA V3, the underlying verifier used for performing reachibility analysis was Veda, an Estelle based tool from which the *Object*GEODE simulator and verifier were derived; the verifier used in the work reported here is *Object*GEODE.

A key element in TVEDA's applicability to all sorts of large-scale specifications is that it never performs a raw reachability analysis on the whole specification. When we compare with TGV which also uses reachability analysis, TGV drastically reduces the complexity of the search by taking into account the sole part of the behaviour that matches a given test purpose (as will be explained below, in the case of TGV, on-the-fly generation is a key ingredient for a drastic reduction of the complexity). In the case of TVEDA, since we were keen on generating test purposes, we had to find other ways of reducing the complexity of the reachability analysis to avoid state space explosion.

This is done in several ways. Firstly, TVEDA uses a static dataflow analysis to detect those parts of the specification that contribute to reaching targeted transitions (e.g. we remove variables that do not contribute directly - or indirectly by transitive closure - to transition firing conditions). Similar techniques have been used with *Object*GEODE [3]. Secondly, TVEDA performs only limited (bounded) searches. If it fails to reach a given condition within a tailorable limit (typically 30000) on the number of states explored in the reachability graph, then it gives up and uses other heuristics. The basic heuristic is to restart a search from a configuration that has already been reached and retained (because it is a starting point for a transition). It turns out that combining limited search and heuristics provides most (over 90% usually) desired configurations. Once the preambles have been computed, other searches are then performed to compute test kernels and postambles. Again, the search space is much reduced by constraining the behaviour of the specification using observers that focus on a targeted transition (and there is one bounded search for each targeted transition).

2.1.3. Applications

TVEDA has been quite a success in CNET. In [12] we reported on our experience with more than twenty real-size applications of TVEDA. TVEDA is now in use in CNET for deriving tests from SDL specifications of protocols (ATM, IN etc) and services (mainly IN services). However, it has been developed with aging technologies. Integrating its main algorithms and heuristics within *Object*GEODE along with the accurate and efficient algorithms developed for TGV will contribute to reinforce and extend the application of automatic test generation within France Telecom and other organizations.

2.2. TGV

TGV is a prototype tool developed in collaboration by the Pampa project of IRISA/INRIA Rennes and Verimag Grenoble [9,10,7,14,3]. Its aim is to automatically generate conformance test cases starting from a formal specification of the system and test purposes allowing to select test cases according to conformance requirements. The main features of TGV are the correctness and quality of test cases and the efficiency of their generation. They are explained below.

2.2.1. Testing theory

TGV is based on a well defined testing theory based on the model of labelled transition systems (LTS for short) e.g. [20]. Specifications, implementations, test cases and test purposes are defined by a special class of LTS named IOLTS where a distinction is made between inputs (observable events), outputs (controlable events) and internal events. TGV uses a conformance relation relating specifications to correct implementations. This conformance relation which is very similar to the **ioco** relation of Tretmans et al. [20] says that an implementation conforms to a specification if after an observable trace of the specification, outputs of the implementation are included in outputs of the specification and the implementation is allowed to block (due to a deadlock, a livelock or absence of output) only if the specification is also allowed to block. TGV insures by construction that produced test cases are unbiased. This means that the rejection of an implementation by a test case through the occurrence of a fail verdict during test execution proves that it is not conformant to the specification w.r.t **ioco**. Conversely, TGV only ensures a "theoretical" exhaustiveness as complete exhaustiveness is a myth for realistic specifications and implementations. The property says that if an implementation is not conformant to its specification, there exists a test purpose for which TGV can produce a test case which, when executed repetitively, will reject the implementation, assuming that the implementation behaves in a fair way (due to non-determinism) and that timers values are appropriate (for the detection of blocking situations).

2.2.2. On-the-fly generation

TGV computes a test case from a specification of the system and a test purpose. A test purpose characterizes an abstract property that the system should have and that one wants to test. In TGV it is simply formalized by a finite automaton labelled with internal or observable events of the specification (internal actions are necessary in order to generate test cases for testing in context). This automaton has Accept and Reject states. Accept states are used to select a test case among all possible behaviours of the specification, Reject states are used to prune the search. The specification is supposed to be given in a language which operational semantics allows to represent the set of possible behaviours of the specification by an IOLTS.

In most test generation methods (except syntactic methods), one has to build the complete state graph of the specification which is subject to the classical state explosion problem. As conformance testing only considers traces, internal actions are abstracted and reduced, the resulting graph is determinized and sometimes minimized before the main test generation algorithm is applied. TGV tries to avoid the state explosion problem in performing these operations (except minimization) on-the-fly [14]. The principle is to synthesize a test case while constructing, in a lazy strategy, a part of the state graph guided by the test purpose and which is necessary for the test case generation. The advantage of this method is to allow to generate test cases for large specifications with very large and even infinite state graphs while most other test generation methods fail. Moreover, the frequent limitation of automatic tools to mono-process specifications does not apply to TGV.

In order to be applicable, TGV must be linked with an API of a simulation tool which provides some basic functions for the traversal of the implicit state graph, namely the functions which computes the initial global state, fireable transitions, the successor relation, a state comparison function and a storage function. This has been done with CADP [8] and *Object*GEODE [15] allowing respectively to generate test cases from LOTOS and SDL.

2.2.3. Main algorithms

The two main algorithms of TGV are adaptations of the same classical algorithm of Tarjan [19] which computes the set of maximal strongly connected components of a graph. Tarjan's algorithm is based on a depth first search and is linear in the size of the graph. This partly explains the efficiency of TGV.

Abstraction and determinization

Abstraction, reduction of internal actions and determinization [14] are applied on the synchronous product of the (implicit) state graph of the specification and a test purpose. The use of Tarjan in this step is necessary in order to capture loops of internal actions (i.e. livelocks) in the specification. The possibly costly phase of TGV is determinization which has exponential complexity in the size of the graph. It is performed by a classical subset construction (see e.g. [13]) during reduction using synthesized information on fireable observable events. This is another argument for on-the-fly generation as the cost of determinization is applied only on a part of the state graph.

Controlability of the test cases

The result of the previous algorithm is an implicit graph of observable events with Accept (meta-)states. It is used by another algorithm named TGV_loop. This algorithm can be understood as a model-checking algorithm for the property which is the negation of the property specified by the test purpose. The graph represents a complete diagnosis of the property giving all counter-examples. This graph is not a test case in general because it is not controlable: a test case controls its outputs and thus should never have a choice between two outputs or between inputs and outputs. Without the abovementionned option, controlability conflicts are solved in two phases. TGV_loop solves all the conflicts which can be solved when a state is popped during the depth first search. This does not necessarily reduce all conflicts but often allows to prune the traversal, thus saving time. Resulting conflicts are solved by a breadth traversal starting from accepting states using the predecessor relation, ensuring that all states (except Inconclusive states) of the resulting graph can still reach Accept states.

A side effect of this algorithm is the reduction of Inconclusive verdicts due to the conservation of loops and confluent sequences. We can prove that for a given test purpose and a given specification, among unbiased test cases, TGV generates the maximal ones in the sense that the occurrence of Inconclusive verdicts is minimized.

3. *TestComposer* tool architecture

The implementation of the *TestComposer* tool corresponds to the complete rewriting of the current *Object*GEODE's test generator tool, TTCGEN. *TestComposer* integrates some principles of TVEDA, and the main algorithms of TGV. The resulting tool works with three phases, depicted in figure 1. TVEDA principles are implemented in the Test Purpose generation phase, and correspond to the Test Purpose computation box. The algorithms of TGV are part of the test case Generation engine.

TestComposer takes as inputs a SDL specification, a specification of the test environment and a possibly empty set of user defined test purposes. These user defined test purposes can be built interactively using the simulator, or written using MSC or GOAL observers. In the sequel, we will call these test purposes "test MSCs" or "GOAL test observers".

The tool then completes the set of test purposes by computation of new test purposes according to structural coverage. Then the generation engine is fed with each test purpose, and produces test cases which are stored in the test case database. Finally, through the test case database API, the test suite is build and written in a TTCN-mp file.

3.1. The SSCOP protocol example

In order to illustrate the workings of the tool, we will use a standard protocol of the ATM family. The SSCOP protocol tends to be a classical example for test generation tools as it was experimented with TVEDA [6] and TGV [3]. It was also the support example for other tools such as TestGen from INT [4] and SAMSTAG from the university of Lübeck [11].

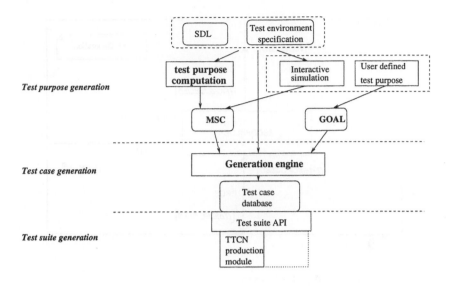

Figure 1. Functional architecture of the *TestComposer* tool

3.2. The SSCOP protocol

The SSCOP protocol is standardized under reference ITU-T Q2110 [17]. Originally, it was conceived to reliably transfer data between two high bandwidth network entities. Although its design makes it ready to treat significant volumes of data, currently its use is confined in the indication layer of the ATM. However, it is reasonable to think that it will be employed to transfer high volumes of data in future applications. SSCOP is one of the under-layers of the layer AAL (ATM Adaptation Layer). The main role of AAL is to adapt the service provided by the ATM physical layer to the type of data passing by connections established between two ends.

3.3. SDL reference specification

The SDL specification is the central item for efficient test generation. This SDL specification is generally not used for the generation of the code of the Implementation Under Test (IUT), but rather for describing what is the correct behavior of the IUT, from an external view point. In that sense, the SDL specification may not even reflect the internal structure of the Implementation Under Test.

Another important point to describe is the test architecture : an IUT is generally not directly reachable, one must interpose communication layers and SAPs. Furthermore, more than one tester are sometimes needed for testing distributed systems. In order to model various test architectures, we choose to integrate its description into the SDL specification. A complete SDL specification for test generation thus corresponds to the description of the System Under test : the IUT embedded into its test architecture. An example of test architecture is given in figure 2.

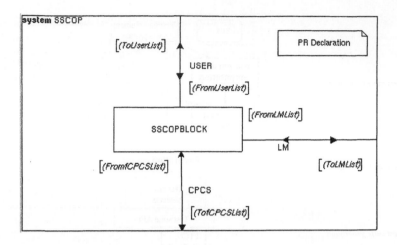

Figure 2. Test architecture for the SSCOP

Test architecture of the SSCOP protocol

The test architecture chosen is described in the SDL specification of the protocol and is shown in figure 2. It is a remote architecture with three PCOs, one of these being a delaying channel (CPCS), and the other a channel for the upper tester (User).

3.4. Test environment specification

SDL allows to design open systems, i.e. systems whose description is in some sense incomplete, as part of the behavior depends on its interactions with its environment. Using *Object*GEODE simulator, the basic assumption is to consider that the environment does nothing. Then the user can provide an abstract description of the environment using the following means:

The output command is used to issue one signal just once from the environment to the system. A sequence of outputs can be collected into the scenario file format, which is replayable by the simulator.

the feed command is used to describe what kind of signals the environment is ready to send to the system at any time. This is combined with the **reasonable feed** parameter which specifies if the environment should wait for the system to complete all its internal signal exchanges before issuing a new signal or let the time progress. This parameter corresponds to an assumption which says that the system reacts much faster than the environment. Another parameter option is the **loose-time** parameter which is meant for lessening the **reasonable feed** parameter, in the sense that time is then allowed to progress as an alternative to any actions, even actions internal to the system.

the MSC **and** GOAL **observers** come generally in complement to `feeds`, as they are usually used to filter signals so they occur only under specific conditions. For example, a MSC can be used to model the signals interchange of a connection protocol, and then a GOAL [2] observer to model the data transfer. By using appropriate MSC and GOAL observers combination, one can effectively control the simulation. In addition, GOAL observers have access to all internal elements of the specification, and can also change the values of variables or the contents of queues. So GOAL observers can be used for more elaborate simulations, involving fault injections for example.

All of these are parts of the test environment specification. This means in particular that MSC and GOAL observers can be combined with test MSC and GOAL test observers, for a more efficient or more directed test case generation.

3.5. Principles of the generation of test purposes

The principles of test purpose generation follow the simulation approach of TVEDA, they are based on a structural coverage of the specification. However, the TVEDA approach was meant to deal with single process specifications, so some adaptations were defined, in particular what is the coverage unit, and more crucial, what is an appropriate relationship between these coverage units and the test purposes. Structural coverage relates in some sense to white box testing, as it needs information internal to the Implementation Under Test. However, the test cases we want to build are conformance tests, i.e. black box tests. In black box testing, only observable events count and structural units are usually not observable. So we must introduce black box testing concerns in the choice and computation of the test purposes we generate.

The coverage unit we choose is the basic block, i.e. the biggest block of SDL instructions without branching instructions. Starting from the SDL specification of the SUT, we want to generate a set of test purposes which cover a given set of basic blocks. A basic block is not observable in the testing sense : most do not include instructions linked directly to observable events (INPUT or OUTPUT of messages with the environment). Even if a basic block contains such instructions, it is generally impossible to distinguish with black-box tests two basic blocks with the same observable events. This has two main consequences :

- Computing one test purpose for each basic block to cover would lead to many identical test purposes, when basic blocks do not contain observable events. This kind of basic blocks is especially numerous when working with multi-processes systems.

- When dealing with non deterministic systems (and even deterministic IUT can yield non deterministic systems in an embedded Test architecture), it is impossible to guarantee that a successful test case has covered one particular basic block, even if this block is observable, as there can be other behaviors of the SUT exhibiting strictly the same observable events, yet corresponding to the execution of different transitions.

To address these two problems, we define the observation step as the basis for test purpose computation. An observation step is a sequence of events leading from one

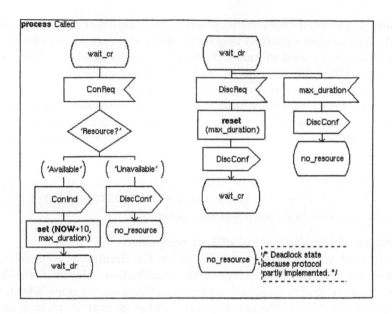

Figure 3. Observation step examples

stable testing state to another stable testing state. A stable testing state is defined as an IUT state where the only possible actions are the input of an observable test event, or the timeout of an internal timer (i.e. the IUT work does not progress without external stimulation or the progress of time). Each test purpose computed will correspond to an observation step and each observation step corresponds to the coverage of one or many basic blocks, as shown in the example 3.

In this example, only the signals ConReq and DiscConf are observable (i.e. are used on channels linked to the environment). So only wait_cr and no_resource are stable testing states. wait_dr is not a stable testing state , as it can progress without receiving an observable signal (as DiscReq is an internal one). If we consider the basic blocks of these transitions, there are 5 basic blocks to cover, as shown in the figure. However, there are 3 observation steps for covering these 5 basic blocks :

```
1 <wait_cr>- input ConReq - output DiscConf - <no_resource>
2 <wait_cr>- input ConReq - output ConInd - <wait_dr> - input DiscReq -
output DiscConf - <wait_cr>
3 <wait_dr>- output DiscConf - <no_resource>
```

The use of the observation step into the test purpose computation allows to alleviate the problem of non observable basic blocks, but not to solve it: when dealing with non deterministic systems, an observation step can still correspond to several paths of the SDL specification. One way to solve this problem is to compute Unique Input-Output sequences, for the identification of states, but even if an UIO exists, its computation is generally too costly, especially for a multi-process system.

3.6. Test purpose generation modes

Technically, the generation of test purposes with *TestComposer* is done using one of the two following modes :

the automatic mode in this mode the system is explored up to a given percentage of coverage. Each time a basic block not covered by a previously generated test purpose is found, then a new test purpose is computed and generated.

the interactive mode where the user uses the simulator to simulate step by step the system. Once the user thinks that the current sequence is an interesting test purpose, he asks the simulator to compute the complete observation step. The basic block coverage table is updated accordingly.

Moreover experienced users, or users wanting to design by themselves more complex test purposes than simple sequences, can use the graphic GOAL language[2]. Test purposes described in GOAL can be complete automata, and can refer to internal signal exchanges and data transformations.

3.6.1. Abstraction in test purposes

Whatever the generation modes, a test purpose can represent the complete observable signal interchange needed for the test case computation, but can also be more abstract for the outputs, i.e. contain only all the inputs (i.e. the needed stimulations from the tester) and some outputs. It can also be completely abstract, describing only some of the desired inputs or outputs. It is then the job of the generation engine to fill the gaps, by computing all the possible signal interchanges needed to go from one test purpose event to another. This abstraction is often useful, notably for reducing the occurrence of inconclusive verdicts in the test case. For example, even if the system sends some signals in a given order, the use of different communication channels combined with delays implies that they can be received in any order. If the test purpose imposes an order, then the generated test case, will reflect this and produce an inconclusive verdict for any other order. To alleviate this, *TestComposer* exploits the description of the test architecture in the SDL specification, and abstract test purposes, in order to generate test cases where all possibilities are explored to see if they lead to the test completion.

Another interesting point with abstract test purposes, is linked with the maintenance of the test generation items. With completely defined test purposes, any modification the SDL specification having impact on the observable behavior of the system, implies modification of the test purposes. Using more abstract test purposes, one can avoid this kind of maintenance problem.

Using all the possibilities, the user can build a set of test purposes, complete not only with respect to structural coverage, but also to functional coverage, as the interactive mode and the writing of MSC or GOAL test observers allows to add additional test purposes illustrating the key functions of the system.

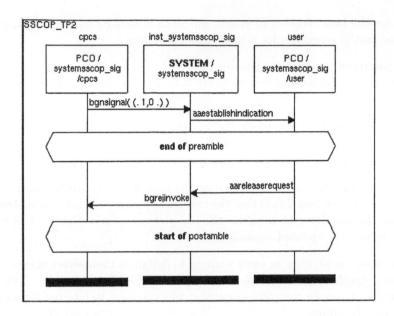

Figure 4. Example of test purpose for the SSCOP protocol

3.6.2. Methodological aspects

A SDL specification is often built in parallel with a set of MSCs, these MSCs usually describing the key functions of the system (nominal behaviors, error handling behaviors, ...). These MSCs can usually be used as a basis for interactive test purpose building, giving a starting point with respect to structural coverage. Then the next step is to apply the automatic mode, in order to obtain the highest possible coverage rate. It is generally not possible to obtain one hundred per cent straight away, as the exhaustive exploration can be very resource consuming or impossible (due to infinite size of queues, for example). Then again the interactive mode, combined with the visualization of the coverage table, can be used to build test purposes for the basic blocks not covered so far. Finally, for more elaborate or tricky behaviors, GOAL test observers can be designed and added to the set of test purposes.

3.7. From test purposes to test cases

The algorithms of TGV, as described in section 2.2.3 provide the basis for the test case generation engine. The main characteristics of this engine are:

On the fly generation the ability to work on the fly is a key to the efficiency of the tools. It also provides the basis for a test oriented simulation mode, where a simulation step would go from one set of externally observable events to another. This kind of simulation requires the abstraction of non observable events, and also the determinization of the resulting behavior, just for the part of the behavior of a simulation step. This kind of test oriented simulation would allow to design interactively test purposes and test cases, without having to bother with interactions internal to the system.

Lazy exploration As the generation engine computes part of the controllability on the fly, it explores effectively only a subset of the behavior of the system. This is especially important when dealing with abstract test purposes, where the exploration is not as constrained as with complete test purposes.

Computation of a complete test graph In order to minimize the number of Inconclusive verdicts, the engine explores all alternative paths (respecting controllability) leading to the Pass verdict. Moreover, it also compute loops, which are another major cause of Inconclusive verdicts.

Again, this engine can be run either interactively, or in batch. The interactive mode correspond to the building of one sequence using interactive simulation, then asking the simulator to generate the corresponding test case, thus bypassing the test purpose generation. The batch mode takes as inputs the current set of test purposes and produces all the corresponding test cases.

3.7.1. Postamble computation

The test purpose usually gives hints on the preamble and test body content. However it is usually not used to describe also the postamble (although it could be used for this with *TestComposer*). The postamble computation is often a difficult task for automated test generation techniques. A postamble can be used for several aims :

- A state check sequence, which allows to identify the last state of the test. Strictly speaking, a check sequence should be part of the test body. Check sequences relate to e.g. UIO, which are generally very costly to compute,

- An initializing sequence, which gets the system back in a state where it can execute the next test case. This kind of state can be of course the initial state of the system, but these states usually are no more reachable after the system start. Other states of interest are the *initial stable states*, i.e. the states where the system ends in, when started with no external stimulation.

With *TestComposer* the postamble goal can be user defined in the sense that the user can define the characteristics of the state the postamble should go to. Two default choices are the initial stable states or the next stable states. As an observation step ends in a stable state, the second option means no postamble computation, as the test body already ends up in a correct state.

3.8. From test cases to the test suite

The test cases produced are stored into a database. This database is accessible through an Application Programming Interface which provides access to the following items :

- general informations about the test suite such as the PCOs, the timers used, the signals and their characteristics (controllable or observable)

- informations about the messages, such as the values and types of parameters. These information are provided by the actual API to the SDL specification[21] for the types and a new API to the *Object*GEODE's simulator for the values.

- information on the test cases structures. The test suite database allows to structure test cases into test steps (following the partitioning of a test case into preamble, test body and postamble).

3.9. TTCN production

TestComposer provides a test suite production module whose output is the standard TTCN language. Most constituent parts of TTCN can be obtained using the test suite API i.e. PCOs and timers declaration, types and constraints declaration, description of the test cases behavior. However, the test suite structure (grouping of test cases based on protocol function, or control states, ...) can not be extracted from the SDL specification, as this kind of information is usually highly user dependent.

Z-105 to ASN.1 translation

SDL and TTCN support ASN.1 as a common language for data types definition. However, they support it with their own restrictions. Furthermore, each language brings its own data type language. For SDL its own ACT-ONE based language is combined with ASN.1 into a standard called Z-105. This international standard is currently supported by *Object*GEODE. On the TTCN side, one can also use the TTCN tabular form. For *Test-Composer*, we chose to concentrate on ASN.1 for the types description in TTCN, and use the tabular form only for the declaration of ASP and PDUs. Thus we integrated into *Test-Composer* a translation module taking all Z-105 (i.e. ACT-ONE + ASN.1) declarations and translating them into ASN.1 acceptable by the TTCN standards.

4. Conclusion

We have presented *TestComposer*, an automated test generation tool for conformance testing, which becomes a module of the *Object*GEODE toolset. It is the result of the rewriting of the current TTCGEN tool, together with the integration of two state of the art test generation tools TVEDA and TGV. The development of the tool has been funded by France-Telecom-CNET. The resulting tool will be commercially available as part of *Object*GEODE, during 1999.

We believe that this tool stays in line with a constant concern which governed the development of TVEDA and TGV, that is to automate manual and proven practices, rather than try to impose a theoretically complete, but practically hard to use method. The generation of test purposes is done according to current practices in the telecommunications world, and additional test purposes can be easily built interactively. The test suite are structured into test cases, which rely themselves on the use of test steps.

However, this tool goes further, as it allows to compute more complete test cases which would be hard to design by hand. It also allows the test designer to work on a high

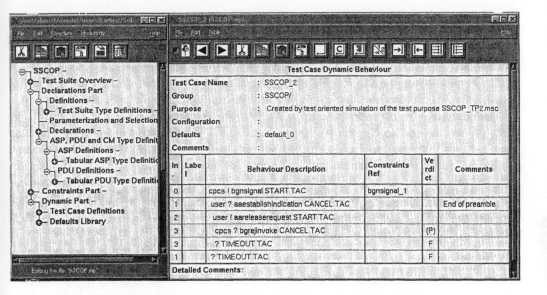

Figure 5. Excerpt of the TTCN suite, with Sema Group TED editor

level SDL specification, a more practical way to describe the IUT structure and behavior than TTCN which requires to keep in a separate format information on the internal SUT structure or behavior, for correct test cases writing. Furthermore, maintenance of large test suites is easier at the SDL level when combined with automatic generation, than at the TTCN level where most of the test cases or constraints have to be revised for any evolution.

A test generation tool would not be complete without links to test edition and execution environments. One project, near completion, aims at developing a test execution flexible environment, dedicated to SDL generated application within the *Object*GEODE framework. The test suites are described using ad-hoc extensions of the TCL language, allowing for a rapid prototyping of user specific test execution environments. Another project aims at offering a complete TTCN environment. It is based on the coupling of the *TestComposer* tool with the TTCN editor Ted from Sema Group, and the TTCN execution environment TTCN toolbox from DANET.

Perspectives

Only some of TVEDA concepts have been integrated into the tool. Other principles of TVEDA based on the static analysis of the specification are considered, such as the data flow analysis of variables to compute their domain of values, and where in the specification is a variable active or useless. These kind of information are needed for different aims, such as choosing test purposes based on data informations instead of behavior informations or reducing the size of the graph to explore for test generation and verification, by eliminating locally useless variables. We already explored this track with good results [3].

Another point of interest is the integration of so called symbolic techniques into the test generation techniques. One major source of complexity in these techniques is the handling of variables, or the treatment of time progression and timer constraints. Some research results propose techniques to represent and manipulate these kinds of informations by the way of formulae, instead of discrete values. These kind of symbolic techniques, although generally delicate to implement, allow to limit the so called explosion problem and to go further into the test and verification processes. This is especially an hot topic for applications with strong real time constraints, such as multimedia applications with strict Quality of Services requirements. The ongoing national project Proust, led by Verilog and supported by France-Telecom-CNET, Sema Group and Verimag, aims at providing solutions for the specification, verification and test generation for such strongly temporized applications. In particular, one aim is to propose sound and coherent time related extensions to SDL, MSC and TTCN.

Thanks

Many thanks to the teams of four different places, who, by working smoothly together, allowed to produce this illustration of the state of the art in test generation. In particular, we wish to thank Marylène Clatin, Nathalie Risser and Daniel Vincent from France-Telecom-CNET, Hakim Kahlouche and Pierre Morel from IRISA, Jean Claude Fernandez from VERIMAG, and the development team Jean-Louis Colaco, Philippe Coucaud, Marc Galibourg, Carole Haudebourg and Yves Lejeune from VERILOG.

Many people worked on TGV and TVEDA, so a complete list should include at least fifteen additional people. For more complete lists, please refer to [12] for TVEDA and [9,3] for TGV.

REFERENCES

1. ISO/IEC International Standard 9646-1/2/3. OSI-Open Systems Interconnection, Information Technology - Open Systems Interconnection Conformance Testing Methodology and Framework - Part 1 : General Concept - Part 2 : Abstract Test Suite Specification - Part 3 : The Tree and Tabular Combined Notation (TTCN), 1992.
2. B. Algayres, Y. Lejeune, and F. Hugonnet. GOAL: Observing SDL Behaviors with GEODE. In *SDL forum'95*. Elsevier Science (North Holland), 1995.
3. Marius Bozga, Jean-Claude Fernandez, Lucian Ghirvu, Claude Jard, Thierry Jéron, Alain Kerbrat, Pierre Morel, and Laurent Mounier. Verification and test generation for the SSCOP protocol. *Journal of Science of Computer Programming, Special Issue on The Application of Formal Methods in Industry Critical Systems*, To appear, 1999.
4. A. Cavalli, B.-H. Lee, and T. Macavei. Test generation for the SSCOP-ATM networks protocol. In *Proceedings of SDL forum'97*. Elsevier Science (North Holland), 1997.
5. M. Clatin, R. Groz, M. Phalippou, and Richard Thummel. Two approaches linking a test generation tool with verification techniques. In A. Cavalli and S. Budkowski, editors, *Proceedings of IWPTS'95 (8th Int. Workshop on Protocol Test Systems, Evry, France)*. INT, sep 1995.
6. I. Dinsenmeyer, S. Gauthier, and L. Boullier. L'outil TVEDA dans une chaîne de production de tests d'un protocole de télécommunication. In G. Leduc, editor, *CFIP'97 : Ingénierie*

des Protocoles, pages 271–286. Hermès, sept 1997.

7. L. Doldi, V. Encontre, J.-C. Fernandez, T. Jéron, S. Le Bricquir, N. Texier, and M. Philippou. Assessment of automatic generation methods of conformance test suites in an industrial context. In B. Baumgarten, H.-J. Burkhardt, and A. Giessler, editors, *IFIP TC6 9th International Workshop on Testing of Communicating Systems*. Chapman & Hall, September 1996.

8. J.-C. Fernandez, H. Garavel, A. Kerbrat, R. Mateescu, L. Mounier, and M. Sighireanu. CADP: A Protocol Validation and Verification Toolbox. In Rajeev Alur and Thomas A. Henzinger, editors, *Proceedings of the 8th Conference on Computer-Aided Verification, CAV'96 (New Brunswick, New Jersey, USA)*. LNCS 1102 Springer Verlag, August 1996.

9. J.-C. Fernandez, C. Jard, T. Jéron, and C. Viho. Using On-the-fly Verification Techniques for the Generation of Test Suites. In R. Alur and T.A. Henzinger, editors, *Proceedings of the 8th Conference on Computer-Aided Verification, CAV'96, (New Brunswick, New Jersey, USA)*. LNCS 1102 Springer Verlag, aug 1996.

10. J.-C. Fernandez, C. Jard, T. Jéron, and C. Viho. An Experiment in Automatic Generation of Test Suites for Protocoles with Verification Technology. *Science of Computer Programming*, 29, 1997.

11. J. Grabowski, R. Scheurer, and D. Hogrefe. Applying SAMSTAG to the B-ISDN Protocol SSCOP. Technical Report A-97-01, part I, University of Lübeck, January 97.

12. R. Groz and N. Risser. Eight years of experience in test generation from fdts using tveda. In T. Mizuno, N. Shiratori, T. Higashino, and A. Togashi, editors, *Proceedings of FORTE-PSTV'97*. Chapman & Hall, sep 1997.

13. J.E. Hopcroft and J.D. Ullman. *Introduction to automata theory, languages, and computation*. Addison-Wesley series in computer science, 1979.

14. T. Jéron and P. Morel. Abstraction, τ-réduction et déterminisation à la volée: application à la génération de test. In G. Leduc, editor, *CFIP'97 : Ingénierie des Protocoles*. Hermes, sept 1997.

15. A. Kerbrat, C. Rodriguez, and Y. Lejeune. Interconnecting the *Object*GEODE and CÆSAR-ALDÉBARAN Toolsets. In *Proceedings of SDL forum'97*. Elsevier Science (North Holland), 1997.

16. M. Phalippou and R. Groz. Evaluation of an empirical approach for computer-aided test cases generation. In I. Davidson, editor, *Proceedings of IWPTS'90 (3rd Int. Workshop on Protocol Test Systems, McLean VA, USA)*. Corporation for Open Systems, oct 1990.

17. ITU-T Recommendation Q.2110. B-ISDN - ATM Adaptation Layer - Service Specific Connection Oriented Protocol (SSCOP), 1994.

18. ITU-T Recommendation Z.500. Formal methods for conformance testing, 1997.

19. R. Tarjan. Depth-first search and linear graph algorithms. *SIAM J. Comput.*, 1(2):146–160, June 1972.

20. J. Tretmans. Test generation with inputs, outputs and repetitive quiescence. *Software—Concepts and Tools*, 17(3):103–120, 1996. Also: Technical Report No. 96-26, Centre for Telematics and Information Technology, University of Twente, The Netherlands.

21. VERILOG. ObjectGeode SDL/API Reference Manual. Technical report, VERILOG, 1996.

SDL'99 : The Next Millennium
R. Dssouli, G.v. Bochmann and Y. Lahav, editors
©1999 Elsevier Science B.V. All rights reserved

Methods and Methodology for an Incremental Test Generation from SDL Specifications

Athmane TOUAG [a] [*] and Anne ROUGER [b]

[a] Université de Paris 6, LIP6/MSI/SRC, 4 Place Jussieu 75005 Paris, FRANCE
E-mail : Athmane.Touag@lip6.fr,   Tel : 33 1 4427 8817

[b] France Telecom CNET DSV/SCA, 38-40 rue du Général Leclerc, 92794 Issy Moulineaux Cedex, France, E-mail : anne.rouger@cnet.francetelecom.fr, Tel : 33 1 4529 6134

This paper presents new results concerning test generation methods based on SDL specifications. Our purpose is to deal with the problem of the of the states space explosion when generating test scenarii. We propose a methodology that links several methods, by joining the advantages of some already existing methods with new ideas. The methodology relies on an incremental computation of test scenarii from a set of test purposes automatically computed from the SDL specification. Four methods are sequentially applied, mainly based on constraints solving techniques and an on-the-fly exploration of system behaviours. We also make the point of taking advantages of the structural form of the test purposes.

keywords : Test generation, On-the-fly techniques, Constraints solving, ACT, Reachability graph.

1.   INTRODUCTION

Test generation methods generally rely on the use of mathematical models, such as : Finite State Machines FSM [1], and Labelled Transition Systems LTS [2, 3]. A shared drawback of these mathematical models is the inadequacy to take into account systems of industrial size, where data are widely used.

Thereafter, research studies have focused on test generation methods from compact representations, based on these mathematical models extended with data and related concepts such as (parameters, variables, operation on data, predicates on data, ...). The well known one is the EFSM (Extended Finite State Machine) which is the basis semantic representation of Formal Description Techniques such as SDL. Test generation methods from EFSM can be classified according to three approaches : static, symbolic and dynamic.

Static methods such as [4, 5, 6] select transitions sequences from the EFSM. On the outcomes transitions sequences, neither the data values are computed nor the predicates are evaluated. Therefore, a considerable human effort is required, on one hand, to set the data values for satisfying the predicates and on the other hand, to complete the behaviours of the

---

[*] This work has been supported by France Telecom CNET.

iteration loops. The results are executable transitions sequences that we call *test scenarii*. A test case is built by considering the input and output signals sequence from each test scenario.

Symbolic methods such as [7, 8, 9] automate the production of the data values and of the iterative loops behaviour by using constraints solving and symbolic execution techniques. These methods have the advantage to work on the compact representation. However, their application requires some hypotheses on the loops and the predicates. Hence, in a given specification, only the parts that come up to these hypotheses are considered.

Dynamic methods are based on the reachability analysis where all the behaviours with all the data values are enumerated. First, a model representing all allowed behaviours by means of a reachability graph or an Asynchronous Communication Tree (ACT) is computed [10]. An ACT assumes the communication to be asynchronous between the system processes and the system environment. Then, specific behaviours (test scenarii) which will be tested on the real implementation of the system are extracted from the model. The main problem of these methods is that the computation of test scenarii does not fully succeed when applied to real telecommunication systems. Very often, the models have a real big size. This leads to a combinatory explosion of the states space and to a storage memory overflow.

Since the end of the eighties, several ideas have been proposed in order to face the states space explosion. [11] and the European project [12] have proposed to make assumptions when building the ACT. However, even though the ACT is reduced (thanks to these assumptions), the complete construction of the ACT is still confronted to the explosion of the states space. In addition, even if the ACT can be completely built, too many test scenarii are generated. This raises a question : how to select representative test scenarii among the whole set of the generated ones ?

That is why, at the beginning of the nineties, some studies have focused on the computation of test scenarii when exploring the ACT. The idea has been introduced for the test generation aim in [13] and improved later in [14]. First of all, a set of test purposes is defined. This set is considered as a basis set for which test scenarii have to be computed. A test purpose represents an incomplete description of the system behaviour we want to test. While previous methods build the complete model before extracting test scenarii, this method generates test scenarii *on-the-fly* at the same time the ACT is explored. The underlying technique is based on the parallel simulation of the SDL specification and a test purpose. During the exploration, only one test scenario of the ACT is kept in memory at a time. Hence the whole ACT is not stored. Moreover, in order to face the storage memory overflow problem, the exploration depth of the ACT is bounded. Another advantage of the method is that it includes the construction of test purposes it self : this approach reflects practical uses of the validation world. Its benefit lies in the automatic computation of sets of test scenarii corresponding to predefined tests purposes. However, the test purposes are manually supplied.

At the middle of the nineties, another principle has emerged in [15]. The idea focuses on the automatic computation of test purposes from the SDL specification (or a compact representation). The aim is first, to avoid the human errors that can be introduced when defining the test purposes and second, to get at low cost a set of test purposes. By automatically producing a set of test purposes (and consequently, a set of test scenarii), the test teams can concentrate their efforts on the production of specific test scenarii that are difficult to get automatically (i.e. the specific behaviours for which no general algorithm is suitable). The method is based on the reachability graph building technique.

In [16] we propose a method which, first, links the two principles : the on-the-fly exploration [13] and the automatic computation of the test purposes [15]. By this link, we gather in one method their respective advantages : storage memory overflow avoidance and definition time reduction of the test purposes. Second, while [15] defines a test purpose as one SDL transition, [16] defines a test purpose as a syntactic *path* of the SDL specification (i.e. a sequence of SDL transitions). By considering a test purpose as a path instead of one single SDL transition, a best coverage of the SDL specification is obtained.

In this paper, we extend the work presented in [16] by taking advantage of the structural form of the test purposes. There are two major advantages in defining the test purposes as SDL paths :

- the structural form of these test purposes gives the opportunity to apply static and symbolic methods. Thus, some complete test scenarii are computed by relying only on these test purposes (without exploring the reachability graph).

- the structural form of these test purposes contains information that allows to drive the computation of test scenarii during the on-the-fly exploration. Hence, thanks to this driving, we gain time by only exploring the relevant part of the reachability graph.

We make the point on the storage memory overflow problems and the long computation time needed to enumerate the reachability graph states. As already said, the on-the-fly exploration techniques can solve the first point by bounding the exploration depth of the ACT. The second one is still carried on. Since the exploration time grows exponentially depending on the depth of the reachability graph and because of the economic limitation to test a system during a restricted time, a reachability graph is only explored during a restricted time and consequently, with a restricted depth. As a result, test purposes corresponding to test scenarii of a length higher than the reached depth are not treated.

In this paper we show how taking advantage of the structural form of the test purposes allows to drive the on the fly exploration and reduce the computation time. We also propose a methodology that links static, symbolic and dynamic methods in order to take advantage of each of them and enhance the test purposes handling. The methodology relies on an incremental computation of test scenarii from test purposes extracted from the specification by means of four methods we describe in the paper.

2. METHODOLOGY CONTENTS

The methodology is based :
- on the computation of a finite set of test purposes from EFSM,
- on an incremental computation of the test scenarii from this set of test purposes. The computation relies on a successive application of four methods, which progressively enhance the set of the test scenarii. Each time a method is applied, a subset of the test scenarii is obtained from a subset of the test purposes. Hence, the set of the test purposes decreases and the next method is applied to the remaining test purposes.

Notations : G denotes the method for the test purposes generation, TP denotes the initial set of the test purposes, M_i ($i = 1, ..., 4$) denotes a method, TS denotes the set of the test scenarii and TS_i the subset of the test scenarii obtained with method M_i and that results from the computation of a subset TP_i of set TP of the test purposes.

G generates the initial set *TP* of test purposes for which M_i ($i = 1..4$) compute test scenarii. Each time M_i is applied the number of test scenarii is incremented and the number of the test purposes is reduced (the test purposes dealt with are suppressed). As final results, a set of test scenarii $TS=(\cup_{i=1..4} TS_i)$ is produced. The remaining test purposes correspond to $TP - (\cup_{i=1..4} TP_i)$. In the following, we will see that the test purposes can be classified according to the complexity to deal with them. Each M_i tries to cope with the test purposes that the methods M_k ($k<i$) cannot treat.

In the methodology the three approaches are linked. G and M_1 are static ones, M_2 is a symbolic approach based and M_3 and M_4 are both based on a dynamic approach. This link becomes possible because of the choose of the test purpose structure as a path. Static and symbolic methods are applied first to obtain test scenarii at a low cost i.e. without being faced to the explosion of the states space. Then, the remaining test purposes are treated with the dynamic methods. In order to face the problem of the states space explosion and gain exploration time, we propose here a new dynamic method (heuristic) which takes advantage of the test purposes structure. An optimisation is made by driving the exploration thanks to the information contained within the test purposes themselves.

The following of the paper focuses on these four methods which are fully detailed. Before introducing each of them, we briefly sum up the general framework of the methodology and give some important assumptions and definitions.

2.1. General framework

The four methods are applied on the SDL specification already transformed into a specific extended finite state machine called SDL_EFSM. This last one, has a reachability graph semantically equivalent to the one of the initial SDL specification. Before defining the SDL_EFSM, let us first introduce the assumptions that we make on the SDL specification and its environment.

2.1.1. Assumptions

Regarding the SDL specification, we assume that the initial specification is composed of only one SDL process. This process does not contain any concepts such as signals save, join or procedure calls. However, the process can contain all the SDL concepts about the triggering conditions of the transitions. That includes the input signals with parameters, the enabling conditions and continuous signals (which are predicates). We also assume that variables (and parameters) are defined over finite and countable domains. Finally, we assume that the system does not send any signal to itself.

Regarding the SDL process environment, we assume that the SDL process behaves under the Reasonable Environment (RE) hypothesis [11] : The environment is supposed behaving likewise the process in the SDL system. The literature [12, 14] proposes different interpretations of this hypothesis and analysis about its application. Our interpretation is based on [12]. First of all, we assume the environment does not anticipate signal sending. This means, when the process is executing an atomic transition (occurs between two states), the environment does not send any signal. Second, at a current process state, the environment only sends an expected signal to the process. This avoids the implicit consumption of signals in that state (SDL semantics). This also means that if all trigger conditions are continuous signals in a state, the environment will not send any signals in that state. Considering Figure 1(a), in state S_i, the environment may only send I_1 and will not send I_2 until the process reaches S_j or S_p. According to this assumption, we avoid the computation of test scenarii with signals that would be implicitly consumed.

2.1.2. SDL_EFSM computation

The transformation of the SDL process into a SDL_EFSM mainly consists in considering a SDL decision node as a specific state of the SDL_EFSM (we call it decision state), and SDL decision responses as specific trigger conditions of SDL_EFSM transitions. These specific trigger conditions are semantically equivalent to SDL continuous signals. Figure 1(b) gives an example of Figure 1(a) decision node transformation. The hypotheses described before are also assumed for the SDL_EFSM.

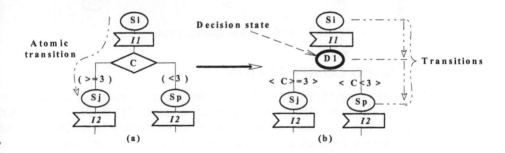

Figure 1 : Transformation of SDL process to SDL_EFSM

The behaviours of the SDL process reachability graph and the those of the SDL_EFSM are equivalent. The proof consists (for each SDL process and SDL_EFSM transition) in showing that the SDL process queue has the same content as the SDL_EFSM queue and vice-versa.

2.1.3. SDL_EFSM definition

We formally define the SDL_EFSM as $< S \cup DS,\ S_0,\ Stop,\ I,\ O,\ V \cup P,\ Pr,\ A,\ T >$, where :
- S is a set of states (SDL states), DS is a set of decision states,
- S_0 and $Stop$ ($S_0,\ Stop \in S$) are respectively the initial and the final states,
- I and O are respectively two sets of input signals symbols and output signals symbols,
- V is the set of internal variables and P the set of signals parameters,
- Pr is a finite set of predicates defined over V and P (the predicates correspond to the expressions of enabling conditions and continuous signals of the SDL_EFSM),
- A is a finite set of actions that operate on V and P,
- $T : (S \times I \times Pr) \cup (DS \times Pr) \longrightarrow (O \cup A)^* \times (S \cup DS)$ is a transition function.

Figure 2 shows an example of a SDL_EFSM, in which the output signals are omitted (in order to make the representation clearer). These outputs are not prerequisite for the transition triggering. A transition is named with an *italic* font. We assume the variable *received* has an initial value equal to 0.

158

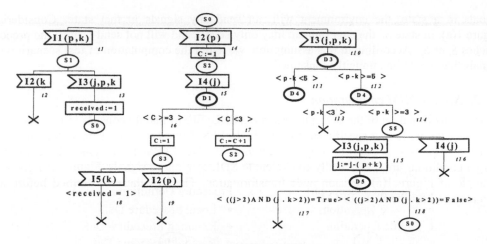

Figure 2 : SDL_EFSM specification

3. TEST SCENARII COMPUTATION

The steps of our methodology follow what the validation teams do when they test a system. Since the system behaviours generally involve an infinite number of tests, the test designer, thanks to its expertise, only considers a finite sample of behaviours he estimates to be representative. First, these behaviours are expressed as a finite set of test purposes. Then, these test purposes (which are incomplete descriptions of behaviours) are specified as tests scenarii. A test scenario is an executable sequence of transitions starting from the initial state S_0 and ending in a *stop* state or returning to S_0.

3.1. Generation of the test purposes (G)

Our computation of test purposes is based on SDL_EFSM coverage criteria by means of static paths strategies. Static means that when computing paths (i.e., SDL_EFSM transitions sequences), neither the data values are computed nor the predicates are evaluated. The algorithm directly splits the graph of the SDL_EFSM into a set of static paths according to some criteria. Each path defines a test purpose which is generally an incomplete behaviour and which is non-executable for two reasons :

- input parameters are not computed and predicates are not evaluated ;
- some behaviour parts may be missing because the static computation does not consider the behaviours related to iteration loops.

For the methodology we do not stress on the paths selecting criteria. Different ones can be designed according the classes of behaviours we want to test from the specification (control based criteria, data based criteria and so on). The meaningful concept (for the methodology) is that the structure of the resulting test purposes should be defined as paths.

We choose for our work one criterion proposed in [5] that computes every path starting from the initial SDL_EFSM state then returning to the initial state or ending up in a *stop* state. The computation equally splits the graph at states (SDL states and decision states) and takes care of preventing loops on states through each path. The only allowed loop is the one on the initial state. Figure 3 shows the paths that we obtain from the SDL_EFSM of Figure 2.

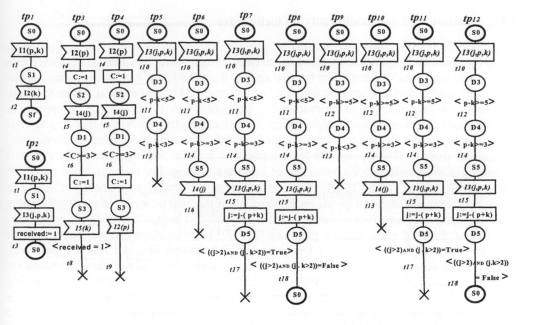

Figure 3 : test purposes in structure of path

3.2. Method M_1 : computation of test scenarii in a static way

The input of M_1 is the computed set TP of test purposes defined as paths. A subset TP_1 of test purposes in TP is identified. This set TP_1 corresponds to the one for which M_1 can compute a set ST_1 of test scenarii. From the point of view of M_1, the test purposes can be classified according to their structural form into two classes : test purposes without any predicate, called *simple test purposes* and test purposes containing predicates.

M_1 deals with the simple test purposes. Since they do not contain predicates, input parameter values have no influence on the triggering of the transitions. Transitions are only triggered on the receipt of an input signal. Hence, in order to produce test scenarii, M_1 arbitrary chooses the values on the definition domains of the parameters. tp1 and tp2 are examples of such test purposes (Figure 3).

The simplicity of M_1 shows the importance of defining the structure of the test purposes as paths. The question naturally to ask is : how many test purposes can be treated by M_1 ? That depends on the writing style of the specification. The more the specification holds transitions without predicate, the more simple test purposes may be computed and then treated by M_1. Protocols of low layers in OSI model, are examples where this writing style can be used, because these systems frequently transmit messages to the higher layers protocols without examining the parameter values.

To conclude, M_1 identifies a set of simple test purposes TP_1 for which it computes a corresponding test scenarii set ST_1. The remaining test purposes $TP- TP_1$ are passed on to the following methods.

3.3.   Method M_2 : constraints solving techniques

Method M_2 applies constraints solving techniques to some of the remaining test purposes $TP - TP_1$. These techniques solve a set of constraints on data values (predicates) expressed as a set of linear equations. We want here to draw up how a symbolic test generation technique can be incorporated within a general methodology of incremental tests production, where the main techniques are dynamic (based on reachability analysis). For that reason, M_2 is applied to specific predicates holding simple constraints. Nevertheless, other studies in this area such as [8, 9] may bring new elements for improving M_2, in order to handle more complex predicates.

Because method G computes the test purposes in a static way, the parts of transitions sequences corresponding to the behaviour of loops are missing. For instance, on Figure 3, in test purpose $tp_4 : (t_4, t_5, t_6, t_9)$ there is a missing part. t_6 holds a predicate ($C \geq 3$). The satisfaction of this predicate depends on the iteration of the loop (t_7, t_5) incrementing the value of C. The transitions sequence of this iteration is not included in tp_4.

From M_2 point of view, the test purposes $(TP- TP_1)$ can be classified according to their structural form into two classes : test purpose without missing part and test purposes with missing parts. A test purpose with missing parts is not stand-alone : since some transitions are omitted, predicates associated to these transitions are missing and constraints solving techniques are not applicable. On the contrary, a test purpose with no missing part is stand-alone : it contains all the set of predicates needed to compute the parameter values and to generate a test scenario. The parameter values are computed by applying constraints solving techniques on the set of the test purpose predicates.

In M_2 two criteria are applied to select from $TP - TP_1$ a subset TP_2 that M_2 can treat. The first criterion concerns the selection of test purposes which do not contain any missing part. For that purpose, we consider test purposes which have no predicates on internal variables but only on input signals parameters. Moreover, we assume that predicates on input parameters are only part of the transition triggered on the receipt of the input signal containing the parameter. The second criterion is used to select only test purposes with simple constraints. By simple constraints we assume, on one hand that, the value of a parameter is not assigned between its receipt (in an input signal) and the predicate where it appears, and on the other hand, the expressions of the predicates are linear.

tp5 constraints	tp6 constraints	tp9 constraints	tp10 constraints
$\begin{cases} \text{p-k} < 5 \\ \text{p-k} < 3 \end{cases}$	$\begin{cases} \text{p-k} < 5 \\ \text{p-k} >= 3 \end{cases}$	$\begin{cases} \text{p-k} >= 5 \\ \text{p-k} < 3 \end{cases}$	$\begin{cases} \text{p-k} >= 5 \\ \text{p-k} >= 3 \end{cases}$

Figure 4 : Test purposes constraints

For instance, test purposes tp_5, tp_6, tp_9 and tp_{10} match these specific criteria. Figure 4, shows the different constraints (system of inequalities) for each selected test purpose. Test purposes $tp3$ and $tp4$ are not selected by method M_2 because the predicate (continuous signal) associated to the decision state D_1 contains an internal variable C. Test purposes tp_7, tp_8, tp_{11}, tp_{12} are not selected either. Their predicates expressions are not linear.

The computation of test scenarii is performed in two steps. At a first step, for each system of inequalities related to a given test purpose, constraints solving techniques are applied to compute input parameters values. At a second step, these parameters are injected through the test purpose assignments in order to compute output parameters values.

To conclude, a subset TP_2 of test purposes is selected from the set $TP - TP_1$. Then, a set TS_2 of test scenarii is computed. TS_2 constitutes the second set of test scenarii, which is added to the first one already produced by method M_1, $TS = TS_1 \cup TS_2$.

3.4. Method M_3 : On-the-fly search

Method M_3 deals with the remaining set $TP - (TP_1 \cup TP_2)$ of test purposes left by the static and symbolic methods M_1 and M_2. This set includes the test purposes with missing parts and/or those which do not match the properties of simple constraints (predicates with linear expression, ...)

The method is based on the simulation and the observation principles introduced in [13] for the test generation aim. With M_3 [16], these principles are adapted to test purposes automatically defined as paths. The behaviour of the SDL_EFSM is simulated and explored in an on-the-fly way in order to compute for each test purpose a test scenario that covers and matches the sequence of transitions of the test purpose. Therefore, the resulting test scenario includes the behaviour of the missing parts of the test purpose, and the parameters values of input signals that satisfy the predicates over the test purpose.

For the needs of the method we adopt the observer language GOAL (Geode Observer Automata Language) [17]. The concepts of this language have initially been developed by the CNET (France Telecom) in the framework of the VEDA tool [18]. A GOAL observer is an extended automaton model mainly used to define properties (like a sequence of events, ...) that we want to observe. During the simulation of the synchronous product of a specification with a GOAL observer, the GOAL observer can :

- *observe* the execution by scrutinizing the input and/or output events, the firing of the transitions and the current values of variables of the specification. Hence, in an observer, the triggering conditions of a transition may refer to observations of the executions of the specification.

- *control* the execution of the specification by modifying the variables values, and then influence the triggering conditions of the specification transitions.

These principles are respectively applied to our SDL_EFSM and our test purposes. First, each test purpose is translated into a goal observer. Second, the execution of the synchronous product of the SDL_EFSM with the **whole** set of observers is simulated. The behaviour of the SDL_EFSM is explored on-the-fly, in a "depth first" mode with a bounded depth.

Let Fired(Transition_name) be a function used in the enabling condition of the observer transitions. The function returns «True» if the SDL_EFSM transition whose name is «Transition_name» is fired during the last simulation step (see below).

After the translation, the resulting automaton of the observer is a single path similar to the test purpose, where each observer transition corresponds to a test purpose transition and each observer state corresponds to a test purpose state. The triggering condition of each observer transition relies on the firing observation of the corresponding transition of the test purpose (Figure 5). All states of the observer are declared as « accepting states », except the final state, which is declared as « success state ». This state corresponds, in the test purpose, either to a *stop* or to the initial state.

162

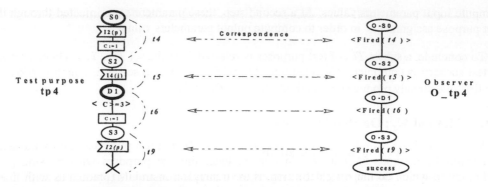

Figure 5 : Translation of a test purpose into a Goal observer

We simulate the synchronous product of the SDL_EFSM with the whole set of the observers. During the simulation, the progression of the observers is driven by the SDL_EFSM execution. Initially, the SDL_EFSM and the observers are in their initial states.

Each observer being in an acceptance state behaves as follows. Each time a SDL_EFSM transition t_i is executed (during a simulation step) :

- if the observation of this transition firing is expected at the current observer state then, the enabling condition <Fired(t_i)> of the observer transition is satisfied. Hence, the observer progresses to a new accepting state, or a success state (within the same simulation step).
- otherwise, the observer remains in its current state ;

In case a success state is reached, the complete execution scenario of SDL_EFSM (going from its initial state to the state corresponding to this success state of the observer) is saved in a file on the disk during the simulation. Since this scenario matches the transitions sequence of the test purpose (the corresponding observer), the scenario necessarily includes the missing parts of the test purposes and sets the parameters values in a way to satisfy the test purpose predicates. This scenario is then a test scenario corresponding to the test purpose. For instance, for the test purpose (t_4, t_5, t_6, t_9) of Figure 5, the complete test scenario corresponds to the transitions sequence $(t_4, t_5, t_7, t_8, t_7, t_5, t_6, t_9)$ where the missing loop of the "static" test purpose has been completed.

The exploration is performed in k-bounded depth first mode. Accordingly, the exploration of the reachability graph covers the execution scenarii of length k. Since the exploration is on-the-fly, at a given time, only one execution scenario of length k is kept in memory (Random Access Memory). Hence, with this mode, memory overflow problems cannot not occur. During the exploration, each time a test scenario ts is found for a given test purpose tp, ts is added to TS_3, tp is suppressed from $TP - (TP_1 \cup TP_2)$ and the exploration continue to find other test scenarii. At the end, ST is incremented to $TS_1 \cup TS_2 \cup TS_3$ and the test purposes set is reduced to $TP - (TP_1 \cup TP_2 \cup TP_3)$.

As previously mentioned in the paper, in practice test designers only produce test scenarii during a restricted time. Of course, the same restriction holds for test generation methods. The dynamic methods, such as M_3, are known as being time consuming methods (the time grows exponentially with the depth of the exploration). Hence, we have to apply M_3 during a restricted time. Let *Time* be the time allowed for applying M_3. Therefore, M_3 is performed as follows. Initially, M_3 is applied with a depth bound k equal to the minimal length of the test purposes of TP - $(TP_1 \cup TP_2)$. When all the behaviours of length k are explored, k is incremented ($k := k+1$) then M_3 is applied once more and so on, until *Time* is consumed. The increment one by one of the exploration depth bound is chosen in order to ensure for each test purpose a minimal solution (a shortest test scenario).

To conclude, M_3 computes a set TS_3 of test scenarii of length less or equal than the final reached depth k. Hence, once again, we increment the number of the test scenarii : $TS = TS_1 \cup TS_2 \cup TS_3$. Because of the limitation of time, a set of test purposes ($TP-(TP_1 \cup TP_2 \cup TP_3)$) is still left by M_3. This is partially due to the fact that when the exploration is performed, test purposes act as passive observers whereas test purposes contain some information which could drive the exploration. For this reason we propose method M_4 in order to gain time by giving an active role to the test purposes.

3.5. Method M_4 : On-the-fly search driving

Method M_4 deals with the remaining set TP - $(TP_1 \cup TP_2 \cup TP_3)$ of test purposes left by M_1, M_2, M_3. When compared to $TP_1 \cup TP_2$, these remaining test purposes hold missing parts and non-simple constraints (non linear expression, ...). And when compared to TP_3, test scenarii corresponding to these remaining test purposes have lengths higher than the ones of TP_3.

With M_4, we propose once again to take advantage of the test purposes structure to drive the exploration. The idea is to force and constrain the exploration to only specific parts of the reachability graph. Thus, it prevents from exploring some parts of the reachability graph in which corresponding test scenarii could not be included. The gained time can be used to explore depths higher than the one reached by M_3.

The literature proposes different optimisations of the computation of the whole system behaviour, such as by using the Reasonable Environment hypothesis, see for [12]. The distinctive feature of our method is that only relevant parts of the system behaviours (ie, those corresponding to the test purposes themselves) are explored during the simulation. The method takes advantage of the information contained within the test purposes. We already compared above our test purposes definition with the one of [15]. Concerning a test purpose of [13, 14], it describes an exchanging of input and/or output signals. The system states where these signals should be received or sent are not defined. Test purposes of our methodology hold more information. Each test purpose, defined as a path, is a **contiguous** sequence of SDL_EFSM transitions from which we can extract the following information :

- the input signals needed to trigger the test purposes transitions and **especially**,
- the states of the specification where these input signals should be received.

These are the key information that we use to develop the driving technique. Method M_4 is composed of three steps : transformation of the SDL_EFSM, transformation of the remaining observers and execution of the driving exploration.

SDL_EFSM transformation. The SDL_EFSM is automatically transformed into an equivalent one which allows the exploration driving. This modification only affects the transitions starting from a SDL state (and not the ones starting from a decision state). For each transition 't_i' of a SDL_EFSM, we add a new predicate P_t_i into the transition condition part. If the condition part already contains a predicate P, the resulting predicate will be (P **AND**

164

P_t_i) after the modification. The predicate P_t_i is an expression of the boolean variable P_t_i that we introduce (automatically) into the internal variables set V of the SDL_EFSM. These variables (we call them *driving variables*) are initialised to 'TRUE' and their values are not modified (by assignment) through SDL_EFSM. Consequently, the firing conditions of the transitions are not influenced by the modification that we apply. The behaviour of the resulting SDL_EFSM remains unchanged. Let SDL_EFSM' be the modified SDL_EFSM. Figure 6(a) shows how some of these new predicates are added to the SDL_EFSM.

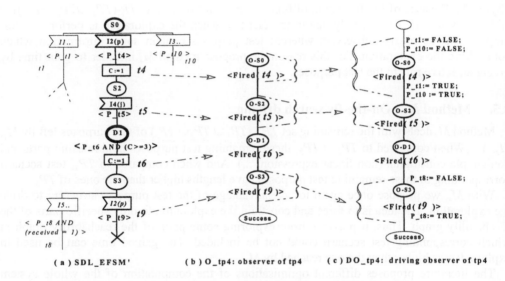

Figure 6 : Computation of a driving observer

Observer transformation. Each remaining observer is rewritten in such a way that it drives the on-the-fly exploration. This can be done thanks to the Goal observer language which gives access to the SDL_EFSM' variables, and allows the modification of their values during the simulation. Therefore, an observer can influence the triggering conditions of the SDL_EFSM' transitions (the predicates) and then, it can drive the exploration during the simulation. For the driving technique that we introduce, the observers are transformed into ones that act on the driving variables added to the SDL_EFSM. The resulting observers are called *driving observers*.

The driving principle is the following : each time the SDL_EFSM' and the observer reach similar states[1], the observer has to force the exploration to only fire the SDL_EFSM' transition which is expected in the observer.

Let $O\text{-}S_i$ be an observer state and Fired(t_i) the enabling condition at $O\text{-}S_i$ that expects the firing of the SDL_EFSM' transition t_i at state S_i (where $S_i \notin DS$). Let $Trans(S_i)$ be the set of transitions that can be fired from state S_i. Since, at state $O\text{-}S_i$ the observer expects the firing of t_i and not the other transitions ($\forall t_j \in Trans(S_i)$ where $t_j \neq t_i$), we transform the initial observer into another one which sets to 'FALSE' the driving variables P_t_j (where $t_j \in Trans(S_i)$, $t_j \neq t_i$)

---

[1] Since the observer is computed from the SDL_EFSM, an observer state $O\text{-}S_i$ corresponds to the SDL_EFSM state S_i.

on the observer transition that leads to state $O\text{-}S_i$. This setting has the effect to disable the triggering condition of the transitions t_j (where $t_j \in Trans(S_i)$ and $t_j \neq t_i$) and then to avoid the exploration of the behaviour part depending on the firing of these transitions. In other words, the driving forces the simulation to only explore the behaviour corresponding to transition t_i. As soon as Fired(t_i) is observed, the driving variables $\mathbf{P}\_t_j$ (where $t_j \in Trans(S_i)$ and $t_j \neq t_i$) are set to 'TRUE' because the related transitions can be executed afterwards. Figure 6(c) illustrates the driving observer DO_tp_4 obtained from the observer O_tp_4.

Simulation of SDL_EFSM' with each driving observer. Because driving observers influence the exploration, the exploration is performed for each of them. Hence, several simulations are executed (in k-bounded depth first mode) : one for each synchronous product of the SDL_EFSM' and a driving observer.

Within M_3 the observers have only a passive role on the execution running : they only observe the progression of the SDL_EFSM. On the contrary within M_4, each driving observer plays an active rôle : for every simulation, on one hand, the observer progresses by observing the firing of SDL_EFSM' transitions (as explained in section III.4) and on the other hand, the observer drives the execution of the SDL_EFSM' every time the SDL_EFSM' and the observer reach similar states. The driving technique forces the simulation to execute precise transitions. Hence, by avoiding the exploration of some behaviours parts of the reachability graph, time is gained when searching scenarii for a given driving observer.

Note that the driving technique is applied only when the transition starting from $O\text{-}S_i$ has a triggering condition that refer to a SDL_EFSM transition t_i which should be necessarily triggered by an input signal reception. The reason is that the system environment (the tester) can control the execution of this transition by sending the related input signal. On the opposite, the driving cannot be applied in case the triggering condition of t_i is a predicate on variables (continuous signal), because the environment has no access to the system variables. Accordingly, no driving is done when the observer reaches a state that corresponds to a decision state of the SDL_EFSM'.

For each driving observer, M_4 is performed with the execution mode of M_3: on-the-fly in the bounded depth first mode. As in M_3, the depth bound is incremented until the allowed time is consumed (for the driving observer). The starting depth bound is equal to the depth reached with M_3.

For instance, let us follow step by step, the execution of the synchronous product of the observer DO_tp_4 (Figure 6(c)) and the SDL_EFSM' corresponding to the SDL_EFSM (Figure 2). The Figure 6(a) shows the relevant parts of SDL_EFSM'. Note that, as already stated, the satisfaction of the predicate ($C \geq 3$) of transition t_6 depends on the execution of an iteration loop on decision state D_1. This behaviour is missing in the test purpose tp_4. To simplify the illustration we explain the applying of M_4 with the depth bound equal to 8. No solution is found with depths less than 8.

After the initialisation step, DO_tp_4 sets to 'FALSE' the driving variables P_t_1 and P_t_{10} of SDL_EFSM'. Thus, when the system is at the state S_0 the triggering conditions of transitions t_1 and t_{10} are disabled. Hence, the observer explicitly prevents the exploration of all the behaviour parts that depend on the execution of these two transitions (see Figure 7). Therefore, the simulation is driven to only explore the remaining transition t_4. When this transition is fired, SDL_EFSM' reaches state S2. Likewise, DO_tp_4 progresses from state $O\text{-}S_0$ to state $O\text{-}S_2$ and resets to 'TRUE' P_t_1 and P_t_{10}.

At the next simulation step the transition t_5 is executed, then the SDL_EFSM' reaches the decision state D_1 and the observer DO_tp_4 progresses to state $O\text{-}D_1$. At $O\text{-}D_1$, the observer DO_tp_4 expects the firing of the SDL_EFSM' transition t_6. Since the triggering condition of t_6 is a predicate, no driving is done. The simulation goes on and explores several scenarii until t_6 is fired (the depth is bounded to 8). In that case, the predicate ($C \geq 3$) of t_6 is satisfied. It means that the scenario which fired t_6 completes the missing part related the loops behaviour. When t_6 is fired the SDL_EFSM' reaches state S_3. Likewise, the observer progresses from $O\text{-}D_1$ to $O\text{-}S_3$ and sets to 'FALSE' the driving variable P_t_8. This setting allows once again the driving of the simulation to only explore the behaviour part related to the transition t_9. When t_9 is executed the observer reaches a success state and then the whole execution scenario is saved into a file. The scenario starts from the initial state to the final state and includes the behaviour of the missing part.

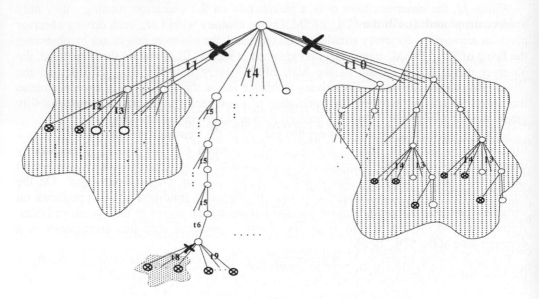

Figure 7 : driving the reachability graph exploration

The driving technique gives up the exploration of specific reachability graph parts in order to gain time when searching test scenarii. For a given test purpose seen as a sequence of SDL_EFSM states and transitions $(S_0, t_1, S_1, t_2, \ldots S_j, t_j, \ldots)$, the driving technique is faster than M_3 exploration if $\forall\ t_j$ at state S_j, the execution of t_j is independent of all the behaviours given up at states S_k preceding S_j (these behaviours are unnecessary to the test scenario composition). However, if $\exists\ t_j$ (at state S_j) whose execution depends on a given up behaviour at states S_k preceding S_j, this implies that test scenario may not be found for this test purpose. For example, see the test purpose tp_3 and its predicate (*received =1*) on transition t_8. The satisfaction of this predicate depend on the execution of the transitions sequence (t_1, t_3). Unfortunately, during the driving exploration this behaviour is given up at state S_0. The occurrence of this problem can be reduced by giving specific writing rules to specifications. It is necessary to avoid loops on states which corresponds to a preliminary sequence of transitions. The only allowed loops on states must be iterations ones.

4.   DISCUSSION & FUTURE WORKS

This paper describes a test generation methodology that tries to cope with the problem of the combinatorial explosion of the states space and to enhance the number of the treated test purposes. We illustrate how static, symbolic and dynamic methods can be linked in order to generate test scenarii in an incremental way. Thus, we combine the advantages of the three methods. Moreover, we show the benefit to define a test purpose as a static path extracted from the SDL specification. Due to the structure of the test purposes, we can, on one hand, apply constraints solving techniques and on the other hand, improve the on-the-fly exploration technique.

The proposed sequencing of the four methods in the methodology, allows for more and more complex test purposes to be taken into account. M_1 deals with the simple ones which do not contain any predicates. M_2 deals with the ones holding predicates. However, the structure of these test purposes have to comply with some hypotheses (no missing parts, simple constraints, ...). M_1 can be seen as a particular case of M_2 with trivial "True" constraints. However, these two methods are distinguished in our methodology to emphasize the importance of choosing the structure of the test purposes. In case of path structure, it is not worth using complex methods such as constraints solving techniques ones, when some test purposes can be obtained at low cost with M_1. Then, M_3 and M_4 consider the remaining test purposes, i.e., those with a more complex structure (with missing parts and non simple constraints). M_4 is an improvement of M_3 where the treated test purposes are those for which correspond test scenarii with lengths higher than the ones M_3 can computes.

Methods M_1 and M_2 are applied first because they work on a compact representation. Hence, contrary to the dynamic methods, they avoid the problem of the explosion of the states space. Besides, M_1 and M_2 reduce the number of test purposes to be treated by the dynamic methods. Method M_3 is applied before method M_4 because of computation time. Method M_3 is based on the synchronous product of the SDL_EFSM with **all** the test purposes (observers) at once. On the contrary, M_4 is applied for **each** test purpose. Hence, in order to reduce the computation time of M_4 it is necessary to reduce the number of test purposes by applying M_3 before. Moreover, when the size of the system is not too big, M_3 may be sufficient for computing the major part of the test scenarii.

An advantage of the dynamic methods is that their applicability is not restricted by hypotheses on the structure of the test purposes (such as the linearity of the predicates). However, since the computation time grows exponentially with the depth of the exploration, the length of the computed test scenarii is bounded. On the opposite, the static and the symbolic methods M_1 and M_2 are only applied on test purposes that match some hypotheses on the structure of the test purposes. However, no restriction is made on the length of the test purposes. Hence, the four methods are complementary.

Future work consists in studying how results of symbolic methods can contribute to improve the driving of the on-the-fly exploration technique. The key idea is the following. With M_4, no driving is performed when searching a missing part of a test purpose. Based on symbolic analysis of the SDL_EFSM, we propose to identify a set of SDL_EFSM cycles (of transitions sequences) that can be candidates to complete the missing parts of the test purposes. When applying the driving technique, the simulation can be driven to explore first these candidates. A similar approach is described in [Chanson 93] in the area study of the symbolic approaches.

A second extension of our work is to incorporate in the methodology the possibility of considering test purposes based on functional coverage (described in MSC for example) in addition to the test purposes based on structural coverage. A key idea is to compute for these functional based test purposes corresponding structural based test purposes, i.e., SDL-EFSM paths for our methodology. Then, we apply the four methods with the candidates paths. However, we have to answer to the question : for which classes of functional based test purposes can we compute paths on the SDL-EFSM ?

REFERENCES

1. K. Sabnani, A.Dahbura, A protocol test generation procedure -Computer Networks ISDN Systems, North-Holland, no, 15, pp 285-297, 1988.
2. E. Brinksma, A theory for derivation of tests, proceedings of 8th PSTV 1988.
3. J. Tretmans A formal approach to conformance testing, PhD. thesis, Twente university, 1992.
4. B. Sarikaya, G. V. Bochmann, E. Cerny, A Test Methodology for Protocol Testing. IEEE Trans. on Software Eng., Vol. SE-13, NO. 5, May 1987.
5. A. Rouger, P. Combes, Exhaustive validation and test generation in ELVIS. SDL Forum'89.
6. G. V. Bochmann, A. Petrenko, O. Bellal, S. Maguiraga, Automating the processof test derivation from SDL specifications, SDL Forum'97, Paris, September 1997.
7. W. Chun, P. Amer, Test Case Generation for Protocols Specified in Estelle. FORTE, 1990, Madrid.
8. S. T. Chanson, J. Zhu. A Unified Approach to Protocol Test Sequence Generation. In Proc. IEEE INFOCOM, 1993
9. C.Bourhfir, R.Dssouli, E. Aboulhamid, N. Rico, Automatic executable test case generation for extended finite state machine protocols. IFIP 9th IWTCS, Korea September 1997.
10. D. Hogrefe. Automatic generation of test cases from SDL specifications. SDL-Newsletter. CCITT 88.
11. L. Bromstrup, D. Hogrefe. TESDL : Experience with Generating Test Cases from SDL Specifications. SDL'89.
12. Enhanced Methodology for Computer Aided Test Generation. RACE project R1084 PROvision of VErification December 1992.
13. J. Grabowski, D. Hogrefe, R. Nahm, Test case generation with test purpose specification by MSCs. In, 6th SDL Forum, O. Færgemand, A. Sarma, Darmstad (Germany), 1993.
14. J. Fernandez, C. Jard, T. Jéron, G. Viho, Using on-the-fly verification techniques for generation of conformance test suites. Conference CAV, New Jersey, USA. 1996.
15. M. Clatin, R. Groz, M. Phalippou, R. Thummel, Two approaches linking a test generation tool with verification techniques. IFIP 8th IWPTS, France, September 1995.
16. A. Touag, A. Rouger, Génération de tests à partir de spécifications LDS basée sur une construction partielle de l'arbre d'accessibilité. Proceedings of CFIP'96 Octobre 1996. Rabat.
17. B. Algayres, Y. Lejeune, F. Hugonnet, GOAL: Observing SDL behaviours with GEODE, in SDL'95.
18. C.Jard, R.Groz, J. F. Monin, Development of VEDA : a prototyping tool for distributed algorithms, IEEE, Trans. on Software Eng., March 1989.

Session V

SDL and MSC for the Next Millennium

this session includes the following presentations not included in the proceedings :

1. MSC-2000 presentation

2. SDL-2000 presentation

SDL'99 : The Next Millennium
R. Dssouli, G.v. Bochmann and Y. Lahav, editors

Towards a New Formal SDL Semantics based on Abstract State Machines

U. Glässer[a], R. Gotzhein[b] and A. Prinz[c]

[a]Heinz Nixdorf Institute, Paderborn University, Dept. of Math. & Computing Science,
D-33102 Paderborn, Germany, glaesser@uni-paderborn.de

[b]Computer Networks Group, University of Kaiserslautern, Dept. of Computing Science,
D-67653 Kaiserslautern, Germany, gotzhein@informatik.uni-kl.de

[c]DResearch GmbH Berlin, D-10319 Berlin, Germany, prinz@dresearch.de

With the year 2000 approaching, a new version of SDL called SDL-2000 is currently reaching maturity, and is expected to pass the standardization bodies shortly. Apart from the usual language maintenance, SDL-2000 will offer new features for exception handling and object-oriented data types. To capture these features formally, a new formal SDL semantics is being devised. In several meetings of ITU-T SG10/Q6, the essential design objectives have been clarified, and an outline of the behaviour model for SDL has been presented and discussed. A major concern in this discussion has been the demand for an executable model, which calls for an operational formalism with readily available tool support. Subsequent investigations have shown that *Abstract State Machines (ASMs)* meet this and all other design objectives, and therefore have been chosen as the underlying formalism. In this paper, ASMs are applied to define the behaviour model of a sample SDL specification formally, thereby illustrating the approach in general.

1. INTRODUCTION

In 1988, a formal semantics for SDL has been added as Annex F to the Z.100 SDL standard of ITU-T [12]. Along with the efforts to improve SDL, this semantics has been revised several times since then. Essentially, Annex F defines a sequence of Meta IV programs that take an SDL specification as input, determine the correctness of its static semantics, perform a number of transformations to replace several SDL language constructs, and interpret the specification. It has been argued that this style of defining the formal semantics is particularly suitable for tool builders.

With the ongoing work to improve SDL, and a new version called SDL-2000 to pass the standardization bodies shortly, it has become apparent that a decision concerning the SDL semantics needs to be taken. Based on the assessment that the existing Meta IV programs will be too difficult to maintain, there is a strong tendency towards defining a new formal semantics. In several meetings of ITU-T SG10/Q6, the essential design objectives of such a semantics have been clarified (see also [7]). Among the primary design objectives is *intelligibility*, which is to be achieved by building on well-known mathematical models and notation, a close correspondence between specification and underlying model, and by a concise and well-structured semantics document. Of similar importance and causally dependent on intelligibility is *maintainability*, since SDL is an evolving language. Language modifications currently under consideration include exception handling, hierarchical states, dynamic block creation, object-oriented data types, real time expressiveness beyond timers, and the removal of some obsolete language features. Therefore, the semantic model has to be sufficiently rich and flexible.

During the discussions within ITU-T SG10/Q6, it has turned out that a prime design objective is the demand for an *executable semantics*. This calls for an operational formalism with readily available tool support. Subsequent investigations have shown that *Abstract State Machines* (ASMs) meet this and all other design objectives, and therefore have been chosen as the underlying formalism. In this paper, we show how ASMs are applied to define the behaviour model of a sample SDL specification formally. More specifically, we develop a behaviour model that can be understood as ASM code generated from an SDL specification. This approach differs substantially from the interpreter view taken in previous work (see also [5,4]), and will enable SDL-to-ASM compilers.

We define a distributed execution model for SDL based on the formalism of *multi-agent real-time ASM*. The behaviour of active SDL objects is described in terms of concurrently operating and asynchronously communicating ASM agents directly reflecting the intuitive understanding of Z.100. Due to its abstract operational view, one obtains a clear and concise formalization of the dynamic semantics of SDL at a natural level of detail and precision.

For the purpose of illustrating the approach, a formal behaviour model of a sample SDL system specification is presented (cf. [7]). Section 2 gives an overview of the modeling approach and illustrates the ASM representation of SDL specifications which serves as a starting point for defining the dynamic semantics in Section 3 (signal flow model) and Section 4 (control flow model). Section 5 contains the conclusions.

2. BACKGROUND AND OVERVIEW

The material of this section is intended to provide an informal overview of the modeling approach, without going into detail. For a rigorous definition of the mathematical foundations, the reader is referred to [8,9]. A comprehensive treatment of methodological aspects of ASM-based modeling and validation of complex systems can be found in [2].[1]

2.1. Associating ASM models with SDL specifications

The dynamic semantics associates with each SDL specification, represented as an abstract syntax tree (AST), a particular multi-agent real-time ASM. Intuitively, an ASM consists of a set of *autonomous agents* cooperatively performing *concurrent machine runs*. The behaviour of agents is determined by *ASM programs*, each consisting of a set of *transition rules*, which define the set of possible runs. Each agent has its own *partial view* on a given global state, on which it fires the rules of its program. According to this view, agents have a *local state* and a *shared state* through which they can interact.

---

[1]For a comprehensive overview on ASM applications and other available material see also the annotated ASM bibliography [1] as well as the following two URLs: http://www.uni-paderborn.de/cs/asm/ and http://www.eecs.umich.edu/gasm/.

It is pointed out that there are strong structural similarities between SDL systems and ASMs, which is a prerequisite for intelligibility and maintainability. These structural similarities are now exploited by identifying ASM agents with certain SDL units. For instance, agents will be introduced for processes, process sets, blocks, and channel segments. Agents can be created during the system initialization phase as well as dynamically, which allows, e.g., to directly represent dynamic process creation in the underlying model.

The execution of a system starts with the creation of a single agent for the SDL unit "system". This agent then creates further agents according to the substructure of the system as defined by the specification, and associates a view and an ASM program with each of them. ASM programs are determined by the kind of the SDL unit modeled by a given agent and the AST of a given SDL specification.

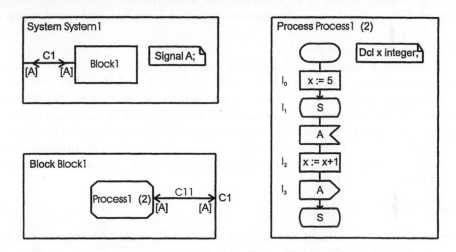

Figure 1. An SDL system specification

Example In Figure 1, a system consisting of a single block Block1 and a delaying channel segment C1 is specified in SDL. The dynamic semantics defines that execution of this system starts with the creation of an agent for System1 with an associated ASM program. This program consists of a rule that, when fired, leads to the creation of two further agents, one agent for Block1 and another for C1. After this rule has been fired and the system has reached an initial state, the agent modeling System1 becomes inactive.

Agents modeling SDL units with a substructure such as block, process set, or process, create further agents modeling the SDL units of this substructure. The ASM program associated with these agents determines the set of agents to be created and their behaviour. Starting with the agent modeling the SDL unit "system", this is repeatedly done until leaf units of the SDL specification such as process or service are reached.

Example In Figure 1, Block1 is substructured into a process set and a channel segment C11. These SDL units are modeled by two corresponding ASM agents. The execution of the ASM agent modeling the process set then leads to the creation of two additional agents, each modeling an instance of Process1. All created processes fire transition rules to reach a specified initial state. This completes the system initialization phase.

Once the initial system structure has been built up by creating a set of agents and associating, with each agent, a view and an ASM program, the actual system execution starts. The behaviour of agents during system execution is determined by their ASM programs defining the set of possible runs. During a run, further agents may be created, and existing agents be terminated, according to the transitions of the SDL processes.

Example The actual execution of the system specified in Figure 1 starts when the agents modeling System1, Block1, C1, C11, and the process set as well as the instances of Process1 have been created and reached their initial state. The behaviour of both process instances is formally defined by an ASM program that is derived from the process graph. It is one of the tasks of the formal semantics definition to make this derivation precise.

2.2. Real-Time Behaviour

By introducing a notion of global system time and imposing additional constraints on machine runs, one obtains a restricted class of ASM, called multi-agent real-time ASM, with agents performing *instantaneous* actions in *continuous* time. For the purpose considered here, it is important that agents fire their rules at the moment they are enabled.

SDL uses the expression **now** to represent the global system time, where the possible values of **now** are given by the predefined SDL sort $Time^2$. The machine model is therefore extended by a nullary dynamic function *now* taking values in a corresponding domain *TIME*.

$$now: \quad TIME, \quad TIME \subseteq \mathbb{R}$$

It is intended that the value of *now* changes dynamically without being affected by the machine model. Intuitively, *now* represents physical time.

2.3. The External World

Following an *open system view*, interactions between a system and the external world, e.g. the environment into which the system is embedded, are modeled in terms of various interface mechanisms. Regarding the reactive nature of distributed systems, it is important to clearly identify and precisely state

- assumptions and constraints on the expected behaviour of the external world, and

- how external conditions and events affect the transition behaviour of an ASM model.

This is achieved through a classification of *dynamic* ASM functions into three categories, namely *controlled*, *monitored* and *shared* functions. By definition, controlled functions can only be altered by an ASM agent, whereas monitored functions exclusively belong to the external world and are *read-only* functions within an ASM program. A monitored function may nevertheless change its values from state to state (e.g., the function *now*).

---

[2] *Time* values are actually real numbers with restricted operations (see Appendix D to Z.100); in particular, SDL does not define a notion for scaling time (it is merely assumed that the same scale of time is used throughout an entire system description).

Shared functions may be altered by the environment as well as by the machine model. Hence, a reasonable *integrity constraint* on shared functions is that no interference with respect to mutually updated locations must occur. Assuming that the external world itself acts like an ASM agent (or a collection of ASM agents), this is ensured by the underlying model of concurrency[3].

2.4. ASM Representation of SDL Specifications

SDL specifications are represented in the ASM model based on their AST. In Figure 2, an excerpt of the AST for the running example is shown. This AST is then encoded by a finite collection of ASM objects from a static domain *DEFINITION* in combination with various functions defined thereon. By means of these functions, the definitions are related to each other and the relevant information can be extracted. Emphasizing the tight relation between SDL specifications and their ASM representation, the terminology and the notation of the AS are reused here. That is, function names denoting AST components in the machine model are identical to the non-terminals used in the AS definition:

$$
\begin{array}{lll}
\textit{System-definition} & : & \textit{DEFINITION} \\
\textit{System-name} & : & \textit{DEFINITION} \rightarrow \textit{NAME} \\
\textit{Block-definition-set} & : & \textit{DEFINITION} \rightarrow \textit{DEFINITION}\text{-set} \\
\textit{Block-definition} & : & \textit{DEFINITION} \rightarrow \textit{DEFINITION} \\
\textit{... etc.}
\end{array}
$$

2.5. Composition of the Dynamic Semantics

Following an abstract operational view, behaviour is expressed in terms of *SDL abstract machine runs*. The formal definition of the dynamic semantics is restricted to specifications that comply with the static semantics of SDL. Previous work on an ASM semantics for SDL (see [5,4]) provides a conceptual framework which is partly reused here.

Starting with the native ASM formalism, the dynamic semantics of SDL is defined in two steps. Firstly, an SDL oriented ASM formalism called BSDL (former work on BSDL is reported in [11]) is given (see Section 3). BSDL can be seen as a kernel containing certain fundamental SDL mechanisms, such as signals, gates, channels, signal consumption, and timers. These mechanisms are collectively referred to as "signal flow model", and are independent of a particular SDL specification.

Secondly, the semantics of SDL is defined based on the signal flow model (see Section 4). Starting point is an ASM representation of SDL specifications as outlined in Section 2.4. ASM modules that determine the behaviour of different kinds of SDL components are provided and used to define the execution model of the SDL specification shown in Figure 1. This is collectively referred to as "control flow model".

2.6. Notational Conventions

For an improved readability, complex transition rules are defined in a stepwise manner by means of *macros* (with parameters). Formally, macros are syntactic abbreviations, i.e. each occurrence of a macro in a rule is to be replaced textually by the related macro definition (replacing formal parameters by actual parameters). For further details, see [6].

---

[3]For details, see the notion of *partially ordered run* in [8].

176

System-definition
    System-name
       System1

    Block-definition-set
      Block-definition
      (include AST of block Block1 here)

    Process-definition-set

    Channel-definition-set
      Channel-definition
        Channel-name
          C1
        Channel-path
          Originating-entity
            Block1
          Destination-entity
            ENVIRONMENT
        Signal-identifier-set
          Signal-identifier
            A

        Channel-path
          Originating-entity
            ENVIRONMENT
          Destination-entity
            Block1
        Signal-identifier-set
          Signal-identifier
            A

    Signal-definition-set
      Signal-definition
        Signal-name
          A

    Data-type-definition

    Syntype-definition-set

Figure 2. Abstract Syntax Tree of the SDL Specification of System1

3. SIGNAL FLOW MODEL

This section introduces *Base SDL (BSDL)* as a kind of kernel language for dealing with certain fundamental features of SDL at a more abstract level. The main focus here is on signal flow aspects, in particular, on the definition of a basic process pattern stating how *active objects* communicate through signals via *gates*. Also, certain structural aspects are covered here.

3.1. Units

To deal with the various types of behavioural SDL objects (systems, blocks, processes) in a uniform way, the concept of *behavioural units* (*units* for short) is introduced. The intention is that behavioural units look the same from their outside (interface) regardless whether they represent direct behaviour, e.g. as processes, or structural aspects, e.g. as systems. Units communicate asynchronously by means of signals via gates, where the gates are interfaces (see Section 3.3).

There is a domain *PLAINUNIT* of plain units with direct behaviour representation. Furthermore, there is a domain *STRUCTURALUNIT* of structural units, which are composed of plain units or structural units.

$$UNIT \equiv PLAINUNIT \cup STRUCTURALUNIT$$

$$subunits : STRUCTURALUNIT \rightarrow UNIT\text{-set}$$

Plain units usually represent behaviour in the sense of *AGENT*s, whereas structural units usually do not have a behaviour of their own. Instead, their behaviour is defined by the behaviour of their internal units. Internal units communicate with each other and with the outside via their gates. The enclosing structural unit unifies the gates of its internal units and its own gates, thus enabling communication.

3.2. Signals

A static domain *SIGNAL* denotes the set of *signal types* occurring in an SDL specification. Dynamically created *signal instances* (*signals* for short) are given by a dynamic domain *SIGNALINST*, where each element of *SIGNALINST* is uniquely related to an element of *SIGNAL*. Finite *sequences* of signals belong to a domain *SIGNALINST** with a distinguished element *empty* denoting the empty sequence of signals.

To each signal a (possibly empty) list of *signal values* is assigned. Since the type information and concrete value is immaterial to the dynamic aspects considered here, signal values are abstractly represented in a uniform way as elements of some static domain *VALUE*. We introduce values at this point unstructured and with no type information.

$$name : SIGNALINST \rightarrow SIGNAL, \quad values : SIGNALINST \rightarrow VALUE^*$$

Additional functions on signals are *sender*, *toArg*, and *viaArg* specifying the sender process, the destination and optional constraints on admissable communication paths. The meaning of these functions is detailed in subsequent sections.

3.3. Gates

Exchange of signals between scope units (such as processes, blocks or a system and its environment) is modeled by means of *gates*. A gate forms an interface for *serial* and *unidirectional* communication between two or more units. The same gate may have the role of an *input gate* for one unit and the role of an *output gate* for another unit. To every unit a set of input gates and a set of output gates is associated.

$$ingates, outgates: \ UNIT \rightarrow GATE\text{-set}, \quad \forall a \in UNIT: \ ingates(a) \cap outgates(a) = \emptyset$$

3.3.1. Discrete Delay Model

A gate must be capable of holding signals that arrived there. Hence, to each gate a (possibly empty) *signal queue* is assigned, as detailed below. Moreover, signals need not reach their destination instantaneously but may be subject to delays. That means, it must be possible to send signals to arrive in the future. Although those signals are only available for disposal when their arrival time has come, they are represented within gates.

To model this behaviour, each signal S which is in transit (not yet arrived) has its individual *arrival time*, i.e. the time at which S eventually reaches a certain gate.

$$arrival \ : \ SIGNALINST \rightarrow TIME$$

One can now represent signals which are in transit to a gate g by means of a *schedule* specifying the respective *signal arrivals* at the gate. More generally, in a given state of the abstract machine model, one can associate to every gate g in $GATE$ some finite sequence of signals, called $schedule(g)$, such that $schedule(g)$ specifies all those signals S which are currently in transit (with destination g).

A reasonable integrity constraint on $schedule(g)$ is that signals in $schedule(g)$ are linearly ordered by their arrival times. That is, if $schedule(g)$ contains signals S, S' and $arrival(S) < arrival(S')$ then $S < S'$ in the order defined by $schedule(g)$.

Intuitively, a signal S in $schedule(g)$ does not arrive at gate g before $now \geq arrival(S)$. In other words, S remains 'invisible' as long as it is in transit. Thus, in every given state of the abstract machine model, the visible part of $schedule(g)$ forms a possibly empty signal queue, denoted as $queue(g)$, which is defined as follows (see also Figure 3).

$$schedule, \ queue \ : \ GATE \rightarrow SIGNALINST^*$$

$$queue(g) \ \equiv \ \langle s : s \ in \ schedule(g) \wedge now \geq arrival(s) \rangle$$

3.3.2. Operations on Schedules

To ensure that the order on signals is preserved when new signals are added to the schedule of a gate, there is a special insertion function on schedules.

$$insert \ : \ SIGNALINST \times TIME \times SIGNALINST^* \rightarrow SIGNALINST^*$$

The result of inserting some signal S with arrival time t into a schedule *seq* is defined as follows.

$$insert(S, t, seq) =$$

$$\begin{cases} \langle S | seq \rangle, & \text{if } seq = empty \text{ or } t < arrival(seq.head), \\ \langle seq.head | insert(S, t, seq.tail) \rangle, & \text{otherwise.} \end{cases}$$

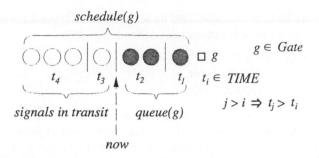

Figure 3. Signals at a gate

Analogously, a function *delete* (with an obvious meaning) is used to remove an item from a schedule.

$$delete \ : \ SIGNALINST \times SIGINST^* \to SIGINST^*$$

As shorthands for operations on schedules to be used in subsequent rules the following two macros are defined.

$$\text{INSERT}(S, t, g) \ \equiv \ schedule(g) := insert(S, t, schedule(g)), \quad arrival(S) := t$$
$$\text{DELETE}(S, g) \ \equiv \ schedule(g) := delete(S, schedule(g)), \quad arrival(S) := undef$$

3.4. Channels

Channels are decomposed into individual channel paths having the role of connection primitives with associated gates. More specifically, a channel path forms a unidirectional point-to-point communication link for the transport of signals from its ingate ($from$) to its outgate (to). Channel paths declared in an SDL specification are formally represented by the elements of a static domain *LINK*.

$$LINK \subseteq AGENT$$

SDL considers channels as reliable and order-preserving connections. A channel may however delay the transportation of a signal for an *indeterminate* and *non-constant* time interval. Although the exact delaying behaviour is not further specified, the fact that channels are reliable implies that all delays must be finite.

Signal delays are modeled through a monitored function *delay* stating the dependency on external conditions and events. That is, *delay* dynamically associates time intervals from a domain *DURATION* to the elements of *LINK*, where the length of a time interval is determined by the environment. Taking into account that there are also non-delaying channels, a reasonable integrity constraint on the function *delay* is that the result value on non-delaying channel paths is always 0.

Channel paths are further characterized by a set of signal types they are able to convey. This constraint is stated by a function *with* defined on *LINK*.

$$
\begin{array}{lll}
from, to & : & LINK \rightarrow GATE \\
with & : & LINK \rightarrow SIGNAL\text{-}\mathbf{set} \\
delay & : & LINK \rightarrow DURATION
\end{array}
$$

Channel Behaviour

A link agent l performs a single operation: signals received at $from(l)$ are forwarded to $to(l)$. That means, l continuously watches ingate $from(l)$ waiting for the next deliverable signal in $queue(from(l))$. Whenever l is applicable to a signal S identified by the head of $queue(from(l))$, it attempts to discard S from $queue(from(l))$ in order to insert S into $schedule(to(c))$. Note that this attempt need not necessarily be successful as, in general, there may be several link agents competing for the same signal S.

How does a link agent l know whether it is applicable to a signal S? Now, this decision depends on the values of $toArg(S)$, $viaArg(S)$, $name(S)$ and $with(l)$. In other words, l is a legal choice for the transportation of S only, if $name(S) \in with(l)$ and there is an admissible path connecting $to(l)$ to a valid destination of S. Abstractly, this decision can be expressed using a predicate *Compatible* as stated below.[4]

The behaviour of channel paths is specified by the module Link_Module below, where an auxiliary function *last_time* defined on *LINK* states the accumulated delays as required to ensure that the transfer of signals is *order-preserving*.

Link_Module:

```
FORWARDSIGNAL
  ≡ if Self.from.queue ≠ empty then
      let S = Self.from.queue.head in
        if Applicable(Self, S) then
          DELETE(S, Self.from)
          INSERT(S, Delay(Self), Self.to)
          Self.last_time := Delay(Self)
  where
    Applicable(Self, S)
      ≡ S.name ∈ Self.with ∧ Compatible(Self.to, S.name, S.toArg, S.viaArg)
    Delay(Self)
      ≡ max(now + Self.delay, Self.last_time)
```

3.5. Processes

A static domain *PROCESS* represents the *process definitions* as introduced by an SDL specification, where properties associated with elements of this domain are stated by various functions defined on *PROCESS*.

---

[4]Clearly, there is quite some amount of complexity hidden in this predicate *Compatible* performing the computations as defined with the reachability rules of [12]. However, all involved functions are computable and could (and probably will) be refined down to the level of detail and precision stated in [12].

Individual process instances are represented by a dynamic domain *PROCESSINST*, *PROCESSINST* ⊂ *AGENT*, which grows and shrinks dynamically as new process instances are created at run time respectively old ones cease to exist. Each process instance has a unique *process instance identifier – PId* from a dynamic domain *PID* as stated by a corresponding function *self* defined on process instances. Input ports of process instances are modeled as finite sequences of signals in terms of a gate.

$$self \ : \ PROCESSINST \rightarrow PID, \quad inport \ : \ PROCESSINST \rightarrow GATE$$

Process instances are organized in *process instance sets*, where all members of a process instance set share the same sets of input gates and output gates. A process instance set is abstractly represented by an element of a dynamic domain *PROCESSSET*. The relation between process instances and process sets is modeled by a dynamic function *owner*. Signals received at an input gate of a process set are appended to the input port of a process instance depending on the value of the *toArg*. Simultaneously arriving signals which match the same process instance are appended, one at a time, in an order chosen non-deterministically. Signals are discarded whenever no matching receiver instance exists. Notice that SDL allows the following syntactic ambiguity (where the value of *toArg* may also be undefined).

$$toArg \ : \ SIGNALINST \rightarrow PID \cup PROCESS$$

Process agents frequently check their input gates for new signals as specified in terms of a rule macro HANDLESIGNALS.

HANDLESIGNALS
  ≡ choose s : $Arrived(S) \wedge Matches(S)$
        INSERT($Self.buffer, S.arrival, S$)
    // discard zombie signals
    choose S : $Arrived(S) \wedge PostMortem(S)$
        DELETE($Self.buffer, S$)
    where
        $Arrived(S) \equiv \exists g : g \in Self.ingates \wedge S = g.queue.head$
        $Matches(S) \equiv S.toArg = Self.pid \vee S.toArg = Self.owner$
        $PostMortem(S)$
            $\equiv S.toArg \in PID \wedge (\forall p \in PROCESSINST : pid(p) \neq S.toArg)$

3.5.1. Signal Consumption

Consider a process agent denoted by *Self* consuming input signals from its input port *Self.inport.queue*. The input operation is modeled below, where the parameters *InputSet* and *SaveSet* specify the set of valid input signals and the set of signals to be saved depending on the current state node. Note that an *input node* is defined by a triple (*Signal, Vars, Trans*) identifying a *signal type*, a (possibly empty) list of *variable names* and a resulting *transition*. The value of *Trans* specifies the label of the transition rule to be executed in the next machine step, as explained in Section 4.

An auxiliary function *extract* (defined below) checks the input port for a suitable input signal S returning *undef*, if no such signal exists. A monitored predicate *Spontaneous* indicates a spontaneous transition event.

> CONSUMEINPUTSIGNAL(*InputSet, SaveSet*)
> $\equiv$ if *Spontaneous* then
>   choose *node* : *node* $\in$ *InputSet* $\wedge$ *node* = $\langle$*none, empty, Trans*$\rangle$
>   *label*(*Self*) := *Trans*
>   else
>   if *Self.inport.queue* $\neq$ *emptyQ* then
>   let S = *extract*(*Self.inport.queue, SaveSet*) in
>   if $S \neq$ *undef* then
>   DELETE(S, *Self.inport*)
>   let $\langle$*S.name, Vars, Trans*$\rangle$ $\in$ *InputSet* in
>   *label*(*Self*) := *Trans*
>   ASSIGNVALUES(S, *Vars, Self*)

The auxiliary function *extract* is defined recursively as follows.

$extract(Q, SaveSet) =$

$$\begin{cases} undef, & \text{if } Q = empty, \\ S, & \text{if } Q = \langle S|RestQ\rangle \wedge name(S) \notin SaveSet, \\ extract(RestQ, SaveSet), & \text{if } Q = \langle S|RestQ\rangle \wedge name(S) \in SaveSet, \end{cases}$$

3.5.2. Timers

A particular concise way of modeling timers is by identifying timer objects with respective timer signals. More precisely, each *active* timer is represented by a corresponding timer signal in the schedule associated with the input port of the related process instance.

$$TIMER \subseteq SIGNAL, \quad TIMERINST \subseteq SIGNALINST$$

Timer signals of a given process are uniquely identified by their timer name in combination with a list of timer values as stated by the following function.

$$tsig \ : \ PID \times TIMER \times VALUE^* \to TIMERINST$$

The information associated with timers is accessed using the functions defined on *SIGNAL* with their usual meaning (where both *toArg* and *viaArg* have the value *undef*).

To indicate whether a timer instance is active or passive, there is a corresponding predicate *Active*. For a given process *PId* and a given timer t, the value of *Active* is defined as follows.

$$Active(PId, t) \equiv t.arrival > now \vee t \text{ in } PId.inport.queue$$

The macros below model the operations *set* and *reset* on timers as executed by a process agent of the abstract machine model. An SDL **set** will be transformed into a reset operation immediately followed by a set operation.

$$\text{SETTIMER}(\textit{TName},\ \textit{TValues},\ \textit{Time})$$
$$\equiv \texttt{let}\ \ S = \textit{tsig}(\textit{Self},\ \textit{TName},\ \textit{TValues})\ \ \texttt{in}$$
$$\quad\quad \texttt{if}\ \ \textit{Time} = \textit{undef}\ \ \texttt{then}$$
$$\quad\quad\quad // \text{ set default duration}$$
$$\quad\quad\quad \text{INSERT}(S,\ \textit{defaultTime},\ \textit{Self.inport})$$
$$\quad\quad \texttt{else}$$
$$\quad\quad\quad \text{INSERT}(S,\ \textit{Time},\ \textit{Self.inport})$$
$$\quad \texttt{where}$$
$$\quad\quad \textit{defaultTime} \equiv\ \textit{now} + \textit{duration}(\textit{TName})$$

$$\text{RESETTIMER}(\textit{TName},\ \textit{TValues})$$
$$\equiv \texttt{let}\ \ S = \textit{tsig}(\textit{Self},\ \textit{TName},\ \textit{TValues})\ \ \texttt{in}$$
$$\quad\quad \texttt{if}\ \ \textit{Active}(\textit{Self},\ S)\ \ \texttt{then}$$
$$\quad\quad\quad \text{DELETE}(S,\ \textit{Self.inport})$$

4. CONTROL FLOW MODEL

Building on the signal flow concepts of BSDL, defined in Section 3, this section complements the semantic definition by fixing the missing control flow aspects.

4.1. SDL Abstract Machine Model

Behavioural properties of ASM agents are expressed in terms of transition rules defined by a finite collection of program *modules*. A module is identified by its module name from a static domain $MODULE$. A dynamic function Mod specifies for each agent the module to be executed in the next step of the SDL abstract machine.

$$Mod\ :\ AGENT \rightarrow MODULE$$

An SDL abstract machine run splits into two basically different phases, an *initialization phase* followed by an *execution phase*. Accordingly, there are two kinds of transition rules, namely *initialization rules* and *execution rules*, as identified by two categories of modules.

$$MODULE\ \equiv\ INITMODULE \cup EXECMODULE$$

Initialization modules are denoted by a fixed set of module names as given by the following static domain.

$$INITMODULE \equiv \{\ \text{Init\_Block\_Module},\ \text{Init\_Process\_Set\_Module},\ \text{Init\_Process\_Module}\ \}$$

Execution modules are denoted by the elements of a static domain $EXECMODULE$. Note that the particular set of execution modules depends on the underlying SDL specification. More specifically, there is one execution module for each type of process. This relation is stated by a static function *execmod*.

$$\textit{execmod}\ :\ PROCESS \rightarrow EXECMODULE$$

The compilation of SDL processes into ASM transition rules handles control flow information through a *labeling* of process graph nodes. Resulting node labels relate individual process operations to transition rules in the machine model. The effect of state transitions of processes is modeled by firing the related transition rules in an analogous order.

Labels are abstractly represented by a static domain *LABEL*. A dynamic function *label*, defined on process agents, is used to model dynamic rule selection. That is, *label* identifies for each process agent the rule to be fired in a given machine state.

$$label \; : \; PROCESSINST \rightarrow LABEL$$

4.2. Preinitial System State

This section states requirements on the initial state S_0 of the abstract SDL machine model. Formally, S_0 is defined by a set of first-order formulas $\varphi_1, \ldots, \varphi_n$ such that $S_0 \models \varphi_1 \wedge \ldots \wedge \varphi_n$. For brevity, it is assumed that dynamic functions (predicates) yield the value *undef* (*false*) on those locations which have not explicitly been initialized with some other value. With regard to dynamic domains that means that their default interpretation is the empty set.[5]

STARTLABEL denotes a set of distinguished *start labels*, one for each process type. The assignment of start labels to process types is stated by a static function *startlabel*.

$$startlabel \; : \; PROCESS \rightarrow STARTLABEL, \quad STARTLABEL \subset LABEL$$

Initial Agents

Agents have two basic operation modes as stated by a static domain *MODE*. A unary dynamic function *mode* defined on agents indicates the mode of an agent in a given abstract machine state.

$$MODE \equiv \{ initial, \; starting \}, \quad mode \; : \quad AGENT \rightarrow MODE$$

Initially, there is a single agent *system* denoting a uniquely determined system instance from $SYSTEMINST = \{ system \}$.

$$Mod(system) = \mathsf{Init\_Block\_Module}, \quad mode(system) = initial$$

A unary function *ref* defined on agents identifies for each agent an AST (sub-) definition to be processed during the initialization phase.

$$ref \; : \; AGENT \rightarrow DEFINITION, \quad ref(system) = System\text{-}definition$$

Gates at system level are to be created during the initialization phase. The two sets of system gates are initialized accordingly.

$$ingates(system) = outgates(system) = \emptyset$$

---

[5]Technically speaking, ASM states form many-sorted structures on top of elementary structures modeling domains through unary predicates.

4.3. System Initialization Phase

Starting from S_0 the initialization rules describe a recursive *unfolding* of the specified system instance according to its hierarchical structure. Each initialization step may create several object instances simultaneously.

An auxiliary function *owner*, defined on units, is introduced in order to state the relation between individual system parts and their constituent components. More specifically, an agent a is considered as owner of another agent b if the component modeled by b actually is a subcomponent of the component modeled by a.

$$owner \quad : \quad UNIT \to UNIT$$

4.3.1. System and Block Level Initialization

The initialization of systems and blocks is defined by the module Init_Block_Module, where *Self*, depending on the context, either denotes a system agent or block agent.

Init_Block_Module:

INITBLOCK
$\equiv$ if $mode(Self) = initial$ then
    $mode(Self) := starting$
    CREATEBLOCKS($Self, Self.ref.Block\text{-}definition\text{-}set$)
    CREATEPROCESSSETS($Self, Self.ref.Process\text{-}definition\text{-}set$)
    CREATECONNECTIONS($Self, Self.ref.Channel\text{-}to\text{-}channel\text{-}connection\text{-}set$)
  else
    CREATECHANNELS($Self, Self.ref.Channel\text{-}definition\text{-}set$)
    // switch to execution phase
    $Mod(Self) := undef$

Block Creation

A block instance is represented by an agent of type $BLOCKINST$. The initialization behaviour of block instances is specified by the module Init_Block_Module.

CREATEBLOCKS($Owner, Items$)
$\equiv$ do forall $item : item \in Items$
    // create block agent
    CREATEBLOCKAGENT($Owner, item$)

CREATEBLOCKAGENT($Owner, Ref$)
$\equiv$ extend $BLOCKINST$ with b
    $ref(b) := Ref$
    $mode(b) := initial$
    $owner(b) := Owner$
    $ingates(b) := \emptyset$
    $outgates(b) := \emptyset$
    $Mod(b) := $ Init_Block_Module

Process Set Creation

A process set is represented by an agent of type *PROCESSSET*. The initialization behaviour of process sets is specified by the module Init_Process_Set_Module.

CREATEPROCESSSETS(*Owner, Items*)
≡ do forall *item* : *item* ∈ *Items*
    // create process agent
    CREATEPROCSETAGENT(*Owner, item*)

CREATEPROCSETAGENT(*Owner, Ref*)
≡ extend *PROCESSSET* with *ps*
    ref(*ps*) := *Ref*
    mode(*ps*) := *initial*
    owner(*ps*) := *Owner*
    ingates(*ps*) := ∅
    outgates(*ps*) := ∅
    Mod(*ps*) := Init_Process_Set_Module

Connection Creation

For each connection declared in a *Channel-to-channel-connection-set* associated with a certain scope unit, depending on whether this connection is unidirectional or bidirectional, either one or two gates of the scope unit need to be created.

An auxiliary function *directions* when applied to a connection determines the specified direction(s).

directions : *DEFINITION* → *DIRECTION*-set

CREATECONNECTIONS(*Owner, Items*)
≡ do forall *item* : *item* ∈ *Items*
    // create one gate per direction
    do forall *direction* : *direction* ∈ *directions*(*item*)
        CREATEGATE(*Owner, direction*)

CREATEGATE(*Owner, Direction*)
≡ extend *GATE* with *g*
    owner(*g*) := *Owner*
    if *Direction* = *in* then
        ingates(*Owner*) := *ingates*(*Owner*) ∪ { *g* }
    if *Direction* = *out* then
        outgates(*Owner*) := *outgates*(*Owner*) ∪ { *g* }

Channel Creation

Channels are modeled through unidirectional channel paths. Each channel path is represented by an agent of type *LINK*.

CREATECHANNELS(*Owner, Items*)
≡ do forall *item* : *item* ∈ *Items*
    do forall *path* : *path* ∈ *Channel-paths*(*item*)
        CREATECHANNELPATH(*Owner, item, path*)

4.3.2. Process Set Level Initialization

The initialization of process sets is defined by the module Init_Process_Set_Module, where *Self* denotes any process set agent.

Init_Process_Set_Module:

INITPROCESSSET
$\equiv$ // create process set gates
  CREATEPROCESSSETGATES(*Self, Self.owner.ref*)
  // create initial process instances
  do forall $i: i \in \{1 .. Self.ref.Initial-number-of-instances\}$
    CREATEPROCESSINSTANCE(*Self, Self.ref*)
  Mod(*Self*) := *undef*

CREATEPROCESSINSTANCE(*Owner, Ref*)
$\equiv$ extend *PROCESSINST* with *p*
  ref(*p*) := *Ref*
  mode(*p*) := *initial*
  owner(*p*) := *Owner*
  Mod(*p*) := Init_Process_Module

4.3.3. Process Level Initialization

The initialization of process instances is defined by the module Init_Process_Module, where *Self* denotes any process agent.

Init_Process_Module:

INITPROCESS
$\equiv name(Self) := Self.ref.Process\text{-}name$
  $label(Self) := Self.owner.startlabel$
  CREATEPROCESSGATES(*Self*)
  CREATEPROCESSVARIABLES(*Self, Self.ref*)
  // switch to execution module
  Mod(*Self*) := *execmod*(*Self.owner*)

4.4. System Execution Phase

This section extends the description of the behaviour of process agents from the previous Section by introducing another rule, called EXECPROCESS, as given by the corresponding execution module for a process type. This additional rule defines the behaviour of process agents during the execution phase. Notice that these are the only agents running during the execution phase.

Example Specification

The value of *execmod*(*Process1*) is defined to be Process1_Module. By setting the value of *Mod* to *execmod*(*Process1*), the final step of the initialization of processes, as stated by the INITPROCESS rule, effectively switches the two process agents resulting from the initialization phase to the execution phase.

By means of an appropriate labeling of control flow graph nodes in the graphical representation of Process1 (see Figure 1), we can directly relate the execution of individual operations to the resulting rules in the machine model.

$$PROCESS = \{\, \text{Process1}\,\}$$

$$execmod(\text{Process1}) = \text{Process1\_Module}$$

$$LABEL = \{\, l_0, \ldots, l_3 \,\}, \quad startlabel(\text{Process1}) = l_0, \quad inputlabels(\text{Process1}) = \{\, l_1 \,\}$$

Process1_Module:

EXECPROCESS
  $\equiv$ if $label(Self) = l_0$ then
        ASSIGNVALUE$((x, Self), eval(5, Self))$
        $label(Self) := l_1$

    if $label(Self) = l_1$ then
        CONSUMEINPUTSIGNAL$(\{(A, \langle\rangle, l_2)\}, \emptyset)$

    if $label(Self) = l_2$ then
        ASSIGNVALUE$((x, Self), eval(x + 1, Self))$
        $label(Self) := l_3$

    if $label(Self) = l_3$ then
        OUTPUTSIGNAL$(A, \langle\rangle, Env, undef)$
        $label(Self) := l_1$

    if $label(Self) \notin inputlabels(Self)$ then
        HANDLESIGNALS

4.5. Interaction with the Environment

In Table 1, we summarize some interfaces to the external world. Signals, for instance, may either be introduced by the system or by the environment extending the domain $SIGNALINST$ accordingly. Notice also that by declaring $SIGNALINST$ as shared, functions defined on $SIGNALINST$ are shared as well.

Regarding time related aspects, one can reasonably assume that values of *now* increase monotonically. Similarly, one can characterize all other interfaces, stating the expected behaviour of the external world (where the degree of detail and precision clearly depends on the underlying abstraction level).

Identifier	Type	Intended Meaning
SIGNALINST	shared	dynamically created signal instances
PID	shared	dynamically created PId's
now	monitored	global system time
delay	monitored	delaying behaviour of channels
schedule	shared	signal queues of (system) gates
Spontaneous	monitored	indicates spontaneous transitions

Table 1
Classification of dynamic ASM functions/predicates

5. CONCLUSIONS

In this paper, we have applied ASMs to define the dynamic semantics of a sample SDL specification formally. ASMs meet the design objectives of the dynamic part of the formal SDL semantics and have therefore been chosen as the underlying formalism. In addition, the static semantics as well as the data model have to be defined and combined with the behaviour model.

A particularity of the dynamic semantics is the compiler view, which — in conjunction with ASMs — yields an extremely concise behaviour model and will enable SDL-to-ASM compilers. Once such a compiler is available, existing ASM-tools can be used to execute the semantic model of any given SDL specification.

Readability of the semantic model is supported by a structure that mimics SDL structuring mechanisms. As a novelty, we have integrated the structured modeling of SDL communication links. This further improves readability and makes the semantics even more flexible w.r.t. future language development.

Two important observations concerning our modeling approach are in place:

- The SDL view of distributed systems with real-time constraints and the semantic modeling concept of multi-agent real-time ASM clearly coincide; essential properties of the underlying computation models — namely, the notions of concurrency, reactivity and time as well as the notion of states — are so tightly related that the common understanding of SDL can directly be converted into a formal semantic model avoiding any formalization overhead.

- Even without direct support of object-oriented features in ASMs, the resulting ASM model of the dynamic semantics is particularly concise, readable and understandable. Furthermore, this model can easily be extended and modified as required for an evolving technical standard. Beyond the purpose addressed here, ASM models can be utilized for defining a bridging semantics in order to combine SDL with other domain specific modeling languages.

ACKNOWLEGEMENTS

We take this as an opportunity to thank Joachim Fischer and his group for actively supporting our endeavour to define a new formal SDL semantics. We also thank Anders Olsen, Rick Reed, and Thomas Weigert for their advise and encouragement.

REFERENCES

1. E. Börger and J. Huggins. Abstract State Machines 1988-1998: Commented ASM Bibliography. *Bulletin of EATCS*, 64:105–127, February 1998.
2. E. Börger. High Level System Design and Analysis using Abstract State Machines. In D. Hutter, W. Stephan, P. Traverso and M. Ullmann, editors, *Current Trends in Applied Formal Methods (FM-Trends 98)*. Lecture Notes in Computer Science, Springer-Verlag, Berlin Heidelberg New York (1999)
3. G. Del Castillo. The ASM Workbench: an Open and Extensible Environment for Abstract State Machines. In U. Glässer and P. Schmitt, editors, *Proc. of the 5th International ASM Workshop*, TR, pages 139–155, Magdeburg University, 1998.
4. U. Glässer. ASM semantics of SDL: Concepts, methods, tools. In Y. Lahav, A. Wolisz, J. Fischer, and E. Holz, editors, *Proc. of the 1st Workshop of the SDL Forum Society on SDL and MSC (Berlin, June 29 - July 1, 1998)*, volume 2, pages 271–280, 1998.
5. U. Glässer and R. Karges. Abstract State Machine semantics of SDL. *Journal of Universal Computer Science*, 3(12):1382–1414, 1997.
6. U. Glässer, R. Gotzhein and A. Prinz. SDL Formal Semantics Definition. Technical Report tr-rsfb-99-065, Department of Mathematics and Computing Science, Paderborn University, 1999.
7. R. Gotzhein, B. Geppert, F. Rößler, and P. Schaible. Towards a new formal SDL semantics. In Y. Lahav, A. Wolisz, J. Fischer, and E. Holz, editors, *Proc. of the 1st Workshop of the SDL Forum Society on SDL and MSC (Berlin, June 29 - July 1, 1998)*, volume 1, pages 55–64, 1998.
8. Y. Gurevich. Evolving Algebra 1993: Lipari Guide. In E. Börger, editor, *Specification and Validation Methods*, pages 9–36. Oxford University Press, 1995.
9. Y. Gurevich. ASM Guide 97. CSE Technical Report CSE-TR-336-97, EECS Department, University of Michigan–Ann Arbor, 1997.
10. Y. Gurevich and J. Huggins. The Railroad Crossing Problem: An Experiment with Instantaneous Actions and Immediate Reactions. In *Proceedings of CSL'95 (Computer Science Logic)*, volume 1092 of *LNCS*, pages 266–290. Springer, 1996.
11. St. Lau and A. Prinz. BSDL: The Language – Version 0.2. Department of Computer Science, Humboldt University Berlin, August 1995.
12. ITU-T Recommendation Z.100. *Specification and Description Language (SDL)*. International Telecommunication Union (ITU), Geneva, 1994 + Addendum 1996.

Session VI

UML in Collaboration with MSC and SDL

SDL'99 : The Next Millennium
R. Dssouli, G.v. Bochmann and Y. Lahav, editors
©1999 Elsevier Science B.V. All rights reserved

Towards a Harmonization of UML-Sequence Diagrams and MSC

Ekkart Rudolph[a], Jens Grabowski[b], and Peter Graubmann[c]

[a]Technical University of Munich, Institute for Informatics, Arcisstrasse 21, D-80290 München, Germany, eMail: rudolphe@informatik.tu-muenchen.de

[b]Institute for Telematics, University of Lübeck, Ratzeburger Allee 160, D-23538 Lübeck, Germany, eMail: jens@itm.mu-luebeck.de

[c]Siemens AG, ZT SE 2, Otto-Hahn-Ring 6, D-81739 München, Germany, eMail: Peter.Graubmann@mchp.siemens.de

Sequence Diagrams as part of UML play an important role within use case driven object oriented (OO) software engineering. They can be seen as OO variants of the ITU-T standard language Message Sequence Chart (MSC) which is very popular mainly in the telecommunication area. Both notations would benefit from a harmonization. A more formal and powerful notation for Sequence Diagrams may arise, on the one hand. On the other hand, the application area of MSC might be considerably enlarged. In this context, it has to be noted that the acceptance of a language in the OO community essentially depends on a clear visualization of constructs typical for OO modelling. It is argued that Sequence Diagrams can be transformed into MSC diagrams if some enhancements of MSC are introduced. Such a transformation demonstrates the big advantage of MSC concerning composition mechanisms, particularly, in comparison with the rather obscuring branching constructs in Sequence Diagrams. At the same time, such a transformation may be used for a formalization of Sequence Diagrams in UML since MSC has a formal semantics based on process algebra.

Keywords: MSC, UML, OO, software engineering, distributed systems, real time systems, telecommunication

1. Introduction

Sequence Diagrams in UML [10] resulted from two sources: Ivar Jacobson's interaction diagrams (Objectory) [3] and the 1992 version of the MSC language (MSC-92)[1] [11]. From MSC-92 first an OO variant, called OMSC, was developed at Siemens [2] which essentially combined a subset of MSC with constructs typical for OO design, in particular, the construct for method calls. Sequence Diagrams are a further development and adjustment of OMSC. They do not claim to have the same degree of formality yet as MSC. This refers

---

[1]The terms MSC-92, MSC-96 and MSC-2000 refer to the 1992, 1996 and 2000 versions of the MSC recommendation Z.120. MSC without version indication refers to the actual 1996 language definition [11].

to both syntax and semantics. The syntax is not equally fixed in UML as in the ITU-T Recommendation Z.120 [12]. Therefore, different authors referring to UML use slightly different variants and take over some more constructs from MSC.

Sequence Diagrams and use cases are closely related within UML [1,10]. Sequence Diagrams are derived from use cases. A use case diagram shows the relationship among actors and use cases within a system. A use case diagram is a graph of actors, a set of use cases enclosed by a system boundary, communication associations between the actors and the use cases, and generalizations among the use cases. A given use case is typically characterized by multiple scenarios. Scenarios are described by means of Sequence Diagrams.

Sequence Diagrams are used whenever dynamic aspects are considered. The interaction between objects always arises from methods or processes being attached to objects. Such processes need time, have to be ordered possibly with respect to other processes, can be called only under certain guards, need parameters and provide results. Sequence Diagrams are useful whenever such correlations shall be visualized without showing the concrete programming code of a special programming language. Thereby, an abstraction of details of the later implementation is essential. Often, only a rather coarse overall view of the interplay of the concerned objects is important. Nevertheless, in its strongest refinement, Sequence Diagrams in OO systems can take over a similar role which in a procedural paradigm flow diagrams can play.

MSC is an ITU-T standard trace language for the specification and description of the communication behaviour of system components and their environment by means of message exchange [12]. In general, MSC applications can be attached to the area of reactive and distributed systems, and its main application area lies in the field of telecommunication systems. Traditionally, MSC is used primarily in connection with SDL. Indeed, it also arose from the same ITU-T study group as SDL. Contrary to Sequence Diagrams, MSC is a rather advanced language with a well defined syntax and semantics [4,6,9,12,13].

After the 1996 edition, MSC has been considered several times by Rational as a candidate for the trace description of object interaction in UML. A main obstacle essentially was the missing notion of flow of control in MSC. A harmonization of MSC and Sequence Diagrams certainly will enhance the application area of MSC by bringing it more to the attention of the OO community. However, the introduction of flow of control into MSC is more than a pure marketing strategy. It also pays attention to the fact that traditional telecommunication developing methods and OO techniques grow together. Beyond that, the introduction of flow of control to MSC appears as a challenging and promising subject in itself. The explicit representation of flow of control, in addition to the message flow representation, offers a completely new view of the implicit event trace which may contribute considerably to transparency and expressiveness of the description. It is also a natural place to introduce new·communication mechanisms into MSC, e.g., synchronous communication, remote procedure call, etc. [8]. Though the role of flow of control in MSC appears to be not yet completely settled, it may be looked at already as a description, supplementary to the message flow. In this paper the role of flow of control within MSC will be clarified and the benefits of its explicit representation will be explained. A particular problem is how and on which level flow of control patterns can be embedded into the MSC language. Last not least, an intuitive graphical representation is crucial.

Within Chapter 2, the constructs of Sequence Diagram are presented and compared with corresponding constructs in MSC. In Chapter 3, a proposal for the introduction of flow of control into MSC is given and an interpretation of flow of control based on event structures is presented. The possible interpretation as critical region in case of shared resources is mentioned. Chapter 4 contains concluding remarks and an outlook.

2. Sequence Diagrams and MSC

Sequence Diagrams are an advanced form of Ivar Jacobson's interaction diagrams [3]. Sequence Diagrams, however, now go much beyond the purely sequential interaction diagrams. The following sections provide a more detailed comparison of Sequence Diagrams and MSC.

2.1. General remarks

Sequence Diagrams and MSCs represent different views of system modelling and also refer to different application areas. Sequence Diagrams offer a software oriented view where the target program normally is running on one processor and the flow of control is passing between various program modules.

Contrary to that, MSCs are typically applied to the description of logically and physically distributed systems with asynchronous communication mechanisms. The specification by means of MSCs normally refers to a fairly high level of abstraction focusing on the causal relations between the contained events. The introduction of control flow to these highly concurrent behaviour descriptions appears much less obvious than in the case of Sequence Diagrams. The harmonization of MSC and Sequence Diagrams is intended to connect the software oriented view of Sequence Diagrams with the distributed conception of MSC.

The MSC example in Figure 2 which is obtained by translating the UML example in Figure 1 into MSC-96 clearly shows that the information of control flow is missing. The complete diagram in Figure 2 seems to be rather disconnected in comparison with Figure 1. In addition, the return message is not distinguished graphically from the calling message (a corresponding construct is missing in MSC-96). An advantage is that the MSC diagram is not overloaded by symbols.

2.2. Diagram area

For describing the interworking of several entities in a graphical form, the constructs of Sequence Diagrams and MSC have to be arranged according to the syntax rules in a diagram area.

Sequence Diagrams: The diagram area of Sequence Diagrams (Figure 1) has two dimensions: the vertical dimension represents time, in the horizontal dimension different objects are described. Usually, merely the ordering of events in time is shown. However, for real time applications, the time axis may actually show a metric. In comparison with MSC, the diagram area of Sequence Diagrams is not bounded by a frame.

MSC: Also the diagram area of MSC, e.g., Figure 2, is two-dimensional with the vertical dimension representing time and the horizontal dimension representing different instances.

196

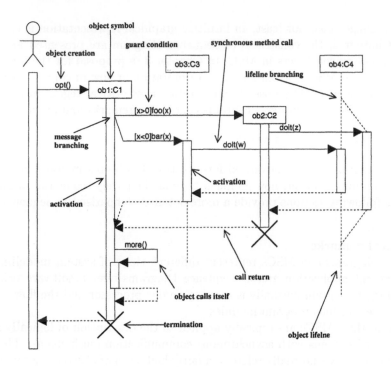

Figure 1. A Sequence Diagram example from the UML1.1 reference manual

Within MSC-96, only time ordering is provided. In MSC-2000, means for real time descriptions is expected. The diagram area of MSC is surrounded by a frame which represents the system environment. In contrast to instances (Section 2.3), no ordering of communication events is assumed at the environment.

2.3. Objects and instances

The entities which interwork are called *objects* in Sequence Diagrams and *instances* in MSC.

Sequence Diagrams: An object denotes a unique instance of an object class and is meant to be an entity to which a set of operations can be applied and which has a state that stores the effects of the operations. Graphically, an object in Sequence Diagrams is described by an *object symbol* and an *object lifeline*.

An object symbol is represented by a rectangular box which is drawn on top of a life line containing the object name and class name separated by a colon (e.g., ob1:C1 in Figure 1). An object lifeline is shown as a vertical dashed line. The lifeline represents the existence of the object at a particular time. In contrast to MSC instance axes, object lifelines do not possess an explicit end symbol unless the termination of the respective object shall be expressed.

Objects may create other objects and may terminate. If an object is created within a Sequence Diagram, then the message that causes the creation is drawn with its arrow head

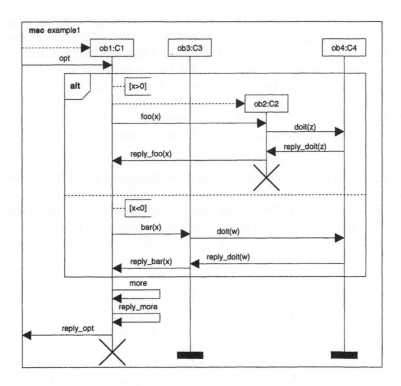

Figure 2. Sequence Diagram example in Figure 1 translated into MSC-96

attached to the object symbol of the created object. Contrary to MSC, create messages in Sequence Diagrams have the same syntax as normal messages, i.e., they show as solid lines with, possibly, names and parameters. An example of object creation can be found in Figure 1, the creation of ob1:C1 is the result of the creation message opt() coming from the system environment.

An object may terminate itself or its termination may be caused by a destroy operation called from some other object. The termination of an object is indicated by a cross symbol at the end of the object lifeline. In Figure 1 the objects ob1:C1 and ob2:C2 terminate themselves. In order to indicate the call of a destroy operation the termination symbol may be the target of a message arrow.

MSC: An MSC instance consists of an *instance head,* an *instance axis* and either an *instance end* or an *instance stop symbol.* The instance head is graphically represented by a rectangular box. Within the instance head, an entity type may be specified in addition to the instance name. An MSC instance axis corresponds to an object lifeline in Sequence Diagrams. Instances are shown by vertical lines or, alternatively, by columns. The instance axis line is solid to indicate the total ordering of events. A coregion may be attached to the instance axis in form of a dashed line. The instance end in an MSC diagram is indicated explicitly by an instance end symbol, i.e., a small solid rectangular box.

An instance can terminate itself by executing a stop event. The termination of an instance is graphically represented by a stop symbol in form of a cross at the end of the instance axis. In contrast to Sequence Diagrams, the stop event is not allowed to be the target of a message. This is due to the fact that the termination of an MSC instance by another instance is not considered a valid concept within MSC.

An MSC instance may be created by another MSC instance. The MSC *create symbol* is a dashed horizontal arrow which may be associated with a parameter list. A create arrow originates from a parent instance and points at the instance head of the child instance.

2.4. Communication

Communication among the entities in Sequence Diagrams and MSC are described in form of arrows. Different types of arrows are used to denote different types of communication. Generally, we may distinguish between synchronous and asynchronous communication. Synchronous means that the involved parties have to meet and during the meeting the communication is performed. Asynchronous means that the communication partners exchange messages which are buffered, i.e., the sending of messages and their consumption are decoupled.

Sequence Diagrams: The communication in Sequence Diagrams is based on *method calls*. Methods are attached to objects and can be compared to procedures in imperative paradigms. The call of a method is only possible from another method, but, calling and called method can be attached to different objects.

Method calls may be synchronous or asynchronous. In case of a synchronous method call, the calling object is suspended until the called object has performed the called method and has given back the result of the method. This can be seen as passing program control from the calling object to the called object and back. In case of an asynchronous method call, the calling object will not be suspended, i.e., may perform other actions during the execution of the called method, and may not wait for an answer about the success of the called method from the corresponding object.

In Sequence Diagrams, a synchronous method call is described by a solid arrow with a full arrow head. The return is shown as a dashed arrow with a thin arrow head. On the called side, both, method call and return message normally are connected by a vertical bar (thin vertical rectangle) representing the activated method. There are several variants admitted. Method call and return message may be combined to one bi-directional arrow with one full arrow head in the direction of the call and one thin arrow head in the return direction in case where no special activity is shown. In a procedural flow of control, the return message may be omitted, otherwise it is mandatory. In case of an asynchronous method call, the arrow describing the call message is solid and drawn with a half arrow head. The arrows of synchronous and asynchronous method calls are labelled with the call name and argument values (in parentheses).

Method calls in general are nested. An object may call itself directly or indirectly. In this case, the nested method symbols (vertical bars) are drawn slightly to the right of the previous one.

A method call in a Sequence Diagram normally is shown as a horizontal solid arrow from the lifeline of one object to the lifeline of another object. The horizontal arrow indicates that the duration required to call the method is atomic, that means, it is brief compared to the granularity of the interaction and nothing else can happen during the call transmission. If the method call requires some time to arrive, during which something else can occur (such as a method call in the opposite direction) then the call arrow is slanted downward.

Method calls in Sequence Diagrams contain some additional concepts which are not contained in the MSC message concept: a call in Sequence Diagrams may contain sequence numbers (to show the sequence of the method call in the overall interaction) and guard conditions by placing Boolean expressions in braces.

MSC: MSC only provides a means to describe asynchronous communication. A construct for synchronous communication is still missing.

Communication in MSC is performed by the exchange of *messages*. One message represents two events, namely message sending and reception. A message is graphically represented by a solid arrow with a full arrow head. A message name is attached to the message arrow. To the message name, a parameter list may be assigned in parentheses.

Messages in MSC may be horizontal or have a downward slope and may be bent. The special form has no additional semantics, no concrete timing semantics is connected with the special graphical form. The message name, if necessary, with a parameter list in parantheses, is attached to the message arrow.

2.5. Methods and activation

The concepts of *methods* and the *activation of methods* are related to the OO view of the world. Denoting that a method is activated means that it has control and is performing some tasks. In case of a synchronous call the activation ends when the method decides to give the control back to the calling object, i.e., during the activation the calling party is suspended. For the asynchronous case, the called object decides itself when it returns into passive state.

Sequence Diagrams: The activation of a method graphically is shown as a tall thin rectangle whose top is aligned with its initiation time and whose bottom is aligned with its completion time.

The top of the activation symbol is attached to the arrow representing the method call, and, if there is a return message, the base of the symbol is attached to the tail of the return message. For example, in Figure 1 the object ob1:C1 is activated by the call opt() from the environment and remains activated throughout the entire Sequence Diagram. The object ob1:C1 terminates itself and returns some results to the environment. During the described communication behaviour, ob1:C1 may call a method in ob3:C3.

Activations may be nested, if a method of an object with already existing activations is called. In this case, the new activation symbol is drawn slightly to the right of the previous one, so that it appears to stack up visually. This can be seen on the lifeline of ob1:C1 in Figure 1. By means of the call more() the object calls a method which is owned by itself. Please note, that the existence of nested activations does not necessarily describe concurrency.

Actions being performed during an activation may be described in text next to the activation symbol or in the left margin, alternately the method call may indicate the action with its name.

MSC: The UML-terms method and activation do not have an immediate counterpart in MSC. However, for inclusion of such concepts into MSC-2000 a corresponding proposal has been made. It will be presented in Section 3 [8].

2.6. Branching, iteration and other structural concepts

Both in Sequence Diagrams and MSCs, some structural concepts have been introduced for a compact representation of either complex situations or more than one communication behaviour. Contrary to MSC, the structural concepts contained in Sequence Diagrams are rather limited and concern alternatives and iteration only.

Sequence Diagrams: A Sequence Diagram can exist in two forms: a *generic form* and an *instance form*. In the generic form which may contain branches and loops it describes several communication behaviours. In the instance form it describes one actual behaviour.

In generic Sequence Diagrams, object life-lines may branch and merge, thus showing alternatives (e.g., ob4:C4 in Figure 1). The branching of a method call is also allowed: it is represented by multiple arrows emanating from one common origin. The guards for messages included in Sequence Diagrams can be interpreted as an if-statement, without else-part. An example of a method call branching protected by guards can be seen in Figure 1. The choice of the method calls foo(x) and bar(x) by ob1:C1 depends on the fulfilment of the gate conditions [X>0] and [X<0].

A connected set of method calls in a Sequence Diagram may be enclosed and marked as an iteration.

MSC: Within MSC, the branching and iteration constructs can be described by inline expressions. Their clarity is an advantage of MSC. A corresponding construct for method call guards, however, is missing. The inclusion of guards for alternatives is planned together with the inclusion of formal data descriptions for MSC-2000. Even then, as is shown by the example in Fig. 6, local data attached to one object cannot be simply translated into guards within the inline expression which in general refers to several objects. The problem of non-locality of choices in MSC has been pointed out already before [5].

2.7. Real time specification

In Sequence Diagrams and MSCs, usually only time ordering of events is described. For real time applications, however, the time axis may have an actual metric and time specifications and constraints may be added to the diagram.

Sequence Diagrams: Various labels indicating timing marks can be shown either in the margin or near the transitions or activations that they refer to. These labels may be used to indicate the transition time for messages: One label (e.g., a in Figure 3) may be attached to the tail of a method call representing the sending time, another label (e.g., b) may be attached to the arrow head indicating the reception time. These labels may be used in constraint expressions (e.g., [b - a < 5 sec]).

MSC: A corresponding explicit notation for the indication of time and time constraints does not exist in MSC-96. Time annotations can be provided in form of comments, but from a formal point of view the time annotations in Sequence Diagrams may also be seen as some sort of comments. A syntax definition for time descriptions in MSC-2000 is in preparation.

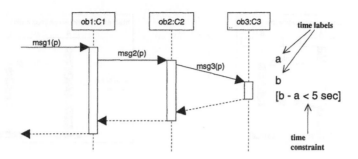

Figure 3. Sequence Diagrams with time labels

2.8. MSC concepts, not supported in Sequence Diagrams

MSC concepts, not or only partially supported in Sequence Diagrams, are *MSC reference*, *High level MSC* (HMSC), *inline expression, coregion, generalized ordering, instance decomposition, gates, special timer constructs, action symbols* and *conditions*.

MSC reference, HMSC, inline expression: MSC references and HMSC are not supported by Sequence Diagrams in UML 1.1. Inline expressions partially enter Sequence Diagrams. According to the UML 1.1 manual, a connected set of messages may be enclosed and marked as an iteration which is very close to the idea of inline expressions. For a scenario, the iteration indicates that the set of messages can occur multiple times. However, no concrete syntax showing the graphical representation of this iteration construct is provided.

Coregion and generalized ordering: Sophisticated ordering constructs like coregion and generalized ordering are not supported in Sequence Diagrams. A total ordering of events along each object lifeline is assumed.

Instance decomposition: Instance decomposition admitting refinement of instances is not supported.

Gates: As already said before, Sequence Diagrams do not contain an explicit environment and therefore also no explicit gates. The environment may be represented by an additional environmental lifeline, like the leftmost lifeline in Figure 1, or by messages with no lifeline as target or source.

Special timer constructs: Special timer constructs are not part of the UML Sequence Diagram syntax. MSC includes language constructs for expressing the setting, resetting and time-out of timers.

Action: An explicit action symbol containing informal text is not included in Sequence Diagrams. An action being performed may be labelled in text next to the activation symbol or in the left margin, alternately the name of a method call may indicate an action.

Condition: Condition symbols indicating initial, final, intermediate, global and non-global states do not exist in Sequence Diagrams.

202

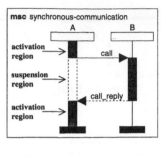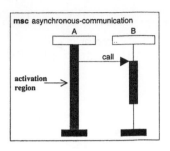

(a) synchronous call   (b) asynchronous call

Figure 4. Synchronous and asynchronous calls in MSC

3. Introduction of flow of control into MSC

In this section we make a proposal for the introduction of flow of control into MSC. For this we assume that objects and method calls of Sequence Diagrams can be translated into instances and messages in MSC.

3.1. Definition of flow of control for plain MSCs

Within Sequence Diagrams the notion of *flow of control* plays an important role. A strict distinction is made between passive objects which do not have control and active objects which have control. "Having control" means that an object which has control is able to execute its program code independently from other objects. An active object may calculate some data, may communicate asynchronously with other objects or may call other methods.

Thus, only active objects can call a method whereas passive objects can be activated by a method call. In the simplest case of a sequential program and synchronous communication, only one object has the control at a time. By means of a synchronous method call, the control is passed from one object to another.

In concurrent systems, the control may be distributed over several objects, i.e., several objects may have control at the same time. Depending on the level and purpose of specification the control flow in Sequence Diagrams may be indicated explicitly in graphical form whereby the active part is represented by the activation construct (Section 2.5).

The possibility to explicitly indicate the flow of control in a similar way seems to be essential for the acceptance of the MSC language for OO modelling. It certainly offers a significant new visualization of the processes occurring in the system. Because of that, a corresponding activation construct, the *activation region*, has been proposed recently within ITU-T for MSC-2000 [8]. An activation region indicates the activity carried out due to a synchronous or an asynchronous method call. It also indicates the flow of control in an MSC since the activation denotes which instance has control.

It turns out that the activation region alone is not sufficient for a clear definition of flow of control in MSC. For the detailed specification of the flow of control, two regions are employed (Figure 4a):

Activation region: The *activation region* may be explicitly represented by a tall thin vertical shadowed rectangle like in Sequence Diagrams. An activation region describes that an instance has been activated.

Suspension region: The *suspension region* indicates the blocking state of a synchronous call which is explicitly represented by a tall thin vertical white rectangle with dotted vertical border lines. The suspension region has no counterpart in Sequence Diagrams. It has been suggested to clearly distinguish the blocking state within a synchronous call from the activation region. In Sequence Diagrams, a suspension is graphically indicated as an activation which is rather misleading.

For modelling method calls in MSC, two kinds of calls are used: synchronous calls with blocking mechanism for the calling instance and asynchronous calls without blocking mechanism. It should be noted that the term *synchronous call* used in this context refers to the blocking mechanism and does not mean that the communication is atomic. A synchronous call is represented by a normal message and a message reply in form of a dashed arrow (Figure 4a). The asynchronous call is represented by a normal message (Figure 4b). Due to the suspension region, synchronous and asynchronous calls are sufficiently distinguished so that no special arrow head symbols are necessary as is the case in Sequence Diagrams. As shown in Figure 5a the mixture of synchronous and asynchronous calls is also possible and does not lose transparency for the reader.

It should be noted that the specification of the control flow should be left as an option to the user depending on the purpose and on the stage of design. In particular, no uniform representation is demanded, i.e., even within one MSC diagram it should be admitted to indicate the flow of control only for certain parts.

On *normal* instances, i.e., outside of activation and suspensions regions, we assume the usual syntax rules for message events [12] with few extensions concerning synchronous calls: Synchronous calls are also allowed from and to normal instances. As a static semantics rule, it is requested that no events may occur between a synchronous call and the corresponding call reply.

The description of the flow of control for plain MSCs is governed by few relatively simple rules:

1. An activation region starts with a call input or with the instance begin (see also Rule 13).

2. In case of a synchronous call, the activation region is terminated by the sending of the corresponding call reply.

3. In case of an asynchronous call, the activation region terminates before the reception of the subsequent new call input.

4. Both, asynchronous and synchronous calls can start from an activation region.

5. If a synchronous call starts from an activation region, the region goes over to a suspension region.

6. If an asynchronous call starts from an activation region, the region remains active.

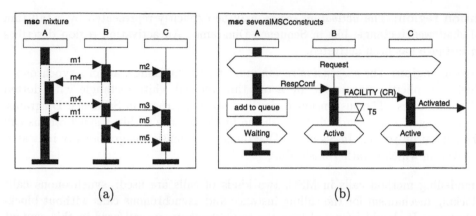

(a)   (b)

Figure 5. Use of flow of control in MSC

7. Call inputs must not enter activation regions.

8. A suspension region starts with a synchronous call from an activation region.

9. A suspension region is terminated by the reception of the corresponding call reply.

10. No calls may start from a suspension region.

11. Call inputs must not enter suspension regions apart from a direct or indirect synchronous call of the instance to itself in which case the suspension region goes over to an activation region. The activation region is then drawn slightly shifted above the suspension region which indicates that the suspension region is only interrupted.

12. Other orderable events like create output, action, timer set and reset may be attached to an activation region. Time-out should be treated like call inputs.

13. We allow activation and suspension regions to be split between different MSCs, in analogy to timer events. If an activation or suspension region is continued in a subsequent MSC, it finishes at the instance end of the first MSC and starts at the instance begin of the second MSC. As a special case, an instance may start with an activation region from the very beginning (*start instance*).

In order to get an intuitive idea, the activation region may be compared with SDL state transitions triggered by message inputs (Figure 5b). The SDL start transition corresponds to the *start instance*. A formal syntax and semantics description may be derived from these rules.

In the following, the integration of a syntax description for the flow of control into the MSC syntax is sketched only. For the synchronous communication, a return message (graphically represented by a dashed arrow line) has to be introduced in addition to the existing message construct. Incomplete return messages should be introduced in analogy to incomplete messages. The return message events should be added to the list of orderable events. Return message events follow the same syntax rules as the normal message events, but a number of new static semantics rules has to be added, e.g., a return message input has to occur always after the corresponding message output. Activation regions and suspension regions may be integrated into the MSC syntax description similarly to coregions, i.e., in the graphical syntax an activation symbol has to be introduced containing an activation event area, and a suspension symbol containing a suspension event area. Activation regions optionally may follow a message input, suspension regions always have to follow synchronous message outputs within activation regions. Activation regions also may contain higher order language constructs like inline expressions and MSC references. Finally, activation regions and suspensions regions have to be added to coregions. The inclusion of flow of control into the structural concepts of MSC will be discussed in Section 3.3.

3.2. Interpretation of flow of control

Within the ITU-T MSC standardization group, the formal definition of flow of control and its semantics has attracted special attention. The following definition has been given in terms of event structures abstracting from special regions:

> *"Flow of control can be understood as a sequence of events also distributed over several instances, but still representing the accomplishment of one behavioral purpose.*
>
> *The sequence of events should be such that two events following each other in the flow of control either are events following each other on the same instance axis or are the two events of the same message.*
>
> *Flow of control may be forked to a flow of control tree / graph, and several flow of controls may be present in an MSC. A fork then 'produces' a new flow of control that needs a new identification.*
>
> *One instance may be involved in more than one flow of control. Independence of flow of control must be defined. It is clear that two flow of controls do not share the same event (other than possibly the forking event). Other restrictions do not seem to be needed or desirable."*

This formulation of flow of control certainly gives a completely new view within MSC: A flow of control appears as a special kind of event flow whereby emphasis is put on the *independence* of different flows of control. At present, this *independence* only refers to the exclusion of shared events since MSC is defined in terms of event structures. Intuitively, control structures also have the interpretation of *critical regions* with respect to shared resources. Depending on the role which in the future the inclusion of formal data concepts within MSC will play, this provides a special semantics of control structures already on the MSC level or only on later stages of design and implementation. Without data concepts, flow of control seems to have no special dynamic semantics but it implies several static semantic rules and it contributes strongly to the intuition.

3.3. Inclusion of structural concepts

In the following, a generalization of the flow of control to structural concepts is sketched. It should be noted that the inclusion of structural concepts certainly needs further elabora-

206

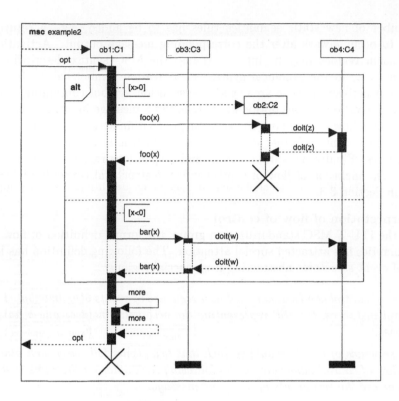

Figure 6. MSC in Figure 2 extended by flow of control

tion. In particular, the representation of flow of control within nested structural concepts, e.g., inline expressions, poses special problems since it soon loses transparency.

MSC references and inline expressions: The definition of flow of control for plain MSCs can be generalized to MSC references and inline expressions in a straightforward manner. The rules stated in Section 3.1 have just to be applied to individual inline sections or to the plain MSCs referred to by MSC references. An illustrations for the inclusion of flow of control is provided for inline expressions by Figure 6.

Instance decomposition: MSC offers the possibility of instance refinement by means of decomposed instances. This mechanism can be used within OO modelling to describe objects including other objects and communication behavior caused by the encapsulation, i.e., reading and changing encapsulated data structures by calling special access functions [7]. By that, the behavior of systems can be modelled on different levels of abstraction. The flow of control on the decomposed instance may be specified according to the same rules as on normal instances (Figure 7a). However, no formal mapping to the flow of control of the refining MSC (Figure 7b) is assumed.

Coregion and generalized ordering: MSC provides several means for the specification of parallel activities within one instance. Apart from parallel operator expressions, the

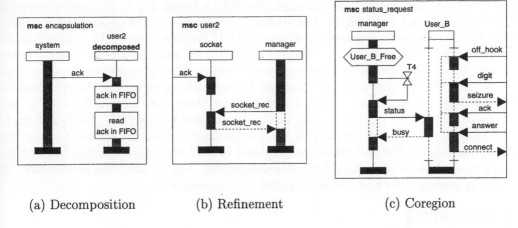

(a) Decomposition   (b) Refinement   (c) Coregion

Figure 7. Instance decomposition, instance refinement and coregion (generalized ordering)

coregion and generalized ordering constructs are tailored for this purpose. Such constructs allow the specification of logically and causally independent tasks in a form where no time ordering between them is provided. Such a specification is ideally suited on early stages of design where decisions concerning implementation are not yet made. An introduction of the concept of flow of control to coregions and generalized ordering constructs imposes some additional restrictions due to the static semantics rules stated in Section 3.1. In case of an explicit specification of activation and suspension regions, we assume a total event ordering along these regions. Figure 7c shows the case where activation regions are embedded in a coregion. The activation regions are partially ordered by means of generalized ordering constructs graphically represented by dotted lines. The example demonstrates that one object may be able to cope with several method calls in parallel. The order of execution of events is left open apart from the prescribed generalized ordering and the total order imposed by the activation regions themselves.

In case of non-explicit representation of flow of control, some ordering consistency rules have to be obeyed within the coregion since otherwise reception and sending of method calls might be arbitrarily interchanged. These ordering rules can be derived from the static semantics rules provided in Section 3.1.

4. Conclusion and outlook

It the preceding chapters, it has been shown that flow of control can be integrated consistently into MSC. Therefore, the representation of the flow of control should be included in MSC-2000. Within this paper, the most important features of flow of control have been tackled. As can be seen from Figure 6 in Chapter 3, some constructs in Sequence Diagram have no immediate counterpart in MSC: At present, there are no formal means in MSC to express guard conditions, a deficiency which hopefully will be removed in MSC-2000. Since the create construct in Sequence Diagrams implies a method call, e.g., in Figure 6 the creation of object ob2:C2 has been described by a create message followed by a MSC method call message. Possibly, a better way of harmonization with UML may be found in the future. In addition, the different kinds of messages need further elaboration. Certainly, one also needs special MSC language constructs to discriminate between asynchronous and synchronous messages in the sense of atomic or non-atomic events. Concerning the two regions proposed in Section 3, we have restricted ourselves to simple flow of control descriptions governed by basic syntax rules. For the specification of flow of control within highly concurrent systems, these rules may turn out to be too stringent. Therefore, a generalization has been proposed by the ITU-T MSC standardization group whereby also call inputs and asynchronous replies are allowed to enter the activation region. The usefulness and graphical form of such more complex flow of control descriptions certainly need further investigations. Beyond that, the development of a formal semantics for flow of control is still in a beginning state.

REFERENCES

1. M. Andersson, J. Bergstrand. *Formalizing Use Cases with Message Sequence Charts.* Master Thesis, Lund Institute of Technology, 1995.
2. F. Buschmann, R. Meunier, H. Rohnert, P. Sommerlad, M. Stal. *A System of Patterns, Pattern Oriented Software Architecture.* John Wiley & Sons, New-York 1996
3. I. Jacobson et al. *Object-Oriented Software Engineering, A Use Case Driven Approach.* Addison-Wesley, 1994.
4. O. Haugen. *The MSC-96 Distillery.* In SDL'97: Time for Testing - SDL, MSC and Trends, Proceedings of the 8th SDL Forum in Evry, France (A. Cavalli and A. Sarma editors), North-Holland, Sept. 1997.
5. P.B. Ladkin, S. Leue. *Four issues concerning the semantics of message flow graphs.* Formal Description Techniques VII, FORTE 94 (D. Hogrefe and S. Leue editors), Chapman & Hall, 1995.
6. S. Mauw. The formalization of Message Sequence Charts, In: Computer Networks and ISDN Systems - SDL and MSC) (Guest editor: O. Haugen), Volume 28 (1996), Number 12, June 1996.
7. A. Rinkel. *MSC: A universal tool for describing and analysing communication structures.* Technical Report, ITU-T Experts Meeting St. Petersburg, April 1995.
8. E. Rudolph. *Control flow for synchronous and asynchronous calls, a unifying approach (UMSC).* Technical Report, ITU-T Experts Meeting Sophia Antipolis, October 1998.
9. E. Rudolph, P. Graubmann, J. Grabowski. *Tutorial on Message Sequence Charts (MSC-96).* Forte/PSTV'96, Kaiserslautern, October 1996.
10. J. Rumbaugh, I. Jacobson, G. Booch. *The Unified Modelling Language, Reference Manual Version 1.1.* Rational 1997.
11. ITU-T Rec. Z.120 (1993). *Message Sequence Chart (MSC).* Geneva, 1994.
12. ITU-T Rec. Z.120 (1996). *Message Sequence Chart (MSC).* Geneva, 1996.
13. ITU-T Rec. Z.120 (1998). *Message Sequence Chart (MSC),* Annex B. Geneva, 1998.

SDL'99 : The Next Millennium
R. Dssouli, G.v. Bochmann and Y. Lahav, editors
©1999 Elsevier Science B.V. All rights reserved

Three Scenarios for combining UML and SDL 96

Kurt Verschaeve[a] and Anders Ek[b]

[a] System and Software Engineering Lab, Vrije Universiteit Brussel, Pleinlaan 2, B1050
Brussel, Belgium. kaversch@info.vub.ac.be

[b] Telelogic AB, P O Box 4128, S-203 12 Malmö, Sweden. anders.ek@telelogic.se

UML and SDL both have their own merits and form a strong alliance when combined in one methodology. In this paper we describe three scenarios for combining UML and SDL: Forward Engineering, Reverse Engineering and Round-Trip Engineering. The foundation that makes these scenarios possible is a detailed mapping between UML & SDL'96 concepts. We also explain the mapping is used to implement a two-way translation between UML and SDL.

1. Introduction

This paper describes in three scenarios how UML and SDL could be brought together to make a strong combination. We define a detailed mapping of concepts between UML and SDL and use this to translate and update from UML to SDL and the other way round.

The basic assumption we make is that SDL is suited to implement the targeted system. Good examples are real-time systems and reactive systems, bad examples are database applications and mathematics libraries. The main question we answer here is: in which way can UML [BR95] improve the development or maintenance of a system and how can it be combined with SDL in the best possible way. A good introduction of how UML is used to model real-time systems can be found in [Dou98]. Previous research has been done for combining OMT and SDL in [HWW96].

Our goal is to get the maximum profit of the advantages of both UML and SDL. UML and SDL share a number of qualities, like having a graphical notation, good readability and good tool support. They also incorporate object orientation and state machines, which make UML and SDL suitable to work together. But each of them also has enough advantages to make it worthwhile to use them both in one methodology. Below we list the most important advantages.

Main advantages of UML over SDL:

- Generic Concepts
- Smooth transition from Use Cases, Conceptual Model and Sequence Diagrams to Class Diagrams and State Chart

- Multiple Views on the same information, i.e. a class can be viewed in several diagrams.
- Little constraints during modeling, more flexibility

Main advantages of SDL over UML:

- Specialized Concepts
- Formal definition and semantics
- Simulatable and executable
- Both graphical and textual syntax

Comparing the diagrams available in UML and SDL, we come to the same conclusion that UML and SDL is a good alliance. Figure 1 shows the diagrams or information available in UML and SDL. They share the specification for the static structure, behavior and scenarios. Unique for UML is the use cases and the collaboration diagrams. In SDL the type specification and the transitions can be implemented in full detail. Note that UML Sequence Diagrams and MSC's both are used to specify scenarios, but are not dealt with in our round-trip engineering.

The cross-section of Figure 1 shows the part of UML and SDL for which we have a mapping. Based on this mapping we can build support for three different scenarios:

1. Forward Engineering: This scenario is followed for new projects. The requirements analysis and system design is done in UML. The system design model is then translated to SDL, where the development continues with the round-trip scenario.

2. Reverse Engineering: This scenario is followed in the case that there is already an SDL specification available. The specification is translated to UML, either for documentation purposes or for reengineer purposes.

3. Round-trip Engineering: After either scenario 1 or 2, there is UML and SDL available for the same system. From then on the two models are kept synchronous by forwarding the changes made on the other side.

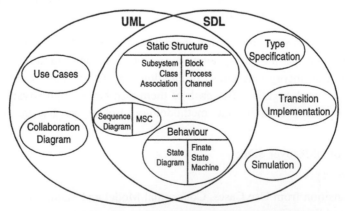

Figure 1. Comparison of Features of UML and SDL

Structure of the paper. Section 2 gives an in-depth description of each of the three scenarios. We will elaborate on the different phases of each scenario. Section 3 presents the mapping of all the common concepts in UML and SDL. Complex parts of the mapping are highlighted with an example. Section 4 then shows how the mapping relates to the translation and iteration processes needed to support the three scenarios. Section 5 concludes the paper and tells something about the future.

2. Three Scenarios

2.1 Forward Engineering

In this first scenario, the developer starts building a new system. UML offers many advantages to start building a system from scratch. Figure 2 shows an overview of the activities in this scenario.

The set of external objects and their interaction with the system form the basis for the requirements analysis of the system [Dou98]. Use-case diagrams and collaboration diagrams are especially suited for this task. These, together with sequence diagrams, allow a smooth transition to system analysis.

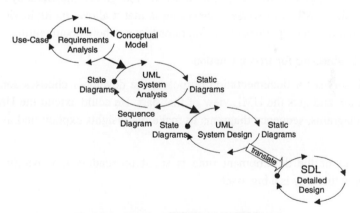

Figure 2. Forward Engineering Scenario

The goal of system analysis is a static and behavior model of all the important components in the system. Starting from the requirements, the analyst must identify the key objects and classes and their relationships within the system. Using the first set of classes, a sequence diagrams is made for a number of use-cases, possibly detecting missing classes. The classes can also be extended with operations now; each message the class needs to understand becomes an operation.

The last step before the translation to SDL is system design. Still a lot of design decisions need to be taken here. First, the classes need to be grouped into subsystems and packages can be split. All attributes and operation parameters must be given a type and undefined types must be defined. If state charts are used, all concepts that cannot be translated, like history states

212

and concurrency, must be eliminated. It should also be checked whether all signals that are sent are also declared as reception in another class and is used in the state diagram of that class.

During detailed design the developer can continue development based on the generated SDL. Typically this encompasses activities like –but not limited to– filling type declarations, improving channel definitions, completing details on transitions, process initialization, creating timers, adding formal parameters, etc. In other words, anything that cannot be expressed in UML, although everything may be changed. Note that this is more than only filling in the details, it is a continuation of the design.

At this stage we enter the round-trip scenario because we have a UML model and an SDL specification of the same system. From hereof, most changes one side can automatically be reflected on the other side. Please see section 2.3 for the continuation of the development life cycle.

2.2 Reverse Engineering

The primary reason to reverse engineer an SDL system is to get a different, more abstract view on the system. This view can either be used as documentation to give better insights into the system or as a basis to refactor, restructure or reengineer the SDL system. The main advantages of using UML for reverse engineering is that it allows multiple views on the same information and that it incorporates other diagrams that can help documenting the system.

2.2.1 Reverse Engineering for Documentation

If the UML serves for documentation purposes, the developer chooses some parts of the SDL specification and gets the UML view of that part. He could extend the UML model with collaboration diagrams, sequence diagrams to make his insights explicit and available to other developers.

If a large part of the development time is spent on reading the specifications, creating documentation in this way is a big asset.

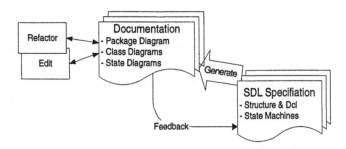

Figure 3. Reverse Engineering for Documentation

2.2.2 Reverse Engineering for Round-trip Engineering

In this case the developer intends to make modification to the SDL system based on the UML model. The kind of the modifications can vary from behavior preserving refactoring to total restructuring for re-engineering.

For this purpose, the complete SDL specification is reverse-engineered to UML. Although some round-trip support could be given on partial UML models, it would be very error prone because there is no context information about signals, declarations, packages, etc. Therefor the entire SDL specification is translated as complete as possible. The developer then improves the generated diagrams and creates more diagrams for specific views on the system. Now we have a UML model of our system, so we can continue with the round-trip scenario in chapter2.3.

2.3 Round-trip Engineering

In this scenario, the developer already has an UML and SDL model of his system and he would like to keep them synchronized. In this way he can profit from the advantages of UML and SDL during the whole development and maintenance life-cycle.

The main advantages of UML in a round-trip scenario is that it allows multiple views on the system and thus can give a abstract view on the system as well as the details on certain topics and relationships between classes in different sub-systems. It is also easier to make structural changes, because there are less limitation in how you can edit. And of course the developer can still use all the UML diagrams to extend the requirements or continue the system analysis.

The main issue in round-trip engineering is of course that no matter which model is modified, the common information in both models is kept up to date. Although any change may be made in either model, there is a difference in the typical changes you make in UML or SDL. Figure 4 shows the interaction between the different activities during round-trip

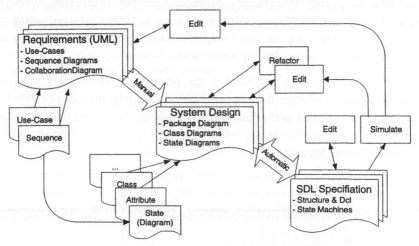

Figure 4. Information flow during Round-Trip Engineering

engineering.

UML is better suited for high level changes. For example, for new requirements, you start creating one or more use cases and examine how it influences the class model and state diagram. Or as the system become bigger, it is probably a good idea to restructure the system on the analysis level. And new design insight might lead you to refactor the class and state diagram, e.g. splitting a class in two classes or applying a design pattern.

SDL is better suited to get all the details right. The first goal is usually to make the SDL specification ready for simulation. So first of all the things that could not be expressed in UML must be added, e.g. timers, sorts specification, creation of process and Pid handling. The generated SDL specification can also be optimized from an SDL point of view, e.g. merging channels, moving signal declarations, creating signal lists, etc. And most important, the SDL system can be simulated, giving a valuable feedback to the design and implementation. By observing the running system, you will find errors, missing parts or extra requirements, making the circle round.

3. Mapping UML and SDL Concepts

The mapping between UML and SDL concepts is an essential part of our research. The mapping definition determines how the information in the UML model relates to information in the SDL system. Most mappings are syntax oriented, e.g. a UML class maps on an SDL process, but some mappings are more semantically, e.g. communication between classes maps on communication between processes. The translation of complete models or changes in the model is based on this mapping.

The mapping is deliberately kept as simple and as intuitive as possible, with many one on one mappings. This is desirable because the user needs to understand the generated system and should be able to predict the changes happening on the other side during round-trip engineering. Thanks to UML's various concepts, there is almost no overloading of different mappings on one concept. Still, the list of mappings is long (more than 60 items) and require quite some study and practice to get acquainted with.

The mapping definitions are presented in the form of tables. Starting from table 3, the middle column indicates whether the mapping hold in both directions ⟺) or only holds when going from UML to SDL (⟹) or the other way round (⟸).

3.1 Mapping of Static Structure

The basic building blocks of a model in UML are packages, subsystems and classes, where the classes represent the active components. In SDL the basic building blocks of a system are packages, blocks, processes and possibly services. This gives us the mapping table shown in Table 1.

UML	SDL
Model	Specification
Package	Package/System
Subsystem[1]	Block
Class	Process

Table 1: Mapping of basic structures

For each of the three SDL constructs system, block and process, there is also a typed version (e.g. block type). The corresponding UML notation is to make the subsystem or class abstract. The rationale behind this mapping is that an SDL process type, just like an abstract class, cannot be instantiated directly, instead a type based process must be created first.

UML	Subsystem	Class
Normal	Block	Process
Abstract	Block type	Process Type

Table 2: Mapping of SDL types

Another aspect of the static structure is the relationship between classes. Basically, associations map on communication in SDL and aggregation maps on nested structure. But in fact, things are a bit more complicated than this, because on the UML side we have different kind of aggregations and on the SDL side we have different kinds of communication.Table 3 shows an overview of the mapping of the relationships.

The mapping of communication needs some elaboration. The basic rule is that for every association between two non-abstract classes, there must be a communication route between the corresponding process. However, this can be achieved in different ways. For two processes in the same block, there is no problem, the association maps on one single signal route between the two processes. But in order to connect two processes in a different block, we need two partial signal routes (i.e. signal routes to the environment) and a number of channels connecting the two signal routes. In order to maintain readability in bigger systems, channels are merged as much as possible. SeeFigure 5 for an example of merged channels.

---

[1] In UML 1.1[Rat97] the subsystem is defined as an entity that inherits the properties from both the package and the classifier. Most tools, however, do not support it as such. In that case we use the combination of a package and a class with same name and with stereotype «subsystem».

216

UML Concept		SDL Mapping
Composite Aggregation (♦—)	⇒	Type based instance set
Navigable Aggregation (◊—)	⇒	Pid pointer
Generalization	⇔	Inheritance
Association between Abstract Classes	⇒	Gate
Association between Classes	⇔	Signal Route and/or Pid variable
Association between Subsystems	⇔	Channel(s)
Role of Association	⇔	Gate
Output(X) ∩ Reception(Y)	⇒	Signals on Channel from X to Y
«interface»	⇒	Signal list

Table 3: Mapping of UML relationships

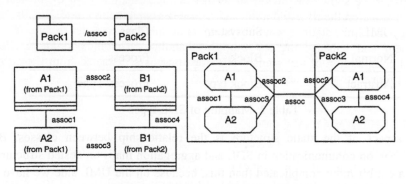

Figure 5: Translation of Communication

3.2 Mapping of Declarations

Other aspects of the mapping are the signal, type and variable declarations. UML allows the declaration of signals in a package, either as a class with stereotype «signal» or as textual declaration. It is clear that this maps on the SDL signal declaration. Furthermore, an operations in an UML class that corresponds with a signal, is actually a signal reception, i.e. the class i able to receive that signal. The set of receptions of an UML class maps on the input signal set of an SDL process or class. Table 4 gives an overview of the declaration mappings.

UML Concept		SDL Mapping
Signal definition	⇔	Signal definition
Signal Reception	⇐	Signal in signal set
Set of Receptions	⇔	Input signal set
Attribute	⇔	Process Variable
• Public		• Exported & Remote

Derived		Imported
Operation (¬ reception)	⇔	Procedure Definition
• Private Operation		• Local Procedure Def.
• Public Operation		• Exported Procedure Def.
• NA		• Remote Procedure Def.
• NA		• Procedure in Procedure
• Parameter		• Formal Parameter

Table 4: Mapping of Declarations

We illustrate the mapping of the static structure by showing the UML and SDL model of a simplified version the toffee vendor example of [EHS97].Figure 6 shows the combined view of the package diagram and class diagram of a toffeevendor. The model contains two subsystems: Dialogue and the abstract (in italic) *WMgr*. The subsystem Dialogue contains a class Control, an abstract class CoinHdlr and a component CoinH. The actor User serves as the environment and has an association to the non-abstract classes and to theWareManager.

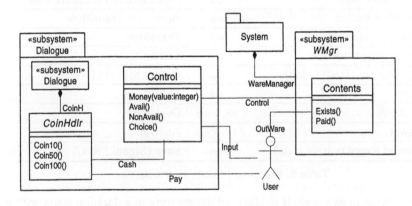

Figure 6. Static Structure of Toffeevendor example

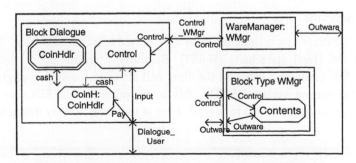

Figure 7. SDL translation of of Toffeevendor example

Figure 7 shows an overview of the SDL system after translating the UML model inFigure 6. The abstract subsystem WMgr maps on the Block Type WMgr and has two gates, one for each association to WareManager. WareManager is a block defined by the typeWMgr and uses the gates to connect two channels.

3.3 Mapping of Statecharts

The mapping of UML state diagrams on SDL state diagrams are rather straight forward, except for nested state diagrams and entry and exit actions.

UML Concept		SDL Mapping
State Diagram	⇔	Final State Machine
Initial State	⇔	Start
State	⇔	State
Final State	⇔	Stop
Nested State Diagram	⇒	State lists and/or Flattening
Submachine State	⇔	Procedure & Procedure Call
Entry/Exit Action	⇒	Action on Transition
Outgoing Transition	⇔	Transition
Internal Transition	⇔	Transition to –
Output Event (Destination)	⇔	Output Signal (To Pid)
Action	⇔	Action
Decision	⇐ ∨ ⇔	Decision
Answer	⇐ ∨ ⇔	Answer
Deferred Event (within state)	⇔	Save (Signal / RPC)

Table 5: Mapping of state charts items

The decision maps in two ways if in UML all the answers in a decision starts with the same expression or equals else (e.g. [x<0], [x>=0], else). Otherwise there is only a translation from SDL to UML.

Nested State Diagrams

The UML state diagrams include the notion of nested hierarchical states. This concept is inherited from the Harel statecharts [Har87]. Basically it mean that a state can contain substates and while being in a substate, the class will also fire transitions originating from the superstate. In the current version of SDL, this is not possible, but SDL has the notion of statelists. A transition can be added to several states at the same time by listing the states in the state symbol.

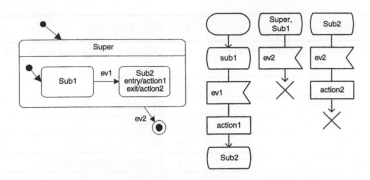

Figure 8: Flattening a State Diagram with Entry & Exit actions

It can be shown that a hierarchical UML state diagram can be correctly translated to SDL using statelists when none of the substates have exit actions. In the other case, the substates containing exit actions, must be excluded from the statelist and get a duplication of all the transitions. Figure 8 shows an example of a nested state diagram in UML and SDL. Note that, unlike the exit action, the entry action in state Sub2, does not cause the duplication of transitions.

UML differentiates between 6 events, each of which has a different mapping as shown in Table 6. In UML, an event is what triggers a transition. There is always exactly one event for each transition, possibly guarded with a guard-condition. Please refer to the UML semantics definition for a comprehensive explanation of all different events.

In UML, an action is anything that happens on a transition. Compared to OMT, UML differentiates between many kinds of actions, which makes it easy to achieve a detailed mapping, see Table 7.

UML Event		SDL Mapping
Call Event	⇔	RPC input
Guard on Event	⇔	Enabling Condition
Change Event (e.g. [x < 10])	⇔	Continuous Signal
Time Event (e.g. after 5 sec)	⇒	Action on Transition
Signal Event	⇔	Input
Empty Event (or lambda transition)	⇔	Spontaneous Transition
Deferred Event (within state)	⇔	Save (Signal / RPC)

Table 6: Mapping of Events

UML Action	⇔	SDL Mapping
Send : target.event(parameter)	⇔	Output event(parameter) TO target
Call	⇔	RPC Call
Local Invocation	⇔	Procedure Call
Create	⇔	Create
Terminate	⇔	Stop
Destroy	⇔	Output "destroy" signal
Return from submachine	⇔	Return
Uninterpreted • With ":=" • With SDL keyword • Other	⇔	SDL Expression • Assignment • Expression • TASK "

Table 7: Mapping of Action

A number of UML concepts cannot be mapped to SDL because there is no equivalent and it would be too difficult to translate them. First, there are the history and deep-history states. Translating the history state to SDL would require duplicating the complete state diagram, which is unacceptable. Second, there are the concurrent and non-concurrent composite states. Composite states introduce concurrency within one class, but it is impossible to have concurrency in one SDL process. Related to this the fork and join states are not mapped either.

On the other side, there are a lot of SDL constructs that cannot be expressed in UML. For example the body of a newtype declaration, signal lists, connection of multiple channels, timer in general and priority. But there is one SDL feature that is particularly difficult to translate, namely the join. The join, together with the decision, allows one transition to have different paths and merge after some actions. On a translation from SDL to UML, all actions after the join must be duplicated, resulting in a many on one mapping.

4. The Mapping in Action

The mapping presented in the previous section defines how UML and SDL concepts relate to each other. It does not define, however, how to translate a complete UML model to SDL or the other way around. We realize that the practical usage of the presented mapping largely depends on tool support. In this section we discus how the mapping is used to support the three scenarios. The instructions given below, can either be used as guidelines for someone doing the translation by hand, but are actually intended as a roadmap for building automated tools for translation and round-trip engineering. The translators can then be integrated in existing UML and SDL tools and called from a menu.

4.1 Use Mapping for One way translations

The first usage of the mapping definition, is the translation of an UML model to an SDL96 definition. To do this, each mapping is interpreted as a translation rule. Starting from an UML model, an SDL specification can be generated by translating each UML entity in the correct order and in the correct context. For example, first a subsystem is translated into a block and then the classes in the subsystem are translated into process within the block. However, there are many exceptions to this rule. For example, signals must be defined in higher scope than the process, possibly at system level. And the translation of an association can be spread over many levels, as explained in section3.1. There are a couple of other tricky issues that must be resolved to get all the details right. Hierarchical statechart must be flattened, nameless associations must be assigned a default name, name collisions must be resolved, etc. Most of the solutions described in [VJW96] can be reused, because these issues are the same in the translation from OMT to SDL.

The most difficult part, however, for implementing a complete translator based on current UML tools, is working around the missing details in the UML datastructure. For example, most UML tools will not support all different kind of actions, shown inTable 7. Therefor the translator must first identify the meaning for each action.The same holds for operations and events on transitions. This requires an analysis of the system, e.g. to find whether an operation is used as an event or as a procedure in the state diagrams. We expect that tools will improve as UML stabilizes for a longer period.

4.2 Use Mapping for Reverse Engineering

When using the mapping for reverse engineering, all mapping rules that have a reverse arrow ($\Leftarrow$ or $\Leftrightarrow$) can be used as reverse translation rules. The static SDL structure is easy to translate in a hierarchy of packages and classes. But from that point of things get trickier. We give a non-exhaustive list how to interpret the mappings for reverse engineering:

- Do not translate Pid variables, as the type of their destination is not known.

- Generate an association for each normal signal route and each pair of partial signal routes with the same name.

- Generate additional (derived) associations, based on channels and gates. It is difficult to find a general approach and probably depends on the specific situation.

- Use the input signal set of a process to generate the list of operations.

- Translate signal definitions as signal receptions (operation) in the classes that receive that signal.

- Try to reconstruct nested state diagrams based on the state lists.

- Entry and Exit actions cannot be recovered in general.

- SDL decisions are less general than UML decisions and thus can always be translated.

222

- Transitions with labels and/or join are very difficult to translate. Actually this is the trickies problem. The only general solution is to duplicate the part of the transition after the join, which might results in unreadable state diagrams. Leaving out the actions on those transitions might be useful.

- Translate the SDL actions that do not have a direct UML counterpart as text.

Apart from these guidelines it also depends for what purpose the reverse engineering is performed. If the generated UML is used for documentation purposes, other techniques can be used to create extra diagrams with other views on the system. If it used as a basis for round-trip engineering, it is better to leave out some details in the state diagram to avoid conflicts during iterations.

4.3 Use Mapping for Round-Trip Engineering

Once the SDL specification is generated, the developer will start modifying the specification, for example to fill is missing declarations or to enhance the statecharts. The mapping can now be used to update the SDL whenever the UML model is modified or, the other way around, to update the UML model, whenever the SDL is modified. Note that any of these update operations should remove as little information as possible. For example when the name of class changes, the corresponding process should simply be renamed and not regenerated. This can be achieved by comparing the previous version of the UML model with the current version UML model and translating the changes instead of the complete model. For technical description of the iteration process, please see [Ver97].

The mapping is used to maintain hierarchical links between the UML model and the SDL specification. Whenever a change on one side is detected, the corresponding entity must be found on the other side to translate and apply the change. For this reason there is a link between each UML entity that has a mapping, except actions, and its corresponding SDL

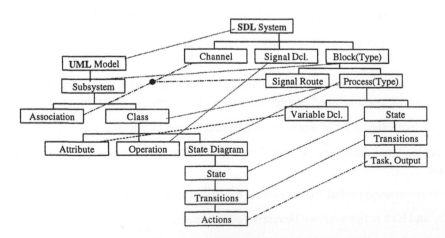

Figure 9. Hierarchical Links between UML and SDL

entity or entities. See Figure 9 for a visual representation of the links. These links can either be stored explicitly or can be recovered based on the name. We call these links hierarchical links, because they are situated on different levels in the model hierarchy. For example there can only be a link between an attribute and a variable declaration when there exists a link between the class of the attribute and the process of the variable. Another approach for maintaining links is the ImpLink concept of the SOMT method [And95].

Three factors complicate achieving a correct update. First, for some UML entities, there is a one-on-many mapping to SDL entities, instead of a one-on-one mapping. For example, one association is mapped on two signal routes. So what happens if only one of the signal routes changes? Second, small changes on one side can result in big changes on the other side. For example adding an aggregation between two subsystems, results in a complete block and all the channels towards it to be moved. Third, it is not always possible to update a hierarchical state diagram to correctly reflect the changes in the SDL state machine. Therefor we made the following restrictions to support iteration:

Restriction from UML to SDL

- Actions are not updated, they are only translated together with transitions.

Restrictions from SDL to UML

- No support for actions.

- Pid variables are not translated.

- Associations are only updated for new classes.

5. Conclusion & Future Work

In this paper we presented a mapping between UML and SDL'96. The profoundness of the mapping definition shows that UML and SDL have grown toward each other. As well in the object diagram and in the state diagram of UML many new concepts, as compared to OMT, have contributed to coherent mapping.

The mapping definition forms the basis for a translation for UML to SDL and the other way round and for tool support for synchronizing a UML model and an SDL specification. This in turn makes it possible to combining UML and SDL is three scenarios: forward engineering, reverse engineering and round-trip engineering.

In [Ver97] we described how to automate the iteration between OMT* and SDL. In this paper we built on those results to accomplish a round-trip engineering and at same time provide the means for new users to get on track by applying forward engineering or reverse engineering. Moreover, since our previous work, the mapping is updated from OMT to UML and from SDL'88 to SDL'96.

In the future UML and SDL will continue to grow toward each other. SDL 2000 is expected to really target the integration with UML. For example, the SDL specification could partially be presented with UML syntax. Also some annoying restriction will be removed like the fact that block and process cannot be next to each and the difference between channel and signal route will disappear. In extreme case, UML and SDL could be become the same language, only with a different semantics.

6. References

[And95]   E. Anders. *The SOMT Method.* Preliminary product information, Telelogic. September 19, 1995.

[BR95]   G. Booch, J. Rumbaugh. *Unified Method for Object-Oriented Development.* Rational Software Corporation, 1995.

[Har87]   D. Harel. *Statecharts: a Visual Formalism for Complex Systems.* Science of Computer Programming 8, 1987, 231-274.

[Dou98]   B. Douglass. *Real-Time UML, Developing Efficient Objects for Embedded Systems.* Addison-Wesley, Massachusetts, 1998

[EHS97]   J. Ellsberger, D. Hogrefe, A. Sarma. *SDL, Formal Object-Oriented Language for Communicating Systems.* Prentice Hall, London, 1997.

[HWW96] E. Holz, M. Wasowski, D. Witaszek, S. Lau, J. Fischer, P. Roques, K. Verschaeve, E. Mariatos, and J.-P. Delpiroux. *The INSYDE Methodology.* Deliverable INSYDE/WP1/HUB/400/v2, ESPRIT Ref: P8641, January 1996.

[Rat97]   Rational Software Corporation, et al. *UML 1.1 Semantics.*

[Ver97]   Kurt Verschaeve. *Automated Iteration between OMT* and SDL.* 8th SDL Forum, Paris, 1997.

[VJW96]   K. Verschaeve, V. Jonckers, B. Wydaeghe, L. Cuypers. *Translating OMT* to SDL, Coupling Object-Oriented Analysis with Formal Description Techniques.* Method Engineering 96 proceedings, p.126-141. IFIP, Atlanta, USA, 1996.

SDL'99 : The Next Millennium
R. Dssouli, G.v. Bochmann and Y. Lahav, editors

Automatic synthesis of SDL models in Use Case Methodology

N. Mansurov[a] and D. Zhukov[b]

[a,b]Department of CASE tools, Institute for System Programming (ISP), 25 B. Kommunis-
ticheskaya, Moscow 109004, Russia; email {nick,dmjr}@ispras.ru

Formal description techniques (FDT's) supported by computer-aided software engineering
(CASE) tools are rapidly evolving as a response to the new challenges of the telecommunications industry, especially the need to improve "*time-to-market*" of software products. In this
paper we summarize our experience in using *automatic synthesis* of formal models in ITU-T
standard Specification and Description Language (SDL) to *speed-up* the software development
process. Suggested *accelerated methodology* requires formalization of functional scenarios
(use cases) using another ITU-T standard - Message Sequence Charts (MSC) extended with
data operations. Our Moscow Synthesizer Tool (MOST-SDL) provides a *bridge* from MSC
models to SDL executable specifications which can be simulated using SDL tools to provide an
early *feedback* for the phases of requirements analysis, system analysis or system design. We
present our synthesis algorithm, provide comparison with related work and discuss the results
of a few case studies where the Moscow Synthesizer Tool was used together with Telelogic
SDL tools for an accelerated MSC-based prototyping which involved incremental synthesis,
validation and simulation of the formal model.

1. Introduction

Modern telecommunications industry hosts highly successful software development organizations, but as new requirements and technologies arrive and more players enter the competition, there is a constant need for improvements [1,2]. In particular, "*time-to-market*" is
becoming the dominating factor of industrial success. Other goals are more traditional and
include higher quality of products, better price/performance and lower development costs [1].
It is generally recognized that the use of formal description techniques (FDT's) supported by
computer-aided software engineering (CASE) tools is an important prerequisite for achieving
these goals.

ITU-T Specification and Description Language (SDL) [4] is one of the most successful telecommunications standard FDT [8]. Industrial-strength commercial tools exist which are able to
analyze SDL specifications, perform validation of SDL specifications based on state-explora-
tion algorithms, automatically generate abstract TTCN test cases from SDL specifications and
also automatically generate implementations for real-time operating systems [6]. A number of
industrial case studies has been recently completed, claiming improved quality, much lower
development costs and speedup in time-to-market up to 20-30% due to the use of SDL-based
CASE tools. "Success stories" of using SDL in industry mention the phases of system design,
detailed design, automatic generation of implementations [19] as well as testing [8].

However, the early phases of the software development process require different approaches. Use case based methodologies are becoming predominant in software development [2,1,3,11]. Use case based methodologies share the common way of capturing customer requirements as *scenarios*. Message Sequence Charts (MSC) [5] or Sequence Diagrams of the Unified Modelling Language (UML) [20] can be used to model use cases. The MSC language is especially attractive as an FDT for the early phases of the software development process because it is well accepted in the telecommunications industry and also because it has a well-defined formal semantics. However much less support is provided by existing CASE tools for MSC modelling as compared to SDL.

We believe that significant improvements of the time-to-market can be gained by expanding the use of FDT-based CASE tools to the early phases of the software development process. The key idea of the suggested accelerated methodology is to use *automatic synthesis* of executable SDL specifications from MSC models.

In this paper, we summarize our experience in using automatic synthesis of SDL models to speed-up the use case based development process. Our accelerated methodology requires formalization of use cases using MSC extended with data operations. We have developed the synthesis algorithm and the corresponding tool called the Moscow Synthesizer Tool (MOST-SDL[1]) which provides a bridge from MSC models to executable SDL specifications. Existing SDL tools can be used to simulate the synthesized models. Additional scenarios can be generated during the simulation of the synthesized SDL model. Thus the automatic synthesis of SDL models enables *tool-aided iterative development* at the early phases of the software process. The timely *feedback* between SDL and MSC models is the prerequisite for the speed-up.

We discuss two possible ways of incorporating the MOST-SDL tool into a use case based methodology. One strategy is to use the MOST-SDL tool to speed-up the *requirements analysis* phase. The feedback provided by SDL tools allows to quickly discover inconsistencies and incompleteness of the requirements model. Another strategy is to use the MOST-SDL tool at the *system analysis* phase when the architecture of the system is being defined and independent groups of developers produce system scenarios for each architecture component. In this case the MOST-SDL tool will produce an executable architecture model of the system by synthesizing the behavior of each component and integrating it into an aggregate model. Automatically derived relationships between components can be compared to the intended ones. Exploration of the executable architecture model allows to uncover system analysis faults. We discuss the results of a few case studies where Moscow Synthesizer Tool was used in conjunction with Telelogic SDL tools [6] for an accelerated MSC-based prototyping of telecommunications-like systems which involved incremental synthesis, simulation and validation of the formal model.

The rest of the paper has the following organization. In Section 2 we discuss methodological issues of using automatic synthesis in a use case based software development process. In Section 3 we present our MSC extensions for capturing data flows over the use cases. In Section 4 we describe the details of the synthesis algorithm of the Moscow Synthesizer Tool, outline the overall structure of the synthesized SDL models and provide an illustrative example. In Section 5 we provide comparison with related work. In Section 6 we summarize our experience and make some conclusions.

---

1. The word *"MOST"* means *"bridge"* in the russian language.

2. Methodological issues

Use case based methodologies are becoming predominant in software development. The main concepts of a use case methodology are *actors* and *use cases* [2]. An *actor* represents an entity external to the system under development. An actor interacts with the system in order to achieve certain *goals*. A *use case* is a description of a typical (illustrative) interaction between one or many actors and the system, through which one of the actors achieves a specific goal. One use case can cover several sequences of events, called *scenarios*. Several use case based methodologies were proposed [1,2,3,10,11].

Use case driven methodologies share the common way of capturing customer requirements as functional scenarios but differ in ways of how scenarios are represented. Overview of use cases, actors and their relationships are captured in the form of informal pictures [2,20], scenarios are captured using tabular forms [11], plain text [1,3] or UML Sequence Diagrams [20]. Formalization of use cases using MSC diagrams was suggested in [12].

A overview of a typical use case methodology is presented in Figure 1. This figure shows the *phases* of the methodology (right column), the most important *models* (boxes) as well as the most important information *feedbacks* provided by SDL tools (dashed lines). Relationships and feedbacks between the behavioral and the structural models at the same phase are omitted. Also omitted are the feedbacks between the models at any subsequent phases. We also emphasize two different modelling perspectives [20,3,13], namely the *behavioral path* (left sequence of boxes) and the *structural path* (right sequence of boxes). The structural path describes what entities constitute the software at the given level of abstraction and what are the relationships between them. The behavioral path describes how entities interact in order to achieve the given functionality.

An information feedback is very important because it is a prerequisite for *iterative development*. An accelerated development process can be based on such iterations. Thus the key idea of our approach is to move the use of FDTs to the earliest possible phases of the traditional development process in order to enable tool-aided iterative development.

FIGURE 1. Overview of a use case based methodology

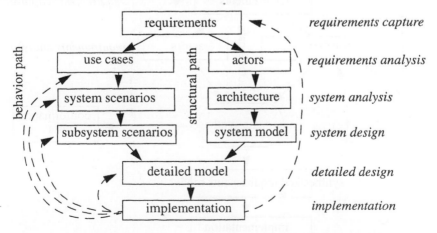

228

In a typical telecommunications oriented industrial process formalization starts at the detailed design phase. The *system model* (Figure 1) is represented as several SDL block diagrams and the *detailed model* is represented as the corresponding set of SDL process diagrams [6]. Transitions between all phases are done manually, except for the transition from the detailed model to the implementation which is done by SDL tools. The only useful feedback provided by SDL tools is the one from the implementation back to the detailed model. Other feedbacks are less useful, because the corresponding models are not formalized and also because the transition to the detailed SDL model is usually too costly for any iterations to be feasible.

2.1 Automatic synthesis at the requirements analysis phase

We suggest two ways of using the automatic synthesis to speed-up the traditional process depending on the phase to which formalization is extended. The most ambitious strategy is to synthesize an SDL model at the requirements analysis phase (Figure 2). The only input at this phase is the use case model which in our case should be formalized using MSC. The only structural information available at this phase consists of the set of external actors and the system (represented as distinct instances in the MSC model). Use cases and their control-flow relationships provide additional structural information which can be used by the synthesis algorithm. The behavioral information is available in the form of (incomplete) functional scenarios representing the typical interactions between the external actors and the use cases within the system. Important behavioral information can be additionally captured in the form of *data flows over the use cases* using our data extensions (see Section 3). The so called *synthesized requirements model* (SRM) is the projection of the information captured at the requirements analysis phase down to the detailed design (and the implementation) phase. All feedbacks shown in Figure 2 become useful because they are provided in a timely manner as the requirements model is being created, enabling the *iterative development* of the latter.

FIGURE 2. Automatic synthesis at the requirements analysis phase

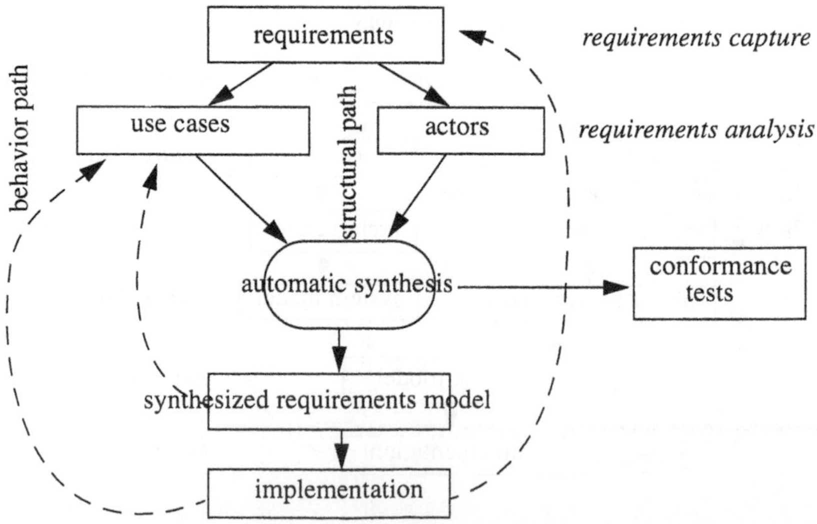

The synthesized requirements model can be used to *generate additional scenarios* which are *longer* than the original scenarios of the requirements model and therefore provide better understanding of the requirements [17]. Simulation of the synthesized requirements model allows to quickly discover inconsistencies and incompleteness of the requirements because the synthesized model will generate many variations of the original scenarios, including abnormal behavior. Such scenarios are likely to be less well understood by the developers.

The synthesized requirements model can be used to automatically generate test cases [8] (which at this phase of the development process correspond to conformance or acceptance tests).

2.2 Automatic synthesis at the system analysis phase

Another strategy is to use the automatic synthesis at the system analysis phase when the architecture of the system is being defined and independent groups of developers produce system scenarios for each architecture component (Figure 3). The input at this phase is a set of system scenarios. Normally a system scenario will be a projection of the corresponding use case from the requirements analysis phase. The structural information available in the system scenarios consists of the set of external actors and the architecture components (represented as distinct instances in the MSC model). The behavioral information is available in the form of functional scenarios representing the typical interactions between the architectural components as well as between external actors and the architectural components. Additional behavioral information can be captured in the form of the data flows over the system scenarios. The automatically synthesized model created at this phase is called the *synthesized architecture model* (SAM). The feedbacks provided by SDL tools through the SAM go both to the system scenarios as well as to the architecture model (Figure 3). In this case the SAM will reproduce the architectural components of the system by deriving them from the collection of system scenarios, synthesize the behavior of each component and integrate the model. Automatically derived relationships between components can be compared to the intended ones (described in the architecture model). In our experience the synthesized architecture model is helpful in uncovering system analysis faults.

FIGURE 3. Automatic synthesis at system analysis phase

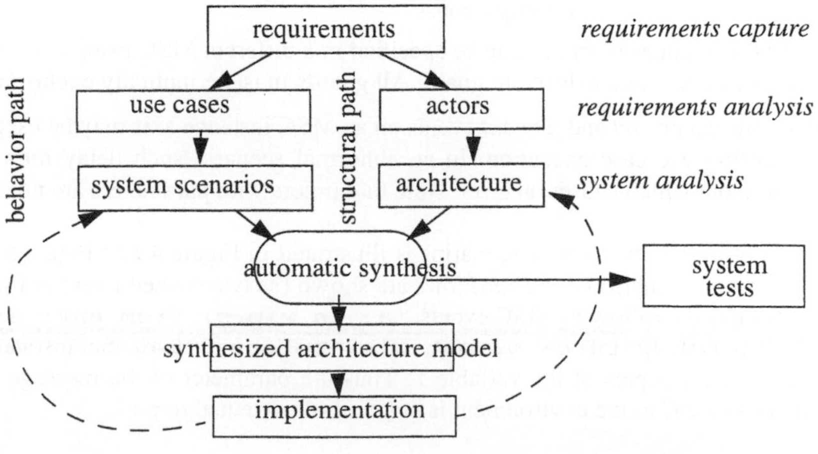

3. Formalization of Use Cases using extended MSC

We use extended Message Sequence Charts (MSC) language [5] to formalize *scenarios*. Each *use case* is formalized by a high-level MSC (HMSC) which represents control-flow relationships between scenarios of the use case. Our extensions to the MSC language describe the *flows of data* through individual scenarios (local data flows) as well as data flow dependencies between scenarios (global data flows).

1. **Variable definitions**. We allow to define variables of different types. SDL semantics is assumed. Variable definition is placed into a text symbol in any MSC diagram. A local copy of each variable is propagated to each actor. Simplified SDL syntax is used for variable definitions:

   variable definition ::=   dcl name type;

2. **Actions**. We allow MSC action symbols to contain operations on local variables. SDL semantics is assumed. Simplified SDL syntax is used for actions:

   assignment ::=   var := expr

   function call ::=   func (expr$_1$, ..., expr$_n$)

3. **Message parameters**. We allow messages to have parameters. We restrict the syntax of message parameters to variable names. SDL semantics is assumed for parameter passing.

4. **Create parameters**. Actors are allowed to have parameters which are passed from the parent instance to the child instance during the create event. We restrict the syntax of create parameters to variable names. SDL semantics is assumed.

5. **Local conditions**. We allow to specify local decisions using boolean expressions over instance variables. Syntactically, local decisions are specified as local conditions on the axis of the corresponding instance. The boolean expression is written in a comment box attached to the local condition. Semantics of such condition is that the subsequent events are considered only when the value of the boolean expression is true. Boolean expressions are restricted to the following syntax:

   boolean expression::=   var <op> var

   var <op> const

   Alternative sequences of events can be specified in a different MSC using a local condition with the same name and a different guard. All guards must be mutually exclusive.

6. **Timers**. Subsequent *set* and *timeout* events on an MSC instance axis may be used to specify a delay during use case execution. In an abnormal scenario such delay may specify an expired timeout which causes an error. Note that timers with parameters are not supported.

The concept of data flows over scenarios is illustrated in Figure 4 and Figure 5. Two local data flows through scenario *LocalDataFlows* are shown (as two dashed lines) in Figure 4. The first flow contains the following MSC events: a: **in** x(p,q) **from env**; a: **create** b(p,q); b: **out** y **to** c; c: **out** z(r) **to env**; Note, that instances B and C use different (local) copies of the variable r. Thus the parameter of the message z which is sent by the instance C to the environment is not necessarily equal to p+1.

The second flow contains the following MSC events: a: **in** x(p,q) **from env**; a: **create** b(p,q); b: **action** 'r:=p+1'; b: **out** w(r) **to env**;

Note that the instance C will send message z(r) to environment only when condition q>0 is true. Alternative events for the instance C can be specified using the local condition chck_1 with a different guard. Global conditions in the HMSC graph will be required when alternative events involve other instances.

FIGURE 4. Local data flows

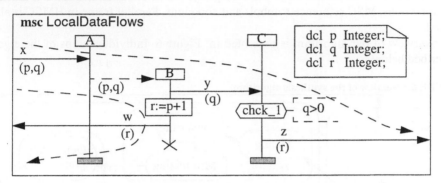

Figure 5 illustrates the specification of global data flows between use cases. In Figure 5 parameters of the message *value* returned by the use case *UC_POP* as a reaction to the message *get* depends on the events in the use case *UC_PUSH*. push and pop are assumed to be user-defined SDL procedures with in/out parameters implementing typical stack operations.

FIGURE 5. Global data flows

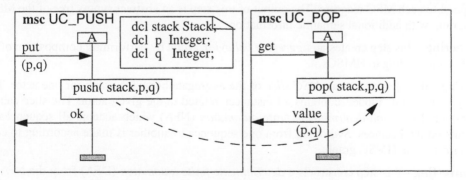

Our main motivation in adding data extensions to MSC is to allow more accurate specifications of functional requirements. However the same data sub-language turns extended MSC into a powerful FDT for design phases.

232

4. Synthesis Algorithm

4.1 Overview of the algorithm

In this section we describe our algorithm of synthesizing an SDL model from an (H)MSC model. The input to our algorithm is a set of HMSCs and the corresponding referenced bMSCs in the event-oriented textual form. bMSCs can contain data extensions described in the previous section. Restrictions on the input MSC language are as follows: bMSCs can not contain inline expressions, MSC reference symbols and coregions. Parallel frame in HMSC is also not supported.

The overview of our algorithm is presented in Figure 6. Individual steps of the algorithm are described below.

FIGURE 6. Overview of the synthesis algorithm

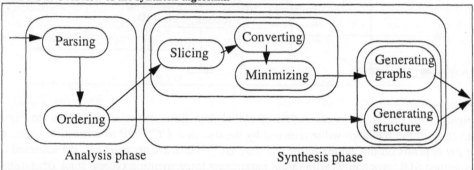

1. **Parsing** - this step performs syntax and semantic analysis of the MSC model. This step is applied to each MSC diagram. The output of this step is an abstract syntax tree of the MSC diagram with additional semantic information.

2. **Ordering** - this step creates an *aggregate behavior graph* by performing composition of all bMSCs according to HMSCs.

3. **Slicing** - this step creates an *MSC slice* of the aggregate behavior graph for one actor. The slice of the MSC model contains all instances related to the given actor. The slice can be considered as a *non-deterministic finite automaton* (NFA) which accepts all sequences of events on its instances. Switching from one sequence to another is made according to connections in the HMSC graph.

4. **Converting** - this step constructs a *deterministic finite automaton* (DFA) from the NFA. A well-known *subset construction* algorithm [7] is used. Only *useful* subsets are constructed, which allows to avoid the exponential growth of the number of states in the original NFA in most cases.

5. **Minimizing** - this step minimizes the DFA, produced at the previous step. Converting and minimizingsteps are performed for each MSC slice independently.

6. **Generating** - this step produces the resulting SDL model from a minimized DFA. SDL graphs are generated from the DFA, while SDL structure is generated directly from the aggregate behavior graph.

4.2 MSC Events and Finite Automata

Our synthesis algorithm constructs *finite automata* corresponding to MSC instances. The *input symbols* for the finite automata constructed by our algorithm are *MSC events*. We distinguish between *input* and *active* events.

Input events include the following MSC events:

- message inputs *in(m,i)* for all message names *m* and instances *i*;
- timeouts *timeout(t)* for all timer names *t*.

Active events include the following MSC events:

- message outputs *out(m,i)* for all message names *m* and instances *i*;
- MSC actions *action(a)* for all assignments and function calls *a*;
- set timer actions *set(t,d)* for all timer names *t* and duration values *d* (*d* may be omitted);
- reset timer actions *reset(t)* for all timer names *t*;
- stop action *stop*;
- local conditions *check(C)* where *C* is a boolean expression;

A *non-deterministic finite automaton* (NFA) is a tuple $A=(Q,E,q_0,\delta,\varepsilon)$ where

- Q is the set of *states*;
- E is the set of *events*;
- q_0 is an element of Q called the *start state*;
- $\delta : Q \times E \to 2^Q$ is the *transition function* (which maps set-event pairs to sets of states). For any state q and event e the value of $\delta(q,e)$ is the set of all possible states to which the automaton can go from state q. Each transition is *labeled by* an event e. We will write $q \to_{(e)} q'$ if q' belongs to $\delta(q,e)$.
- $\varepsilon : Q \to 2^Q$ is the *idle transition* function. An "idle" transition without any event is allowed from state q to q' if q' belongs to $\varepsilon(q)$. To denote this fact we will write $q \to_{(\lambda)} q'$ where λ is an empty sequence of events.

A *deterministic finite automaton* (DFA) is a special case of a NFA in which

- no state has an idle transition, i.e. $|\varepsilon|=0$
- for each state q and event e, there is at most one transition labeled e leaving q, i.e. $|\delta(q,e)| \leq 1$ for each state q in Q and for each e in E.

Automata will be represented diagrammatically by *transition graphs* in which the nodes are states and the labeled edges represent the transition function (see Figure 8 and Figure 9).

We define an *MSC slice* (with respect to an instance i) as a non-deterministic finite automaton NFA_i which is constructed according to the following rules:

1. The set of NFA states contains a state for each symbol in the HMSC graph. Lines connecting symbols are mapped to idle transitions between the corresponding states.

2. For each bMSC m a sequence of states is created that performs the sequence of events along the instance i in bMSC m. For each reference to bMSC m the corresponding state is replaced by the new sequence of states. If the bMSC m does not contain instance i then the new sequence of states is empty.

3. The start state of the NFA corresponds to the start symbol of the HMSC.

By construction, the language recognized by an MSC slice is equivalent to the set of all valid event traces for the corresponding MSC instance.

4.3 Generating SDL graphs

SDL graphs are generated from a minimized deterministic finite automaton $DFA_i=(Q,E,q_0,\delta)$. Active events are mapped onto SDL statements. DFA states are mapped to SDL states and free actions according to the following rules:

1. States which have outgoing transitions labeled only by input events are mapped to SDL states. Input events of this DFA state are mapped to the input stimuli of the SDL state. An *asterisk save* statement is added to each state to prevent deadlocks [12].

2. States which have a single outgoing transition labeled only an active event are mapped to SDL free actions.

3. States with multiple outgoing transitions labeled only by active events are mapped onto free actions starting with a non-deterministic choice between transitions using SDL *decision(any)* statement.

4. States which have multiple outgoing transitions labeled by both input and active events are mapped to SDL free actions starting with a non-deterministic choice between the active events. Additional alternative contains an SDL *nextstate* into another SDL state corresponding to input events (see rule 1).

5. Each state which has transitions labeled by events $check(C_1)$, ..., $check(C_n)$ is mapped to a chain of SDL *decision* statements which select a transition with a satisfied condition. We impose the following restrictions on the usage of local conditions:

- If a state has an outgoing transition labeled by a *check(C)* event then all outgoing transitions from this state must have *check* events.

- If a state has outgoing transitions with events $check(C_1)$, ..., $check(C_n)$ then expressions C_1, ..., C_n must be mutually exclusive.

4.4 Generating SDL structure

We attempted to synthesize flexible typebased SDL models in order to facilitate refinement of the model and better reusability of its components (see example in Section 4.5). The synthesized model includes one SDL package and an SDL system. The synthesized package contains one process type for the system actor and one process type for each external actor (Figure 11). The package contains synthesized definitions of SDL signals for all messages used in the MSC model (Figure 11). Each process type has separate gates for incoming and outgoing signals. Start transitions are generated as *virtual* to allow redefinition in subtypes (Figure 10).

The package also contains a block type specifying instantiations of actors and the collaboration between external actors and the system (Figure 11). This block type contains a typebased process instance for each actor in the model. Process instances are connected by explicit channels. Process types for actors are made *virtual* within the block type. In order to do that additional virtual process type definitions are provided within the block type (Figure 11). These additional process types simply inherit the corresponding process types generated for actors.

We also generate an SDL system which contains a single typebased instance of the block. The generated SDL system imports definitions from the generated package (Figure 12). Redefinitions of the synthesized model can provide subtypes of the synthesized block type (Figure 12). SDL graphs for actors can be reused by directly inheriting from synthesized process types (Figure 10).

4.5 Example

We are illustrating our algorithm by considering a simple MSC model shown in Figure 7. It contains two use cases *Wait* and *Reply* where each of them has only one scenario. The instance *R* corresponds to the system actor and the instance *S* is an external actor. MSC slices for this MSC model are shown in Figure 8.

FIGURE 7. Example MSC model

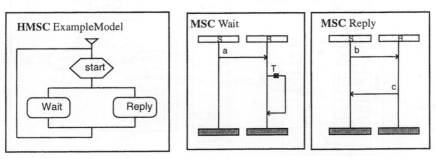

Note that according to the definition of an MSC slice (Section 4.2) slices NA_R and NA_S in Figure 8 have the same structure as the HMCS *ExampleModel* in Figure 7.

FIGURE 8. MSC slices

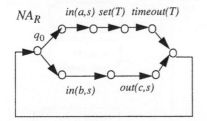
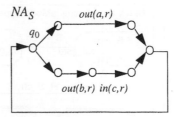

236

FIGURE 9. Synthesized finite automata

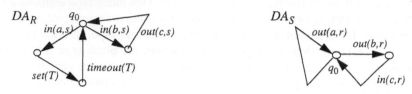

Synthesized DFA for this example are shown in Figure 9. Note that although DA_S is deterministic in automata terms (Section 4.2), it specifies a *non-deterministic behavior* in terms of MSC events: outgoing transitions from the state q_0 are labeled by active MSC events $out(a,r)$ and $out(b,r)$ which are not caused by any external stimuli. As can be observed from the original MSC model (Figure 7), DA_S specifies the behavior of an external actor where messages a and b initiate use cases. We generate a non-deterministic SDL graph (Figure 10).

FIGURE 10. Generated SDL graphs

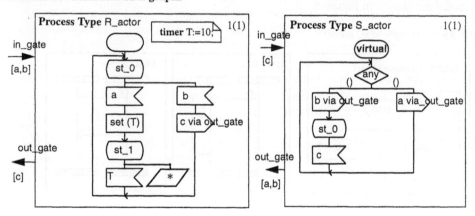

FIGURE 11. Generated SDL package

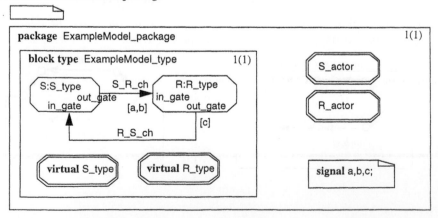

FIGURE 12. Generated and redefined SDL systems

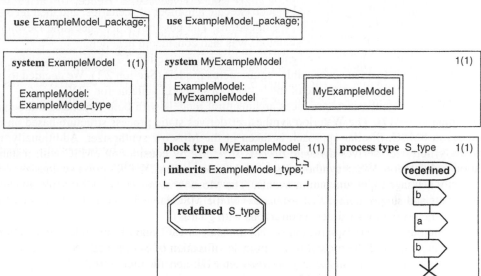

5. Comparison to related work

Automatic synthesis of executable models from scenarios is an active research field. Much work has been done on the subject of translating MSC to other languages [13,17,18]. Synthesizing SDL specifications from MSC is addressed in [12]. Survey of work on a more general subject of protocol synthesis is available in [15].

Methodological issues of generating a formal executable specification from a set of use cases are addressed in [13]. This paper summarizes experience in manually developing a LOTOS specification of a telecommunications standard on the basis of use cases provided by industry. LOTOS tools were used to validate the specification and generate all original use cases as well as additional ones. The main motivation of the project was to use LOTOS tools to analyze and maintain a set of use cases. The benefit of using the formal executable specification for prototyping purposes was emphasized.

The University of Montreal synthesizer [18] translates scenarios with timing constraints into timed automata. The main motivation of the project is to provide formalization of scenarios and ensure the accuracy of requirements analysis.

The Waterloo synthesizer [17] translates MSC models into ROOM specifications. The main motivation of this project is to create an executable architectural model supporting design phases. Firstly, an executable architecture model was considered useful for prototyping purposes. Synthesized ROOM models can be simulated by ObjecTime Developer tool with the possibility to visualize execution sequences as bMSCs. According to [17], the MSC traces are useful for visualizing execution sequences that are longer that the bMSC scenarios in the original MSC specification and therefore provide a better overview and understanding of the system. Executable architecture models were considered helpful in supporting communication and education of new team members. Secondly, automatic synthesis of architectural models was considered useful in evolutionary prototyping by providing refinements to the model. Designers can modify the synthesized model, execute a number of scenarios, and then feed the results back into the domain of MSC specifications. The possibility of ObjecTime Developer to automatically generate C++ code skeletons was also considered beneficial.

The motivation of the Moscow synthesizer is similar (Section 2.2), however we also use automatic synthesis to create executable requirements models (Section 2.1). We decided to use SDL as the target language because of the better tool support available for SDL.

The Waterloo synthesizer produces architectural models with both structural and behavioral components [17]. The Waterloo synthesizer derives static process structure based on the instances in bMSC. Similar approach is taken in the Moscow synthesizer. Additionally, the Moscow synthesizer derives *dynamic process structure* by considering bMSC with instance creation and deletion. When synthesizing behavior components, the Waterloo synthesizer considers only message input and output events. The Moscow synthesizer additionally considers timer events and supports *data flow extensions* to the MSC language (variables, message and create parameters, actions and local conditions with guards).

The Concordia University synthesizer [12] translates MSC models into SDL specifications. The main motivation of the project is to eliminate validation of SDL specifications against the set of MSCs by ensuring consistency between the SDL specification and the MSC specification through automatic synthesis [12]. The main characteristic of the Concordia synthesizer is that the architecture of the target SDL specification is required as an input to the synthesis algorithm and the question of implementability of the given set of MSCs within the given SDL architecture is addressed [12]. Thus the Concordia synthesizer produces only behavioral components. Composition of bMSCs using HMSC was not addressed in [12] although it was considered as a direction for future work.

Although the Moscow synthesizer was developed independently, some of the technical decisions are similar, e.g. the use of SDL save statement to avoid deadlocks in the synthesized SDL models. However the motivation of the Moscow synthesizer is somewhat different. The Moscow synthesizer produces both the behavioral and the structural components (similar to [17]) which allows us to synthesize executable requirements models (similar to [13]) as well as executable architecture models [17]. Consideration of data flows in the Moscow synthesizer allows more accurate capture of the functional requirements as well as more accurate capture of the architectural issues.

6. Conclusions

We have shown how automatic synthesis of SDL models can be used to speed-up the use case based software development process. Our main motivation is to extend the use of formal description techniques to the early phases of the development process. Our accelerated methodology uses MSC with data extensions to formalize use cases. The speed-up is achieved through enabling tool-aided iterative development and rapid transition from requirements analysis to design and validation. Automatically synthesized requirements models and architecture models are executable and can be simulated using existing SDL tools. Data extensions are essential to provide accurate capture of the functional requirements.

MSC language with data extensions can be used as an accelerated prototyping language. Using MSCs for forward engineering combines high descriptive power of a specification language with fast code generation.

The Moscow Synthesizer Tool was applied to several small-sized case studies of telecommunications-like software systems, in particular the ToolExchange project, described in [9].

The Moscow Synthesizer Tool was also used at the Moscow State University in the undergraduate course "Formal specification methodologies: MSC and SDL" [10]. The course introduces a use case based software development methodology. MSC are used to formalize use cases. SDL is used to capture the results of architectural analysis [2] as well as to perform system and detailed design. The course involves practical assignments, where each student is presented with a realistic case study. Each assignment involves going through all phases of the development process and constructing a series of formal models, driven by the original use cases, up to the point when a complete executable SDL model of the case study is developed. In parallel, we experimented with the MOST-SDL tool. The MOST-SDL tool was applied to the formalized use case model as soon as it became available. Later, the automatically synthesized SDL models were compared with the models developed manually by students. Results of this comparison show, that the automatic synthesis of SDL models allows more than 40% reduction of the development time, and a dramatic improvement of the quality of SDL models.

In our experience, the MOST-SDL tool has a good potential as a training tool, because students or new developers can inspect (rather non-trivial) SDL models produced by the tool, while specifying functionality in a "low learning curve" MSC formalism.

Simulation of the synthesized models provided very useful feedback to the analysts. In particular, we discovered that the non-deterministic SDL graphs of the external actors resulted in excellent test suites. Additional scenarios, generated during the exploration of the synthesized model, yielded a high number of problems in the original requirements and architecture models. Tool-aided iterations between formal models in MSC and executable SDL specifications resulted in considerable speed-up. Automatic derivation of test cases from the synthesized SDL models is a promising future research direction.

The Moscow Synthesizer Tool described in this paper was used for re-engineering of legacy telecommunications software [9]. Probe traces were dynamically collected from a suitably instrumented legacy system. The traces were then converted into MSCs. An SDL model of the system was then obtained by applying the MOST-SDL tool. Detailed description of our dynamic scenario-based approach to re-engineering of legacy is presented in [9].

Our experience with Moscow Synthesizer Tool shows that automatic synthesis of SDL models from scenarios has a good potential in allowing significant reductions of the time-to-market for a "real-world" telecommunications industry. It also offers a very cost-efficient way of introducing MSC and SDL-based formal methodology into an industrial environment.

7. References

[1] B. Regnell, A. Davidson, From Requirements to Design with Use Cases - Experiences from Industrial Pilot Projects, in Proc. 3rd Int. Workshop on Requirements Engineering - Foundation for Software Quality, Barcelona, June 16-20, 1997

[2] I. Jacobson, M. Christerson., P. Jonsson, G. Overgaard, Object-Oriented Software Engineering: A Use Case Driven Approach, Addison-Wesley, Reading, MA, 1992.

[3] A. Jaaksi, A Method for Your First Object-Oriented Project, JOOP, January 1998.

[4] ITU-T (1993), CCITT Specification and Description Language (SDL), ITU-T, June 1994

[5] Z.120 (1996) CCITT Message Sequence Charts (MSC), ITU-T, June 1992

[6] TeleLOGIC AB, TeleLOGIC ORCA and SDT 3.4, Telelogic AB, Box 4128, S-203 12 Malmoe, Sweden, 1998

[7] A. Aho, R. Sethi, J. Ullman, Compilers: Principles, Techniques and Tools, Addison-Wesley, 1988

[8] A. Ek, J. Grabowski, D. Hogrefe, R. Jerome, B. Koch, M. Schmitt, Towards the Industrial Use of Validation Techniques and Automatic Test Generation Methods for SDL Specifications, in Proc. of the 8-th SDL Forum, Evry, France, 23-26 September, 1997, Elsevier Science Publishers B.V. (North-Holland), pp. 245-261

[9] N. Mansurov, R. Probert, Dynamic scenario-based approach to re-engineering of legacy telecommunication software, in Proc. of the 9th SDL Forum, Montreal, Canada, 21-25 June 1999, Elsevier Science Publishers B.V. (North-Holland), 1999

[10] N. Mansurov, O. Majlingova, Formal specification methodologies: MSC and SDL languages, lecture notes and tutorial, (in Russian), Moscow State University, Department of Computational Mathematics and Cybernetics, 1998

[11] A. Cockburn, Using Goal-Based Use Cases, JOOP, November/December, 1997, pp. 56-62

[12] G. Robert, F. Khendek, P. Grogono, Deriving an SDL specification with a given architecture from a set of MSCs, in Proc. of the 8-th SDL Forum, Evry, France, 23-26 September, 1997, Elsevier Science Publishers B.V. (North-Holland), pp. 197-212

[13] R.Tuok, L. Logrippo, Formal specification and use case generation for a mobile telephony system, Computer Networks and ISDN Systems, 30 (1998), pp. 1045-1063.

[14] M. Andersson, J. Bergstrand, Formalization of Use Cases with Message Sequence Charts, MSc Thesis, Lund Institute of Technology, May 1995

[15] R. L. Probert, K. Saleh, Synthesis of communication protocols: survey and assessment, IEEE Transactions on Computers, 40(4), pp. 468-475, April 1991

[16] B. Regnell, K. Kimbler, A. Wesslen, Improving the Use Case Driven Approach to Requirements Engineering, in Proc. 2nd IEEE Symposium on Requirements Engineering, York, March 1995

[17] S. Leue, L. Mehrmann, M. Rezai, Synthesizing ROOM Models from Message Sequence Chart Specifications, University of Waterloo, Technical Report 98-06, 1998

[18] S. Some, R. Dssouli, and J. Vaucher, From scenarios to timed automata: Building specifications from user requirements, In Proc. 2nd Asia Pacific Software Engineering Conference, IEEE, December 1995.

[19] R. Singh, J. Serviss, Code Generation using GEODE: A CASE Study, in Proc. of the 8-th SDL Forum, Evry, France, 23-26 September, 1997, Elsevier Science Publishers B.V. (North-Holland), pp. 539-550

[20] J. Rumbaugh, I. Jacobson, G. Booch, The Unified Modelling Language Reference Manual, Addison-Wesley, 1999

SDL'99 : The Next Millennium
R. Dssouli, G.v. Bochmann and Y. Lahav, editors
©1999 Elsevier Science B.V. All rights reserved

Integrating Schedulability Analysis and SDL in an Object-Oriented Methodology for Embedded Real-time Systems

J. M. Alvarez, M. Díaz, L. M. Llopis, E. Pimentel, J.M. Troya
{alvarezp,mdr,luisll,ernesto,troya}@lcc.uma.es

Dpto. Lenguajes y Ciencias de la Computación. University of Málaga
Campus de Teatinos - 29071. Málaga - SPAIN

The usage of object oriented methodologies in conjunction with formal description techniques has arisen as a promising way of dealing with the increasing complexity of embedded real-time systems. These methodologies are currently well supported by a set of tools that allow the specification, simulation and validation of the functional aspects of these systems. However most of these methodologies do not take into account non-functional aspects as hardware interaction and real-time constraints, which are especially important in the context of this kind of systems. In this paper, we present a new methodology for the design of embedded real-time systems. This methodology is based on a combination of ideas from different existing methodologies (UML, OCTOPUS,...) together with the integration of rate-monotonic analysis in the context of the SDL Formal Description Technique development cycle. The methodology pays special attention to the transition from the object model to the task model, taking into account real-time and hardware integration issues. In addition to the presentation of the methodology, we also describe its application to a real-life example as the development of a multi-handset cordless telephone.

1. INTRODUCTION

Embedded software has special characteristics that make it different from other kinds of software. This software has to cope with concurrent events, real-time constraints, memory and processing limitations, etc. In addition to this, requirements are getting more and more complex and they are difficult to manage with the traditional methodologies used by real-time developers.

The joint use of object-oriented technologies and Formal Description Techniques (FDTs) has been proposed as a promising alternative for the development of this kind of systems [1]. Object-oriented methodologies are widely used to cope with complexity in any kind of system, but most of them lack of a formal foundation that allows for the analysis and verification of designs, that is one of main requirements to deal with the complexity of concurrent and reactive systems. On the other hand, FDTs provide the basis for an automated design process, allowing simulation, validation and automatic code generation from the specifications. These FDTs were originally developed for the design of telecommunication systems and, for this reason, they were designed to cope with the characteristics of this kind of systems (concurrency, reactivity,...) that are common to embedded real-time systems.

One of the most widely used FDTs is SDL [2]. The "Specification and Description Language" (SDL) is an ITU standard and is currently well supported by commercial tools like SDT [3] and Object-Geode [4]. SDL is based on Extended Finite State Communicating Machines and can be used through all the development cycle, from specification to implementation, although it is better suited for design purposes. Current object-oriented methodologies based on SDL, as SOMT [2], use UML [5] in the requirements phase, jointly with some other formalisms to express external dynamic behavior, like Message Sequence Charts (MSCs) [6]. MSCs are another ITU standard that can be used in combination with SDL to simulate and verify the system design. The main problem of these methodologies, as it is also in other object-oriented methodologies not based on SDL, is the gap between the object model obtained from the requirement analysis and the final process model. This step can not be automated and its success depends heavily on the experience of the designer.

Rate-Monotonic Analysis (RMA) [7] provides a collection of quantitative methods that enable to analyze and predict the timing behavior of real-time systems. This analysis can help us to organize processes and resources in our design to make it possible to predict the timing behavior of the final system. In this sense, RMA will help us to save the gap between the object model and the task model in other object-oriented methodologies, including the ones proposed for the SDT and Object-Geode tools.

In this paper we present a new methodology based on the integration of RMA in the context of the SDL FDT development cycle. In order to achieve this integration, we have defined a new predictable execution model for SDL. The semantics of SDL includes non-determinism, like unpredictable ordering of messages or unpredictable process activation, and can not be directly used to model real-time behavior. In addition, interactions with the system (including hardware devices) are always asynchronous and are not included in the design model. Our new model allows the specification of hard real-time constraints and interaction with hardware devices is also included as an important model feature. However, it is still consistent with standard SDL semantics, allowing the use of standard simulation and validation tools.

The rest of the paper is organized as follows. In the next subsection we survey some related work on object-oriented methodologies for real-time systems. In section 2 we present the real-time execution model for SDL. The methodology based on this model is presented in section 3. An application of the defined methodology to the development of a cordless telephone system is presented in section 4. Finally, some conclusions and future work are discussed in section 5.

1.1 Object technology and real-time embedded systems

There exist many proposals that try to use object technology for the development of real-time systems, but most of them do not take into account other characteristics of embedded systems, like hardware interaction or performance and memory limitations. With respect to real-time, two main features have to be considered in order to analyze the existing methodologies: the support for timing analysis and whether they are formal founded or not.

HRT-HOOD [8], for example, includes the explicit definition of application timing constraints and integrates appropriate scheduling paradigms with the design process, but lacks of a formal foundation that allows to simulate and validate the designs in the early phase of the development cycle. In addition, it remains strongly attached to a procedural view of a multitask application. OCTOPUS [9] is an object-oriented method for real-time systems based on OMT [10] and Fusion [11]. It also lacks a formal foundation, but it is more object-oriented, in the sense that objects and not tasks (as in HRT-HOOD) are the main concern of the designs. In this methodology, an implicit concurrency model is used, delaying the design of concurrency until we are near of the implementation phase. It provides some rules for deriving process priorities, but it does not allow schedulability analysis.

With respect to methodologies with a formal foundation, we will consider two different approaches: ROOM [12], that is based in the actor paradigm and Object-Geode and SDT, which are based on the SDL FDT. Both are well supported by commercial tools, that provide all the elements for simulation and rapid prototyping. The main drawback of these methodologies is that they do not allow any kind of timing analysis.

Some work is being carried out to try to integrate this kind of analysis in a SDL model. For example, in [13] an earliest deadline semantics is given for SDL, allowing a mapping from a SDL specification to an analyzable task network. However, they do not integrate this analysis in the rest of the development cycle, nor take into account hardware interaction or real-time anomalies as priority inversion. Another working line in this context is the one of supplementing SDL with load and machine models, as the ones described in [14], that use queuing theory to calculate job and message queuing times and processor peak and average workloads. We think that these works can be complementary and useful in the first phases of design, but a final schedulability analysis have to be done for real-time systems and, in order to achieve this, it is necessary to provide SDL with a predictable execution model.

2. A REAL-TIME MODEL FOR SDL

In this section we describe a predictable execution model for SDL. With this model we try to eliminate non-determinism from the SDL semantics and to make possible the real-time analysis of the implementations derived directly from an SDL design. This implementation will be automatically generated and will run on the final target either with an autonomous SDL run-time library (without operating system support, as the SDT Cmicro library [3]) or using a real-time operating system to implement the SDL execution model. In both cases, a predictable SDL execution model will be necessary if we want to be able to analyze real-time behavior.

When defining an execution model for embedded real-time systems we have to take into account at least the following aspects:

- Process scheduling. In real-time systems processes have to be scheduled in the appropriate way in order to meet real-time constraints. In our model we will use preemptive scheduling with fixed priorities that is the base of RMA.
- Process communication mechanisms. SDL uses asynchronous message-passing as the basic mechanism for process communication, although in SDL-92 remote procedure call has been integrated as an alternative communication mechanism.
- Hardware interaction model. Hardware interaction is not considered explicitly in SDL. All the interactions with the system environment have to be achieved by means of asynchronous signal interchange.

In addition, we need to be able to express real-time constraints in the language context (SDL). Although SDL has mechanisms to express real-time constraints (timers) it is necessary to analyze if they are powerful enough and if they can be easily managed in the context of the execution model. Our objective is to introduce as few modifications as possible to the language, maintaining the semantics of timers as close as possible to the standard semantics.

244

In the rest of this section we first analyze the problems in expressing real-time constraints and the real-time anomalies that the SDL standard execution model introduces and later, we describe our proposal.

2.1 Expressing real-time constraints

In SDL there are two main mechanisms to express real-time constraints:

- A global clock that can be accessed by means of the *now* function. This function returns a *TIME* type value that represents the time in seconds since system initializations.
- Timers: they are special objects that support the *SET(time, Timer)* and *RESET(Timer)* operations.

Figure 1 shows an example of how a periodic process can be specified with these operations. The expressiveness of these constructions can be enough, but it depends on the underlying execution model. For example, with the standard FIFO semantics of signal reception, time-out signals are received after all the signals that were in the process queue when the timer expired. With this semantics it is impossible to activate a process exactly when the timer expires and henceforth it is impossible, for example, to specify a periodic process or an exact delay.

Another problem with the SDL semantics of time is the difficulties of expressing real-time constraints involving the sending and reception of signals. There is no way of knowing when a signal was really sent or received. If we want to know in figure 1 when a signal was received we can not use the *now* function. Since process scheduling can be preemptive, a lot of time could have elapsed between the signal reception and the invocation of the *now* function.

In order to avoid these difficulties we have included two minimum extensions to SDL:

- *Process and transition priorities*. We will assign priorities to process transitions, depending on the events they are involved and following RMA criteria. Process priorities are calculated taking into account the signals in the process queue and the possible transition on the current state (see section 2.2). Processes can have a default priority that it is specified in the process declaration. Both signal and process priorities can be specified with the keywords **with priority P.**
- *Signal Time-stamps*. Every signal instance will have two time-stamps: one recording when the signal was sent and another one recording when the signal was received. These Time-stamps can be accessed by means of two predefined functions: time_sent and time_received both functions are referred to the signal that activated the transition. With these time-stamps it is easy to specify real-time constraints relative to signal sending and reception, as input or output jitter.

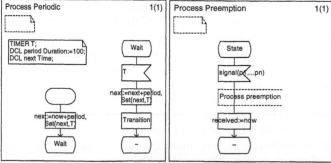

Figure 1. Real-time requirements in SDL

In addition to real-time expressiveness, SDL presents other real-time anomalies common to other message based models. For example, data cannot be directly shared among processes and it has to be encapsulated in a server process and, as it is known, this can cause priority inversion. For example, priority inversion can occur when different clients with different priorities try to access the same server at the same time. In this case, if the standard FIFO semantics is maintained, process with higher priority can be starved. Priority inheritance protocols have to be used in order to avoid these situations.

Precedence constraints can also influence real-time response. In message-based systems, the treatment of any event may involve different related processes in some precedence order. For example, consider two simple external events (Senv1 and Senv2) that are processed by a chain of three processes ProcessH, ProcessM and ProcessL.

The external event Senv1 is initially processed by *ProcessH* that sends a signal to *ProcessM*, that, in turn, sends another signal to *ProcessL*. The other event, *Senv2*, is processed in a similar way but the precedence relation is reverse. That is, *ProcessL* receives Senv2 and sends a signal to *ProcessM*. Then, *ProcessM* sends another signal to *ProcessH*. Let us suppose that we assign priorities to processes and that *priority(ProcessH) > priority(ProcessM) > priority(ProcessL)*. When *Senv1* is processed the behavior of the processes is correct, but when *Senv2* is received its processing can be starved, since *ProcessM* and *ProcessH* could also be involved in the processing of other events. This problem occurs due to assigning fixed priorities to processes. If a process can receive signals caused by events with different timing requirements, its priority cannot remain the same for attending the different signals.

Finally, another SDL characteristic that has to be taken into account is hardware interaction. All the interactions with the environment are achieved by means of signals to and from the environment. For this reason hardware drivers have to be active process independent of the SDL design. In embedded systems, hardware interaction conforms a great part of the system and should be considered in the design. In addition, if we want to obtain an analyzable model, hardware timing requirements and driver timing behaviors have to be considered.

2.2 An analyzable execution model

There are some prerequisites which have to be satisfied in order to be able to define an analyzable execution model: we do not consider dynamic process creation and we assume that there is no implicit signal consumption. The execution model is based on fixed priority preemptive scheduling, however, we do not assign fixed priorities directly to processes but to process transitions. Process priorities can vary from one state to another depending on the transitions that it can carry out in the current state (taken into account the queued signals). Processes are scheduled according to these dynamic priorities, although the schedulability analysis is based on the transition priorities, which are fixed. Transitions can be preempted by higher priority ready transitions of other processes, but never by a transition of the same process, i.e. if a process transition with higher priority become ready while it is executing another transition, this transition is delayed until the current one has finished. This may cause an increment of the response time of events, but this constraint is necessary in order to maintain SDL process execution semantics. Assuming this, processes are preemptively scheduled according to its dynamic priority. In order to show how process priorities are calculated we first define the following sets and functions:

- `Process`, `States` and `Signals`: the set of system processes, process states and signals.

- The function `sig` defined as `sig: Process × States → ℘(Signals x N)`. It returns pairs `(signal,priority)` indicating the signals that can be received and the priority assigned to the transition associated to that signal.
- The function `received` defined as `received: Process → Signals`, where `received(P)` returns the signals that are currently in process P queue.

Priorities are calculated as follows:

- Initially, every process has its default priority or the priority assigned to its START transition.
- Every time a signal s is received in the state e by process P, the priority change according to the following rule:

$$pri(P) := \begin{cases} max\{pri(p),p\} & if\ (s,p) \in sig(P,e) \\ pri(P) & otherwise \end{cases} \qquad (1)$$

The new priority is the maximum between the current priority and the priority of the transition enabled by the signal reception, but only if that signal can be accepted in the current state. If the process was inactive, it can become active interrupting the current executing process, ant if it was active it continues its execution with the new priority. In this case, this priority change can be considered a kind of priority inheritance between the transition currently under execution and the next transition to be achieved by that process.

- When process P change to state e:

$$pri(P) := max\{p:(s,p) \in sig(P,e)\ and\ s \in received(P)\} \qquad (2)$$

Every time a process finishes a transition, its priority is recalculated for being equal to the priority of the higher priority enabled transition.

Assigning priorities in this way, we always execute the transition with higher priority, except when that transition belongs to the current executing process. In this case, we have to consider the executing transition time as blocking time for the new high priority task. However, this effect can be minimized during design time trying to avoid having processes attending to possibly concurrent events. We will discuss this issue section 3.

2.2.1 Assigning priorities to transitions

Timing requirements are specified with respect to external events, considering timer expirations as external events too. For each event in the system we consider the sequence of signals exchanged among the SDL processes. This sequence is constructed from the external event adding to the sequence the signals sent for subsequent processes. If every process only sends a single signal to another process, we obtain a sequential string of transitions, corresponding to actions that have to be carried out on the event occurrence. For instance, for the precedence constraint example we obtain a sequential sequence string for both external events: *Senv1 →S1 →S2; Senv2 →S3 →S4.*

The actions achieved for the different processes can be considered equivalent to actions achieved by a single sequential task and, henceforth, all the transitions involved in the same sequential string will have the same priority. This priority will be determined by rate monotonic or deadline monotonic assignment based on the timing requirements of the external event. If a process can send more than one signal in a single transition, each of the signals is considered a new (internal) event, that have to be taken into account in the timing analysis. The priority of the transitions involved in the treatment of this new event will be determined by the ones of the external event. However, there exist situations in which signals are sent to other processes conditionally. In these cases, the time requirements may be adjusted depending on how often the conditions occur to cause the sending of the message.

Another aspect to take into account is transition sharing. In some systems, transitions may be shared by two or more events, however a transition can be executing only on behalf of one event at a time. In this situation priority inversion can occur if we assign the transition priority arbitrarily. A possible solution to this synchronization problem is to use the highest locker protocol [15]. In this protocol all shared resources have a ceiling priority, that is the highest priority among the processes that can access the resource. Any process trying to access the resource changes its priority to one level higher than the resource priority ceiling. In this way, any other process that also wants to use it will not preempt the process that is accessing the resource. This protocol can be directly used to solve the problem of shared transitions, considering the transition itself as a shared resource. In this sense, the transition priority will be one level higher that the maximum priority corresponding to the events in which it is involved, avoiding possible priority inversion problems.

2.2.2 Sharing Resources

As we analyze in section 2.1, resource sharing in SDL can lead to priority inversion situations. This situation can be avoided by using the execution model described above, but data and resource sharing can be very inefficient and difficult to analyze, since it may involve several message exchanges and process context switches. In our model, shared data and resources will be encapsulated into a special kind of processes. These processes are, externally, normal SDL ones, but its behavior is limited as follows:

- They act as passive server processes, i.e. they do not initiate any action by themselves.
- They only use RPC as communication mechanism, i.e. they are always waiting for receiving RPCs from other processes.
- Blocking during transition execution must be bounded.

Each of these processes has assigned a priority ceiling, that is the maximum of the priorities among all the other process transitions where the resource is accessed. In this way we avoid possible priority inversion in data access and blocking time in shared data access is predictable.

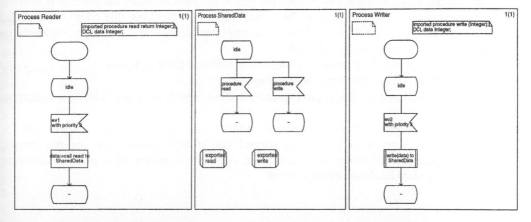

Figure 2. Resource sharing example

Mutual exclusion is also guaranteed, since all the process transitions will be executed at the higher priority between all the processes that shared the resource. In the figure 2 we show an example of how a reader and a writer process access shared data using this schema. The priority ceiling of the *SharedData* process will be 3, since it is accessed from two different transitions with priority 2 and 3, respectively.

In addition, using this schema for modeling data sharing has another important advantage: it can be implemented very efficiently. Although in the SDL model data are encapsulated in a process, this is not really translated to a real process in the implementation. Each of these processes can be mapped into a set of procedures, one for each transition, inside a module in the target language. These procedures will be called by the processes that share the data after changing its priority to the priority ceiling of the resource.

2.2.3 Hardware Integration

As we discussed in section 2.1, hardware control software must be included in the SDL design. Here, we provide a simple general model for the integration of hardware in an SDL design. Every hardware component is modeled by two different processes:

- A passive process as the ones introduced for data sharing. These processes execute transitions only as a result of a hardware interruption or when their associated driver processes call them. Their priority ceiling will be a hardware level priority and will be system dependent. Only critical hardware operations will be achieved inside this process and with this high hardware priority.
- An active driver process that will interact with the passive one and that will provide the access interface to the rest of the processes in the system. Interaction with this driver process can be asynchronous or synchronous. Its priority will be determined by the same rules that the rest of the processes in the system (i.e. depending on the external events they deal with).

Hardware registers are described in terms of SDL data types and they will be mapped onto the physical ones during the final implementation phase. These registers are all encapsulated in the passive process.

Hardware interruptions will be modeled by external SDL signals that will be received by the passive processes. The interrupt priority will be indicated in the transition that will attend to that interruption. This transition will be the only one in the state in which the process is waiting for the interruption (in order to prevent the possible interrupt blocking that could occur if the process is attending any call from the driver). Interrupt notifications are sent asynchronously to the driver process (so they can be buffered).

With this interrupt-handling model, we have three different priority levels:

- The highest one for attending the interrupt.
- The one indicated by the passive process ceiling, which indicates hardware operation priorities.
- The driver priority, that will be determined by the priority of the events it deals with.

In this way the amount of computing carried out at high priority can be minimized, increasing system schedulability. In figure 3 we show the structure of a passive hardware process and a standard hardware configuration.

2.3 Timing Analysis

The timing analysis is based on the analysis technique presented in [15]. With this technique it is possible to calculate the response time for each event in the system. For each transition we need to know the worst case execution time (Ci) and the blocking time (Bi). A transition is blocked if its execution is delayed by a lower priority one. In our model this can occur under the following circumstances:

- If a lower priority transition of the same process is under execution. In this case, the worst execution time among all the lower priority transition has to be considered as blocking time.
- If a shared resource is accessed within the transition. The worst execution time among the resource procedures used by lower priority processes has to be considered as blocking time.

In both cases this time is bounded, since we use immediate priority inheritance as we described above. We also have to consider as blocking time SDL atomic action (timer handling and signal sending and reception). We will consider as blocking time the worst time among the possible blocking sources described above. From this data, we can calculate the response time for each event taking into account the transition event string. If all the priorities of the transitions are the same, they can all be considered part of the same sequential process and the response time (Ri) can be calculated with the well-known iterative method given by:

$$R_i = C_i + B_i + \sum_{j \in hp(i)} \left\lceil \frac{R_i}{T_j} \right\rceil \cdot C_j \tag{3}$$

If there are transitions with different priorities (i.e. the same transition is shared by different events) the method described in [15] has to be used. This method groups together transitions with the same priorities defining segments with different priorities within the same event string. Other timing characteristics as release jitter, scheduling overheads, etc. can also be easily included in the analysis, but this will be dependent of the SDL run-time system implementation.

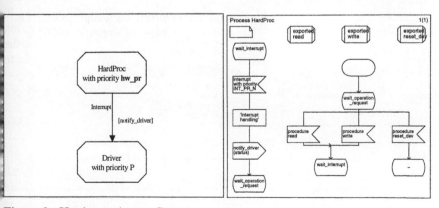

Figure 3. Hardware Access Process.

3. THE METHODOLOGY

Our proposal is conceptually based on the approach already used in other methodologies (SOMT, Octopus). However, partial solutions are provided to some of the problems that are presented in the methodologies mentioned above. Special attention is paid to the existing gap between the object model and the process model, which presents a special interest in the context of real-time embedded systems. Thus, an approach to move the object model into a process model is provided, in such a way that the real-time constraints can be predictable. This way to map objects into processes is, perhaps, the most innovative aspect of our proposal. From our experience in developing real-time embedded systems, two other lessons arise. Firstly, the object model can be refined a bit more than other methodologies recommend, and in some occasions this finer object-oriented design is encouraged. And secondly, this refinement can be better exploited if a good correspondence between elements in the object model (UML) and elements in the process model (SDL) is obtained.

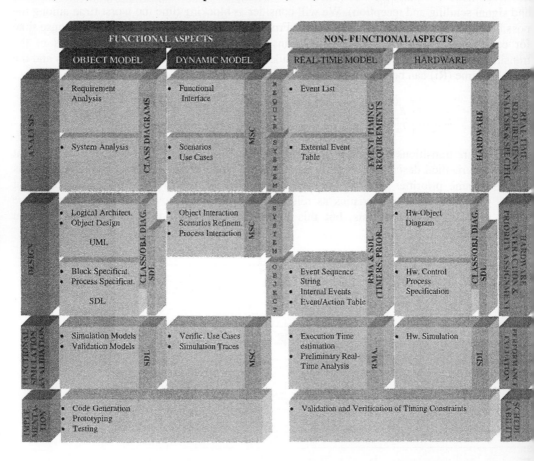

Figure 4. Methodology overview

The primary focus of this method is, like in other proposals, on system development using object-oriented analysis and design, and providing real-time analysis with SDL. The methodology proposed is basically divided into four phases: Analysis, Design, Validation and Implementation. In every phase both the functional and the non-functional aspects are considered in two different, but complementary, views of the system. This distinction allows capturing the real-time features and the hardware peculiarities of the system, with (relative) independence from the functional requirements (object and dynamic models), but keeping track of the level where the specific requirements are arisen. The different phases for each aspect are shown in figure 4.

The analysis phase starts at a high-level of abstraction (general requirements), and the design one (hardware interaction, priority assignment) finishes in a detailed object (event) description. The third phase is devoted to simulate and validate the functional design of the system, and to evaluate the performance of this design. Finally, during the implementation-schedulability phase the code generation is made, and the timing constraints are analyzed to decide whether the processes are schedulable or not.

For a better understanding, an example of a multihandset cordless telephone is developed explaining the different phases of the methodology. For the sake of clarity, only a part of the whole system will be considered and only examples of the most relevant documents exposed.

3.1 Analysis and Real-Time Requirements Specification

3.1.1 Analysis

This is the activity where the problem domain and the user requirements on the system are captured and analyzed. Basically, during this phase there must be established a first object model and preliminary use cases of the system. Two graphic notations are proposed to support both activities: OMT (or UML) to capture the object-oriented description, and MSC to describe the dynamic model. There are two abstraction levels inside this phase: the requirement analysis and the system analysis.

3.1.1.1 Requirement Level

Usually, the requirement analysis is based on a textual document, presenting the user requirements on the system to be built. As it is usual, the textual documents are combined with other more technical documents and a data dictionary is used to fix a common vocabulary and terminology.

3.1.1.2 System Level

In the system analysis phase the system to be constructed is analyzed using an object-oriented method, in order to provide the architecture of the system, and to identify the objects to be implemented to obtain the required functionality (figure 5). From an object-oriented perspective, the main aim during the requirement analysis phase is to define the problem that the system has to solve, the purpose of the system analysis is to describe the system itself. From a use-case perspective, at the system level, the MSCs detected during the requirement analysis have to be refined (figure 6).

252

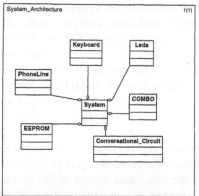

Figure 5. System Object Architecture.

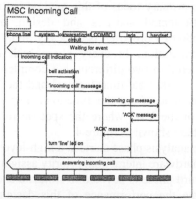

Figure 6. MSC for Incoming Call scenario

3.1.2 Real-Time Requirements Analysis and Specification

A real-time system responds simultaneously to random occurrences of events and gives the desired responses within the required time limits. Thus, this phase will focus on the detection of external events (specially input events) produced by the hardware interaction and other subsystems. The result is a table with the external events, where the following information is given for each event: event name, involved classes, and real-time requirements (rate, deadline, jitter, ..).

3.2 Design, Hardware Interaction and Priority Assignment

3.2.1 Design
System Level

At this level, the system architecture is designed by (basically) using an object-oriented approach. Although the logical structure of the classes in the system already appears during the analysis phase, a precise definition of this structure is made during the system design. On the other hand, the dynamic model is refined to obtain the description of the object and process interaction. See figures 7 and 8.

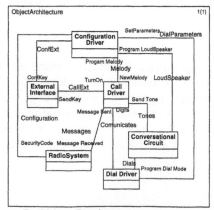

Figure 7. Object Design.

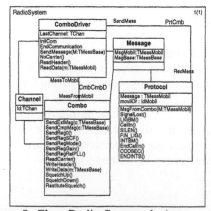

Figure 8. Class Radio System design.

3.2.1.1 Object Level

The object design is made mainly in SDL. However, the class/object diagrams are still used until the last stages of this phase. Thus, during this design level, blocks and processes are specified in SDL, taking as starting point a rather refined object design. Perhaps, this is the activity mostly influenced by the real-time and hardware requirements, which are analyzed in the following section. Nevertheless, independently on these non-functional requirements, a number of new strategies and criteria to map objects into processes are also proposed, learned from the previous experience in developing real-time embedded systems. In particular, a sophisticated way to map elements from the object model into SDL entities is proposed. Some of these strategies correspond to the mapping between associations (in the object model) and signal routes (in SDL), or the mapping of active and passive objects into different kinds of processes in SDL. Concerning the first issue, a mechanism to associate subsets of methods (of a class) with associations is established. This makes the translation to signal routes and signal lists easier. On the other hand, objects are mapped into processes attending to certain criteria as the following ones. Active object are always moved to one process at least; in some situations more than one process have to be considered (e.g. when the object is involved in two parallel events which cannot fulfill some time constraints; in this case, it is necessary to define one process for each event). Passive objects not shared by different active objects are modeled as internal data types defined in the client process. If the passive object is shared, the limitations established in the section 2.2.2 have to be considered. Finally, the classes which model the hardware behavior are treated, and the distinction between active processes (hardware drivers) and passive processes (directly modeling the hardware) is proposed (see section 2.2.3). The system specification and a more detailed block specification are shown on figures 9 and 10.

In the system developed, process COMBO, representing the radio circuit, is the passive process modeling the hardware device and its features will be accessed by means of RPC calls. All the interactions will be carried out through the active process corresponding to its driver. However, it is necessary to split the driver process in two (DcomboIn, DcomboOut) since it deals with parallel events (simultaneous send and receive messages) and this situation introduces a blocking delaying time making the system no schedulable. As a consequence of this, it is also necessary to add a passive process to encapsulate, as shared resources, part of the object internal state. These shared resources are the table of channels and the active reception and transmission channels. The arrival of a message from a handset is dealt with as an interruption, so a signal route between Combo and DComboIn is added.

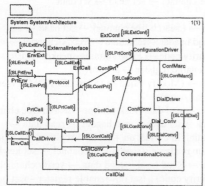

Figure 9. SDL System Specification.

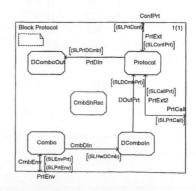

Figure 10. Block Protocol Specification

254

3.2.2 Hardware Interaction and Priority Assignment

3.2.2.1 System Level

Concerning the non-functional issues, the design has to capture how the hardware interacts with the system. In this sense, each hardware component must be modeled in one object; therefore, a class has to be defined in order to represent the corresponding physical component. Thus, the activities to be developed in this phase are similar to the ones proposed in other methodologies, e.g., Octopus. However, the guidelines to group the classes modeling the hardware present substantial differences with respect to the approach promoted by Octopus. In fact, as it was mentioned in section 2.2.3, instead of grouping all these classes in only one subsystem, we propose to distribute the hardware classes among the different subsystems that have been generated during the analysis phase. This promotes a more natural and reasonable design, because the classes representing every hardware component are located where they will be needed. Basically, the notation proposed at this level is OMT/UML (class-object diagrams).

3.2.2.2 Object Level

The object level of this phase is devoted to design the hardware interaction, such as it was discussed in section 2.2.3, distinguishing, for each hardware component, a passive process and a driver process. The first process models the direct hardware component access, and the second one implements the protocol demanded by the system requirements. All this is specified in SDL. Other activities are carried out. On the one hand, the event sequence string is completed, associating objects to events, or fixing the priorities of the actions--transitions (see sections 2.2.1 and 2.2.3). On the other hand, the passive process ceilings are assigned as it was described in previous sections. Finally, a table must be constructed, showing the correspondence between every event and the related sequence of actions. The table 1 shows the event/action table for a subset of the application events.

Table 1. Event/actions table.

Event Name	Type	Arrival Pattern (ms)	Time Req. (ms)	Response/ Action
Keyboard reading	I	P, 7.82	H, 7.82	read key → read key → read key → verify key
Turn LED on	I	P, 500	S, 100	set on → enable register → set port
Turn LED off	I	P, 500	S, 150	set off → disable register → set port
Scan channels	I	P, 0.122	H, 0.122	get scan ready → set squelch level → change channel
Messages to handset	I	P, 1000	H, 500	search free channel → set head → set data
Check line	I	P, 0.122	H, 0.01	check line
Incoming call	E	P, 700	S, 700	check line → (search free channel → set head → set data→ Read header →read data → verify channel → verify security code)→ Programming speaker registers ‖ (set on → enable register → set port)
New security code	E	P, 600	S, 400	New Code → (Modify value → (Save EEPROM ‖ (set header → set data)))
Outgoing call	E	P, 1100	S, 1100	read header→read data→ask for line→search free channel → set head → set data→ read header → read data → (Programming line ‖ (set on → enable register → set port)
Intercommunication	E	P, 1200	S, 1200	get intercom ready → ((search free channel → set header → set data → Read head →read data → verify channel → verify security code) ‖ (set on→enable register →set port))

3.3   Simulation, Validation and Performance Evaluation

In this phase, simulation models to analyze quantitative measures like throughput and response time are used. This analysis can also be carried out with existing commercial tools, although the integration of performance evaluation in SDL has not been fully established. Concerning the hardware interaction, hardware must be simulated by SDL processes. When the system is implemented, the hardware will be accessed by means of C functions embedded in the code and generated from the design; during this phase, the SDL specification has to be completed with SDL processes modeling the hardware behavior. This allows to simulate and validate the whole system, also taking into account the interaction with the hardware. Another stage is the preliminary real-time analysis, which will be based on the event/action table and a rate-monotonic analysis. Table 2 calculates the response time in the different functional modes.

Table 2. Response time for operating mode actions.

Event name	Deadline	Response Time for Idle mode	Response Time for Incoming Call Mode	Response Time for Outgoing Call Mode
Keyboard reading	7.82 ms.	5.850 ms.	0.053 ms.	
Turn LED on	100 ms.	76.370 ms.	0.190 ms.	0.156 ms.
Turn LED off	150 ms.	77.590 ms.	0.200 ms.	0.166 ms.
Scan channels	0.122 ms.	0.121 ms.		
Check line	0.01ms.	0.005 ms.		0.005 ms.
Incoming call	700 ms.		515.920 ms	
Outgoing call	1100 ms.			1067.370 ms.

3.4   Implementation and Schedulability Analysis

The operating system or SDL runtime system must provide certain characteristics in order to support the implementation of our real-time execution model: at least, fully preemptive scheduling based on fixed priorities, and some form of priority inheritance. In addition, the hardware model should be adapted to the provided one (if any).

Current commercial code generators can be divided into two groups: the ones that use an existing operating system and which adapt the SDL execution model to it and the ones that are based on a customizable runtime system. For this approach to embedded systems, the second option seems more suitable, since it allows a more direct translation of the execution model and a tighter integration of hardware devices in the SDL design. A prototype of a runtime system support for a subset of SDL that implements the real-time execution model has been developed. With this support, the implementation phase is mainly devoted to completing hardware access functions and a successive design refinement.

Schedulability analysis must be accomplished jointly with the final phases of the design and implementation. As soon as some estimation of transition execution times can be obtained, they should be used in order to obtain estimations of event response times. This information can be very useful and it can deeply influence the final design. In order to achieve an accurate schedulability analysis several factors must be included in the analysis model. For example, aspects such as timer implementation, process and signal queue management, interrupt handling, etc. must be taken into account. All these factors are very system dependent and they should be measured and adjusted in order to obtain a reliable model.

4. CONCLUSIONS AND FUTURE WORK

The contributions of this paper could be summarized in three main aspects. On the one hand we integrate Rate Monotonic Analysis in the SDL development cycle, paying special attention to the transition between the object and the process models. This integration help us to fulfil the gap existing between both models, which is particularly important in embedded real-time systems. On the other hand, a new predictable execution model for SDL has been presented. This model is based on transition priority assignment and priority inheritance, and it considers subjects as precedence constraints, priority inversion and hardware integration. Finally, we combine all these aspects to propose an object-oriented methodology for embedded real-time systems, and we detect the activities to be carried out in each of the four phases. To illustrate the most relevant details of our proposal, we have also analyzed a case study, corresponding to the software development for a cordless telephone application.

The conclusions presented at this work are the result of particular experiences of the authors developing embedded real-time software. As a future work, we want to evaluate the advantages and inconveniences of applying this methodology to a wider range of problems. We are also interested in constructing automatic tools to support all the proposed techniques. To do this, we have two possibilities: to extend existing tools, which already support the functional aspects, or construct new ones. We have already developed a prototype of a runtime system support for a subset of SDL, which implements the real-time execution model described in section 3.3.

REFERENCES

1. Terrier, F., Barroca, L. "Object Technology and Real-time: Problematic and Trends". Object-oriented Technology. ECOOP 97 Workshop Reader. Bosch, J., Mitchell, S eds., 417-433. 1997.
2. ITU recommendation Z. 100. "Specification and Description Language (SDL)". 1994.
3. Telelogic "SDT 3.4 Manuals". 1998.
4. Leblanc, P. et al.. "Object-Geode: Method Guidelines". Verilog S.A.. 1996.
5. Booch, G. et al. "Unified Modeling Language". Notation Guide version 1.0. Rational Software Corporation. 1997.
6. ITU recommendation Z. 120. "Message Sequence Chart (MSC)". 1996.
7. Klein, M.H. et al. "A Practitioner's Handbook for Real-time Analysis". Kluwer Academic Publishers. 1993.
8. Burns, A., Wellings A. "HRT-HOOD: A Structured Design Method for Hard Real-Time Ada Systems". Real-time Safety Critical Systems. Vol. 3. Elsevier. 1995.
9. Awad, M. et al. "Object Oriented Technology for Real-Time Systems". Prentice Hall. 1996.
10. Rumbaugh J. et al.. "Object-Oriented Modeling and Design". Prentice Hall. 1991.
11. Coleman D. et al. "Object-Oriented Development – The Fusion Method". Prentice Hall. 1993.
12. Sellic B. et al. "Real-Time Object-Oriented Modeling". John Wiley Publisher. 1994.
13. Kolloch T., Färber G. "Mapping an Embedded Hard Real Time Systems SDL specification to an Analyzable task network – A case Study. LCTES'98, Montreal, Canada, 19 - 20 June 1998. Springer-Verlag.
14. Mitschele-Thiel, A. Müller-Clostermann, B. "Performance Engineering of SDL/MSC Systems". Workshop on Performance and Time in SDL and MSC. University of Erlangen. 1998.
15. González M. et al. "Fixed Priority Scheduling of Periodic Tasks with Varying Execution Priorities". Real Time Systems Symposium. 1991.

Session VII

Code Generation

SDL'99 : The Next Millennium
R. Dssouli, G.v. Bochmann and Y. Lahav, editors
©1999 Elsevier Science B.V. All rights reserved

COCOS - A Configurable SDL Compiler for Generating Efficient Protocol Implementations[*]

Peter Langendoerfer, Hartmut Koenig

Brandenburg University of Technology at Cottbus, Department of Computer Science
PF 101344, D-03013 Cottbus, Germany, email: {pl,koenig}@informatik.tu-cottbus.de

Current FDT compilers do not achieve the efficiency of advanced implementation techniques as activity threads and integrated layer processing. The integration of these techniques into FDT compilers is difficult due to semantic constraints of the specification techniques and the lack of language features to flexibly adapt to a given implementation context. In this paper, we present the SDL compiler COCOS that provides such features. COCOS is a configurable compiler that includes different implementation techniques. Currently, it supports the server model and the activity thread model. COCOS possesses a variable implementation model that permits to adapt the code generation to the given implementation context. The adaption process is controlled by means of the implementation-oriented annotation iSDL which allows it to introduce implementation-related information into the specification. In the paper, we describe the motives for the design of COCOS and give an overview of its main features. We explain the inclusion of different implementation techniques and give examples for the use of iSDL. The measurements we present show that by applying the activity thread approach the efficiency of the generated code can be increased up to 50 per cent compared to the Cadvanced code generator of the SDT tool. Further, we show that by avoiding copy operations the efficiency of the generated code can be further increased.

Keywords: Formal description techniques, SDL, automated protocol implementation, activity threads, variable implementation model, implementation specification, configurable FDT compiler

1 Motivation

Formal description techniques (FDTs) have been successfully applied to increase the quality of protocol developments and telecommunication systems. Their application, however, is mainly focused on design, specification, verification, testing, and recently performance prediction. The implementation phase still represents a gap in this chain of development steps. The main reason for this is that code automatically generated by an FDT compiler is mostly inadequate for application in a real-life environment [7], [8], [15]. Therefore, automatically derived implementations are usually used for prototyping rather than for product implementations. Real-life protocol implementations are mainly hand-coded. This process is lengthy and requires a lot of implementation decisions which are not covered by formal verification and can be only

* The research described is supported in part by the *Deutsche Forschungsgemeinschaft* under grant Ko 1273/11-1.

validated by a thorough protocol test. Automated protocol implementation, on the other hand, may bring some remarkable benefits: a considerable reduction of the duration of the implementation process, independence of subjective implementation decisions, better conformance to the specification, and simplification of changes.

Formal description techniques will be only accepted in large scale in practice if they support a continual application of the FDT in all phases of the protocol development process including the implementation phase. As long as protocol engineers are forced after finishing the design and verification phase to "rewrite" the protocol in C or another implementation language in order to get an efficient implementation, they will scarcely be willing to apply an FDT. This process often takes almost the same time as specifying the protocol in an FDT (usually several weeks or months). For a thorough application of the FDT in the whole protocol development process, techniques for deriving sufficiently efficient implementations from formal descriptions are indispensable.

The inefficiency of automatically derived protocol implementations is caused by following reasons [8]:

(1) design of the implementation model during tool development phase,

(2) lack of capability of the code generator to adapt to the given implementation environment,

(3) overhead due to the FDT semantics,

(4) lack of integrating protocol layers.

In recent years several approaches have been proposed to improve the efficiency of automated implementation techniques. These approaches cover a wide range of proposals from improving the mapping strategies over parallelism to including hand-coding techniques [2], [5], [6], [8], [12]. An overview on these works is given in [9], [10]. All these techniques more or less focus on one single approach. They only in part overcome the shortcomings of automated implementation. Protocol implementation techniques, on the other hand, have meanwhile become very sophisticated. They can be optimized according to the requirements of the implementation context (i.e. the given implementation environment) and take aspects into account which as, for instance, memory accesses are not covered by formal specifications at all [4]. Thus, the gap between the efficiency of hand-coded and automatically generated implementations becomes even larger. We believe that automated implementation techniques will be only then successfully applied for real-life implementations if their efficiency comes despite the given constraints close to that of manually coded implementations. This requires the integration of means

(1) to adapt FDT compilers to different implementation contexts, and

(2) to apply advanced implementation techniques in FDT compilers.

In this paper, we present with the configurable SDL compiler COCOS an approach which follows this way. COCOS possesses a variable implementation model that permits to adapt the code generation to the given implementation environment. It supports different implementation techniques. Beside the server model, which is usually applied to FDT compilers, it allows generating activity thread implementations as proposed in [9], [10]. Other implementation techniques will be added later. The code generation is controlled by means of an implementation-oriented annotation, called iSDL, to introduce implementation-related information into the specification.

The remainder of the paper is organized as follows. In Section 2, we give a short overview of the design objectives of COCOS. Section 3 describes the structure of the COCOS compiler and the supported implementation techniques. Section 4 introduces iSDL and gives examples for its application. In Section 5, we present measurements of the application of COCOS to a client/server specification using a TCP/IP protocol stack. Section 6 discusses the avoidance of copy operations. In the final remarks, we give an outlook on the next research steps.

2 Design objectives of COCOS

The main design objetive of COCOS (*Configurable Compiler for SDL*) has been to develop a tool that generates code the efficiency of which comes close to that of hand-coded implementations. This has been done by combining two concepts: a variable implementation model and advanced implementation techniques. In contrast to hand-coded implementations which can individually adapated to the given implementation environment during the coding process, the implementation model* of the FDT compiler has to be designed during the tool development phase. It remains unchanged for all implementations derived with that tool. To make automatically derived implementations more flexible we adopted the idea of a variable implementation model proposed in [8]. COCOS is a configurable compiler which can be adjusted to the given implementation context. Further, it contains features which allow it to take parameters of the target system into account and to automatically configure a tailored runtime system. This is done by means of the implementation-oriented annotation iSDL which refines a given SDL specification by all information on the implementation context needed for deriving an implementation and for controlling the code generation process.

Current FDT compilers apply the server model [9] (see also below). They do not support advanced implementation techniques as activity threads and integrated layer processing (ILP) [3], [4], [16]. COCOS supports several implementation techniques. It gives the implementor the possibility to select the implementation model which is most appropriate for his purposes. In the first development stage, COCOS supports the server model and the activity thread model. Other implementation techniques as the ILP approach will be introduced in the next stage. COCOS also includes techniques to avoid the copying of data packets.

3 The COCOS compiler

3.1 Structure of the compiler

The COCOS compiler consists of three main components: the analyser, the intermediate format analyser (*IF-analyser*), and the synthesizer. The structure is depicted in figure 1.

The basis for the code generation is an SDL protocol specification which has been refined with implementation-related information presented in iSDL (see below). We call this text implementation-oriented specification in the following. The implementation-oriented specification is input in the analyser for syntax checking. The *analyser* consists of two parsers - one for the SDL text and one for the iSDL annotation. It outputs code in an intermediate format in which the SDL constructs are denoted by an implementation-oriented representation or a cor-

---

* The implementation model describes the logical structure of the implementation, their components and the interactions between them [8]. It defines the set of rules applied in the code generator for mapping the formal specification into the implementation. Thus, it determines the architecture of the generated implementations.

responding default value. The intermediate representation is used for computations needed to detect semantics violations and to optimize the performance. These computations are performed by the *IF-analyser*. Examples for such computations are:

(1) the detection of cyclic process call sequences which may occur during runtime so that the activity thread model cannot be applied,

(2) the avoidance of data copy operations, and

(3) the identification of the receiving process instances if they are not explicitly given.

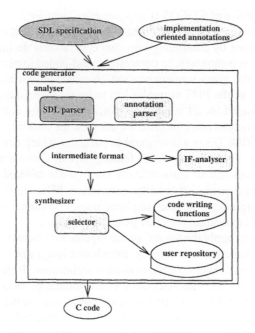

Figure 1: Structure of the COCOS compiler

If semantics violations are detected the code generation is stopped and the respective errors are indicated. Otherwise, the intermediate code including the analysis results is input in the synthesizer for final code generation.

The *synthesizer* consists of three parts: the selector, a set of code writing functions and a user repository. The selector is controlled by a set of mapping rules between iSDL and C. For each mapping rule, a separate code writing function was implemented. The selection of the concrete rules is determined by the iSDL specification. The selector identifies the mapping rule and calls the respective code writing function. For certain SDL statements, e.g. the *output* statement, several mapping rules exist. For example, in activity thread implementations *output* is mapped on a procedure call, whereas in server model implementations *output* has to be implemented as a buffered handing over of references. The code segments provided in the user repository are inlined by the selector at the places where their use is specified.

3.2 Supported implementation techniques

In its current version, COCOS supports two process models[*]: the server model and the activity thread model.

Server Model

Basic pinciple: The server model implements [16] the protocol entities by a cyclic task (process or thread of the operating system or runtime system). This task reads analogously to a driver an incoming event from its input queue, analyzes it and switches to the code segment which handles the event. The code segment represents a transition of an extended finite state machine (EFSM). Using the server model each SDL process instance can be mapped on such a server that processes signals and other events (e.g. timeouts, continuous signals or spontaneous transitions). After handling the event a possible output is written in the input queue of the receiving server and the process returns to the beginning to read the next event. The servers are usually executed in a round robin fashion so that every process instance can proceed. The automatic derivation of code is straight-forward, because the server model corresponds to the communication paradigm of SDL. Most SDL compilers apply this process model. The server model, however, exhibits heavy overhead for storing the events between the protocol entities and for process management so that it limits the generation of efficient code (see [9], [10]).

COCOS implementation strategy: In COCOS we use a common FIFO queue for the input which is called *procedure call list* (see Section 3.4). A common queue increases the efficiency of the generated code as shown in [8]. It is used by the runtime support system to determine the next instance to be executed.This implementation strategy optimizes the scheduling of the processes since each executed process instance in fact has an input signal or timer to process. If the common input queue is empty the process instances are scheduled in round robin fashion to detect whether continuous signals or spontaneous transitions have to be processed.This execution strategy combines the advantages of the basic server model with advantages of the activity thread model approach as presented in [9].

Activity Thread Model

Basic Principle: The activity thread model [3], [16] implements a protocol entity as a set of procedures. A procedure usually executes a transition of the EFSM. The active elements in this model are the events or signals in SDL, respectively. An incoming signal activates the respective procedure which immediately handles the event and executes the transition. If the transition contains an output the respective procedure of the next protocol entity is called. The sequence of inputs and outputs (input→output→input ... input→output ...) results in a sequence of procedure calls - the *activity thread*. By this, the term activity thread denotes the execution path an event takes through the protocol stack. The activity thread model provides an essentially more efficient implementation strategy, but its semantic model (synchronous computation and communication) differs considerably from the semantic model of SDL. Internal transitions, however, cannot be handled by this approach. They must be removed by refining the specification.

COCOS implementation strategy: In COCOS we apply the approach proposed in [9]. It implements each process instance by a set of procedures, one procedure for each input signal. In cer-

---

[*] The process model describes the manner how the specification is mapped on the process structure of the implementation environment or operating system, respectively [16].

264

tain cases, this may cause semantics conflicts: when cyclic process call sequences occur during runtime, if the executed transition performs actions after an *output* statement, or by multiple outputs. In [9] we proposed to buffer these procedure calls. COCOS implements the *output* statements as last actions of a transition (see Section 3.3). This solves most of problems discussed in [9] and avoids the overhead for buffering of the procedure calls.

3.3 Implementation of SDL processes

In order to simplify the code generation according to the requirements of different process models we split up each SDL process into a *reentrant procedure*, which implements the behaviour of the process, and a so-called *instance control block* (ICB), which contains the data of the process (see figure 2).

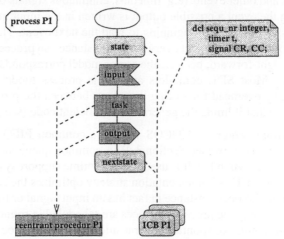

Figure 2: Implementation of SDL processes

Instance Control Blocks: The ICBs contain the following data:

(1) all variables of the process,

(2) all internal information like *offspring, parent, self* and *sender*,

(3) a list of all saved signals,

(4) the actual state.

Each process instance has its own ICBs. Consequently, the execution of *create* consists only in generating a new ICB.

Reentrant Procedures: The implementation of the reentrant procedures depends on the chosen implementation technique. When the server model is applied one procedure is implemented for each SDL process type. In activity thread implementations, a procedure for each input signal is generated. This simplifies the handing over of parameters. All reentrant procedures are extended by a function that checks whether the *save* list in the ICB is empty or not. In the latter case, the elements of the *save* list are executed first.

To avoid semantic conflicts in activity thread implementations in connection with *output* statements (see above) COCOS generally appends *output* statements as last segment to the generated code of the transition. In case of multiple outputs additional measures have to be taken using the procedure call list in which the *output* statements are buffered (see Section 3.4).

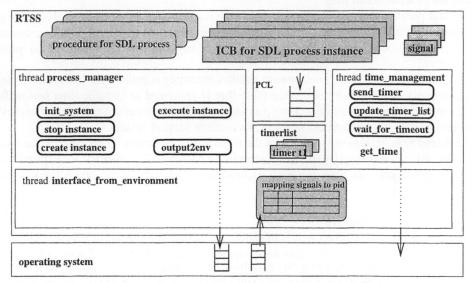

Figure 3: Structure of the generated implementation

3.4 Runtime support system

The *runtime support system* (RTSS) of the code generator has to simultaneously support the different implementation strategies (see figure 3). It is implemented by three operating system threads the *process_manager,* the *time_management,* and the *interface_from_environment* which are located in one single operating system process.

The thread *process_manager* is responsible for the generation of new process instances, for the communication with the environment and among the process instances, and for the execution of the process instances. The communication among the process instances is implemented by a buffered handing over of pointers to the corresponding signals. The pointers are buffered in a global list named *procedure call list (PCL)*. It has the following structure:

(1) identity of the receiving process instance

(2) identity of the sending process instance

(3) identity of the signal

(4) pointer to the data of the signal

(5) pointer to the next entry

The length of the procedure call list is determined by the sum of the length of all input queues defined in iSDL (see below). The procedure call list can be either used for communication between protocol instances implemented in different process models, i.e. between server-based and activity thread-based instances, or for communication between process instances implemented in the same model. The main difference in the runtime support of both implementation strategies consists in the execution procedure. Server model-based instances are executed periodically even when no input signals exist or when they are addressed as the receiving instance in the head of the procedure call list. Activity thread model-based instances are directly executed when a procedure is called or when they are the receiving instance addressed in the head of the procedure call list.

The later planned inclusion of the ILP technique does not require an additional runtime support, because the ILP approach only concerns the implementation of data manipulation operations. ILP loops can be used inside server-based and activity thread-based process instances.

The thread *interface_from_environment* handles incoming signals. It first determines the receiving process instance using a routing table that is generated at compile time and updated during runtime. Then it creates the corresponding entry in the procedure call list and copies the signal and its data into the address space of the runtime support system.

The thread *time_management* manages the timer list. It generates a new entry when a timer is set. The *time_management* periodically checks all entries of the timer list for expired timers using the system call *get_time*. For each expired timer, an entry in the procedure call list is created.

3.5 Supported SDL features

As the main focus of our research is to show how advanced implementation techniques can be used for automated code generation we currently do not support the full scope of SDL. The COCOS parser accepts the full SDL' 92 language. The code generation supports SDL' 88 with exception of macro calls and the axiomatic definition of data types. Additionally, the following SDL' 92 constructs are supported: packages, procedures with formal parameters, no delay channels. The object orientation introduced by SDL' 92 is not supported.

4 iSDL

A configurable compiler requires a language to support the selection of the components of the variable implementation model and to control the code generation process. For this, the implementation-oriented annotation iSDL [13] has been proposed to add implementation-related information to the SDL specification. The refined specification is the input for the automated code generation. In the following, we can only give a short overview of the main features of the annotation. The full definition of iSDL is given in [14].

4.1 Embedding of iSDL

iSDL annotations are syntactically included as comments in the SDL specification (SDL/ GR: comment and text symbols, SDL/PR: comments). The use of comments for the iSDL statements does not interfere the processing of the specification with existing SDL tools such as SDT [17] and Geode [18] and simplifies the reuse of the implementation-oriented specification. The iSDL annotation inside an SDL comment are marked by the keywords **iSDL** and **iSDLend,** or for short by **${** and **}$**. The iSDL statements are separated by a semicolon.

iSDL annotations may be introduced at any level of an SDL specification. Annotations at system or block level are applied to all substructures. iSDL descriptions given at system level may be refined or changed at block level.

4.2 iSDL elements

Currently, iSDL provides features to support the following implementation decisions and requirements:

Implementation-oriented features

- *Mapping on the target hardware*

  iSDL assists to control the mapping of processes of the implementation on processor clusters, e.g.

  > **define cluster** cluster1 processor1, processor2 **shared memory**;
  > **mapping** process_1, process_2 **on** cluster1;

  The implementation of the signal exchange depends on the underlying hardware. If SDL processes are mapped on processors with distributed memory message passing is applied for signal exchange. If shared memory is used the signals are exchanged by means of references via a FIFO queue. Note that shared memory allows more efficient implementations.

- *Selection of the process model*

  iSDL allows the implementor to select between the supported process model, e.g

  > ***process model*** server;

  The server model can be used independently of the memory organization of the target hardware. The activity thread model may be only applied for SDL processes mapped on target systems with shared memory.

- *Support of ILP implementations*

  iSDL also supports the later inclusion of ILP. It provides means to specify ILP loops, i.e. to specify the transitions which are supposed to be included in the loop. Further, it allows selecting so-called word filters, e.g.

  > **define** ILP loop_1;
  > ...
  > input sig1 **belongs to** loop_1;
  > **word filter** one_to_two;

  Word filters have to be specified wherever data is exchanged between data manipulation functions that operate on different word length. Word filters are used to adapt the length of the word which the data manipulation functions in an ILP loop are supposed to operate on. For example, a word filter is needed to decompose the 32 bytes words of an encryption function into 1 byte words for the CRC chuckles calculation. Since it is not possible to predefine all variants of word filters needed, the implementor may define own word filters and include the respective code in a special repository.

- *Definition of time units*

  As time units are not provided by SDL but needed for a correct implementation iSDL supports the specification of time units. Predefined time units are *sec, msec, μsec*.

- *Definition of the queue length*

  In SDL, the length of an input queue is unlimited. For the generation of efficient implementations, it is necessary to know the length of the input queues to initialize the input queues when setting up the SDL system. Thus, no time is lost for allocating additional entries to the input queues during runtime.

  > ***input queue*** 30;

  For the same reason, iSDL also supports the definition of the length of a *save* queue. The distinction between input and *save* queues is necessary, because activity thread implementations do not use input queues at all.

Features for performance prediction

iSDL provides means to define performance requirements and to define monitoring points. Both features can be used to analyze the performance of implementations generated with COCOS.

- *Definition of performance requirements*

  With iSDL sequences of signals can be defined. We call such a sequence signal chain. For each signal chain, the maximal computation time can be specified.

  > **define signal chain** tcp_ip_stack: tcp_packet, ip_packet ;
  > **computation time** tcp_ip_stack 50 *msec*;

  The computation time defines the time between the sending of the first and the last signal of the signal chain. Monitoring points for signal chains are inserted automatically.

- *Inserting monitoring points*

  Monitoring points can also be defined and set explicitly using *mstart* and *mstop* to start and stop the measurement. Explicit monitor points are used when the performance inside of SDL processes is of interest.

  > **define monitoring point** add_IP_header;
  > **mstart** add_IP_header;
  > **mstop** add_IP_header;

4.3 Example

To demonstrate the features of iSDL we give a short example (see figure 4). Figure 4a) depicts an implementation-oriented specification of a client/server application that includes the TCP/IP protocol stack (see also Section 5). The structure of the resulting implementation is shown in figure 4b). The whole system is implemented on a cluster of two processors with shared memory (fig. 4a)). This forces COCOS to set up the runtime support system only once and to integrate all SDL processes into the runtime system (see fig. 3)). The specification is mapped as follows. The *application* and the *network* process instance are implemented according to the server model, while for the socket, the TCP, and the IP protocol layer the activity thread model is applied[*]. Since shared memory is specified no message passing techniques have to be applied. For the signal exchange between the processes of different process models, the compiler generates a FIFO queue.

5 Measurements

To evaluate the performance of the COCOS compiler we compared it with the *Cadvanced* code generator of the SDT tool version 3.2 [17]. We applied both tools to generate implementations for the SDL specification of a client/server application based on a TCP/IP protocol stack of [11]. The structure of the specification is depicted in figure 5.

The *client* generates data which have to be transmitted to the *server* site. The client process has to ask for a socket before it can open a TCP connection. The server process initiates a passive open to the *socket* layer. Then it listens. The socket process forwards the application data to the TCP process and vice versa.

---

[*]   Note that this structure is typical for such implementations, because every activity thread implementation must be enclosed by an asynchronous interface with the environment.

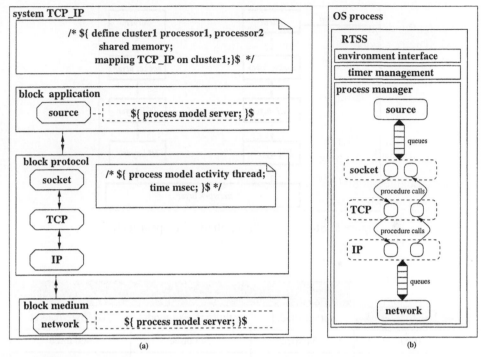

Figure 4: An iSDL specification and the resulting implementation structure

The process *TCP* contains the description for the protocol automaton of TCP. Its main functions are:

(1) to break down application data into TCP segments,

(2) to set a timer for each packet so that it can be retransmitted if the acknowledgement is not received in time, and

(3) to discard duplicated IP packets.

It further provides flow control using the sliding window mechanism, cyclic redundancy check, and congestion control.

The process *IP* supports all existing TCP connections, builds valid IP datagrams and routes them to the receiver. In this specification IP does not contain fragmentation. The *network* layer models the transmission of the IP datagrams to the server site.

COCOS as well as *Cadvanced* implement the whole specification by a single operating system process. Thus, the interfaces between the generated code and the operating system did not influence the results. With COCOS, we generated a server model implementation and a activity thread model implementation. Note that in the activity thread implementation the processes *sokket*, TCP, and IP were mapped on activity threads, whereas the processes *client*, *server*, and *network* were implemented according to the server model (see figure 4).

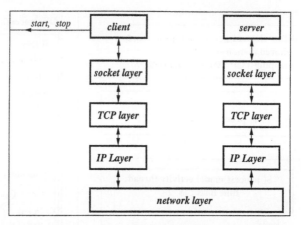

Figure 5: Structure of the applied SDL specification

	COCOS		SDT(cadvanced)
number of packets	server model	activity thread model	1024byte/packet
1000	354 msec	243 msec	466 msec
10 000	3353 msec	2152 msec	4382 msec
20 000	6700 msec	4189 msec	8 757 msec

Table 1: Measurements of different implementation strategies

The COCOS and *Cadvanced* implementations were compiled by means of the *gcc compiler* without any optimizing options. The measurements were made on a Sun Sparc 20 workstation with four processors and Solaris 2.5 as operating system.

We measured the time needed to transmit a fixed number of packets from the client to the server. The measurement started when the first packet was sent and stopped when the client received the acknowledgement of the last packet. To ensure an equivalent overhead for the measurements in both implementations we did not use the iSDL monitoring points. Instead we extended the specification with the signals *start* and *stop* which were sent from the client to the environment. These signals were used to trigger the measurement function. We repeated each measurement 50 times. To exclude exceptional behaviour extreme good and extreme bad measured values were eliminated and then the arithmetic middle of the remaining measured values was calculated. The results are given in table 1 and figure 6.

The results show that the implementation generated by COCOS achieves a 25-50 per cent better performance than those of *Cadvanced*. For the server model implementation, the performance gain is achieved by using a predefined length of the individual input queues and due to the data flow driven scheduling (see Section 3.4). The activity thread based processes do not use the procedure call list for communication. No additional entries into the procedure call list are needed during runtime. Further, the activity threads have not to be scheduled by the runtime support system. This brings another performance gain of 25 per cent.

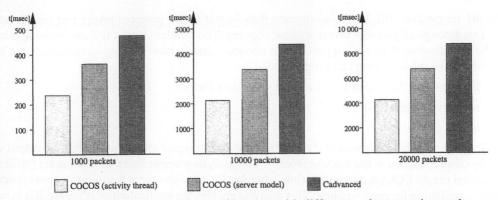

Figure 6: Measurements of the specification with different code generation tools

6 Avoiding copy operations

The copying of data packets within protocol stacks can considerably decrease the efficiency of protocol implementations. It is a well-known rule for protocol implementations that copy operations should be avoided whenever possible. Considering an SDL specification one notices that signals are several times copied even within the specification. Normally, an SDL signal is copied at least three times:

(1) from the sending process instance into the communication structure (signalroute/channel),

(2) from the communication structure into the input queue of the receiving process instance,

(3) from the input queue to local variables of the process instance (*copy on input*), and

(4) depending on the specification also between local variables of the process instance.

We presented an approach to minimize the number of data copy operations in [9]. It was called *data referencing*. The data referencing concept proposes to split up the signals into a control and a data part. The control part contains the signal identifier and a reference to the data part. It is passed to the receiving process instance, while the data part is copied into a common data area. The main objective of this approach has been to avoid the copying of signals according to case (1) and (3) of the above given situations. In COCOS, we apply a slightly modified solution. We use the global *procedure call list* (see Section 3.4) instead of implementing signalroutes, channels and individual input queues. This allows it to combine the copy operations (1) and (2) into a single copy operation, thus saving at least one of four possible copy operations. We call this combined operation *copy on output* in the following.

In [9], it was stated that *copy on input (3)* may be omitted in any case. Meanwhile, we detected that this statement is not always correct. When data of input signals are not only used in the transition the signal has triggered but also in other transitions, a local copy of these data is required, because the data may be destroyed by other processes. To decide whether *copy on input* may be omitted it must be determined which transitions access to the data of the input signal. This is done by means of a liveness analysis of the variables at compile time as applied in modern programming language compilers [1].

To avoid *copy on input, copy on output*, and copy operations inside of SDL processes (case (4)), the concept of *Integrated Paket Framing* (IPF) has been introduced in [9]. The IPF applies the off-set method [16]. It uses a common data format for all protocol layers and passes data packets through all protocol layers without copying. The problem is that IPF cannot be applied if the specification does not support such a common data format. IPF implementations can be applied when the following conditions hold:

(1) the input and the output signal use the same data format,

(2) no *copy on input*, and

(3) no *copy on output*.

The latter can be only avoided if the data of the output signal are not used after the output or in any other transition of the sending process. The analysis whether these conditions are fulfilled is carried out by COCOS at compile time whereby for *copy on output* a similar liveness procedure is applied as for *copy on input*. This analysis enables the application of IPF even if it is not explicitly intended by the user. In some cases, the common data format is inherently given by the problem, e.g. for multiplexers and to certain extend for routers.

The reduction of copy operations does not depend on the selected process model, but it can only be applied if the sending and the receiving process instances are implemented on processors with shared memory.

We measured the performance gain that can be achieved by reducing data copy operations using again the SDL specification from [11]. In the experiment we compared two COCOS server model implementations, one with and one without copy operations (see table 2). The used data formats allowed it only to remove *copy on input* operations. The measurements were carried out in exactly the same manner as described in Section 5.

number of packets	COCOS	
	with copy on input	without copy on input
1000	354 msec	275 msec
10 000	3353 msec	2676 msec
20 000	6700 msec	5348 msec

Table 2: Comparison of implementations with and without *copy on input*

The measurements show that a performance gain of about 25 per cent can be achieved by eleminating copy operations. Compared with implementations derived by means of the *Cadvanced* compiler (see table 1) the performance gain is even between 40 - 50 per cent (see figure 7).

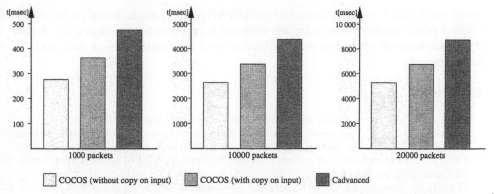

Figure 7: Measurements with avoiding of copy operations (server model)

7 Final remarks

In this paper, we have presented the configurable SDL compiler COCOS which has been designed for generating efficient protocol implementations. COCOS possesses a variable implementation model and supports different implementation strategies, currently the server model and the activity thread model. It also has functions to reduce data copy operations. The configuration concept gives the implementor the opportunity to select the most appropriate implementation model and to generate a tailored runtime support system for the given implementation context. Thus, we overcome one of the main shortcomings of automated protocol implementation the rigid implementation model designed during the tool development phase.

The concept of COCOS is based on the use of an intermediate specification level that refines the protocol specification to add needed information about the implementation and the target system. To present this information we have defined the implementation-oriented annotation iSDL.

The introduction of an implementation-oriented specification level brings several benefits for the implementation process:

(1) It refines the protocol specification with respect to the target system for which the implementation is planned and provides all needed information about the system.

(2) It documents implementation design decisions at specification level what facilitates the reuse of both the implementation-oriented specification and the implementation.

(3) It assists to improve the quality of the implementation by features to evaluate its performance.

The measurements we have presented show a considerable increase of the efficiency compared to the *Cadvanced* compiler. Efficiency improvements from 25 up to 50 per cent depending on the applied technique show that there is still a large range of possibilities to improve the performance of automated code generation.

The current implementation of COCOS comprises the functionality described in this paper. The implementation of the integrated layer processing concept will be finished in few months. After that, we plan to further evaluate our tool by also comparing it with other code generation

274

tools and hand-coded implementations of the TCP/IP protocol stack. Based on the results we will define performance measures for the different implementation strategies which shall be used for performance prediction at specification level to facilitate design decisions for the implementor.

REFERENCES

1.   Appel, A. W. : Modern Compiler Implementation in C. Cambridge University Press, 1998.
2.   Catrina, O.; Lallet, E.; Budkowski, S.: Automatic protocols implementation using Estelle Development Toolset (EDT). Institut National des Télécommunications (INT) Evry, Rapport de Recherche, 1997.
3.   Clark, D. D.: The structuring of systems using upcalls. Proc. 10 th ACM SIGOPS Symp. Oper. Syst. Principles, 1985, pp. 171-180.
4.   Clark, D. D.; Tennenhouse, D. L.: Architectural considerations for a new generation of protocols. *ACM SIGCOMM*, 1990, pp. 200-208.
5.   Fischer, S.; Effelsberg, W.: Efficient Configuration of Protocol Software for Multiprocessors. In Puigjaner, R. (ed.): High Performance Networking VI, Chapman & Hall, 1995, pp. 195-210.
6.   Gotzhein, R. et al: Improving the Efficiency of Automated Protocol Implementation Using Estelle. Computer Communications 19 (1996), 1226-1235.
7.   Hakansson, P.-O.; Karlsson, J.; Verhaard. Combinig SDL and C. In Cavalli, A.; Sarma, A. (eds.): SDL'97 Time for Testing. Elsevier, 1997, pp. 383-396.
8.   Held T.; Koenig, H.: Increasing the Efficiency of Computer-aided Protocol Implementations. In Vuong, S., Chanson, S. (eds.): *Protocol Specification, Testing and Verification XIV*, Chapman & Hall, 1995, pp. 387-394.
9.   Henke, R.; König, H.; Mitschele-Thiel, A.: Derivation of Efficient Implementations from SDL Specifications Employing Data Referencing, Integrated Packet Framing and Activity Threads. In Cavalli, A.; Sarma, A. (eds.): SDL'97 Time for Testing. Elsevier, 1997, pp. 397-414.
10. Henke, R.; Mitschele-Thiel, A.; Koenig, H.: On the Influence of Semantic Constraints on the Code Generation from Estelle Specifications. In Mizuno,T. et al. (eds.): *Formal Description Techniques and Protocol Specification, Testing and Verification*, Chapman&Hall, 1997,pp. 399-414
11. Hintelmann, J.; Westerfeld, R.: Performance Analysis of TCP's Flow Control Mechanisms Using Queueing SDL . In Cavalli, A.; Sarma, A. (eds.): SDL'97 Time for Testing. Elsevier, 1997, pp. 69-84
12. Lallet, E.; Fischer, S.; Verdier, J.-F.: A New Approach for Distributing Estelle Specifications. In Bochmann, G., Dssouli, R., Rafiq, O. (eds.): Proc. 8th Int. Conf. on Formal Description Techniques, Montreal, 1995, pp. 439-448.
13. Langendörfer, P.; König, H.: Improving the Efficiency of Automatically Generated Code by Using Implementation-specific Annotations. Proc. HIPPARCH'97 Workshop, Uppsala, June 1997.
14. Langendörfer, P.: Definition of the implementation-oriented annotation iSDL. Preprint I-04/1998, BTU Cottbus, 1998.
15. Mansurov, N.; Chernov, A.; Ragozin A. Industrial Strength Code Generation from SDL. In Cavalli, A.; Sarma, A. (eds.): SDL'97 Time for Testing. Elsevier, 1997, pp. 415-430.
16. Svobodova, L.: Implementing OSI Systems. IEEE Journal on *Selected Areas in Communications*, 7(1989) 7, 1115-1130.
17. Telelogic Malmö AB: SDT 3.2 User's Guide, SDT 3.2 Reference Manual. 1998.
18. Verilog Toulouse: Geode User's Guide, Reference Manual. 1995.

SDL'99 : The Next Millennium
R. Dssouli, G.v. Bochmann and Y. Lahav, editors
©1999 Elsevier Science B.V. All rights reserved

Using declarative mappings for automatic code generation from SDL and ASN.1

Nikolai Mansurov and Alexei Ragozin

Department for CASE tools,

Institute for System programming, Russian Academy of Sciences

25 B. Kommunisticheskaya, Moscow, 109004, Russia

email: {nick,ar}@ispras.ru

We present the concept of declarative mappings between specification and implementation languages. The main idea of a declarative mapping is to represent the properties of run-time entities rather than their implementations. Transformation of the declarative description into a "real" implementation is postponed until the run-time of the system. We call this additional run-time phase the start-up time of the automatically generated code. Delayed building of run-time structures brings much control of the appearance of the generated code. Declarative approach allows to generate very readable programs which are more attractive for code inspections, debugging and maintenance. Additional degree of control of the generated code can be used to significantly improve its external interfaces so that is can be easily integrated with legacy code or ported to different target platforms and environments. Delaying the transformation of the generated code allows to build very efficient run-time structures. We demonstrate how the concept of declarative mappings can be applied to SDL and ASN.1.

1. BACKGROUND

Automatic code generation from specification languages becomes more and more accepted within the telecommunications industry. This paper summarizes some of our four-year experience [1,2,3] in developing advanced automatic code generation techniques for telecommunications standard specification languages such as SDL [6] and ASN.1 [7]. The main motivation of our research is to generate understandable, readable C++ programs from SDL specifications. In [1] we defined readability as preserving the appearance of the original specification in the generated program. Industry-driven research [3] demonstrated that several other structural characteristics of the generated code are also important. The mapping between the specification language and the target language as well as the code generator in general should support the evolution of the generated program such as its refinement, customization and integration with hand-written (legacy) code. Our projects required additional degrees of control over the structural properties of the generated code, which could not be easily provided by traditional code generation techniques [10].

The key ideas of a declarative mapping for SDL were first introduced in [1]. Later we realized that this technique is quite general and that it allows to solve several problems of code generation:

- size and readability of generated programs;

- separate compilation of large specifications;
- integration of a generated program with different support systems, platforms and tools;
- in some cases reduction of the size of executable code;
- reduction of the effort on design of the mapping and development of the code generator.

The paper has the following organization. Section 2 describes the concept of declarative mappings and compares it to traditional imperative mappings. In section 3 we discuss our experience of applying declarative mappings to SDL, ASN.1 and a toy language for specification of finite state machines. Several illustrative examples are considered. Examples in Section 3 are used to further highlight the differences between declarative and imperative mappings. Section 4 considers quality and performance of the programs generated using dĕclarative mappings. Results of our measurements and comparisons with imperative mappings are presented. We demonstrate that a declarative mapping does not bring any serious performance degradation and that in some cases it can reduce the size of the executable code. Section 5 discusses advantages and limitations of declarative mappings. Section 6 concludes the paper.

2. DECLARATIVE VS. IMPERATIVE MAPPINGS

In this section we introduce the general concept of declarative mappings and compare declarative mappings with traditional imperative mappings.

Let's define some terminology. We consider *automatic code generation* from a formal specification language (called the source language) onto a high-level imperative implementation-oriented language (called the target language). Examples of source languages are SDL, ASN.1, ACT ONE, TTCN. Examples of target languages are C, C++, Pascal, Modula-2, CHILL. The major challenge of the automatic code generation is to develop a *mapping* for a given pair of languages. The mapping is a set of interrelated decisions specifying how the constructs of the source language are represented by the target language constructs. When a complete specification in the source language is generated into the target language the corresponding target program should be syntactically and semantically correct and should preserve the meaning of original specification. We distinguish between *executable* and *structural* constructs of a language.

Traditional *imperative mappings* [10] (in [1] we called it *direct mappings*) can be defined by the following rules:

- Executable constructs of the source language, which have semantically close equivalents in the target language, are represented directly by those equivalents (e.g. loops, conditional operators, exact control passing).
- Executable constructs of the source language, which don't have any equivalents in target language, are modeled by groups of target structural and executable constructs. Usually such groups are encapsulated in the library of run-time support. Examples from SDL include remote procedure call, signal input with guard.
- Structural constructs of specification languages, which have semantically close equivalents in the target language, are represented directly by those equivalents (e.g. objects, procedures, modules, packages).
- Those structural constructs, which have no direct counterpart in the target language (examples in SDL include communication scheme, axioms, timers), are either transformed during translation or modeled using a suitable combination of structural and executable constructs of the target language.

The concept of *declarative mappings* (in [1] we called it *indirect mappings*) allows to represent semantically distinct structural constructs of the specification language without direct modeling them in the target code. The key idea of a declarative mapping is to use *executable statements (directives)* as a uniform representation for semantically distant constructs. The generated executable directives are used to control the building of the internal run-time structures for the specified system. This allows to completely separate decisions regarding the appearance of the generated code from decisions regarding the organization of the internal run-time structures. Building of the run-time structures is thus postponed until the start of generated program.

Declarative mappings assume that the execution process for generated program consists of two basic parts: start-up time and run-time. Start-up time is used to perform generated directives and build the internal representation of the system. This internal representation is then used by the support system during the "real" execution.

Generated code for the source specification within a declarative mapping consists of two separate parts:
- code which is performed only once at start-up, and
- code for executable statements of a source language.

Declarative mappings solve the *problem of glue constructs* in the generated code [1]. The composition of structural and executable constructs within the target language programs should satisfy specific syntactic and semantic constraints of the target language. This means that it is not sufficient to design the mapping for each source language construct. The main challenge of the mapping design is to provide glue constructs, which will ensure that all fragments of the target program fit together. Usually syntactic constraints of the target language will lead to a considerable fragmentation of the generated segments [1]. In our experience declarative mappings allow much more control over the structure of the generated program because this approach uses executable directives which require considerably less glue than any other constructs in a typical target language.

3. CASE STUDIES

To demonstrate different aspects of declarative mappings we used three different specification languages: a toy FSM language, SDL and ASN1. Our first example demonstrates a declarative mapping for specification of an FSM. Second example concentrates on declarative mapping for SDL communication. The third example shows how declarative mappings can be applied to generating encoders, decoders and other service functions for ASN.1 specifications of data types. Memory consumption and performance of the generated code will be discussed in the next section.

3.1. FSM specification language

As our first illustration of declarative mappings let's consider a small example using a toy language. The language describes communicating finite-state machines. The example is intended to demonstrate two basic approaches to mapping for a simple hypothetical language. Below is a specification of an FSM.

module M;	modulebody;	state ST2;	receive S2;
inputset S1,S2;	receive S1;	send S3;	state ST1;
outputset S2,S3;	state ST1;	nextstate ST1;	nextstate ST2;
stateset ST1,ST2;	send S2;		state ST2;
startstate ST2;	nextstate ST1;		stop;

FSM M has two input signals (S1,S2), two output signals (S2,S3) and two states (ST1,ST2). FSM can send asynchronous signals to the environment when it performs a transition to another state.

Table 1

Alternative mappings for specification of an FSM

Imperative mapping	Declarative mapping
Void run_M(void)	**Support system:**
{	*typedef struct {*
tSignal CurrentSignal;	*int CurrentState,*
tState CurrentState = stateST1;	*tStateList StateSet,*
while((CurrentSignal = GetSignal())	*tSignallist InputSignalSet,*
!= NoSignal){	*tSignallist OutputSignalSet,*
switch(CurrentSignal){	*tFunction** Table}*
case sigS1 :	*tModule;*
switch (CurrentState){	**Generated transitions:**
case stateST1:	*tModule M;*
SendSignal(sigS2);	*Void m_S1_ST1(tModule* desc){*
CurrentState = stateST1;	*SendSignal(sigS2);*
continue;	*Nextstate(desc,stateST1);*
case stateST2:	*}*
SendSignal(sigS3);	*void m_S1_ST2(tModule* desc){*
CurrentState = stateST1;	*SendSignal(sigS3);*
continue;	*Nextstate(desc,stateST1);*
}	*}*
case sigS2 :	*void m_S2_ST1(tModule* desc){*
switch(CurrentState){	*Nextstate(desc,stateST2);*
case stateST1:	*}*
CurrentState = stateST2;	*void m_S2_ST2(tModule* desc){*
continue;	*Stop(desc);*
case stateST2:	*}*
Stop();	**Generated executable directives:**
return;	*void InitModule_M(tModule* desc){*
}	*DeclareInputSet(desc,sigS1,sigS2,0);*
}	*DeclareOutputSet(desc,sigS2,sigS3,0);*
}	*DeclareStateSet(desc,stateST1,stateST2,0);*
}	*DeclareStartState(desc,stateST2);*
	DeclareReaction(desc,sigS1,stateST1,m_S1_ST1);
	DeclareReaction(desc,sigS1,stateST2,m_S1_ST2);
	DeclareReaction(desc,sigS2,stateST1,m_S2_ST1);
	DeclareReaction(desc,sigS2,stateST2,m_S2_ST2);
	}

Table 1 demonstrates alternative mappings from the FSM language to the C language. The left column presents typical imperative mapping solution. The right column shows a declarative mapping.

In a typical imperative program FSM is represented by a loop containing two nested switches. The control flow does not leave the function *run*_M except to call library functions *SendSignal* and *Stop*. FSM reads incoming signals either until it stops or until the input port becomes empty. Any additional functionality can not be easily added to the generated function without direct changes in the generated code.

The declarative mapping of the FSM has at least three parts:
- support system (data definitions for internal run-time representation of the FSM and functions for manipulating the FSM);
- generated FSM transitions (each transition as a separate function);
- generated executable directives for building the internal run-time representation of the FSM at the start-up time.

Generated functions have the same structure as the source specification. Implementation details are removed from the generated code. Note that such generated code requires more support from the library support system.

3.2. Mapping SDL communication

Declarative mapping for SDL was presented in [1]. Comparisons with other implementations demonstrated that the application of declarative mapping allowed to:
- significantly improve appearance of generated programs,
- provide direct and efficient support for complex SDL constructs (inheritance, FSM extensions, etc.),
- achieve a good execution speed of the generated programs.

In this paper we will consider a declarative mapping for SDL communication. Mappings of the communication scheme onto implementation languages usually involve non-trivial transformations of the source specification structure. Transformations are necessary to model SDL links using target language constructs. Usually SDL links are transformed into tables of routing information and/or exact specification of the destination process (for some kinds of OUTPUT statement) in the generated program [2,7]. Delivery of a signal uses the generated tables to find out the destination. In some cases destination process is assigned by a code generator. For the reasons listed below we believe that such deep translation of specification is inconvenient:
- Many implementations select the destination process for an OUTPUT statement statically at compile-time. Such solution restricts SDL communication scheme [6]. When OUTPUT to PID value is used it is necessary to make a dynamic check of signal availability from sender to receiver. Some implementations omit these checks.
- Deep transformation of the communication structure significantly decreases the readability of the generated program. Channels, signalroutes, gates and connect statements are replaced by some lower level tables with complex structure. The mapping for SDL communication is complex which makes it very hard for the user to understand and to integrate manually written fragments with the generated code.
- Routing tables are generated explicitly and can not be changed. Explicit representation of the routing tables in the generated code makes the implementation inflexible. For example, it is hard to reuse a part of the generated code (e.g. for a chosen block) when routing tables are provided for the whole system and can not be split.

At the same time routing tables are very appropriate for the implementation of communication in SDL. To combine the advantages of the traditional routing table approach with the requirement to ensure readability and flexibility of the generated code we have applied declarative mappings (see Table 2). Declarative SDL-oriented directives look quite natural for an SDL designer. Each SDL link (channel, signalroute, gate) is mapped to a separate object. For each scope unit containing communication paths, constructor of contained links is called at start-up (when the constructor for this scope unit is executed). This constructor receives complete information about the link (endpoints, signallists, etc.). A CONNECT statement is mapped to a method call which connects two given links. When all links of the SDL system are created, a special algorithm performs creation of the routing tables. Dynamically created routing tables are used later by signal delivery methods. The code generated for OUTPUT statement is very simple: one method call with the same parameters as in the source specification.

A very similar approach to mapping SDL communication onto an object-oriented language is described in [9].

Table 2

Declarative mapping for SDL communication onto C++

SDL	Generated C++ (declarative mapping after preprocessing)
SYSTEM TYPE S: /* BLOCK B1 : B1TYPE */ CHANNEL C1 from B2 to B1 via G1 with S1,S2;	sytS::sytS : chnC1=new SDLChannel("Ch1", iblkB2,((bltB2TYPE*)iblkB2)->gatNoGate, iblkB1, ((bltB1TYPE*)iblkB1)->gatG1, newSDLSignallist(sigS1::Id,sigSig2::Id,0));
BLOCK B2: SIGNALROUTE R from P to env with S1,S1;	BltB2::bltB2 : SgrR=new SDLSignalroute("R", iprcP,((prcP*)iprcP)->gatNoGate, iprcENV,((prcENV*)iprcENV)->gatNoGate, newSDLSignallist(sigS1::Id,sigSig2::Id,0));
BLOCK B2: CONNECT C1 and R;	BltB2::bltB2 : SgrR->Connect(&((((sytS*)SystemAddr)->chnC1));
PROCESS P: OUTPUT S1 via C1;	CurrentGraph->Output(new sigS1(Self()), ((sytS*)SystemAddr)->chnC1);

As demonstrated in Table 2, the C++ code generated for SDL communication using declarative mappings does not depend on the representation of routing tables in the implementation of the corresponding support system. It has exactly the same structure as the source SDL. Remote procedures (usually transformed to communication scheme) in our mapping are also represented declaratively. This means that all standard transformations, including generation of new channels, signalroutes, states and inputs, are performed only during the start-up time of the system.

The mapping rules for SDL communication require a minimum effort in the SDL translator. There is no need to synthesize routing tables and perform standard transformations for RPC and import. Code generator requires only an abstract syntax tree of the SDL specification with a few semantic attributes (reference to point of definition).

The run-time support system should be extended with the functionality for creating routing tables. In our opinion the implementation of the transformation algorithms within the

run-time system is easier than within the translator or the code generator. We believe that localizing transformations inside the support library is a good design decision:
- It does not impact the mapping.
- It allows to separate requirements of generating correct code from concrete implementation solutions.
- It gives an opportunity to replace implementation of routing without changing the mapping (e.g. inter-process socket connection, scrambled connection, special support for RPC etc.) and even to dynamically reconfigure SDL communication links.

3.3. Coders for ASN.1

ASN.1 specifications of types and values are traditionally mapped to directly equivalent data definitions in the implementation language (SDL, C, C++, JAVA). It is a very well defined area and it's hard to suggest any reasonable improvements in mapping. At the same time ASN.1 specifications are also used for automatic generating of encoding and decoding functions which translate data between an application format and sequences of bits. The application format of data is based on the generated data definitions. The representation of ASN.1 values as a bit sequence is driven by encoding rules (BER, CER, DER, etc.), which are standardized by ITU [8]. Encoders and decoders perform a simple translation from one representation of a data type to another. Recursive-descend parsing is used.

Typically separate encoding and decoding functions for each ASN.1 type are generated. Encoding function takes a data value in the application format and returns its equivalent in the encoded representation. A decoding function performs the reverse operation by decoding each component of the data type. Encoders and decoders for predefined ASN.1 types are implemented manually. The mapping from ASN.1 into encoding/decoding functions is also quite natural. It is determined by both the representation of a data type in implementation language and by encoding rules. The run-time support library is usually used for the implementation of coders for predefined types, dynamic memory management, buffering (for encoded data), error handling.

We have applied the concept of declarative mappings to generate encoders, decoders and other services (e.g. printing functions, memory allocators) for ASN.1 data in an implementation language (which is C). The basic idea of the declarative mapping for ASN.1 data is that encoders, decoders and other service functions for each ASN.1 type are not generated *at all*. Instead, we generate executable statements declaring the structure of ASN.1 types. These statements are used as directives for a special Coder Framework (CF). The CF is a kind of a run-time support system which in addition to the functionality described above independently performs encoding and decoding of all ASN.1 types. The CF uses executable directives to configure an internal table of ASN.1 types with complete information about each ASN.1 type: its structure, tag, tag kind, etc. Additionally, the table of types can be extended with more information: size of data value for type, reference to redefined encoder/decoder function, etc. The structure of the type table is very similar to syntactic structure of the source ASN.1 specification. All type declaration directives are executed when an appropriate ASN.1 module starts to use it. This is the only moment when the generated functions work. The rest of the functionality is provided by the CF.

The table below demonstrates an example of declaration directives for a simple ASN.1 sequence type. Note that the target language type definitions are generated separately and are not presented here.

Table 3

Declarative mapping for ASN.1 type definitions

ASN.1	Declarative style C (beautified by macros)

PersonalRecord::= SET{
  Name OPTIONAL,
  age [0] INTEGER,
  children[1] set of IA5STRING
}
	SET_TYPE_DEF(PersonalRecord)
	SEQUENCE_COMPONENT(TYPE_REF(Name),
	   OPTIONAL,Name,IS_REF)
	SEQUENCE_COMPONENT(
	   IMPLICIT_TAGGED_TYPE(
	     PRIVATE_TAG,0,TYPE_REF(INTEGER)),
	   PRESENT,age,IS_VAL)
	SEQUENCE_COMPONENT(
	   IMPLICIT_TAGGED_TYPE(
	     PRIVATE_TAG,1,
	
	IMPLICIT_SET_OF_TYPE(TYPE_REF(IA5STRING))),
	   PRESENT,children,IS_REF)
	END_SET_TYPE_DEF;

The CF contains two general-purpose functions for each encoding rule: *<Encoding rule>Encode* and *<Encoding rule>Decode*, where *<Encoding rule>* is *{BER, CER, DER etc}*. These functions have one additional parameter – a type identifier which is assigned when the ASN.1 type is initialized in the CF. The type identifier is used to find an appropriate record in the type table which contains the description of the corresponding type structure. When the type description is found, the function performs interpretation of the application data value (when encoding) or the encoded data value (when decoding). Encoding and decoding functions in the CF generally look like a switch statement factored by the encoded/decoded type. For example, a separate case label exists for all ASN.1 sequence types. The case contains a recursive call of the encoder/decoder for each component (from the list of components present in the type information for each ASN.1 sequence type). Coding functions from the CF :

- encapsulate the algorithm of encoding/decoding (i.e. the source and the target representation of data);
- determine the internal run-time representation of encoded data;
- perform memory allocation for the decoded data;
- perform error handling.

Traditionally, all this functionality is distributed through the generated encoder/decoder functions.

We emphasize the following advantages of using declarative mappings for generating service functions for ASN.1 data types.

1. **Flexibility**. Executable type declaration directives are used only to configure ASN.1 type representations. These directives are the only place, which contains information about the ASN.1 type structure (except for C declarations of ASN.1 types). The process of encoding and decoding of ASN.1 values (or any other operation with them) is driven by the type information, which is stored as data, not as functions. Such representation of the type information is much more flexible than the executable code because data can be changed dynamically. Below we list some manifestations of flexibility:

- Many encoding rules are defined in ASN.1 standards. Although quite different in some detail they are very similar to each other in general. Executable type declaration directives allow not to generate different encoders/decoders for different encoding rules. It is sufficient to have a single function to initialize the ASN.1 module and different variations of manually written encoder/decoder functions in the Coder Framework.

- There is a good opportunity for the dynamic configuring of ASN.1 types. All properties of an ASN.1 type can be modified if it is necessary. E.g. someone can override standard encoder and decoder functions for any ASN.1 type. There is a special opportunity in the CF, which allows to register user-supplied coders in the type table. Encode and decode functions check the user-supplied coders before they apply any default coding methods.

- Other service functions are very often generated for each ASN.1 type. Explicit run-time type information allows not to generate separate functions for each type. Printing functions, garbage collectors and other utilities can be implemented within the Coder Framework controlled by the type table.

- The Coder Framework together with the generated executable type declaration directives can be used for symbolic debugging of ASN.1 data types in terms of the source specification. All necessary information is available in the type table.

- The type table can be used to implement semantic consistency checking of ASN.1 values represented in the application-specific format.

- Actually, it is not absolutely necessary to attach the CF to a concrete representation of an ASN.1 data type in the application. The same CF and the same executable type declaration directives can work with different models of data if generic model of the ASN.1 data representation is applied and special interface functions are supplied. These interface functions translate data values from the generic representation to the application-specific representation of data. Interface functions should be provided by the application and should be stored in the type table in the same way as user-supplied coders.

2. **Readability**. Generated executable declarations of ASN.1 data types are very compact and quite readable. Executable declarations are structured in the same way as the source specification. Generated code does not contain any additional implementation details. To increase readability level even further macrodefinitions can be used. Thus the declarative mapping preserves the structure of the source specification.

3. **Ease of generator implementation**. Technically it is quite easy to write a generator of ASN.1 executable declaration directives, because declarations have exactly the same structure as the abstract syntax tree for the ASN.1 specification (which is the input for the generator).

4. **Efficiency**. Performance issues are very important in the area of telecommunication applications. They are discussed separately in section 4.

Alternative approaches to mapping for ASN.1 service functions can be considered. Some of them are quite different from the traditional function-oriented approach and also somewhat different from the approach discussed above. ASN.1 type declarations can be mapped to meta-data describing the types of the source language. Such meta-data can be represented in two basic ways:

- As binary data in any format in the generated file;

- As data definitions in the generated code in the implementation language.

The first approach is implemented in the SNACC compiler [4]. The type table (separate for each module) is generated by the SNACC ASN.1 Compiler and written to disk. Appropriate type declarations are generated as a C header file. When the application needs to deal with an ASN.1 module it loads the type table into memory and dynamically configures the type information. After that the table-driven encode, decode, print functions can be used to work with the data types defined in that module.

The second approach (which is a variation of the declarative mapping) is to generate a C implementation file containing only variable declarations. These declarations are intended to statically build the type table.

Both ways of type representation are very similar to what we suggested above. In all cases there is no need to generate any service functions for ASN.1 types. Generic functions are used instead and the run-time type representation is used to drive generic functions. The only difference is in the life time of the type table in memory. In our approach and in the case of loadable type information: from the moment when ASN.1 module is used first time until the moment when it becomes unnecessary. In the case of static variable declarations the type table lives throughout the lifetime of the program.

We have chosen dynamic executable declarations for ASN.1 types for the following reasons:

- Compared to a binary type table on disk, generated executable declarations are more readable and easier to check and even to modify.
- Compared to a static type table, our approach is more flexible because the type table is built in dynamic memory, it can be dynamically destroyed and modified.

4. MEASUREMENTS OF GENERATED CODE

This section discusses the quality of the generated programs emphasizing performance characteristics, the size of the executable program and memory usage. Readability of the generated programs is also discussed.

4.1. FSM dispatching

Let's consider performance characteristics of SDL systems. The key mechanisms in SDL implementation are process scheduling, FSM dispatching and communication handling. Let's evaluate different implementations of FSM dispatching.

As it was outlined in example mappings for the toy FSM language (section 2), there are two alternatives to implement FSM dispatching: double switching (one – by state, one – by signal) and table-driven dispatching. The first approach is typical for imperative mappings. Table-driven dispatching is well suited for declarative mappings because the table of transitions is initialized dynamically at start-up time and is used at run-time.

We compared three implementations of FSM: 1) double switching, 2) transition table with addresses of functions implementing transitions and 3) transition table with jump addresses of transitions. The third implementation of FSM dispatching is described in [1]. This method uses the standard C library of non-local control passing <setjmp.h> to store addresses of transitions in the table. All transitions of the FSM are located in a single function.

Table 4 summarizes execution speed, size of the object file and memory usage for all three implementations of FSM. Compilation of programs was done using of GNU C++ 2.7.2 compiler. SUN ULTRASPARC-1 (147MHz) machine with Solaris 2.6 was used as the run-time platform for measurements. Two FSMs were used for measurements: one with 10 states and 10 transitions in each state and another one with 40 states in 40 transitions in each state. One million of transitions was performed by each FSM.

Table 4

Comparison of FSM implementations

Implementation method	Execution time (seconds)		Object file size (bytes)		Memory usage (bytes)	
FSM size	10x10	40x40	10x10	40x40	10x10	40x40
Double switching	0.194	0.195	12008	159728	8	8
Table of function addresses	0.118	0.119	19764	303336	412	1612
Table of jump addresses	0.838	0.841	37068	565908	5218	83212

The use of function addresses results in the fastest code. It is 64% faster than double switching because control is passed via direct addressing which is more effective than double switch statements. Non-local control passing is less effective since each long jump restores all register values (it is enough to restore address counter and stack pointer). For the above reasons the transition table for jump addresses requires more memory.

The object file size is 64%-89% shorter for double switch implementation. This is because table-initializing statements also require some start-up code and each transition is implemented as a separate function. In table-driven implementations the memory is used for storing transition tables.

4.2. ASN.1 coders

Declarative approach to generation of encoding and decoding functions from ASN.1 specifications (Section 3) was compared with traditional imperative mapping implemented in the SNACC compiler. We used a simple ASN.1 specification consisting of :

- one *choice* type,
- one *sequence* with two components,
- two *set*s with six and three components respectively,
- one *set of* type,
- eight *tagged* types.

IA5String type with average string length of eight symbols was used to store string information.

Table 5 summarizes different characteristics of the generated code: execution speed of encoding/decoding (10000 repetitions of encoding/decoding for a given type), size of object file for the generated coders, usage of memory and readability metrics [1]. The object file size is taken instead of the full executable size because the support library (which is always linked) has fixed size while the volume of coders depends on the size of an ASN.1 specification. Readability metrics E (coefficient of generated text expansion compared to source), F (average fragmentation of mapping for source constructs) and U (expansion of source names usage in the generated program comparing to source) are defined in [1].

Table 5

Comparison of mappings for ASN.1 coders

Implementation	Execution time (milliseconds)	Object file size (bytes)	Memory usage (bytes)	Readability		
				E	F	U
Declarative mapping	54	5164	920	1.9	3	1.8
SNACC	45	20244	0	25.3	2	11.8

Conditions for measurements are the same as for FSM dispatching (section 4.2).
Speed degradation (20%) in our implementation is predictable since a general function for all ASN.1 types is used instead of a specialized coder for each ASN.1 type. This degradation becomes smaller when longer string values are coded. At the same time object file size in our implementation is significantly smaller (approximately **4 times**). Dynamic memory is used by declarative mapping to store the ASN.1 type table. Readability metrics demonstrate that declarative mapping for ASN.1 coders allows to dramatically reduce the volume of the generated program text (**13 times**) and makes it more suitable for inspections and maintenance.

5. DISCUSSION

This section summarizes advantages and limitations of declarative mappings.

5.1. Advantages of declarative approach

The major difference between imperative and declarative mappings can be summarized by the phrase: **"what** instead of **how"**. Imperative mappings generate statements which exactly specify *how* the code should work, which data structures and algorithms should be applied. Within the declarative approach to mapping the generated code specifies *what* is the structure of specification while decisions about the data structures and algorithms are postponed until the start-up time. Declarative approach to code generation requires start-up initialization. Start-up procedures are usually not necessary when an imperative mapping is used.

Readability

Declarative mapping omits most of the low-level details of system execution. Those details are transferred into the support system. This is the major reason why programs mapped in a declarative manner are more readable and compact. At the same time declarative mapping preserves the source structure of the specification in the automatically generated implementation. Compactness and readability of generated programs makes it easier to inspect them by the people who are familiar with the source specification but not familiar with implementation details. Debugging and maintenance of generated systems is also simplified when generated program is compact and preserves source specification structure. Compactness of generated programs is an important factor for volume-critical real-time and embedded applications.

The next major advantage is that the generated code within the declarative approach is more *universal*. Below we list different aspects of universality.

Configurability

Most implementation details are hidden within the support system. Generated program has a clear interface with the run-time support system: at the beginning it sends information about its own structure to the support system and then the support system calls the appropriate generated functions (methods). More control is moved into the support system which means that the same generated code can be configured to work with different implementations, on different target platforms, in different run-time configurations. The generated program, e.g. for an SDL specification, can be easily configured to work as a stand-alone application under a real-time operating system or to be managed by a simulator or a validator. The appearance of the generated code in all these cases remains the same.

Another interesting feature is the possibility to dynamically change the configuration of the running system. Basically, executable declarations of the generated system perform at the start-up time before the real execution starts. It is possible to change some parameters of the system at run-time without regenerating, recompiling and reloading the system. E.g. for the toy language suggested above it is possible to dynamically extend FSM and change reactions on signals.

Integration with legacy

Declarative mappings bring advantages in integrating generated programs with legacy code or existing libraries. There are two possibilities:
1) Manual integration when the generated code is adjusted to work together with the external code. This is much easier within suggested approach since the generated program is more readable and compact and it is easier to inspect and understand it.
2) Integration when the generated code is not modified.
   Declarative mapping allows to integrate external code with the generated program via the support system. The support system in this case looks like an application framework. The rest of the code (generated or hand-written) is connected to this framework. The control flow usually comes from the framework to the generated code (framework is primary). Details of the implementation are not hard-coded in the generated program. Instead they can be defined in external libraries.
   Declaratively generated code can be easily embedded into existing applications. E.g. for the toy example language described in section 3.1 the declarative mapping makes it possible to change FSM dispatching, to launch more FSMs, etc. The major prerequisite is that control comes from the support system to the generated code. Imperative mapping for some languages is not so flexible.

Symbolic debugging and verification

Within the declarative mapping a generated program contains full information about its structure during the execution time. This information is primarily used by the support framework. At the same time the internal representation of the running system can be used for the purpose of debugging because it has the same structure as the source specification. Source level debugging can be organized on top of the internal representation. Availability of the internal representation at run-time allows to mix static analysis (which is usually build around an abstract syntax tree of the specification) with dynamic analysis (which is embedded into the executing system). E.g. internal representation brings additional opportunities for verification and testing of the specification.

Simplicity of mapping design

It is easier to develop declarative mappings than imperative mappings. Declarative executable statements replace complex data structures (type definitions and data definitions). For most of implementation-oriented programming languages it is better to map a construct into an executable operator (function call) than to generate data structures because:
- syntactically function call is more flexible than a data definition;
- time of invocation is under control;
- function call has dynamic nature (parameters are dynamically computed);
- functionality is encapsulated while type definitions and data initializations can not be encapsulated.

Another aspect simplifying the development of declarative mappings is that the mapping design is divided into three more or less independent activities:
1) design of the target language representation for each source construct;
2) design of the internal representation for the generated program (type definitions);
3) design of support system functions.

Within imperative mappings activities 1) and 2) are very much interrelated since the internal representation appears in the generated program. The mixture of activities requires additional development time.

One more positive aspect of declarative mappings is that they assume direct support for most of source language constructs. There is no need to implement complex transformation algorithms inside the translator. The structure of the code generator is quite simple: it just makes few traverses of the abstract syntax tree. The code generator requires a minimum of semantic information.

5.2. Limitations

There are a few limitations of declarative mappings. The limitations are described below.
- Declarative mappings allow representation of semantically distant constructs which have no direct counterpart in the implementation language. But in case when a construct of the source language more or less directly corresponds to *executable statements* of the target language the declarative mapping does not always bring any advantages. E.g. there is not much advantage to map SDL transitions in declarative style. There exists direct correspondence between transition actions and target language executable statements. It seems that the best way is to mix declarative and imperative approaches depending on the source language construct.
- The start-up phase of the system execution requires extra time and certain memory resources (executable code, dynamic memory). As it was demonstrated in section 4 this overhead is not very big and brings reduction of the size of the executable file. But when the generated system is invoked frequently and works for a short period of time the start-up overhead can become critical. Another issue is the volume of the run-time support system. Declarative mapping requires more functionality of the support system so its volume grows. When the generated system is rather small, the part of the support system

(which is always constant) is rather large and brings overall growth of the size of the executable code.

- Declarative mapping style makes the generated code more flexible and readable, simplifies integration with external code, debugging and maintenance. But probably it is not always necessary to have such great opportunities. It is not reasonable to apply declarative mappings for constructing highly specialized or highly optimized systems with extreme requirements on speed and memory usage. The situation with the application of the declarative style in code generation is in some way similar to migration from programming in assembly language to high-level programming languages. This migration resulted in some performance degradation and expansion of executables but the efficiency of the software development process has increased.

6. CONCLUSION

We have introduced the concept of declarative mappings between a specification and an implementation. Applications of declarative mappings were demonstrated for standard telecommunications languages SDL and ASN.1. Declarative mappings represent an attempt to increase the semantic level of the generated code, its readability and usability. The basic characteristic of declarative mappings is the presence of the start-up phase. Start-up phase is used to separate decisions regarding the appearance of the generated program from decisions regarding the internal structures of the implementation. This brings the following benefits:

- clearly understandable generated code;
- more opportunities to change the underlying support system;
- easy integration of the generated code into existing manually written applications;
- code generator becomes more simple and thus can be developed faster.

Advantages of the declarative style of code generation are very much similar to requirements for code generation described in [5]. Interfacing with legacy, customization, readability, portability, trace facilities are very important for successful usage of generated code and can be achieved using declarative mappings.

Our measurements of the generated code demonstrate the following:

- There is almost no performance degradation compared to examples of code generated with imperative mapping.
- Executable code size is some cases grows (additional start-up executable statements), in some case decreases (functionality is transferred to support system) but in general there is no tendency to expansion of executable.
- Memory usage grows because the internal run-time system representation is always in memory.

We believe that the use of declarative approach to mapping from specification languages can stimulate wider introduction of automatic code generation into industrial software product development.

7. ACKNOWLEDGEMENTS

This research is partly supported by SDL Forum Society grant and by RFBR grant 97-01-00494. We would also thank to Tord Andreasson and Federico Engler from Telelogic AB (Sweden) for supporting our research.

REFERENCES

[1]   N. Mansurov, A.Ragozin, "Generating readable programs from SDL" in SAM98 Workshop, June 29-July 1,1998, Berlin, pp.151-160.

[2]   N. Mansurov, A. Kalinov, A. Ragozin, A. Chernov, "Design Issues of RASTA SDL-92 Translator", in R. Braek, A. Sarma (Eds.) SDL'95 with MSC in CASE, Proc. of the 7-th SDL Forum, Oslo, Norway, 6-29 September, 1995, Elsevier Science Publishers B. V. (North-Holland), pp. 165—174.

[3]   N. Mansurov, A. Ragozin, A. Chernov, "Industrial strength code generation from SDL", in A. Cavalli, A. Sarma (Eds.) SDL'97: TIME FOR TESTING – SDL, MSC and Trends, Proc. Of the 8-th SDL Forum, Evry, France, 23-26 September, 1997, , Elsevier Science Publishers B. V. (North-Holland), pp. 415—430.

[4]   M. Sample, "SNACC 1.1: A High Performance ASN.1 to C/C++ Compiler", University of British Columbia, Canada, July 1993.

[5]   Rajit Singh, Jerry Serviss, "Code generation using GEODE: A CASE Study", in A. Cavalli, A. Sarma (Eds.) SDL'97: TIME FOR TESTING – SDL, MSC and Trends, Proc. of the 8-th SDL Forum, Evry, France, 23-26 September, 1997, Elsevier Science Publishers B. V. (North-Holland), pp. 539-550.

[6]   CCITT, CCITT Specification and Description Language (SDL), Recommendation Z.100, 1992 .

[7]   ISO/IEC 8824: Specification of Abstract Syntax Notation One (ASN.1) (1989).

[8]   ISO/IEC 8825, Specification of Basic Encoding Rules for ASN.1 (1989).

[9]   J. Fischer et. al. , A Run Time Library for the Simulation of SDL'92 Specifications., Proc. of the 6-th SDL Forum.

[10]   R. Braek, O. Haugen, "Engineering Real-Time Systems", Prentice-Hall BCS Practitioner Series, 1993.

Session VIII

Metric

SDL'99 : The Next Millennium
R. Dssouli, G.v. Bochmann and Y. Lahav, editors
©1999 Elsevier Science B.V. All rights reserved

Using Design Metrics to Identify Error-Prone Components of SDL Designs*

W. M. Zage, D. M. Zage, J. M. McGrew and N. Sood

Department of Computer Science, Ball State University
Muncie, IN 47306-0450
USA

The goal of our design metrics research is to support the design process of software development by providing validated metrics that can be used to highlight error-prone components in a software design and to determine overall design quality. We have developed a metrics approach for analyzing software designs that helps designers engineer quality into the design product. Two of the design metrics developed are an external design metric, D_e, that focuses on a module's external relationships to other modules in the software system, and an internal design metric, D_i, that incorporates factors related to a module's internal structure. Over a nine-year metrics evaluation and validation period, on study data consisting of university-based projects and large-scale industrial software, these design metrics consistently proved to be excellent predictors of error-prone modules.

This paper presents the results of a two-year study of SDL designs and error report data from Motorola Corporation. Our collaboration with Motorola was to develop an appropriate mapping from SDL artifacts to design metrics primitives that reflects the experience of industrial software developers, and that will then assist them in identifying error-prone components of their SDL designs. Once the mapping was completed, the design metrics D_e and D_i were computed on SDL designs of existing communications products. We then determined if the stress points identified by the metrics were those SDL components that were either identified by developers as difficult or were indeed error-prone as indicated by error reports produced at Motorola. The results indicate that design metrics can be applied to SDL models to identify error-prone components.

1 INTRODUCTION

This paper is a product of the research being conducted as part of the Software Engineering Research Center (SERC) project entitled Metrics Directed Verification of SDL Designs funded by Motorola Corporation. The goal of this project is to apply our proven

---

*This research was supported, in part, by a grant from the Software Engineering Research Center at Purdue University, a National Science Foundation Industry/University Cooperative Research Center (NSF Grant No. ECD-8913133).

design metrics technology to identify stress points in SDL designs, and assess the utility and effectiveness of our design metrics in identifying error-prone SDL components.

We present here the results of a two-year study of SDL designs and error report data from Motorola. The goal of the study has been to develop an appropriate mapping between design metrics primitives and SDL artifacts, that reflects the experience of industrial software developers, and that will then assist them in identifying error-prone components of their SDL designs. SDL designs of existing communications products at Motorola were analyzed using the design metrics, D_e and D_i, and this analysis was verified against actual error reports produced by the original testing teams at Motorola.

In what follows, we describe the mapping of the SDL artifacts to the primitive components of D_e and D_i and the subsequent refinement of the design metrics model as it applies to SDL designs. In a first study, we analyzed the effectiveness of our design metrics in pinpointing SDL components that were considered difficult by the SDL model developers. In a second study, we investigated the applicability of the design metrics in identifying error-prone modules. The data from these industrial SDL applications suggest that design metrics can be used by practitioners to make early design decisions and modifications.

2 THE DESIGN METRICS MODEL

The design metrics research team at Ball State University has developed a metrics approach for analyzing software designs that helps designers engineer quality into the design product. The primary objective is to employ these metrics to identify troublesome modules, or stress points, in the structure of the software. The software designer can then make changes in the software design that make the resulting product less error-prone as well as easier to understand and maintain.

We began analyzing software systems to determine if identifiable traits of error modules could be uncovered during design. Our selection criteria were that the metrics capturing such traits must be objective and automatable. As presented in [ZAGE90] and [ZAGE93], the first three design metrics developed were called D_e, D_i and $D(G)$. The external design metric D_e is defined as

$$D_e = e_1 * (inflows * outflows) + e_2 * (fan\text{-}in * fan\text{-}out)$$

where

inflows is the number of data entities passed to the module from superordinate or subordinate modules plus referenced external data entities,

outflows is the number of data entities passed from the module to superordinate or subordinate modules plus changed external data entities,

fan-in and fan-out are the number of superordinate and subordinate modules, respectively, directly connected to the given module, and

e_1 and e_2 are weighting factors.

The term *inflows* * *outflows* provides an indication of the amount of data flowing through the module. The term *fan-in* * *fan-out* captures the local architectural structure around a module since these factors are equivalent to the number of modules that are structurally above and below the given module. This product gives the number of invocation sequences through the module. D_e focuses on a module's external relationships to other modules in the software system.

The internal design metric D_i is defined as

$$D_i = i_1(CC) + i_2(DSM) + i_3(I/O)$$

where

CC, the Central Calls, is the total number of subordinate module invocations;

DSM, the Data Structure Manipulations, is the number of references to data entities of complex types that use indirect addressing;

I/O, the Input/Output, is the number of external device accesses,

and

i_1, i_2 and i_3 are weighting factors.

There were many candidates related to a module's internal structure to select from for incorporation into D_i. Our aim was to choose a small set of measures that would be easy to collect and would highlight error-prone modules. During the analyses of errors for the projects in our database, our research team identified three areas as the locations where the majority of errors occurred. These were at the point of a module invocation, in statements including complex data structure manipulations, and in input/output statements. Thus we selected three measures, CC, DSM and I/O to form the components of D_i.

$D(G)$ is a linear combination of the external design metric D_e and the internal design metric D_i and has the form

$$D(G) = D_e + D_i$$

The metrics D_e and D_i are designed to offer useful information during two different stages of software design. The calculation of D_e is based on information available during architectural design, whereas D_i is calculated when detailed design is completed. For examples showing the calculations of D_e, D_i and $D(G)$, see [LI97].

To corroborate the effectiveness of the metrics as predictors of error-proneness, the design metrics team reexamines the software when error reports are available to determine to what extent the stress-point modules were indeed error-prone. Over a nine-year metrics evaluation and validation period, on study data consisting of university-based projects and large-scale industrial software, our design metrics consistently outperformed classical, well-known metrics such as LOC, V(G), and information flow metrics, as predictors of error-prone modules [ZAGE93].

SDL is a standard language for the specification and description of systems. Its more recent versions contain object orientation, remote procedure calls and non-determinism [ELLS97]. SDL is used in the telecommunications area, as well as in other real-time, distributed and communicating systems to increase productivity, reduce errors and improve maintainability. Mappings from SDL to code have been developed [FLOC95]. One of our initial objectives in this research was to map SDL artifacts to design metrics primitives so that D_e and D_i can be computed for the components of SDL models.

3   IDENTIFYING THE FUNDAMENTAL SDL UNIT OF DE-SIGN AND CORRESPONDING DESIGN ARTIFACTS

Our research team members met with Motorola personnel at the Land Mobile Products site in Schaumburg, IL to obtain a sample SDL model. The document obtained describes the functionality of the SRS Horizon demonstration pager. A mapping of SDL artifacts to design metrics primitives was completed using the pager documentation.

In conventional procedural programming languages, such as C, the basic unit on which metrics are computed is the module or function/procedure unit. In SDL, the corresponding programming unit can be the system, a block, a process, a service, a state, an individual state transition or a procedure. For purposes of this report, we restrict the scope of the term *module* to refer to either an SDL state, state transition or procedure.

Our aim was to pinpoint the stress points in SDL designs in order to reduce the amount of effort needed to reexamine the resulting stress points while maximizing the benefit to the designer. However, the design metrics can also be calculated on higher levels of design abstraction (e.g., systems, blocks, processes, etc.) depending on the stage of development of the design.

The term *data entities passed* in SDL refers to procedure parameters, signals and signal parameters. By *external data entities* we mean variables and constants declared in an enclosing scope. A *superordinate module* can be a state transition which calls the current procedure or a state which initiates a transition to the current state. Similarly, the term *subordinate module* refers to a state (the nextstate of a transition), a procedure called within a state transition, or a process to which a signal is output.

4   MAPPING SDL ARTIFACTS TO DESIGN METRICS PRIMITIVES

To compute the design metrics D_e and D_i , we must count the metrics fan-in, fan-out, inflows, outflows, central calls, data structure manipulations and I/O. To accomplish these tasks for SDL, we have adopted the following conventions:

Fan-in for an SDL state (the current state) is the number of SDL states that transition to the current state. The fan-in for a state transition is the same as the fan-in for its originating state. For a procedure, the fan-in is the sum of the number of SDL state transitions and procedures that invoke it.

Fan-out for an SDL state is the sum of the number of states to which it can transition plus the number of procedures called. Fan-out for a state transition is the number of procedures called plus the number of nextstates to which it can transition. Fan-out for a procedure is the number of called procedures.

Inflows is the number of data entities passed to the module from superordinate and/or subordinate modules plus referenced external entities. For an SDL state, this includes the parameters of called procedures changed by the procedure called, referenced external data entities, return values from procedure calls and input signals received by the state. For a procedure, the input parameters of the procedure are also counted. This metric is a composite of primitive metrics according to the following formula:

$$
\begin{aligned}
\textit{Inflows} \;=\; & \textit{formal parameter list * adjusted fan-in (for procedures)} \\
+\; & \textit{arguments changed by subordinate modules} \\
+\; & \textit{returns from subordinate modules} \\
+\; & \textit{external data entities used} \\
+\; & \textit{input signals (for states) * adjusted fan-in (for states)}
\end{aligned}
$$

where *adjusted fan-in* $= max\{fan\text{-}in, 1\}$.

Formal Parameter List is the total number of parameters of the module. This applies only to procedures, since states and state transitions do not have parameters.

Arguments Changed by Subordinate Modules refers to the number of unique arguments passed to subordinate modules that are changed by those modules.

Returns from Subordinate Modules is the total number of return values from subordinate modules that are used in the current module.

External Data Entities Used is the total number of unique variables or synonyms used within a module but which are not declared within the scope of that module.

Input Signals for a module is the total number of input signals for which that module state has a nonempty action.

Outflows is the number of data entities passed from the module to superordinate and/or subordinate modules plus the number of changed external entities. This includes changed external data entities, changed formal parameters, arguments to subordinate modules, and returns to superordinate modules. It is a composite of primitive metrics according to the formula given below.

$$
\begin{aligned}
\textit{Outflows} \;=\; & \textit{changed formal parameters * adjusted fan-in (for procedures)} \\
+\; & \textit{sends return * adjusted fan-in (for procedures)} \\
+\; & \textit{subordinate module's argument list} \\
+\; & \textit{external data entities changed} \\
+\; & \textit{output signals (for states)}
\end{aligned}
$$

Changed Formal Parameters refers to the total number of those parameters counted in the input parameter list metric that were changed either by the module itself or by any of its subordinate modules.

Sends Returns has a value of 1 if the current module returns a value to a superordinate module. It is 0, otherwise. Notice that for SDL states, this value is always 0.

Subordinate Module's Argument List is the total number of arguments for each subordinate module.

External Data Entities Changed is the total number of unique changed variables not declared within the scope of the procedure or the state.

Output Signals is the number of distinct SDL signals which are ouput from a module.

Data Structure Manipulation is the total number of accesses or changes to the fields of a complex data structure. Examples of DSMs include: any modifications to a timer in SDL; an access of an element in an array; or a reference to a member of a structure.

Central Calls refers to the total number of procedure calls plus the number of state transitions. Multiple transitions to the same state are included in the count.

Input/Output is the number of input signals for which there are nonempty actions plus the number of output statements. Notice that this differs from the definition of *Input/Output* in the basic metrics model, which refers only to external device accesses. However, signals in SDL can be used to pass messages to the environment (e.g., possibly some external I/O device) as well as for passing messages between components within a system.

5 VALIDATING THE DESIGN METRICS MODEL ON THE STUDY DATA

Having identified the mapping of SDL artifacts to the design metrics primitives, we collected the primitive values for each state transition and procedure in the pager model. The procedures were then ranked from highest to lowest by each of the metrics D_e, D_i and $D(G)$. A detailed analysis of this demonstration pager SDL model can be found in [ZAGE98].

The highest-ranking modules (typically the top 10–15%), based on the values of D_e, D_i and $D(G)$, are characterized as stress points by our design metrics. The next step was to determine if these stress points were (1) the difficult components, as identified by the SDL practitioners,   and   (2) the error-prone components, as determined through the

Table 1
Distribution of the Rated Pager Modules

Rating	Number of Modules
5	3
4	9
3	20
2	36
1	168
0	2

Table 2
Comparing Practitioners' Rankings and Metric Counts for Stress-Point Modules

Ranking	D_e		D_i		$D(G)$		NCNB		Fan-in		V(G)	
	#	%	#	%	#	%	#	%	#	%	#	%
5	3	100	3	100	3	100	3	100	0	0	2	67
4	6	67	6	67	6	67	7	78	1	11	6	67
3	11	55	11	55	11	55	11	55	9	45	7	35
2	9	25	9	25	9	25	10	28	4	11	11	31
1	3	2	3	2	3	2	1	1	18	11	6	4
0	0	0	0	0	0	0	0	0	0	0	0	0
5,4 or 3	20	63	20	63	20	63	21	66	10	31	15	47

evaluation of error reports obtained from Motorola. The developers of this SDL model determined a rating for each of the 238 pager modules ranging from 0 to 5, with 5 being the most difficult to implement. Although this rating scale was a subjective one, it was based on the experience of those most closely involved with the implementation of the modules. Table 1 provides the distribution of the ratings for the 238 pager modules.

Table 2 is a comparison of practitioners' rankings and metric counts for modules identified as stress points by the design metrics D_e, D_i, $D(G)$, as well as the metrics $NCNB$, Fan-in and $V(G)$ used for comparison purposes. We chose the top 13% of the modules (32 modules) in this study because the number of modules with the rating of 5, 4 or 3 totaled 32. Naturally, the best result would occur if all of the modules ranked 5, 4 or 3 were identified as stress points and no stress point modules were from those with difficulty levels 1 or 2.

As one can see from Table 2, all of the design metrics perform equally well in identifying 63% of the modules rated as difficult. Only NCNB performed slightly better. However,

Table 3
Classification Table Using D_i on Pager SDL Model

	Predicted		
Observed	*Easy*	*Difficult*	**Percent Correct**
Easy	169	35	82.8%
Difficult	5	27	84.4%
Overall			**83.1%**

if early identification of difficult modules is desired and can be performed, then D_e is the metric of choice.

We also performed statistical analyses of the metric data. To determine how well our metrics predicted the difficulty of these modules we grouped the modules with ratings of 1 or 2 into one category, called the "easy" modules, and those with ratings of 3, 4 or 5 into another category, called the "difficult" modules. A series of logistic regression on the metrics data was completed. The first test used only D_e and D_i, and the regression selected D_i as the more significant metric in predicting the level of difficulty of the modules, with D_e not adding any significant information to the analysis.

The results, summarized in Table 3, showed that D_i could predict easy modules 83% of the time and could predict difficult modules 84% of the time. Another observation from this analysis is that the probability of a module being easy was .97 when $D_i < 5$ and the probability of a module being difficult was .8 when $D_i > 19$. These ranges may be useful as a first pass when evaluating a module's difficulty level.

Our second test used all of the metrics gathered on the modules, excluding only $D(G)$. (See [ZAGE98].) A logistic regression on these data selected the following component metrics, in order of significance:

1. $NCNB$ (Number of non-comment/non-blank lines of code);

2. Comments (Number of lines within the module that contained comments);

3. Fan-out (Number of distinct modules called);

4. Calls (Number of actual calls to modules, not necessarily distinct modules); and

5. $V(G)$ (McCabe's cyclomatic complexity metric).

These combined to give the following formula for predicting the difficulty of a module:

$$M - 11.0497 = \log \frac{P}{1-P},$$

where

$$M = 1.7106 * (Fan\text{-}out) - 0.5117*(Calls)$$
$$+ 0.6436*NCNB + 1.1179*(Comments) - 0.7437*V(G),$$

and P is the probability that a given module is difficult. Thus the dividing line between difficult and easy modules is the value $M = 11.0497$.

In arriving at this result we used half of the modules chosen at random as training modules to produce the formula and then tested the formula on the other half of the modules. The prediction rate of the training modules is shown in Table 4. In Table 5 we see that for the testing set the formula gave us a better than 81% success rate in correctly predicting difficult modules and a better than 98% rate in correctly predicting easy modules.

Although this is an excellent logistic regression model, at least one of its underlying conditions is questionable. Notice that in the logistic regression equation, $V(G)$ has a negative multiplier, which implies that increased cyclomatic complexity decreases a module's chance of being classified as difficult. This model's predictive qualities have been tested on another SDL system, and the results are shown in the next section.

Table 4
Classification Table for the Training Set of Pager Modules

Observed	Predicted		
	Easy	*Difficult*	**Percent Correct**
Easy	95	1	98.96%
Difficult	1	20	95.29%
Overall			**98.29%**

Table 5
Classification Table for the Testing Set of Pager Modules

Observed	Predicted		
	Easy	*Difficult*	**Percent Correct**
Easy	104	2	98.11%
Difficult	2	9	81.58%
Overall			**96.58%**

6 VALIDATING THE METRICS MODELS ON THE PRODUCTION SDL STUDY DATA

Through our collaborative efforts with Motorola, we were able to obtain a second SDL model to review — a production SDL model consisting of over 48,000 *LOC* and 56 states, complete with error data documentation. We computed metrics primitives on the SDL states and procedures, mapped defect information back to its origin in the model, and reviewed the effort required to fix the defects. Our goal was to determine if stress points identified by our design metrics were indeed the SDL components that had high concentrations of errors. We also wanted to determine if the logistic regression model described in the previous section accurately identified error-prone modules.

To provide a comparable framework with the previous study, we will present the metrics analysis on SDL procedures. Since we are dealing with error-proneness in this section instead of practitioners' ratings of modules as easy or difficult, we categorized a module as *problematic* if it contained four or more errors, and categorized it as *simple* if it contained less than four errors. Placing the cutoff at four allowed us to select a number of problematic modules that was comparable to the number of difficult modules identified in the pager model. The complex metrics regression model derived from the SDL pager system was applied to these new data. In Table 6, we see that the regression model identified 100% of the problematic (difficult) modules correctly, but it also had developers looking at 94 false positives. The regression model success rate at identifying modules as problematic or simple was only 24%.

We now turn our attention to the applicability of the design metrics to identifying error-prone SDL components. As in previous studies, the modules with the top 13% of the design metric values for D_e and D_i were identified as the stress points. As shown in Table 7, the stress points determined by D_e identified 67% of the problematic modules while only giving 13 false positives. Overall, however, D_e correctly categorized 86% of the modules. Recall that when D_e was used to identify the most difficult modules as determined by developers of the pager model, it identified 63% of the difficult modules. However, in the regression analysis of the design metrics for the pager model, D_e was not selected as an important candidate, whereas the internal design metric D_i was significant. A conclusion that can be drawn from these data is that the difficulty rating by developers

Table 6
Regression Model Applied to the Production Study Data

Observed	Predicted		
	Simple	*Problematic*	*% Correct*
Simple	17	94	15.32%
Problematic	0	12	100%
Overall			**23.58%**

is concentrated on the internal complexity. Error-proneness is also affected by external complexity of a module (see Table 7), something that is not always clearly identifiable by the developer.

The results of a similar study using D_i are given in Table 8. Note that D_i alone identified 58% of the problematic modules with only 10 false positives and an overall correct identification rate of 88%.

Table 7
D_e as a Predictor of Simple/Problematic Modules in the Production Study Data

	Predicted		
Observed	Simple	Problematic	% Correct
Simple	98	13	88.29%
Problematic	4	8	66.67%
Overall			**86.18%**

Table 8
D_i as a Predictor of Simple/Problematic Modules in the Production Study Data

	Predicted		
Observed	Simple	Problematic	% Correct
Simple	101	10	90.99%
Problematic	5	7	58.33%
Overall			**87.80%**

Table 9
D_e and D_i as a Predictor of Simple/Problematic Modules in the Production Study
Data

	Predicted		
Observed	*Simple*	*Problematic*	*% Correct*
Simple	98	13	88.29%
Problematic	1	11	91.67%
Overall			**88.62%**

Table 9 demonstrates the effectiveness of using both D_e and D_i to identify error-prone modules. If a module is in the top 13% of either the D_e or D_i metric values it is considered problematic. This model produced a 92% success rate of selecting the problematic modules, with only 13 false positives. It also selects correctly 88% of the simple modules, giving the model an overall success rating of 89%.

7 CONCLUSIONS

It is well known that design and code inspections for each module can reduce the total number of errors in a system by as much as 70% [JONE78]. Applying the design metrics during design can have even more significant benefits. As seen here, stress points, as determined by the design metrics, contain 92% of the modules with high concentrations of errors detected in the system studied. Thus, the calculation of the design metrics is an efficient approach to determining error-prone components of a design. This information can be used to focus the inspections on the modules with the highest likelihood of error. Furthermore, the cost of incorporating design metrics into a systems development plan is minimal, whereas the potential benefits of reducing total errors can be substantial.

8 FUTURE DIRECTIONS

Future work will include the analysis of additional SDL models and supporting documentation to further validate the metrics models already developed. In addition, we plan to develop metrics guidelines to assist practitioners in making decisions on where testing effort should be focused in an SDL model.

References

[ELLS97]   Ellsberger, J., D. Hogrefe and A. Sarma, *SDL, Formal Object-oriented Language for Communicating Systems*, Prentice Hall Europe, 1997.

[FLOC95]   Floch, J., "Supporting Evolution and Maintenance by Using a Flexible Automatic Code Generator", *Proceedings of the International Conference on Software Engineering '95*, Seattle, WA, 1995.

[JONE78]   Jones, T.C., "Measuring Programming Quality and Productivity," *IBM Systems Journal*, 17, 1, 1978.

[LI97]   Li, J.J., E. Wong, W. Zage, and D.M. Zage, "Validation of Design Metrics on a Telecommunication Application", SERC Technical Report TR-171-P, April 1997.

[ZAGE90]   Zage, W.M. and D.M. Zage, "Relating Design Metrics to Software Quality: Some Empirical Results", SERC-TR-74-P, May 1990.

[ZAGE93]   Zage, W.M., D.M. Zage, "Evaluating Design Metrics on Large-Scale Software", *IEEE Software*, Vol. 10, No. 4, July 1993.

[ZAGE98]   W.M. Zage, D.M. Zage, J.M. McGrew, N. Sood, "Using Design Metrics to Identify Stress Points in SDL Designs", SERC Technical Report TR-176-P, March, 1998.

SDL'99 : The Next Millennium
R. Dssouli, G.v. Bochmann and Y. Lahav, editors

Application of SDL metric suite through development phases

Yury Chernov

ECI Telecom Ltd., Hasivim 30, Petah Tikva, 49133, Israel
e-mail: yury.chernov@ecitele.com

This paper presents a software metric suite which intends for formal estimation of the SDL design. The suite includes the tuple of metric characteristics applied through development cycle from requirements specification to detailed design phases. However the main challenge is to apply the SDL metric suite at early stages of design. This increases the quality of the software by means of measurement and improvement of the current design and a proper choice between candidate designs. Although the presented metric suite is based on SDL methodologically it might be applied to arbitrary real-time/embedded systems.

1. INTRODUCTION

Software measurement is an integral part of development process [5, 8]. It is used for:
- Prediction of development efforts
- Understanding what happening during development and maintenance
- Control of development processes
- Improvement of processes and products.

The well-known problem with software metrics is that majority of models are intended for measurement of completed code. Software specification and design metrics are less developed or, to be more exact, are less applicable. However only measurement at early development stages may actually stimulate design improvement.

Specification Description Language (SDL), being one of the formal description techniques, combines both specification and implementation features. It has proved to be an efficient technique for unambiguous software specification and design. SDL covers all stages of software design for event-driven systems [4]. It is a good basis for building a consistent metric suite for real-time software. However, to date, there are very few works and results related to formal specification metrics in general and SDL metrics in particular. We can just mention [2, 3, 7].

The present work introduces SDL-based metric suite and some aspects of its implementation. Measurement in the SDL software metric suite is performed along three dimensions:
- Development cycle
- Structural object
- Measured characteristic

Development cycle includes well-known software engineering design phases - requirement specification, high level design and detailed design. The SDL model building is mapped onto these phases according to existing methodologies [1]. One of the major objectives of the present work is to show how to measure a software design consequently through development phases. Development phase activities reflect actual state of a project rather than formal content of the related document.

Structural objects represent structural hierarchy of the SDL specification. The highest level is the system. It is composed of processes which can be considered as real-time tasks. Processes themselves are composed of states and transitions. Processes are grouped into blocks. Measurement of design characteristics of various SDL objects has two objectives. The first is improvement of their inner design. The second is enabling the calculation of some higher level metric indices as a composition of lower level characteristics. It should be mentioned that the same metric indices being applied at distinct hierarchical levels may have different interpretation and be calculated differently.

Characteristics included in the presented software metric suite actually measure various aspects of software complexity [12]. From the 1970s onwards, software complexity measurement has been developed intensively. However, most of obtained results have shown that no one metric is complete and representative enough to characterize the software complexity. Following the fundamental software metrics works [5, 10, 11] and taking into consideration the specifics of the real-time domain, basic SDL metrics were introduced [2]. In the present paper this set of metric indices is refined and software complexity is regarded actually as a multi-tuple characteristic based on these indices.

The present paper includes description of SDL metric suite regarding development phases, SDL objects and metric characteristics. Then two case studies are presented. They illustrate basic properties of the metric suite. Finally, major aspects of metric suite implementation are studied.

2. DEVELOPMENT CYCLE

Software requirements specification includes definition of functionality and required properties of product's software and formulation of its basic concepts. The requirements can be put by customers or might be arisen by the product environment. Some properties are general, while others are specific for the system. Functional requirements which define the product behavior are distinguished from non-functional ones which put constrains on the implementation. This phase mainly covers those aspects of the product that are relevant for its external representation and use.

In the SDL design this phase includes definition of major structural elements: blocks, processes, channels and signal routes. Signal interchange for both environment and inner communication is defined. However, refinement of signal parameters is not included at this phase. Building of processes and interactions between them actually defines functionality of individual processes. Definition of behavior aspects of SDL design (inner process structure) is deferred for later phases.

High level design includes description of basic behavior of the product and its functional parts, synchronization between individual functional parts and complete definition of the structure including its dynamic changing.

In the SDL specification states of individual processes and transitions from state to state are built, dynamically created processes are indicated and procedure signatures at all structural levels are defined. Process transition include mainly "informal text". However, decisions, loops and other logical structure are refined. Formalized are signal consumption and signal sending (including timers). Major data elements are defined. This includes data sorts, signal parameters, synonyms, timers and basic variables.

Detailed design phase includes refinement of behavior and data all over the system. Correspondingly the SDL design is refined. That is, processes and procedures are completely defined. "Informal text" is replaced by formal definitions. All necessary variables are added. From the software metrics point of view the finalized SDL code is developed at this phase.

SDL specification design through the system development phases is summarized in Table 1. This summary allows to better understand what and how can be measured during the product development and what elements of the SDL model are available at various development phases. Building of specific metric indices is based upon these elements.

Table 1
SDL Design through Development Phases

Elements of SDL model	Development phases		
	Specification Requirements	High Level Design	Detailed Design
Structure			
Blocks	+		
Processes	+		
Procedure signatures		+	
Dynamical creation of processes		+	
Communication			
Channels	+		
Signal routes	+		
Environment signals	+		
Inner signals	+		
Behavior			
Process states		+	
Transitions		+	+
Signal consumption		+	
Signal sending		+	
Procedure body			+
Data			
Data sorts and synonyms		+	
Environment signal parameters		+	
Inner signal parameters		+	
Timers		+	
Variables		+	+

3. DESIGN OBJECTS

The basic theoretical model of the SDL specification is built of communicating finite state machines. Typically state machines are presented by separate tasks or threads (SDL processes). Processes communicate by means of discrete messages - signals. This theoretical model is preserved for the metric suite. Following the SDL structural hierarchy we assume system as the highest-level object. The measurement at this level is relevant at all development phases. The SDL measurement does not include the block concept of SDL since the later practically does not influence functional and implementation aspects.

The next level includes the complexity of the processes themselves. Processes are composed of states and transitions. States consume incoming signals (including expired timers and remote procedure calls) and transitions send outgoing signals (including remote procedure calls). Some process characteristics can not be measured at the requirement phase, because there is still no relevant information. So the process-level metrics are relevant mainly for the high level and detailed designs.

The last level includes states and transitions themselves. While the state measurement is applicable at high level design, the transition measurement is applicable at this design phase only partly.

Besides inherent structural objects, functional services are introduced. Functional services represent the basic functions of the system defined at the software requirement specification. Metric indices related to functional services are estimated at all development phases.

4. METRIC INDICES

As was mentioned before metric characteristics reflect various aspects of complexity of the software under measurement. The metric suite includes the following six characteristics:
- Size
- Control complexity
- Data flow complexity
- Structural coupling
- Functional cohesion
- Performance

These metrics are known in the software practice. However, in the present work we address real-time systems. So our interpretation of the indices might differ from the traditional one. More than this, it may differ from object to object. In details this is described in the following parts of the article. Before detailed description of the metric suite two remarks should be given. Firstly, some of presented indices are rather trivial. Our aim is to present a complete suite rather than an elaborated research of specific characteristics. The second remark relates to the formulas for specific indices. The discussion about their basis and comparison of various alternatives is out of the scope of the present paper. Formulas are based upon the design characteristics that can be obtained at specific phases. They are empirical with mainly a common sense behind them.

Lets briefly describe six basic characteristics.

Size of the system is a statically measured attribute. The most popular size measure is the number of lines of code. Design size index for SDL reflects the number of various components included into specification (processes, signals, decisions or tasks). This index can be relevant not only for a system in whole, but for SDL blocks as well. Blocks compose a set of processes and typically represent sub-systems. Besides design size, an implementation size is defined. It is the size of the load file received after automatic code generation and compilation. This index is relevant for the system in whole and only at the detailed design phase.

Control complexity typically reflects algorithmic complexity. The traditional logic is that the more loops, jumps and selections a program contains the higher is its control flow complexity, because it is more complicated for understanding. This traditional interpretation is applicable only at the level of an individual transition. At the process and system level more important are the number and consequence of components (processes or states) involved in the processing of incoming signals. So the control flow complexity is actually the signal processing complexity.

Flow complexity reflects the data (signal parameters) circulation and processing. Flow complexity characterizes the intensity of processing of data incoming into a process from other processes and from the environment. There are two major results of this processing: process inner data updating and sending of outgoing signals with parameters. Our flow complexity relates to the later one. The concept of flow complexity differs form the well-known information flow complexity [6, 10], which mostly characterizes module coupling. However, the approach was inherited from mentioned works.

Structural coupling was defined as "the degree of interdependence between modules" [12]. It is usually an attribute of pairs of modules. We replace modules by SDL objects - processes, states and transition. This is relevant with the finite state machine concept. Structural coupling has two aspects. First one, intra-coupling, reflects the coupling between inner components of an analyzed object. The second aspect, inter-coupling, relates to the connectivity of the object with peer ones.

Functional cohesion reflects the extent to which individual components are involved in performance of the same function or task. In our context these tasks are represented by mentioned functional services and components are represented by processes, states and transitions.

Performance includes two indices: real-time required to perform individual functional services and the context switching index. The later can be received even at the high level design, when all interactions and protocols between processes are defined.

Table 2 shows which metric characteristics at what development phases are calculated. R denotes requirement specification phase, H - high level phase, D - detailed design phase. When an index is marked at an earlier phase and is not marked at a later phase, than it is not refined and the previously calculated value is accepted at the later phase. If an index is marked through consequent phases, than it is refined at a later phase.

Introduced indices are described below phase by phase. When certain index is omitted, this means that its model has not changed from the previous phase or that its estimation is not relevant yet. We focus mainly at the early phases and at the system level. Process, state and transition indices are described briefly.

Table 2
SDL Metric Characteristics

Metric Characteristics	System			Process			State			Transition			Functional Service		
	R	H	D	R	H	D	R	H	D	R	H	D	R	H	D
Size	x	x		x	x		x					x			
Control complexity	x	x		x	x		x				x				
Data complexity					x						x				
Structural coupling	x			x	x		x				x				
Functional cohesion	x			x									x		
Performance		x	x									x		x	x

4.1. Requirement phase

4.1.1. Size

At the requirement phase the SDL specification includes signals and processes with no inner structure defined. Design size is a function of both factors. Sensitivity of design size to the number of signals should be less than sensitivity to the number of processes, since typically there are much more signals than processes. The most intuitive expression which reflects this is a straightforward multiplication:

$$DS(y) = P(y) * M(y) \qquad (1)$$

where $DS(y)$ - design size of the system; $P(y)$ - number of processes in the system; $M(y)$ - total number of signals in the system. Expression (1) reflects linear dependency of $DS(y)$ upon $P(y)$ and $M(y)$. The linear model is very sensitive to variances of $P(y)$ and $M(y)$. This results, for instance, in inadequate difference between design size values for alternative architectures, when they preserve the same functionality and differ mainly in number of processes into which the system is broken. The second drawback is that systems with different basic size have equal variance when $P(y)$ or $M(y)$ vary. More relevant seems a non-linear model where the same delta to $P(y)$ or $M(y)$ tends to influence less with the growth of the system size. This can be defined as:

$$DS(y) = \log_2(P(y) * M(y)) \qquad (2)$$

An additional aspect here is whether all the signals including environment and inner ones should be considered or environment signals alone. We think the first alternative is preferable since it reflects the complexity of inner interactions between individual processes and this affects the actual size of the system.

Process size is expressed by the following formula:

$$DS(p_i) = \log_2(M(p_i)) \qquad (3)$$

where $DS(p_i)$ - design size of the i-th process, $M(p_i)$ - total number of incoming and outgoing signals of the i-th process.

4.1.2. Control complexity

The logic behind control complexity at this development phase is that the number of inter-process signals defined to support environment signals is bigger for systems with higher control complexity. In other words, if one environment input or output requires many interactions by means of inter-process signals, the control is more complicated. So, the control complexity index is given by:

$$CC(y) = 1 - M^E(y) / M(y) \tag{4}$$

where $CC(y)$ - control complexity of the system; $M^E(y)$ - number of environment signals. Formula (4) does not take into consideration the control complexity of processes. This results in higher values of the control complexity index for systems with "good architecture" (strong decoupling of functionality) over systems with "spaghetti" design. To improve this the following model is used:

$$CC(p_i) = M^I(p_i) * M^O(p_i) \tag{5}$$

where $CC(p_i)$ - control complexity of the i-th process; $M^I(p_i)$ and $M^O(p_i)$ correspondingly number of incoming signals and outgoing signals of the i-th process. It is supposed that there is always at least one incoming and one outgoing signal in a process.

Control complexity of the system is given by:

$$CC(y) = \sum_{i=1}^{P(y)} CC(p_i) / P(y) \tag{6}$$

where $P(y)$ - total number of processes in the system. This model still has the same drawback as the previous one, since "good architecture" typically includes switching functionality where incoming signals are plainly transferred to a proper target. According to (5) these processes will have high control complexity. However, this effect is strongly reduced. At lower level design the drawback will be fixed with inclusion of more adequate process control complexity expression. For a preliminary estimation at the requirement phase both models are good enough. In particular, we shall show this in our case studies.

4.1.3. Structural coupling

Structural intra-coupling at the system level relates to the connectivity between processes. This connectivity is represented by the signal interchange and dynamic creation of processes. However at the requirement phase dynamic creation is nor defined yet. So only the first component is included. Refined expression for coupling is (20). More important is the fact itself whether there is signal connection between two processes or not, rather than number of sent signals between these processes. Inter-coupling of the i-th process is presented by:

$$SC^{Inter}(p_i) = P^M(p_i) / P(y) \tag{7}$$

where $P^M(p_i)$ denotes number of processes with which th i-th process have signal interchange.

Structural intra-coupling of the system, $SC^{Intra}(y)$, is calculated as:

$$SC^{Intra}(y) = \sum_{i=1}^{P(y)} SC^{Inter}(p_i) / P(y) \tag{8}$$

Inter-coupling at the system level characterizes the interactions with the environment. This especially important for the portability of the system. Structural inter-coupling of the system, $SC^{Inter}(y)$, is defined as:

$$SC^{Inter}(y) = P^E(y) / P(y) \tag{9}$$

where $P^E(y)$ denotes number of processes that have signal interaction with the environment.

4.1.4. Functional cohesion

Functional cohesion is defined on the basis of functional services. Its value does not require refinements at the later development phases.

$$CH(y) = \sum_{j=1}^{F(y)} \lambda_j * P(f_j) / P(y) \tag{10}$$

where $CH(y)$ - functional cohesion of the system; $P(f_j)$ - number of processes involved in the j-th functional service; $F(y)$ - number of defined functional services; λ_j - weight (importance) of the j-th functional service. The sum of λ_j is equal one, so that functional cohesion varies from zero to one. Ratio $P(f_j) / P(y)$ actually defines cohesion of the j-th functional service.

Functional cohesion can be defined per process as well. It is calculated as:

$$CH(p_i) = F(p_i)/F(y) \tag{11}$$

where $F(p_i)$ is the number of functional services to which the i-th process is involved.

4.2. High level design phase

4.2.1. Size

At the high level design phase the size index can be defined for the system, processes and states. The state size of the j-th state in the i-th process, $DS(s_{ij})$, is calculated as:

$$DS(s_{ij}) = R(s_{ij}) * M^I(s_{ij}) \tag{12}$$

where $R(s_{ij})$ - number of transitions coming out of the state; $M^I(s_{ij})$ - number of signals consumed in the state.

The size index for the i-th process, $DS(p_i)$, is defined as followers:

$$DS(p_i) = M(p_i) * (S(p_i) + R(p_i)) \tag{13}$$

where $M(p_i)$ denotes number of signals of the i-th process; $S(p_i)$ - number of states in the i-th process; $R(p_i)$ - number of transitions in the i-th process. The second multiplier in (13) is actually the size of the process state machine graph, where states are nodes and transitions are arcs.

The system size is the sum of the process size indices:

$$DS(y) = \sum_{i=1}^{P(y)} DS(p_i) \tag{14}$$

4.2.2. Control complexity

At the high level design phase control complexity can be estimated for states, transitions, processes and system. Control complexity of a state reflects the complexity of states connectivity as a result of signal consumption. The more is the quantity of states which are connected to the current state by both outgoing (next states) and incoming (previous states) transitions the higher is its control complexity. When the incoming and outgoing connections are well decoupled the control complexity is lower. This logic is expressed by the following model:

$$CC(s_{ij}) = S^{N \cap P}(s_{ij}) / S^{N \cup P}(s_{ij}) \tag{15}$$

where $S^{N \cap P}(s_{ij})$ - number of states which belong to the intersection of the next state set with the previous state set; $S^{N \cup P}(s_{ij})$ - number of states which belong to the union of two sets.

Control complexity of an individual transition is based on the flowgraph concept [11]. The most popular flowgraph-oriented metric is McCabe cyclomatic complexity[5]. It is calculated as $e - n + 2$, where e denotes number of arcs of a flowgraph and n - number of its nodes. Arcs are linear sequences of operators. For SDL this includes task, consumption, sending, save and procedure call. Nodes are points of branching - SDL decisions. McCabe cyclomatic complexity measures how close is the program graph to a tree-like structure. For pure trees cyclomatic complexity equals one. When cyclomatic complexity exceeds ten it is commonly to confirmed that the program might be problematic. Standard McCabe measurement does not seem appropriate for the SDL metrics because its value is unlimited and linearly depends upon number of arcs and nodes. So, for instance, addition of one arc increases the complexity value by one for both small and large flowgraphs. Actually large flowgraph should be less sensitive.

Lets represent transition as a set of logical branches. Each branch is a linear sequence of operators from the input state to the next state. Each decision is expanded into additional logical branches. Different branches typically have common parts of SDL code. Each branch has a target state which is one of the next states of the transition. Our logic is that control complexity is higher when more branches have the same target state, and control complexity is lower when each branch ends at individual target state. This is expressed in the following formula:

$$CC(r_{ik}) = 1 - S^T(r_{ik}) / B(r_{ik}) \tag{16}$$

where $CC(r_{ik})$ - control complexity of the k-th transition of the i-th process; $S^T(r_{ik})$ - number of target states; $B(r_{ik})$ - number of logical branches.

Model (16) actually expresses the idea identical to McCabe cyclomatic complexity. For tree-like transitions expanded to logical branches $S^T(r_{ik}) = B(r_{ik})$ and $CC(r_{ik}) = 0$.

Process control complexity is a function of both number of signals and complexity of processing of these signal. The first component is expressed by (5), the second one is the mean state and transition complexity. The later is the sum of the mean state complexity and the mean transition complexity divided by two to preserve its normalized form. So, the final model is given by:

$$CC(p_i) = 0.5 * (M^I(p_i) * M^O(p_i)) * (\sum_j CC(s_{ij})/ S(p_i) + \sum_k CC(r_{ik}) / R(p_i)) \qquad (17)$$

Control complexity of the system is calculated by (6).

4.2.3. Data flow complexity
Data flow complexity is relevant for transitions and processes. Lets define the size of a signal as the summary number of elementary fields of all parameters of this signal. Elementary fields are obtained by expansion of more complex types to the level of SDL predefined types. Lets denote the size of signal m_ξ by $SZ(m_\xi)$. Data complexity for the i-th process is calculated as:

$$DC(p_i) = \sum_\xi SZ(m_\xi) * \sum_\eta SZ(m_\eta) \qquad (18)$$

where ξ runs over all incoming $M^I(p_i)$ and η runs over all outgoing $M^O(p_i)$ signals of the i-th process.

At transition level we have an expression similar to (18) which involves incoming and outgoing signals of a measured transition.

4.2.4. Structural coupling
State coupling is expressed by ratio of the number of states to which or from which transitions exist to the total number of states in the i-th process:

$$CP(s_{ij}) = S^{N \cup P}(s_{ij}) / S(p_i) \qquad (19)$$

Transition coupling does not make sense.

Inter-coupling of a process is calculated by means of refined formula (7). Now it includes dynamic process creation coupling as well. The expression looks as followers:

$$SC^{Inter}(p_i) = (\alpha * P^M(p_i) + (1-\alpha) * P^C(p_i)) / P(y) \qquad (20)$$

where $P^M(p_i)$ and $P^C(p_i)$ correspondingly number of processes with which th i-th process have signal interchange and which are dynamically created from it; α - weight of the signal coupling over creation coupling ($0 \leq \alpha \leq 1$), defined expertly.

Process intra-coupling is a mean state coupling:

$$CP^{Intra}(p_i) = \sum_j CP(s_{ij}) / S(p_i) \qquad (21)$$

4.2.5. Performance
The context switching index reflects the number of times the control is being transferred from one process to another during performance of a specific functional service. The system context switching is a weighted sum of functional service values:

$$CS(y) = \left(\sum_{j=1}^{F(y)} \lambda_j * CS(f_j)\right) / F(y) \tag{22}$$

where $CS(f_j)$ denotes the context switching index of the j-th functional service.

The context switching index can be calculated at the requirement phase as well. However at the high level design phase with defined states and signal consumption it can be calculated automatically in the simulation mode.

4.3. Detailed Level Design

4.3.1. Size

Transition size is estimated at this phase as number of SDL operators included in the transition. This is a code-oriented characteristic similar to the lines of code. Correspondingly process size can be represented as the number of SDL operators. It does not equal to a summary transition length, since various transitions may have the same parts accessed by means of "goto". However the previously defined expression for process size (13) seems to be more informative.

At the detailed design phase the code size is obtained after code generation and compilation.

4.3.2. Performance

The generated code is used to estimate the real-time required for various functional services. This can be obtained on a target or in a host environment. The performance real-time index is calculated as weighted through functional services:

$$RT(y) = \sum_{j=1}^{F(y)} \lambda_j * RT(f_j) / P(y) \tag{23}$$

5. CASE STUDIES

We consider two case studies. The major objective is to show that the SDL metric suite can be consistent through development phases. That is, indices which were calculated at the earlier stages and are refined later basically preserve their ranking. For instance, the scaling of processes by control complexity calculated at the specification phase preserves after refinement at the high level design. This means that estimations at the requirement phase are good enough and can be used for design decisions. It is clear that the earlier we can make design decisions the more efforts can be saved.

The first case study is a protocol converter card. The card stands between a public switch and a local exchange. The interface to the public switch is a standard channel associating signaling (CAS) protocol. The local exchange interacts by several proprietary protocols. The function of the converter card is to translate to both sides incoming control signals. Besides its direct function the card also receive some maintenance commands from the control device, reports about major events and performs periodic testing.

The second case study is a session server of a broadband ATM multiplexer for high-quality TV telecommunications services. The system allows switched subscriber-to-subscriber communication. The session server is responsible for validation of available resources and for managing of individual sessions.

Table 3
Case Studies. Basic Characteristics

Project	Process		Project Characteristics				
		States	Transitions	Incoming Signals	Outgoing Signals	Process Creation	Process Commu-nication
Protocol	PH_Ctrl	1	8	7	7	3	7
Converter	PH_C_Intr	1	8	8	9	0	3
	PH_P_Intc	1	6	6	6	0	3
	PH_Chnl	9	17	19	15	0	4
	MMI_Ctrl	1	7	7	6	0	2
	Mtc_Ctrl	2	5	4	5	0	3
	Tst_Ctrl	2	6	4	2	1	2
	Tst_Perf	1	3	2	3	0	3
Session	Server	4	23	35	25	2	8
Server	Sess_Srv	19	67	30	31	0	7
	Mon_Srv	1	1	10	10	0	6
	Srv_Ctrl	1	3	12	12	1	6
	Srv_Hndlr	5	10	16	16	0	6
	Conn_Ctrl	4	16	28	33	2	7
	Sess_Conn	1	18	27	29	0	5
	Mng_Conn	1	1	1	1	0	1
	Bisdn_Sig	5	19	26	19	0	2

Table 4
Case Studies. Metric Indices

Case Study	Process/System	Metric Indices					
		Size		Complexity		Coupling	
		R	H	R	H	R	H
Protocol	System	8.92	50.76	65.75	11.80	0.86	0.35
Converter	Process PH_Ctrl	3.79	6.96	49.0	12.25	0.88	0.78
	Process PH_C_Intr	4.07	7.24	72.0	21.60	0.38	0.30
	Process PH_P_Intc	3.57	6.38	36.0	10.44	0.38	0.30
	Process PH_Chnl	5.07	9.77	285.0	25.65	0.50	0.40
	Process MMI_Ctrl	3.69	4.56	42.0	15.96	0.25	0.20
	Process Mtc_Ctrl	3.17	5.97	20.0	5.00	0.38	0.30
	Process Tst_Ctrl	2.58	5.57	8.0	2.00	0.25	0.23
	Process Tst_Perf	2.31	4.31	6.0	1.50	0.38	0.30
Session	System	11.27	76.18	500.8	206.0	0.59	0.44
Server	Process Server	5.90	10.66	875.0	271.3	0.89	0.68
	Process Sess_Srv	5.93	12.35	930.0	176.7	0.78	0.56
	Process Mon_Srv	4.32	5.32	100.0	50.0	0.67	0.48
	Process Srv_Ctrl	4.58	6.58	144.0	136.8	0.67	0.50
	Process Srv_Hndlr	5.00	8.90	256.0	117.8	0.67	0.48
	Process Conn_Ctrl	5.93	10.25	924.0	323.4	0.78	0.60
	Process Sess_Conn	5.80	10.05	783.0	540.3	0.56	0.40
	Process Mng_Conn	1.00	2.00	1.0	0.5	0.11	0.08
	Process Bisdn_Sig	5.49	10.07	494.3	237.1	0.22	0.16

Both case studies are taken from industrial projects developed with SDT tool from Telelogic. Basic characteristics of both case studies are presented in Table 3.

Calculated SDL metric for both case studies are presented in Table 4. We have chosen a subset of metrics space, which include the size, control complexity and structural coupling indices for the process and system level. The indices cover the requirement specification (R) and high level design (H) phases.

The major objective of the case studies is to show that indices calculated at the requirement specification phase are rather reliable for the analysis of the design. The basic relations between index values are preserved at the later phases. To better illustrate this two graphics were built. Figure 1 presents the protocol converter case study, Figure 2 - the session server case study. The graphs contain three groups of charts. The first group reflect the size index, the second - control complexity and the third - coupling. Size and control complexity are included in a normalized form.

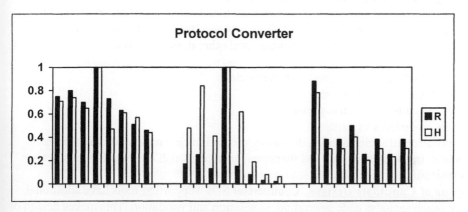

Figure 1. Protocol Converter. Metric Indices.

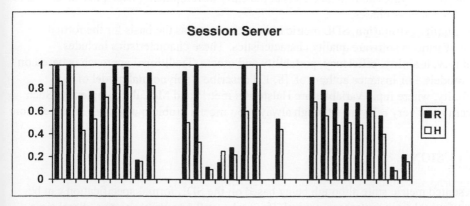

Figure 2. Session Server. Metric Indices

It can be seen that by exception of three processes in the second case study's control complexity all indices clearly preserve proportions.

6. IMPLEMENTATION OF METRIC SUITE

The principle objective of the SDL metric suite is to improve design quality through the lifecycle of developing software. Software quality has various aspects. Below we address some of them where SDL metric indices are especially appropriate.

Measurement. The SDL metric suite allows the measurement of a project in order to predict some very important characteristics. Among them are:
- development, testing and maintenance efforts;
- reliability of the software;
- portability and ease of implementation in various environments.

Improvement. The SDL metric suite being applied at various development phases allows to improve the design. The improvement relates both to the macro structure (breaking of system into processes and building of interactions between them) and to the micro design aspects. The later includes inner process structure and other design decisions. Some examples are listed below:
- additional signals vs. signal with parameters;
- additional intermediate states;
- remote calls vs. specific signals;
- new procedures vs. cloning.

Besides evaluation of various design decisions, metric indices can identify fault-prone processes, states, transitions, signals and functional services which can be problematic when testing and maintaining the product.

Comparison of Candidate Designs. Commercial SDL supporting tools have additional functionality which includes code generation, simulation and validation. This makes design of several candidate alternatives feasible even under the pressure of industrial development cycles with their time-to-market restrictions. Each alternative can be quickly built, tested and loaded into a target. SDL metric suite allows to formally compare them and to choose the best one. This process requires additional efforts at the early development phases, but saves lots of efforts and time at later phases.

Formal quality estimation. SDL metric indices can serve as the basis for the formal calculation of various software quality characteristics. These characteristics includes maintainability, usability, efficiency, portability and others. Traditional approach is based on statistical models. For instance authors of [8, 13] describe a polynomial model of maintainability, where input variables are Halstead's metric and McCabe complexity. Such models seem to be very relevant although always you meet a problem of proper interpretation.

7. CONCLUSION

The presented metric suite although being based on the SDL formal specification can be appropriate for real-time systems in general. If we take well-known properties of real-time

Table 5
Measurement of Real-time Software Properties

Metric Characteristics	Real-time Software Properties				
	Reactiveness	Timeliness	Concurrency	Dyn. Structure	Distribution
Size					+
Control	+				
Complexity					
Coupling				+	
Cohesion			+		+
Flow Complexity	+				
Performance		+	+		

software [9], we can see that they are reflected by presented metric characteristics. These relations are shown in Table 5.

REFERENCES

1. Brak, R., Haugen, O. Engineering Real Time Systems. Prentice Hall, 1993.
2. Chernov, Y., Lahav, Y. Basics for the SDL metrics. Proc. of the 1st Workshop of the SDL Forum Society on SDL and MSC, Berlin, 1998, 221-230.
3. Chernov, Y., Lahav, Y., Kahana, A. Evaluation of Software Quality of Event-driven Systems at Early Development Stages. Proc. of the Twelfth International Conference of The Israel Society for Quality, Jerusalem, 1998.
4. Ellsberger, J., Hogrefe, D., Sarma, A. SDL. Formal Object-oriented Language for Communicating Systems. Prentice Hall, 1997.
5. Fenton, N.E., Pfleeger, S.L. Software Metrics, A rigorous and Practical Approach. PWS, 1997.
6. Henry S., Kafure, D. Software Structure Metrics based on Information flow. IEEE Transactions on Software Engineering, SE-7(5) (1981) 510-518.
7. Huang,. S.J., Lai, R. On measuring the complexity of an Estelle specification. Journal Systems and Software, 40 (1998) 165-181.
8. Oman, P., Hagemeister, J. Constructing and Testing of Polynomials Predicting Software Maintainability. Journal of Systems and Software, vol. 24(3), March (1994) 251-266.
9. Selic, B., Gullekson, G., Ward, P. Real-Time Object-Oriented Modeling. John Willey & Sons, 1994.
10. Shepperd, M. Foundations of Software Measurement. Prentice Hall, 1995.
11. Shepperd, M., Ince, D. Derivation and Validation of Software Metrics. Clarendon Press, Oxford, 1993.
12. Yourdan, E., Constantine, L.L.: Structured Design. Prentice Hall, 1979.
13. Zhuo, F., et al., Constructing and testing software maintainability assessment models. Proc. Of the First International Software Metrics Symposium, IEEE Computer Society Press, 1993, pp. 61-70.

Session IX

Applications II

SDL'99 : The Next Millennium
R. Dssouli, G.v. Bochmann and Y. Lahav, editors
©1999 Elsevier Science B.V. All rights reserved

Dynamic scenario-based approach to re-engineering of legacy telecommunication software[1]

N. Mansurov[a] **and R. Probert**[b]

[a]Department of CASE tools, Institute for System Programming (ISP), 25 B. Kommunis-ticheskaya, Moscow 109004, Russia; email: nick@ispras.ru

[b]Telecommunications Software Engineering Group (TSERG), School of Information Technology and Engineering, University of Ottawa; Ottawa, Ontario, Canada K1N 6N5; email: bob@site.uottawa.ca

Large amounts of legacy software create a "barrier" for adoption of formal description techniques in the telecommunication industry. To overcome this barrier, algorithms and methods for automated re-engineering of legacy telecommunication software into formal specifications are required.

In this paper we present a "dynamic scenario-based" approach to re-engineering of legacy telecommunication software into SDL specifications. Our approach is iterative and is based on 1) dynamically deriving scenarios from the legacy software and 2) automatically synthesizing an SDL model from these scenarios. For the latter purpose we use the Moscow Synthesizer Tool (MOST-SDL) which is capable of synthesizing an SDL-92 model from a set of extended Message Sequence Charts (MSC). The paper provides detailed descriptions of our re-engineering methodology, emphasizing dynamically deriving both conformance and functional scenarios from legacy. A case study is discussed where our dynamic scenario-based methodology was applied to re-engineer a small-sized telecommunications-like software system, called the ToolExchange.

1. Introduction and Background

The demand for high-quality, efficient communications systems and the rate of change of requirements for such systems continues to increase rapidly. As a result, development time or "time to market" has become as important to industrial success as product quality, price/performance, and development cost. Though Computer-Aided Software Engineering (CASE) technology and Formal Description Techniques (FDT's) have offered promising means of

---

1. Partially supported by research grant 97-01-00494 "Algebraic approach to automatic generation of test cases for object-oriented programs", Russian Foundation for Basic Research (RFBR) and by Natural Sciences and Engineering Research Council of Canada, (NSERC) and by Communications and Information Technology Ontario (CITO)

delivering better systems sooner, up to now the promises have not been fulfilled. The current situation, however, is showing significant signs of improvement.

First, a small number of scalable, industrial-strength CASE tools have won substantial acceptance in industry. These include TAU from Telelogic [7,11], ObjectGEODE from Verilog, UML-RT from ObjecTime [14], and Rose from Rational Software. These tools provide designers with powerful analysis, modelling, and fast-prototyping capabilities which enable early verification and validation of designs, usually by simulation, with some dynamic state-space exploration features also offered in the first three toolkits. The tools are stable, and support standard modelling languages and notations for specifying system requirements, designs, and tests.

Secondly, the FDT SDL (Specification and Description Language), used primarily for representing protocols and system design specifications, has now gone through several releases as an international standard language[4], together with the corresponding scenario description language MSC [6]. Moreover, among the FDT's supported by ITU, SDL is by far the most widely adopted for industrial use. The evolution of the widely accepted languages and notations such as SDL, MSC, and Tree and Tabular Notation (TTCN) [5] has been accelerated by the symbiotic evolution of the industrial-strength CASE tools listed above.

A number of very successful industrial case studies have been recently completed, claiming improved quality, much lower development cost, and decreases in time to market costs of 20% to 50% . Some of this increased designer productivity and system quality comes directly from the use of design toolkits or environments - documentation is generated as development proceeds, design decisions are traceable to requirements represented as MSCs (scenarios), code is generated automatically, designs can be simulated before production code is produced, test cases can be produced semi-automatically or automatically in some circumstances, and so on. We believe that more savings in development time actually come from better designs produced with the use of these industrial-strength design and development tools, since better designs will require substantially less rework and redesign. In addition, in a recent pilot study by TSERG and Mitel Electronics [10], it was found that a CASE-based approach could be used to develop functional test specifications for complex telecommunications systems several times faster than current technologies allow. Thus, CASE-based approaches (often using SDL tools) offer significant improvements in quality, productivity, and time to market.

However, in order for CASE-based communications software engineering to become common practice, it is necessary to provide cost-effective methods for integrating CASE-produced components and systems with older, "legacy" base software. Legacy software systems were produced with older development methods, often involving a blend of higher-level code, and system-level code, with heterogeneous languages, architectures, and styles, and often very poorly documented. Up to now, this fact has constituted a "*legacy barrier*" to the cost effective use of new development technologies.

In order to overcome the "legacy barrier", there is an increasing demand for developing automatic (or semi-automatic) re-engineering methods which will significantly reduce the effort involved in creating formal specifications of the base software platforms. Cost-effective methods for producing SDL models of the base software platform will allow the following benefits:

- better understanding of the operation of the legacy software through dynamic simulation of the SDL model, which often produces more intuitive results and does not involve the costly use of the target hardware;

- automated generation of regression test cases for the base software platform;
- analysis and validation of the formal specifications of the new features built on top of the SDL model of the base software platform;
- feature interaction analysis including existing and new features;
- automated generation of test cases for new features;
- automatic generation of implementations of the new features. Such implementations are retargetable for different implementation languages (e.g. C, C++, CHILL) as well as for different real-time operating systems (e.g. pSOS, VxWorks, etc.).

All the above is a motivation for a joint research and development work conducted by Department of CASE Tools, Institute for System Programming, Moscow, Russia and Telecommunications Software Engineering Research Group (TSERG), School of Information Technology and Engineering, University of Ottawa. The TSERG group performs active research in testing methodologies for telecommunications software [5], including high yield testing methods [10] as well as methods of instrumenting software by probes [12,13]. The Department of CASE Tools performs research in reverse engineering methodologies [1,2,15], development of reverse engineering tools in collaboration with industry [15], as well as development of forward engineering tools for SDL and MSC languages [3,8,9]. Upon completion of a forward engineering project which involved automatic synthesis of SDL models from MSC [3] we realized that this technology has the potential for reverse engineering provided that scenarios can be derived from legacy software. After the presentation of this technology at TSERG a joint project has emerged, which benefited from the expertise of each group.

In this paper we present our methodology of *dynamic scenario-based* re-engineering of legacy telecommunications systems into a system design model expressed in SDL, and illustrate our approach by applying it to a case study, namely a small-sized telecommunications-like software system, called the ToolExchange.

Our approach consists of

- placing semantic probes [12] into the legacy code at strategic locations based on structural analysis of the code,

- selecting key representative scenarios from the regression test database and other sources,

- executing the scenarios by the legacy code to generate probe sequences, which are then converted to MSCs with conditions and

- synthesizing an SDL-92 model from this set of Message Sequence Charts (MSCs) using the Moscow Synthesizer Tool [3].

This process is repeated until the SDL design model satisfies certain validity constraints. This SDL model is then used to assess and improve the quality and coverage of legacy system tests, including regression tests. The approach may be used to re-engineer and re-test legacy code from a black-box (environment), white-box (source code), or grey-box (collaborations among subsystems) point of view [12,13].

The rest of the paper has the following organization. Section 2 provides an overview of our dynamic scenario-based re-engineering methodology. Detailed steps of the methodology are described in Section 3 Section 4 contains a brief presentation of the Moscow Synthesizer

Tool. In Section 5 we summarize our experience gained during a case study: we demonstrate how our dynamic scenario-based methodology was used to re-engineer a ToolExchange system. Section 6 contains some comparison to related approaches and conclusions.

2. Methodology Overview

Dynamic scenario-based re-engineering of legacy software into SDL models is a process, where an SDL model is synthesized from *probe traces* [12], collected from *dynamically* executing the *instrumented* legacy system (see Figure 1). More specifically, in the process of scenario-based re-engineering, the SDL model is synthesized from a higher-level representation - *extended MSC-92 model* (later referred to simply as MSC model) which is abstracted from probe traces. The execution is driven by a *test suite*.

The enabling technology for our dynamic scenario-based re-engineering process is automatic synthesis of SDL models from a set of MSCs [3]. So far automatic synthesis of SDL models from MSC was considered only as a forward engineering technology. In our dynamic scenario-based re-engineering process we exploit the duality of MSCs as both a requirements capturing language and a trace description language which allows us to treat probe traces as requirements for the SDL model.

An alternative approach to re-engineering of legacy software into SDL models, the so-called *direct* automatic re-engineering [1,2] is also shown in Figure 1. In contrast, the direct re-engineering approach derives an SDL model statically from the source code by performing semantic-preserving translation [2]. Detailed comparison of re-engineering approaches is contained in Section 6.

FIGURE 1. Dynamic scenario-based re-engineering

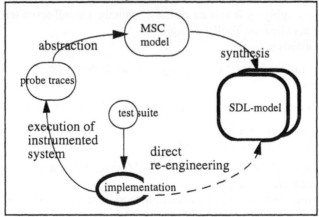

Our methodology is an *iterative* process, consisting of the following four *phases*.

1. Preparation

2. Dynamic collection of probe traces

3. Synthesis of SDL model

4. Investigation of the SDL model

Each phase involves a few *steps*. Iterations are controlled by *validity criteria*, which are checked during the last phase. An overview of all steps of the methodology is shown in Figure 2. In Figure 2 the methodology is presented as a dataflow diagram. Important *artifacts* are represented as rectangles; methodology steps (sub-processes) are represented by ovals. Five artifacts, which were already mentioned in Figure 1, are highlighted. Lines in Figure 2 represent flows of data, which determine the sequence of methodology steps. A detailed description of methodology steps is contained in the next section.

FIGURE 2. Methodology overview

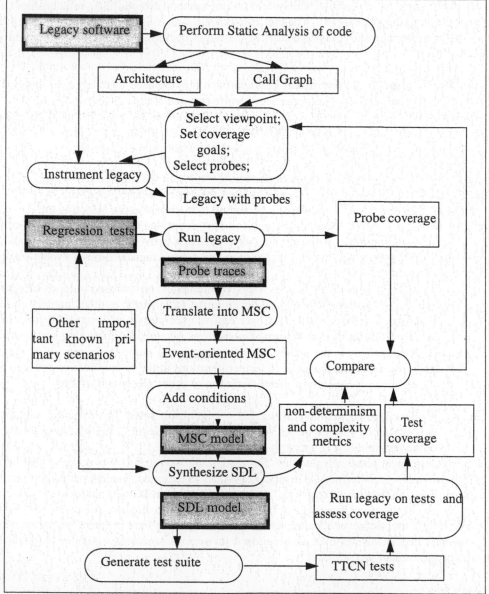

3. Detailed steps in the methodology

3.1. Preparation phase

This aim of this phase is to develop a *probe placement strategy* and select the set of scenarios which will drive execution of the instrumented system and resulting probe trace capture.

Step 1. **Analyze code.** This step uses well-known methods of static structural analysis to select probe placements. Two models of software can be used as guidelines for probe placement - the *architectural model* of the system (major components and their relationships) and the *call graph* of the system [15]. The call graph of the system should identify *external interfaces* of the system (usually - system calls of the target operating system, or assembly inline code).

Step 2. **Select modeling viewpoint.** Our approach may be used to re-engineer and re-test legacy code from a *black-box* (environment), *white-box* (core code), or *grey-box* (collaborations among subsystems) point of view. Viewpoint determines the structure of the resulting SDL model. It also affects the level of details in traces and thus (among other things) the amount of adaptation work for automatically generated a test suite [7] (see also step 11).

Step 3. **Set coverage goal and select probes**. At this step we finalize probe placement by selecting particular locations in the source code of the system where probes are to be placed, and defining the format of the information generated by each probe. By selecting the coverage goal we control the level of details in traces and thus determine the external interface of the model. The external interface of the model is determined in terms of locations on the architectural model of the system and the call graph, such that probes register desired events and collect desired data.

Semantic probing [12] is assumed. Coverage requirement is not phrased in terms of syntactic entities such as statements or branches, but in terms of semantic entities, namely *equivalence classes* of program behavior [12]. These equivalence classes of program behavior are determined solely from the system design. Probe traces obtained by executing instrumented code can be related directly to the system design. Inspection of probe traces may drive modification of semantic probes and thus lead to further iterations of the re-engineering process. See Section 5, "ToolExchange case study" for illustration of probe placement strategy.

Step 4. **Collect known primary scenarios + regression tests.** The dynamic capture of probe traces is driven by the *test suite*. We suggest that the (legacy) regression test suite be used to drive the first iteration of scenario-based methodology.

Let us introduce some terminology for discussing *scenarios*. We make a distinction between *primary scenarios* (normal, everything works as expected, success paths) and *secondary scenarios* (alternative, exceptional, race conditions, collisions, known pathological sequences of client/system interactions, fail paths). All *functional scenarios* (scenarios which describe how a user achieves a particular service or capability) are primary, scenarios which describe how he/she was thwarted are secondary. In general, scenarios which are essential and desired by a customer are primary.

Primary scenarios are denoted "*low-yield*" since they describe situations and actions which are generally well understood. The yield (detected or anticipated error count) is therefore low. Secondary scenarios, on the other hand are denoted *moderate* or *high-yield*, since they describe situations and interactions which are generally not well documented, and therefore are not well understood. The associated yield for such scenarios is high because designer choices are likely to differ from client choices, or to be non-deterministic.

We start our iterative re-engineering process with regression tests. *Regression tests* consist of a blend of *conformance tests* (usually success paths and therefore low-yield), primary scenarios (low-yield), and a few known important secondary scenarios (moderate to high yield). We continue with additional functional (primary) scenarios as required to improve the semantic capture of our SDL model. As our iterations converge, the resulting SDL model is used to produce TTCN test cases (using SDL tools, according to known techniques [11]). During this process we are more interested in secondary higher-yield scenarios.

3.2. Dynamic collection of probe traces

The aim of this phase is to capture the set of probe traces, which correspond to the probe placement strategy and selected scenarios.

Step 5. **Instrument legacy.** Suitable *probing infrastructure* for generation and collection of probe traces needs to be established. Probes need to be inserted into the source code according to the placement strategy. Discussion of the technical details of instrumenting legacy is outside of the scope of this paper.

Step 6. **Run legacy code to generate probe traces.** The legacy system needs to be built and executed on a test suite. The target or simulated environment together with the existing testing infrastructure are used. The result of this step is a collection of *probe traces*. Another result of this step is the measurement of *probe coverage* of the system by the current test suite.

3.3. Synthesis of SDL model

This is the key phase in our methodology. The aim of this phase is to synthesize an SDL model of the legacy system.

Step 7. **Translate probe traces into event-oriented MSCs.** This step was introduced into the methodology in order to separate two different concerns - dynamically capturing scenarios from legacy and synthesizing SDL models from scenarios. This step performs a (simple) translation between traces and MSC. This step is determined mostly by the differences between the format of probe traces (as defined at the instrumentation step), and the format of input to the synthesizer tool.

Step 8. **Add conditions to MSCs.** This step was described as "abstraction" in Figure 1. The aim of this step is to identify transaction-like sequences of interactions, corresponding to requirement use cases. Then linear MSCs (corresponding to traces) are converted into an MSC model, which corresponds to requirement use cases. This is done by inserting conditions [6] into places where loops or branching are possible. Note, that we are using an extended event-oriented MSC-92 notation as the input to the MOST-SDL tool. In MSC-96 this corresponds to creating an HMSC.

FIGURE 3. Example of adding conditions to MSC

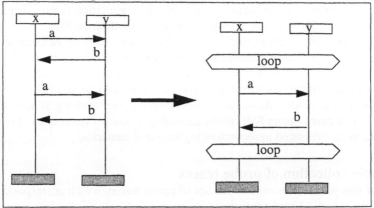

This process is illustrated in Figure 3. The MSC at the left side does not contain any conditions. This MSC describes a single trace. However, we can identify a transaction-like sequence of interactions such as:

x: **out** a **to** y; y: **in** a **from** x; y: **out** b **to** x; x: **in** b **from** y;

Two such sequences are repeated. Provided we know that this sequence can be arbitrarily repeated, we can add conditions before and after this sequence as demonstrated at the MSC at the right side. The MSC at the right side describes an infinite number of traces (including the one described by the MSC at the left side). Thus adding conditions to MSCs can significantly improve the amount of information, contained in MSCs which will lead to synthesis of models with more interesting behavior.

Step 9. **Synthesize SDL model.** This step is done automatically by applying the Moscow Synthesizer Tool (MOST-SDL). Synthesizer technology is briefly described in the next section. A more detailed description is contained in [3].

The outputs of this step are the 1) synthesized SDL model; and some complexity metrics of the model: 2) number of states in SDL model and 3) *non-determinism metric* of the model. The later metric is an *indirect termination criteria* for the re-engineering process. A non-deterministic choice is generated each time when two or more input scenarios have different behavior on the same external stimulus. In practice this often means that behavior of the system is determined by the previous history, but the traces captured during the previous steps do not contain enough data. High values of the non-determinism metric should lead to further iterations of the re-engineering process.

3.4. Investigation of SDL model

The aim of this phase is to update the original test suite by using automatic test case generation from the SDL model and to check termination criteria by comparing the probe coverage and the test coverage (as well as the non-determinism metric).

Step 10. **Generate TTCN test cases.** Using an SDL model for automatic generation of test cases is one of our ultimate goals. Techniques for automatic generation of test cases form SDL models are described elsewhere [11].

Step 11. **Execute tests on legacy and assess coverage.** Execution of the automatically generated test case may require some *adaptation* (conversion of abstracted interfaces into original interfaces) [7]. Adaptation of test interfaces to system interfaces is shown in Figure 4. Probe traces and the corresponding automatically generated test cases use *abstracted interfaces* of the system (according to selected *probe placement strategy*).

FIGURE 4. Adaptations of test interfaces

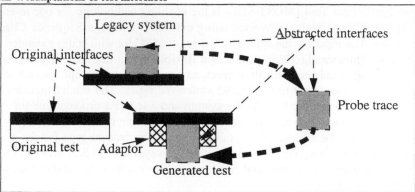

An abstracted interface consists of internal functions (grey box) within the system, which are not necessarily accessible from the environment of the legacy system. In Figure 4 this is illustrated by a grey cavity inside of the rectangle representing the legacy code.

Original tests use original interfaces of the system. The original interface consists of externally accessible functions (black box). In Figure 4 this is illustrated as the outer bottom layer of the legacy code. The functionality of the *adaptor* (illustrated as hatched area) is to convert an abstracted interface back into the original one.

Our experience demonstrates that some compromise should be found between the "depth" of the abstracted interface and the simplicity of the adaptor. An abstracted interface at the logical level greatly simplifies probe traces and leads to more meaningful generated SDL models. In some cases a special-purpose direct access to the internal functionality should be provided for the ease of implementing an adaptor.

Step 12. **Terminating criteria.** We need to make sure that the generated model adequately captures the behavior of the legacy system. This may require several iterations of the re-engineering process. Inadequate behavior of the model may be caused by at least two factors: 1) some important primary scenario is not captured in (legacy) regression tests; 2) an abstracted interface of the system is incorrectly selected (missing probe or incorrectly placed probe).

A probe can be incorrectly placed when it a) does not correspond to a desired behavior equivalence class (e.g. two different probes are placed in the same equivalence class); b) probe is placed into correct behavior equivalence class, but is placed in an incorrect syntactical place

- into a code location which is not executed when at least some locations of the desired behavior class are executed (e.g. probe is placed into only one branch of a conditional statement).

In our experience, incorrectly placed probes result in errors in probe coverage. Missed probes on input interfaces result in high values of the model non-determinism metric. Missed probes on output interfaces result in errors in generated test coverage. Thus when the probe coverage, non-determinism metric and generated test coverage together are satisfactory the iterations can be terminated.

4. Moscow Synthesizer Tool

Moscow Synthesizer Tool (MOST-SDL) is the enabling technology for our re-engineering process. Synthesis methodology involves using extended Message Sequence Charts to formalize use cases. The input for the synthesis is a set of MSC-92 with states extended with data operations. The synthesis algorithm produces a flexible object-oriented SDL-92 model. The model is syntactically and semantically correct, and complete with respect to the input set of MSCs. The model extensively uses SDL-92 structured types. The model includes one SDL package consisting of a process type for the system and a separate process type for each actor in the model. The package also contains the block type showing instantiations of processes and collaboration between the system and its environment. The process type for the system consists of several service types, one per each use case. The synthesized SDL model is ready to be simulated and validated by commercial SDL tools. More complete presentation of MOST-SDL tool can be found in [3].

5. ToolExchange case study

We have applied our methodology to re-engineer a small-sized telecommunications-like system, called the ToolExchange. The ToolExchange was developed at the Department for CASE Tools, Institute for System Programming, Moscow.

5.1. Description of the ToolExchange system

The ToolExchange implements *an integration mechanism* for extensible multi-component CASE environments. ToolExchange provides *interoperability* between loosely connected *interactive tools* by allowing them to perform remote *services*.

The ToolExchange supports the following model. Each tool has a unique *symbolic name*. When a tool dynamically connects to the ToolExchange it is registered at the ToolExchange as a "*subscriber*" with unique *identifier*. A *service* can be requested either based on a symbolic name or a unique identifier. When the service is requested via symbolic name, the ToolExchange first checks, if there is any *active* subscriber with such name. If an active subscriber exists, the ToolExchange sends the service request to it. If no active subscriber exists, the ToolExchange *launches* the tool using the "*tool command line*" for a particular symbolic name. When the service is requested via the unique identifier, the ToolExchange checks if the particular subscriber is still *connected* and sends the service request to it. The ToolExchange establishes a temporary connection between the service requestor and the service provider, by sending the unique identifier of the service requestor to the service provider, so that the later can send back the *reply*.

ToolExchange implements a simple lightweight text-based protocol for communication between tools (as opposed to e.g. CORBA [16]).

5.2. Analysis of the system and probe placement strategy

The architecture of the ToolExchange is presented in Figure 5. Rectangular boxes represent architecture components. Lines represent relationships between components (usually implemented via function calls; each line can represent several function calls; direction of lines represent the direction of function calls). Lines between components and the frame of the picture represent external interfaces of the system. Each external interface has a name (to the left of the corresponding line). Components are arranged according to their logical level (low-level components are at the bottom, higher-level components are at the top). Such architecture diagrams can be produced e.g. using inSight reverse engineering tool [15] from the source code of the system.

FIGURE 5. Architecture of ToolExchange

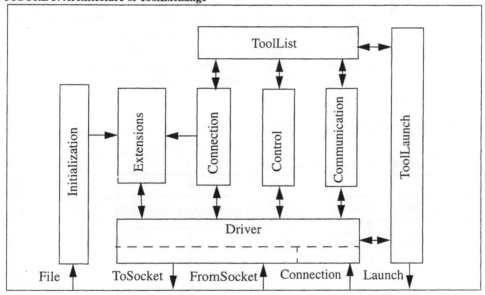

The Driver component implements the low-level protocol based on *sockets*. The Driver contains the main event loop which handles messages from already opened sockets (interface **FromSocket**) as well as new connections (interface **Connection**). It also encapsulates sending messages to sockets (interface **ToSocket**). The Driver component consists of several modules: low-level socket communication, socket connections, interpreter of the low-level message format, etc. The Initialization component allows reading an initial sequence of requests from a file (interface **File**). ToolLaunch component implements the protocol for launching new tools (interface **Launch**).

The ToolList component represents the key abstraction of the ToolExchange - the list of current subscribers. This list is used to search for an active subscriber with a given name. Elements of this list can be marked as active or locked based on requests from Control component, which implements the logic of processing requests performed internally by the

ToolExchange. The Connection components represents the logic of adding new subscribers. The Communication component represents the logic of handling service requests. The Extensions components represents the logic of handling events and customizable menus (outside of the scope of this case study).

Implementation of the ToolExchange system consists of 14 modules in C++ language. The implementation contains 110 functions. The total size of the implementation is 1128 LOC. There exists a small regression test suite, consisting of 15 test cases.

5.3. Deriving scenarios

The external interface of the ToolExchange consists of the following UNIX operating system calls: *socket, bind, listen, accept, connect, close, recv, send, fputs, fopen, fprint, select, fgets, fork, execv*. Most important are calls *recv* and *send* (interfaces **ToSocket** and **FromSocket**).

Function *recv* received one character at a time from a socket *sock* into a variable *ch*. Function *send* sends a string of length *len* into a socket *sock*. Analysis of the call graph of the ToolExchange (see Figure 6) shows that *send* and *recv* functions are wrapped into higher-level *sioReceive* and *sioSend* functions. Function *sioReceive* fills in an internal buffer by reading information from socket *sock* by calling function *recv* several times until a message terminator is read. Function *sioSend* sends the contents of an internal buffer into socket *sock* by calling function send once. There exists a higher-level interface consisting of functions *sendMessage* and *processMessage* (see Figure 6).

FIGURE 6. Fragment of the call graph of the ToolExchange

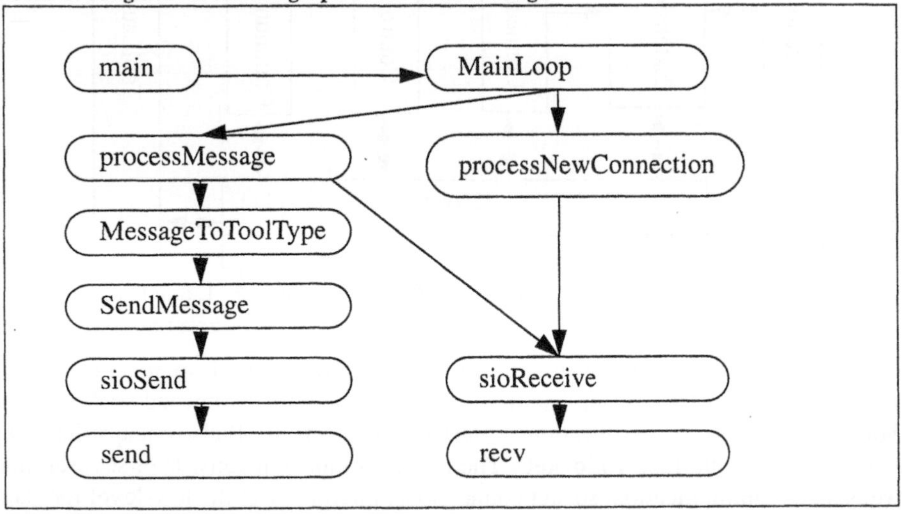

The ToolExchange waits for service requests and connections in a loop in function *MainLoop* (Driver component). When a service request arrives it is processed by *processMessage->sioReceive->recv* functions. Then the service request is analyzed by *processMessage* function of the Driver component. The *processMessage* function calls one of the higher-level functions in components Communication, Control, Connection or Extensions. Most service requests will be forwarded to some other tool. Sending requests via tool name is done by the Communication component which will later again call some functions of the Driver component: *process-Message->MessageToToolType->SendMessage->sioSend->send.*

The previous paragraph presented a typical call sequence. Other call sequences are possible. All call sequences originate in the Driver component. Most call sequences go into one of the higher-level components (Communication, Connection, Control or Extensions), then visit the ToolList component and then go back to the Driver component.

Some call sequences after going into ToolList component will go into ToolLauncher component and terminate by issuing a "launch request". A special call sequence originates in the Driver component, then goes into the ToolLauncher component and then goes back into the ToolList, one of the higher-level components and then back into the Driver component. This allows the ToolExchange to launch a new tool, wait until it connects and then send the request to it.

We have experimented with three different probe placement strategies using the same test suite (see Table 1).

TABLE 1. Probe placement strategies

Iteration	Name	Description	MSC (LOC)
1	Medium	probes inserted inside the Driver component (at sioSend, sioReceive functions)	610
1	High	probes inserted at high-level interface of the Driver component (SendMessage, ProcessMessage functions)	408
2	Low	probes inserted at the operating system interface	44852
2	Medium	probes inserted at complete medium level (12 more functions added)	10000
2	High	probes inserted at complete high level (2 more functions added)	1600

Table 1 gives brief explanation of each probe placement strategy and shows the volume of the generated MSC models (converted from probe traces) for each probe placement strategy. The volume of the trace is roughly the product of the number of events and the amount of data handled by each event. As expected, traces of the higher level protocol have less volume than the lower level protocol. Investigation of the probe coverage after the first iteration allowed us to place probes on some additional functions which significantly improved the coverage (and hence the volume of the trace).

Table 2 shows the resulting probe coverage of components. Most of the probe hits are inside the Driver component. It is interesting to observe that moving to a low-level placement strategy from a medium-level one did not increase the coverage of the high-level components (Communication, Connection, Control, Extensions, ToolList and ToolLauncher).

TABLE 2. Probe hits per component

Component	High	Medium	Low
Driver	286	1553	9840
Communication	37	74	74
Connection	14	186	186
Control	2	14	14

338

Component	High	Medium	Low
Extensions	47	89	89
Initialization	0	122	186
ToolList	0	80	80
ToolLauncher	0	71	71

5.4. Applying Moscow Synthesizer Tool to derived scenarios

We applied Moscow Synthesizer Tool to MSC models, captured at the previous step. We also examined MSC models and added conditions. Table 3 summarizes synthesized SDL models. Table 3 shows the volume of the synthesized SDL models, the number of states in each SDL model and the non-determinism metric (# any) of each SDL model (see step 12 of the methodology).

TABLE 3. Synthesized SDL models

Iteration	MSC model	SDL (LOC)	# states	# any
1	Medium-level probes, no conditions	554	68	11
1	Medium-level probes, simple loop conditions	120	7	4
1	High-level probes, no conditions	250	12	6
1	High-level probes, loop conditions	155	1	11
2	Medium-level probes, no conditions	9784	1391	14
2	High-level probes, no conditions	1653	227	10

Analysis of Table 3 shows that high level probes cause less non-determinism compared to medium level probes (lines 1 and 3, also lines 5 and 6). Adding conditions to medium level probes resulted in folding loops which lead to dramatic reduction in the size of the synthesized model (lines 1 and 2 and also lines 3 and 4).

We experienced that higher level probes result in more meaningful models. This happens because more logical information becomes available as probes are inserted higher in the call graph of the system: low level functions *send*, *recv* operate with socket identificators; *sioSend*, *sioReceive* functions operate with connection identificators; *processMessage*, *sendMessage* functions operate with tool identificators. It is easier to relate high level information to the architectural and logical models of the system.

6. Relation to other approaches and conclusions

We presented dynamic scenario-based approach to re-engineering legacy telecommunications software. Our approach consists of

• placing semantic probes into the legacy code at strategic locations based on structural analysis of the code,

• selecting key representative scenarios from the regression test database and other sources,

- executing the scenarios by the legacy code to generate probe sequences, which are then converted to MSCs with conditions   and

- synthesizing an SDL-92 model from this set of Message Sequence Charts (MSCs) using the Moscow Synthesizer tool [3].

This process is repeated until the SDL design model satisfies certain validity constraints. This SDL model is then used to assess and improve the quality and coverage of legacy system tests, including regression tests. The approach may be used to re-engineer and re-test legacy code from a black-box (environment), white-box (core code), or grey-box (collaborations among subsystems) point of view.

The alternative approach to re-engineering of legacy software into SDL models is the so-called direct automatic re-engineering. Direct re-engineering approach derives SDL model statically from the source code by performing semantic-preserving translation [1,2]. Thus the direct SDL model contains *at least the same* amount of information as the implementation itself. In fact, directly generated SDL models contain on average *8-12 times more* information than the implementation, because the mapping from a conventional language to SDL is *divergent*, as demonstrated in [2]. In contrast, SDL models which are synthesized according to our dynamic scenario-based approach always contains *less* information than the implementation.

Both kinds of SDL models are *trace-equivalent* with respect to the traces, produced by the test suite. However, a directly generated SDL model is capable of producing more traces, than those produced by the original test suite, while a scenario-based SDL model is fully defined by the original test suite.

On the other hand, traces produced by two SDL models have different *levels of detail*. Traces produced by directly generated SDL model contain all implementation detail, plus some additional detail, introduced by the mapping [2]. The level of detail of directly generated SDL models can controlled by selecting external interface of the implementation. Traces, produced by scenario-based SDL model are expected to contain much less detail. As demonstrated above, the level of detail of the scenario-based model is controlled by the *probe placement strategy*.

The direct approach has certain advantages: it is independent of (legacy) regression tests, and it is usually easier to achieve complete semantic coverage of the legacy. However, there are some disadvantages as well: direct mapping has to handle larger volumes of base software platform source code, therefore - SDL tools need to handle larger SDL models. The biggest advantages of scenario-based approach as compared to direct approach, is the flexibility to produce a broad range of distinct models by varying input scenarios and probe placement strategies. In general, scenario-based approach yields more abstract models, which are free from implementation detail. Thus SDL tools could be easier applied to such models.

In our experience, the use of dynamic scenario-based re-engineering methodology combined with subsequent use of SDL tools allows between 20 and 30 % speedup in time-to-market for a typical telecommunication system. The use of tools in a related project was found to yield a 20-25% improvement in time-to-market; therefore the estimate above is likely quite conservative.

As compared to a direct static re-engineering approach, dynamic scenario-based approach has greater potential for creating abstract SDL models thus avoiding the confusion and complexity of existing "spaghetti code" in legacy systems. Dynamic derivation of scenarios is a cost-effective way of capturing data manipulations within the base software platform.

340

Our methodology provides an efficient means of improving understanding of both legacy code and regression test suites. Automatic re-engineering of legacy telecommunication software into SDL models is the key prerequisite for adoption of SDL methodology in industry thus our approach appears to be a cost-effective means of removing barriers to full adoption of SDL in industry.

7. References

[1] N. Mansurov, A. Ragozin, A. Laskavaya, A. Chernov, On one approach to using SDL-92 and MSC for reverse engineering, (in Russian), in Problems of Cybernetics, Vol. 3, 1997, Moscow.

[2] N. Mansurov, et. al., Direct approach to automatic re-engineering of legacy telecommunication software, (in Russian), in Problems of Cybernetics, Vol. 6, 1999, Moscow

[3] N. Mansurov, D. Zhukov, Automatic synthesis of SDL models in Use Case Methodology, in Proc. 9th SDL Forum, Montreal, Canada, June 21-26, 1999, Elsevier Science Publishers B.V. (North-Holland).

[4] ITU-T (1993), CCITT Specification and Description Language (SDL), ITU-T, June 1994.

[5] R.L. Probert, O.Monkewich, TTCN: the international notation for specifying tests for communications systems, Computer Networks, Vol. 23, No. 5, 1992, pp. 417-738

[6] Z.120 (1996) CCITT Message Sequence Charts (MSC), ITU-T, June 1992.

[7] Telelogic (1998), Telelogic ORCA and SDT 3.4, Telelogic AB, Box 4128, S-203 12 Malmoe, Sweden, 1998.

[8] N. Mansurov, A. Kalinov, A. Ragozin, A. Chernov (1995), Design Issues of RASTA SDL-92 Translator, in Proc. of the 7-th SDL Forum, Oslo, Norway, 26-29 September, 1995, Elsevier Science Publishers B.V. (North-Holland), pp. 165-174.

[9] N. Mansurov, A. Ragozin, Generating readable programs from SDL, in Proc. SAM'98 workshop, 29 June-1 July, 1998, Humboldt University, Berlin, 1998.

[10] R. Probert, H. Ural, A. Williams, J. Li, R. Plackowski, Experience with rapid generation of functional tests using MSCs, SDL, and TTCN, submitted to Special Issue of Formal Descriptions Techniques in Practice of Computer Communications, 1999

[11] Anders Ek, Jens Grabowski, Dieter Hogrefe, Richard Jerome, Beat Koch, Michael Schmitt, Towards the Industrial Use of Validation Techniques and Automatic Test Generation Methods for SDL Specifications, in Proc. of the 8-th SDL Forum, Evry, France, 23-26 September, 1997, Elsevier Science Publishers B.V. (North-Holland), pp. 245-261.

[12] R. Probert, Life-Cycle/Grey-Box Testing, Congressus Numeratium, Vol. 34 (1982), pp. 87-117.

[13] R. Probert, Optimal Instrumentation of Software by Probes, IEEE Trans. on Software Engineering, Vol. 16, No. 1, 1982, pp. 17-29.

[14] B. Selic, G. Gullekson, P. Ward, Real-Time Object Oriented Modelling, John Wiley & Sons, Toronto, 1994.

[15] N. Rajala, D. Campara, N. Mansurov, inSight Reverse Engineering CASE Tool, in Proc. of the ICSE'99, Los Angeles, USA, 1998.

[16] A. Pope, The CORBA Reference Guide, Addison-Wesley, 1998

)L'99 : The Next Millennium
Dssouli, G.v. Bochmann and Y. Lahav, editors
1999 Elsevier Science B.V. All rights reserved

pecification, Validation and Implementation of ATM UNI Signaling Protocols in

DL

ong Yuping[a], Lu Yinghua[a] and Gao Qiang[b]

raining Center of Beijing University of Posts & Telecommunications, 100876, Beijing,
R. China[*]

VT International Validation & Testing Corp. P.O. Box, 32115, 1386 Richmond Road, Ottawa,
ntario, Canada.

We are involved in an industry project to build an ATM network access system. During the rst phase of our project, we used conventional way of writing C code manually. We were able implement ATM access signaling protocols. However, the code is not reliable, a lot of efforts ere spent on testing the codes and fixing the bugs during the integration phase. During the :cond phase, we switched to formal design technique SDL (Specification and Description anguage)[7] and we used the ObjectGEODE [5] CASE tool. We formally specified the otocols in SDL, we validated their logical correctness and we automatically generated the C de, and targeted the code on hardware. We reached a significant improvement on software lality, reliability and time to market.

In this paper, we present our approach in the use of the formal SDL methodology in real life rotocol developing which have general industrial application value, and our experience to nplement the ATM UNI signaling protocols. Several key aspects including interpreting system onfigurations, modeling UNI signaling protocols in SDL, validating, implementing and sting the protocols are addressed respectively.

. Introduction

The ATM system aims at accessing different applications in the existing communication etworks. It will extend ATM to the normal user of the existing networks and plays an nportant role in making ATM the leading technology in the next century.

Supported by China National 863 Program
* Supported by BUPT-IVT Collaboration Project

We are involved in an industrial project building an ATM network access system. During the first phase of our project, we used the conventional way of writing C code manually. We were able to implement the ATM access signaling protocols. However, the code is not reliable. A lot of efforts were spent to test the code and fix the bugs during the integration phase. Despite our efforts, it was still difficult to say that the system did what it was supposed to do and to prove quickly in front of our customers.

SDL (Specification and Description Language) is an international standard for formal description of communication systems. SDL is based on Extended Communicating Finite State Machine (ECFSM). Modeling a protocol based on SDL provides a mean for formal validation of protocols correctness and automatic generation of its implementation in C code.

Therefore, during the second phase of our project, we switched to the formal design technique using SDL in order to implement the UNI signaling protocols in our ATM access system. We observed a significant improvement on software quality, reliability and productivity.

Rest of the paper is organized as follows. In Section 2, we present an approach for the use of formal design techniques in real life protocol development. In Section 3, we explain our hardware environment. In Section 4, we describe the UNI signaling protocols in SDL. In Section 5, we introduce the validation and simulation procedure. In Section 6, we present the implementation of ATM UNI signaling part on the ATM access system. In Section 7, we describe the testing that we have taken. In Section 8, we summarize our experience and discuss the advantage and disadvantages of using SDL and C language in protocol design. This paper is concluded in Section 9.

2. Methodology for Developing Real Size Protocols using SDL

Formal description techniques, such as SDL, have been proposed for protocol engineering to produce systems of the highest quality by applying state-of-the-art verification (does the system work) and validation (does the system do what it is supposed to) techniques at the earliest possible stage in the development cycle. In the following we present our approach for developing real size protocols using SDL methodology.

Defining Requirements: This phase consists of designing the formal (SDL) model of the service to be provided and all features to be satisfied by protocols and systems. For protocols this is called the service description. The purpose is to model and to understand the user requirements in the real world environment. We capture the static and dynamic aspects of the systems to be developed from the customer requirements document. However, we do not need to write a full service description. We can restrict ourselves to the verification of selected properties for particular interest.

We use Message Sequence Chart (MSC)[6] and operators such as parallel operators, sequential operators, and choice operators to describe the dynamic aspects of services.

Modeling: Given a system or a protocol described in natural language or in a pseudo-code fashion, we should first make a formal description of it in SDL. We need to clarify the problem to be solved and to remove any ambiguities in the textual requirements. Elementary scenarios can be expressed with the help of MSCs, and they can be organized using temporal operators such as "parallel", "sequence", "choice", etc. into a functional model. In this way the complete set of service expected from the system is clearly defined before starting the modeling phase. This is very important because crucial choices made during this stage will greatly influence the ability to detect certain kinds of errors.

Validation by Simulation: We checked the modeled behavior against properties thanks to the simulation technique. Once a system has been partially designed, rapid prototyping or verification and validation of the concurrent parts of the system was performed using the ObjectGEODE SDL Simulator. We were able to simulate incomplete models and thanks to the richness of the graphical interface we performed rapid prototyping very early in the development process, ensuring early detection of errors and inconsistencies between requirements and design.

Validation by Interactive Simulation: In this phase we "debug the SDL code". It starts with verifications (syntax, cross-references etc.) and some preliminary simulations (random simulation) just to check that the formal model can be executed, and it is a faithful representation of the system or the protocol. At this point, we are not looking for a formal proof. It continues with some basic tests trying to reproduce, with the interactive facilities of the simulator, the expected behavior. It is useful to know how much of the formal specification has been covered in the process of running a few typical examples, and the tool give the coverage rate for transitions and states (rate of executed SDL transitions/states and number of never-executed SDL transitions/ states). Ideally, those should be 100%; however, this level may not always be easy to reach.

Validation by Random Simulation: In this phase, validation proceeds through long random simulation runs in order to detect errors when the system reaches a deadlock, or when a stop condition becomes true, or when a dynamic error occurs, or when an observer detect a success or an error, etc. In this way, by replaying the scenario automatically generated by the simulator we can fix "bugs".

Verification: Its purpose is to detect design errors in order to answer to the question "Are we building the system right?" We detected design errors such as deadlocks, unknown receiver processes, array overflow, etc

Implementation: After simulation and validation, there are no errors in the model. Then t⯑ application can be automatically generated into C code. This automatically generated code ⯑ independent of the target. And then, it is integrated into the target environment using run-tim⯑ libraries relevant to the operating system used. These libraries could be customized for differe⯑ operating system needs or constraints.

Testing: Test design is performed in parallel with architectural and software design. Th⯑ activity aims to produce test suites used for object integration. At process and class level, te⯑ suites are used for unit testing, and at SDL structuring entity level, they serve for integrati⯑ testing. Test consists of conformance test and performance test. In this phase, the who⯑ application will run in real environment. *Conformance* testing is done to ensure that t⯑ implemented protocol conforms to the international standard. It is done thanks to a protoc⯑ tester which accepts in input conformance test suites. *Performance* testing is done to test th⯑ whole system's performance in real environment.

3. Hardware Environment

Hardware Environment is a set of electronic devices where ATM access system realizes t⯑ function of ATM NT2 [8]. According to ITU-T's specification, NT2 should not only have t⯑ UNI user side interface to public network, but also the UNI network side interface to the loc⯑ user. So the signaling software of ATM access system should implement the functions of U⯑ user side signaling protocols as well as the UNI network side protocols separately.

The configuration of our access system is shown in Figure 1. It consists of two main module⯑ One is the application access module, the other is the switching module. Many applicatio⯑ access modules, which access different applications, such as ISDN, LAN, Frame Relay, a⯑ VOD (video on demand) etc, are connected to the switching module through optical cable⯑ And the switching module is connected to the public network. On each interface, there is⯑ signaling channel (VPI/VCI=0/5). There is only one CPU on each module. The operati⯑ system on these CPU's is the multi-task operating system known as VxWorks[13].

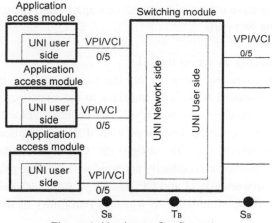

Figure 1. Hardware Configuration

According to the hardware configuration, there should be two implementations of ATM UNI ignaling software in this system. One is applied on each application access module and ccesses different applications. The other is for switching module, implementing the functions f local exchange and providing the standard UNI interface to the public network side.

1. Modeling ATM access system signaling protocols in SDL

We designed the signaling software of the access system according to ITU-T ATM UNI ignaling protocol Q.2931 and Q.2971 [11][12] whose main functions are call control. ccording to them, we divided the call control function into five processes: Coordination rocess, Call Control process (CC), Party Control process (PC), Restart process (RS) and Restart Response (RR), as shown in Fig. 2.

Coordination process (CO) distributes primitives received from upper and lower layer to elated processes, establishes and maintains the link with SAAL [9][10] on which messages are exchanged with remote signaling entity.

Call Control processes (CC) setup, maintain, and release connections for user communications.

Party Control processes (PC) setup, maintain, and release leaves in point to multi-point connections.

Restart process (RS) and Restart Response process (RR) restart the established connections if necessary.

With consideration of the hardware configuration, signaling software of the access module

and the switching module have other unique functions apart from the call control function a
described in the following two parts.

Modeling signaling protocols on access module

The main function of signaling software on the access module is to access differen
applications and provide standard ATM UNI interface to the switching module. The softwar
can be divided into two blocks: one is CC_U (call control) block, the other is AP_
(Application User side) block which interfaces with different applications such as Q.93
(ISDN), Q.933 (Frame relay), etc. To design the CC_U independently from differe
applications, thus new application can be easily accessed without changing the CC_U block, w
specified the primitives between AP_U and CC_U. AP_U translates call control messages c
different application into these primitives. As a result, reusability of the signaling software
improved.

The CC_U block is divided into five processes according to Q.2931 and Q.2971 as shown i
Fig2.

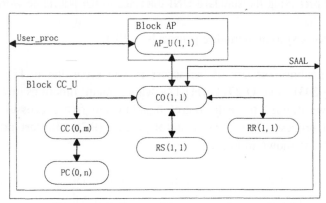

Figure 2. Software Diagram on Access Module

There is only one CO instance for the lifetime of the system. CC instances are created by C
instance. One CC instance corresponds to one call. When CO receives a new call by receivin
a *setup.req* primitive from AP_U or a *SETUP* message from SAAL, it creates a CC instance
Later it routes the subsequent messages and primitives of the call to this CC instance accordin
to CR (call reference) which is included in the messages and primitives. In addition, CC
collects the primitives and messages coming from every CC instance and transfers them t
AP_U or SAAL. PC instances are created by CC, corresponding to one leaf in a point
multi-point connection. Whether RS or RR has only one instance for the lifetime of the system

Modeling signaling protocols on switching module

According to the access system configuration described in Section 3, signaling on switching
module should provide UNI network side signaling function to the access module, and UN

ser side signaling function to the public network side. So the signaling protocol on the witching module is divided into three blocks. They are CC_N block (Call Control Network ide) which processes the local call connection, CC_U_N block (Call Control User side aterface with public Network) which processes the outgoing call connection with the public etwork, and AP_N block (Application on Network module) which analyzes called number and elps to do call accept control (CAC).

CC_N block and CC_U_N block have the same functions as CC_U block in the access nodule. They are also divided into five processes as those in CC_U block. However, AP_N lock is different from AP_U block in the access module. AP_N block performs call number nalysis and implements call accept control (CAC) function. When it receives primitive *etup.ind* which indicates a call coming from CC_N block, it communicates with CAC part of ae system to judge whether the remaining resource of the system can satisfy the request of the all. If the request is not satisfied, AP_N asks CC_N to release the call; otherwise, AP_N nalyzes the called number of this call to see if the call is a local call or an outgoing call. If it is local call, AP_N directs CC_N block to establish the call with access module. If the call is an utgoing call, AP_N requests CC_U_N to establish the call with public network. After the call s established, AP_N informs the switch control on the network module to rewrite the switch able. After the call is released, AP_N should also inform switch control to change the switch able. The SDL model of the signaling software in the switching module is shown in Fig. 3.

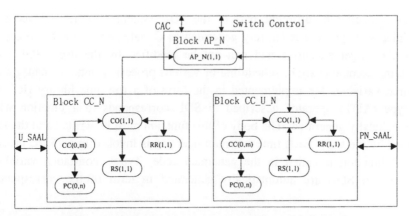

Figure 3 Software Diagram on Switching Module

5. Simulation and Validation

The model can be simulated using the ObjectGEODE Simulator [5] for verification and rapid prototyping purposes. The Simulator allows simulating the execution of the program. Validation work is performed by developers by simulating the behavior of the system. The Simulator can be regarded as a sort of "SDL debugger", as it can simulate the description step by step, undo/redo execution steps, set break points and watch contents of variables and queues.

Three modes of simulation are provided: interactive, random, and exhaustive as described
Section 2. Errors such as deadlocks, live locks, or dead code can be detected throu
simulation.

6. Implementation

6.1. Code Generation and Integration
A SDL description is composed of a hierarchy of structural objects. The physic
implementation of the SDL description is derived from this architecture and consists of
hierarchy of the following objects:
-   Node: All software controlled by a multi-task real time operating system
-   Task: A unit of parallelism of the operating system
-   Process instance: A process instance is a unit of parallelism in SDL sense.

A task can be mapped to one of the following SDL objects:
-   a process (Task/Process (TP) mapping). One task corresponds to one SDL process.
-   a process instance (Task/Instance (TI) mapping). One task corresponds to one SDL proces
    instance.
-   a block (Task/Block (TB) mapping). One task corresponds to one SDL block.
-   the whole system (Task/System (TS) mapping). One task corresponds to the whole system

During C code generation, different part of the SDL system is generated according t
different principle. SDL process is entirely generated as C statements, which are complete
independent of the target executive and can not be modified by the user. SDL dynami
semantics involving communication, scheduling of various process instances, management o
timers and shared variables are implemented in the form of a run-time library (RTL). Eac
abstract data type (ADT) operator described in SDL corresponds to a function whose
interface is automatically generated. The body of this function must be written and the functio
must be compiled by the user. Each time when an operator is invoked in an SDL process, t
corresponding C function is called in the generated code. Types, constants, variables an
operators declared in SDL are automatically generated in term of the corresponding
definitions.

Source code including makefile are generated from ObjectGEODE for Vxworks in th
Task/Process mapping mode, complied and linked to obtain a downloadable binary on the las
machine. And the the binary is downloaded onto the target board. Since signaling protoco
needs the support of AAL5 and ATM sublayer to transmit the information in ATM cell
signaling software should be integrated with external tasks, such as transmitting and receivin
tasks of AAL5 PDU.

.2. Performance Optimization

fter generating and integrating the source code, signaling software can be run in the real time vironment which helps us to find performance problems. Once a problem is located, erformance optimization has to be taken. Here is a example that call setup time was shorten ter performance optimization was taken.

hrough analysis, the time spent on data copying between processes is the main factor to fluence the speed. Two methods were taken to optimize the performance.

irst, TB mapping instead of TP mapping was used in code generation. The number of actual nning tasks decreased greatly. Thus the copy times is reduced.

/e found that the first method was still not effective enough. The second method was taken to ange the communication mechanism in RTL (Run Time Library) for data exchange. Message ueue is the default communication mechanism in RTL. In the message queue mechanism, hen one process wants to send data to another process, it allocates a block of memory space or the data and copies the data to this data space, then passes the pointer of the data space to the eceiver by a message queue. The receiver receives this pointer from the message queue and opies the content pointed by the pointer to its own data space. After that, the data space located by the sender is released. Thus in one data exchange, data is copied twice. As the ontent of one message is exchanged among two or three processes during one message passing ccording to the protocol, so there are too many copy actions of the almost same content. herefore, shared memory mechanism was used to replace the message queue in the same node. /hen one message comes from SAAL, CO allocates a data space for the message. This data pace will not be released until the last process finished processing content of this message. The rocesses just modify the content according to their own needs in this data space and pass the ointers. With the second method, the copy time of message content is decreased dramatically. hus the call setup time is shorten accordingly.

. Testing

Testing is necessary before the new system can be connected to the public network. It was nplemented in two steps. Step one is the conformance testing which checks if the realized ignaling protocols conform to the standards. Step two is performance testing which tests the eliability of the signaling software by generating load to the access system.

Conformance Testing: The aim of conformance testing is to interconnect the new system with ther provider's ATM equipment. It is carried out in real hardware environment thanks to a ester. After the executable code is downloaded onto the target board, a tester is connected with e target board directly. First, the access module was tested by configuring the tester as etwork. Second, switching module was tested by configuring the tester as user. Then, the testing can be done by executing the conformance testing suites step by step against the new system.

Performance testing: Load can be simulated by a protocol tester. Protocol tester can be appropriately set to generate calls continuously with different average speed, for example, at 1 calls/second, and can be released after some time. Thus, a real environment is simulated. We configured the tester to simulate actual user and let it generate calls in different speed with different distribution functions to test the performance of our signaling software. Performance testing can evaluate the efficiency of the signaling software and help to optimize the communication mechanism and code generating control. For example, in real environment, call setup time does not depend on the signaling process time only. It depends on different process time of different parts in the whole system. Through performance testing, we improved the call setup frequency from 3 to 9 calls/second.

8. Discussions

We have applied the ObjectGEODE toolset and the methodology to the development of the ATM UNI Signaling Protocol and found that it is more efficient, comparing with the conventional method of writing C code. As it is impossible to achieve a fault-free system at the first life cycle of development, we have found some errors in our model while using ObjectGEODE Simulator. These errors mainly occurred in CO (Coordination) process. Due to the limitation of space, we cannot detail the causes of the errors and the solutions. Instead, we summarize our experience and discuss the implementation of protocols in SDL and in C.

Comparison between the Implementation designed in SDL and the Manually written C program

We have done two versions of UNI signaling software user side in different phases. One implemented directly in C. The other is implementing using SDL. Each approach has its advantages and disadvantages.

- Productivity, "time-to-market"

Development in SDL is much more efficient than in C. It takes one people-year to implement ATM UNI signaling user side signaling protocol in C program. While it only takes nine man-month to implement the ATM UNI signaling user side protocol. And it takes another six man-month to extend it to network side protocol.

- Portability

Since the code can be generated automatically with several RTL, the software developed using SDL can be easily ported to different operating systems. For example, we can easily transplant the signaling software on PC which is useful in LANE (LAN Emulation).

Readability

The graphic interface of SDL is more easily understood than a program in C. It is easier for
her person to continue the former's work.

Reliability

Using validation methodology of SDL, the deadlock is fewer in SDL than in C. Thus the
liability of the software is very good using SDL.

Code Efficiency

Code generated automatically in SDL is not so efficient than manually written C Code. We
ve realized UNI user side signaling in about 7,000 lines in C, while the code generated in
DL is about 20,000 lines (1% comments). The size of generated C code is larger than that of
anaually written C code. And the execution speed of generated C code is slower than that of
anually written C code.

Program Optimization

It is easy to optimize a program in C, because they are all written by the programmer himself.
at to optimize a program generated from SDL is not so easy, because the code is generated
tomatically and the customization of RTL needs much knowledge on the operating system.

Dynamic Table Using

Dynamic table is very useful in memory saving. C language provides rich operations on
inters to realize dynamic table, while SDL does not have such powerful functions.

DL for Modeling Signaling Protocols

Although SDL has some disadvantages comparing with C language, it is very good for
gnaling protocol development.

Since signaling protocols are defined using Extended Communicating Finite State Machine
CFSM) while ECFSM is also the base of SDL, they match with each other very well.

Modeling a protocol based on SDL provides a means for formally validating the correctness
protocols and automatically generating their implementation in C code.

But the running speed of the software which will affect the performance of the signaling
ftware needs to be improved by optimize the communication mechanism as explained in
ction 6.

Conclusion

SDL is a technique widely used in communication protocol development. Through the two

phases of signaling protocol development in manually writing C and in SDL separately, w
have realized that developing communication protocols using the SDL language is much mor
efficient. The method provided by the SDL development CASE tools in simulation an
validation improves the reliability of the software, reduces the time to market and maintenanc
costs in a very significant way. The portability of the SDL system is also good. All these give
confidence in developing protocol software in SDL.

ATM UNI signaling protocol is the base for many other ATM applications. We have use t
user side UNI protocol in our LANE (LAN Emulation) server and client. We are planning
integrate it into our VOD equipment in the future.

REFERENCES

1. Uyless Black, ATM: Signaling in broadband networks, Prentice Hall PTR (1996).
2. Bahiya Hatim, Mairtin O Droma, Telecommunication Software Development using SDL-9.
   Practical experience, Proceedings of the IEEE International Conference on Engineering (
   Complex Computer Systems, ICECCS Proceedings of the 1996 2nd IEEE Internationa
   Conference on Engineering of Complex Computer Systems Oct 21-25 1996.
3. Nogueira Martins, Paulo; Carrapatoso, Eurico Manuel, Method to create graphical u
   interfaces in telecommunication services specified in SDL, Proceedings - IEEE Conventio
   of Electrical & Electronics Engineers in Israel Proceedings of the 1996 19th Convention (
   Electrical and Electronics Engineers in Israel Nov 5-6 1996.
4. Lin, Guochun, Integrated modeling and simulation of signalling protocols at B-ISDN UNI o
   an SDL'92-based platform for performance evaluation, IEEE Symposium on Computers an
   Communications - Proceedings Proceeding of the 1997 2nd IEEE Symposium on Computer
   and Communications Jul 1-3 1997.
5. ObjectGEODE V1.2 manuals, Verilog, SA, 1998.
6. Oystein Haugen, SDL'95 with MSC in CASE Tutorials 95.09.25, Sep, 1995.
7. ITU-T Recommendation Z.105, "SDL Combined with ASN.1", Geneva, 1996
8. ITU-T Recommendation I.321: B-ISDN Protocol Reference Model and its Application
   ITU-T(1992).
9. ITU-T Recommendation Q.2110: B-ISDN Signalling ATM Adaptation Layer (SAAL),ITU
   T(1994).
10. ITU-T Recommendation Q.2130:B-ISDN Signalling ATM Adaptation Layer-Service
    Specific Coordination Function for Support of Signalling at the User Networl
    Interface(SSCF at UNI), ITU-T(1994).
11. ITU-T Recommendation Q.2931: Broadband Integrated Services Digital Network (B
    ISDN)-Digital Subscriber Signalling System No.2(DSS2)-User Network Interface(UNI)
    Layer 3 Specification for Basic Call/Connection Control, ITU-T(1995).
12. ITU-T Recommendation Q.2971: Broadband Integrated Services Digital Network (B

ISDN)-Digital Subscriber Signalling System No.2 (DSS2)-User Network Interface(UNI)-Layer 3 Specification for Point to Multipoint Call/Connection Control, ITU-T(1995).

13. WindRiver System, VxWorks Programer's Guide 5.3.1(1997).
14. Qiang. Gao, "On the Design, Validation and Implementation of Distributed Rendezvous Algorithms," Ph.D. Thesis, University of Montreal, Dept. IRO, November, 1995.
15. G. J. Holtzmann, Design and Validation of Computer Protocols, Prentice Hall, 1991.

SDL'99 : The Next Millennium
R. Dssouli, G.v. Bochmann and Y. Lahav, editors
©1999 Elsevier Science B.V. All rights reserved

Using Metapatterns with SDL

Torben Worm

*The Maersk Mc-Kinney Møller Institute for Production Technology, Odense University,
Campusvej 55, DK-5000 Odense M, Denmark*
tworm@mip.sdu.dk

Abstract

This article describes how SDL can be used to model systems using the concept of
metapatterns[13]. Metapatterns are abstractions over the general design pattern[4]
concept. According to [13] seven metapatterns exist and these seven patterns provide the necessary modeling power to express other design patterns, e.g. those
found in [4]. In this article we investigate the language constructs of SDL suitable
to support the metapatterns concept and we provide examples of their usage.

Key words: metapatterns, patterns, frameworks, architecture, language concepts

1 Introduction

Software systems are growing larger and larger which implies that the importance of system structure and this structure's impact on system qualities
such as reduction of complexity and increase in maintainability is becoming
more evident.

Recently there has been an increasing focus on the usage of design patterns[1,2,4,15] in conjunction with SDL and how to adapt these patterns to
specific needs and protocols[6].

The general assumption underlying design patterns is that they are design
descriptions that exist independently of the concrete implementation language. In general design patterns are based on object oriented languages

---

[1] Odense University is part of University of Southern Denmark
[2] This work is supported by Ericsson Diax A/S and The Danish Academy of Technical Sciences (ATV), grant number EF-659

and thus it is important to explore the object oriented capabilities of SDL with respect to support of the patterns concepts. In this article we focus on the language constructs in SDL that supports the notion of *metapatterns*.

Metapatterns is a general and powerful concept that can be used as a basis for framework design and for the design of reusable components[13]. It is thus important to investigate the SDL language with respect to metapatterns. If we are able to utilize SDL directly in conjunction with metapatterns we are able to express design patterns more directly in the language.

Section 2 of this article describes the notion of software architecture and explains some of the important implications a more architecture centered software development model could have on the perception of the software.

Section 3 discusses the impact the metapattern concept can have on the software development process in terms of changing the process from an application oriented development process to a framework oriented process.

Section 4 describes the concept of metapatterns and the language concepts necessary to support this abstraction. The section focuses on the basic principles *template* and *hook* underlying the metapatterns. The seven metapatterns of [13] are briefly described.

Section 5 analyses the language constructs in SDL that may be used as means for utilizing metapatterns. The interesting language constructs of SDL are the Abstract Data Type, the procedure, and the process. The advantages and liabilities of these three concepts are discussed through schematic exploration and examples.

Section 6 is the conclusion.

2 Software Architecture

Software Architecture is becoming more important as the size and complexity of software systems increase because the structure of the systems are becoming more important than the algorithms and data structures[5].

Many of the architectural descriptions existing today are on a very general level e.g. the *pipes-and-filters* and *layer* architectural patterns of [1]. In this article we focus on *micro-architecture* on the pattern level as an important basis for the higher level architectural descriptions.

In general software can be viewed from two different but closely related points of view: the *functional* view and the *non-functional* view, typically expressed as two kinds of requirements on the software.

The *functional* requirements express the functionality of the software or more specifically the *correctness* of the software. This is purely a notion of whether the software does what is it supposed to do or not.

The *non-functional* requirements deal with the aspects of the software that has nothing to do with the functionality, i.e. changing the non-functional requirements does not affect the correctness of the software. Typical examples of non-functional requirements are performance, space-requirements, maintainability, quality.

Software architecture is a means to fulfill these requirements. The structure of the system is very important in order to fulfill especially the non-functional requirements but also increasingly the functional requirements as more flexibility is demanded from the software. It might be a functional requirement that the software is flexible in some respects and thus the architecture of the system becomes evident.

In this article we focus on the structural aspects of software architecture as a means to support both the functional and non-functional requirements. We do not explicitly address the architectural aspects of using SDL but indirectly through metapatterns. We do this by focusing on the structural implications the usage of metapatterns have on the usage of SDL.

Design patterns and architectural patterns all focus on structure and the soft requirements are only briefly described in the accompanying text (and often forgotten in the implementation). Design patterns is a step in the right direction because there is also a description of advantages and disadvantages of using a specific pattern. Metapatterns is no exception in this respect.

3 Framework Centered Software Development

One of the major arguments for using object-oriented programming has always been that we can reuse parts of our code by means of inheritance and thus develop software faster and cheaper[10]. The view on reuse seems to shift from the code-reuse view to a more architectural based view, e.g. through the use of frameworks and design patterns. One of the means to realize an architectural approach to software development is to use frameworks.

A framework is a means to reuse both code and the design because it is typically designed with the use of a number of patterns, and the code is

358

directly reused in derived applications. A framework for a particular application domain consists of a number of (possibly unfinished) building blocks that can be combined and refined to constitute the final application.

The core concept of a framework is that it contains carefully chosen design decisions with respect to what to keep flexible and what to keep fixed in this particular application domain. According to Pree[13, p. 224] the models used for FW-centered software are radically different from traditional methods as illustrated in Figure 1(b).

A framework can be viewed as consisting of a number of fixed structures called *frozen spots* indicated in Figure 1(a) by the white color and a number of flexible, adaptable areas called *hot spots* (the gray areas in the figure)[13, p. 228].

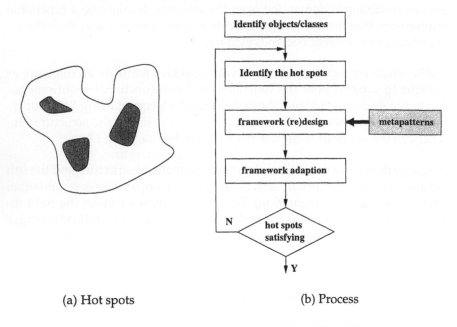

(a) Hot spots   (b) Process

Fig. 1. Hot spot driven approach[13, p. 228–230]

The core activity of framework centered software development is to identify the stable structures and the variable structures of a given application domain. A suggestion for this process is shown in Figure 1(b) where the process starts by identifying the objects and classes in the application domain e.g. with the aid of domain experts and other methods.

When the classes and objects are found the hot spots of the application area must be identified. This activity is conducted by domain experts and the software engineers. When the hot spots are identified metapatterns and/or other pattern approaches can be used to reach the desired degree of flexibility.

The framework is then adapted to the actual application and evaluated to decide whether the chosen hot-spots satisfies their purposes. This spiral is repeated until the hot spots are adequate.

4 Metapatterns

Both if development process is a "per application" process or a framework centered approach design patterns[4,1] are an important aid in constructing well structured software. Patterns are especially helpful in constructing frameworks because they often focus on the hot spots of some specific problem, e.g. the Strategy pattern[4, p. 315] where the hot spot is some particular algorithm.

Metapatterns is a general and powerful concept that can be used as a means for modeling reusable components[13]. Metapatterns is an abstraction over the object-oriented features in object-oriented languages and the modeling methods used to model and implement flexible software.

As stated by [13]: "We introduce the term *metapattern* for a set of design patterns that describes how to construct frameworks independent of a specific domain. Actually constructing frameworks by combining the basic object-oriented concepts proves quite straightforward. Thus these metapatterns turn out to be an elegant and powerful approach that can be applied to categorize and describe any framework example design pattern on a *metalevel*. So metapatterns do not replace state-of-the-art design pattern approaches, but complement them"[13, p. 105] In this context the term *framework example design pattern* means design patterns in the [4] sense.

Metapatterns is thus a concept we can use to build frameworks and a technique to describe the design patterns we know from e.g. [4]. The point here is, that if the language we use directly support the concepts that metapatterns are abstractions over, then it will be easier to implement the patterns we know because it is possible to express these patterns in terms of the metapatterns.

4.1 Language support

The metapatterns concept is basically an abstraction over the object oriented concepts *inheritance, virtuallity*, and *dynamic binding and polymorphy*

```
class Equip {
private:
  List<Parts> part_list;
  Price sum;
public:
  ...
  Price calc_price(void) {
    foreach p in part_list {
      sum += p->GetPrice();
    }
    return sum;
  }
}
```

Fig. 2. A C++ like example on the usage of template an hook methods

and thus the language used to implement the design made through the usage of metapatterns must support these concepts.

4.2 Template and hook

The basic principle on which the metapatterns concept builds is the notion of *template* and *hook* methods and corresponding classes. The class containing the template method is called a *template class* and the class containing the hook method is called a *hook class*.

A *template* method is a skeleton for a method in which parts of the method must be kept flexible, i.e. a template method implements some frozen spot of an application.

A *hook* method is a method that the template method depends upon in order to do its task, i.e. the hook method implements the flexible (hot) spots of the template method.

As an example of the usage of template and hook methods consider the calculation of the price of some composed equipment (aggregated from many parts). In this calculation the method outlined above in Figure 2 is an example of a template method where the frozen spot is the algorithm and the actual prize of some equipment is the hot spot.

In general template methods are based on hook methods, which are either abstract methods, regular methods or template methods[13, p. 107]. Template methods implement the frozen spots and hook methods implement the hot spots of an application.

In order to explore the SDL language mechanisms necessary to support metapatterns it is important to look at the relationship between the template and hook classes. Whether a class is a template or a hook class depends on the viewpoint because classes may contain methods that are hooks for some classes and templates for others at the same time.

There are three ways the template and hook classes can be related. The template class is based on one or more hook methods which can be defined[13, p. 112]:

- within the same class as the template method
- in one of the superclasses of the class where the template is defined
- in another class

If inheritance between the template an hook class exist the template class is always a descendant of the hook class[13, p. 121–122].

Fig. 3. Unified template and hook classes[13, p. 122]

These three types of relations between the template and the hook classes can be shown graphically as depicted in the following figures (3, 4, 5).

The notation used is a subset of the notation used by OMT[14] and thus should be familiar. A solid line between to classes represents 1 : 1-relationship, a diamond at the beginning of a line represents aggregation, and a dot on the line represents 1 : N-relationship, a triangle represents inheritance.

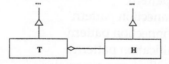

Fig. 4. No inheritance relationship between template and hook classes[13, p. 121]

In Figure 3 the template and hook method are defined in the same class and related either without or with a reference. If we wish to change the hook method in this case it can only be done by sub classing the unified class. This implies that we lose the flexibility to change the behavior of the template at runtime[13, p. 133].

Fig. 5. Template and hook classes related by inheritance[13, p. 122]

Figure 4 shows the relationship between the template and hook classes if no inheritance relationship exists between the classes. If there is no inheritance relationship between the template and hook classes it is not possible to construct recursive structures. A typical example of this type of patterns is the *Strategy* pattern from [4, p. 315] in which the e.g. the actual algorithm used in a calculation is determined by the use of an appropriate strategy class that can be changed at runtime.

Figure 5 shows the template and hook classes related by inheritance. In this situation it is possible to construct recursive structures. A well known example of a recursive structure is the implementation of the folder and document metaphors of modern graphic displays in which folders may contain either folders or documents recursively.

4.3   The seven metapatterns

The template and hook classes are (if we exclude the unification metapattern) related by a reference from the template class to the hook class. This relation can be of either 1 : 1 or 1 : N cardinality. If the cardinality of the relation is combined with the possible recursiveness of the hook class we end up with seven metapatterns:

(1) Unification pattern
(2) 1 : 1 Connection pattern
(3) 1 : N Connection pattern
(4) 1 : 1 Recursive Connection pattern
(5) 1 : N Recursive Connection pattern
(6) 1 : 1 Recursive Unification pattern
(7) 1 : N Recursive Unification pattern

It is not the purpose of this paper to discuss the different purposes and consequences of these seven patterns, but they are mentioned here for completeness. In the next section we investigate the language constructs of SDL that support these seven patterns.

5   SDL and Metapatterns

In order to use SDL in conjunction with metapatterns we must investigate the SDL language constructs that support the necessary concepts that metapatterns are based on. As mentioned in Section 4 these concepts are: *virtuallity, inheritance,* and *polymorphy and dynamic binding.*

There are three concepts in SDL that are candidates for for the implementation of template and hook methods: *Abstract Data Types (ADT), procedures,* and *processes.* These constructs all contain one or more of the concepts necessary to support metapatterns.

One of the important principles the metapattern approach is build upon is the narrow inheritance interface principle which states: "Behavior that is spread over several methods in a class should be based on a minimal set of methods which have to be overwritten"[13, p. 113].

This is a general design principle which means that as few as possible methods in the subclass should be rewritten in order to adapt a template method. We will later see that this principle is important when we use processes as our base for the realization of metapatterns in SDL.

5.1 Abstract Data Type

SDL does not have the same object/class concept as normally found in object-oriented languages; in stead SDL operated on types and instances of those types which is a richer concept.

The concept in SDL that is nearest to the class/object concept found in object-oriented languages is the Abstract Data Type (ADT). The Abstract Data Type is the basis for object-oriented programming[11] and in SDL it is possible to build inheritance hierarchies from ADTs.

```
NEWTYPE HookAdt
OPERATORS
  hook: HookAdt->HookAdt;
ENDNEWTYPE;

NEWTYPE TemplateAdt
INHERITS HookAdt
ADDING
OPERATORS
  hook: HookAdt->HookAdt;
  temp: TemplateAdt->TemplateAdt;
ENDNEWTYPE;
```

Fig. 6. SDL ADT used to implement metapattern

An ADT in SDL is an abstract description of a data object and its associated operations with possible inheritance of the data and operations. The ADT concept in SDL has some serious shortcomings compared to the normal class concept because it lacks the possibility to make operations virtual and the ability to overwrite operations in subtypes.

An example of an attempt to use ADT's to implement patterns—or in this case a simple polymorphic method is shown in Figure 6. The problem here is, that it is not possible to redefine the hook method in the template ADT. This is no surprise because the ADT concept in SDL is meant to be an abstraction for data and not an object/class abstraction.

5.2 Procedure

The procedure concept in SDL resembles the procedure concept found in most programming languages with the exception that the procedure can be declared virtual in e.g. a process type and later refined in a subtype. This means that the procedure concept in SDL can be used in transitions to adapt their behavior.

One of the problems we face when using the procedure is that we can only implement 1 : 1 relationships between the template and hook class because an actual instance of a procedure will be tied to one particular instance of a process and thus it is not possible to address a set of procedures without doing it through a set of process instances.

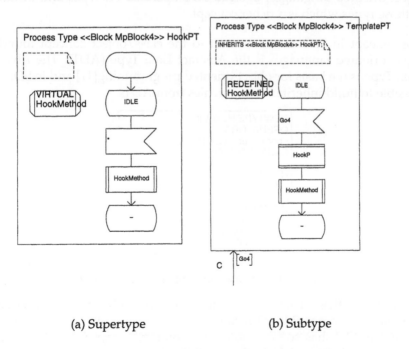

(a) Supertype   (b) Subtype

Fig. 7. SDL procedure used to implement metapattern

Figure 7(a) shows the process supertype's transitions if procedures are used to implement the hook class. In this case the class is the SDL process and it is specialized by means of the virtual procedure as shown in Figure 7(b).

Procedures can be utilized in two different ways: either as part of a process where they are specialized in specializations of the process as shown above or "stand-alone" where one template procedure uses one or more other virtual procedures as hook procedures.

5.3 Process

Processes are suitable to implement the metapatterns concept but the principle is different from the normal usage of classes, objects, and methods in object-orientation due to the usage of signals and virtual transitions. If we use processes to model the objects the template process must specify virtual transitions to implement the virtuallity.

In SDL, if we look at the process case, not all transitions are virtual and thus not all methods are virtual in the metapattern sense. This does however not constitute a problem because it forces us to design our frameworks very careful since we can only adapt transitions that are meant to be adapted. This point stresses the importance of the narrow inheritance interface principle with respect to SDL.

In this section we investigate the SDL language first with respect to the $1 : 1$ relation between template and hook class in order to keep the discussion of the basic mechanisms simple. Next we discuss the implications $1 : N$ relationships will have on the usage of SDL. We discuss the three different inheritance relations in the $1 : 1$ case (Section 4.2) in the first part and the $1 : N$ implications on these relations in the next part.

In general the class and method concepts of ordinary object-oriented languages are mapped to processes and transitions in the SDL language, i.e. classes are mapped to process types, objects to process instances and methods to transitions.

5.3.1 Unification Metapattern

In the unification metapattern the template and hook methods are located in the same class which implies that hook methods must be redefined in subclasses.

In SDL this behavior can be obtained by using the *virtual process* concept. We define a block type in which the process containing the template and hook transitions is declared to be virtual as shown in Figure 8.

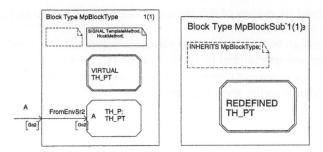

Fig. 8. SDL block for the super and sub processes of the unification metapattern

Figure 9(a) shows the general structure of the transition graph of the unification metapatterns super process type. The *Go2* signal is just used in the simulation to start the process from the outside.

The template method is shown here in a very schematic way but the essence is that somewhere in the transition the `HookMethod` method is called by sending the signal *HookMethod* to its own instance. It would of course be possible to insert a state and wait for an answer from the hook method and thus the behavior would be identical to the normal object-oriented behavior.

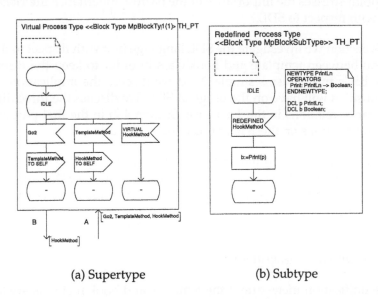

(a) Supertype   (b) Subtype

Fig. 9. Transition graph for the unification metapattern process type

The *HookMethod* transition is declared *virtual* in order to be able to redefine it in the redefinition of the process. In the sub process type the *HookMethod* is *redefined* to conduct the desired behavior. In this case it just calls an operator on an instance of an abstract data type.

When the unification metapatterns is used in this form, it is done by instantiating an instance of the subblock. This subblock will then contain a process with the redefined behavior for the hook method.

5.3.2 1 : 1 *Recursive Connection Metapattern*

The recursive metapatterns are characterized by the inheritance relationship between the template and the hook classes. This inheritance relationship enables the possibility to build recursive structures.

In this section and the next section we will use the principal block shown in Figure 10. It consists of two process types which in this section are related by inheritance and in the next section are unrelated. There is one instance of each class.

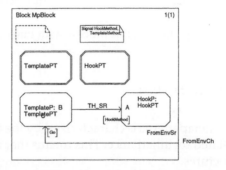

Fig. 10. SDL block for the inheritance metapattern

In the recursive case the template class inherits from the hook class. In SDL this can be expressed as shown in Figure 11(a) where the transition graph of the template process type is shown.

The template process type implements the *TemplateMethod* transition. This transition uses the *HookMethod* signal to invoke the *HookMethod* transition in the super type. In this case the *HookMethod* signal is sent to self which effectively makes this implementation a unification metapattern. If the *HookMethod* signal instead is sent to an instance of the hook process type the implementation is a 1 : 1 recursive connection metapattern.

The hook process type shown in Figure 11(b) simply implements the *Hook-Method* transition. This transition could also be virtual if there is a need to redefine the hook method. This redefinition could take place in the template process type because the template process type is a descendant of the hook process type, or in another descendant of the hook process type.

368

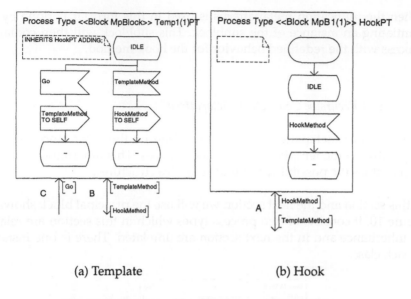

(a) Template   (b) Hook

Fig. 11. Template and hook process with inheritance

5.3.3 1 : 1 *Connection Metapattern*

The 1 : 1 connection metapatterns is characterized by the template and hook classes not being related by inheritance. This means that it is not possible to make recursive structures.

The implementation is analog to the implementation of the 1 : 1 recursive connection pattern. We define a template process type and a hook process type but in this case we cannot redefine the *HookMethod* in the template process type but only within its own inheritance hierarchy.

The template process contains the same transitions as the case with the recursive connection pattern. In this case we also create the hook process in order to know its process identification (PId). We later use this PId to invoke the HookMethod method in the hook process. In this simple case we do not need to save the hook PId (but we do it anyway) because the hook process only exists in one instance and thus the *HookMethod* will always reach the right process.

The hook process simply contains the hook method. The same holds for this implementation as for the recursive case that the *HookMethod* could be virtual if there is a need to redefine this transition.

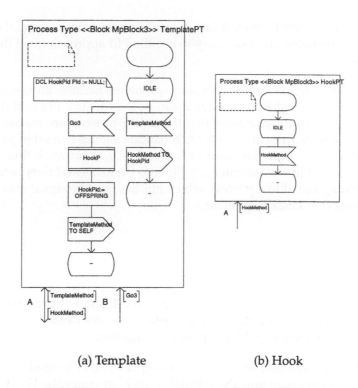

(a) Template   (b) Hook

Fig. 12. Template and hook process without inheritance

5.3.4   1 : N Connections

The $1 : N$ connections differ from the $1 : 1$ connections with respect to how many hook methods are called from the template method. In the $1 : 1$ case there is only one instance of both the template and the hook process, but in the $1 : N$ case there is up to N instances of the hook process. A typical template method iterates over these instances.

We must thus look at how SDL implements references to objects (or processes) because the whole metapattern approach is closely tied to how objects are referenced.

In SDL we have two means for referencing processes: either through the static description on the structural level or through PId's.

The structural description has a kind of type checking because it is possible to analyze the program statically with respect to which signals can be received. The problem with the static description is that a signal route may point to a process set, and it is not possible on the structural level to point out a particular instance in the process set. Thus if we need more than one process instance we must address this instance through its PId. The PId method is necessary because it is not possible to broadcast a signal to a set of process instances. It is necessary to use the PId approach in all the $1 : N$ patterns.

The PId approach also introduces some problems because any legal (i.e. if its declared on a signal route) signal can be sent to any PId and thus the static analysis cannot guarantee that the right processes are reached when particular signals are sent. In order to broadcast signals to a set of processes we must save the PId's for these processes in e.g. an array. If this array is just an array of PId we can enter any PId into the array and thus potentially send a wrong signal to a process, which implies that the signal may be lost or causing other kinds of problems.

5.4   Other issues

There is a number of other issues we can investigate with respect to SDL and the usage of (meta)patterns. These aspects are not treated in this article but could be made a target for further investigation.

There is no class/object and method concepts in SDL. Instead we use the process type/instance and the (virtual) transition concepts. What are the implications of this rather different approach to object-orientation compared to the classical view?

There is no such concept as an abstract process in SDL and thus all processes must have well defined behavior (even though this behavior may be empty transitions). It is the task of the programmer to ensure that an "abstract" class isn't instantiated. This is of cause a problem with respect to the modeling of systems since we cannot make abstract implementations and be certain that these abstract implementations aren't instantiated.

6   Conclusion

In this article we have investigated the SDL language concepts suitable for supporting the concept of metapatterns.

SDL has three language constructs that may be utilized to implement metapatterns: the Abstract Data Type, the procedure, and the process.

The abstract data type is not suitable to support metapatterns because of the lack of virtuallity and redefinability of the operators of the ADT.

The procedure is suitable to implement 1 : 1 connection and the unification metapatterns, but is unable to support the 1 : N connection patterns because the procedures are tied to particular process instances.

The process is the most powerful SDL concept and it seems to be powerful enough to support the object-oriented concepts necessary to utilize metapatterns. The necessary object-oriented concepts are *inheritance, virtuallity,* and *dynamic binding and polymorphy.* These concepts are supported in the SDL process type and thus the metapatterns concept can be utilized in SDL.

References

[1] Frank Buschmann, Regine Meunier, Hans Rohnert, Peter Sommerlad, and Michael Stal. *Pattern-Oriented Siftware Architecture. A System of Patterns.* John Wiley and Sons Ltd., 1996.

[2] James O. Coplien and Douglas C. Schmidt, editors. *Pattern Languages of Program Design,* volume 1. Addison-Wesley Publishing Company, Inc., 1995.

[3] Jan Ellsberger, Dieter Hogrefe, and Amardeo Sarma. *SDL. Formal Object-oriented Language for Communicating Systems.* Prentice-Hall International Editions, 1997.

[4] Eric Gamma, Richard Helm, Ralph Johnson, and John Vlissides. *Design Patterns. Elements of reuseable Object-Oriented Software.* Addison-Wesley Publishing Company, Inc., 1995.

[5] David Garlan and Dewayne E. Perry. Introduction to the special issue on software architecture. *IEEE Transactions on Software Engineering,* 21(4):269–274, April 1995.

[6] Birgit Geppert, Reinhard Gotzhein, and Frank Rößler. Configuring communication protocols using sdl patterns. In A. Carvalli and A. Sarma, editors, *SDL '97: Time for Testing - SDL, MSC and Trends.* SDL-Forum, Elsevier Science B.V., 1997.

[7] Hermann Hüni, Ralph Johnson, and Robert Engel. A framework for network protocol software. In *OOPSLA '95 Proceedings,* pages 358–369, 1995.

[8] ITU-T. *Z100 Standard.* ITU-T, 199X.

[9] Norman L. Kerth and Ward Cunningham. Using patterns to improve our architectural vision. *IEEE Software,* 14(1):53–59, January/February 1997.

[10] Ole Lehrmann Madsen, Birger Møller-Pedersen, and Kristen Nygaard. *Object Oriented Programming in The BETA Programming Language.* Addison-Wesley Publishing Company, Inc., 1994.

372

[11] Bertrand Meyer. *Object-Oriented Software Construction*. Prentice-Hall International Editions, second edition, 1997.

[12] Anders Olsen et al. *Systems Engineering Using SDL-92*. Elsevier, 1994.

[13] Wolfgang Pree. *Design Patterns for Object-Oriented Software Development*. Addison-Wesley Publishing Company, Inc., 1994.

[14] James Rumbaugh, Michael Blaha, William Premerlani, Frederick Eddy, and William Lorensen. *Object-Oriented Modeling and Design*. Prentice-Hall International Editions, 1991.

[15] John M. Vlissides, James O. Coplien, and Norman L. Kerth, editors. *Pattern Languages of Program Design 2*, volume 2. Addison-Wesley Publishing Company, Inc., 1996.

SDL'99 : The Next Millennium
R. Dssouli, G.v. Bochmann and Y. Lahav, editors

External communication with SDL Systems

Gerd Kurzbach[a], Martin v. Löwis of Menar[b], Ralf Schröder[c]

[a] Siemens AG, ICN CA IN, Siemensdamm 50-54, D-13629 Berlin, Germany

[bc] Humboldt Universität zu Berlin, Institut für Informatik, Lehrstuhl für Systemanalyse, Unter den Linden 6, 10099 Berlin, Germany
loewis@informatik.hu-berlin.de
r.schroeder@informatik.hu-berlin.de

The formal description technique SDL is used for the documentation and verification of complex distributed communication systems. SDL tools are able to transform a specification automatically to a prototype implementation or even to a software product. The generated program is not isolated in a real system environment. However, the communication aspect with a system environment is not standardized. Hence, there are only tool specific solutions. With the standardization of interface description techniques, e.g. ASN.1 and IDL and even the combination of SDL with these techniques, the external communication aspect of SDL should be investigated. Scenarios with different start points are discussed, some of them are applied within an industrial software project.

KEYWORDS

SDL, ASN.1, IDL, Basic Encoding Rules, Common Data Representation, CORBA, environment communication, interface

1. Introduction

Distributed systems specified and implemented using SDL need to communicate using existing infrastructure and communication protocols. Often, such SDL systems also need to integrate with systems not specified in SDL.

In 1995, a combination of SDL with ASN.1 [X.208] was standardized [Z.105] by ITU-T. It is expected that in 2000 there is a standardized mapping of an ITU extension of OMG IDL to SDL [Z.130]. Both languages are interface languages with a well defined encoding scheme for data values and they are key technologies in various application areas. For example, ASN.1 is extensively used to communicate operations in the Intelligent Network [Q.1228] by means of the Basic Encoding Rules [X.209]. OMG IDL is tightly integrated with the CORBA standard [CORBA], which defines the Common Data Representation and relies on TCP/IP [Pos81].

Even though these integration techniques combine the different notations on a semantic level, they do not integrate SDL with the infrastructure. There are two basic scenarios:

1. The SDL system is given, e.g. as standard, a program is generated from that formal specification using any SDL tool. Such an SDL based program has provides a vendor specific and often specification dependent interface for external communication. The typical way is to use SDL signals to the system environment. It would be helpful for the further development process to use well known interface description techniques for that kind of communication. This scenario is discussed in chapter 2.

2. The interface description or even an implementation is given and an SDL system has to be developed using that description. Applications are access to custom specific libraries and hand implementation of SDL entities - typically data - for run time optimization. Chapter 3 is dedicated these problems.

The technical background of this work is based on SDL tools, which are implemented at Humboldt University [SITE]. These tools are known as SDL Integrated Tool Environment (SITE). Some of the presented features were implemented for research only; others have been used in deployed applications.

2. Signal Exchange

There are SDL systems with channels to the system environment. Typical examples are protocol layer specifications. If such a system is part of a larger software system, the exchange of signals can be seen as communication between program modules. This approach has the advantage of supporting the complete set of SDL communication concepts, but restricts communication peers to "SDL-aware" entities. The asynchronous communication with the SDL system environment via channels has no formal semantics. But practical applications have some natural assumptions:

1. A snapshot of all communicating software instances can be considered as blocks in one SDL system connected with implicit channels. It is a snapshot only, because programs can be started and killed, and dynamic block creation is not part of SDL.

2. An outgoing signal is an information object consisting of the signal instance (signal identification and parameters), the sender identification, an optional receiver identification and optional routing information (e.g. the outgoing channel). An incoming signal should provide the same set of information.

3. Possibly, the channel structure of the SDL system is ignored by external applications. So, it is useful to provide a communication peer, which represents the unification of all channels to the system environment.

Current SDL tools provide a tool specific application interface (API). Often the user has to fill and read tool specific structures. If these structures are described with an interface description technique, e.g. IDL or ASN.1, well known technologies could be used for the management of these application interfaces. The most natural approach is the use of ASN.1 because the combination of SDL with ASN.1 is well defined. Today IDL is another well-known interface description technique. So it is useful to consider the specification of interfaces with IDL, too. Programming communication infrastructure it would be very helpful, if tool vendors provide this kind of API in one of the known techniques on user request.

2.1 ASN.1 approach

The combination of SDL and ASN.1 is established in the SDL community. ASN.1 provides an encoding scheme BER [X.209] to map data values to a byte stream and vice versa. If the SDL program supports the connection between its internal data structures and encoded values, any ASN.1 tool, e.g. Snacc [SaNe], could be used to read or write the data values of SDL signals.

This assumes that signal parameters are ASN.1 data only or that SDL data structures are mapped to ASN.1 definitions. As a consequence of the BER encoding, the tagging scheme of the ASN.1 data must be correct. This is not a requirement of the Z.105 standard! The SITE tool set is able to check the correct tagging as well as to generate suitable coding functions for ASN.1 data definitions and selected SDL structures. The use of SDL data without direct ASN.1 representation is not recommended, because of the tool specific mapping. Such data are Array and SDL struct constructs, or even the simple sorts *PId* and *Time*.

The standardized coding is not enough, however. The byte stream must be transmitted somehow and a suitable addressing scheme has to be provided, too. Normally, the generated software is embedded into a communication system, e.g. a proprietary TCP implementation, which is able to transmit a byte stream to a certain communication partner. Often such an interface is not developed for the communication with more than one communication instance per endpoint, so that the SDL specific sender and receiver information has to be coded into a PDU somehow. The ASN.1 description

```
SignalPDU ::= SEQUENCE {
   signal_identification ID,
   sender PId,
   receiver PId OPTIONAL,
   route PATH OPTIONAL,
   encoded_parameter OCTET STRING
}
```

could encapsulate the signal parameters, where the definitions of the data type *ID*, *PId*, and *PATH* are tool-dependent. Of course, a library specific PDU could be used, too. SITE code generation supports two socket based libraries, which were provided by the tool users.

One was used for a demonstration platform for advanced multimedia teleservices, based on a sophisticated broadband network and signalling system [BGKS+]. Most of the B-ISDN protocol layers was specified using SDL systems, ATM hardware driver and user applications was programmed in C++. Here the signal identification was a static assignment to numbers, each external channel was mapped to a connection oriented communication peer of the socket library and PId values are represented by locally unique numbers. The connection of two SDL systems was managed without user configuration assuming equal channel and signal names. A non SDL program could use a name service to establish the connection even across operating system boundaries, e.g. between VxWorks, Solaris and WinNT. The figure 1 demonstrates the connection scenario of two SDL systems, a name service and a central time server.

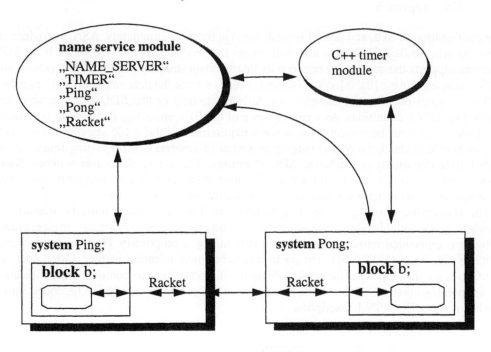

figure 1

The other library is part of a IN run-time-environment developed by SIEMENS. This application is in production use. Here the communication infrastructure can be configured dynamically with a management information base (MIB)[CFSD]. The configuration includes the mechanism of the transport because available protocol implementations, e.g. libraries for interacting with TCAP or SNMP. The mapping of communication primitives to SDL signals is implemented either in the run-time system directly, or using mapping rules from ASN.1 specifications where appropriate.

A third solution for the communication library was the use of a CORBA implementation of ORBacus [OOC98] for the transport of PDU's. Here an IDL interface is provided for channel endpoints, PId's, signals and the system. The initial connection is established with an extra name service. Because of the two levels of encoding data parameters - BER for parameters and CDR for signals with the encoded data parameter - a direct encoding of data with CDR is desirable. This technology described in [Bie97]. This library was used for the prototype development of alternative transport protocols (B-ISDN [Q.2931]) of CORBA implementations [AIGN+].

Instead of using TCP or CORBA, any other infrastructure capable of messaging could be used to transmit signal PDU's (e.g. ROSE).

2.2 CORBA approach

The consequent continuation of using CORBA as a transport for signal PDU's is the encoding of signal parameters with CDR directly. A straight-forward support for ASN.1 parameters comes from [XoJIDM]. For the remaining core SDL communication concepts IDL representations are provided by the SDL tool, i.e. tool uses a partial mapping from SDL to IDL.

This is an SDL-centric viewpoint. The mapping from IDL to SDL as defined in a draft standard [Z.130] is the reverse direction and is discussed in chapter 3. Such a mapping is useful if the designer is able to start with the interface description, i.e. the system is developed from scratch. In the telecommunication area, the SDL specification or at least the signal description is often fixed, e.g. by standards, so that the development from scratch is impossible. Therefore a possibly standardized mapping from SDL to IDL is useful. It is not necessary that the SDL to IDL mapping is compatible with the IDL to SDL mapping.

One outline of an SDL to IDL mapping is presented in *table 1:SDL-IDL communications mapping*. With such a mapping, it is possible to connect different SDL systems, as long as they share the same set of signals, and as long as all provide the necessary IDL interfaces at run-time. Since CORBA encapsulates implementations, it is also possible for non-SDL entities to send and receive signals to and from an SDL system.

In the mapping, each SDL system acts as a well-known object, which can be used to navigate to individual channels. Hence, a program has to know the object reference in order to send signals to the SDL system. The channels, in turn, can receive incoming signals, and support an attached peer for outgoing signals. Here the object reference of the receiver has to be registered, so an SDL bidirectional channel has both roles: server and client. Remote procedure calls would be transmitted using signals as defined in the model [Z.100].

SDL	IDL

system s	exception NoRoute { };
	interface System{ };
	interface s:System{
	   Channel get_<c>; //for each channel
	};

channel c	interface Channel{
	   void set_peer(in Channel remote);
	   void transmit(in Signal s);
	};

signal s
<parameter>
	valuetype Signal {
	   public PId sender;
	   public PId receiver;
	};
	valuetype s:Signal{
	   <mapping for parameters>
	};

remote procedure p	mapping to signals according to the SDL model
data subset	as defined in the ASN.1 to IDL mapping

PId	interface PId {
	   System get_system();
	};

table 1: SDL-IDL communications mapping

Technology

An SDL tool has to generate IDL descriptions for all necessary entities. This would allow the use of that interface with non-SDL software, e.g. Java applets. The SDL tool has two options:

○ An IDL compiler is used to generate target code. The SDL tools generate target code based on the CORBA vendor's IDL compiler output. With respect to code generation this approach is simple. The problem is that the scheduling system of the SDL system has to work together with the used CORBA library.

○ The SDL tools are able to generate the CDR encoding themselves and the communication system of the target library supports CORBA conform transports exactly as it is needed. The tools become more complex, but the vendor of the SDL target library has the complete control over the design.

The CDR encoding is not yet supported by SITE tools. There are plans to test this approach with a simulation library for SDL systems, because the connection between the simulator and the SDL program is CORBA based already.

The technology presented here does not deal with the bootstrapping process of the distributed application, and how initial object references are communicated. There are a number of approaches known to deal with this issue; mandating a specific one is not desirable because tool vendors often supports different strategies for that problem.

3. Integrated interface descriptions

This section discusses some ways how an SDL system can be adapted to a given communications interface description. This is the case if an SDL system can be developed from scratch or if parts of the SDL system have to be connected with a given library interface.

3.1   Beyond Z.105

For the use of ASN.1 in SDL a new language was designed and has to be maintained [Z.105]. This is a bad solution because:

○ it is a special solution for ASN.1 and not applicable to other languages.

○ it is a compromise for both languages: SDL and ASN.1. There are syntactic and with respect to ASN.1 even semantics changes. For example there are multiple problems with the following Z.105 description:

>   *Set ::= integer{ one(1), two(2), three(3), unknown(-1) }*
>   *RetValues ::= integer{ timout(1), invalid_argument(2), unknown(3) }*

The type *Set* has an SDL keyword as name. This example is artificial but there are many hits for field names in real ASN.1 specifications. The value *unknown* is mapped to a synonym description according to Z.105. It is defined twice. Because of the conflict with the operation '-' the correct ASN.1 name *invalid-argument* cannot be used directly.

A syntactic isolation of the external notation is useful, provided the implicit mapping to SDL is intuitive:

```
asntype
    -- here ASN.1 syntax is accepted only --
    Set ::= INTEGER{ one(1), two(2), three(3), unknown(-1) }
    RetValues ::= INTEGER{ timout(1), invalid-argument(2), unknown(3) }
endasntype;
```

This solution only solves syntactic problems of the direct use of ASN.1 specifications. Semantic problems have to be solved by improving the mapping rules. Of course, ASN.1 expressions cannot be used in SDL tasks now. But practical experiences with the SITE tool set show, that it is sufficient to use SDL-like expressions with two small exceptions: optional field elements in complete structure initialization and choice initialization.

An analog notation, which is already supported by SITE tools on syntactic level, is the ITU-ODL integration:

```
odltype
    module ExternalRPC {
        interface SDLGate {
            long Fibonacci(in long argument)
    } };
endodltype;
```

Here the future mapping rules of ITU-ODL to SDL could be implemented for the semantic interpretation. The syntactic approach is not restricted to interface descriptions. An implementation can be given, too:

```
cplusplustype
    int Fib(int i) { return i<=1 ? 1 : Fib(i-1)+Fib(i-2); }
endcplusplustype;
```

The external notation has to be analyzed so, that the SDL tool knows the defined symbols. The combination of SDL tools with several external analysis tools can be a good solution for the implementation of the external descriptions. There are two typical semantic backgrounds of external notations:

1. The external description is mapped to SDL. E.g. the integration of ASN.1 assumes the mapping of all constructs to SDL, i.e. the external constructs are interpreted according to the semantics of SDL. This is a good idea with respect to the formal background of SDL.

2. The external construct is mapped to an interface description only, e.g. a sort definition with signature but without behavior. Formally, such an SDL specification is not correct because, the semantics of the external constructs remains undefined. The user is responsible for any good or bad use of these constructs. This semantic approach has to be applied if the "foreign" notation does not fit easily into the formal SDL semantics but the user needs the interworking property. Pointer constructions are a typical example.

An extension of an SDL tool could be to provide the mapping from the external notation to SDL directly, i.e. the user has not to know the mapping rules in detail. This is useful for mappings of type 1, e.g. ITU-ODL to SDL. However, it is dangerous for mappings of type 2 because the user sees normal SDL constructs with non SDL behavior.

3.2 ASN.1 in current infrastructures

OSI standards [X.200] provide the notation Remote Operation Service Elements [X.219] together with suitable protocols. Using these constructs, signatures for remote operations can be specified in ASN.1. An ASN.1 combination with SDL should allow a direct use of remote operations and as a consequence at least the error descriptions, too. This is not an academic view, many protocol descriptions in the telecommunication area, e.g. the intelligent network [Q.1228], provides ASN.1 specifications with remote operation definitions. Capability Set 2 of the IN specification uses constructs provided by the new ASN.1 definition [X.680]. For a suitable integration, the mapping of ASN.1 constructs to SDL must be enhanced. Here the concepts with implementation background are discussed only.

Predefined macro applications

At least the macro applications (or equivalent X.680-style information objects) OPERATION and ERROR should be supported by the mapping because these constructs are used by protocols. Useful is a mapping of macro values (object instances) to SDL signals, e.g. the specification

```
op OPERATION
    ARGUMENT INTEGER
    RESULT BOOLEAN
    ERRORS { timeout, unsupported }
 ::= localValue 42

timeout ERROR PARAMETER REAL ::= localValue 1001

unsupported ERROR ::= localValue 1002
```

introduces multiple SDL signals implicitly:

```
signal op(ROSE_ARG,Integer), op_RESULT(ROSE_RES,Boolean),
    timeout(ROSE_ERROR, Real),
    unsupported(ROSE_ERROR);
```

Contrary to the first intuition of SDL users, the ASN.1 OPERATION macro is *not* expressed as a remote procedure in SDL. The protocol stack used (TCAP, [Q.771]) defines different operation classes, e.g. an operation might "succeed" if there was no error in a certain period of time. Also, a service might need to invoke multiple operations simultaneously, which are then transmitted in a single PDU. Fine-tuning control flow based on remote procedures would not be possible.

The additional parameter is based on practical experience: a real world library for remote operations, e.g. an SS7 stack implementation, expects additional protocol information (e.g. invoke identifications). The exact contents of the parameter is specific to the application area.

This functionality is supported for the SIEMENS specific SDL library of chapter 2 to connect SDL specifications with an SS7 stack implementation of an other vendor. The application runs on call control units.

Like ERROR and OPERATION, other information object definitions of the new ASN.1 standard could be directly supported by SDL in combination with ASN.1.

Rules of extensibility

These rules are an encoding enhancement for better version control of PDU's. The essence is, that the encoder has to skip and store unknown encoded fragments and the decoder has to include the stored unknown arguments again. The unknown encoded strings have to be stored in placeholders of data structures. Possibly this place holder is hidden or can be accessed by suitable operations. At least, it must be assignment transparent:

```
Arg1 ::= sequence{
    i Integer,
    ...
}
Arg2 := sequence {
    my_addr PId,
    pdu Arg1
}

signal sig1(Arg1), sig2(Arg2);

...

input sig(arg1);
    task arg2 := (. self, arg1 .);
    output sig2(arg2);
    ...
```

This specification should be able to receive an encoded value of type

```
Arg1-version2 ::= sequence {
    i Integer,
    ...,
    b Boolean
}
```

The additional field b is also part of the encoded value for signal sig2. Choices and enumerations are straight forward, e.g.:

```
        Version ::= enumerated { one(1), two(2),...}
        dcl v Version;
        ...
        decision v;
            (one) : ...
            (two): ...
            else : /* unknown versions */
        enddecision;
```

ASN.1 ANY

The interpretation of the ASN.1 type ANY is given in Z.105:

```
        newtype Any_type
        endnewtype Any_type;
```

Obviously, this sort is not helpful, there are no values. A more convincing solution is already discussed in [Schr94]: the definition of *Any_type* depends on all defined data of the specification and provides operations to convert from and to a specific sort:

```
        Seq ::= sequence {
            kind Integer,
            parameter any defined by kind
        }
        dcl seq Seq, b Boolean, i Integer;
        ...
        decision seq!kind;
            (0): task b := Boolean(seq!parameter);
            (1): task i := Integer(seq!parameter);
            else : call ErrorMsg('some error...');
        enddecision;
```

In context of ASN.1 there is a natural technical solution for the conversion: it is the application of the encoding rules. If conversion to the requested type fails, an exception is raised. The exception concept will be part of the SDL language revision in 2000.

3.3   IDL Mapping

In a CORBA environment, distribution is based on interfaces designed prior to implementing the functionality behind the interfaces. Just as an ASN.1 specification defines nothing but on-the-wire representation, the IDL definition, together with the GIOP specification, defines how operation invocations are communicated between remote entities.

Since the CORBA RPC concepts are more similar to SDL RPC than ASN.1/ROSE is, [Z.130] defines that IDL/ODL operations map to remote procedures. Once the exception concept [TDB609] is available in SDL, designing CORBA clients and servers is very natural in SDL.

From a tool viewpoint, integration between the CORBA and SDL run-time systems is a difficult issue. Typically, CORBA run-time systems provide native support for a few selected languages, such as C++ and Java. As outlined in section 2.2, design alternatives include integration of stubs of a foreign language into the run-time system, and complete implementation of a CORBA run-time system within the SDL run-time. The authors are currently investigating the latter option.

4. Summary

Many of the interface aspects presented here are driven by an industrial project in the telecommunication area. In particular, the features relating to ASN.1 have been used in implementing IN SCP functionality by one of the authors. This paper presents a broader view, so that some proposed concepts are not implemented with SITE, for example CDR support for code generation.

SDL applications have to interwork with foreign technology in different infrastructures, which impose different requirements on the application. Further work (both research and standardization) is necessary to integrate SDL with these infrastructures, while at the same time maintaining the high abstraction level of SDL.

5. Literature

AIGN+   AT&T, Iona, GMD Fokus, Nortel, Teltec DCU, Alcatel, Deutsche Telekom, Ericsson Telecommunications, Humboldt University of Berlin, Object Oriented Concepts, Open Environment Software, Telenor: Interworking Between CORBA And TC Systems, document telecom/98-10-13, OMG, 1998.

BGKS+   Ulf Behnke, Michael Geipl, Gerd Kurzbach, Ralf Schröder, Nils Fischbeck, Renee Mundstock: Development of broadband ISDN telecommunication services using SDL'92, ASN.1 and automatic code generation. In Participation Proceedings of 8th international conference of Formal Description Techniques for Distributed Systems and Communication Protocols FORTE'92, Montreal,1995.

Bie97   Frank Bielig: Implementierung einer SDL-Laufzeitbibliothek auf CORBA-Basis, Diplomarbeit, Humboldt-Universität, Institut f. Informatik, Berlin, 1997.

CFSD   J. Case, M. Fedor, M. Schoffstall, J. Davin: A Simple Network Management Protocol (SNMP), RFC 1157, 1990.

CORBA   OMG: The Common Object Request Broker: Architecture and Specification, formal/98-02-33, Framingham, 1998.

OOC98   OOC: ORBacus for C++ and Java, Object-Oriented Concepts, Inc, 1998.

Pos81   Jon B. Postel: Transmission Control Protocol, IETF, RFC 793, Arlington, 1981.

Q.771   ITU: Functional Description of Transaction Capabilities, Recommendation Q.771, Genf, 1997.

Q.1228   ITU: Interface Recommendation for intelligent network Capability Set 2, Geneva, 1997.

Q.2931   ITU: Recommendation B-ISDN-DSS2-UNI-Layer 3 specification for basic call / connection control, Genf.

SaNe   Michael Sample, Gerald Neufeld: Snacc 1.0: A High Performance ASN.1 to C/C++ Compiler. University of British Columbia, Vancouver, Canada, 1993.

Schr94   Ralf Schröder: SDL'92 data handling in combination with ASN.1. master thesis, Department of Computer Science, Humboldt University Berlin, Germany, March 1994.

SITE   SDL Integrated Tool Environment of Humboldt University Berlin: http://www.informatik.hu-berlin.de/Themen/SITE.

TDB609   Q.2/10 rapporteur: New Constructs for Exception Handling, ITU-T, Berlin, 1998.

X.200   CCITT: Data communication networks open system interconnection (OSI) model and notation, service definition. Blue Book Recommendation X.200, Melbourne, November 1988.

X.208   CCITT: Specification of Abstract Syntax Notation One (ASN.1), In Open Systems Interconnection [X.200] - Basis Reference Model. International Standard Recommendation X.208, conform with ISO8824, Melbourne, 1988.

X.209   CCITT: Specification of Basic Encoding Rules of Abstract Syntax Notation One (ASN.1). In Open Systems Interconnection [X.200] - Basis Reference Model. International Standard Recommendation X.209, conform with ISO8825, Melbourne, 1988.

X.219   CCITT: Data communication networks open system interconnection (OSI) Remote operations: model, notation and service definition. In Blue Book Recommendation X.200, Melbourne, November 1988.

X.680   ITU-T: Data networks and open system communications, OSI networking and system aspects - Abstract Syntax Notation One (ASN.1): Specification of basic notation, ITU-T Recommendation X.680,1995

XoJIDM   Joint X/Open-NMF Inter-Domain Management (XoJIDM) Task Force, Inter Domain Management: Specification Translation, X/Open Preliminary Specification, May 1997.

Z.100   ITU: CCITT Specification and Description Language, Recommendation Z.100, Genf, 1993.

Z.105   ITU: SDL in combination with ASN.1, Recommendation Z.105, Genf, 1997.

Z.130   ITU: ITU-ODL - ITU Object Description Language, Draft International Standard Recommendation Z.130, Genf,1998.

Session X

Testing II

SDL'99 : The Next Millennium
R. Dssouli, G.v. Bochmann and Y. Lahav, editors
©1999 Elsevier Science B.V. All rights reserved

SDL and MSC Based Test Generation for Distributed Test Architectures

Jens Grabowski, Beat Koch, Michael Schmitt, and Dieter Hogrefe

Institute for Telematics, University of Lübeck, Ratzeburger Allee 160, D-23538 Lübeck, Germany, eMail: {jens,bkoch,schmitt,hogrefe}@itm.mu-luebeck.de

Most of the SDL and MSC based test generation methods and tools produce non-concurrent TTCN test cases only. If the test equipment itself is a distributed system, the implementation of such test cases is a difficult task and requires a substantial amount of additional work. In this paper, we explain how concurrent TTCN test cases can be generated directly from SDL system specifications and MSC test purposes. To do this, explicit synchronization points have to be indicated in the MSC test purposes, and information about the existing test components and their connections has to be provided.

Keywords: SDL, MSC, TTCN, distributed systems, distributed test systems, conformance testing, test generation.

1. Introduction

Supporting simulation, validation, code generation and test generation are the most important reasons for using SDL [4,15] as system specification language and MSC [12, 16] as requirement specification language within the software life-cycle for distributed systems. Validation, simulation and code generation tools for SDL and MSC descriptions are commercially available and heavily used in industry [1,11,14].

Contrarily, the use of test generation tools is not very popular yet. There are a lot of reasons for this: Fully automatic test generation methods mainly fail due to complexity. Even for toy examples, they calculate an amount of test cases which cannot be handled in practice. Pragmatic problems are related to the fact that specification based test generation is not applicable equally in all stages of the software life-cycle: In most cases, no detailed SDL specification is developed for small and medium sized software modules and therefore, SDL based test generation methods cannot be used for software module testing and software integration testing.

However, tools which follow a pragmatic approach, such as AUTOLINK, SAMsTAG, TGV, TTCgeN or TVEDA, are used increasingly in industry, research and standardization [2,3,6,7,10,13]. Most of them provide generation of test cases guided by test purposes. SDL is used for system specification; MSC or observer processes are used for test purpose description and the *Tree and Tabular Combined Notation* (TTCN) [9] is used for the representation of the generated test cases.

The current tools compute test cases for one global tester process controlling and observing the entire *System Under Test* (SUT)[1]. Thus, the test cases are described in the non-concurrent form of TTCN. The use of such test cases is problematic if the SUT is a distributed system with components at different locations. In that case, the test equipment itself forms a distributed system, and a test case can be seen as a program running on the distributed test system. It is obvious that the implementation of a non-concurrent TTCN test case on distributed test equipment is a complicated and error-prone task. The use of concurrent TTCN, which directly supports the distribution of test cases among test components, would be more appropriate.

The generation of concurrent TTCN instead of non-concurrent TTCN is not trivial, because additional information is needed which cannot be deduced from an SDL specification. In this paper, we present our ideas of generating concurrent TTCN test cases based on SDL system specifications and MSC test purposes. Throughout the paper, we describe our approach by using the terminology defined in the international standard *'Conformance Testing Methodology and Framework'* (CTMF) [8].

This article is structured in the following manner: In Section 2, we give an introduction to the concepts of concurrent TTCN. Section 3 presents methods for the definition of test component configurations and the synchronization of test events. In Section 4, an algorithm for the generation of concurrent test cases is described. Finally, Section 5 contains a summary and an outlook on our future plans.

2. Concurrent TTCN

In 1996, TTCN [9] has been extended with mechanisms for specifying test suites for distributed test systems. In this section, we introduce the most important concepts of concurrent TTCN.

2.1. Test component configuration

In TTCN, a test system is structured into a number of *test components*. In the non-concurrent case, only one *Main Test Component* (MTC) exists which is defined implicitly. In the concurrent case, one MTC and one or more *Parallel Test Components* (PTCs) exist. The MTC is responsible for the creation of the PTCs and the computation of the final test verdict.

The test components may or may not communicate with the SUT via *Points of Control and Observation* (PCOs). A PCO is exclusively assigned to one test component. Communication at PCOs is bidirectional and asynchronous, i.e., the model for a PCO is a combination of two infinite FIFO buffers. The messages exchanged at PCOs are either *Protocol Data Units* (PDUs) or *Abstract Service Primitives* (ASPs). In the following, we will just use the term ASP, but this could be exchanged with PDU at all places.

Communication between two test components can be performed by an asynchronous exchange of *Coordination Messages* (CMs) at *Coordination Points* (CPs). Similar to a PCO, a CP can also be understood as a combination of two infinite FIFO buffers.

Even if there is no CP specified between the MTC and a PTC, two types of implicit communication are defined: (1) PTCs assign their test verdict to the global result variable which is used by the MTC to compute the final test verdict, and (2) the MTC can check

---

[1] All abbreviations can be found in an appendix at the end of this paper.

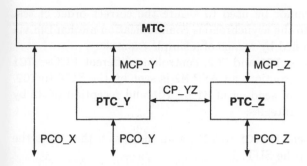

Figure 1. Example test component configuration

whether a PTC has terminated.

The relations between the MTC, the PTCs and the SUT are described by a *test component configuration*. A test suite may contain several test component configurations. For each concurrent test case, one test component configuration has to be chosen. Figure 1 shows a test component configuration: The MTC is connected with the PTCs through the coordination points MCP_Y and MCP_Z. In addition, the MTC controls one PCO (PCO_X). PTC_Y communicates with the SUT through PCO_Y. PTC_Z controls and observes the SUT through PCO_Z. Finally, PTC_Y and PTC_Z may exchange CMs through coordination point CP_YZ.

2.2. Behavior description in concurrent TTCN

The behavior description in concurrent and non-concurrent TTCN is basically identical. The behavior of an MTC is described by using a *Test Case Dynamic Behaviour* table. PTCs are specified as test steps. The behavior of these test steps may be defined as *local trees* within the *Test Case Dynamic Behaviour* table or by using separate *Test Step Dynamic Behaviour* tables.

An example of a concurrent TTCN test case is shown in Figure 10. The behavior of the MTC is specified by the main behavior tree. The PTC descriptions are included as local trees. The MTC creates all PTCs by calling the corresponding behavior descriptions with the CREATE construct (line 1). The termination of the PTCs is checked by means of DONE events (lines 7 and 11).

Communication among test components is treated the same way as communication with the SUT. In Figure 10, statement MCP_2!Proceed(Sync2,Y) on line 6 denotes the sending of CM Proceed(Sync2,Y) via CP MCP_2 to PTC PTC_2. The corresponding receive event of the PTC can be found on line 24.

2.3. Synchronization of test components

The synchronization of test components may be done implicitly or explicitly. Implicit synchronization is performed at the start and the termination of the test case execution: The MTC creates all PTCs and is able to check their termination. Explicit synchronization can be performed by exchanging CMs between test components.

The exchange of CMs can only be used to coordinate the actions of test components controlling different PCOs. But it cannot be used to ensure the correct order of test events at different PCOs. This is due to the asynchronous communication mechanism via infinite FIFO buffers and can be explained by means of a simple example:

Assume we have two test components, TC1 and TC2, controlling different PCOs. TC1 sends an ASP M1 to the SUT and as a reaction, an ASP M2 is sent by the SUT to TC2. We can try to ensure the correct order of sending of M1 by TC1 and reception of M2 by TC2 by using one of the following two strategies:

1. A coordination message CM1 is sent by TC1 to TC2 as an indication that M2 is the next message to be received from the SUT.

2. TC2 knows that M2 is the reaction to M1 sent by TC1 and therefore sends a coordination message CM2 to TC1 as a request to send M1.

In the first case, M2 may overtake CM1 and TC2 will interpret this as a failure although the actual order was correct. In the second case, neither TC1 nor TC2 will detect if the SUT sends M2 during the transmission of CM2 (i.e., before M1 has been sent), and an incorrect order will pass the test. Thus, neither of the strategies can be used to ensure the correct order of sending M1 and receiving M2. Assuming additional knowledge about the transmission time of messages does not help either: According to CTMF, "the relative speed of systems executing the test case should not have an impact on the test result".

3. Test purpose specification for distributed test architectures

Test purpose description with *system level MSCs* has proven to be an effective and intuitive method for tool-supported TTCN test generation from SDL specifications [5]. In a system level MSC, there is one instance for the SUT[2] and one instance for every PCO, where all channels to the environment of the SDL system are considered to be PCOs. For the generation of test cases in the concurrent TTCN format, additional information has to be provided. This information concerns the test component configuration and the synchronization of test components.

3.1. Defining test component configurations

An SDL specification defines the functionality of a system by describing its dynamic behavior. The concrete and finally implemented system architecture, including the distribution of the different components, is not described. The use of structural SDL concepts, e.g., blocks, processes, services, or procedures, may give some hints about the system architecture, but they are only means for structuring the specification. Whether two blocks or processes execute on the same or on several computers at different locations is not described. Therefore, it is not possible to determine an appropriate test component configuration by an analysis of the SDL specification for which we intend to generate test cases. Additional information has to be provided which identifies

1. the test components and their roles (either MTC or PTC),

---

[2]The restriction that the entire SUT is represented only by one instance can be weakened without problems. Due to our experience [13], we keep it here.

2. the assignment of PCOs to test components (connections between test components and SUT),

3. the CPs, and

4. the assignment of CPs to test components (connections among test components).

This information may be provided in a graphical form, e.g., in form of an SDL system or block diagram, in form of the corresponding TTCN tables, or in form of a tool specific command language. A more sophisticated tool may also be able to calculate a default configuration automatically, e.g., a test component configuration where each PTC handles one PCO only and the MTC is responsible for PTC creation, synchronization, and computation of the final test verdict.

In order to implement the automatic generation of concurrent TTCN test cases from SDL system specifications and MSC test purposes, we have to restrict ourselves to a certain class of test component configurations. Therefore, we require that each PTC handles at least one PCO and that it is connected directly to the MTC with a CP. The MTC primarily controls and synchronizes the PTCs. It does not have to handle PCOs on its own, but we require that it is able to exchange CMs with all PTCs.

3.2. Synchronization of test components and test purpose descriptions

For test specification, we distinguish two types of synchronization: Implicit and explicit synchronization.

3.2.1. Implicit synchronization

Implicit synchronization is done at the start and may be done at the end of a test case by the MTC. The corresponding CREATE constructs and DONE events can be generated automatically by a tool.

Further synchronization is needed if it has to be guaranteed that the first send event happens after the creation of all PTCs or if the PTCs should indicate their termination to the MTC. For these cases, one of the explicit synchronization mechanisms has to be used.

3.2.2. Explicit synchronization

During the execution of a concurrent TTCN test case, a test component is not aware of the state of the other test components. If the execution of a test event PCO_X!DataReq by a test component TC_A should happen after the execution of a test event PCO_Y!ReleaseReq by test component TC_B, then TC_A and TC_B have to exchange CMs to accomplish the execution of PCO_X!DataReq and PCO_Y!ReleaseReq in the correct order.

The points in the control flow of the test components at which such a synchronization should take place cannot be calculated automatically, because they may depend on the intention of the test designer. For example, for the situation described above, the test designer intends to test the appropriate treatment of a DataReq during the release of a connection. Without additional information, a test generation tool will not care whether the ReleaseReq is sent before DataReq or not. As a consequence, for such cases the synchronization of test components has to be specified explicitly by the test designer within the MSC test purpose.

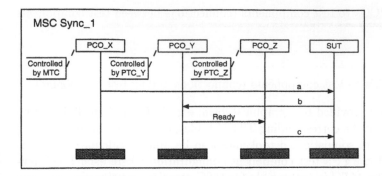

Figure 2. Explicit synchronization by means of a coordination message

Depending on the number of test components involved and test events to be coordinated, the CM exchange which is necessary for an explicit synchronization may become very complex. To cope with simple as well as complex situations, we provide two means for the specification of explicit synchronization. First, it can be done by describing the CM exchange directly and secondly, by using MSC conditions for the definition of synchronization points. For the latter case, the exchange of CMs among the test components is generated automatically.

Explicit synchronization with coordination messages. Defining explicit synchronization by describing the exchange of CMs within the MSC test purpose is not as easy as it seems to be at first glance. The reason is that in the MSCs we use for test purpose description, the instances represent PCOs and not the test components controlling the PCOs.[3] However, CMs are exchanged between test components and therefore the actual sender and receiver processes of the CMs are not represented in the MSC test purposes.

Nevertheless, we allow to specify CMs between PCO instances and interpret them as follows: A coordination message CM1 with an origin at PCO instance PCO_A and a target at PCO instance PCO_B coordinates test events at PCO_A and PCO_B. The origin refers to the send event of CM1 by the test component controlling PCO_A. The target refers to the corresponding receive event by the test component controlling PCO_B. The order of events (including send and receive events of CMs) along a PCO instance has to be preserved by the test component controlling the PCO. It should be noted that no graphical distinction between CMs and ASPs has to be made in the MSC test purposes. Origin and target of a CM arrow have to be PCO instances. For ASPs, either the origin or target has to be the SUT instance.

Figure 2 shows an MSC test purpose description. The corresponding test component configuration is the one presented in Figure 1. The MSC includes the CM Ready drawn by the test designer. It has to be interpreted as follows: PTC_Y should send the CM Ready after the reception of ASP b at PCO_Y, and PTC_Z should send ASP c after the reception of CM Ready. In this case, the CM Ready forces the test components to perform exactly

---

[3]Note that a test component may control and observe more than one PCO.

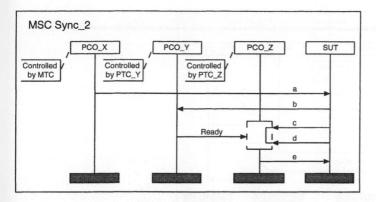

Figure 3. Complex explicit synchronization by means of coordination messages

the order PCO_X!a → PCO_Y?b → PCO_Z!c of test events during their communication with the SUT.

However, the specification of CMs by the test designer becomes difficult if more than two test components are involved, and if receive events of CMs are alternatives to the reception of ASPs.

Figure 3 provides a test purpose example for the same test component configuration as in the previous example (Figure 1). The test run should execute as follows: First, PTC_X sends ASP a via PCO_X to the SUT, which in turn answers with ASPs b, c and d to be observed at PCO_Y and PCO_Z, respectively. ASP e should be sent via PCO_Z after the reception of b, c and d. To ensure this, the reception of b has to be confirmed by means of CM Ready sent by PTC_Y.

ASPs c and d are received via the same FIFO queue PCO_Z, and their order is given by the test purpose. The CM Ready is received by PTC_Z via a second FIFO queue, i.e., the CP between PTC_Y and PTC_Z. It cannot be predicted if the CM Ready is received before, after or between the reception of c and d. Thus, a coregion with generalized ordering has to be used to specify all possible orders of reception.

It is obvious that the manual drawing of CMs becomes increasingly complicated if even more test components, CMs and CPs are involved. In order to ease the test specification, we present another possibility to describe explicit synchronization in the next paragraph.

Explicit synchronization with conditions. In order to get a simple but robust and consistent mechanism to specify synchronization, we use MSC conditions. The conditions used for test synchronization purposes should only cover PCO instances. We call them *synchronization conditions*. They define common *synchronization points* within the message flow at the different PCOs.

Figure 4 shows an MSC test purpose description with a synchronization condition. The desired effect of the synchronization is the same as in Figure 3: PTC_Z should send ASP e not before the ASPs b, c and d have been received.

During test case generation, the synchronization conditions are used to calculate the

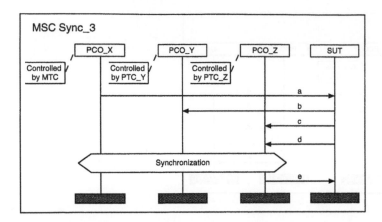

Figure 4. Explicit synchronization by means of a condition

actual exchange of CMs between test components. There are several possibilities to perform a synchronization by means of message exchange, but a discussion about the advantages and disadvantages of the different possibilities would go beyond the scope of this paper.

For an implementation, we have decided to support one mechanism only which allows to synchronize the ASP exchange of an arbitrary number of PCOs. The synchronization is managed by the MTC, and the principle of the mechanism is simple: As already stated above, synchronization conditions define common synchronization points within the ASP exchange at different PCOs. A PCO can be seen as a sequential process, and the test component handling the PCO as the process manager. If a PCO reaches a synchronization point, this is reported to the MTC, and the PCO goes into a waiting state. If the test event following the synchronization point is the reception of an ASP, the PCO waits for the ASP. If it is a send event, the PCO has to wait for a CM from the MTC to get the permission to send the next ASP to the SUT. This mechanism assures that all PCOs involved in the synchronization reach the synchronization point before the execution of the test case continues.

By applying this mechanism, the CM exchange shown in Figure 5 is generated automatically for the condition in Figure 4. The Ready CMs are used to indicate that the synchronization point has been reached, and the CM Proceed is used to allow the sending of ASP e.

4. Test case generation procedure

In this section, we will show how a test case specified in concurrent TTCN can be derived from an SDL specification and an MSC test purpose. Two algorithms are presented for the computation of the behavior trees of an MTC and PTCs. Explicit exchange of CMs is not considered; instead, we will explain the way synchronization conditions can be treated.

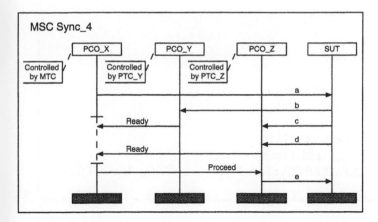

Figure 5. Automatically generated CM exchange for the condition in Figure 4

4.1. Simulator requirements

The test generation algorithm is based on the basic functionality provided by a general purpose state space exploration tool which allows the combined simulation of an SDL specification and an MSC test purpose [7,11,14]. In particular, we require that the following two functions are available:

next_events($state_{sim}$) – Given a state $state_{sim}$, **next_events** returns a set of all events which may occur next. State $state_{sim}$ describes both the current global state of the simulated SDL system (i.e., the state, timers and variable values of each individual process, queue contents etc.) and the progress in the MSC (i.e., the events which are to be simulated next at each instance). If **next_events** returns the empty set, we assume that the MSC has been verified completely, i.e., a path through the reachability graph of the SDL system has been found which satisfies the MSC.[4]

next_state($state_{sim}$,e) – Given a state $state_{sim}$ and an event e, **next_state** returns the state which is obtained if e is executed in $state_{sim}$.

There are several different types of events that might happen during simulation. Some of them may only refer to the SDL system (e. g., internal events that are not represented in the MSC), while others may only refer to the MSC (e. g., messages related to synchronization conditions). During test generation, we consider four types of events which are listed below. All other events which might be reported by the simulator engine are skipped during test generation. This means that they are executed in order to get to the next system state, but they are not transformed into TTCN events.

Event 'Send from SDL environment' ($pco!sig$) – ASPs sent from the environment into the SDL system during simulation become TTCN send events. In order to be able

---

[4]For simplicity, we neglect the possibility that a deadlock occurs or the simulation is stopped because the behavior of the SDL system does not comply to the MSC.

```
(1)   testgen
(2)   {
(3)      for i = 1 ... n do
(4)      {
(5)        root_{ptc_i} := new_start_node();
(6)        testgen_ptc(i, root_{sim}, root_{ptc_i})
(7)      }
(8)      root_{mtc} := new_start_node();
(9)      testgen_mtc(root_{sim}, add_trans(root_{mtc},
(10)                    CREATE(PTC_1:TestPTC_1, ..., PTC_n:TestPTC_n)))
(11)  }
```

Figure 6. Invocation of the test generation for the PTCs and the MTC

to specify a send event, the simulator is required to return both the complete signal and the channel (PCO) through which the ASP was sent.

Event 'Send to SDL environment' ($pco?sig$) – ASPs sent by the SDL system to its environment become receive events in the TTCN test case. In analogy to send events, the simulator has to report both the PCO and the ASP.

Event 'Enter synchronization' (enter_sync(id, pco, Cur, All)) – Whenever an instance in the MSC test purpose may reach a synchronization condition, a special event called enter_sync has to be returned by function next_events. enter_sync has four parameters: id denotes the unique identifier of the condition; pco is the name of the PCO instance which reached the synchronization condition; Cur is the set of instances that have reached the condition so far; and All denotes the set of all instances which are involved in the synchronization.

Event 'Leave synchronization' (leave_sync(id, pco)) – When all instances engaged in a synchronization have entered the condition, the simulator skips the condition silently. However, for all instances in the MSC which send a message directly after the condition, an additional notification is required to indicate that the message is allowed to be sent now. To find out whether such an event has to be created by the simulator engine, an initial static analysis of the MSC is sufficient.

4.2. Test generation algorithms for MTC and PTCs

There are two approaches to generate a distributed test case based on a given SDL specification and an MSC test purpose: On the one hand, a complete behavior tree may be generated first which covers all signals exchanged between the tester and the SUT, plus additional information about synchronization. Based on this sequential test description, single behavior trees for all PTCs and the MTC can be derived. Alternatively, separate behavior trees for the PTCs and the MTC may be created immediately at the time of the simulation of the SDL specification. The test generation algorithms for both approaches

```
(1)    testgen_ptc(i, state_sim, state_test)
(2)    {
(3)       E := next_events(state_sim);
(4)       if (∃e ∈ E : e = pco!sig ∧ pco ∈ PCO_i)
(5)       {
(6)          nextstate_test := add_trans(state_test, e);
(7)          testgen_ptc(i, next_state(state_sim, e), nextstate_test);
(8)       }
(9)       else if (∃e ∈ E : e = enter_sync(id, pco, Cur, All) ∧
(10)                  pco ∈ PCO_i ∧ (PCO_i ∩ All) ⊆ Cur ∧ All ⊄ PCO_i)
(11)      {
(12)         nextstate_test := add_trans(state_test, MCP_i!Ready(id));
(13)         testgen_ptc(i, next_state(state_sim, e), nextstate_test);
(14)      }
(15)      else for all e ∈ E do
(16)      {
(17)         if (e = pco?sig ∧ pco ∈ PCO_i)
(18)            nextstate_test := add_trans(state_test, e);
(19)         else if (e = leave_sync(id, pco) ∧ pco ∈ PCO_i)
(20)            nextstate_test := add_trans(state_test, MCP_i?Proceed(id, pco));
(21)         else
(22)            nextstate_test := state_test;
(23)         testgen_ptc(i, next_state(state_sim, e), nextstate_test);
(24)      }
(25)   }
```

Figure 7. Test generation algorithm for PTC_i

are basically the same. For the sake of simplicity, we present a solution for the latter approach.

In Figures 6, 7 and 8, the construction of the behavior trees for the PTCs and the MTC is explained. Figure 6 describes the invocation of the test generation functions. In Figures 7 and 8, the core algorithms are presented.

The algorithms for the MTC and the PTCs are structurally similar. To a certain extend, the algorithm for the MTC is the inverse of the algorithm for the PTCs. For example, if a PTC sends a message to the MTC, a corresponding receive event has to be added to the MTC behavior description. In addition, CREATE constructs and DONE events have to be added to the root and the leaves of the MTC behavior tree (line 10 in Figure 6 and line 5 in Figure 8). Due to the similarity of both algorithms, we will concentrate on the description of the PTC generation in the following.

We assume that the PTCs are numbered ($i \in \{1..n\}$). The set of all PCOs which belong to a parallel test component PTC_i is defined as PCO_i.

The PTC algorithm is invoked with three parameters: i denotes the number of the

```
(1)    testgen_mtc(state_sim, state_test)
(2)    {
(3)        E := next_events(state_sim);
(4)        if (E = ∅)
(5)          nextstate_test := add_trans(state_test, ?DONE(PTC_1,...,PTC_n))
(6)        else if (∃e ∈ E : e = pco!sig ∧ pco ∈ PCO_MTC)
(7)        {
(8)          nextstate_test := add_trans(state_test, e);
(9)          testgen_mtc(next_state(state_sim, e), nextstate_test);
(10)       }
(11)       else if (∃e ∈ E : e = leave_sync(id, pco) ∧
(12)                ∃i ∈ {1..n} : pco ∈ PCO_i)
(13)       {
(14)         nextstate_test := add_trans(state_test, MCP_i!Proceed(id, pco));
(15)         testgen_mtc(next_state(state_sim, e), nextstate_test);
(16)       }
(17)       else for all e ∈ E do
(18)       {
(19)         if (e = pco?sig ∧ pco ∈ PCO_MTC)
(20)           nextstate_test := add_trans(state_test, e);
(21)         else if (e = enter_sync(id, pco, Cur, All) ∧
(22)                  ∃i ∈ {1..n} : pco ∈ PCO_i ∧ (PCO_i ∩ All) ⊆ Cur ∧
(23)                  All ⊄ PCO_i)
(24)           nextstate_test := add_trans(state_test, MCP_i?Ready(id));
(25)         else
(26)           nextstate_test := state_test;
(27)         testgen_mtc(next_state(state_sim, e), nextstate_test);
(28)       }
(29)   }
```

Figure 8. Test generation algorithm for the MTC

PTC; $state_{sim}$ is the current node in the reachability graph of the SDL system (initially the root node; see line 6 in Figure 6) and $state_{test}$ is the current node in the behavior tree to be constructed.

At first, all possible next events are requested from the simulator engine by function **next_events** (line 3 in Figure 7). Then it is checked whether the PTC can send either an ASP to the SUT (line 4) or a coordination message to the MTC (lines 9 and 10). Whenever a test component can send a signal, we assume that it should do so immediately. In this case, no other alternatives are taken into account. Instead, the send event is added to the behavior tree (lines 6 and 12) and the algorithm is invoked recursively with the successor node of $state_{sim}$ and $nextstate_{test}$ (lines 7 and 13). Only if the PTC cannot send a signal, all possible events have to be considered, as indicated by the loop in lines 15–24.

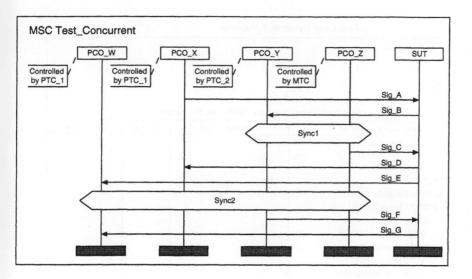

Figure 9. MSC Test_Concurrent used for test generation

If an event has to be appended to the behavior tree, a transition to a new node ($nextstate_{test}$) is inserted into the tree (lines 6, 12, 18 and 20). Otherwise, $nextstate_{test}$ is set to $state_{test}$ (line 22). By invoking itself recursively, testgen_ptc explores the whole state space of the SDL specification. Due to the interleaving semantics of SDL, the algorithm might reach a state where it wants to add an already existing edge to the behavior tree. In order to handle this, function add_trans($state, e$) has been introduced. If an edge from $state$ labelled with e exists, it simply returns the successor node; otherwise a new successor node is added.

There are two CMs used for the communication between a PTC and the MTC: CM Ready(id) is sent from a PTC to the MTC in order to indicate that all relevant instances of the PTC have reached synchronization condition id (line 12). It is only sent, if (1) an enter_sync event is reported by the simulator engine, (2) all instances of the PTC which are involved in the synchronization have already reached the condition $((PCO_i \cap All) \subseteq Cur)$ and (3) there are other TCs which are also involved in the synchronization ($All \not\subseteq PCO_i$) (lines 9 and 10). In reverse, CM Proceed(id, pco) is received from the MTC and indicates that the PTC is allowed to send further ASPs via pco (line 20).

4.3. Example

The test generation is illustrated by the following example. In Figure 9, an MSC test purpose is shown for which a test case is to be generated. For this MSC, a test configuration with two PTCs and an MTC is defined. PTC_1 controls two different PCOs (PCO_W and PCO_X), whereas PTC_2 communicates with the SUT only via PCO_Y. The MTC exchanges signals both with the PTCs via MCP_1 and MCP_2 and with the SUT via PCO_Z.

Figure 10 shows the behavior descriptions for both the MTC and the two PTCs (named Test_PTC_1 and Test_PTC_2). As can be seen, only one synchronization message is sent

		Test Case Dynamic Behaviour			
Test Case Name		: Test_Concurrent			
Group		:			
Purpose		:			
Configuration		: Conf			
Default		:			
Comments		: The tester consists of a Main Test Component and two Parallel Test Components			
Nr	Label	Behaviour Description	Constraints Ref	Verdict	Comments
1		CREATE(PTC_1:Test_PTC_1, PTC_2:Test_PTC_2)			
2		MCP_2 ? Ready(Sync1)			
3		PCO_Z ! Sig_C	C_Sig_C		
4		MCP_1 ? Ready(Sync2)			
5		MCP_2 ? Ready(Sync2)			
6		MCP_2 ! Proceed(Sync2,Y)			
7		?DONE(PTC_1,PTC_2)		R	
8		MCP_2 ? Ready(Sync2)			
9		MCP_1 ? Ready(Sync2)			
10		MCP_2 ! Proceed(Sync2,Y)			
11		?DONE(PTC_1,PTC_2)		R	
		Test_PTC_1			
12		PCO_X ! Sig_A	C_Sig_A		
13		PCO_X ? Sig_D	C_Sig_D		
14		PCO_W ? Sig_E	C_Sig_E		
15		MCP_1 ! Ready(Sync2)			
16		PCO_W ? Sig_G	C_Sig_G	(P)	
17		PCO_W ? Sig_E	C_Sig_E		
18		PCO_X ? Sig_D	C_Sig_D		
19		MCP_1 ! Ready(Sync2)			
20		PCO_W ? Sig_G	C_Sig_G	(P)	
		Test_PTC_2			
21		PCO_Y ? Sig_B	C_Sig_B		
22		MCP_2 ! Ready(Sync1)			
23		MCP_2 ! Ready(Sync2)			
24		MCP_2 ? Proceed(Sync2,Y)			
25		PCO_Y ! Sig_F	C_Sig_F	(P)	
Detailed Comments :					

Figure 10. A concurrent TTCN test case for MSC Test_Concurrent

to the MTC for each PTC. The size of an MTC mainly depends on the number of PTCs which are involved in a synchronization, since the MTC must be able to receive Ready CMs in every possible order.

5. Summary and outlook

In this paper, we have presented our approach to automatic generation of test cases in concurrent TTCN format. To do this, a test component configuration and information concerning the synchronization of test components has to be provided. If the synchronization is specified by means of conditions, a corresponding exchange of CMs between test components can be generated automatically. We have provided the corresponding algorithms and presented a small example explaining the output of the algorithms.

The implementation of our approach has already been started and the results of the first experiments have been promising. If our approach proves its applicability to real world examples, we also intend to implement it in the Autolink tool.

Acknowledgements

We would like to thank Stefan Heymer for valuable comments on earlier drafts of this paper and for careful proofreading.

REFERENCES

1. Cinderella SDL product description. http://www.cinderella.dk
2. M. Clatin, R. Groz, M. Phalippou, R. Thummel. *Two Approaches Linking a Test Generation Tool with Verification Techniques*. Proceedings of *IWPTS'95*, Evry, 1995.
3. L. Doldi, V. Encontre, J.-C. Fernandez, T. Jéron, S. Le Bricquir, N. Texier, M. Phalippou. *Assessment of Automatic Generation Methods of Conformance Test Suites in an Industrial Context*. Testing of Communicating Systems, vol. 9, Chapman & Hall, 1996.
4. J. Ellsberger, D. Hogrefe, A. Sarma. *SDL – Formal Object-oriented Language for Communicating Systems*. Prentice Hall, 1997.
5. ETSI TC MTS. *CATG Handbook*. European Guide, ETSI, Sophia-Antipolis, 1998.
6. J. Grabowski, D. Hogrefe, R. Scheurer, Z.R. Dai. *Applying SAMSTAG to the B-ISDN Protocol SSCOP*. Testing of Communicating Systems, vol. 10, Chapman & Hall, 1997.
7. J. Grabowski, D. Hogrefe, R. Nahm. *Test Case Generation with Test Purpose Specification by MSCs*. In "SDL'93 – Using Objects" (O. Færgemand, A. Sarma, editors). North-Holland, October 1993.
8. ISO. *Information Technology – OSI-Conformance Testing Methodology and Framework – Part 1: General Concepts*. ISO IS 9646-1, 1994.
9. ISO. *Information Technology – OSI-Conformance Testing Methodology and Framework – Part 3: The Tree and Tabular Combined Notation (TTCN)*. ISO IS 9646-3, 1996.
10. H. Kahlouche, C. Viho, M. Zendri. *An Industrial Experiment in Automatic Generation of Executable Test Suites for a Cache Coherency Protocol*. Testing of Communicating Systems, vol. 11, Kluwer Academic Press, 1998.
11. ObjectGEODE product description. http://www.verilog.fr
12. E. Rudolph, P. Graubmann, J. Grabowski. *Tutorial on Message Sequence Charts (MSC-96)*. Forte/PSTV'96, Kaiserslautern, October 1996.
13. M. Schmitt, A. Ek, J. Grabowski, D. Hogrefe, B. Koch. *Autolink – Putting SDL-based Test Generation into Practice*. Testing of Communicating Systems, vol. 11, Kluwer Academic Press, 1998.
14. Telelogic TAU product description. http://www.telelogic.se
15. ITU-T Rec. Z.100 (1996). *Specification and Description Language (SDL)*. Geneva, 1996.
16. ITU-T Rec. Z.120 (1996). *Message Sequence Chart (MSC)*. Geneva, 1996.

404

Appendix: List of abbreviations

ASP	Abstract Service Primitive
CM	Coordination Message
CP	Coordination Point
CTMF	Conformance Testing Methodology and Framework [8]
FIFO	First-In First-Out
MSC	Message Sequence Chart [16]
MTC	Main Test Component
PCO	Point of Control and Observation
PDU	Protocol Data Unit
PTC	Parallel Test Component
SDL	Specification and Description Language [15]
SUT	System Under Test
TTCN	Tree and Tabular Combined Notation [9]

SDL'99 : The Next Millennium
R. Dssouli, G.v. Bochmann and Y. Lahav, editors
©1999 Elsevier Science B.V. All rights reserved

A test case generation tool for conformance testing of SDL systems[*]

C. Bourhfir[a], R. Dssouli[a], E. Aboulhamid[a], N. Rico[b]

Département d'Informatique et de Recherche Opérationnelle, Pavillon André Aisenstadt, C.P.
6128, succursale Centre-Ville, Montréal, Québec, H3C-3J7, Canada.
E-mail: {bourhfir, dssouli, aboulham}@iro.umontreal.ca.

Nortel, 16 Place du commerce, Verdun, H3E-1H6

This paper presents a set of tools for automatic executable test case and test sequence generation for a protocol modeled by an SDL system. Our methodology uses a unified method which tests an Extended Finite State Machine (EFSM) based system by using control and data flow techniques. To test an SDL system, it extracts an EFSM from each process then the system is tested by incrementally computing a partial product for each EFSM C, taking into account only transitions which influence (or are influenced by) C, and generating test cases for it. This process ends when the coverage achieved by the generated test cases is satisfactory or when the partial products for all EFSMs are tested. Experimental results show that this method can be applied to systems of practical size.

Keywords

CEFSM, Partial product, Reachability analysis, Control and data flow testing, Executability

1. INTRODUCTION

To ensure that the entities of a protocol communicate reliably, the protocol implementation must be tested for conformance to its specification. Quite a number of methods and tools have been proposed in the literature for test case generation from EFSM specifications using data flow testing techniques and/or control flow testing techniques [Ural 1991, Huang 1995, Chanson 1993, Bourhfir 97]. However, these methods are applicable when the protocol consists only of one EFSM. For CEFSM specified protocols, other methods should be used. To our knowledge, very few work has been done in this area, and most existing methods deal only with communicating finite state machines (CFSMs) where the data part of the protocol is not considered. An easy approach to testing CFSMs is to compose them all-at-once into one machine, using reachability analysis, and then generate test cases for the product machine. But we would run into the well known state explosion problem. Also, applying this approach to generate test cases for CEFSMs is unpractical due to the presence of variables and conditional statements. To cope with the complexity, methods for reduced reachability analysis have been

_____
[*] This work is supported by Nortel grant.

proposed for CFSMs [Rubin 1982, Gouda 1984, Lee 1996]. The basic idea consists in constructing a smaller graph representing a partial behavior of the system and allowing one to study properties of communication. In this paper, we present a methodology which can be used to test a CEFSM based system or a part of it after a correction or enhancement. Our method does not compose all machines but decomposes the problem into computing a partial product (defined later) for each CEFSM and generating test cases for it. Another problem is that most existing methods generate test cases from specifications written in the normal form [Sarikaya 96] which is not a widely used specification approach. For this reason, our test generation method should start from specifications written in a high level specification language. Since we are interested in testing communication protocols and since SDL is the most used specification language in the telecommunication community, our method starts the test generation process form SDL specifications.

The objective of this paper is to present a set of tools which can be used to generate automatically executable test cases for SDL systems and to show the architecture of each tool.

The organization of this paper is as follows. Section 2 presents some existing tools for test generation from SDL systems most of which are semi-automatic. Section 3 describes the EFSM and CEFSM models. Section 4 presents our methodology for test generation from SDL systems. This latter uses the EFTG tool which is presented in section 5 and which generates test cases for EFSM based systems. Section 6 presents the TEST CASE GENERATOR which generates test cases for CEFSM based systems. In section 7, we present the results obtained by applying CEFTG on a real communicating system. Finally, section 8 concludes the paper.

2. SOME TEST GENERATION TOOLS FROM SDL SPECIFICATIONS

Over the past ten years, tools have become available that seek to automate the software testing process. These tools can help to improve the efficiency of the test execution process by replacing personnel with test scripts that playback application behavior. However, it is the up-front process of deciding what to test and how to test it that has the dominant impact on product quality. Likewise, the cost and time to develop tests is an order of magnitude greater than that required for test execution. Today, manual methods are still the primary tools for this critical stage, however, tools exist which automate some parts of the testing process. In the following, some existing tools for test case generation or tools that help the test suite developer in the test generation process are presented.

TESDL [Bromstrup 1989] is a prototype tool for the automatic generation of test cases from SDL specifications in the context of the OSI Conformance Testing Methodology and Framework. TESDL implements a heuristic algorithm to derive the global behavior of a protocol as a tree, called Asynchronous Communication Tree (ACT), which is based on a restricted set of SDL diagrams (one process per block, no two processes are able to receive the same kind of signal, etc.). The ACT is the global system description as obtained by reachability analysis by perturbation. In the ACT, the nodes represent global states. A global state contains information about the states of all processes in the specification. Tests are derived from the ACT of a specification by a software tool, called TESDL. Input for the tool is

.n SDL specification (SDL-PR), the output are the test cases in TTCN-Notation.

TTCN Link (LINK for short) [ITEX 1995] is an environment for efficient development of TTCN test suites based on SDL specifications in SDT3.0 (SDL Description Tool) [SDT 995]. LINK assures consistency between the SDL specification and the TTCN test suite. It ncreases the productivity in the development by automatic generation of the *static parts* of the est suite and specification-based support for the test case design. The intended user of the LINK tool is a TTCN test suite developer. His inputs are an SDL specification and a test suite tructure with test purposes and his task is to develop an abstract TTCN test suite, based on his input. This tool is semi-automatic.

SAMSTAG [Grabowski 93, 94] is developed within the research and development project 'Conformance Testing a Tool for the Generation of Test Cases" which is funded by the Swiss 'TT. The allowed behavior of the protocol which should be tested is defined by an SDL pecification and the purpose of a test case is given by an MSC which is a widespread mean or the graphical visualization of selected system runs of communication systems. The aMsTaG method formalizes test purposes and defines the relation between test purposes, rotocol specifications and test cases. Furthermore, it includes the algorithms for the test case eneration.

TOPIC V2 [Algayres 1995] (prototype of TTC GEN) works by co-simulating the SDL pecification and an observer representing the test purpose. This co-simulation enables to xplore a constrained graph, i.e., a part of the reachability graph of the specification, which nables to use this method for infinite graphs. The observer is described in a language called GOAL (Geode Observation Automata Language). In order to facilitate the use of TOPIC, it is ossible to generate the observers from MSC's. From the constrained graph, some procedures re executed in order to generate the TTCN test.

Tveda V3 [Clatin 1995] is a tool for automatic test case generation which incorporates everal features:

A modular architecture, that makes it possible to choose between the specification languages (Estelle or SDL), test description languages (TTCN or Menuet) and test selection strategy (single transition, extended transition tour, etc.)

A semantic module, which can be called from the strategy modules to compute feasible paths.

Functional extensions, such as hypertext links between tests and specification, test coverage analysis, etc.

To compute execution paths, two techniques can be used, symbolic computation techniques or eachability analysis. Symbolic computation techniques put strong restrictions on which onstructs are accepted and the path computation requires an exponential computation with espect to the length of the path to be computed. On the contrary, reachability analysis puts lmost no restriction on the Estelle or SDL constructs which are accepted, and it is implemented y interfacing Tveda with a powerful commercial tool for reachability analysis, Véda.

Since we are interested in testing SDL protocols, we present, in the next section, the EFSM nd CEFSM models which are the underlying models for SDL systems.

3. THE EFSM AND CEFSM MODELS

Definition1. An EFSM is formally represented as a 8-tuple $<S, s_0, I, O, T, A, \delta, V>$ where

1. S is a non empty set of states,
2. s_0 is the initial state,
3. I is a nonempty set of input interactions,
4. O is a nonempty set of output interactions,
5. T is a nonempty set of transitions,
6. A is a set of actions,
7. δ is a transition relation $\delta: S \times A \rightarrow S$,
8. V is the set variables.

Each element of A is a 5-tuple t=(initial_state, final_state, input, predicate, block). Here "*initial_state*" and "*final_state*" are the states in S representing the starting state and the tail state of t, respectively. "*input*" is either an input interaction from I or empty. "*predicate*" is a predicate expressed in terms of the variables in V, the parameters of the input interaction and some constants. "*block*" is a set of assignment and output statements.

Definition2 . A communicating system is a 2k-tuple $(C_1, C_2,...,C_k, F_1, F_2,..., F_k)$ where

- $C_i = <S, s_0, I, O, T, A, \delta, V>$ is an EFSM
- F_i is a First In First Out (FIFO) for Ci, i=1..k.

Suppose a protocol Π consists of k communicating EFSMs or CEFSMs for short: C_1, $C_2,...,C_k$. Then its state is a 2k-tuple $<s^{(1)}, s^{(2)},..., s^{(k)}, m_1, m_2,...,m_k>$ where $s^{(j)}$ is a state of C_j.and m_j, j=1..k are set of messages contained in $F_1, F_2,...,F_k$ respectively. The CEFSMs exchange messages through bounded storage input FIFO channels. We suppose that a FIFO exists for each CEFSM and that all messages to a CEFSM go through its FIFO. We suppose in that case that an internal message identifies its sender and its receiver. An input interaction for a transition may be internal (if it is sent by another CEFSM) or external (if it comes from the environment). The model obtained from a communicating system via reachability analysis is called a global model. This model is a directed graph G = (V, E) where V is a set of global states and E corresponds to the set of global transitions.

Definition 3. A global state of G is a 2k-tuple $<s^{(1)}, s^{(2)},..., s^{(k)}, m_1, m_2,...,m_k>$ where m_j, j=1..k are set of messages contained in $F_1, F_2,...,F_k$ respectively.

Definition 4 . A global transition in G is a pair t = (i, α) where $\alpha \in A_i$ (set of actions). t is firable in s = $<s^{(1)}, s^{(2)},..., s^{(k)}, m_1, m_2,...,m_k>$ if and only if the following two conditions are satisfied where α = (initial_state, final_state, input, predicate, compute-block).

- A transition relation $\delta_i (s,\alpha)$ is defined

- $input = null$ and $predicate = True$ or $input = a$ and $m_i = aW$, where W is a set of messages to C_i, and $predicate = True$.

After t is fired, the system goes to $s' = <s'^{(1)}, s'^{(2)},..., s'^{(k)}, m'_1, m'_2,...,m'_k>$ and messages contained in the channels are m'_j where

- $s'^{(i)} = \delta(s^{(i)},\alpha)$ and $s'^{(j)} = s^{(j)} \ \forall(j \neq i)$

if $input = \emptyset$ and $output = \emptyset$, then $m'_j = m_j$

if $input = \emptyset$ and $output = b$ then $m'_u = m_u b$ (C_u is the machine which receives b)

if $input \neq \emptyset$ and $output = \emptyset$ then $m_i = W$ and $m'_j = m_j \ \forall(j \neq i)$

if $input \neq \emptyset$ and $output = b$ then $m_i = W$ and $m'_u = m_u b$

In the next section, our test case generation methodology is presented.

. OUR METHODOLOGY FOR TEST GENERATION FROM SDL SYSTEMS

Our methodology uses a set of tools developed at Université de Montréal. Some of the tools use an underlying FSM model and were adapted so that they can be used for an underlying EFSM model.

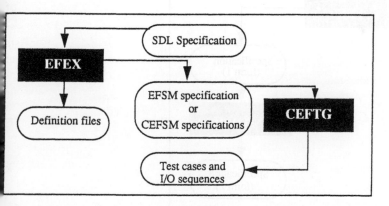

FIGURE 1. The process of test case generation from SDL specifications

Figure 1 shows the process of generating test cases from SDL systems. First, the EFEX tool is applied to the SDL system in order to extract the corresponding EFSM when the SDL system is made of only one process or the corresponding CEFSMs otherwise. At the same time, files containing SDL declarations of interactions (or signals) and channels are created, as for CEFTG, it generates automatically executable test cases for CEFSM based systems.

4.1. The EFEX tool

EFEX is the EFsm EXtractor. It is based on the FEX tool [Bochmann 97]. This latter wa developed at Université de Montréal in order to extract an FSM representing a partial behavio of an SDL system by applying a normalization algorithm. One or more transitions in the generated FSM correspond to a given input at a given state in the SDL specification. This is due to the fact that the tool uses partial unfolding to preserve constraints on the values of message parameters. In addition, FEX generates additional files that can be used in order to complete the test cases. For these reasons, and due to the availability of FEX, we decided to use FEX and to modify the output of FEX so that it can be processed by CEFTG. Even though FEX wa originally built to extract an FSM from an SDL system, it can also extract the corresponding EFSM from it. In [Bochmann 97], the output file generated by FEX contains assignmen statements as well as the predicates of the transitions but these were not used by the too described in the same paper, while this information will indeed be used by CEFTG. EFEX generates an EFSM (or CEFSM) for each process of the SDL system.

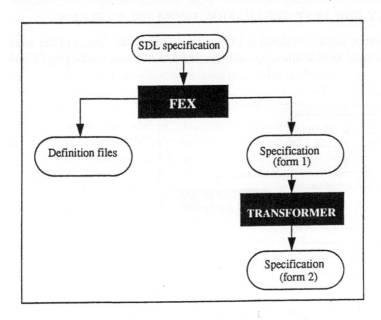

FIGURE 2. The EFEX tool

As we already mentioned before, the input of CEFTG is a specification in the normal form, which is different from the output generated by FEX. For this reason, the output of FEX, Specification (form 1), is processed by TRANSFORMER and transformed to the normal form

Specification (form 2)).

Figure 3 below shows an example of an SDL specification, the output generated by FEX and the input accepted by CEFTG.

```
SDL Specification:
state S0;
    input I1;
    output O1;
    nextstate S1;

    input I2(n);
    decision n;
    (0): output O2;
        nextstate S2;
    (1): output O3;
        nextstate S3;
    enddecision;

Transitions generated by FEX:
S0?I1!O1 > S1;
S0?I2(n = 0)!O2 >S2;
S0?I2(n = 1)!O3 >S3;

Transitions generated by Transformer and accepted by CEFTG:

When I1
From S0
To S1
Name t1: Begin
Output(O1);
End;

When I2(n)
From S0
To S2
Provided (n = 0)
Name t2: Begin
Output(O2);
End;

When I2(n)
From S0
To S3
Provided (n =1)
Name t3: Begin
Output (O3);
End;
```

FIGURE 3. Example of an SDL specification and its corresponding form1 and form2

The next section presents the CEFTG tool. This latter generates executable test cases for CEFSM based systems by generating test cases for each CEFSM in context.

412

4.2. The CEFTG tool

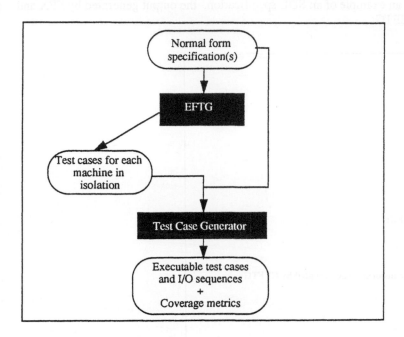

FIGURE 4. The CEFTG tool

CEFTG is the CEFsm Test Generator and can generate test cases for systems modeled by one EFSM using the EFTG tool. For CEFSM based systems, the user can generate test cases for the global system by performing a complete reachability analysis, i.e., taking into consideration all transitions of all CEFSMs, and generating test cases for the complete product (or reachability graph). CEFTG can also generate test cases for each CEFSM in context. In that case, the process ends when the coverage achieved by the generated test cases is satisfactory or after the generation of the test cases for the partial products of all CEFSMs.

CEFTG includes all the activities starting from the specification and leading to the test cases and to the input/output sequences. The first task performed by CEFTG is to generate test cases for each CEFSM in isolation, i.e, without considering its interaction with the other CEFSMs. During this first phase, the tool EFTG is applied in order to generate test cases for each normal form specification in isolation. The next section presents the EFTG tool presented in [Bourhfir 1997] which is now a part of the CEFTG tool. This latter uses control flow testing techniques, data flow testing techniques and symbolic evaluation to generate test cases for systems modeled by one EFSM.

5. THE EFTG TOOL

The tool EFTG (Extended Finite state machine Test Generator) generates executable test cases for EFSM specified protocols which cover both control and data flow. The control flow criterion used is the UIO (Unique Input Output) sequence [Sabnani 1986] and the data flow criterion is the "all-definition-uses" (or def-use for short) criterion [Weyuker 1985] where all the paths in the specification containing a definition of a variable and its uses are generated. A variable is defined in a transition if it appears at the left hand side of an assignment statement or if it appears in an input interaction. It is used if it appears in the predicate of the transition, at the right hand side of an assignment statement or in an output interaction.

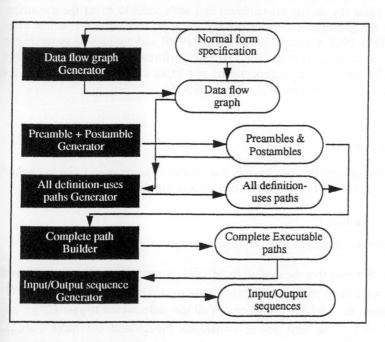

FIGURE 5. The EFTG tool

EFTG performs the following steps in order to generate executable test cases for an EFSM based system:

Step 1: From the normal form specification of the CEFSM, a dataflow graph is built. During this step, all definitions and uses of all variables are identified.

Step 2: For each state S in the graph, EFTG generates all its executable preambles (a preamble is a path such that its first transition's initial state is the initial state of the system and its last transition's tail state is S) and all its postambles (a postamble is a path such that its first transition's start state is S and its last transition's tail state is the initial state). To generate the "all-def-use" paths, EFTG generates all paths between each definition of a variable and each of its uses and verifies if these paths are executable, i.e., if all the predicates in the paths are true. To evaluate the predicates along each transition in a definition-use path, EFTG interprets symbolically all the variables in the predicate backward until these variables are represented by constants and input parameters only. If the predicate is false, EFTG applies a heuristic in order to make the path executable. The heuristic uses "Cycle Analysis" in order to find cycles (a sequence of transitions such that the start state of the first transition and the ending state of the last transition are the same) which can be inserted in the path so that it becomes executable. After this step, EFTG removes the paths which are included in the already existing ones, completes the remaining paths (by adding postambles) and adds paths to cover the transitions which are not covered by the generated test cases. EFTG discovers more executable test cases over the other methods [Ural 1991, Chanson 1993, Huang 1995] and enables to generate test cases for specifications with unbounded loops. The first task performed by CEFTG is to apply the EFTG tool to each CEFSM in order to generate its test cases in isolation, i.e., when the communication of this CEFSM with the others is not considered.

6. TEST CASE GENERATOR

Before presenting the choices that the user have in the second step, we would like to explain what a partial product for one CEFSM is and how it can be computed.

6.1. Computing a partial product

The following steps summarizes the process of computing a partial product for one CEFSM:

Step 1: Marking process. Suppose that the system to be tested is modeled by $C_1, C_2,...,C_k$ and suppose that we want to test the machine C_n in context. We use the test cases generated by EFTG, for each machine in isolation, to mark the transitions in all the paths which trigger C_n (or are triggered by C_n). We shall call the first set of transitions $Pr(C_n)$ and the latter $Po(C_n)$. Determining $Pr(C_n)$ and $Po(C_n)$ can be very costly if exhaustive reachability analysis is considered. For this purpose, our method uses the test cases generated by EFTG for each machine in isolation as a guide. If a transition in C_n receives (sends) a message from (to) a CEFSM C_i and since this message is sent (received) by some transitions in C_i which belong necessarily to test cases generated by EFTG for C_i in isolation, we mark all the transitions in these test cases. By marking all the transitions in each test case, we insure that transitions preceding (following) the transition which sends (receives) the message participate in the partial product generation. When the test case which contains the transition sending (receiving) a message to (from) C_n is marked, we verify if it contains transitions receiving (sending) messages from (to) other CEFSMs. If this is the case, for each such transition T, the same procedure is repeated in order to mark the paths n the machine sending (receiving) the message received (sent) by T.

At the end of this step, all marked transitions will participate in the generation of the partial product.

Step 2: Partial product generation.

After the marking process, the partial product for C_n is performed. This step is similar to a reachability analysis. At each time, among the possible transitions which can be picked to build the reachability graph, only the marked ones are chosen. The partial product is the reachability graph computed with the marked transitions only. The unmarked transitions do not participate in the partial product computation because they do not influence the machine under test.

.2. Testing the partial product

After the partial product for C_n is computed, its test cases are generated automatically with EFTG since the partial product of C_n is also an EFSM. These test cases cover both control and data flow in the partial product and we guarantee the coverage of the "all-def-use + all transitions" criterion in the partial product.

.3. Testing the global system

To test the global system (set of several CEFSMs), CEFTG generates executable test cases incrementally by generating test cases for the partial product for each CEFSM until the desired coverage is achieved. The process of generating test cases for the global system may stop after generating the partial product for some CEFSMs. In that case, these test cases cover the all def-use criterion for the partial product machines (this include all transitions in the CEFSM as well as transitions in other CEFSMs). In term of transition coverage, these test cases cover 100% of the transitions for each CEFSM for which a partial product was computed and p% of the transitions of each other CEFSM, where $p = (marked - transitions)/(all - transitions)$ for some CEFSM.

.4. Test case generator

The test case generator asks the user to make a choice among the following:

Generate executable test cases for a certain CEFSM M in context: the marking process explained in section 6.1 is performed. Once this process is over, a reduced reachability analysis is performed considering only marked transitions. The result of this analysis is a partial product which is tested using EFTG. The generated test cases enables to test the machine M when its context is considered, unlike the test cases generated for M in isolation.

Generate test cases for the complete product of all CEFSMs of the system: in that case, the marking process is not called because all transitions of all CEFSMs participate in the reachability analysis. CEFTG builds the complete product using a classical reachability

416

analysis algorithm and generates test cases for the complete product using EFTG. Thi
option is used when the CEFSMs as well as the complete product are small. However, Th
test case generation for the complete product may be impossible due to state explosion.

•   Generate test cases for each CEFSM in context until the generated test cases reach a certai
    coverage or until test cases are generated for each partial product: this choice can be take
    when the user wants to generate test cases which cover each transition of each CEFSM
    instead of each global transition (of the global system). In that case, CEFTG generates th
    partial products, starting by the CEFSM which has less interactions with the other machines
    The goal here is to avoid generating large partial products. Each time, test cases ar
    generated for a partial product, the tool computes the coverage achieved in order t
    determine how many transitions are covered by the generated test cases. If the user i
    satisfied with the coverage, the algorithm ends. Otherwise, CEFTG computes another partia
    product and generates test cases for it until the user is satisfied or all partial products ar
    generated.

Once test cases for the partial products are generated, input/output sequences are extracte
and used to test the conformance of the implementation against the specification. For the inpu
and output messages with parameters, symbolic evaluation is used in order to determine thei
values.

7. EXPERIMENTATION

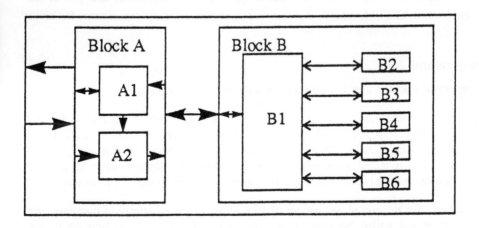

FIGURE 6. Architecture of a communicating system

We tried CEFTG on a real SDL system whose architecture is similar to that of figure 6 and we obtained the following results: the first CEFSM of the system, with 2 states and 17 transitions, communicates with all other CEFSMs and when computing its partial product, all transitions were marked. Its partial product is also the complete product, i.e., the reachability graph for the global SDL system, and this latter could not be computed due to state explosion. The second CEFSM has 1 state and 3 transitions and its partial product has 8 states, 13 transitions and 9 executable def-use paths. The third CEFSM has 4 states, 10 transitions and its partial product has 24 states, 55 transitions and 43 executable def-use paths. The fourth machine has 5 states, 12 transitions, and its partial product has 75 states,139 transitions and 95 executable all-use paths. The fifth CEFSM has 11 states and 24 transitions. Its partial product has 1027 states and 3992 transitions. CEFTG could not generate test cases for the partial product.This is because the criterion used by CEFTG, the all-def-use criterion is too expensive. For this reason, weaker criteria should be implemented so that test case generation may be possible for large systems or for large partial products. In fact, this solution may be more practical for the industry.

3. CONCLUSION

In this paper, we presented a methodology for test generation from SDL systems. Unlike other methods or tools, our method is completely automatic and does not need any assistance from the user. Our method enables the user to generate the complete reachability graph of the system. The user can also test the SDL system by testing each of its processes in context. Also, he can test one process in context after a modification or enhancement without testing the entire system. Another advantage of CEFTG is that it can compute the coverage achieved by the generated test cases. We are currently working in transforming the test cases generated by CEFTG in TTCN to test the implementation under test. The next step consists in improving the EFEX tool so that more complex SDL systems are processed by CEFTG. We also intend to link our tool to a set of tools such as ObjectGeode [Verilog 93] or SDT.

418

References

Bernard Algayres, Yves Lejeune, Florence Hugonnet (Verilog), "GOAL: Observing SDL behaviors with ObjectGeode", 7th SDL Forum, Oslo, Norway, 26-29 September 1995.

G. v. Bochmann, A. Petrenko, O. Bellal, S. Maguiraga (1997), "Automating the process of test derivation from SDL specifications", SDL forum, Elsevier, pp. 261-276.

C. Bourhfir, R. Dssouli, E. Aboulhamid, N. Rico (1998), "A guided incremental test case generation method for testing CEFSM based systems", IWTCS, Kluwer Academic Publishers, pp.279-294.

C. Bourhfir, R. Dssouli, E. Aboulhamid, N. Rico (1997), "Automatic executable test case generation for EFSM specified protocols", IWTCS, Chapman & Hall, pp. 75-90.

Lars Bromstrup, Dieter Hogrefe, "TESDL: Experience with Generating Test Cases from SDL Specifications", Fourth Proc. SDL Forum, pp. 267-279, 1989.

Chanson, S. T. and Zhu, J.(1993) "A Unified Approach to Protocol Test Sequence Generation", In Proc. IEEE INFOCOM.

Marylene Clatin, Roland Groz, Marc Phalippou, Richard Thummel, "Two approaches linking a test generation tool with verification techniques", International Workshop on Protocol Test Systems (IWPTS), Evry, 4-6 September, 1995.

M. G. Gouda, Y. T. Yu (1984), "Protocol Validation by Maximal Progressive Exploration", IEEE Trans. on Comm. Vol. 32, No. 1, January.

Jens Grabowski, Dieter Hogrefe, Robert Nahm (1993), "A Method for the Generation of Test Cases Based on SDL and MSCs", Institut fur Informatik, Universitat Bern, April.

Jens Grabowski (1994), "SDL and MSC Based Test Case Generation: An Overall View of the SaMsTaG Method", Institut fur Informatik, Universitat Bern, May.

Huang, C.M. Lin, Y.C. and Jang, M.Y. (1995) An Executable Protocol Test Sequence Generation Method for EFSM-Specified Protocols (IWPTS), Evry, 4-6 September.

"ITEX User Manual", Telelogic AB, 1995.

David Lee, Krishan K. Sabnani, David M. Kristol, Sanjoy Paul (1996), "Conformance Testing of Protocols Specified as Communicating Finite State Machines- A Guided Random Walk Based Approach", IEEE Trans. on Comm. Vol. 44, No. 5, May.

Monien, B. (1983) "The complexity of determining paths of length k", Proc. Int. Workshop on Graph Theoretical Concepts in Computer Science, Trauner B Verlag, Linz, 241-251.

J. Rubin, C. H. West (1982), "An Improved Protocol Validation Technique", Computer Networks, 6, April.

"SDT User Manual", Telelogic Malmö AB, 1995.

Ural, H. and Yang. B. (1991) A Test Sequence Selection Method for Protocol Testing. IEEE Transactions on Communication, Vol 39, No4, April.

K.Sabnani, A.Dahbura (1985), "A new Technique for Generating Protocol Tests", ACM Comput. Commun. Rev. Vol 15, No 4, September.

Verilog, Geode Editor- Reference Manual, France, 1993.
Weyuker, E.J. and Rapps, S. (1985) Selecting Software Test Data using Data Flow Information. IEEE Transactions on Software Engineering, April.

Session XI

Time, Performance and Simulation

SDL'99 : The Next Millennium
R. Dssouli, G.v. Bochmann and Y. Lahav, editors
©1999 Elsevier Science B.V. All rights reserved

IF: An Intermediate Representation for SDL and its Applications

Marius Bozga[a], Jean-Claude Fernandez[b], Lucian Ghirvu[a*], Susanne Graf[a], Jean-Pierre Krimm[a], Laurent Mounier[a] and Joseph Sifakis[a]

[a]VERIMAG, Centre Equation, 2 avenue de Vignate, F-38610 Gières,
e-mail: Marius.Bozga@imag.fr, http://www-verimag.imag.fr/DIST_SYS/IF

[b]LSR/IMAG, BP 82, F-38402 Saint Martin d'Hères Cedex,
e-mail: Jean-Claude.Fernandez@imag.fr

We present work of a project for the improvement of a specification/validation toolbox integrating a commercial toolset *Object*GEODE and different validation tools such as the verification tool CADP and the test sequence generator TGV.

The intrinsic complexity of most protocol specifications lead us to study combinations of techniques such as static analysis and abstraction together with classical model-checking techniques. Experimentation and validation of our results in this context motivated the development of an intermediate representation for SDL called IF. In IF, a system is represented as a set of timed automata communicating asynchronously through a set of buffers or by rendez-vous through a set of synchronization gates. The advantage of the use of such a program level intermediate representation is that it is easier to interface with various existing tools, such as static analysis, abstraction and compositional state space generation. Moreover, it allows to define for SDL different, but mathematically sound, notions of time.

Keywords:
SDL, Time Semantics, Validation, Model-Checking, Test Generation, Static Analysis.

1. INTRODUCTION

SDL and related formalisms such as MSC and TTCN are at the base of a technology for the specification and the validation of telecommunication systems. This technology will be developing fast due to many reasons, institutional, commercial and economical ones. SDL is promoted by ITU and other international standardization bodies. There exist commercially available tools and most importantly, there are increasing needs for description and validation tools covering as many aspects of system development as possible. These needs motivate the work for enhancement of the existing standards undertaken by ITU and ETSI, in particular.

Among the work directions for improvement of SDL, an important one is the description of non functional aspects of the behavior, such as performance and timing. Finding a

---

*Work partially supported by Région Rhône-Alpes, France

"reasonable" notion of time is a central problem which admits many possible solutions depending on choices of semantic models. This is certainly a non trivial question and this is reflected by the variety of the existing proposals.

Choosing an appropriate timed extension for SDL should take into account not only technical considerations about the semantics of timed systems but also more pragmatic ones related to the appropriateness for use in a system engineering context. We believe that the different ideas about extensions of the language must be validated experimentally before being adopted to avoid phenomena of rejection by the users. Furthermore, it is important to ensure as much as possible compatibility with the existing technology and provide evidence that the modified standard can be efficiently supported by tools.

Another challenge for the existing technology for SDL to face the demand for description and validation of systems of increasing size, is to provide environments that allow the user to master this complexity. The existing commercial tools are quite satisfactory in several respects and this is a recognized advantage of SDL over other formalisms poorly supported by tools. However, it is necessary to improve the existing technology to avoid failing to keep up. Mastering complexity requires a set of integrated tools supporting user driven analysis. Of course, the existing tools such as simulators, verifiers, automatic test generators can be improved. Our experience from real case studies shows that another family of tools is badly needed to break down complexity. All the methods for achieving such a goal are important ranging from the simplest and most "naive" to the most sophisticated.

In this paper we present work of a project for the improvement of a specification and validation toolbox interconnecting *Object*GEODE[1] and different validation tools such as CADP[2] developed jointly with the VASY team of Inria Rhône-Alpes and TGV[3] developed jointly with the PAMPA team of IRISA. The project has two complementary work directions. The first is the study and the implementation of timed extensions for SDL; this work is carried out in cooperation with Verilog, Sema Group and CNET within a common project. The second is coping with complexity by using a combination of techniques based on static analysis, abstraction and compositional generation. Achieving these objectives requires both theoretical and experimental work. Experimentation and validation of our results in this context motivated the development of an intermediate representation for SDL called IF. IF is based on a simple, and semantically sound model for distributed timed systems which is asynchronously communicating timed automata (automata with clocks). A translator from a static subset of SDL to IF has been developed and IF has been connected to different tools of our toolbox. The use of such an intermediate representation confers many advantages.

- IF to implement and evaluate different semantics of time for SDL as the underlying model of IF is general enough to encompass a large variety of notions of urgency, time non determinism and different kinds of real-time constructs.

- IF allows a flattened description of the corresponding SDL specification with the possibility of direct manipulation, simplification and generally application of analysis algorithms which are not easy to perform using commercial tools which, in general, are closed.

- IF can be considered as a common representation model for other existing languages or for the combination of languages adopting different description styles.

Related work

After its standardization in the eighties, a lot of work has been done concerning the mathematical foundations of SDL. The first complete semantics was given by the annex F to the recommendation Z.100 [4,5] and is based on a combination of CSP [6] and META-IV [7]. Even if it is the reference semantics of SDL (about 500 pages), it is far from being complete and contains many inconsistencies and obscure points.

In [8] is given a semantics for SDL based on *streams* and *stream processing functions*. It deals with a subset of SDL and the timing aspects are simplified. An *operational semantics* which covers SDL systems, processes, blocks and channels is given in [9]. It defines a method to build labeled transition systems from SDL specifications. The approach is relatively complete, however in this case too, time is not handled in a satisfactory manner. An important work is done in [10,11] which gives a semantics based on *process algebra* to a rather simple subset of SDL, called φ^-SDL. A method is given, for translating each SDL system into a term of PA_{drt}^{psc}-ID which is a discrete time process algebra extended with propositional signals and conditions, counting process creation operator, and a state operator. Finally, we mention the work of [12] which proposes an axiomatic semantics based on *Duration Calculus* and the work of [13] which uses *abstract real time machines*.

Our aim is somewhat different from the one of the above mentioned works, as it is not only to present a sound semantics, especially concerning timing aspects, but also to make forward a step concerning verification of SDL specifications: we give a program level intermediate representation into which a large subset of SDL and also other specification formalisms can be translated — by preserving its semantics — and which is the input language of an open verification environment.

The paper is organized as follows. In the next section, we present an example used throughout the paper to illustrate our work. Then, we describe the main features of the IF formalism used as an intermediate representation for SDL. Finally, we present an open validation environment for SDL specifications and illustrate its usefulness by means of some experimental results.

2. AN EXAMPLE: A DISTRIBUTED LEADER ELECTION ALGORITHM

We present a simple example used throughout the paper to illustrate the introduced formalisms and verification methods. We consider a *token ring*, that is a system of n stations $S_1, \ldots, S_n$, connected through a circular network, in which a station is allowed to access some shared resource R only when it "owns" a particular message, the *token*. If the network is unreliable, it is necessary to recover from token loss. This can be done using a *leader election algorithm* [14,15] to designate a station responsible for generating a new token.

Formal specifications and verifications of these algorithms already exist and we consider here an SDL version of the one described in [16]. Figure 1 shows the system view of the specification. The signals **open** and **close** denote the access and the release of the shared resource (here part of the environment). The signals **token** and **claim** are the messages circulating on the ring.

All stations S_i are identical and modeled by the SDL process of Figure 2. On expiration

426

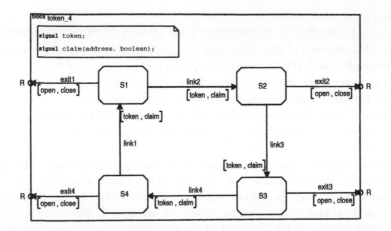

Figure 1. The *token-ring* architecture

of the timer `worried` token loss is assumed: this timer is set when the station waits for
the token, and reset when it receives it. The "alternating bit" `round` is used to distinguish
between valid claims (emitted during the current election phase) and old ones (cancelled
by a token reception). In the `idle` state, a station may either receive the token from its
neighbor (then it reaches the `critical` state and can access the resource), receive a timer
expiration signal (then it emits a claim stamped with its `address` and the current value
of `round`) or receive a claim. A received claim is "filtered" if its associated `address` is
smaller than its own address and transmitted unchanged if it is greater. If its own valid
claim is received, then this station is elected and generates a new token.

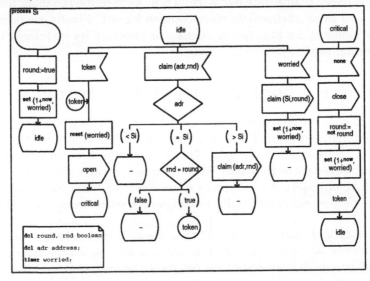

Figure 2. The behavior of station S_i

In the SDL specification, message loss must be modeled explicitly (for instance by introducing a non deterministic choice when a token or claim is transmitted by a station). Using the intermediate representation IF, message loss can be expressed simpler by means of lossy buffers, for which exist particular verification techniques.

3. IF: AN INTERMEDIATE REPRESENTATION FOR SDL

In the following sections, we give a brief overview of the intermediate representation IF, its operational semantics in terms of labeled transition systems and the translation of a rather extended subset of SDL into IF. A more complete description can be found in [17]. In particular, we do not present the rendez-vous communication mechanism here.

3.1. An overview on IF

In IF, a system is a set of *processes* (state machines as SDL processes) communicating *asynchronously* through a set of *buffers* (which may be lossy/reliable and bounded/unbounded). Each process can send and receive messages to/from any buffer. The timed behavior of a system can be controlled through *clocks* (like in timed automata [18,19]) and *timers* (SDL timers, which can be set, reset and expire when they reach a value below 0).

3.1.1. IF system definition

A system is a tuple $Sys = (glob\text{-}def,\text{PROCS})$ where

- $glob\text{-}def = (type\text{-}def,sig\text{-}def,var\text{-}def,buf\text{-}def)$ is a list of global definitions, where $type\text{-}def$ is a list of type definitions, $sig\text{-}def$ defines a list of parameterized signals (as in SDL), $var\text{-}def$ is a list of global variable definitions, and finally, $buf\text{-}def$ is a list of buffers through which the processes communicate by asynchronous signal exchange.

- PROCS defines a set of processes described in section 3.1.2.

3.1.2. IF process definition

Processes are defined by a set of local variables, a set of control states and a set of control transitions. A process $P \in \text{PROCS}$ is a tuple $P = (var\text{-}def, \text{Q}, \text{CTRANS})$, where:

- $var\text{-}def$ is a list of local variable definitions (including timers and clocks)

- Q is a set of control states on which the following attributes are defined:
    - $stable(q)$ and $init(q)$ are boolean attributes, where the attribute $stable$ allows to control the level of atomicity, which is a useful feature for verification: only $stable$ states are visible on the semantic level.
    - $save(q)$, $discard(q)$ are lists of `filters` of the form
      `signal-list in buf if cond`.
      $save(q)$ is used to implement the **save** statement of SDL; its effect is to preserve all signals of the list in `buf`, whenever the condition `cond` holds.

      $discard(q)$ is used to implement the implicit discarding of non consumable signals of SDL. When reading the next input signal in `buf`, all signals to be discarded in `buf` preceding it are discarded in the same atomic transition.

- CTRANS is a set of control transitions, consisting of two types of transitions between two control states $q, q' \in Q$:

– input transitions which are triggered by some signal read from one of the communication buffers as in SDL:

$$q \xrightarrow[(u)]{g \mapsto \textbf{input} \; ; \; body} q'$$

– internal transitions depending not on communications:

$$q \xrightarrow[(u)]{g \mapsto body} q'$$

Where in both cases:

- g is a predicate representing the *guard* of the transition which may depend on variables visible in the process (including timers, clocks and and buffers, where buffers are accessed through a set of primitives).

- body is a sequence of the following types of atomic actions:
  – *outputs* of the form "**output** *sig(par_list)* **to** *buf*" have as effect to append a *signal* of the form "*sig(par_list)*" at the end of the buffer *buf*.
  – usual *assignments*.
  – *settings* of timers of the form "**set** *timer* := **exp**". This has the effect to activate **timer** and to set it to the value of **exp**. An active timer decreases with progress of time. SDL timers expire when they reach the value 0, but in IF any timer tests are allowed. Clocks are always active and they increase with progress of time.
  – *resettings* of timers and clocks, which have the effect to inactivate timers and to assign the value 0 to clocks.

- The attribute $u \in \{\textbf{eager}, \textbf{delayable}, \textbf{lazy}\}$ defines the urgency type of each transition. **eager** transitions have absolute priority over progress of time, **delayable** transitions may let time progress, but only as long as they remain enabled, whereas **lazy** transitions cannot prevent progress of time. These urgency types are introduced in [20] and lead to a more flexible notion of urgency than in timed automata, where enabled transitions become urgent when an *invariant* — depending on values of timers and ordinary variables — associated with the starting state q becomes **false**. For compatibility with timed automata we allow also the definition of an attribute *tpc*(q) representing such an invariant (defining a necessary condition for time progress). Notice also that

  – the concept of urgency defines a priority between ordinary transitions and time progress which moreover may vary with time. Thus the concept of urgency is orthogonal to the usual concept of priority between ordinary transitions.
  – urgency and *tpc* attributes are only relevant in *stable* states, as only *stable* states are visible at the semantic level, and therefore only in *stable* states interleaving of transitions (ordinary ones as well as time progress) is possible.

- input is of the form "**input** **sig**(*reference_list*) **from** buf **if** cond" where
  – **sig** is a signal,
  – *reference_list* the list of references[2] in which received parameters are stored,

---

[2]that is an "assignable" expression such as a variable or an element of an array

- buf is the name of the buffer from which the signal should be read
- cond is a "postguard" defining the condition under which the received signal is accepted; cond may depend on received parameters.

Intuitively, an input transition is enabled if its guard is true, the first signal in buf — that can be consumed according to the *save* and *discard* attributes — is of the form $\text{sig}(v_1, ...v_n)$ and the postguard cond holds *after* assigning to the variables of the *reference_list* the corresponding values $v_1, ...v_n$.

That means that the input primitive is — as in SDL — rather complicated, but if one wants to translate the SDL input primitive by means of a simpler primitives, one needs to allow access the elements of the buffer in any order. This means that the input buffer becomes an ordinary array and no specific analysis methods can be applied.

3.2. Semantics of IF

We show how with a process can be associated a labeled transition system, and then, how these process models can be composed to obtain a system model.

3.2.1. Association of a model with a process

Let P= (*var-def*, Q, cTRANS) be a process definition in the system Sys and:

- Let TIME be a set of environments for timers and clocks (for simplicity of the presentation, we suppose that these environments are global, that is, applicable to all timers and clocks occurring in Sys). An environment $\mathcal{T} \in$ TIME defines for each clock a value in a time domain T (positive integers or reals), and for each timer either a value in T or the value *"inac"* (represented by a negative value) meaning that the timer is not active. Setting or resetting a timer or a clock affects a valuation $\mathcal{T}$ in an obvious manner. Progress of time by an amount δ transforms the valuation $\mathcal{T}$ into the valuation $\mathcal{T} \boxplus \delta$ in which the values of all clocks are increased by δ, and the values of all timers are decreased by δ (where the minimal reachable value is zero).

- Let BUF be a set of buffer environments $\mathcal{B}$, representing possible contents of the buffers of the system, on which all necessary primitives are defined: usual buffer access primitives, such as *"get the first signal of a given buffer, taking into account the save and the discard attribute of a given control state"*, *"append a signal at the end of a buffer"*,... and also *"time progress by amount δ"*, denoted by $\mathcal{B} \boxplus \delta$, is necessary for buffers with delay.

- Let ENV be a set of environments $\mathcal{E}$ defining the set of valuations of all other variables defined in the system Sys.

The semantics of P is the labeled transition system $[P] = (Q \times \text{VAL}, \text{TRANS}, \text{TTRANS})$ where

- $Q \times$ VAL is the set of states and VAL= ENV $\times$ TIME $\times$ BUF is the set of data states.

- TRANS is the set of untimed transitions obtained from control transitions by the following rule: for any $(\mathcal{E}, \mathcal{T}, \mathcal{B}), (\mathcal{E}', \mathcal{T}', \mathcal{B}') \in$ VAL and input transition (and simpler for an internal transition)

$$q \xrightarrow[\text{(u)}]{\quad g \mapsto (\text{sig}(x_1...x_n),\text{buf},\text{cond}) \; ; \; body \quad} q' \in \text{cTrans} \qquad \text{implies}$$

$$(q,(\mathcal{E},\mathcal{T},\mathcal{B})) \xrightarrow{\ell} (q',(\mathcal{E}',\mathcal{T}',\mathcal{B}')) \in \text{Trans}, \qquad \text{if}$$

- the guard g evaluates to true in the environment $(\mathcal{E},\mathcal{T},\mathcal{B})$
- the first element of buf in the environment $\mathcal{B}$— after elimination of appropriate signals of the discard attribute and saving of the signals of the save attribute — is a signal $\text{sig}(v_1...v_n)$, and the updated buffer environment, after consumption of $\text{sig}(v_1...v_n)$, is $\mathcal{B}''$
- $\mathcal{E}''=\mathcal{E}[v_1...v_n/x_1...x_n]$ and $\mathcal{T}''=\mathcal{T}[v_1...v_n/x_1...x_n]$,are obtained by assigning to x_i the value v_i of the received parameters,
- the postguard cond evaluates to true in the environment $(\mathcal{E}'',\mathcal{T}'',\mathcal{B}'')$
- $\mathcal{E}'$ is obtained from $\mathcal{E}''$ by executing all the assignments of the body,
- $\mathcal{T}'$ is obtained from $\mathcal{T}''$ by executing all the settings and resettings occurring in the body, without letting time progress,
- $\mathcal{B}'$ is obtained from $\mathcal{B}''$ by appending all signals required by outputs in the body,
- ℓ is an appropriate labeling function used for tracing.

- TTRANS is the set of *time progress transitions*, which are obtained by the following rule which is consistent with the intuitively introduced notion of urgency: in any state $(q,(\mathcal{E},\mathcal{T},\mathcal{B}))$, time can progress by the amount δ, that is

$$(q,(\mathcal{E},\mathcal{T},\mathcal{B})) \xrightarrow{\delta} (q,(\mathcal{E},\mathcal{T} \boxplus \delta, \mathcal{B} \boxplus \delta)) \in \text{TTRANS} \qquad \text{if}$$

1. q is *stable* and
2. time can progress in the state $(q,(\mathcal{E},\mathcal{T},\mathcal{B}))$, and
3. time can progress by steps until δ: whenever time has progressed by an amount δ' where $0 \le \delta' < \delta$, time can still progress in the reached state which is $(q,(\mathcal{E},\mathcal{T} \boxplus \delta',\mathcal{B} \boxplus \delta'))$.

Time can progress in state $(q,(\mathcal{E},\mathcal{T},\mathcal{B}))$ if and only if the following conditions hold:

- the time progress attribute $tpc(q)$ holds in $(\mathcal{E},\mathcal{T},\mathcal{B})$
- *no* transition with urgency attribute **eager** is enabled in $(q,(\mathcal{E},\mathcal{T},\mathcal{B}))$
- for each **delayable** transition tr enabled in $(q,(\mathcal{E},\mathcal{T},\mathcal{B}))$, there exists a positive amount of time ϵ, such that tr cannot be disabled while time progresses by ϵ.

3.2.2. Composition of models

The semantics of a system $Sys = (glob\text{-}def,\text{PROCS})$ is obtained by composing the models of processes by means of an associative and commutative parallel operator $\|$.

Let $[P_i] = (Q_i \times \text{VAL},\text{TRANS}_i,\text{TTRANS}_i)$ be the models associated with processes (or subsystems) of Sys. Then, $[P_1] \| [P_2] = (Q \times \text{VAL},\text{TRANS},\text{TTRANS})$ where

- $Q = Q_1 \times Q_2$ and $\begin{cases} init((q_1,q_2)) & = & init(q_1) \wedge init(q_2) \\ stable((q_1,q_2)) & = & stable(q_1) \wedge stable(q_2) \end{cases}$

- TRANS is the smallest set of transitions obtained by the following rule and its symmetrical rule:

$$\frac{(q_1, \mathcal{V}) \xrightarrow{\ell} (q_1', \mathcal{V}') \in \text{TRANS}_1 \text{ and } \neg stable(q_1) \vee stable(q_2)}{((q_1, q_2), \mathcal{V}) \xrightarrow{\ell} ((q_1', q_2), \mathcal{V}') \in \text{TRANS}}$$

- TTRANS is the smallest set of transitions obtained by the following rule:

$$\frac{(q_1, \mathcal{V}) \xrightarrow{\delta} (q_1, \mathcal{V}') \in \text{TTRANS}_1 \text{ and } (q_2, \mathcal{V}) \xrightarrow{\delta} (q_2, \mathcal{V}') \in \text{TTRANS}_2}{((q_1, q_2), \mathcal{V}) \xrightarrow{\delta} ((q_1, q_2), \mathcal{V}') \in \text{TTRANS}}$$

3.3. Translation from SDL to IF

We present the principles of the translation from SDL to IF considering the structural and the behavioral aspects. We do not present the translation of data aspects, and in particular the object oriented features, as they do not interfere with our framework.

3.3.1. Structure

SDL provides a complex structuring mechanism using blocks, substructures, processes, services, etc, whereas IF systems are *flat*, that is consisting of a single level of processes, communicating directly through buffers. Therefore, a structured SDL system is flattened by the translation into IF. Also, the structured communication mechanism of SDL using channels, signal routes, connection points, etc is transformed into point to point communication through buffers by computing for every output a statically defined unique receiver process (respectively its associated buffer).

All predefined SDL data types, arrays, records and enumerated types can be translated. For abstract data types, only the signatures are translated, and for simulation, the user must provide an appropriate implementation.

In SDL all signals are implicitly parameterized with the pid of the sender process, therefore in IF all signals have an additional first parameter of type pid.

3.3.2. Processes

Basically, for each instance of an SDL process, we generate an equivalent IF process and associate with it a default input queue. If the number of instances can vary in some interval, the maximal number of instances is created.

Variables: Each local variable/timer of an SDL process becomes a local variable/timer of the corresponding IF process. We define also variables sender, offspring and parent which are implicitly defined in SDL. Remote exported/imported variables declared inside an SDL processes become global variables, declared at IF system level.

States: All SDL states (including *start* and *stop*) are translated into *stable* IF control states. As IF transitions have a simpler structure than SDL transitions, we introduce also systematically auxiliary non stable states for each *decision* and each *label* (corresponding to a "join") within an SDL transition. For each *stable* IF state we define the *save* and *discard sets* to be the same as for the corresponding SDL state.

Transitions: For each *minimal path* between two IF control states, an IF transition is generated. It contains the triggers and actions defined on that path in the same order.

All the generated transitions are by default *eager* i.e. they have higher priority than the progress of time; this allows to be conform with the notion of time progress of the tool *Object*GEODE; more liberal notions of time progress can be obtained by using different translations from SDL to IF (see the example below).

- inputs: SDL signal inputs are translated directly into IF inputs, where the sender parameter must be handled explicitly: each signal receives the first parameter in the local variable **sender**.
  Spontaneous input none is translated by an assignment of the **sender** to the pid of the current process. No input part is generated in this case.

- timeouts expirations are *not* notified via timeout signals in IF: each timeout signal consumption in an SDL process is translated into a transition without input, which tests if the corresponding timer evaluates to *zero*, followed by the reset of that timer. The reset is needed to avoid multiple consumption of the same timeout expiration.

- priority inputs: are translated into normal inputs by enforcing the guards of all low priority inputs and the save set of the source state. The guard of each low priority input is conjuncted with a term saying that *"there is no higher priority signal in the buffer"*. All low priority signals are explicitly saved if *"at least one input with higher priority exists in the buffer"*. Such tests can effectively be expressed by predefined predicates on buffers.

- continuous signal: SDL transitions triggered by a continuous signal test, are translated into an IF transition without input, whose guard is equivalent to the SDL continuous signal.

- enabling condition: an enabling condition following an SDL input signal is translated directly into a post guarded input where the received parameters can be tested.

- task: all SDL formal tasks are translated into IF assignments. Informal tasks become comments in the IF specification.

- set and reset: SDL timer sets become IF timer sets, where an *absolute* value *"now + T"* becomes a *relative* value *"T"*. SDL timer resets become IF timer resets.

- output: SDL outputs become IF outputs: if the *to pid-expression* clause is present in the SDL output, the same pid-expression is taken as destination for the IF output. Otherwise, according to *signal routes signature, via restrictions, connections*, etc. we compute **statically** the set of all possible destinations. If this set contains exactly one process instance, it become the IF destination, otherwise, this output is not translated (and a warning is produced). Any output contains as first parameter the **pid** of the sending process.

- decision: each alternative of an SDL formal decision is translated into a guard starting an IF-transition from the corresponding non stable state.

- create: the dynamic creation of processes is not yet handled. But we will translate this construction by using the rendez-vous mechanism of IF: a new instance is created (an "inactive" instance is activated) by synchronizing its first action with the process creating (activating) it. During this synchronization, parameters can be passed between the "creating" and the "created" process, such as the the values of the `parent` and the `offspring` variables, etc.

- procedures: IF does not directly support procedures. But we handle a relatively large class of SDL programs containing procedures by *procedure inlining*, which consists in directly inserting the procedure graph, instead of its call, in the process graph.

Example: translation of the token ring to IF

To illustrate IF, we present the translation of the token ring introduced in Section 2. The translation of the structure is completely straightforward in this example. Figure 3 contains the IF version of the process S_1, where the additional non stable states are dotted.

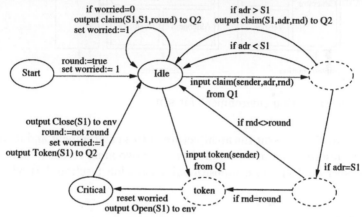

Figure 3. The "graphical" IF description of station S_1

By default, all transitions are **eager**, which leads to the same behavior as in *Object*GEODE. Thus, time can only progress, and the timeout occur, if the token is really lost (that is, no transition is enabled), and therefore a leader election algorithm is only initiated if necessary. In IF, a different notion of time, closer to reality, can be modeled, e.g. by considering the transition from the `critical` state as **lazy**, thus allowing time to pass in this state by an arbitrary amount. In order to limit the time a process can remain in the `critical` state, one can consider this transition as **delayable**, introduce a clock `cl_crit` which is reset when entering `critical` and add to the outgoing transition the guard `cl_crit` ≤ *some_limit*.

4. AN OPEN VALIDATION ENVIRONMENT BASED ON IF

One of the main motivations for developing IF is to provide an intermediate representation between several tools in an "open" validation environment for SDL. Indeed, none of the existing tools provides all the validation facilities a user may expect. Therefore, we want to allow them to cooperate, as much as possible using program level connections. An important feature is the ability of the environment to be open: in particular connections with KRONOS [21] (a model checker for timed automata) and INVEST [22,23] (a tool computing abstractions) are envisaged.

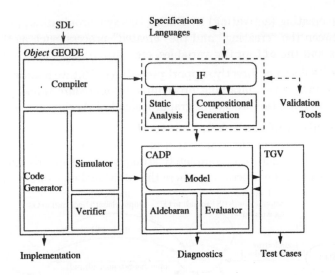

Figure 4. An open validation environment for SDL

In this section, we first present the architecture of this environment and its main components. Then, we describe in a more detailed manner two more recent modules concerning static analysis (section 4.2) and compositional generation (section 4.3) which are based on IF.

4.1. Architecture

The environment is based on two validation toolsets, *Object*GEODE and CADP, connected through the intermediate representation IF. There exists already a connection between these toolsets at the simulator level [24], however using IF offers two main advantages:

- The architecture still allows connections with many other specification languages or tools. Thus, even specifications combining several formalisms could be translated into a single IF intermediate code and globally verified.

- The use of an intermediate program representation where all the variables, timers, buffers and the communication structure are still explicit, allows to apply methods such as static analysis, abstraction, compositional generation. These methods are crucial for the applicability of the model checking algorithms.

*Object*GEODE

*Object*GEODE is a toolset developed by VERILOG supporting the use of SDL, MSC and OMT. It includes graphical editors and compilers for each of these formalisms. It also provides a C code generator and a simulator to help the user to interactively debug an SDL specification. The *Object*GEODE simulator also offers some verification facilities since it allows to perform automatic simulation (either randomly or exhaustively), and behavioral comparison of the specification with special state machines called observers [25].

CADP and TGV

We have been developing for more than ten years a set of tools dedicated to the design and verification of critical systems. Some of them are distributed in collaboration with the VASY team of INRIA Rhône-Alpes as part of the CADP toolset [2,26]. We briefly present here two verifiers integrated in CADP (ALDEBARAN and EVALUATOR) and the test sequence generator TGV [3] built upon CADP jointly with the PAMPA project of IRISA. These tools apply model-checking on behavioral models of the system in the form of labeled transition systems (LTS). ALDEBARAN allows to compare and to minimize finite LTS with respect to various *simulation* or *bisimulation* relations. This allows the comparison between the observable behavior of a given specification with its expected one, expressed at a more abstract level. EVALUATOR is a model-checker for temporal logic formulas expressed on finite LTS. The temporal logic considered is the alternating-free μ-calculus. TGV aims to automatically generate test cases for conformance testing of distributed systems. Test cases are computed during the exploration of the model and they are selected by means of *test purposes*. Test purposes characterize some abstract properties that the system should have and one wants to test. They are formalized in terms of LTS, labeled with some interactions of the specification. Finally, an important feature of CADP is to offer several representations of LTS, enumerative and symbolic ones based on BDD, each of them being handled using well-defined interfaces such as OPEN-CAESAR [27] and SMI [28].

SDL2IF and IF2C

To implement the language level connection through the IF intermediate representation we take advantage of a well-defined API provided by the *Object*GEODE compiler. This API offers a set of functions and data structures to access the abstract tree generated from an SDL specification. SDL2IF uses this abstract tree to generates an IF specification operationally equivalent to the SDL one.

IF is currently connected to CADP via the *implicit model representation* feature supported by CADP. IF programs are compiled using IF2C into a set of C primitives providing a full basis to simulate their execution. An exhaustive simulator built upon these primitives is also implemented to obtain the explicit LTS representation on which all CADP verifiers can be applied.

4.2. Static analysis

The purpose of static analysis is to provide global informations about how a program manipulates data without executing it. Generally, static analysis is used to perform global optimizations on programs [29–31]. Our goal is quite different: we use static analysis in order to perform model reductions before or during its generation or validation. The expected results are the reduction of the state space of the model or of the state vector.

We want to perform two types of static analysis: *property independent* and *property dependent* analysis. In the first case, we use classic analysis methods such as live variable analysis or constant propagation, without regarding any particular property or test purpose we are interesting to validate. In the second case, we take into account informations on data involved in the property and propagate them over the static control structure of the program. Presently, only analysis of the first type is implemented but we are also investigating constraint propagation and more general abstraction techniques. For instance, through the connection with INVEST we will be able to compute abstract IF programs using general and powerful abstraction techniques.

Live variables analysis

A variable is *live* in a control state if there is a path from this state along which its value can be used before it is redefined. An important reduction of the state space of the model can be obtained by taking into account in each state only the values of the live variables.

More formally, the reduction considered is based on the relation $\sim_{live}$ defined over model states: two states are related if and only if they have the same values for all the live variables. It can be easily proved that $\sim_{live}$ is an equivalence relation and furthermore, that it is a bisimulation over the model states. This result can be exploited in several ways. Due to the local nature of $\sim_{live}$ it is possible to directly generate the quotient model w.r.t. $\sim_{live}$ instead of the whole model without any extra computation. Exactly the same reduction is obtained when one modifies the initial program by introducing systematic assignments of non-live variables to some particular value. This second approach is presently implemented for IF programs.

Consider now the token ring protocol example. In the `idle` state the live variables are `round` and `worried`, in the `critical` state only `round` is live, while variables `sender`, `adr` and `rnd` are never live. The reduction obtained by the live reduction is shown in Table 1 (line 3).

Constant propagation

A variable is *constant* in a control state if its value can be statically determined in the state. Two reductions are possible. The first one consists in modifying the source program by replacing constant variables with their value. Thus, it is possible to identify and then to eliminate parts of dead code of the program e.g. guarded by expressions which always evaluates to `false`, therefore to increase the overall efficiency of the program. The second reduction concerns the size of the state vector: for a control state we store only the values of the non-constant variables. The constant values do not need to be stored, they can always be retrieved by looking at the control state.

Note that, both of the proposed reductions do not concern the number of states of the model, they only allow to improve the state space exploration (time and space). However, this kind of analysis may be particularly useful when considering extra information about the values assigned to variables, extracted from the property to be checked.

4.3. Compositional generation

As shown in the previous section, efficient reductions are obtained by replacing a model M by its quotient w.r.t an equivalence relation like $\sim_{live}$. However, stronger reductions can be obtained by taking into account the properties under verification. In particular, it is interesting to consider a weaker equivalence R — which should be a congruence for parallel composition —, able to abstract away non observable actions. The main difficulty is to obtain the quotient M/R without generating M first.

A possible approach is based on the "divide and conquer" paradigm: it consists in splitting the program description into several pieces (i.e., processes or process sets), generating the model M_i associated with each of them, and then composing the quotients M_i/R. Thus, the initial program is never considered as a whole and the hope is that the generated intermediate models can be kept small.

This compositional generation method has already been applied for specification formalisms based on *rendez-vous* communication between processes, and has been shown efficient in practice [32–34]. To our knowledge it has not been investigated within an SDL framework, may be, because buffers raise several difficulties or due to lack of suitable tools.

To illustrate the benefit of a compositional approach we briefly describe here its application to the token ring protocol:

1. We split the IF description into two parts, the first one contains processes S_1 and S_2 and the second one contains processes S_3 and S_4. For each of these descriptions the internal buffer between the two processes is *a priori* bounded to two places. Note that, when a bounded buffer overflows during simulation, a special *overflow* transition occurs in the corresponding execution sequence.

2. The LTS associated with each of these two descriptions are generated considering the "most general" environment, able to provide any potential input. Therefore, the *overflow* transitions appear in these LTS (`claim` and `token` can be transmitted at any time).

3. In each LTS the input and output transitions relative to the internal buffers (Q_2 and Q_4) are hidden (i.e., renamed to the special τ action); then these LTS are reduced w.r.t an equivalence relation preserving the properties under verification. For the sake of efficiency we have chosen the branching bisimulation [35], also preserving all the safety properties (e.g. mutual exclusion).

4. Each reduced LTS is translated back into an IF process, and these two processes are combined into a single IF description, including the two remaining buffers (Q_1 and Q_3). It turns out that the LTS generated from this new description contains no *overflow* transitions (they have been cut off during this last composition, which confirms the hypothesis on the maximal size of the internal buffers).

The final LTS is branching bisimilar to the one obtained from the initial IF description. The gain, obtained by using compositional generation in addition to static analysis, can be found in Table 1 (line 4).

Results

We summarize in the table below the size of the LTS obtained from the token-ring protocol using several generation strategies.

Table 1. LTS obtained for the token ring example

	Generation method	*Number of states*	*Number of transitions*
1	*Object*GEODE	3018145	7119043
2	IF	537891	2298348
3	IF + live reduction	4943	19664
4	IF + compositional generation	1184	4788

The difference between the model generated by *Object*GEODE (line 1) and the one obtained from IF (line 2) are due to the following reasons:

- the handling of timer expirations in *Object*GEODE involves two steps: *first* the time-out signal is appended to the input buffer of the process, and *later* it is consumed, whereas in IF these two steps are collapsed into a single one, bypassing the buffer.

- *Object*GEODE introduces "visible" states for each informal decision, whereas these states do not appear in the model obtained from IF.

The most spectacular reduction is obtained by the live-reduction: the reduced model is about 100 times smaller than the one obtained by direct generation, preserving all properties (models 2 and 3 are strongly bisimilar).

Finally, when considering as visible only the **open** and **close** signals all four LTS are branching bisimilar to the one shown in Figure 5, which proves, in particular, the mutual exclusion property of the protocol.

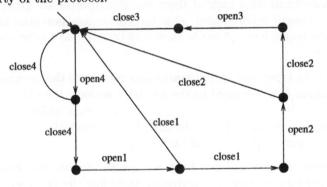

Figure 5. The reduced behavior of the token ring.

5. CONCLUSION AND PERSPECTIVES

We have presented the formalism IF which has been designed as an intermediate representation for SDL, but it can be used as a target language for other FDT as it contains most of the concepts used in these formalisms. The use of IF offers several advantages:

- IF has a formal semantics based on the framework of communicating timed automata. It has powerful concepts interesting for specification purposes, such as different urgency types of transitions, synchronous communication, asynchronous communication through various buffer types (bounded, unbounded, lossy, ...).

- IF programs can be accessed at different levels through a set of well defined API. These include not only several low-level model representations (symbolic, enumerative, ...) but also higher level program representation, where data and communication structures are still explicit. Using these API several tools have been already interconnected within an open environment able to cover a wide spectrum of validation methods.

The IF package is available at http://www-verimag.imag.fr/DIST_SYS/IF. In particular, a translation tool from SDL to IF has been implemented and allows both to experiment different semantics of time for SDL and to analyze real-life SDL specifications with CADP.

A concept which is not provided in IF is dynamic creation of new process instances of processes and parameterization of processes; this is due to the fact that in the framework of algorithmic verification, we consider only static (or dynamic bounded) configurations. However, it is foreseen in the future to handle some kinds of parameterized specifications.

The results obtained using the currently implemented static analysis and abstractions methods are very encouraging. For each type of analysis, it was possible to build a module which takes an IF specification as input and which generates a *reduced* one. This architecture allows to chain several modules to benefit from multiple reductions applied to the same initial specification. We envisage to experiment more sophisticated analysis, such as constraints propagation, and more general abstraction techniques. This will be achieved either by developing dedicated components or through the connections with tools like INVEST.

REFERENCES

1. Verilog. Object*GEODE SDL Simulator - Reference Manual.* http://www.verilogusa.com/solution/pages/ogeode.htm, 1996.
2. J.-C. Fernandez, H. Garavel, A. Kerbrat, R. Mateescu, L. Mounier, and M. Sighireanu. CADP: A Protocol Validation and Verification Toolbox. In *Proceedings of CAV'96 (New Brunswick, USA)*, volume 1102 of *LNCS*, August 1996.
3. J.-C. Fernandez, C. Jard, T. Jéron, and C. Viho. An Experiment in Automatic Generation of Test Suites for Protocols with Verification Technology. *SCP*, 29, 1997.
4. ITU-T. *Annex F.2 to Recommendation Z-100. Specification and Description Language (SDL) - SDL Formal Definition: Static Semantics.* 1994.
5. ITU-T. *Annex F.3 to Recommendation Z-100. Specification and Description Language (SDL) - SDL Formal Definition: Dynamic Semantics.* 1994.
6. C.A.R. Hoare. *Communicating Sequential Processes.* Prentice Hall International, 1984.
7. D. Bjørner and C.B. Jones. *Formal Specification and Software Development.* Prentice Hall Publications, 1982.
8. M. Broy. Towards a Formal Foundation of the Specification and Description Language SDL. *Formal Aspects on Computing*, 1991.
9. J.C. Godskesen. An Operational Semantic Model for Basic SDL. Technical Report TFL RR 1991-2, Tele Danmark Research, 1991.
10. J.A. Bergstra and C.A. Middelburg. Process Algebra Semantics of φSDL. In *2nd Workshop on ACP*, 1995.
11. J.A. Bergstra, C.A. Middelburg, and Y.S. Usenko. Discrete Time Process Algebra and the Semantics of SDL. Technical Report SEN-R9809, CWI, June 1998.
12. S. Mørk, J.C. Godskesen, M.R. Hansen, and R. Sharp. A Timed Semantics for SDL. In *FORTE IX: Theory, Applications and Tools*, 1997.
13. U. Gläser and R. Karges. Abstract State Machine Semantics of SDL. *Journal of Universal Computer Science*, 3(12), 1997.
14. G. Le Lann. Distributed Systems – Towards a Formal Approach. In *Information Processing 77*. IFIP, North Holland, 1977.
15. E. Chang and R. Roberts. An Improved Algorithm for Decentralized Extrema-Finding in

Circular Configurations of Processes. *Communications of ACM*, 22(5), 1979.

16. H. Garavel and L. Mounier. Specification and Verification of Distributed Leader Election Algorithms for Unidirectional Ring Networks. *SCP*, 29, 1997.

17. M. Bozga, J-C. Fernandez, L. Ghirvu, S. Graf, L. Mounier, J.P. Krimm, and J. Sifakis. The Intermediate Representation IF. Technical report, Verimag, 1998.

18. R. Alur, C. Courcoubetis, and D.L. Dill. Model Checking in Dense Real Time. *Information and Computation*, 104(1), 1993.

19. T.A. Henzinger, X. Nicollin, J. Sifakis, and S. Yovine. Symbolic Model Checking for Real-Time Systems. *Information and Computation*, 111(2), 1994.

20. S. Bornot, J. Sifakis, and S. Tripakis. Modeling Urgency in Timed Systems. In *International Symposium: Compositionality - The Significant Difference, Malente (Holstein, Germany)*, 1998. to appear in LNCS.

21. S. Yovine. KRONOS: A Verification Tool for Real-Time Systems. *Software Tools for Technology Transfer*, 1(1-2), December 1997.

22. S. Graf and H. Saidi. Construction of Abstract State Graphs with PVS. In *Proceedings of CAV'97, Haifa*, volume 1254 of *LNCS*, June 1997.

23. S. Bensalem, Y. Lakhnech, and S. Owre. Computing Abstractions of Infinite State Systems Compositionally and Automatically. In *Proceedings of CAV'98, Vancouver, Canada*, volume 1427 of *LNCS*, June 1998.

24. A. Kerbrat, C. Rodriguez, and Y. Lejeune. Interconnecting the *Object*GEODE and CADP Toolsets. In *Proceedings of SDL Forum'97*. Elsevier Science, 1997.

25. B. Algayres, Y. Lejeune, and F. Hugonnet. GOAL: Observing SDL Behaviors with GEODE. In *Proceedings of SDL Forum'95*. Elsevier Science, 1995.

26. M. Bozga, J.-C. Fernandez, A. Kerbrat, and L. Mounier. Protocol Verification with the ALDEBARAN Toolset. *Software Tools for Technology Transfer*, 1, 1997.

27. H. Garavel. OPEN/CÆSAR: An Open Software Architecture for Verification, Simulation, and Testing. In *Proceedings of TACAS'98*, volume 1384 of *LNCS*, March 1998.

28. M. Bozga. SMI: An Open Toolbox for Symbolic Protocol Verification. Technical Report 97-10, Verimag, September 1997.

29. A. Aho, R. Sethi, and J.D. Ullman. *Compilers: Principles, Techniques and Tools*. Addison-Wesley, Readings, MA, 1986.

30. M.N. Wegman and F.K. Zadeck. Constant Propagation with Conditional Branches. *ACM Transactions on Programming Languages and Systems*, 13(2), April 1991.

31. S. Muchnick. *Advanced Compiler Design Implementation*. Morgan Kaufmann Publishers, San Francisco, CA, 1997.

32. S. Graf, G. Lüttgen, and B. Steffen. Compositional Minimisation of Finite State Systems using Interface Specifications. *Formal Aspects of Computation*, 3, 1996.

33. A. Valmari. Compositionality in State Space Verification. In *Application and Theory of Petri Nets*, volume 1091 of *LNCS*, 1996.

34. J.P. Krimm and L. Mounier. Compositional State Space Generation from LOTOS Programs. In *Proceedings of TACAS'97*, volume 1217 of *LNCS*, Enschede, The Netherlands, 1997.

35. R.J. van Glabbeek and W.P. Weijland. Branching-Time and Abstraction in Bisimulation Semantics. CS R8911, CWI, 1989.

SDL'99 : The Next Millennium
R. Dssouli, G.v. Bochmann and Y. Lahav, editors
©1999 Elsevier Science B.V. All rights reserved

PerfSDL : Interface to Protocol Performance Analysis by means of Simulation

Mazen Malek

Conformance Centre,
Ericsson Telecommunication ltd.
Laborc u. 1., 1037 Budapest, Hungary
Tel : (+36-1) 437 7682
Fax : (+36-1) 437 7219
E-mail : mazen.malek@eth.ericsson.se

Abstract

This paper presents a new approach to test the performance of communication systems that contain protocol components. This type of performance testing covers timing properties and identifies performance bottlenecks for range of parameter settings and assesses the measured performance. The general idea of this paper is to integrate protocol performance into system performance by providing appropriate correlation and feedbacks. PerfSDL – an extension of SDL – is an interface to describe protocol components prior to performance testing in a manner that leads to compact testing with maximum benefits of protocol knowledge. The new language adds new constructs that enable the adaptation of SDL systems to the requirements of performance testing by means of simulation without losing speed and efficiency. A powerful simulation tool – PlasmaSIM - was used and first results of the description and execution of performance tests will be presented.

Keywords

Performance testing, SDL, simulation, performance bottlenecks.

1. INTRODUCTION

The development of new protocols requires simulation as means of understanding and debugging the new mechanisms and proofing the applicability to a network. Simulation and visualisation are also needed for the design of elements or a complete domain of communication networks. A wide variety of simulation tools are available in the market, which are used for these simulation needs. Tools that are intended for network simulation have the topology view and simulation control features, and they usually come with a library of some standard network elements. For this purpose, the mostly used products are OPNET, BONeS, and LabVIEW. The TrafficLab of Ericsson at Budapest has developed a network simulator, PlasmaSIM, that applies new techniques in this field. It is a prototype of a network performance analysis tool integrating network simulation, analytical evaluation and optimisation methods in one uniform system. Besides this, PlasmaSIM has a number of advantages over other tools, in particular, its speed that is 10 to 30 times faster. All these tools require the simulated objects, or node models, to be coded in a specific programming language, in PlasmaSIM C++ and TCL languages are used. This lacks the functional description and specification, which is needed during the design and implementation phases of proprietary protocols.

The description abilities of the SDL [1] language offer a lot of advantages that makes it desirable for specification of protocol components [2][3]. Additionally, the system model, together with those components, can be very suitably designed with SDL, exploiting its structural concepts. For simulation and verification of such designs a very good packages are available in the market, like the SDT (Telelogic). They are very powerful in checking errors and inconsistencies in the protocol specifications. The overall performance aspects of a system, which contains protocol entities, can not be inspected on basis of such tools, simply because most of them are not written in SDL. Also, the SDL lacks the suitability for time and throughput measures that are essential in the evaluation of system's performance. A combination of the advantages of SDL and a powerful simulation tool can assist protocol designers with valuable application. This demands special treatment of SDL concepts in order to make them applicable for such task. Within this context, PerfSDL acts as an extension to SDL, which is the new interface to PlasmaSIM for needs of protocol simulations.

The paper will be organised in the following manner. Section 2 will give the terminology behind performance testing. Section 3 gives brief indications on the parts of SDL that need revision and highlights the requirements for a new interface. In section 4 a complete description of the PerfSDL as a new approach to system performance testing including behaviour descriptions. The following section will introduce the adaptations and refinements applied during the development of PerfSDL-PlasmaSIM interface. For purposes of system analysis and studies a mapping between system and protocol performance measures is illustrated in section 6. After that some practical measures will be analysed on a new project that contains some proprietary protocols in section 7. Conclusions highlight the benefits gained by introducing this interface, and some future demands will be sketched.

2. PERFORMANCE TESTING

The main objective of performance testing is to test the performance of network components under normal and overload situations. This load is either an artificial one that is generated by traffic patterns, or a real one that is taken during certain time period. Generally, this testing checks some QoS requirements of the tested component, in particular delays, throughputs and rates. These are the so-called performance-oriented QoS parameters. Performance testing takes place in terms of measurements, which consist of sending time stamped packets through a network and recording delays and throughputs. Once collected, a number of statistics can be computed on the measurement samples.

Simulation is usually employed in performance testing. Other techniques, the empirical and analytical approaches, serve as complementary parts to simulation. Together they build, in an interleaving manner, a complete procedure of providing an accurate model of the system of interest. Simulation process starts by making models of the concerned problem and proceeds with conducting simulations on these models. These models should be as close to the real system as possible. On the contrary, modelling systems should be accomplished with enough simplifications of the system's components having minor impact on the investigated parameters. The simplifications have to be made with sufficient detail of the most relevant parts of the system, without risking losing accuracy of the system behaviour. In addition to that, the simulation time should be kept at a reasonable level. The so-called simulation runs will provide concrete answers on certain questions raised before the simulation. Examples of such questions, regarding the ATM QoS parameters, can be:

- What amount of Statistical Multiplexing Gain can be achieved when turning to VBR-rt service class from CBR service class when transferring a voice-like signal?
- When can we employ bandwidth-allocation other than peak-allocation, and what is the impact on QoS parameters like p-t-p CDV and CLR?

To allow early assessment of performance of communication systems one should consider the protocol design phase. The identification of performance bottlenecks in communication protocols is one aspect of such consideration [4]. To identify it we need to apply statistical evaluation of protocol transitions and detect those with the highest usage. This can guide to improve the system performance. Similar to system performance, questions like the followings may rise.

- What amount of overall performance can be gained by decreasing the time of bottleneck transitions?
- Is it possible to gain better performance by applying different message sequence scenarios?

3. PERFORMANCE SIMULATION AND SDL

3.1. Motivation

As stated earlier, there are needs to apply various kinds of testing during the development cycle of any product in the telecommunication field. Performance testing is the most crucial one for its indication of system's efficiency. Accordingly, product's market-share and life expectancy depend very strongly on those results. Generally, performance aspects are taken into account only after testing the functionality. Only little efforts are utilised at the early stages of development to give estimations on system performance. Thus, protocol development phase is in no direct connection with the performance testing. This phase may be effective in performance improvement if we have a platform that provides the appropriate feedbacks to designers. Some tries were worked out in this direction. In [5] there is a complete application about simulating a complete network domain based on SDL. They used the automatic C code generated from the SDT simulator on a UNIX socket environment. They also introduced a new interface based on Tcl/Tk scripting language for visualisation. The main drawback for such interpretation is the slow execution of the C code. Additionally, it requires the full SDL specification, which does not take into account what may be available in the component libraries most simulation tools provide. Not too far from our approach lies the one introduced in [6]. They build their model on formally specified systems and assess hardware resource needs. They have also introduced probes for statistical evaluation purposes. This has a limited scope in which we can not fit communication protocols.

The adjustability of detail level is of great importance during any simulation scenario. In the case of protocol simulation, functionality and layers should be adjustable during different simulation runs. This would decrease time required for gathering information.

3.2.   Needs in simulation

The main modification that should be applied to SDL is to add more real-time aspects. Such can be the introduction of timed transitions, which reflect the time required for the system to respond to events occur outside it. In an abstract model of the system a transition may include some interworking tasks of internal building blocks. Another important aspect is the handling of concurrency and input queues in SDL. While behaviour processes have to execute in parallel in real time, the simulation of their communication can be performed sequentially that decrease the number of scheduled events. An outgoing signal from a process should be handled to its receiver in one event. In addition to this, one can not simulate a system that has infinite length of buffers.

In simulation there is a need for meters and counters. These are applied and connected to simulated objects without interfering with the behaviour semantics. By using them, we can detect rare and often transitions, and consequently we can identify the bottlenecks in the system. In the following section we will try to sketch a general view of our extension to SDL.

4. PerfSDL

The formal interpretation of PerfSDL is very similar to SDL leaf block level (Those blocks that have only process definitions). Exceptions are the new concepts and the modifications we apply to the basic ones. The main entity of the language is the PerfSDL-process, which can be characterised by the following.

- Set of states, e.g. s_1, s_2, s_3;
- Set of internal variables;
- Set of initial states, e.g. s_0;
- Transition function (a transition can be a set of sub-transitions), e.g. $\mathbf{tr_{12}}$.

This is called the underlying state machine, which requires the availability of a global clock in the system. A trace in this underlying state machine is a sequence of states and transitions.

trace is: $\sigma = s_0\, s_1\, s_2\, s_3\, ...$

transitions are: $\mathbf{tr_{01}}\ \mathbf{tr_{12}}\ \mathbf{tr_{23}}\, ...$

As in figure 1, the environment, where this process runs and communicates, has two types of controlling elements:
- set of signals;
- *schedule* and *time-to-run* events.

The environment acts on process scheduling requests, through *schedule* events, by assigning a time event for performing the task requested. Additionally, it activates relevant processes when there is some task to be handled by them through *time-to-run* events. This synchronisation is performed between each running process and the environment. PerfSDL processes can communicate with each other at block level. All levels higher than leaf block level are described in the simulation environment. The modifications to the base language may be divided into two parts, static and dynamic. By static we mean those additions that do not take part in the behaviour description of the model, but rather reflect some measures in the specification. Dynamic changes are either new concepts or modified ones in the base language.

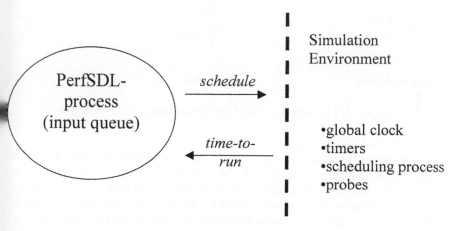

Figure 1. PerfSDL process interactions with the environment.

Static constructs. They are called probes, and have the ability to monitor, count and analyse the applied system. They are new elements that can be included during the design process but may be defined during testing. Here we define two kinds of probes; counters and recorders. A counter counts the number of times certain transition is visited, while recorder records the time when that transition starts executing. A recorder may be accompanied by some relevant information, e.g. the current status of some internal variables.

Dynamic constructs. These are the extension of SDL on syntactic level.

1   Enhancing the SDL machine with time:
This means taking time elapsing in account in each event that uses processor's time. For this purpose *States* will not be considered because they are conceptual. Instead, we redefine a trace in the following way. A trace is a sequence of states and timed transitions:

trace is: $\theta = s_0(t_0) \, s_1(t_1) \, s_2(t_2) \, s_3(t_3) \, ...$
transitions are: $tr_{01}(t_0) \, tr_{12}(t_1) \, tr_{23}(t_2) \, ...$

These times, e.g. t_1, include the consumption of inputs and execution of transitions. Moreover, we allow the recording of events when transitions start execution:

events for transitions: $\tau_0 \, \tau_1 \, \tau_2 \, \tau_3 \, ...$

and we define simple timing property:

446

- time never decreases but possibly increases due to transition execution:

$$\tau_i \geq \tau_{i-1} + t_{i-1}$$

The inequality implies that there could be a time consumed in between transitions, which may simulate additional time for internal events other than transitions. Figure 2 introduces the graphical representation of probes and timed transitions, which will be used when developing a graphical interface to PlasmaSIM.

timed-transition   probe

Figure 2. The introduction of new constructs.

2   Adding the concept of Scheduling:

This concept is the most substantial one during simulation. It specifies the time when the simulator is asked to act on certain change in the state of the model; here we assume the event-driven simulation model. This is not necessarily performed at the time when transitions start. When a process consumes an input signal, it should indicate to the simulator its reaction and when to handle it, also the simulator has to consider the possible interactions that may happen after or during that reaction. In this context we consider the scheduling to be events that should occur after each progress in time, which happens when consuming input or performing a transition. For this purpose we introduced the so-called sub-transitions, which are necessary to discrete the transitions into events that can be scheduled. A sub-transition can be output event or task. Of course, when transitions are so simple there could be no need for reducing them into sub-transitions.

5. APPLICATION OF PerfSDL IN PlasmaSIM

There were a number of simplifications applied during this phase, ranging from applying simple communication to introducing new type of states. Most of the structural concepts of the SDL were integrated into the simulation environment. By other words, instead of considering systems that consist of blocks and channels to be the model nodes, we regard leaf blocks as the only simulated objects to be thought about. Systems in this respect will be collection of leaf blocks and the channels connecting them. This collection is referred to as Container Object in PlasmaSIM, which behaves as a single physical element in the model. The communication between them is totally handled by PlasmaSIM, with its underlying CORBA, except in case of delaying channels we need to define such channels as individual simulation objects. This interpretation implies that the simulation system knows every thing about the environment of a block, which is the reason why the concept of a system is designated to the simulation system. Figure 3 show where to define blocks in the general PlasmaSIM platform, while figure 4 depicts the relation between processes and blocks as applied in object oriented modelling. A block, as being a simulated object, should inherit its communication and scheduling features from a basic model for that purpose. *Simulated Object* is a set of basic features for measuring, scheduling and communication written in C++. Processes, on the other hand, are sorts of behaviour that should be included in the block code that describes its functionality.

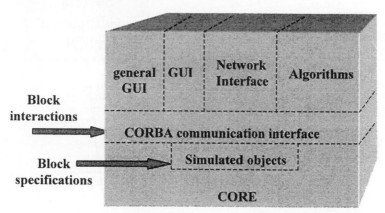

Figure 3. SDL specifications in PlasmaSIM platform.

All sorts of non-determinism should be resolved prior to production of PerfSDL specifications by using random generators. This requires the manipulation of discrete random number generators that have some imperfections and are considered rather pseudo-random. The new interface demands to include a switch that turns the non-determinism on and off during simulation.

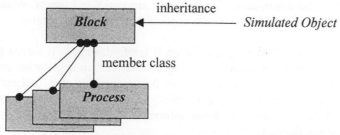

Figure 4. Object Oriented modelling of processes and blocks.

In order to handle decisions we interpret them as unstable states, and apply internal inputs as triggering events for transitions to stable states. The question and the answer of the decision are implied in the internal input that follows the unstable state. The internal inputs, afterward, determine which transition branch is to be taken. The continuous signal and enabling condition can be expressed suitably in terms of internal inputs. This interpretation was needed to uniform the scheduling mechanism of internal and external events; hence we have a single scheduler and a single global clock. Beside the former points, many other simplifications were utilised some of which are following.

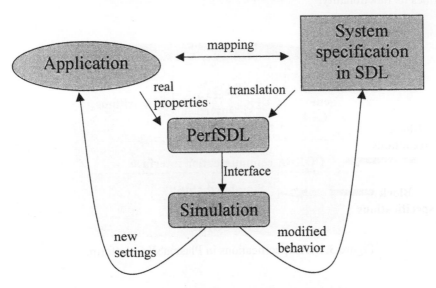

Figure 5. How to make use of the new interface.

- Single-direction channel.

Our simulation tool only handles this type of communication, so for bidirectional channels we assign two unidirectional ones.

- Matrix of states/inputs and the cells are function calls.

The whole implementation of the simulated object code, which contains SDL processes, is based on process matrix. The dimensions of this matrix are states and inputs, while its cells are function calls that handle transitions. For each process there is a single matrix.

The application of PerfSDL during simulation is twofold. Firstly, it assists to present modified behaviour in the tested specification bearing in mind certain application constraints. Secondly, it indicates necessity for new settings in the application due to limitations in behaviour machines. Figure 5 depicts this applicability within the different domains. It is worth noticing that PerfSDL requires two input information streams, from the application domain and the specification domain.

6. RELATION BETWEEN SYSTEM AND PROTOCOL PERFORMANCE

In its wider sense, system performance is a term that contains protocol performance. It is an overall measure of the efficiency of a system, in particular, it gives figures on system's achievement in terms of rates and throughputs. In addition, fulfilment of certain time criteria is checked by realising delays. Protocol performance, on the other hand, shows how efficiently a protocol machine accomplishes its tasks. That's why it is rather an identification of bottlenecks in protocols. Transitions are inspected both from the time and speed point of views, time they take to execute and speed they require to reduce that time. Consequently improvements can be introduced, e.g. decreasing transition time or applying less number of transitions.

To obtain a closer look at the correlation between the two types of performance, we need to get the logical domain prospect of systems and protocols. In figure 6 an overall system function is sketched. Input can either be cell, message, packet or any type of discrete information.

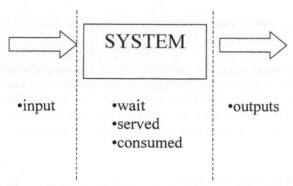

Figure 6. System function for handling arriving information.

The system will respond to this piece of information by consuming it with or without sending outputs. The arrived information can either be waiting or served before it is consumed at a moment. To obtain the system performance a simplified structure and functionality is tested at the level of the arrived information (i.e. packet level for example). As shown in figure 7, some sort of internal message is issued to the protocol component in accordance to the incoming information. This message will be handled due to behaviour rules and some appropriate actions and output messages may be produced.

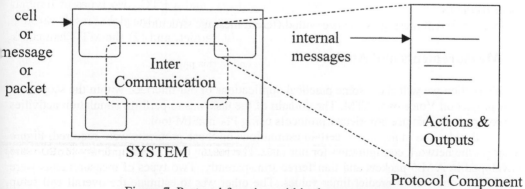

Figure 7. Protocol function within the system scope.

For communicating systems, protocols are usually employed to govern their communication. In this context, a protocol component is installed and accordingly the internal structure is built up. For this reason protocol performance is very decisive in obtaining the entire dimensions of a system. A typical protocol performance metric is the recurrence of transitions and output messages. When trying to get key points in a protocol design that may influence some performance criterion, a relationship should be obtained between system and protocol domains.

Proposal
Assuming functionality is verified:

Each system performance metric can be interpreted as a set of protocol and non-protocol performance metrics.

The foregoing proposal states the interpretation of system performance in terms of protocol performance, and requires the functionality of the system to be verified. Frequently, system performance aspects require measures that include non-protocol components in the system, like maintenance blocks and memory buffers. These can not be obtained in protocol performance evaluation. Following an example of correlating the two terms.

Example
Call Setup Time (CST) in a Transit Exchange.
The time required to handle a call setup message depends on the received information and the availability of links to neighbouring exchanges. After extracting the called party number, an internal database is consulted to get the address of next exchange to forward to. Data base access and other tasks require internal communication between exchange blocks.

Correlation
The signalling protocol in question is responsible for acting in this case, as well as the proprietary protocols used to coordinate the work between the different parts of the exchange. A possible protocol performance metric may be the time required for a certain message sequence between those parts, e.g. to set a call record.

Improvements
applying different message sequence with different message structure.

7. Measurements and Analysis

In this section we will show some practical applications of our interface within the scope of a new project on Voice over ATM. The domain of the task was to perform simulation activities for components that use proprietary protocols using PlasmaSIM tool.
Besides the sanity proof, certain estimations on those protocols were required. Figure 8 shows the network configuration for our task. The messages of the proprietary protocol are enveloped in AAL5 packets and transferred transparently. Two types of measurements were conducted: one was to predict timer values. The other was to estimate the overall call setup time and try to decrease it by modifying certain parts of the proprietary protocol.

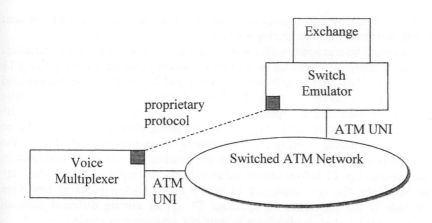

Figure 8. The problem domain.

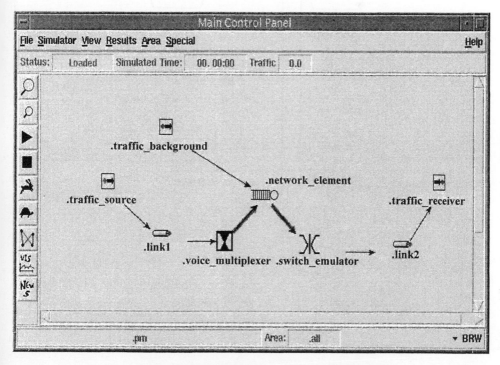

Figure 9. The simulation domain in PlasmaSIM.

To get a view of the influence on protocol timer values that may be introduced by the environment, we conduct a measure on that in figures 9,10 and 11. Figure 9 demonstrates a simplified network domain, while figure 10(a) shows part of the protocol specification that contains the timer T1. The simulation domain contains many estimations on the connecting

452

network that is characterised by two figures of delay and loss rate. The network element object was modelled to simulate the connecting network.

In addition to that, background traffic was used that is based on certain statistical measures. The results of applying variations on T1 versus blocking rate are drawn in figure 11 with three sets of settings. They were as following: curves 1 and 2 were for heavy background traffic with curve 2 being for slower served traffic. Curve 3 was for light background traffic and slow served traffic. In each one, the optimum value for T1 is where the curve reaches its lowest point. The larger T1 value we set the bigger blocking probability we get. This is due to multiplexer resources used during waiting for T1 intervals when messages are lost in the network. When this happens, requests for connection are blocked at arriving to multiplexer. On the other hand, decreasing T1 below certain value will discard reply messages that may arrive a bit later. No doubt, the best choice of T1 is that one with less blocking rate. One important remark here is the difference in optimum T1 values among different network settings. This may be considered as one feedback to protocol development phase.

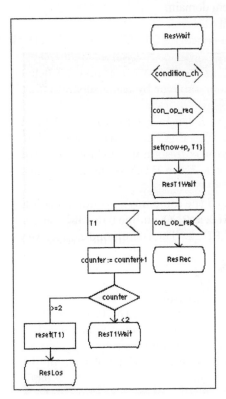

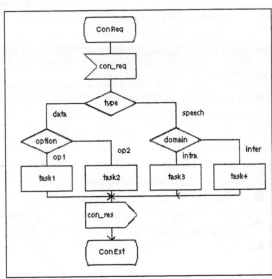

Figure 10. a) On the left, timer T1 and b) on the right, handling of connection options in the SDL diagram of the multiplexer.

The second measurement was on optimising the Call Setup Time (CST), which is the time required for setting a connection between different modules in the network. The two simulated nodes, voice multiplexer and switch emulator, communicate during CST and exchange request and reply messages. We model the CST as including smaller time intervals, like Request Setup Time (RST) that elapses during the communication between the voice multiplexer and switch emulator. RST can be further interpreted as the time consumed during communication between behaviour process of the proprietary protocol installed in those two nodes. Part of this is depicted in figure 10(b). It is the behaviour of voice multiplexer process when receiving a request from the switch emulator. According to the contents of the received request a decision chain is applied to forward it to the proper entity, which is drawn as tasks 1,2,3 and 4. These tasks contain calls to other components in the multiplexer other than the protocol component. By applying our additions to SDL we were able to find the bottleneck of this behaviour. We applied timed transition and counters instead of those tasks, as in figure 12. The times for those transitions were estimations on the time required by the tasks. When applying a certain traffic source, measures on the usage of tasks were obtained. Table 1 shows that task1 got 90% of the processing time relatively to the other tasks. This was repeated for three different cases of traffic sources. The table implies that task 1 is the bottleneck of this process, and decreasing its required time would lead to better performance. Figure 13 demonstrates this. Curve 1 is for relating RST to increment in network load, while curves 2 and 3 are for the same relation when task 2 and task 1 were decreased by 50% respectively. It is obvious that performance improves only when the bottleneck transition time is decreased.

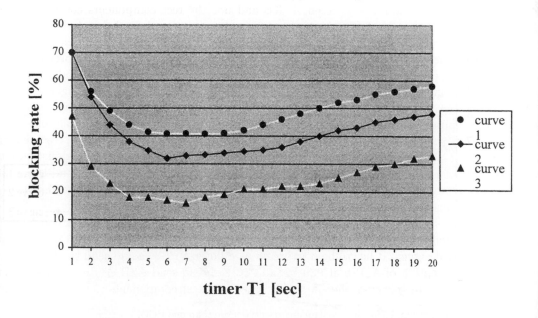

Figure 11. T1 versus blocking rate.

8. Conclusions

In this paper, we have presented a new approach for relating protocol performance to system performance. We also showed a tool for integration of behaviour and performance simulation, which is intended to be used during the development of proprietary protocols.

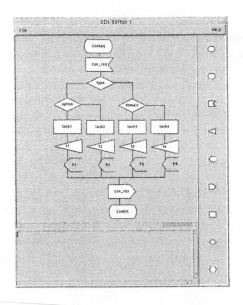

	Case1	Case2	Case3
P1	9231	8897	9011
P2	441	70	53
P3	98	20	60
P4	107	11	31

Table 1. Number of execution of tasks.

Figure 12. SDL specification of figure 10(b) using PerfSDL editor

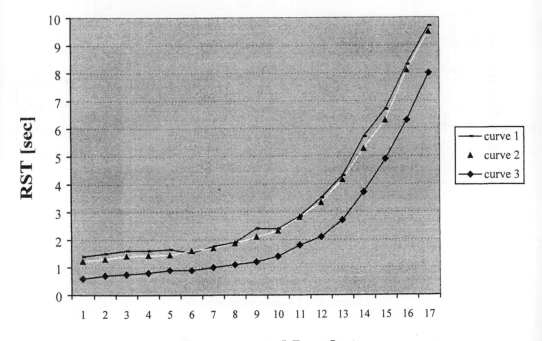

Figure 13. RST versus incremental Load.

System designers can use the interface introduced here to make careful choice of design alternatives. These alternatives can be message length, recurrence of non-replied requests or timer values. Additionally, it is a complementary part to verification tools that show the fulfilment of requirements.

The future work will focus on finding algorithms to identify bottleneck transitions on bases of statistical usage measures without requiring to run separate simulation. It is worth noting that the method applied in this paper for the purpose of bottleneck identification can be performed in step-like manner. Task 1, for example, can be further investigated and its bottleneck transition can be found out.

References

[1] Telecommunication Standardisation Sector of ITU. Specification and description language (SDL). ITU-T Recommendation Z.100, International Telecommunication Union, March 1993.
[2] Dieter Hogrefe, Amardeo Sarma. SDL with applications from protocol specification. Prentice Hall 1991.
[3] R. Braek, O. Haugen. Engineering Real Time Systems. Prentice Hall, UK, 1993.
[4] Sijian Zhang, Samuel T. Chanson. Analysing Performance bottlenecks based on finite state specifications. Testing of Communicating Systems'97, Chapman & Hall 1997.
[5] Andereas Iselt and Achim Autenrierth. An SDL-based platform for the simulation of communication networks using dynamic block instantiations. SDL'97: TIME FOR TESTING- SDL, MSC and Trends.Elsevier Science 1997.
[6] Martin Steppler and Matthias Lott. SPEET – SDL Performance Evaluation Tool. SDL'97: TIME FOR TESTING- SDL, MSC and Trends.Elsevier Science 1997.

SDL'99 : The Next Millennium
R. Dssouli, G.v. Bochmann and Y. Lahav, editors
©1999 Elsevier Science B.V. All rights reserved

Early Performance Prediction of SDL/MSC-specified Systems by Automated Synthetic Code Generation*

W. Dulz[a], S. Gruhl[b], L. Kerber[a] and M. Söllner[b]

[a]Universität Erlangen-Nürnberg, IMMD VII,
Martensstraße 3, D–91058 Erlangen, Germany
{dulz,kerber}@informatik.uni-erlangen.de

[b]Lucent Technologies, Network Systems GmbH, Global Wireless Systems Research,
Thurn-und-Taxis-Straße 10, D–90411 Nürnberg, Germany
{sgruhl,msoellner}@lucent.com

We present a new approach for early performance prediction based on MSC specified systems in the context of SDL. Our approach is integrated into existing design methodologies as proposed by commercial tool vendors where communication software is fully specified in SDL and the final implementation is derived from there. Obviously the structure of the SDL specification will influence the performance of the final system. Thus it is very important to make performance estimates for the target system available at design time to steer important design decisions. The key to performance evaluation is the development of performance models, which are evaluated either with analytical, simulation or monitoring techniques.

Our approach is scenario-based and uses non-functional annotations of MSCs to formalise additional performance attributes. These MSCs are automatically transformed to an SDL specification which yields a prototype implementation via a code generation tool chain. The resulting implementation is executed on the target machines with the target system software from which many performance characteristics can be evaluated using monitoring techniques. We call the implementation "synthetic" since it is artificially derived from MSC specifications and the generated SDL is *not* designed to be subsequently reused through functional refinement. This paper describes the automatic transformation from MSC to the SDL specification and its environment with a special focus on dynamic issues.

1. INTRODUCTION

Today's huge and complex mobile communication networks must be developed and maintained under the continuous pressure of releasing new featured products to the market at time. One approach to attack this problem is to use high level description and

---

*The work described in this paper is part of the cooperation project MONA (MObile Network Analysis) between Lucent Technologies, Network Systems GmbH, Global Wireless Systems Research, and the University of Erlangen-Nürnberg, IMMD VII.

implementation techniques. The standardised languages SDL (Specification and Description Language, [3]) and MSC (Message Sequence Chart, [10]) are today's choice to fit these needs.

MSC focuses on the message exchange between instances, and its use ranges from requirements engineering down to testing. SDL describes the complete functional system behaviour with extended finite state machines. There has been a rapid development in tool and method support for these languages. E.g. moving from the requirements capture to design is supported by tools that allow the semi-automated transformation of MSC descriptions to SDL skeletons; functional properties of the SDL specification can be checked through automated validation tools.

A crucial part in the development process is the automated generation of main parts of the program code for the protocol from the SDL description. This implies that besides the quality of the code generator the structure of the SDL specification also influences the overall performance of the target system. Thus performance aspects are moved to early phases in the protocol engineering live cycle. Having this in mind one might ask himself in the design phase of the project:

- how does the chosen SDL architecture effect the performance of the target system?

- which processes should be merged to gain more performance?

- will the currently chosen hardware match the performance requirements?

Our experience with code generation in the area of GSM-systems shows that major parts of the performance can be "lost" in the middleware implementing the communication for the SDL processes and also in the internal communication and scheduling mechanisms of the UNIX system (see Table 2, Section 2). Moreover the "loss" of performance is *not* linear with the imposed load on the system, which makes the prediction of the performance very challenging and an approach focussing only on (SDL-) transition delays appears not promising.

The main idea is to create a synthetic SDL prototype solely for the purpose of performance prediction. We call the prototype "synthetic" since it is artificially derived from MSC specifications. The generated SDL is *not* designed to be further reused through functional refinement. The aim is to have a synthetic prototype running on the target hardware with the target middleware and to monitor all necessary performance characteristics. The synthetic prototype should have the property that it is an open reactive system, like the target system, which is triggered by a synthetic environment and produces

- the same amount of internal communication load and

- the same load from (SDL-)transitions

as the target system would generate under the given load from the environment. Since the prototype should be available very early in the protocol life cycle, MSCs are the prime candidate to derive the synthetic system from; since the SDL runtime system and the middleware should resemble the same behaviour as the target system, our approach is to use the same code generation tool chain which will implement the real system. Thus we have transformed MSCs to an SDL system, used the tool chain to get executables, and implemented the synthetic system on the target hardware for measurement studies. Using different synthetic environments the system can be evaluated under different load scenarios.

Related work. Most performance evaluation approaches for SDL/MSC specified systems focus on SDL rather than on MSC. Prominent examples are QSDL (Queueing SDL,[4]) and SPECS (SDL Performance Evaluation of Concurrent Systems,[1]) which extend SDL with processors and time consuming transitions and evaluate their system by discrete event simulation. The SPEET (SDL Performance Evaluation Tool,[14]) approach transforms the specification to C code which can be linked to an emulated target environment.

In contrast to these techniques based on functionally complete descriptions our approach can be classified as a scenario based approach in the context of SDL/MSC since MSCs represent the main basis of our performance model. [6] also uses a scenario based approach to evaluate SDL specified systems. For a set of scenarios MSC traces are derived from the specification and transformed to a so-called Layered Queueing Network (LQN) model, a special queueing model for performance analysis. With the LQN model the system response time or the system utilisation can be derived.

Another scenario based analytical technique to evaluate SDL/MSC specified systems is to calculate the utilisation of processors and channels, and the throughput of the system on the basis of MSC as proposed by one of the authors [5]. Its underlying model estimates the utilisation as *linear* with the offered load, which produced too optimistic results and lead us to develop the work presented in this paper.

One of the authors has jointly developed Performance Message Sequence Charts (PMSC) [7] a language to describe performance models on the basis of MSC. The basic ideas of the performance model presented here and those of PMSC [13] are the same.

A transformation from MSC to SDL was also investigated in [11]. Here only partial transformations are considered, because some kinds of MSC could not be transformed to a given SDL architecture. Unlike in this approach we focus on a transformation for the purpose of performance monitoring which allows us to induce certain changes to the system that are valid for our evaluation purpose, but not for the purpose of further refinement. Therefore we do not face any problems of state related ambiguities due to message overtaking. Thus our approach can generate a valid system specifications regardless of the applied system architecture for the described cases in [11].

Structure of the paper. In section two we continue with a short overview of the GSM mobile communication system, because in our case study we have investigated the performance of a GSM base station controller. Next our performance model is introduced with special focus on the augmented MSC semantics for the parallel composition of MSCs. Section four describes the automatic mapping of MSCs to a synthetic SDL system and the creation of the SDL architecture as well as the behaviour of the SDL processes. Several possible solutions are discussed how to guarantee unique messages and how to solve the addressing of multiple instances. In section five we present our concepts for the synthetic environment to enable measurement studies. Finally we close our paper with some concluding remarks.

460

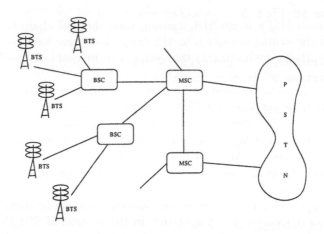

Figure 1. Overview GSM scenario

2. APPLICATION EXAMPLE: GSM

We outline the structure of our case studies to motivate the reasons for our design decisions which are adequate for our application domain.

GSM (Global System for Mobile Communication) is one of the most popular system used for mobile telecommunications especially in Europe and Asia. Figure 1 gives an simplified view of the network architecture with the three main network elements BTS, BSC and MSC. The BTS (Base Transceiver Station) is controlling the radio transmission and the interface to the mobile phones. Several BTS connect to BSC stations (Base Station Controller), while the BSC are connected to the MSC (Mobile Switching Center). These MSC - not to be confused with the "Message Sequence Charts" - provide access to the PSTN (Public Switched Telephone Network), typically ISDN-based.

Table 1
Example traffic characteristics of a Base Station Controller (BSC)

Traffic between MSC and BSC	
Message Rate (1/s)	710
Data Volume transferred (bit/s)	$2.2 \cdot 10^6$
Traffic between BSC and BTS	
Message Rate (1/s)	2600
Data Volume transferred (bit/s)	$7 \cdot 10^5$
Traffic internal to BSC cluster	
Message Rate (1/s)	2200
Data Volume transferred (bit/s)	$1.9 \cdot 10^6$

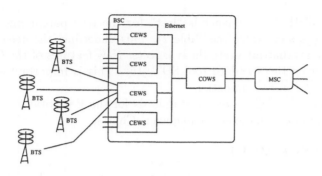

Figure 2. Structure of Base Station Controller (BSC)

From the performance point of view the BSC turned out to be a critical element in the network, because it manages all the signalling traffic and protocol handling for the realtime radio resource management (establishment and release of radio connections, handovers etc.). A typical traffic characteristics of a BSC is given in Table 1.

We examined a realistic BSC software architecture as it is similarly implemented in a commercial product. The unit is implemented as a cluster of several standard UNIX workstations, connected by a 10 MBit Ethernet LAN running TCP/IP (see Figure 2). One workstation, the common workstation (COWS), mainly handles the tasks of a master controller, while the rest, the cell workstations (CEWS), are more concerned with the actual communication services towards the BTS. To allow an adaption to the variable amount of connected BTS this BSC runs server SDL processes for each radio transceiver (simplified). For the performance analysis we assume that the BSC is run in a well planned scenario, where each radio transceiver serves an area of equal mean traffic load. Therefore, equal signalling load is assumed for each of the SDL processes. Note that a different amount of BTS is typically served by one BSC cell workstation which implies that the overall load for the workstations varies.

The BSC application, i.e. the protocol handlers for GSM signalling traffic, is specified in SDL and automatically implemented using proprietary code generation tools. The BSC internal communication is built with a proprietary middleware that offers transparent and absolute addressing of SDL process instances. Measurements at the current BSC show

Table 2

Typical percentage of processor load for common and cell workstations within a BSC cluster at the same external traffic demand

	Radio Side (CEWS)	Net Side (COWS)
SDL Application (Call Handling)	12%	51%
Inter-Process Message Transfer Mechanism	43%	26%
Lower Layer System Calls	(LAPD) 45%	(SS#7) 23%

that major parts of the performance is "lost" for the transparent message transfer for SDL-processes and system calls (see Table 2). This underlines the need for performance evaluation techniques that integrate these aspects. New features of the GSM system will be implemented using the standard tool SDT [15]. This is important since we use this existing tool chain for our examination.

We have specified the GSM protocol standards for the Base Station Controller by use cases with approximately 100 Message Sequence Charts.

3. PERFORMANCE MODEL

When doing performance analysis of computer systems you have to integrate three different aspects:

Traffic : Reactive systems are open systems that react on environmental requests. The traffic model describes when, how often and which type of request is triggered by the environment, probably within specified limits.

Application : The reactive application itself is triggered by the environment and uses the hardware resources. The software architecture and in case of parallel or distributed systems the mapping of software modules to hardware components influences the performance of the overall system.

Machine : The machine model specifies the capabilities offered by the hardware and the system software to the application.

All these aspects build the basis for the performance analysis. Our approach makes use of the target hardware and the system software of the final system. Thus all aspects of the hardware and system software are integrated easily. Therefore no specific machine model is required.

The behavioral aspects of the application are modeled with annotated MSCs that are transformed to an executable synthetic SDL system for the purpose of performance evaluation. The user specifies the amount of consumed CPU time for local actions that are performed beside input and output actions. Moreover the user specifies the length of each message.

Figure 3 shows an example where the client instance produces a 100 byte long *request* message for the server instance which consumes (in mean) 100 μs CPU time to produce a 50 bytes long *reply* message. To keep the following diagrams simple we have skipped these annotations from here on.

Note that the CPU time is of importance here and not the execution time, because the execution time includes also additional waiting times, e.g. due to operating system scheduling mechanisms. The execution time is in fact one of the results of our analysis, while the specification input is the bare duration of CPU time. The CPU time can be measured or estimated for an isolated part, regardless of the overall system load or other delaying influences.

The application itself is seen as a set of independent services that is offered to the environment. Thus, the set of MSCs describing those services on top level run in parallel. From the performance analysis point of view these services are normal machine jobs since their processing needs computation time on the machine.

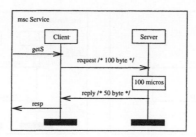

Figure 3. Performance attributes given in the MSCs as annotations

In our current approach each traffic source is characterised by the mean value of its arrival rate assuming equal or negative exponential distributions (as typically used in traffic models for telephone services).

When composing MSCs in parallel the standard semantics from Mauw and Reniers [2] allows the free merge of all events happening on one instance. In Figure 4 for example the following trace is allowed by the system at the *Client* instance:

in(getS1).in(getS2).out(request2).out(request1)...

where in(x) denotes the reception of message x, while out(x) denotes the sending of message x.

Assuming that the input of one message till the next input of another message on the same instance is mapped to one transition in SDL this flexibility in behaviour is not implemented since only transitions might interleave in one SDL process and not actions from different transitions. Thus we have restricted our semantics to the interleaving of

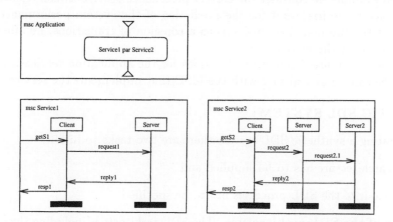

Figure 4. Parallel composed standard MSC

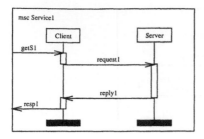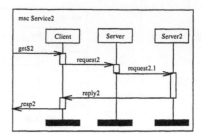

Figure 5. MSCs with transitions

transitions. A transition is bound to an instance and is characterised by the following:

> *There is only one input action in a transition that*
> *is the very first action of the transition. The tran-*
> *sition ends before the next input specified for this*
> *instance.*

The modified example is shown in Figure 5. Here the rectangles define transitions at the instance axis, i.e. atomic regions, where no event from the same instance from parallel MSCs might occur while the region is "active". A transition is active when its first event has occurred, but its last event has not. This implies for the example in Figure 5. that the given trace is not possible.

Note that transitions can contain the sending of none to several messages and the performing of none to several local tasks.

For our GSM example we consider the correct precedence order between transitions on the same instance to be irrelevant for the prediction of the system performance. Thus we can interpret the (normal) instance axis as a coregion of transitions, i.e. there is no precedence imposed by the instance axis.

As a traffic model we use distribution functions for the application services. They are annotated as their mean arrival rate with the MSC that implements the service.

4. SYNTHETIC SDL SYSTEM

When generating a synthetic SDL system there are two tasks to fulfill:

- the SDL architecture has to be supplied and

- the behaviour of the SDL processes has to be specified.

Generation of the SDL architecture. The SDL architecture including the mapping of processes or process sets to operating system processes can be made by the user as with regular SDL specifications. This opens the full flexibility that is available within the given tool set.

block	CS1	contains	Client Server
block	CS2	contains	Client Server
block	SS	contains	Server2

Figure 6. SDL architecture

In addition we have created an architecture specification language that allows us to derive an SDL architecture from the given MSC. The language is especially adopted to the restricted usage of the SDL architecture and the mapping to operating system processes in our particular GSM example, because

- each SDL block is mapped to one operating system process

- there is no more than one SDL process instance of an SDL process type in a block or operating system process.

With this special usage the architecture specification language simply has to relate SDL process types to SDL blocks. Note that it is still possible to assign one process type to different blocks.

The advantage of our language is, that it allows a compact specification for the SDL architecture and an automatic consistency check of the SDL architecture and the MSC. The consistency check for the given set of MSC guarantees the existence of at least one SDL process instance for each MSC instance and the existence of channels and signal routes for all possible communication scenarios.

We have designed our architecture specification language to cover the variety within *our* application architecture. This allows us to evaluate and compare systems with different architectures, while it is true that we do not cover the whole variety of possible SDL architectures. If the power of our language seems inappropriate to the reader please note that this language can be extended or the user can use an explicitly given architecture, where he has the unlimited access to *any* architecture possible within his tool set.

Figure 6 describes one architecture with our architecture specification language for the MSC shown in Figure 5.

Generation of the behaviour of SDL processes. The behavioral parts of the SDL processes are generated from the MSCs. For each MSC instance one SDL process is generated.

Since we assume the order of the atomic transitions within one process to be irrelevant, we do not need to model state dependent behaviour. Such a memoryless process is implemented by a one state machine.

Figure 7 shows such a process generated from the MSCs *Service1* and *Service2* for the instance *Server* from Figure 5.

The system generation involves the composition of the functional behaviour of several MSCs, while the messages in those MSCs do not have to have unique names. Since we found all interchanged messages having a parameter and the actual given parameters of

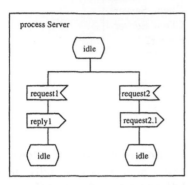

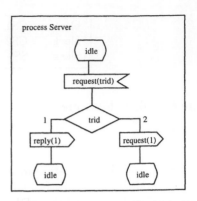

Figure 7. One state SDL process with unique message names

Figure 8. One state SDL process with a two level decision for the transition

the message and the message names are of no importance for the final measurements, uniqueness can mainly be enforced in two ways:

1. renaming of messages, e.g. encoding the MSC name, message name and instance number or

2. providing a unique parameter with the message.

The second alternative was chosen. We have coded the occurrence of the message within an MSC to a unique identifier for the transition posted in a parameter field with the message. Thus the correct transition can be chosen in two steps, first the message name triggers the SDL transition, where different sub-branches are chosen depending on that parameter. Figure 9 shows this in an example and in Figure 8 the corresponding SDL process can be seen. As we aim for performance evaluation we designed our system as a prototype solely for measurements. Therefore our method of turning every message into a unique one is applicable. This guarantees that we can automatically transform the

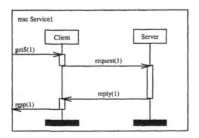

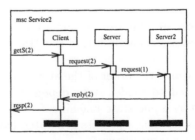

Figure 9. Messages with transition identifiers (trid) as parameters

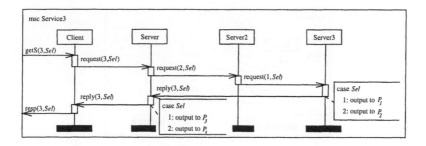

Figure 10. Fixed communication alternatives stored as parameters

given MSC specification regardless of the chosen architecture, as we never face ambiguous states.

Addressing of processes in the presence of multiple instances of one type of process is another issue. MSCs usually are used to specify example traces. Thereby the instances represent some entity in the system. These entities are not necessarily unique, thus multiple entities from the same type with the same behaviour can exist that are modeled by one instance in an MSC. MSC *Service*1 in Figure 4 shows a typical example. A client requests a service from a server. But the actual number of clients and servers is left open by the MSC specification.

Normally an MSC does not provide the information which SDL process instance has to be addressed. It only specifies that one instance is addressed and how it will react.

When the selection of the communication path is made in the environment, the system may be implemented with a set of *predefined communication paths* between the involved instances, while each of the predefined paths gets a unique identifier. The environment of the system will randomly choose one path and by passing the path-id along in the message's parameter field each instance will stick to that path (see Figure 10). This approach allows a probability distributions for several paths even the total restriction of some paths. Due to the large number of possible combinations in a real system, we expect the user to make little use of this feature.

Therefore we decided to use a distributed solution where the paths are dynamically chosen within the system. As long as the probability distribution for an instance selection is independent of the history of the formerly visited instances, it is appropriate to operate with a memoryless and distributed selection mechanism. There is no need to pass information in the parameter field and no memory is required for the local storage of all possible paths, which may be many. This solution is illustrated in Figure 11, where a client instance has many servers to perform its requested service and chooses one of them dynamically.

MSCs often specify situations for an acknowledged service request. Here a reply is passed back the same route where the request was originated. It may not appear appropriate to choose an alternative return route. With predefined communication paths, this is easy to achieve. Our approach of a distributed instance selection during runtime would

468

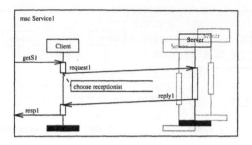

Figure 11. The client instance with decision which server to take

have to be extended to transmit the process ids with the message to allow deterministic instance selection for the return path. This approach is illustrated in Figure 12 where all involved processes store their process id as a parameter. The major drawback of this approach is the possibility to exceed the specified message size.

Architectural information may be used to shape the probability distribution for the instance selection. Investigations for our GSM have shown, that some process pairs which are arranged in one block mainly communicate locally within this block. We therefore shaped the distribution to a deterministic selection of that process instance in the same block. This is only done for this type of communication to this instance type. Note that the selection of communication via other instance types is not affected.

When mapping MSCs to SDL we use quantified values for message length and task duration. Since the synthetic system should carry the same amount of data as in the final application we add "useless" padding as parameters. The execution time for transitions is implemented as a C function that iterates over some multiplication to spend the specified amount of execution time in the transition. The function uses microseconds as parameter and calculates via machine-dependent macro variables the number of iterations of the loop.

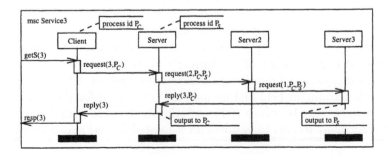

Figure 12. Individual process identifiers stored as parameters

5. ENVIRONMENT AND MEASUREMENT CONCEPT

The environment has to fulfill two tasks in the synthetic system:

- it must stimulate the system with given rates for the different services the system offers and

- it should supply measurement capabilities, such as the measurement of response time.

The environment typically consists of several independent units that communicate with the target system via multiple logical and physical interfaces. One unit might send one signal into the system via one interface while another unit expects the response from the system at another interface. To keep the test system for measurement as simple as possible we have integrated all functionality from the environment on one environment machine. Thus the environment has a global clock available for the measurement of the response time and the environment can be seen as one special MSC instance since all messages to/from the environment are related to one entity on the environment machine.

This special environment instance is also transformed to SDL. It uses the SDL timer mechanism to send messages into the system according to the specified traffic model, i.e. service rates. Up to now we have implemented streams for Poisson and constant rate traffic.

For the measurement of the response time we have added special functionality into the SDL processes. For each message besides the transition identification (trid) a second parameter is created for the purpose of monitoring that holds the measurement identification (mid). The measurement id is copied from all SDL processes in the SDL system, thus the environment can identify the corresponding reply messages from the system. This approach allows a black-box style evaluation of the synthetic system.

Since there are services that specify more than one input from the environment and more than one reply from the system we extend the response time definition as follows:

> The system response time is the elapsed time from
> the last input sent from the environment into the
> system till the last response message from the sys-
> tem has been received by the environment.

Note that the above definition does not imply that all activities from the MSC have finished.

Since the input to the system is within the control of the environment other response times, like "from the first input to the system till the last output from the system" can easily be derived.

If one service specifies multiple replies to the environment the environment has to keep track of the expected messages to match our definition of response time. This is done by some state information in the environment machine counting the total number of received messages with the specific measurement id. We initialise every measurement with the total number of expected replies from the system and perform the response time measurement after the last reply from the system is received. Note the we are investigating a running system where the order of the received messages do not have to be the same as specified in the MSCs.

There exist services that do not show any reply to the environment and thus are not accessible for the response time measurement from the environment machine. For the evaluation of those cases we suggest the introduction of artificial response messages, if the overall execution time - here measured as "response time" - of a particular service is of interest.

Besides the response time the utilisation of the processors and the internal network are of special interest. Since the target system is executed in a standard UNIX environment we can use standard UNIX tools and perform standard LAN monitoring.

6. CONCLUSION

We have presented a new idea how to integrate performance analysis in early phases of the SDL/MSC protocol engineering process. The key idea is to transform annotated MSCs to SDL such that the SDL system can execute all transitions specified in the MSCs. The transition's run time and message lengths given by the user are incorporated into the SDL system. This automatically derived SDL system is automatically implemented with the normal tool chain. In addition an artificial environment is created to trigger this system according to the specified traffic model. This synthetic system is run on the real hardware and measurements of the response time, processor or net utilisation are performed. The main advantages of our approach are, that

- only minimal specification effort is needed to gain the required performance model, since the MSCs can be reused from the functional specification where "only" quantitative values have to be added,

- the influences of the target hardware, target system software and middleware, that implements the transparent communication for the SDL processes, is automatically integrated into the performance measurement, which is very important since this influences are non-linear with increasing load and thus difficult to predict.

The current prototype for these transformations called LISA (Load generation through automatic Implementation of Synthetic Applications) [9] is based on an adopted semantics of MSCs. With LISA we have successfully derived a synthetic prototype from our MSC specified GSM system. In first experiments this prototype has shown non linear behaviour under different load scenarios as we expected from our experience with the existing system. We also monitored significantly varying signal delay with maximum delays up to multiple times the average delay. This is of special interest, as there are hard deadlines for signal responses for the GSM protocol defined.

REFERENCES

1. M. Bütow, M. Mestern, C. Schapiro, and P.S. Kritzinger. Performance Modelling with the Formal Specification Language SDL. In Gotzhein and Bredereke [8], pages 213–228.

2. A. Cavalli and A. Sarma, editors. *SDL '97: Time for Testing - SDL, MSC and Trends*, Evry, France, September 1997. Eighth SDL Forum, Elsevier Science Publishers B.V.

3. CCITT. *Recommendation Z.100: Specification and Description Language SDL, Blue Book*. ITU, Geneva, 1992.

4. M. Diefenbruch, J. Hintelmann, and B. Müller-Clostermann. The QUEST-Approach for the Performance Evaluation of SDL-Systems. In Gotzhein and Bredereke [8], pages 229–244.

5. W. Dulz. A Framework for the Performance Evaluation of SDL/MSC–specified Systems. In A. Javor, A. Lehmann, and I. Molnar, editors, *ESM96 European Simulation Multiconference*, pages 889 – 893, Budapest, Hungary, June 1996. Society for Computer Simulation International.

6. H. El-Sayed, D. Cameron, and M. Woodside. Automated performance modeling from scenarios and sdl designs of distributed systems. In *Proc. of Int. Symp. on Software Engineering for Parallel and Distributed Systems*, pages 127–135, Kyoto, Japan, April 1998. IEEE Press.

7. N. Faltin, L. Lambert, A. Mitschele-Thiel, and F. Slomka. An Annotational Extension of Message Sequence Charts to Support Performance Engineering. In Cavalli and Sarma [2], pages 307–322.

8. R. Gotzhein and J. Bredereke, editors. *Formal Description Techniques IX*. IFIP, Chapman & Hall, Oktober 1996.

9. S. Gruhl. Automatic Generation of Synthetic Load from Formal Use Cases for Performance Evaluation. Diplomarbeit, IMMD7, Universität Erlangen-Nürnberg, November 1998.

10. ITU-TS. *ITU-TS Recommendation Z.120: Message Sequence Charts (MSC)*. ITU, Geneva, 1996.

11. F. Khendek, G. Robert, G. Butler, and P. Grogono. Implementability of Message Sequence Charts. In Lahav et al. [12], pages 171–179.

12. Y. Lahav, A. Wolisz, J. Fischer, and E. Holz, editors. *Proceedings of the 1st Workshop of the SDL Forum Society on SDL and MSC*, Informatik-Berichte. Humboldt-Universität, 29th June – 1st July 1998.

13. L. Lambert. PMSC for Performance Evaluation. In *1. Workshop on Performance and Time in SDL/MSC*, Erlangen, Germany, 1998.

14. M. Steppler. Performance analysis of communication systems formally specified in sdl. In *Proceedings of The First International Workshop on Simulation and Performance '98 (WOSP '98)*, pages 49–62, Santa Fe, New Mexico, USA, 12th–16th October 1998.

15. Telelogic, Malmö AB. *SDT 3.1 User's Guide, SDT 3.1 Reference Manual*, 1996.

SDL'99 : The Next Millennium
R. Dssouli, G.v. Bochmann and Y. Lahav, editors

A simulation model for Message Sequence Charts*

Loïc Hélouët[†]

IRISA, Campus de Beaulieu

35042 Rennes Cedex

helouet@irisa.fr

This article describes a simulation framework for High-level Message Sequence Charts based on a graph grammar representation of MSCs. Normalized grammars allow for asynchronous or synchronized executions of HMSCs, and helps detecting process divergence.

1. Introduction

Specification of distributed systems is a difficult task. Unspecified behaviours can be introduced by unexpected concurrency, and communication media play an important role in the correctness of a protocol (distributed program won't have the same behaviour with asynchronous or synchronous communication media). Message Sequence Charts (MSCs) allow for the specification of distributed systems. They are clear, easy to use, and abstract the communication media from the conception task. MSCs describe a causal order between events of a scenario, and are defined by two types of graphs. Basic Message Sequence Charts (called bMSCs hereafter) define single scenarios. The composition of bMSCs is then done by High-Level Message Sequence Charts, a kind of high-level graph allowing for sequencing and exclusive choice between MSCs. HMSCs are far less intuitive, and can be ambiguous, more especially when a choice between two scenarios is distributed. The official semantics of choices in HMSCs considers that the first instance reaching a choice is responsible for the decision of the scenario to execute, and that all other instances have to perform the same choice. This can result in the storage of an infinite set of history variables (as shown in [1]). A distributed choice can also be treated as a consensus between processes, which involves that the first process able to choose a scenario has to wait for the other's answers. With that interpretation, choices act as synchronizations.

According to the assumed meaning of a choice, the execution of a system specified by an HMSC can be very different. HMSCs appear to be less intuitive than expected. This reinforces the need for formal manipulations of MSCs. Techniques such as model-checking can be used for ensuring the system does not violate critical properties. Unfortunately, MSCs describe infinite behaviours, with infinite state-space, which makes most of the model-checking techniques useless. Another technique for increasing the confidence in the system is simulation. By simulating the behaviour of a distributed program, one can quickly detect undesirable behaviours at an early stage of the specification.

---

*This work was partially supported by Alcatel within the REUTEL project
[†]INRIA

This article proposes a simulation framework for Message Sequence Charts based on the graph grammar representation of MSCs described in [4]. The normalized graph grammars turn out to be a good model for simulation, by reducing the time needed for searching the enabled actions of a system in a given state. Furthermore, the growth of the state size is a good indicator of a divergent specification.

This article is organized as follows: sections 2 defines a partial order semantics for HMSCs. Section 3 describes a graph grammar representation of MSCs and its properties. Section 4 gives an operational semantics for executing a normalized grammar. Section 5 is a complete example. Section 6 concludes, and gives perspectives for further work.

2. Partial order representation of MSCs

This section describes a partial order semantics for MSCs, very close to [6,5]. Partial order semantics models independence of events, while semantics such as [7] models concurrency through an interleaving of actions.

2.1. bMSCs as partial orders

A bMSC (standing for basic MSC) defines a simple scenario, ie an abstraction of a system behaviour. Within bMSCs, processes are called *instances*, and are represented by a vertical axis, along which events are put in a top down order. Message exchanges are represented by arrows labeled by message names from the emitting to the receiving instance. No assumption whatsoever is made about the communication medium. The MSC events can be: communication event (sending, receiving a message), timer events (setting, resetting, or timeout), instance events (creation, stop) or internal actions.

A bMSC defines a precedence relation between events: the emission of a message precedes its reception, and for any event e, all events situated upper than e on the same instance axis are predecessors of e. The order on the axis can be relaxed in some parts of the instance called *co-regions*. These co-regions are represented by dashed parts of the instance axis. Events situated in a co-region are not necessarily concurrent: their order is not specified yet, or is not important for the specification.

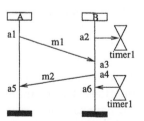

Figure 1. An example bMSC.

Let us consider a bMSC M describing the behaviour of a finite set of instances, called I hereafter. Two events performed by the same instance are ordered according to their coordinates on the instance axis, provided they are not in a co-region. If they are performed by different instances, they are ordered if and only if they are separated by at least one message exchange. So, M defines a partial order between events, and can be formalized by a poset $M =< E, \leq, \alpha, A, I >$ where E is a set of events, $\leq$ is a partial order relation (reflexive, transitive and antisymmetric binary relation) on E called *causal dependence relation*, A is a set of atomic actions names, and α is a labeling function from E to $A \times I$, associating an action name and an instance to each event. In Figure 1, a_1 and a_4 are ordered, but a_1 and a_2 are not.

2.2. HMSCs as partial order families

bMSCs only define simple finite scenarios. Designing communicating systems requires modelling more complex structures. High-level Message Sequence Charts (HMSCs) is a higher-level notation that allows for the composition of bMSCs. The usual syntax for HMSC, called MSC'96 [9] includes sequential and parallel composition of MSCs, loops, choices and inline expressions. This paper only deals with a subset of MSC'96, without inline expressions (which can be formalized by means of higher level descriptions) or parallel composition. Consequently, an HMSC can be seen as a directed graph, the nodes of which are start nodes, end nodes, bMSCs, connection symbols, conditions, or references to other HMSCs. An exemple is shown in Figure 8.

The official semantics of **sequential composition** of bMSCs is defined by a partial order concatenation operation. Let $M_1 = < E_1, \leq_1, \alpha_1, A_1, I_1 >$ and $M_2 = < E_2, \leq_2, \alpha_2, A_2, I_2 >$ be two MSCs. The *concatenation* of M_1 and M_2, written $M_1 \circ M_2$ is defined by:

$$M_1 \circ M_2 = < E_1 \cup E_2, \leq_{M_1 \circ M_2}, \alpha_1 \cup \alpha_2, A_1 \cup A_2, I_1 \cup I_2 >, \text{ where:}$$
$$\leq_{M_1 \circ M_2} = \leq_1 \cup \leq_2 \cup \{(e_1, e_2) \in E_1 \times E_2 \mid$$
$$\exists (e_1', e_2') \in E_1 \times E_2 \wedge \phi_1(e_1') = \phi_2(e_2') \wedge e_1 \leq_1 e_1' \wedge e_2' \leq_2 e_2 \}$$

More intuitively, a concatenation "glues" together two MSCs along their common instance axis. Note that this "weak sequential composition" imposes no synchronization barrier between events of M_1 and events of M_2. This means that in $M_1 \circ M_2$, all events of M_2 may be finished before any event of M_1 is performed. Another vision of sequential composition is "strong sequential composition", which imposes that all event of M_1 must be executed before executing events of M_2. This strong sequential composition is often met in the MSC-related literature, and reduces HMSCs to finite state machines. Yet, the official semantics proposed in norm Z.120 [10] is weak sequential composition.

The **alternative** between two MSCs is an exclusive choice between scenarios. HMSC P_0 in Figure 2-a defines two possible scenarios, represented in Figure 2-b.

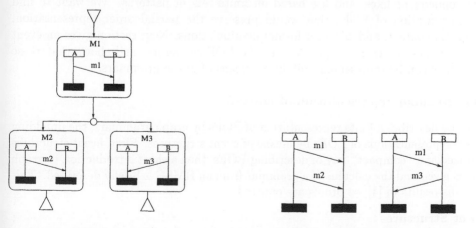

Figure 2. a)HMSC P_0 (with non-local choice). b)Scenarios defined by P_0.

A *path* of an HMSC is a sequence of nodes $n_1.n_2...n_k$ such that $\forall i \in 1..k, n_{i+1}$ is a successor node of n_i. The set of scenarios defined by an HMSC is the sequential composition of partial orders met along the paths of the HMSC. As HMSCs may contain cycles, and as alternatives allows for multiple branchings, an HMSC may describe an infinite number of different path, and infinite paths. So, the set of scenarios defined by an HMSC is a possibly infinite set of possibly infinite partial orders. This set will be called partial order family (or POF for short) hereafter. Let H be an HMSC, the POF defined by H is:

$POF(H) = \{M_1 \circ M_2 \circ ... M_n | \exists$ a path in H going through $M_1, M_2 ... M_n\}$

Definition 1:

An *execution* $w = e_0 e_1 ...$ of an HMSC is a possibly infinite word of E^*. w is *consistent* with respect to an order $M = < E, \leq, \alpha, A, I >$ if and only if:

- $e_0 \in min(M)$ the first event executed is in the minimal events of M,
- $\forall i, j | i < j, e_j \not\leq e_i$ (there is no contradiction between the total order defined by w and the order $\leq$).

Let us consider HMSC P_0 in Figure 2-a. P_0 describes two possible scenarios: $M_1 \circ M_2$ and $M1 \circ M3$. To be consistent with the specification, an execution of P_0 will have to be consistent with the order defined by $M_1 \circ M_2$ or by $M_1 \circ M_3$. Let us note $!m$ the sending of a message m, and $?m$ for it corresponding reception. Consistent executions of P_0 are $w_1 = !m_1.?m_1.!m_2.?m_2$, $w_2 = !m_1.!m_2.?m_1?m_2$ and $w_3 = !m_1.?m_1.!m_3.?m_3$. After the execution of $!m1.?m1$, instance A can decide to perform scenario M_2, and instance B can decide to perform scenario M_3. This situation is be called a *non-local choice*[1]. As the decision to perform M_2 or M_3 is distributed, this can not be done without a synchronization between A and B. Non-local choices can be implemented by means of hidden synchronizations, or distributed consensus mechanisms. However, the simulation of a scenario with non-local choice will suppose that a solution has been implemented, and will only consider conflicts at an abstract level.

HMSCs describe infinite families of potentially infinite partial orders, but these orders may have common prefixes, and are based on finite sets of patterns. We want to find a finite representation of POFs that would preserve the partial order representation, make conflicts apparent, and allow for formal manipulations. Next section gives an event structure semantics to HMSCs equivalent to the POF semantics, and shows that these event structures can be represented finitely by means of graph grammars.

3. Graph grammar representation of HMSCs

This section describes a finite representation of POFs by graph grammars, the unfolding of which are representations of POFs by means of event structures. First, event structures are introduced as a "compact" way of describing POFs, then a short introduction to graph grammars is given and the calculus of a grammar from an HMSC is briefly described. This section recalls results of [4], so proofs are omitted.

3.1. Event Structures

A prime event structure (ES for short) is a 6-tuple $< E, \leq, \sharp, \alpha, A, I >$ where E, A , I, $\leq$ and α have the same meaning than in previous sections, and $\sharp$ is a symmetric anti-reflexive binary relation called *conflict relation*, defining the pair of events that can not appear in the same execution of an ES, and such that:

$\forall e \in E, \forall e' \in E, e \sharp e' \Leftrightarrow \forall e'' \in E, (e' \leq e'' \Rightarrow e \sharp e'')$ (the conflicts are inherited through causality relations).

An event structure defines a domain of *configurations*, that can be seen as possible states of the system. A configuration is a subset C of E that is conflict-free ($\forall e \in C, \not\exists e' \in C \mid e \sharp e'$), and downward-closed ($\forall e \in C, e' \leq e \Rightarrow e' \in C$). An ES defines a family of orders, which are projections of the order relation on its maximal configurations. $POF(ES) = \{max(< E_i, \leq >) | \forall e, e' \in E_i, e \not\sharp e'\}$. For further reading on event structures, consult [8].

The construction of an event structure form an HMSC is straightforward. The partial order relation is built using the weak sequencing operator on the paths of the HMSC. Conflicts are introduced by choices: two events situated in different suffixes of different paths of the HMSC are conflicting events. So, **an execution of an HMSC must not contain events conflicting in its ES representation.**

An event structure can be represented by a graph which associates a vertex to each event, and a typed edge to each conflict and each pair in the order relation. Infinite behaviours lead to infinite graphs. Unfortunately, the resulting graph is not necessarily a regular graph, which means that it can not always be generated by a graph grammar. A first intuitive solution is to represent only minimal conflicts, and the covering of the causality order. The other conflict and causality edges can be deducted from the graph representation, using the conflict inheritance property and the transitivity of the order relation.

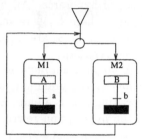

Figure 3. An irregular HMSC.

Even though, graphs obtained from ES may still not be regular: the graph representation for the event structure of HMSC in Figure 3, is the irregular graph in Figure 4-a.

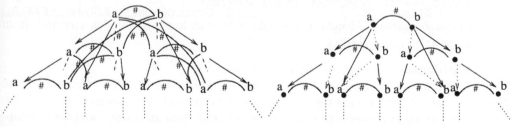

Figure 4. a)Irregular SE graph.   b)Regular covering graph.

In order to solve the problem of regularity caused by conflict edges in the graph representation of an event structure, a new type of edge is defined, and is called conflict inheritance edge. This relation will allow an event e' to inherit all conflicts from an event e, without being causally dependent on e.

An ES can be represented by a *covering graph*: $< E, \longrightarrow, \rightsquigarrow, \sharp_c, \alpha, A, I >$, such that:

- $\longrightarrow = \{(e, e') \in \leq | e \neq e' \wedge \not\exists e'' \in E - \{e, e'\}, e \leq e'' \leq e'\}$ is the covering of $\leq$,
- $\rightsquigarrow$ is an conflict inheritance relation ($\forall (e_1, e_2) \in \rightsquigarrow, \forall e' \in E, e' \sharp e_1 \Rightarrow e' \sharp e_2$),
- $\sharp_c$ is the set of minimal conflicts, i.e. $\{(e, e') \in \sharp | \not\exists e'' \wedge (e'' \leq e' \vee e'' \rightsquigarrow e') \wedge e \sharp e''\}$.

The conflict inheritance relation allows for generating regular covering graphs, that can be represented finitely by a graph grammar.

A covering graph of the event structure of Figure 4-a is represented in Figure 4-b. $\longrightarrow$ is represented by simple arrows, $\rightsquigarrow$ is represented by dotted arrows, and $\sharp$ is represented by an edge labeled by $\sharp$.

For the sake of clarity, the labeling part of covering graphs will be omitted, and a covering graph will be noted $G = < E, \longrightarrow, \rightsquigarrow, \sharp >$.

3.2. Graph grammars

Only a short introduction to graph grammars is given. For further reading, [3] may be consulted. A graph grammar is a grammar in which terminal are vertices and edges, and non-terminals are hyperarcs.

An *hypergraph* G is a pair $(T(G), H(G))$, where $T(G)$ is a finite graph, and $H(G)$ is a set of hyperarcs. An *hyperarc* is a word $ls_1..s_n$, which label l belongs to an alphabet L, and where $\{s_i\}$ are vertices of $T(G)$. On the hypergraph represented in Figure 6, the vertices s_4, s_5, s_6 are linked by an hyperarc labeled by A. Such an hyperarc will then be noted $As_5s_6s_4$.

A *graph grammar* consists in an hypergraph G_0 called the *axiom* of the grammar, and of a set $\mathcal{R}$ of rewriting rules. A rewriting rule is a pair (X, H), where X is an hyperarc, and H is the hypergraph rewritten from X's vertices. We will often write this rule $X \triangleright H$. X will be called the *left part* of the rule, and H the *right part*. For an hypergraph G, we note $G \xrightarrow[G,X]{} G'$ if G can be rewritten into G' by replacing X by H in G. A *direct derivation* of an hypergraph G by a rule $(X, R) \in \mathcal{R}$ is an hypergraph G' such that $G' = G_{[X:=R]}$.

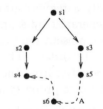

Figure 6: Hypergraph.

We write $G \xrightarrow[G,(X,R)]{} G'$. A sequence of direct derivations $G \xrightarrow[G,(X_1,R_1)]{} G_1 \xrightarrow[G,(X_2,R_2)]{} \cdots \xrightarrow[G,(X_n,R_n)]{} G_n$ is called a *derivation of length n*. We will say that an hypergraph G' is *accessible* from G if there is a derivation leading from G to G'.

3.3. Graph grammar calculus from an HMSC

Section 3.1 has defined a covering graph representation for the POF semantics of an HMSC. As covering graphs are regular, they can be represented by means of graph grammars. These graph grammars can be calculated directly from an HMSC, without developing its POF or it ES representation. As this calculus can be found in [4](p 13-20), we just give a short description. A graph grammar calculus from an HMSC consists in generating rules that will glue together all parts of the covering graph for the SE representation of an HMSC. The right parts of the rules will be either a covering graph without conflict in the case of a single sequencing, and a covering graph with conflicts between minimal events of each bMSC in the case of a choice. The hyperarcs will be sets of maximal events for the order relation. The end nodes will lead to rules that delete hyperarcs. Figure 6 illustrates how MSC features can be transformed into graph grammar rules. From this first step, a normalized grammar can be constructed.

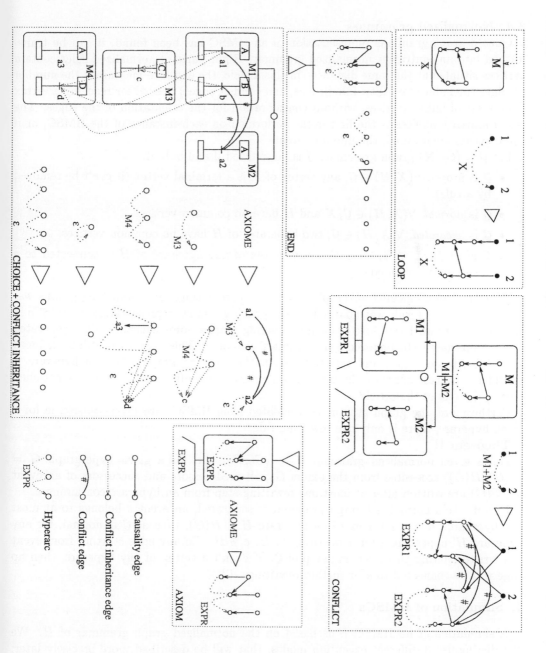

Figure 6. Graph grammar construction from an HMSC.

3.4. Normalized grammars

Once a graph grammar representation of an HMSC has been found, it can be transformed into an equivalent normalized grammar. Right parts of normalized rules contain vertices situated at the same distance. In this article, the distance measure is the number of edges (including causality, inheritance, and conflict edges) needed for reaching a vertex from a set of initial vertices, without consideration for the orientation of the edges. The set of starting vertices is the first event performed on each instance of the HMSC, or if these events are ordered, the minimal events.

Let $\mathcal{G} = (G_0, \mathcal{R})$ graph grammar. $\mathcal{G}$ is normalized if and only if:

- $\mathcal{G}$ is *proper*: $\forall (X, H) \in \mathcal{G}$, any vertex of X is a terminal vertex (it can't be removed by a rule).
- $\mathcal{G}$ is *normal*: $\forall (X, H) \in \mathcal{G}$, X and H have no common vertices
- $\mathcal{G}$ is *separated*: $\forall (X, H) \in \mathcal{G}$, two hyperarcs of H have no common vertices.
- $\mathcal{G}$ is *uniform*: $\forall (X, H) \in \mathcal{G}$, every vertex of any hyperarc of H is connected to a vertex of X by an edge.

A normal form calculus for graph grammars representing finite branching graphs was given in [2]. This result was adapted for the graph grammar representation of HMSCs in [4]. In order to work on finite branching covering graphs, some causality edges generated inside loops have to be removed from the initial grammar. These edges can still be deduced from inheritance edges, and reintroduced in the covering graph when an hyperarc is unfolded. As these edges can be treated easily during unfolding, they won't be mentioned during the rest of the article.

Furthermore, the graph grammars calculated from HMSCs are *deterministic*, ie for a given hyperarc, there is only one rewriting rule.

Theorem 1:

For a given normalized grammar $\mathcal{G} = (G_0, \mathcal{R})$, and for a given hypergraph $G = (T(G), H(G))$ accessible from the axiom G_0, all predecessors and successors of an event $e \in T(G)$ are written after at most one rewriting step from an hyperarc containing e.

Proof: As a normalized graph grammar is separated, an event e belongs to at most one hyperarc. If e is a vertex of an hyperarc $H \in H(G)$, then as $\mathcal{G}$ is normal, for any hyperarc H' appearing after a rewriting of H, $e \notin H'$. So any edge starting from event e is written during this rewriting step of $\mathcal{G}$. If e isn't a vertex of any hyperarc, then no edge will be connected to e by further rewritings. $\square$

4. Simulation of HMSCs

A simulation of an HMSC H is based on the normalized graph grammar of H. We can distinguish 3 different execution modes, that will be described more precisely later: they are called asynchronous, conflict dependent, and consensus execution modes. The main idea of the simulation is to unfold a limited part of the covering graph containing the next executable events. This graph has to be recalculated after the execution of an event: due to the conflict relations, some events are not executable anymore, and have to be removed. This section defines global system states, and then gives 3 semantics of transitions.

4.1. States
Definition 2:

The set of minimal events of a graph $G = <E, \longrightarrow, \rightsquigarrow, \sharp>$ with respect to a relation $\dashrightarrow \subseteq E \times E$ is noted $min(G, \dashrightarrow) = \{e \in E| \not\exists e' \wedge e' \dashrightarrow e\}$.

A *global state* of the system is represented by an hypergraph G, accessible from the axiom of the normalized grammar. This hypergraph represents a part of the event structure's covering graph. From a global state, only minimal actions with respect to an order relation on events can be executed. This order relation can be $\longrightarrow$, for the asynchronous execution and $\longrightarrow \cup \rightsquigarrow$ for the conflict dependent and consensus execution models. In order to make sure that an event is minimal for the hypergraph, it must not be a vertex of an hyperarc. From theorem 1, we know that a single unfolding of hyperarcs containing minimal events ensures that those minimal events are not contained in any hyperarc anymore. Unfolding can create new minimal events, so the calculus of a valid state is an iteration. This iteration stops when there are no more minimal events contained in an hyperarc (in such a case, a valid state was found), or when an unfolding obliges to use a rule twice (in such a case, we can't find a valid state, an though we can not continue the execution of our specification).

An unfolding of an hyperarc h in an hypergraph $G = (T(G), H(G))$ is noted $unfold(G, h)$, and is the hypergraph G' such that $\exists (h, R) \in \mathcal{G} \wedge G \xrightarrow[G,(h,R)]{} G'$ (as our graph grammars are deterministic, (h, R) is unique, and so is G'). A simple algorithm for the calculus of a valid state from an hypergraph G is now defined. Let us call $G_\emptyset = (\emptyset, \emptyset)$ the empty hypergraph, containing no events and no hyperarcs.

```
procedure valid-state(G) =
    G' := G;
    R := {h ∈ H(G)|∃e ∈ min(G, -->) ∧ e ∈ h};
    while R≠ ∅∧G' ≠ G∅ do
        choose h from R; R := R-{h};
        G' := develop-hyperarc(G',{h},h);
    done;
    return G';
end;
procedure develop-hyperarc(G,P,h) =
    G':= Unfold(G, h);
    R :={h ∈ H(G')|∃e ∈ min(G'-G, -->) ∧ e ∈ h};
    while R≠ ∅∧G' ≠ G∅ do
        choose h from R; R := R-{h};
        if h ∈ P then G' := G∅ else G':= develop-hyperarc(G',P∪{h},h);
    done;
    return G';
end
```

Our grammar is proper, which means that no vertex is deleted from a state by rewriting. As our grammar is also separated, there is no intersection between hyperarcs, so developing an hyperarc won't connect edges to the vertices of other hyperarcs in $H(G)$. Consequently, every hyperarc of $H(G)$ can be developed separately.

4.2. Transitions

Once a valid global state G has been calculated, an execution step can be performed. An event e is *executable* if all its predecessors have been executed, and if no event e' such that $e \sharp e'$ have been executed. The execution of an event e from a state G leads to the minimal valid state G', in which e and all events conflicting with e have been removed. This ensures that an execution will never contain conflicting events.

Definition 3:

Let us note $\downarrow (e, G)$ the set containing an event e and its successors in G.
$$\downarrow (e, G) = e \cup \{ \quad e' \in E | \exists e_0, e_1, .., e_n \in E^n, e_0 = e$$
$$\wedge e_n = e' \wedge \forall 1 < i < n(e_i \longrightarrow e_{i+1} \vee e_i \rightsquigarrow e_{i+1})\}$$

Definition 4:

Let us note $G_{|E'}$ the restriction of an hypergraph G to a set E'. For an hypergraph $G = (< E, \longrightarrow, \rightsquigarrow, \sharp >, H(G))$, $G_{|E'} = (< E \cap E', \longrightarrow', \rightsquigarrow', \sharp' >, H'(G))$, where:

- $\longrightarrow' = \{(e, e') \in \longrightarrow | e \in E' \wedge e' \in E'\}$,
- $\rightsquigarrow' = \{(e, e') \in \rightsquigarrow | e \in E' \wedge e' \in E'\}$,
- $\sharp' = \{(e, e') \in \sharp | e \in E' \wedge e' \in E'\}$,
- $H'(G) = \{h \in H(G) | \forall e \in h, e \in E'\}$.

4.3. Asynchronous execution of a MSC

An HMSC might be executed in an *asynchronous* mode, which imposes no constraint on conflicts. An event is executable if it is minimal for the order relation ($\longrightarrow$). Note that this mode implements the meaning of choice recommended by norm Z.120. For any valid state $G = (< E, \longrightarrow, \rightsquigarrow, \sharp >, H(G))$, we have:

$$\frac{e \in min(G, \longrightarrow) \wedge \nexists h \in H(G) \mid e \in h}{G \xrightarrow{e} G'}$$
, where G'=Next-State-Asynchronous(G,

```
procedure Next-State-Asynchronous(G,e)
  G':=G;
  R:= {h ∈ H(G')|∃e'♯e ∧ ∃e" ∈ h ∧ e" ∈↓ (e',G)};
  while R≠ ∅ do
    choose h from R; R:= R−{h};
    if ∃e" ∈ h|∀e♯e', e" ∉↓ (e',G') then G':= unfold(G',h);
    else G':= (T(G'), H(G') − {h});
    R:= {h ∈ H(G')|∃e'♯e ∧ ∃e" ∈ h ∧ e" ∈↓ (e',G')};
  done;
  G':= G'|E'−({e}∪{↓(e',G')|e'♯e});
  Return(valid-state(G'));
end
```

First, any hyperarc $h \in H(G)$ that contain both conflicting and non-conflicting events wrt e is unfolded. The unfoldings stop when any hyperarc of G contains only conflicting events (in that case they will be removed by the restriction on $E - (\{e\} \cup \{\downarrow e'|e'\sharp e\})$), or non-conflicting events (these hyperarcs will be preserved by the restriction). The hypergraph G' obtained is restricted to the set of executable events, and the next valid state reachable from $G'_{|E'-(\{e\}\cup\{\downarrow e'|e'\sharp e\})}$ is calculated.

An HMSC is not always executable in asynchronous mode, and simulation may lead to a deadlock state. Let us consider HMSC H in Figure 7, and its normalized grammar in Figure 8 . Simulating H in an asynchronous mode is impossible. As event a is the only event performed on instance A, and as the event structure representation contains multiple copies of this event that are all minimal events for $\longrightarrow$, it is impossible to find a finite unfolding of the graph grammar where an event labeled by a would be minimal and not contained in any hyperarc. Consequently, the start state for an asynchronous execution of the grammar of Figure 8 is $G_\emptyset$.

Figure 7. a) HMSC H.   b)HMSC H'.

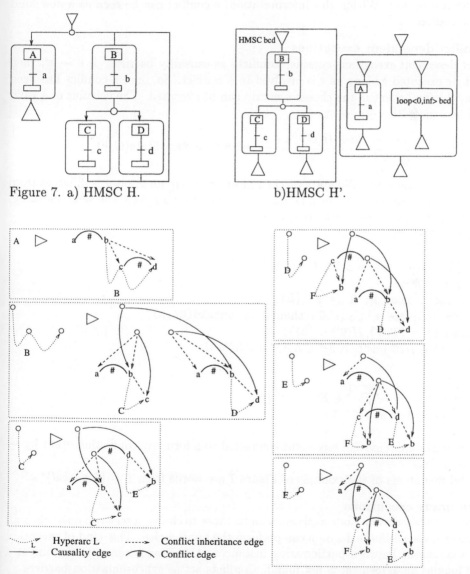

Figure 8. An example of grammar normal form calculated from HMSC in Figure 7.

When an HMSC can not be executed in asynchronous mode, it may be treated by finding an equivalent HMSC (H and H' in Figure 7 have the same POF semantics). Even if scenarios such as H seem to be ill-formed, they express interesting languages and must not be ignored. The language recognized by H is $L = \{w \in A^* || w|_a = 1 \wedge |w|_b = |w|_c + |w|_d\}$. Such an HMSC could be used for defining properties (for example expressing the fact that the number of connections and deconnections in a system must be the same). Most often, the admitted behaviour of the HMSC of Figure 7-a is that a is an exit event for the loop structure. So, the system can perform $b.c$ or $b.d$ an unlimited number of times, until an event a occurs. Within this interpretation, a conflict can be seen as a new kind of synchronization.

4.4. Conflict dependent executions

Conflict dependent executions consider conflicts as causality barriers. If $e \rightsquigarrow e'$, then e' can not be executed as long as e is involved in a conflict. So, once a conflict has been solved, any minimal event in the chosen scenario can be executed. The calculus of a valid state will be done with $\dashrightarrow = \longrightarrow \cup \rightsquigarrow$.

$$\frac{e \in min(G, \longrightarrow \cup \rightsquigarrow) \wedge \nexists h \in H(G) \mid e \in h}{G \stackrel{e}{\longrightarrow} G'} \quad \text{with } G' = \text{Next-State}(G, e)$$

The calculus of the next valid state reached after executing an event e is different from the asynchronous case: the conflict inheritance relation does not have the same meaning, and have to be updated after each transition.

```
procedure Next-State(G,e)
   G':=G;
   R:= {h ∈ H(G')|∃e'♯e ∧ ∃e'' ∈ h ∧ e'' ∈↓ (e',G)};
   while R ≠ ∅ do
      choose h from R; R := R- {h};
      if ∃e'' ∈ h|∀e♯e', e'' ∉↓ (e',G') then G':= unfold(G',h);
      else G':= (T(G'), H(G') − {h});
      R:= {h ∈ H(G')|∃e'♯e ∧ ∃e'' ∈ h ∧ e'' ∈↓ (e',G')};
   done;
   G':= G'|E'−({e}∪↓(e',G')|e'♯e});
   ↝':= {(e', e'') ∈↝' |∃e''' ∈ E' ∧ e'♯e'''};
   Return(valid-state(G'));
end
```

When conflicts are removed, any event connected to a formerly conflicting event by $\rightsquigarrow$ becomes a minimal event.

The valid executions of the example of Figure 7 are words from $L = \{b.c + b.d\}^*.a$.

4.5. Consensus executions

The *consensus* execution mode authorizes an instance to choose a scenario only when all the instances involved in the decision can perform the same choice. This kind of execution requires a consensus between participating instances. An instance can not continue at a choice as long as an agreement is not found. Conflicts act as synchronization barriers.

$$\frac{e \in min(G, \longrightarrow \cup \rightsquigarrow) \wedge \not\exists H \in \mathcal{H} \mid e \in H \wedge \forall e' \mid e' \sharp e, e' \in min(G, \longrightarrow \cup \rightsquigarrow)}{G \xrightarrow{e} G'}$$

with G' =Next-State(G, e)

The calculus of the next valid state is the same that for a conflict dependent execution.

5. Example

Let us consider the simple data transfer protocol defined on Figure 9. First, $User_A$ sends a connection request to $Network_B$. This connection can be accepted or rejected. Once it is accepted, $User_A$ can send data messages to $Network_B$, or close the connection. $Network_B$ forwards received data to $User_B$.

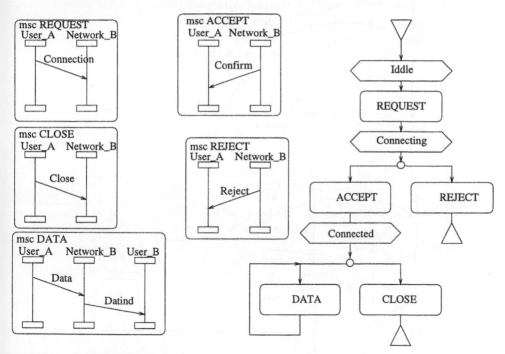

Figure 9. A simple example protocol.

The covering graph of the event structure representation of the HMSC in Figure 9 is represented in Figure 10. We indicated the distance for each event on the graph by drawing frontiers between distant events. One can easily note that the events contained between two frontiers are also events appearing in the same rewriting rule. One can also note that at distance 6, the set of events between two frontiers becomes a regular pattern (it implies that rule F of the normalized graph grammar in Figure 11 can be continued by developing F another time).

Figure 12 shows the different states reached during the asynchronous execution of $w =!connection.?connection.!confirm.?confirm.!data.!data.!data$. The size of the graph

486

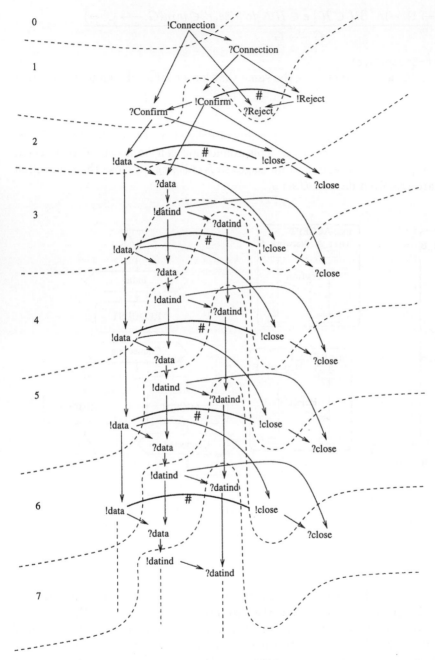

Figure 10. Covering graph for HMSC in Figure 9.

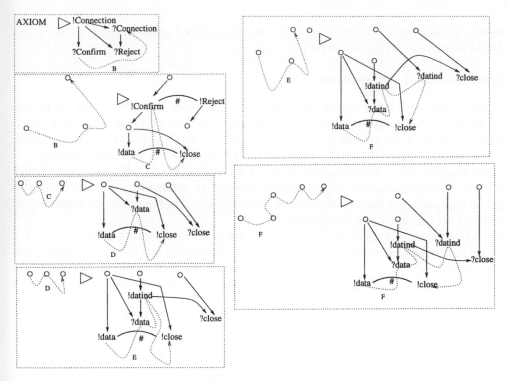

Figure 11. Normalized grammar for HMSC in Figure 9.

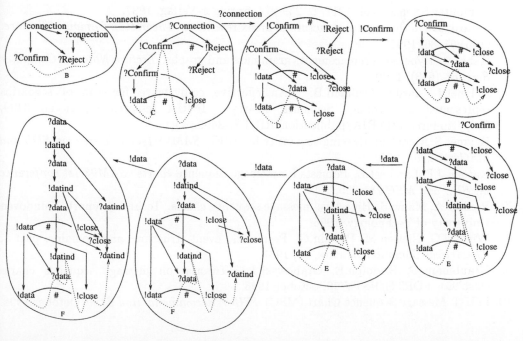

Figure 12. Execution of grammar in Figure 11.

grows in a regular way. This denotes a process divergence between instance $User_A$ and the set of instances $\{Network_B, User_B\}$.

6. Conclusion and perspectives

We have introduced a framework for simulation of scenarios based on graph grammars. Such executions can help detecting undesired behaviours at an early stage of a specification. In addition to providing help in the conception of distributed systems, graph grammars also give useful information about the synchronization of a specification.

Let us consider the communication graph of an HMSC P, $CG(P) = (I, \longrightarrow_P)$ such that $i \longrightarrow_P j$ when instance $i \in I$ can send a message to instance $j \in I$ in P. From this graph we can partition the set of instances into subsets of communicating instances, ie the connected components of the graph $CG(P)$.

From the previous examples, we can see that the size of the states can grow very fast if a set of communicating instances is few synchronized. On the contrary, the size of the states may remain bounded if all the sets of communicating instances are strongly synchronized. This let us think that graph grammar representation could be used to define concurrency measures of HMSCs.

REFERENCES

1. Ben-Abdallah.H,Leue.S Syntactic Detection of Process Divergence and non-Local Choice in Message Sequence Charts in: E. Brinksma (ed.), Proceedings of the Third International Workshop on Tools and Algorithms for the Construction and Analysis of Systems TACAS'97, Enschede, The Netherlands, April 1997, Lecture Notes in Computer Science, Vol. 1217, p. 259-274, Springer-Verlag, 1997.
2. Caucal.D. On the regular structure of prefix rewriting. *Theoretical Computer Science*, (106):61–86, 1992.
3. Habel.A. Hyperedge replacement: grammars and graphs. *Lecture Notes in Computer Science*, (643), 1989.
4. Helouet.L, Jard.C.,Caillaud.B. An effective equivalence for sets of scenarios represented by Message Sequence Charts. INRIA research report no 3499, ftp://ftp.inria.fr/INRIA/publication/RR/RR-3499.ps.gz
5. Heymer.S A non-interleaving semantics for MSC. *SAM98:1st conference on SDL and MSC*,281-290, 1998.
6. Katoen.J.P, Lambert.L, Pomsets for message sequence charts. *SAM98:1st conference on SDL and MSC*,281-290, 1998.
7. Reniers.A, Mauw.S. High-level message sequence charts. Technical report, Heindoven University of Technology, 1996.
8. Winskel.G, Nielsen.M, Plotkin.G. Petri nets, event structures and domains, part 1. *Theoretical Computer Science*, 13, 1981.
9. Graubmann.P, Rudolph.E, Grabowski.J. Tutorial on message sequence charts (msc'96). FORTE/PSTV'96, october 1996.
10. ITU-T Message Sequence Chart (MSC) *ITU-T Recommendation Z120*, October 1996.

Author Index

Page

Printed and bound by CPI Group (UK) Ltd, Croydon, CR0 4YY

03/10/2024

01040419-0012